RANDOM HOUSE

Year
round
crossword
omnibus

edited by Stanley Newman

RANDOM HOUSE

Year round crossword omnibus

edited by Stanley Newman

**Random House
Puzzles & Games**

New York   Toronto   London   Sydney   Auckland

Introduction

Welcome to *Random House Year Round Crossword Puzzle Omnibus*, with 400 warm and wise puzzles from earlier volumes in the handy "Vacation-size" series. Each crossword has a theme, or central idea, running through its longest answers. The title provided at the top of each page will give you a hint as to what the theme is. And the answers are all in the back, just in case.

Thanks to Oriana Leckert and Joan Ginsberg for their help in the preparation of this book.

Your comments on any aspect of this book are most welcome. You can reach me via regular mail or e-mail at the addresses below.

If you're Internet-active, you're invited to my Web site, www.StanXwords.com. It features puzzlemaker profiles, solving hints and other useful info for crossword fans. There's also a free daily crossword and weekly prize contest. Please stop by for a visit.

Best wishes for happy solving!

Stan Newman

Regular mail: P.O. Box 69, Massapequa Park, NY 11762
(Please enclose a self-addressed stamped envelope if you'd like a reply.)

E-mail: StanXwords@aol.com

Join Stan Newman on His Annual Crossword-Theme Cruise!

You'll enjoy a relaxing vacation on a luxurious ship, plus a full program of puzzles, games, and instructional sessions. For complete info on Stan's next cruise, please phone Special Event Cruises at 1-800-326-0373, or visit their Web site, www.specialeventcruises.com/crossword.html.

PUZZLES

1 PUT-ONS

by Randolph Ross

ACROSS

1 Cut wires
5 BBs and bullets
9 Grassy field
12 Wall layer
15 __ and outs
16 Urban sharpie
17 Milk amts.
18 Road warning
19 D.C. VIP
20 Sign of imperfection
22 Marsh plant
24 Does farm work
25 Sticky stuff
28 Grazing areas
32 Wasp
36 Treeless tract
37 Color pros
41 North Carolina locale
43 Celebrants
46 Act angry
47 Actor Mischa
48 "__ Entertainment!"
52 Locks of hair
56 Drs.' grp.
57 Zsa Zsa's sister
60 Coll. club
61 Pioneer
64 Unclose, to the Bard
65 Leftover covering
66 Actor Beatty
67 Slips up
68 Notary's need

DOWN

1 Cultivated earth
2 Its HQ is in Brussels
3 Major ending?
4 Sheriff's band
5 Mimicking
6 Bub
7 Hammer of fiction
8 Unique individual
9 Rye, but not pumpernickel
10 Means of access
11 Size up
12 Dosage units: Abbr.
13 Hightailed it
14 Singing syllable
21 Closes down
22 Film editors, often
23 Clean-air org.
25 Defraud
26 "__ the fields we go . . ."
27 Slangy suffix
29 Official records
30 *Your Show of Shows* routine
31 Camping equipment
33 Kind of exam
34 Help with the dishes
35 Show displeasure
38 Chapter of history
39 Wasn't colorfast
40 JFK jet, once
42 He followed FDR
43 Acts the squealer
44 Part of the Old World
45 Turned sharply
49 Puts an end to
50 Word form for "both"
51 Powder materials
53 Gas-line additive
54 Agatha's colleague
55 German mining region
57 Poet Pound
58 Scaloppine ingredient
59 Dadaist painter
62 Neighbor of Syr.
63 Feeling of wonder

2 SIZES

by Cynthia Lyon

ACROSS

1 Sentry's order
5 Phil Donahue's wife
10 Acclaim
14 *Typee* sequel
15 Like campus walls
16 *The __ American*
17 Harry Kemelman's detective
20 She "cain't say no"
21 Thinly populated
22 Author Sheehy
23 '69 landing site
24 Ruggedly built
27 Flimsy
30 Motorists' org.
31 __-kiri
33 Early Alaska capital
35 Séance operator
39 Iron, in Austria
40 Platter
41 One-fifth of DCCLV
42 Let back in
44 Haunted-house noises
47 *South Pacific* role
48 *Mildred Pierce* author
49 Bad-mouth
52 1910s or 1940s event
56 Jailbreak headline
58 Fails to be, informally

59 Author Remarque
60 Praise to the skies
61 Tacks on
62 Shabby and unkempt
63 NaOH solutions

DOWN

1 Romanian dance
2 *Diary of __ Housewife*
3 Timber wolf
4 Trinidad's neighbor
5 Cinderella's curfew
6 Use
7 Paris' __ Gauche
8 Maui memento
9 Favored, as a bet
10 E.T., for one
11 Ice-cream ingredient
12 What Pandora unleashed
13 Actor Waggoner
18 __ instant (quickly)
19 Ring bearer?
23 What American Plan includes
24 Return-mail expediter: Abbr.
25 Rhino's relative
26 Poker ploy
27 Characteristic
28 New York city
29 Move furtively
32 Accountant's activity
34 Author Kingsley

36 Pragmatic ones
37 Spectrum component
38 A Bergen dummy
43 Fashion
45 Small brook
46 Ultimate purpose
48 Work together
49 Film-rating org.
50 Dry as a desert
51 The Swedish Nightingale
52 Court paper
53 *King Kong* actress
54 Fit of fever
55 National League team
57 Memorable period

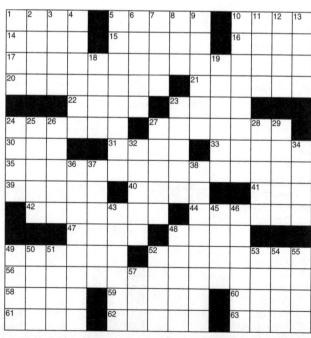

3 WORKING OVERTIME

by Donna J. Stone

ACROSS

1 Yonder folks
5 Shapeless masses
10 Darned thing?
14 Like some buildup
15 Evangelist Semple McPherson
16 Jai __
17 "Excuse me!"
18 Sonia of *Moon Over Parador*
19 Social misfit
20 START OF A QUOTE
23 Mal de __ (seasickness)
24 __ contendere
25 Trunks, for instance
30 Absentee
34 "Wild West" showman
35 Small band
37 It runs through Paris
38 Vein contents
39 MIDDLE OF QUOTE
41 Victory sign
42 TV host Robin
44 Clever remark
45 Bobolink's bill
46 Track events
48 Classical Greek teachers
50 Italian wine region
52 Joplin opus
53 END OF QUOTE
59 Horse's gait
60 "__ Kick Out of You"
61 O'Hara homestead
63 Indian-summer phenomenon
64 Funnel-shaped
65 Writer Hunter
66 Toe the line
67 Squirrel away
68 Resist boldly

DOWN

1 Former United rival
2 "That's a scream!"
3 Small businessman?
4 Al Jolson tune
5 The Yanks' #3
6 Old Italian bread?
7 General Bradley
8 Get cracking
9 Perk up the pot roast
10 Town in a Warwick tune
11 Butter substitute
12 Auto part, for short
13 Clown around
21 Scale notes
22 At __ for words
25 Chew out
26 *She __ Yellow Ribbon*
27 Brainstorms
28 OPEC member
29 Mr. Andronicus
31 Where the bees are
32 __ a time (singly)
33 Pay periods, often
36 Toledo's home
39 More than this?
40 Golf shot
43 Sea dog's ditty
45 Not at all fair-minded
47 Zeno's associates
49 Linden of *Barney Miller*
51 Gold bar
53 Take greedily
54 Percolate
55 Narrow shoe size
56 Elevator inventor
57 Place for pews
58 Big name in tennis
59 Even if, informally
62 Multiple-choice word

4 APT MUSIC

by Karen Hodge

ACROSS
1 Toward the left, at sea
6 Tree branch
10 Not a lot
13 Tougher to find
14 Admired one
15 Getting __ years
17 French flapjack
18 "__ want for Christmas . . ."
19 Beef-grading agcy.
20 Police music?
23 Hardwood tree
24 Big name in theaters
25 Like a pro
28 Olympics org.
31 Memorable period
32 George's big brother
33 Casals' instrument
35 *Ghostbusters* goo
39 Strait music?
42 Cross one's heart
43 Romantic episode
44 __ Lanka
45 Hosp. professionals
47 Pa Cartwright
48 Put up with
49 Baby birds
53 "__ the fields we go . . ."
55 Charitable music?
61 Meal: Lat.
62 Nutritive mineral
63 Tower material
64 It grows on you

65 Straw vote
66 Atlas was one
67 Fort __, NJ
68 Whirlpool
69 Reckless speed

DOWN
1 Foot part
2 __-mutuel betting
3 Pitcher Hershiser
4 Sportscast showing
5 Lock of hair
6 Deceitful one
7 Doing nothing
8 Double agents
9 Coward's __ *Spirit*
10 Ump's call
11 Come next
12 Having more breadth
16 Early political cartoonist
21 "Beggarman" follower
22 College official
25 Puts on TV
26 Furrowed feature
27 Fine fabric
29 Gymnast Korbut
30 Tackle Everest
33 The eyes have it
34 Bassoon's cousin
36 "__ Miracle" (Manilow tune)
37 Goodson of game shows
38 Toledo's lake

40 Lenin's inspiration
41 __-the-mill (ordinary)
46 Skunk feature
48 Miscellaneous facts
49 Scratch the surface
50 In the lead
51 Guardian spirits
52 Hyannis entree
54 Mrs. Bunker
56 Wait on the phone
57 Nothing more than
58 Bons __ (witty remarks)
59 Part of QED
60 "Auld Lang __"

5 M&Ms

by Eric Albert

ACROSS

1 Apollo's twin sister
8 Come through
15 Deadline
16 Venezuelan river
17 *Time* piece
18 With 51 Down, seascape painter
19 Memorable mime
21 Venetian-blind component
22 Greenish blue
23 *L.A. Law* network
26 Electrically versatile
29 Bibliography abbr.
30 Atty.'s title
33 Grille material
36 Detective Wolfe
37 "The Morning After" singer
40 Lendl of tennis
41 Big cheese, maybe
42 Deli bread
43 Prepare salad
44 Assistant
45 __ Lanka
46 Kukla's colleague
49 Folksinger Phil
53 *Some Like It Hot* star
58 Fairly, in a way
60 Broadcast slot
61 Belly

62 Soft-shell clam
63 Elsa was one
64 Santa's elves, e.g.

DOWN

1 First one-term president
2 Part of RFD
3 Tropical fish
4 King's order
5 Ceremonial club
6 "__ never work!"
7 Appear
8 Bridal goods
9 Author Jong
10 Bed sheets or bath towels
11 "Last one __ rotten egg!"

12 Step forward
13 Prefix for system
14 Ticket word
20 Go with
24 Senator Goldwater
25 High-tech replica
26 Poker "bullet"
27 Huntley or Atkins
28 First 007 film
29 Addr. loc.
30 Gives off
31 Really enjoy
32 Hugo character
34 Last year of Queen Victoria's reign
35 "Zounds!"
38 White-hat wearers: Abbr.

39 Indivisible
46 Compose, as a constitution
47 Ceremonial procedures
48 Alda and Arkin
49 Waiting in the wings
50 Nonpaying activity
51 See 18 Across
52 Crystal gazers
54 Elvis __ Presley
55 "One-l lama" poet
56 Tiny bit
57 Hurler Hershiser
58 Good buddy
59 Box-score stat

6 SHORTENED STATES

by Wayne R. Williams

ACROSS

1 One person's opinion
6 Packs away
11 Sylvester, to Tweety Bird
14 Moral principle
15 Pitch
16 Sluggers' stats: Abbr.
17 Middle of Stein's line
18 Board at parties
19 Before, poetically
20 Sherwood Anderson opus
22 Boater or bowler
23 Asian celebrations
24 1990 Oscar winner
26 Strength of character
30 Nebraska river
31 Skier Phil
32 Neil Simon play
35 Three, to Steffi
36 Middle measurement
37 Misfortunes
40 Larry McMurtry novel
42 The Merry Widow
43 Rack partner
45 Fitted together
46 Small wheel
47 Zeus' mother
49 Actress Kaminska
50 Mark Twain book
57 Zilch
58 Adams and Brickell
59 Brimless hat
60 Cable channel
61 Baker's need
62 Unethical one
63 "Oh yeah, __ who?"
64 Fills completely
65 Corrects copy

DOWN

1 Rich Man, Poor Man author
2 Singer of VR.5
3 Unknown auth.
4 Wine attribute
5 Train bridge
6 Nero Wolfe's creator
7 Calendar col. heading
8 Not a dup.
9 Barney Miller character
10 Kenyan language
11 John Irving novel
12 Out-and-out
13 Dangerous fly
21 Quilting party
25 Sines, cosines, etc.
26 C x XXV
27 Musical discernment
28 Alan Cheuse book
29 Mrs. Ed Norton
30 Word after stay or shot
32 Baseballer Ripken
33 Feel poorly
34 Wind dir.
36 Come out on top
38 __ low (stay hidden)
39 Blue
41 Tennis shots
42 Seahawks' home
43 Some collectible art
44 Antiseptic substance
45 Guys
47 Downey costar
48 Party givers
51 Flash of inspiration
52 Italian auto
53 Parka part
54 Prefix for distant
55 Something vital
56 Gets the point

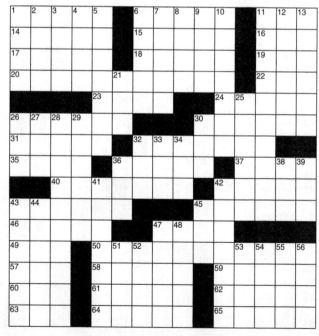

7 ON YOUR METAL

by Karen Hodge

ACROSS

1 Prods, in a way
6 Road feature
10 Bible prophet
14 Limber
15 Neck of the woods
16 Composer __ Carlo Menotti
17 Pittsburgh Steelers' rival?
20 Omit in pronunciation
21 Missile housing
22 Debate side
23 Alluring
25 New England capital
27 Take down a __
30 Runs wild
32 Colonial descendants org.
33 Perched on
35 Mangy mutt
36 Defeats
39 Singer Guthrie
40 Nasal input
42 Make fun of
43 Phone feature
45 Filmdom's Nora Charles
46 Locale
47 Winter bug
48 Can be read effortlessly
50 Moe's hairstyle
51 Düsseldorf dessert
54 Statistical info
56 Great grade
57 "__ restless as a willow . . ."
59 Semidiameters

62 Pewter-maker's directives?
66 Kind of sax
67 Up to the job
68 Wears a hole in the carpet
69 Take five
70 __ good example
71 Criticizes

DOWN

1 Lobbying org.
2 Make eyes at
3 German port
4 "All Shook Up" singer
5 Farm machine
6 Sheep sound
7 Coffeemakers
8 *China Beach* extras
9 Cellist Casals
10 Psyche section
11 Metalworker's motto?
12 Prop for Figaro
13 Put __ to (stop)
18 Word-related
19 Sonata movement
24 "__ Cheatin' Heart"
26 Hauls (off)
27 Carson's predecessor
28 Raison d'__
29 Weather veins?
31 Grimm villain
34 French soldier
36 Disobedient
37 Name in Yugoslavian history

38 Short distance
41 Mind-set
44 Telecast component
48 Like cherries jubilee
49 They take a licking
51 Shankar's instrument
52 Transparent linen
53 Bovary and Samms
55 *Let's Make* __
58 Shaker contents
60 Peruvian ancestor
61 Gossipy tidbit
63 Barracks bed
64 Tchrs.' grp.
65 Draft org.

8 PLACES OF INTEREST

by Eric Albert

ACROSS

1 Copacetic
5 Man and Capri
10 Friday and Columbo
14 Tel __
15 Protester's litany
16 Trim a photo
17 Famous false front
20 Woolly mama
21 Sty cry
22 Keep out of sight
23 Peter Pan pirate
24 Beau Bridges' brother
25 Dulcimer, e.g.
28 Mini-meal
29 E, to Morse
32 Nile city
33 Shoe strip
34 Actor from India
35 Carouse
38 Cub Scout group
39 What the snooty put on
40 *Midnight Cowboy* character
41 Bandage brand
42 Nimble
43 Coded message
44 Parting words
45 Makes lace
46 Tack on
49 "That hurts!"
50 Service charge
53 Police film of '81
56 Toward the dawn
57 Daphnis' love
58 Not quite closed
59 Opening day?
60 J.C. Penney rival
61 Carpet surface

DOWN

1 Taunt
2 Declare openly
3 Windborne toy
4 Actress Arden
5 More distasteful
6 Do very well
7 Long and lean
8 Part of SASE
9 Heel style
10 Musical symbol
11 Kind of hygiene
12 Walt Kelly creation
13 Gush forth
18 Short time
19 Vivacity
23 Beef cut
24 Falters at the altar?
25 *Mothers of Invention* leader
26 Singer who won the Nobel Prize
27 ". . . checking it __"
28 *The Champ* Oscar winner
29 __ Vader
30 Of great weight
31 Henry VIII's house
33 Spins noisily
34 Button alternatives
36 Auto audio accessory
37 Twist out of shape
42 In __ (harmonized)
43 Official seal
44 Predilections
45 One-on-one instructor
46 Mountaintop
47 Brit's baby carriage
48 Tower town
49 *Man __ Mancha*
50 Pacific island group
51 List-shortening abbr.
52 Brontë heroine
54 Bit of resistance?
55 Budget limit

9 SPIRITUALISM

by A.J. Santora

ACROSS

1 Biblical kingdom
5 Overhead-__ engine
8 It may be rattled
13 Shade source
16 Carol start
17 The spirit of the time
18 Sand bar
19 Actress Merkel
20 Eva and Zsa Zsa
22 Volcano name
23 Pat and Vanna's boss
25 Thread holder
27 High-tech scanner
28 Indo-Europeans
31 Appease
33 Tasty tidbit
36 Patronized a casino
37 Team spirit
40 Shorten sleeves, maybe
41 Public opinion, for short
42 Tony Curtis film role
44 Like a bump __
48 Extremity
49 Iwo Jima terrain
52 Actress Singer
53 Years and years
55 Nova __
58 Actor Alastair
59 Divine Comedy writer

61 Philosophical spirit
63 River mammal
64 Florida product
65 Holiday
66 "For shame!"
67 Biol. dept. course

DOWN

1 Simoleons
2 First act
3 Where the bees are
4 Deli order
5 Corn holders
6 Man of morals
7 Dallas-Fort Worth area, e.g.
8 Maritime message
9 Smart
10 Where marines train
11 Arises (from)
12 In the same category
14 Meringue ingredient
15 Scones' partner
21 Scale note
24 Improvised, in jazz
26 South Seas spot
29 Missing in Action star
30 __ Lanka
32 Wrist-related
34 West Indies isle
35 Tokyo's former name

37 Stretch out
38 Tuition payers
39 Nav. officer
40 Leading
43 Emerald Point __ ('80s prime-time series)
45 __ thought (daydreaming)
46 Writer Fallaci
47 Gin drink
50 Parcels (out)
51 TV's Eliot Ness
54 Proofreader's notation
56 S&L payment
57 Ms. Gardner
60 Pitcher's stat.
62 Author Levin

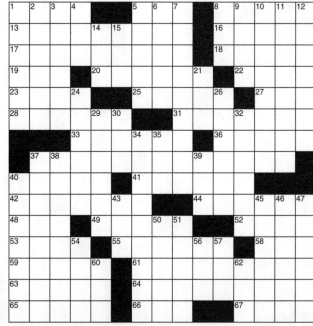

by Emily Cox & Henry Rathvon

ACROSS

1 Redcoat general
5 Passover feast
10 Fairy-tale baddie
14 Something pumped
15 ". . . is as good as __"
16 Campus guys' group, for short
17 Extol
18 Cheesy destiny?
20 Give up the throne
22 Deep chasm
23 State with conviction
24 Buffalo hockey pro
27 African nation
30 Bond of a sort
34 Intrinsically
35 Positive sign
37 Yonder folks
38 Parisian pal
39 Bratlike
42 Three-faced woman?
43 Teaching both genders
45 Film critic James
46 Of longer standing
48 Back up with muscle
50 Lukewarm
52 Man with a Principle
54 Robin Cook book
55 Unexplainable
58 For the few
62 Cheesy fight?
65 "Waterloo" band
66 Pieces' partner
67 Radium researcher
68 Blockhead
69 Shooer's word
70 Office fill-ins
71 Spouses no more

DOWN

1 Arizona river
2 The A of UAR
3 Cheesy exclamation?
4 Salad greens
5 African expedition
6 Send forth
7 Processes veggies
8 BPOE member
9 Fam. member
10 Unconventional
11 Western novelist
12 "Phooey!"
13 Greek letters
19 Have coming
21 Largest asteroid
25 Good-luck charm
26 Army outpost
27 Speedily
28 Clunky car
29 Orbital point
31 Cheesy talker?
32 Carpenter's tool
33 Polishing agent
36 Pinocchio's bane
40 International agreement
41 Bus station
44 Least prudent
47 Summer drink
49 Hazard to navigation
51 French schools
53 Get new guns
55 Suffers recession
56 Leif's dad
57 She was Gilda in '46
59 Lose one's footing
60 Gull's tail?
61 Long-running musical
63 Fall mo.
64 McClanahan of *The Golden Girls*

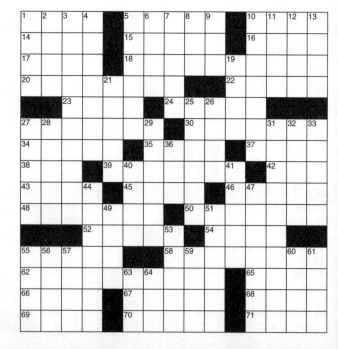

11 BALANCING ACT

by Cynthia Lyon

ACROSS

1 NFL team
6 Allowing a draft
10 Dossier
14 Summarizing paragraph
15 Gossipy info
16 Skunk's weapon
17 What Hillary did
20 Personnel data
21 Con
22 Pursued an office
23 __ move on (rush)
24 Devoid of dirt
27 Dry oneself
31 Music category
32 Boring item
33 Dessert choice
34 Making minimum wage
38 Hula instrument, for short
39 Law-school course
40 Shade sources
41 Mrs. and Mrs.
43 Overall total
45 "I cannot tell __"
46 Actress Caldwell
47 __ the dumps (feeling blue)
50 Snails, squids, etc.
55 How things may be rated
57 Singer/composer Laura
58 Collaborating group
59 Lily variety
60 The yoke's on them

61 Sargasso Sea swimmers
62 "All __ Up" (Elvis tune)

DOWN

1 Not so
2 Pizarro victim
3 Roundish
4 Vincent Lopez's theme
5 __ Nevada mountains
6 Jingle writers
7 Writes (down) quickly
8 Imitate
9 Roeper or Ebert
10 Black-tie affair
11 Germ of inspiration
12 Totally confused
13 Art Deco artist
18 Sigourney role in '88
19 Signs up for
23 "We Got the Beat" group
24 Onetime *Masterpiece Theatre* host
25 Tackle-box contents
26 Large deer
27 Massachusetts university
28 Fiery stones
29 Topics for 9 Down
30 Attorney's earnings
31 Emulated Ederle
32 Come to terms
35 A stressful type?
36 Propose, in a way

37 Corp. bigwig
42 *Cheers* star
43 Greg Norman's game
44 Souvenirs of the past
46 Increases sharply
47 __ harm (be innocuous)
48 Figurine mineral
49 Piece of merchandise
50 Grain product
51 Zion National Park site
52 Fly alone
53 Metric weight
54 Lie in the tub
56 *To Kill a Mockingbird* author

12 *RUSH, RUSH, RUSH*

by Eric Albert

ACROSS

1 Kind of point
8 And the like: Abbr.
11 H. Rider Haggard novel
14 It started about 1000 B.C.
15 Company, it's said
16 Singer Ritter
17 Lana Turner film of '66
18 Badge material
19 Modern music
20 Chap
21 Surf, in a way
23 Stupefy
26 Chinese belief
28 Famous Washington
29 Eye-fooling pictures
31 Boorish
33 Take on tenants
34 Eden character
35 It may be extended
37 Corp. bigwigs
38 Ex-TV E.T.
39 Harmonize
43 Keyless
45 Cornhusker city
46 Butter ringer
49 Ignoble
50 Be suitable
51 J.R. Ewing's foe
53 Check
55 Woods locale?
56 Top-blower of '80
58 Baseball's Brock
60 Zsa Zsa's sister
61 Prepare pancakes
62 Doctorow novel
66 Hitchcock's title
67 "__ Gotta Be Me"
68 Plane part
69 Down
70 Take-home
71 Prepared fowl

DOWN

1 Lower the lights
2 Hurler's stat.
3 Seafood order
4 OLD GERMAN SAYING, PART 1
5 __ Cass Elliot
6 Bond, for one
7 Luthor or Barker
8 Sundance's girlfriend
9 King's smaller version
10 African river
11 Lane success
12 Paradise
13 Old pro
21 MIDDLE OF SAYING
22 END OF SAYING
23 Venetian official
24 High point
25 Western name
27 Secret stuff
30 Try out
32 Do a vet's job
36 "Time __ the essence"
40 Hoop star Archibald
41 Smart
42 Aaron's nickname
44 Watch
46 Haunt one's thoughts
47 Baltic republic
48 Est founder Werner
52 Small and spritely
54 *The Exorcist* star
57 Novgorod negative
59 Impolite look
62 "Awesome, dude"
63 1040 folks: Abbr.
64 Curly's brother
65 Complete

13 3 LITTLE WORDS

by Wayne R. Williams

ACROSS

1 Small snake
4 Belief
9 Ore chore
14 Desktop devices: Abbr.
15 Sank, as a putt
16 Church top
17 Willie Mays' nickname
19 Airport lineup
20 Banquet officiator
21 Yucatan's capital
23 Basketball, essentially
25 Paul Whiteman tune of '27
26 Cir. statistic
27 Nav. rank
28 Singer Sumac
31 No, No, Nanette tune
35 Very impressed
36 Rights grp.
37 Quite devout
39 Cause of ruin
40 Dice toss
41 Make a hasty escape
43 Industrious insect
44 RR stop
45 Pasture plaint
46 The __ Experiment (Rimmer novel)
49 Dramatist Rostand
53 Worthy of a medal
54 Artoo __
55 Revere's co-rider
56 Billboard success
60 Vacuous
61 Where the blissful walk
62 Language ending
63 Pyramid builders
64 Singer James et al.
65 Checkers side

DOWN

1 Church areas
2 Untrustworthy one
3 __ out (intimidate)
4 "Ta-ta!"
5 Western Bean
6 Lodge brother
7 "Agnus __"
8 Fifth wheel
9 The Jetsons' dog
10 Seville's setting
11 Event in the news, 6/67
12 Oratorio piece
13 "You bet!"
18 Attentive
22 Printer's measures
24 O.K. Corral visitor
25 Reversed film
29 Waiter's offering
30 Mideast gulf
31 Scarlett locale
32 A soc. sci.
33 Sinatra tune
34 Hollywood Squares inspiration
35 Belly
38 Just the __ (even so)
42 Silent assenters
44 __ Lanka
47 Sports venue
48 American beauties, e.g.
50 The __ Side of Midnight
51 Sort of pollution
52 Overdid the affection
53 Tennis pro Mandlikova
55 Poorly lit
57 Que. neighbor
58 Butter portion
59 Aunt, in Acapulco

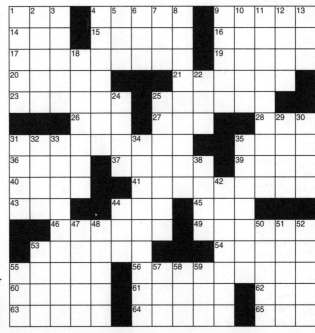

14 NO THYSELF

by Donna J. Stone

ACROSS

1 Fringe benefit
5 Toddler's transport
10 Gripe (about)
14 Mystery writer Rendell
15 Travels by train
16 Forearm bone
17 Actor Sharif
18 START OF A QUIP
20 Enigmatic types
22 "__ dream . . .": King
23 Eshkol's successor
24 Fed
25 PART 2 OF QUIP
28 Order-form word
32 Be superior
33 Oligarchic group
34 GM car
35 Boardwalk structure
36 "Do That to __ More Time" ('79 tune)
37 *Carte*
38 Suffix for form
39 __ *Carats* (Ullmann film)
40 Helicopter part
41 Discipline
43 PART 3 OF QUIP
44 Duck soup
45 Take into account
46 __ alone (solos)
49 Raga musician
53 END OF QUIP
55 How some sit by
56 Knock off
57 Push gently
58 Light filler
59 Heavy weights
60 Nasty look
61 Comic Kaplan

DOWN

1 Old hands
2 Sugar portion
3 The Beehive State
4 Fishing vessel
5 Mrs. Ed Norton
6 Kitchen gadget
7 Lupino and Tarbell
8 Barbie's beau
9 Size up
10 Ninja Turtle, e.g.
11 Norse royal name
12 Green Gables girl
13 Nothing, in Navarre
19 Author Alexander
21 Late singer Carter
24 Sack cloth
25 Animate
26 Send packing
27 Where the buoys are
28 Bartlett bit
29 "__ Kick Out of You"
30 Operatic hero, often
31 "__ telling me!"
33 Novelist Kosinski
36 Humidifies
37 '60s fad
39 Grain implement
40 Perlman of *Cheers*
42 __ *Fables*
43 Not as dry
45 Cabinet part
46 Nitty-gritty
47 In the know about
48 Peter Wimsey's school
49 Marquis de __
50 Brainstorm
51 Mess specialist
52 Actress Daly
54 Flow along

15 SLIPS

by Eric Albert

ACROSS

1 Player
6 Lansbury Broadway role
10 Bushy hairdo
14 Hot stuff
15 Party to
16 Self-admiring
17 SLIP
19 Friend in a fight
20 Orestes' sister
21 Gun-lobby grp.
23 __, lies, and videotape
24 Ball, for one
25 Distinguishing mark
27 Cartoonist Peter
28 As a group
31 Dogpatch creator
34 With polished planes
35 Smelting substance
36 Middle area
39 Brain-wave rdg.
40 *Bounty* crewman
42 Agile
43 Like some protesters
44 ". . . oh where can __?"
47 Not moving
48 Russian inland body of water
52 Mythical beast
54 Patriot descendants' org.
55 Adjective for the Sears Tower
56 Free space
58 SLIP

60 Toning target
61 Fishing fly
62 Monteverdi opera
63 Goat cheese
64 Store-sign abbr.
65 Beasts of burden

DOWN

1 Actress Sharon
2 Santiago's land
3 Forklike
4 Good fellow
5 Mob-scene member
6 Nanki-Poo's father
7 Raggedy one
8 Night light
9 Charm
10 Gardner of *Mogambo*
11 SLIP
12 Raise the dander of
13 Cameo stone
18 Kukla's costar
22 Pitchers?
26 Hood's heater
29 Omen observer
30 Tense
31 Cook book
32 Make __ for it
33 SLIP
34 Debate side
36 Started a pot
37 Within one's tolerance
38 Right-handed, originally

41 ". . . kerchief, and __ my cap"
42 Clouseau portrayer
44 Having headgear
45 Important periods
46 Panama money
49 Vassal's crew
50 Cosmetician Lauder
51 A Musketeer
52 *Carmina Burana* composer
53 Customary function
57 Wharton deg.
59 Museum material

ACROSS

1 Kind of radio
5 Reagan attorney general
10 Gent
14 __ *Richard's Almanack*
15 Also called
16 Playwright David
17 Musical work
18 Gives autographs
19 Scat-singing name
20 According to
21 Wishy-__
22 *60 Minutes* reporter
23 Stand in good __
25 Began to like
27 Bandleader Les or Larry
29 Donald Sutherland's kid
32 Parson __ (Washington biographer)
34 Brought out in the open
36 Egg-yong link
37 Florence's river
38 Shatner's costar
39 Rhine city
40 Taylor or Torn
41 O'Neill's "Emperor"
42 "Semper Fidelis" composer
43 31-game winner in '68
45 Combat zone
47 Optimistic
49 Tears apart
51 Hurry-scurry
53 Meek followers
55 Fall mo.
57 Kick in
58 Bar-mitzvah dances
59 Industrial bigwig
60 Eisenhower's namesakes
61 Not moving
62 Soccer great
63 Make a scene
64 Formative years
65 Hardy boy?

DOWN

1 Each, so to speak
2 Acts apathetic
3 24
4 *The Ghost and __ Muir*
5 Siege site of 73 A.D.
6 Wallach and Whitney
7 24
8 Sony competitor
9 Capital of Somalia?
10 Dream up
11 24
12 Masterly
13 Nectar source
21 Witty ones
22 Lose traction
24 Admiral Zumwalt
26 __-doke
28 London forecast
30 Zillions of years
31 Author Jaffe
32 Open-hearted
33 Leif's pop
35 Climbed
38 "__ but the brave . . ."
39 Blessing
41 Be in harmony
42 Short distance
44 Most relevant
46 Wave heights
48 In unison
50 Parboil
51 "Aquarius" musical
52 Paul the singer
54 Have coming
56 Three-spot
58 Miss' partner
59 Payroll pro: Abbr.

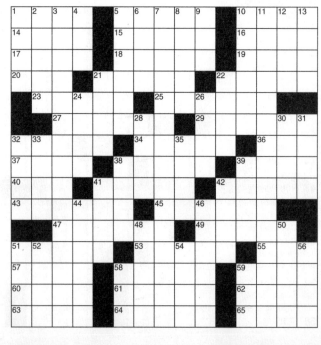

17 CHEF'S SPECIAL

by Eric Albert

ACROSS

1 Super Bowl camera locale
6 Part of a Stein quote
11 Jazz specialty
14 Aviator Markham
15 Shaving accidents
16 Have chits out
17 Administrative charge
19 Cartoonist's staple
20 Missouri mountains
21 Liz role of '63
22 He was caricatured in *The Clouds*
25 Hang together
27 Trudge
28 Bank patron
29 "Me, me!"
30 The ilium
34 Flavor enhancer: Abbr.
37 Cartoon cry
38 Literally, "equator"
39 Discoverer's cry
40 __ Lanka
41 Seasonal worker
42 London area
43 Examines electronically
45 Smell awful
46 Rectangular
48 Candle-wax source
52 Picture of health?
53 Newspaper name
54 Grain holder
55 Banquet VIP
60 Weird
61 City captured by van Gogh
62 Furry Aussie
63 Unseld of basketball
64 Ms. Boop
65 Fortune 500 firm

DOWN

1 Certain ammo
2 Stand for
3 Anger
4 "Goodness gracious!"
5 Shopping center
6 Maestro Previn
7 Takes a chance
8 Folk singer Phil
9 Enjoy Vail
10 Uncommon sense?
11 Whiskey + beer chaser
12 Title holder
13 Indian tea
18 Be a fink
21 Fidel's friend
22 Gets a glimpse of
23 Born first
24 New Zealand territory
25 Nikon rival
26 Out in the open
28 Malt-shop pop
30 Virility personified
31 Cake cover
32 Small dogs
33 Keep out
35 Diaphanous
36 Like newborn colts
44 Affecting innocence
45 1918 World Series winners
46 U-shaped river bend
47 Woman in white
48 Hemmed in
49 Pretentious, in a way
50 Fall veggie
51 Director Edwards
53 Parade command
55 Bill
56 Mine find
57 Put a strain on
58 "Xanadu" rock group, initially
59 Was the manager of

by Wayne R. Williams

ACROSS

1 First name in homespun humor
5 Expensive
9 Hoopster Olajuwon
14 Artery of a sort
15 Exile isle
16 Hal of baseball
17 *Laugh-In* regular
19 Emulate Hamill
20 Elevation standard
21 Working hard
22 Cursor starter?
23 Seditious acts
27 "Mashed Potato Time" singer
31 Model Macpherson
32 __ *Kleine Nachtmusik*
33 Goldfinger's creator
38 Rawls or Reed
39 Diarist Nin
40 Sticky stuff
41 *Same Time, Next Year* star
44 Old-fashioned humor
45 __ carotene
46 Steve Lawrence's partner
49 Dashing young man
53 Actor Wallach
54 Racetrack boundary
55 Franchise holder
60 Vicinities
62 Silents' leading lady
63 Lively dance
64 Get moving
65 Gemini org.
66 Put a stop to
67 Is in the red
68 Author Shirley Ann

DOWN

1 Botches up
2 Memorization method
3 Goya's *The Naked __*
4 Menjou of the movies
5 He was Gilligan
6 Otherwise
7 Like __ from the blue
8 Campaigned (for)
9 Morning hrs.
10 Syndicated deejay
11 Poetic muse
12 Kind of kitchen
13 Bumps into
18 Mrs. Zeus
24 Add polish to
25 Building wings
26 Cakes and __
27 Farmer's locale
28 "Runaround Sue" singer
29 Cold-shoulder
30 Five of a kind
34 Roll-call response
35 Inventor Sikorsky
36 *Cheers* character
37 Vamoosed
39 Dashiell's dog
42 "I'm Just Wild About Harry" composer
43 Fam. member
44 Making money
47 Windshield adornments
48 Highland valley
49 Jam flavor
50 Biblical brother
51 Investor's concern
52 Poke, in a way
56 Frivolous
57 Burn slightly
58 Actress Lanchester
59 Biblical brother
61 Heavy-hearted
62 Good buddy

19 SINGING THE BLUES

by Eric Albert

ACROSS

1 Flying stingers
6 "Hey, you!"
10 Three tsps.
14 Newsboy's cry
15 Hockey great Gordie
16 Jai __
17 Fats Domino tune of '57
19 Nancy of *The Beverly Hillbillies*
20 Garden spots
21 Complain
22 "Pet" complaint
23 Bridge feat
25 Come through
27 Pirate, e.g.
30 Author de Beauvoir
31 Nome home
32 Dyed-in-the-wool
33 Potassium hydroxide solution
36 Steady change
37 Gunning for
39 Mr. Knievel
40 Lawyer's charge
41 Play prize
42 Dickens' __ *House*
43 Accepts, as a credit card
45 Babies do it
46 "Care to dance?"
48 Loud sound
49 Opry greeting
50 Become boring
52 Touch up against
56 Porter's "Well, Did You __!"
57 Dinah Shore tune of '53
59 *Star Wars* role
60 Hairdo for 59 Across
61 Temporary currency
62 Skim along
63 Some NCOs
64 Intrinsically

DOWN

1 Friday's portrayer
2 Wheel shaft
3 Poker variety
4 Sportscaster's place
5 Snead of golf
6 __ Penh
7 Scotch partner
8 Lovely leap
9 Mystery writer Josephine
10 Hoodwink
11 Bobby Vinton tune of '63
12 Soothing substance
13 One who must be paid
18 Barbra's *Funny Girl* costar
22 Walk heavily
24 Count Tolstoy
26 Kuwait's ruler
27 Jazz phrase
28 Sly look
29 Bing Crosby tune of '37
30 Gratifies completely
34 Slangy assent
35 Actress Sommer
37 Take __ (acknowledge applause)
38 Hydrant
39 High style
41 __ the Lonely ('91 film)
42 Pa Cartwright
44 Passé
45 Baby-powder ingredient
46 Book holder
47 Humble home
48 Smile upon
51 Charley had one
53 Roseanne Arnold, nee __
54 *Exodus* author
55 Use a keyboard
57 Airgun ammo
58 Nile slitherer

20 THROUGH THE YEAR

by Trip Payne

ACROSS

1 Roman moralist
5 *Kon-Tiki* material
10 Breakfast-in-bed prop
14 *Hawaii Five-0* star
15 Out of this world
16 Where "you are"
17 Oklahoma town
18 Air sprays
19 Stuffs one's gut
20 MARCH
23 Kimono sash
24 Zilch
25 Pueblo material
28 High __ kite
31 Doll's word
34 Family member
35 Sudden raid
38 Squash potatoes
40 MAY
43 Lamb's pseudonym
44 Sullivan's student
45 Taunter's cry
46 Splinter group
48 Billy __ Williams
49 Televised
51 Bested in the ring
53 Actress Jillian
54 AUGUST
62 Bee, to Opie
63 Had a show of hands
64 Forearm bone
65 Calf-length
66 Dancing Castle
67 Service-club member
68 Pour __ (exert oneself)
69 Fernando of films
70 Diminished by

DOWN

1 Mr. Kadiddlehopper
2 Top-rated
3 Where sines are assigned
4 *Goldfinger* heavy
5 Thumper's playmate
6 Tell __ (falsify)
7 Letter to Santa
8 Clockmaker Thomas
9 Williams of *Happy Days*
10 "Cradle of Texas Liberty"
11 Twenty quires
12 Avant-garde
13 Sportscaster's exclamation
21 Overly large
22 Canyon edge
25 Arthur of tennis
26 Microwave features
27 Actor Davis
28 Ready to fight
29 Subway entrance
30 Pew separator
32 Medieval estate
33 __ crow flies
36 Mork's home
37 Compass dir.
39 Oregon peak
41 Give up
42 Rafsanjani, e.g.
47 Nursery-schooler
50 Completely
52 Prepare eggs, in a way
53 Vicunas' home
54 Call it a day
55 Counteract
56 Copperfield's wife
57 Agenda part
58 Actress Rowlands
59 Netman Nastase
60 Genesis character
61 Rather and Rowan
62 "__ my brother's keeper?"

21 WRITE ON!

by Cynthia Lyon

ACROSS

1 On vacation
4 Back talk
8 Emulate Brian Boitano
13 *South Pacific* role
15 Twice cuatro
16 Courteous
17 START OF A QUIP
19 Writer Cleveland
20 Have no reason to
21 Old hag
22 City on Pearl Harbor's shore
24 Blueprint
25 PART 2 OF QUIP
30 One from Mars
31 What we share
32 Pack away
34 Predetermine the outcome
35 "Enough!", to Enrique
36 Lead to a seat, jocularly
37 Memorized
39 The same
40 Explorer Polo
42 PART 3 OF QUIP
45 Past due
46 Bit of business
47 Cheddarlike cheese
49 Ms. Bloomer
53 Structural
54 END OF QUIP
57 Sun-dried brick
58 Sea shade

59 Auctioneer's cry
60 Hart and Collins
61 Transmit
62 Aye canceler

DOWN

1 Lena of *Havana*
2 Drum partner
3 Actress Alice
4 Tone down
5 Expert
6 Yon maiden
7 Scale member
8 Egyptian amulet
9 What obis accessorize
10 The Bard's river
11 Ersatz swing
12 Ron of TV's *Tarzan*

14 "The will to do, the soul __": Scott
18 Norma Rae's concern
21 Elegance
23 "An oldie, but __"
24 Cheops' edifice
25 David's weapon
26 Princeton mascot
27 Film director Sidney
28 Automotive one-eighty
29 Puccini opera
30 Genesis craft
33 Personal question?
35 Swell

38 Midsize kangaroo
40 Orange Bowl home
41 Shoelace tips
43 Aesop's repertoire
44 In chairs
47 Musical postscript
48 Bloodhound's trail
50 Admired celebrity
51 Kansas city
52 Mayberry sheriff
53 Periodical, for short
54 Home of *Sesame Street*
55 Robin Hood's quaff
56 Baseball score

22 TRADE NAMES

by Wayne R. Williams

ACROSS

1 Wild guesses
6 Run for health
9 Hebrew scroll
14 Classic Gene Tierney film
15 Oklahoma city
16 Wear down
17 Messed up
18 Veteran baseball broadcaster
20 Overacts
22 "My __ Sal"
23 Scalp line
24 Pâté base
27 Doorway side
31 Strikebreaker
32 Contemporary soul singer
34 Prefix for violet
36 __ acids
37 Tenon's complement
40 Waits on
42 Olympics star Zatopek et al.
43 Zurich folk
44 "Night and Day" composer
47 Greek-salad ingredient
51 Farmer, frequently
52 VCR button
53 MacGraw and Baba
54 Shriner's headgear
55 Mother Goose couple
57 Dudley Moore's ex-partner
63 More than enough
64 Martini garnish
65 *Norma __*
66 Some responses
67 Game-show host
68 Hog's home
69 Lock of hair

DOWN

1 Nods off
2 Landing strip
3 Arctic lights
4 Dodgers' #1 hitter in '91
5 Marquis de __
6 Jam holder
7 Poetic piece
8 Handy tool
9 Blue shade
10 Bobby of hockey
11 Stick up
12 Citrus drink
13 __ *Alibi* (Selleck film)
19 Silents vamp
21 Chair parts
25 Regarding
26 By way of
27 Founder of CORE
28 Related (to)
29 Patch up
30 Partnership abbr.
33 Dugout stack
35 Speak like Daffy Duck
37 Engineering branch: Abbr.
38 Melville novel
39 Make angry
40 Overwhelms
41 Road rollers
43 Three before V
45 Cartel in the news
46 Barbershop needs
48 Slip by
49 Auto documents
50 Weigh, in a way
54 At large
56 Mtge. installment
57 "Ulalume" writer
58 "Nightmare" street
59 __ *Tac Dough*
60 Actress Arden
61 Cereal grain
62 Anthem author

by Eric Albert

ACROSS

1 Chili con __
6 Do fingerpainting
10 Make a complaint
14 Liner's "highway"
15 __ facto
16 Singer Fitzgerald
17 Disposes of?
19 *Green Card* director
20 Seeing that
21 What's black and white and Red all over?
23 Falls behind
24 Velvet Underground singer
25 Main road
28 Soup holder
29 Nevada resort
30 Existentialist author
31 In favor of
34 Chance to play
35 Wears a long face
36 Lose energy
37 Pub drink
38 Apartment sign
39 Ground-breaking
40 Paper boss
42 Just
43 Stop-sign shape
45 "The Rape of the Lock" writer
46 Kindergarten book
47 California city
51 Secretary for a day
52 Ecstatic?
54 Fencing need
55 *Dies* __
56 Medium-sized band
57 Laura of *Rambling Rose*
58 Some shortening
59 Deteriorate

DOWN

1 Musical conclusion
2 Old pros
3 Movie division
4 Layered pastry
5 Trap
6 Aria artists
7 *Planet of the* __
8 Halsey's org.
9 Turkish strait
10 Yard-sign start
11 CB radio response?
12 Slur over a syllable
13 Electrical unit
18 Like meringue
22 Bewails
24 Director Sidney
25 "__ girl!"
26 Julia of *The Addams Family*
27 Unfaithful sort?
28 Come to a point
30 List introducer
32 Moundsman Hershiser
33 Bank (on)
35 Service-station supply
36 *Carmen* character
38 Buster Brown's dog
39 Fourth largest planet
41 Make moist
42 Stereo ancestor
43 Made a selection
44 Parisian pancake
45 Went white
47 Lasting impression
48 __ cost (gratis)
49 Pine for
50 Part of A.M.
53 Gun grp.

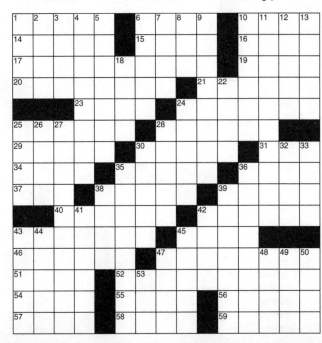

by Matt Gaffney

ACROSS

1 Golf Hall-of-Famer
6 Fortune-teller
12 *Cats* or *King Kong*
13 Bound by affection
15 Spike Lee film of '89
17 "That's amazing!"
18 Top or train
19 B-F link
20 __-Sheikh (former pro footballer)
24 Smart portrayer
26 Life milestones
30 Admits freely, with "up"
31 Hispanic American
32 Wipe clean
34 Arm
37 __ the test (tries out)
43 Air pair
45 Macbeth was one
46 Lacking power
47 Famous Alley
48 Coffee brewer
50 Wash. neighbor
51 Beatles #1 tune of '66
58 Midwestern college town
59 Dine at home
60 December birthstone
61 Make into law

DOWN

1 Police informer
2 Ding-a-lings
3 Ordinal ending
4 Malt beverage
5 Article written by Kant
6 Baseball great Mel
7 Hamelin menace
8 Otto's "Oh!"
9 Jim Belushi's hometown
10 __ a Tenor
11 Beats barely
13 In the past
14 Your ancestor?
15 Tower over
16 "You can do __ you try"
21 Bucks, for instance
22 Enzyme ending
23 Biblical prophet
24 "Just __ suspected!"
25 Actor Dailey
27 Backup strategy
28 __ in "apple"
29 Crush, in a way
33 Go to pieces
34 Candy covering
35 "*Ich bin __* Berliner"
36 Historical period
38 Tony-winner Hagen
39 Useful article
40 Language group
41 Dentyne rival
42 Mr. Hammerstein
43 Amnesiac's question
44 Out-and-out
45 Leon Uris novel
48 Detroit-based org.
49 Victor's partner
52 Computer-keyboard key
53 Carnival locale
54 __ vivant
55 Minuscule
56 Made a getaway
57 "Make __ double!"

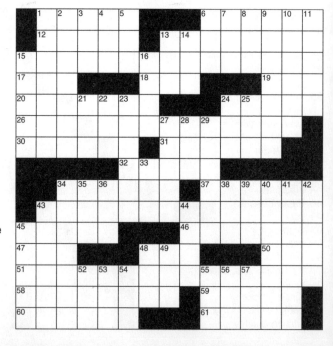

25 PSHAW!

by Mel Rosen

ACROSS

1 Send by truck
5 *Oklahoma!* aunt
10 "Cry __ River"
13 Behan's land
14 "Tough!"
15 Spade's namesakes
16 From a distance
17 Physics branch
19 The little things
21 Nobel's homeland
22 Merchandise
25 Church areas
26 Flock of fish
30 *Mermaids* star
32 Praises highly
33 Literary alias
38 Peace Prize city
39 Irrigate
40 Street performer
41 Northern grouse
43 Mohammed's birthplace
44 Word of regret
45 Kind of descendant
46 Comes out for
50 Hose material
52 Northern hemispheres?
54 Eccentric character
59 Former *Candid Camera* cohost
62 Mixed bag
63 Inventive: Abbr.
64 Brunch choice

65 *Close Encounters* crafts
66 Former Mideast nation: Abbr.
67 Lent a hand
68 Catches some rays

DOWN

1 Clothes line?
2 Old sound system
3 Turkey neighbor
4 Lima's land
5 Observation
6 Astronomical adjective
7 Actor Marvin
8 Ostrich look-alike
9 Dream phenomena: Abbr.

10 Damsels
11 Game-show host
12 NBA and NCAA
15 Short distance
18 Trophy, at times
20 "Terrible" age
23 Rapturous delight
24 Martin of movies
26 Feed the pigs
27 Playbill listing
28 Luau act
29 Bakery enticement
31 Common Mkt. locale
33 Irreligious
34 Seer's signal
35 Good-natured
36 Fitness club
37 Ground grain

39 Wheaton of *Star Trek: The Next Generation*
42 Lodge member
43 Take exception to
45 Kept safe
46 Old-time theater name
47 Athens civic center
48 __ *de Lune*
49 King follower
51 Jeweler's need
53 Humane org.
55 Main event, for one
56 __ Romeo
57 Columbia athlete
58 At a __ for words
60 Work wk. end
61 Showed the way

FILM HAND

by Wayne R. Williams

ACROSS

1 Sharp punch
4 Play the guitar
9 Biblical king
14 *The Name of the Rose* author
15 Lasso
16 Castle or Cara
17 With "*The,*" Heston classic
20 __ Aviv
21 Small bottle
22 Go one better
23 Cruelty, and then some
26 Actress Irving
27 Verse starter?
28 Reynolds film of '83
31 War god
32 Mystery writer Josephine
33 Water pitcher
34 Leather type
35 Laughlin film of '71
38 Store group
41 Ambience
42 Just released
45 Actor Julia
46 Elvis film of '58
49 UFO pilots
50 DC official
51 Something whispered
52 Do something
53 Fiery offense
56 Outer edge
57 Bogart/Hepburn classic
62 Spooky
63 Tour of duty
64 Antelope relative
65 Winding devices
66 Charlie Chan portrayer
67 ABA member

DOWN

1 Black shade
2 Clear plastic
3 Arid
4 Box-office abbr.
5 Cratchit kid
6 Freeway access
7 Present-day Deseret
8 Overzealous one
9 In an indistinct manner
10 "All the Things You __"
11 Business deal
12 Chanted
13 Can't stand
18 Muse of history
19 Myra Hess' title
23 Air France flier, once
24 Goose group
25 Cry like a baby
29 Fam. member
30 Indo-European
31 Razor-billed bird
34 Sudden alarm
35 Puppeteer Baird
36 Moonshine holder
37 Circle sections
38 Brings into being
39 Little axe
40 Forbidding
42 Former leader of Panama
43 Mercury, but not Venus
44 Drenched
46 *From Here to Eternity* actress
47 Be unyielding
48 Brown shade
50 Bank boxes
54 Numerical prefix
55 Tooth partner
58 Prepare to fire
59 Vane dir.
60 Acctg. period
61 Brazil, e.g.

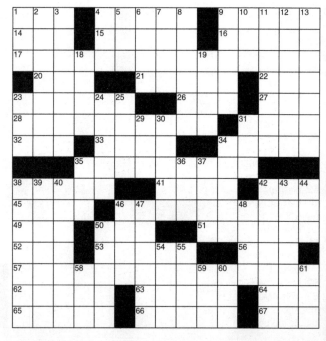

27 SUCCESS DISTRESS

by Donna J. Stone

ACROSS

1 Doorframe part
5 Blind as __
9 Guitarist from Spain
14 *Dies* __ (Latin hymn)
15 Between-meal bite
16 Aficionado
17 Bête noire
18 19-nation grp.
19 Dress style
20 START OF A QUOTE
23 Asleep at the switch
24 Mule's father
25 Lama land
28 Attention-getter
30 Mass expression
34 Airline to Tokyo
35 H.S. jrs.' exam
37 Nome native
39 END OF QUOTE
42 Mechanic's concern
43 Interoffice note
44 Bristol brew
45 Observed
46 Take five
48 __ up (got smart)
50 Wine word
51 Bear lair
52 SPEAKER OF QUOTE
59 Johnson of *Brief Encounter*
60 Well-ventilated
61 "Puttin' on the __"
63 Peel it and weep
64 Sacred cow
65 Buffalo's water
66 Miniskirt Mary
67 "The __ of the Ancient Mariner"
68 Laura of *Mask*

DOWN

1 Mainsail's neighbor
2 King Fahd, e.g.
3 Countless
4 Private Bailey
5 Edifice add-on
6 Gravy holder
7 __ spumante
8 Doubting disciple
9 Crow's toes
10 Trevino's target
11 Tel __
12 Actor Auberjonois
13 Vein contents
21 Old-fashioned sticker
22 Put on a pedestal
25 Subdues Simba
26 Cockamamie
27 Scout's honor
28 Lassie's offering
29 Sunflower supports
30 Rap-sheet abbr.
31 He had a gilt complex
32 Monsieur Zola
33 Big-name
36 Audiophile's equipment
38 April occurrence
40 Wagner's one
41 Dachshund doc
47 Napoleon's cousin
49 Instinctive
50 Barely enough
51 Holmes' creator
52 Course listing
53 *Inter* __ (among other things: Lat.)
54 Pride papa
55 Skirt length
56 *One __ the Heart* (Coppola film)
57 Green land
58 Swizzle
59 *Vin* partner
62 Buddhist sect

28 REPEATERS

by Wayne R. Williams

ACROSS

1 Track circuit
4 Kind of energy
9 Sounded sheepish
14 __ Miss (southern school)
15 Came up
16 Dropped the ball
17 Thorough-going
19 Brings under control
20 Show the pearly whites
21 Giraffe's cousin
23 Joins up
25 Suffix for form
26 Santa __, CA
28 Conks out
29 Kind of combat
33 Lofty poem
34 Soprano Marilyn
35 Mil. address
38 Cheer of a sort
41 Tillis or Tormé
42 Asian capital
44 Genetic letters
45 Gradually
48 Boorish one
52 Short distance
53 __-jongg
54 Provoke passion
56 Fireballer Ryan
58 Spoke and spoke
59 Yonder folks
61 Ruthless competition
65 Bowling alleys
66 April-like
67 Recipe phrase
68 Kasparov's game
69 Van Gogh locale
70 Choice: Abbr.

DOWN

1 Set free
2 Homecoming guests
3 Women's clothing size
4 More rational
5 California fort
6 Old card game
7 Tempe sch.
8 Passed gossip
9 VHS alternative
10 Plains tribe
11 Like strolling lovers
12 Shoebox letters
13 Shingle letters
18 Pub preferences
22 Krazy __
24 Chase away
25 Bring to light
27 __ of Cleves
30 Nav. rank
31 Taunter's cry
32 Penna. neighbor
35 Contented comments
36 Woodland way
37 Basketball variety
38 Strait place: Abbr.
39 SSW opposite
40 Open-mouthed stare
43 Runs against
46 Singer Sumac
47 Dee or O'Connor
48 Ella's style
49 Evans and Blair
50 *My Favorite Year* star
51 Asia's Bay of __
55 They see right through you
57 Not so much
59 RN's specialty
60 Doubter's exclamation
62 Rowing-team member
63 Gerard or Hodges
64 Chemical ending

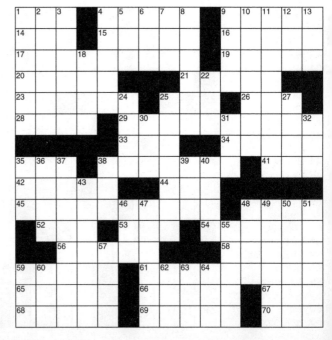

29 ALL AT SEA

by Karen Hodge

ACROSS

1 Do a slow burn
5 Throat-clearing sound
9 Wool-coat owners
13 Hamilton Burger's nemesis
15 Church area
16 Fe, to a chemist
17 Modern prefix
18 Country singer Campbell
19 Utah resort
20 Scottish sailboat?
23 Contemptible sort
24 Quick to learn
25 Chanel's nickname
28 Get ready for dinner
31 Board's partner
34 Garden shrub
36 *Atlantis* org.
38 LaSalle or DeSoto
40 Why ritzy ships are made?
43 Compass dir.
44 "I cannot tell __"
45 __ as the driven snow
46 National League division
48 Something boring
50 Miner's treasures
51 Spherical veggie
53 Hawk
55 Female barge crews?
62 Pavarotti piece
63 Crowd noise
64 Looks leeringly at
66 Breathe hard
67 Bible book
68 Nero's instrument
69 Ultimate objectives
70 Refuse to acknowledge
71 Rag-doll name

DOWN

1 Dallas sch.
2 Powder ingredient
3 Are, to Pilar
4 Timber defect
5 Ms. Lansbury
6 *Let's Make a Deal* host
7 Mr. Knievel
8 The brainy bunch
9 Theater district
10 Guthrie the younger
11 Marquand's sleuth
12 Cereal sound
14 Back of the neck
21 Lament
22 Uses an aerosol
25 Beer purchase
26 Layer in the news
27 __ cropper (failed)
29 Curl the lip
30 "Bali __"
32 Take place
33 Skier Phil
35 Lifts one's spirits
37 Impresario, e.g.
39 Hwys.
41 Clown around
42 Literary justification
47 Sounds of impact
49 Off the track
52 Landed, as gentry
54 Stunt-plane maneuver
55 Appear stunned
56 OPEC member
57 Orange cover
58 Seep slowly
59 Raise a red flag
60 Look ahead
61 Mail out
65 Sauce source

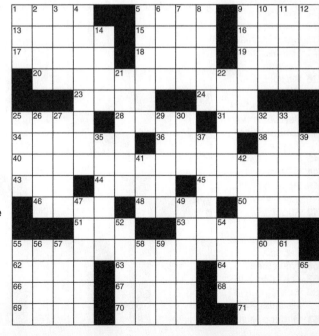

30 COST OF LEAVING

by Eric Albert

ACROSS

1 Temporary currency
6 Lose control
11 Sharp turn
14 Came to power
15 The Jetsons' dog
16 Whitney patriarch
17 START OF A QUIP
19 Ms. Ullmann
20 Fragrant legume
21 Big family
23 Marvin of movies
24 Popular cordial
26 Business patterns
30 Indiana's state flower
31 "Very funny!"
32 Pioneer impressionist
33 Frontiersman Carson
36 MIDDLE OF QUIP
40 Get-up-and-go
41 Ben on *Bonanza*
42 Laundry loss, maybe
43 Fairway flaw
44 Hate heartily
46 Traveling group
49 About 907 kilograms
50 Where you live
51 Supported
56 Wild spree
57 END OF QUIP
60 Take advantage of
61 Girder of a sort
62 Flight part
63 Badminton need
64 *Tootsie* star
65 Expedition

DOWN

1 Fresh talk
2 Cornfield preyer
3 Tiber town
4 "It's clear now!"
5 Grinder
6 Check getter
7 Nonspeaking part in *The Thin Man*
8 Advanced degree?
9 Annuity alternative
10 Gain affection for
11 Allen film of '83
12 Suspect's out
13 Basic assumption
18 Tarzan's neighbors
22 *The Bridge of San Luis __*
24 Touch, for one
25 Leopold's colleague
26 Bloke
27 Ivy League school
28 Block part
29 Run for it
30 Main idea
32 Comic Cohen
33 Running bowline, e.g.
34 Restless desire
35 Toddler
37 Pesto ingredient
38 PBS science show
39 NATO member
43 Dear old one?
44 Weaver's machine
45 Headlong dash
46 Cooking style
47 Humiliate
48 Well-known synonymist
49 Musical motif
51 Kind of carpet
52 Kett of the comics
53 "Buenos __"
54 Troop group
55 Combustible heap
58 Mavericks' org.
59 Hamilton's bill

31 SUCCESSES

by Randolph Ross

ACROSS

1 With suspicion
8 Placing in combat
15 Precarious perch
16 Tuscany, long ago
17 Was successful, in the ring?
19 Begley, Jr. and Sr.
20 Chemistry Nobelist Harold
21 Service charge
22 __ Sea
25 Here: Fr.
26 To-do
27 Was successful, like a pelican?
32 Cable TV's Emmy
33 Civil War shade
34 __ way (sort of)
35 Public platforms
37 Shop machine
41 NBA arbiter
42 Civil unrest
44 Beauty preceder
45 Was successful, at the deli?
48 Circular word
50 Memorable time
51 Kimono accessories
52 Onetime United rival
53 Pérez de Cuéllar's home
55 High-tech banking serv.
57 Was successful, in the air?

63 Treeless region
64 Black eyes
65 Sonnet parts
66 Offers up

DOWN

1 "Eureka!"
2 Charles, to Philip
3 Ship's mph
4 Too
5 Yearn for
6 Train components
7 Hot time in Le Havre
8 *Dick Van Dyke Show* family
9 Spillane's __ *Jury*
10 Low card
11 Oleo holder
12 Easily angered

13 McKinley's hometown
14 Stiff winds
18 Luxembourg, e.g.
22 Worshipper's place?
23 Puerto __
24 Tavern brews
25 "Give __ rest!"
26 Flying standard
28 Leggy bird
29 Working manuscript
30 Once-popular theater name
31 Monogram parts: Abbr.
36 Loyal
38 Swedish auto
39 Culture starter
40 Joins together
42 Second showing

43 "__ Yankee Doodle Dandy"
45 Ms. Barton et al.
46 Day savers
47 Comes __ (is recalled)
48 Assembly instructions
49 In the know
53 Louis XVI, to Louis XVII
54 Polish prose
55 Arthur of tennis
56 Bed size
58 Coll. hoops contest
59 Superlative suffix
60 Society-page word
61 Cur's comment
62 Draft org.

BIRTHDAY BOY

by Mel Rosen

ACROSS

1 Word often mispunctuated
4 Cars for hire
8 Carrot-family spice
13 Big party
15 State openly
16 Sound off
17 Earth sci.
18 Sandwich shop
19 Basic measurements
20 Cult series starring 40 Across
23 "I should say __!"
24 *2001* computer
25 It may be common
27 Likely to be bought
31 Musical combo
35 Greek letter
36 Cotton bundles
39 Do roadwork
40 Actor born March 19, 1928
44 *Aida* piece
45 Reaches new heights
46 Top ranking
47 Doorframe topper
50 Most intimidating
52 Hogan rival
55 Supplement, with "out"
56 Woody's frequent 1980s costar
59 Spy series starring 40 Across
64 Computer-data format

66 It gets high twice a day
67 Cheese choice
68 David's weapon
69 At any time
70 Résumé, for short
71 Family auto
72 Home rooms
73 Heavy weight

DOWN

1 "__ a Kick Out of You"
2 Dash dial
3 Gin flavoring
4 Michigan city
5 Rosary prayers
6 Heavy knives
7 Boars and sows

8 Salad, for one
9 Coffeemaker
10 Most important
11 "Tell __ the judge!"
12 Cozy home
14 __ Centauri
21 Temple leader
22 Printing measures
26 Montreal pro
27 Calyx part
28 Nintendo forerunner
29 Cicero's language
30 Lodge members
32 Resort lake
33 Linda or Dale
34 Article of faith
37 Comic Philips
38 Con game

41 Hamelin pests
42 Receptionists, e.g.
43 Japanese metropolis
48 Annapolis graduate
49 Singer Brenda
51 Israeli desert
53 Played a scene
54 Transmission gear
56 It abuts Vt.
57 Land in the ocean?
58 Low-pH stuff
60 Genesis setting
61 Splice film
62 U.S. alliance
63 Fed. agent
65 Once __ blue moon

33 NO CHANGE

by Cynthia Lyon

ACROSS

1 Comic Conway
4 In need of caulking
9 Kennel cries
13 Indivisible
14 *L.A. Law* role
15 Peter, in Panama
16 Bookkeeper: Abbr.
17 Poison
18 Delight in
19 START OF A FRAN LEBOWITZ QUOTE
22 Job tyro
23 Conditional conjunction
27 Mid.
28 La __ Tar Pits
30 Navigational aid
31 Malt-shop order
34 PART 2 OF QUOTE
37 Lummoxes
39 Rock singer Rose
40 Terry or Burstyn
41 PART 3 OF QUOTE
44 Western wear
45 Pinocchio's undoing
46 Within arm's reach
47 Pierre's pal
49 Chicken
51 Tart in tone
55 END OF QUOTE
58 Trembling
61 Ring championship

62 Dixie st.
63 Stephanie Zimbalist's dad
64 Ibsen's __'s *House*
65 Weightlifting units: Abbr.
66 They're often connected
67 Mead need
68 Loos' Lorelei

DOWN

1 Hoist glasses
2 Bring upon oneself
3 Tourist magnet
4 Hidden
5 Pencil-box contents
6 Ouzo flavoring
7 Well-meaning
8 Himalayan hulk
9 Barbra role
10 N. modifier
11 Paid player
12 Oil source
15 Alias of a sort
20 Noisy bug
21 Where you may see a second helping
24 *South Pacific* character
25 Is frugal
26 Exhausted
28 Popular pooch
29 Rub the wrong way
31 Fishlike
32 Kukla's colleague

33 Wooden peg
35 Sunblock substance
36 __ *Madigan* ('67 film)
38 Like word
42 Does darning
43 Balloon basket
48 Just
50 Personal preferences
51 River of rhyme
52 Cagers' game, for short
53 "__ darned!"
54 Put an end to
56 Logan's locale
57 Rover's playmate
58 Proof letters
59 E.T.'s craft
60 Museum material

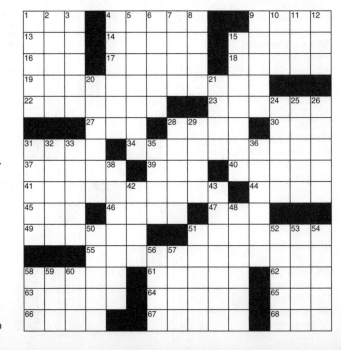

34 GOING METRIC

by Fred Piscop

ACROSS

1 As such
6 Dog-paddled
10 Farm cribs
14 "Hi" or "bye"
15 Rock group Motley __
16 Mary Kay rival
17 Raw __ (crayon color)
18 Auto part
19 *Rikki-Tikki-__*
20 Getting beat
22 Eighth, e.g.
24 A few Z's
25 Metric dessert?
28 Discipline
31 Soprano __ Gluck
32 Boathouse gear
33 Rickenbacker was one
35 "There is many __ twixt . . ."
39 Metric working hours?
44 Alley "oops"
45 Did lunch
46 __ de cologne
47 Moby Dick's foe
50 Dry wine
53 Items at a metric haberdashery?
57 "Am I a man __ mouse?"
58 Native Canadian
59 Droopy-eared dog
63 Engine enclosures
65 Molecule component
67 Type of heating
68 Yemen seaport
69 "Would __ to you?"
70 "Time in a Bottle" singer
71 Nothing
72 Late singer Carter
73 "Casey __ Bat"

DOWN

1 Peter __ Rubens
2 *Blondie* kid
3 Holds up
4 Arab rulers
5 Make money the old-fashioned way
6 Univ. or acad.
7 Off by a mile
8 Arctic sight
9 Intellectual
10 Cave dweller
11 Donald Trump's ex
12 CNN host
13 Take potshots
21 Look in your eye
23 Samms and Lazarus
26 Some time ago
27 Bread or cabbage
28 Gear teeth
29 Lamp part
30 Asian sea
34 Hellenic H
36 Claim against property
37 "__ first you . . ."
38 Tobacco-chewer's sound
40 Tiny container
41 Set of values
42 Use acid, maybe
43 Recovery regimen, for short
48 *Strangers on __*
49 Common bug
51 Mississippi River source
52 Classify
53 Mercury model
54 Wear away
55 *Unsafe at Any Speed* author
56 Apply more lubricant
60 Job opening
61 Price-list word
62 Locust or lime
64 __-Cone (cool treat)
66 Gibson of *Lethal Weapon*

ACROSS

1 *Love __ the Ruins*
6 Gandhi's bane
14 Richards of tennis
15 Pirate-ship post
16 American Leaguer
18 Alts.
19 Transparent gemstone
20 Choice word
21 Arizona State city
22 Army outposts
23 Game judge
26 Inventor Sikorsky
28 Russian river
29 Gymnast Comaneci
31 Supplement, with "out"
34 Turner Field, since 1997
38 Sturgeon-to-be
39 Anatomical pouch
40 "Read 'em and __!"
41 Thin and strong
42 Swell, to Eliza
45 Spongelike cakes
48 __ Peak
49 Piece of steelwork
50 Orthopedist's adjective
52 Dallas sch.
55 NFLer
58 Ups the ante
59 Aaron Copland work

60 Bestowed lavishly
61 *Golden Boy* writer

DOWN

1 Paris landmark
2 Lose solidity
3 Some change
4 Cal. neighbor
5 Old coot
6 Ball's sidekick
7 __-European
8 Getting __ years
9 Mr. Chaney
10 Make beloved
11 Simon and Diamond
12 Break off
13 Fish-eating birds

15 Bob Vila's field
17 Ade flavoring
21 Type starter
22 Big pig
23 German valley
24 Switch suffix
25 Series set at a high school
26 High-minded folks
27 Strait loc.
30 Contented sounds
31 At all times
32 Howard of *Dallas*
33 Catch sight of
35 Sapporo sashes
36 Beethoven's "__ Elise"

37 Leaves openmouthed
41 European capital
43 Give the go-ahead
44 Zipper's descendant
45 Health-spa gear
46 Embarrass
47 Where *el dinero* is
48 Was nosy
50 Old-time autocrat
51 Entr'__
52 Join (with)
53 Have a session
54 Sky sightings
56 Stout alternative
57 Coal carrier

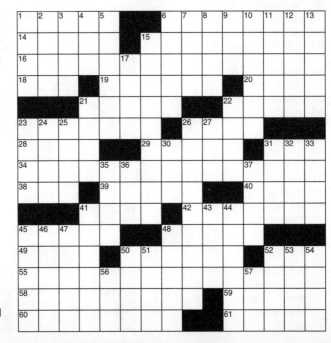

36 HIDDEN ISLANDS

by Wayne R. Williams

ACROSS

1 Nutmeglike spice
5 Rodeo rope
10 Highlander
14 Book after Joel
15 Cast member
16 Race driver Yarborough
17 Fast season
18 Aquanaut hides Caribbean island
20 Ancient Peruvians
22 Stalk topper
23 AAA suggestion
24 Invitees
26 Musical group hides Mediterranean island
29 Ten to one, e.g.
33 Auction unit
34 __ Blair (Orwell)
35 Sharon's nation
37 Supped
38 Musician hides New York island
40 *Little Women* monogram
41 Golf-ball material
43 Novelist Ferber
44 "The Boy King"
45 Roy Rogers' real last name
46 Eastern seaport hides Indonesian island

48 Made over
51 Turned tail
52 Cried out excitedly
55 Greek letter
58 Medicine growers hide Indonesian island
62 Put to sea
63 Dextrous starter
64 Comb, in a way
65 Regarding
66 Catchall cat.
67 Quaking tree
68 Self-images

DOWN

1 Landlocked African nation
2 Prayer conclusion
3 Actually hides Mediterranean island
4 Ritzy home
5 __ Palmas
6 IRA, e.g.
7 R-V hookup?
8 Expressed sorrow
9 Talking tests
10 Use cutters
11 Cleveland team, to fans
12 Spread in a tub
13 Period in office
19 Morse symbol
21 Make a choice
24 Writer Sheehy
25 Sullied
26 Granite blocks
27 Across-the-board
28 La __ Tar Pits

30 Western outlaws hide Pacific islands
31 Hold back
32 Board of education?
35 Doesn't exist
36 Way up
39 Do nothing
42 Type of dancing
46 Letter parts
47 Ann Sothern film role
49 Ecology org.
50 Actress Burke
52 "POW!"
53 Fractional prefix
54 Spheres
56 Spanish painter
57 Pub servings
59 Maple product
60 Mao __-tung
61 Sun Yat-__

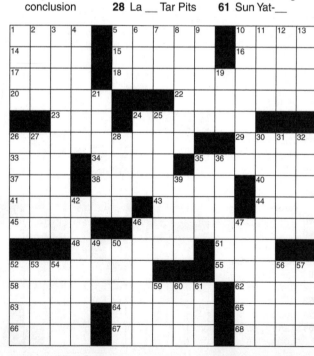

37 THE WORD FOR TODAY

by Mel Rosen

ACROSS

1 Mornings: Abbr.
4 Mr. Marner
9 Copes with
14 Once around
15 "Once upon __ ..."
16 Psi follower
17 Improve, as wine
18 Lead astray
20 Flash's foe
22 Soup ingredient
23 Mao __-tung
24 Creatures of the deep
26 "__ I say ..."
27 Diamond home
29 Stock-market participant
34 Funny Charlotte
37 Battery terminal
39 Bring together
40 Western gullies
42 Bridge boo-boo
44 Hagar's pooch
45 Wesson's partner
47 Stallone's nickname
48 Lofty area
50 "__ the bag!"
52 Actor Holliman
54 "20 Questions" category
58 Cagney costar Clarke
61 Sidekick
63 Lounge around
64 April 1st
67 Pie ingredient
68 *Arroz* partner
69 *Les __-Unis*
70 S.A. country
71 Great buy
72 Country bumpkin
73 Get a load of

DOWN

1 You must remember this
2 Penn and Teller's specialty
3 Went through
4 *Cheers* role
5 *Napoli* native
6 Such as
7 Modified
8 "From __ shining ..."
9 Rick Nelson tune of '63
10 Latin I verb
11 Boston hoopster
12 Hollywood giants?
13 Out of harm's way
19 Imported auto
21 Political initials
25 Act zany
28 Play horseshoes
30 The Beatles' "__ I Love Her"
31 Cutting tools
32 List-shortening abbr.
33 Be certain of
34 Hasty
35 "Rule Britannia" composer
36 "... __ saw Elba"
38 Send forth
41 Special-interest grp.
43 "See you then!"
46 "And __ go before I sleep"
49 Poi source
51 Zilch
53 *The Life of __*
55 Half a '60s singing group
56 Sky blue
57 Narrow shelf
58 Prospectors' drawings
59 "Little Things Mean __"
60 *Glamour* rival
62 Bismarck's loc.
65 Ga. neighbor
66 Fashion monogram

38 SERIES BUSINESS

by Trip Payne

ACROSS

1 Arkbound son
5 Scrub the launch
10 32-card game
14 Cocoon contents
15 No social butterfly
16 *Clair de* __
17 Wallach and Whitney
18 Gladiators' spot
19 It may be pumped
20 Series start
23 Massage needs
24 Thin streak
25 Challenge the polygraph
26 Game-show worker
28 Gift-tag word
29 Banana oil, e.g.
31 Part of TGIF
32 "It's __ for Me to Say"
33 Actor O'Brien
34 Series start
41 Rock singer __ Rose
42 Apt. units
43 &
44 Is without
47 Lots of energy
48 Made pay
50 Author Levin
51 Court order?
53 Outer limit
54 Series start
59 Slightly
60 Computer-screen symbols

61 End in __ (be drawn)
62 Give as an example
63 *On the Beach* author
64 Kind of sign
65 Starr and Kyser
66 "Great blue" bird
67 They're often liberal

DOWN

1 Gush forth
2 Waikiki wiggle
3 Loosely connected
4 Five iron
5 Shepard and Arkin
6 Bjorn of tennis

7 Series start
8 French impressionist
9 Prefix for port
10 Dove into second
11 Late CBS traveler
12 Lawlessness
13 Less relaxed
21 Unkindly
22 Anchor position
26 Graduate deg.
27 Scepter top, often
28 Visibility problem
30 Cardinals' loc.
32 Cardinals' org.
33 Some nightwear
35 Mr. McGrew

36 Special edition
37 Mischief-maker
38 Certain shark
39 Polar to SSW
40 Mighty strange
44 Commandeer
45 Asian peninsula
46 Reason
47 Analyst's concern
48 WPA mastermind
49 *Night of the* __
52 Coffee variety
53 *Barnaby Jones* star
55 Western Indians
56 Word form meaning "within"
57 Free-for-all
58 Cravings

39 HARD LESSONS

by Eric Albert

ACROSS

1 One of the Titans
6 Pugilist's punch
9 Mongol monk
13 Filch
14 Lose one's cool
15 Frankenstein's gofer
16 Casino's video game
17 "__ partridge in a pear tree"
18 Self-centered
19 START OF A QUIP
22 Lawyers' grp.
24 Mag execs.
25 Cotton cloth
26 Toreador's fear
28 Pasty-faced
30 PART 2 OF QUIP
32 Dandy
35 Ancient Peruvian
36 "__ note to follow sol . . ."
37 Zhivago's love
38 Cry of fear
39 PART 3 OF QUIP
43 Tapered boat
44 Ran wild
45 Business bigwigs
48 __ Lingus
49 Is multiplied?
50 END OF QUIP
54 Table extender
55 River in Asia
56 Surpass
59 Cat's-paw
60 Khartoum river
61 Trojan tale
62 Flow forth
63 "Spring forward" period: Abbr.
64 Mother-of-pearl

DOWN

1 Egyptian snake
2 Early afternoon
3 Bob Seger tune of '86
4 Pinnacle
5 Eve's deceiver
6 Songwriter Mitchell
7 Man Friday
8 *A Streetcar Named Desire* character
9 Kind of maid
10 Another time
11 A bit damp
12 Actress Lucie
14 Bullion units
20 Perimeter
21 *Moonstruck* star
22 Texas A&M student
23 Paladin portrayer
27 Director Lupino
28 Has __ (may win in court)
29 Persian ruler
31 Sax range
32 Out of this world
33 Law's partner
34 __ deux
37 Actor Gorcey
39 Healing substance
40 Flawed, in a way
41 ". . . __ saw Elba"
42 Steak cut
43 Closing time
45 Blends together
46 Slightly ahead
47 Run amok
48 Competent
51 *The Haj* author
52 Seagoing sort
53 "Be-Bop-A-__" ('56 tune)
57 Patriot descendants' org.
58 Poem of praise

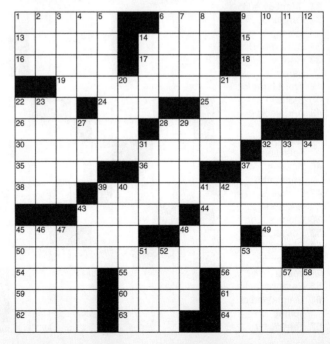

by Trip Payne

ACROSS

1 Women's magazine
5 Ship staff
9 *Star Trek* engineer
14 Needle case
15 Pasta entree
16 West Point senior, at times
17 Cropland unit
18 The Bard's river
19 Hardwood tree
20 Camus novel
23 Cardinals and ordinals: Abbr.
24 Manx cat's lack
25 Tijuana Brass leader
27 *Damn Yankees* tune
29 Tagalong's cry
31 "Monkey suit"
32 Fanatic's feeling
34 Barton or Bow
38 Rock-video parodist
42 Word form for "bone"
43 Anderson of *WKRP*
44 Shelley selection
45 Actress Samantha
47 Persian's weapons
50 Clock sound
53 Forget about
54 Clark's *Mogambo* costar
55 Paraphernalia
61 Maintained a spinet
63 Teensy bit
64 Additional
65 C.S. Lewis' first name
66 Lean-looking
67 All over again
68 No fan
69 Vanilla holder
70 Dozes (off)

DOWN

1 Musical-chairs quest
2 Impress deeply
3 Angler's buy
4 Panama party
5 Alexandra, for one
6 Disraeli, to Gladstone
7 Scholar collar
8 White House section
9 Role for Basil
10 Airport transit
11 Atmospheric layer
12 Voice range
13 Sub-rosa meeting
21 Coal product
22 Have a bite
26 Prince Charles' sport
27 Gradations of color
28 Leave the stage
29 Tom Bradley's title
30 Lively spirit
31 __ for the *Seesaw*
33 Ms. Fitzgerald
35 Declare openly
36 Frees (of)
37 Blackjack card
39 Smell bad
40 Naive reformer
41 Tom, Dick, or Harry
46 Ares or Eros
48 Jar top
49 Tarzan, for instance
50 Concealed drawback
51 Palate neighbor
52 "Be quiet!"
53 Sheet material
56 Cassette alternative
57 Aria, usually
58 Kid's taboo
59 The __ Scott Decision
60 Does needlework
62 Second name?

41 BUZZERS

by Wayne R. Williams

ACROSS

1 Berate
6 Castaway's construction
10 City vehicle
13 Thin candle
14 Lamb's alias
15 Ending for insist
16 Claudius' portrayer
18 Put on TV
19 Bartlett's abbr.
20 Hamlet was one
21 NBA's Archibald
22 *Poltergeist* director
25 Work gang
26 __ good deed
27 Lovers' quarrel
29 Garden sphere
32 Alps river
36 1986 Indy 500 winner
39 Coffee brewer
40 *Do the Right Thing* actress
42 Western Indian
43 *Deliverance* "dueler"
45 Winter wear
46 Critic Reed
47 Farm structure
49 *Viva __ Vegas*
51 Disney dog
53 Centenarian composer
60 Tarbell and Lupino
61 Slaughter of baseball
62 Prayer end
63 *Bonanza* setting: Abbr.
64 *Zoo Story* writer
67 Mr. Whitney
68 Deviate
69 Oceanic ring
70 __ Moines, IA
71 States further
72 Powell/Keeler film of '34

DOWN

1 Office skill
2 Chocolate substitute
3 Bid first
4 Albanian money
5 Erving's nickname
6 Hit the high points
7 *Home __*
8 Cloth makeup
9 Skater Babilonia
10 *Maude* star
11 Make one
12 Scatter about
16 CD's rival
17 Botheration
21 Coll. sports org.
23 Film genre
24 Hawaiian isle
28 Home type
29 Alehouse
30 __ of Good Feelings
31 *The Brady Bunch* actress
33 Dict. notation
34 Bklyn.'s locale
35 Writer LeShan
37 Munched on
38 Tarzan portrayer Barker
41 __ Stanley Gardner
44 Blue birds
48 Had to have
50 Skiing race
51 Paper choice
52 Designer Simpson
54 Single
55 Pig papas
56 Leb. neighbor
57 Take a stroll
58 Hull parts
59 Vane dir.
64 Zsa Zsa's sister
65 Dear old one?
66 Straining __ gnat

NEIGHBORLY ADVICE

by Eric Albert

ACROSS

1 Indian chief?
6 Disconcert
10 __ vu
14 In reserve
15 Midterm, for one
16 Change, often
17 START OF A QUENTIN CRISP QUIP
20 Wonderment
21 Pokes fun at
22 Point of view
23 Vitamin unit
24 Star follower
26 PART 2 OF QUIP
30 German sausage
31 Tamarind and tangerine
32 Keats creation
33 Wild and crazy time
35 Sprat's no-no
38 Small crown
40 Singer Moore
42 PART 3 OF QUIP
46 Sounded like a chick
47 Actress Skye
48 Give a speech
49 Piece of work
50 Not quite oneself
53 END OF QUIP
57 One seeing red?
58 Southeast Asian
59 Make merry
60 X-ray dosage units
61 Chance to participate
62 Sound of impact

DOWN

1 Columnist Barrett
2 Once more
3 Baloney, so to speak
4 Hotshot pilot
5 Vet-turned-author
6 Frail
7 Lumbering needs
8 Heat in a microwave
9 Big bird
10 Depressing experiences
11 Perplexing person
12 Globe-trotter's risk
13 White-faced
18 Potter's oven
19 __ deux
23 Slumberwear
24 The Way We __
25 "Of course!"
26 Company, it's said
27 Western film of '63
28 Preceding, in poems
29 Backbreaker, perhaps
33 "Smooth Operator" singer
34 Stir into action
35 Billie's hubby
36 __ Dhabi
37 Feathers precursor
38 Rides a seesaw
39 Drive forward
40 Micky Dolenz's group
41 Pinkerton logo
42 __ tantrum (got mad)
43 Raised with effort
44 A B vitamin
45 Brit's "Nonsense!"
46 Vivid quality
49 Old autocrat
50 Milky stone
51 Cow : cheddar :: goat : __
52 Guitar ridge
54 Communications corp.
55 Calendar abbr.
56 Eisenhut, e.g.

43 SIBILANCE

by Eric Albert

ACROSS

1 Joint problem
5 Use fingerpaints
10 The third man
14 It's not clear
15 Intoxicating
16 Rex's detective
17 Place for stock talk
20 Practice playing
21 He's light-headed
22 Be a busybody
23 *Strangers on a Train* star
24 Catcher's catch
28 Rapierlike
29 See eye to eye
30 Louise of *Gilligan's Island*
31 Distort, as facts
35 Fight
38 Held on to
39 All-knowing
40 Singer Page
41 Soak in the sun
42 Settle a spat
43 Bright with light
47 Disseminate
48 Young hunk
49 Film-set staffer
54 "My gosh!"
56 The Kingston __
57 Nary a soul
58 Author Kingsley
59 Splinter group
60 Eva or Magda
61 Carry on

DOWN

1 E.g., e.g.
2 Whodunit game
3 Call for quiet
4 Superior companion
5 Four Seasons #1 song
6 Like Oscar Madison
7 Palliate
8 Words from the sponsor
9 Caraway carrier
10 Bruckner or Rubinstein
11 *The Unbearable Lightness of __*
12 Eat into
13 Solo practitioner
18 South Florida city
19 Highlands group
23 Literary category
24 Load luggage
25 Mean sort
26 Onstage phone, for instance
27 Ending for song or slug
28 Brit's phone booth
30 Dickens hero
31 Envelope acronym
32 High-flying toy
33 *Brute* preceder
34 Defeat decisively
36 Last act
37 Produces in profusion
41 Scott of *Charles in Charge*
42 Some felines
43 Flat boats
44 Worship
45 Kind of column
46 Gold brick
47 Pool person
49 Hoity-toity one
50 Kaiser's kin
51 *I Remember __*
52 Similar
53 Hatchling's home
55 Quaid thriller of '88

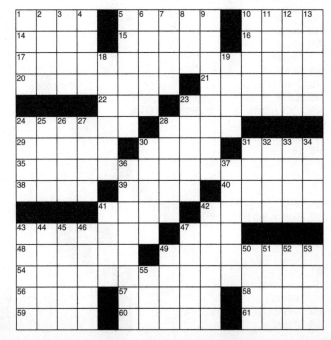

ACROSS

1 Cousin of PDQ
5 Bumps into
10 Kind of tense
14 Theater box
15 God of Islam
16 Pitch-black
17 1963 hit for 32 Across
19 Cut coupons
20 Good-for-nothings
21 Manageable
23 Morning moisture
24 Removes rind
25 To no __ (useless)
29 Cookout remains
32 Singer born April 16th, 1935
35 Do some damage
38 Kadiddle-hopper
39 Deeply felt
40 Comic Kaplan
41 Norm: Abbr.
42 1962 hit for 32 Across
44 Garden flower
45 Set a spell
46 Area code 208
49 Sis' sibling
51 Meal
53 High-steppers
58 Swiss peaks
59 1963 hit for 32 Across
61 Tall story
62 Wimbledon opener
63 Hard to hold
64 Stared at
65 Propelled a gondola
66 Cameo stone

DOWN

1 Church vestments
2 Ford's role in Star Wars
3 Water, to Juan
4 Hammer part
5 Minister's house
6 Pasta shape
7 Building wings
8 Sigma follower
9 Small building
10 Zodiac sign
11 Warbucks' charge
12 Know-how
13 Does word processing
18 In a weird way
22 Ready for business
25 Foundation
26 Electrical unit
27 In the sack
28 Business' "Big Blue"
29 Add on
30 Canonized Mlles.
31 Tel Aviv dance
33 Stringed instrument
34 Not __ many words
35 Engels' colleague
36 Busy as __
37 Comedian Foxx
40 "That's incredible!"
42 Greek letters
43 River through Lake Geneva
44 __ out (discontinued)
46 Ticked off
47 Put off
48 Granny Smith, for one
49 Diacritical mark
50 Made a scene
52 Cookbook qty.
53 Knitting instruction
54 Role for Liz Taylor
55 Roulette bet
56 __ on (trust)
57 Infernal river
60 Composer Delibes

45 STRESS TEST

by Donna J. Stone

ACROSS

1 Chalet shape
7 *The People's Choice* dog
11 Mensa data
14 Compulsive
15 Univ. marchers
16 The word, at times
17 START OF A QUIP
19 Stole style
20 Stable parents
21 Prepare eggs, in a way
23 Arp's art
26 Greases the wheels
29 Border on
30 Put out
32 Old science
34 Photo tint
35 Bountiful setting
36 MIDDLE OF QUIP
41 Breach
42 Gymnast Cathy
45 Maxilla or mandible
49 Bit of wit
51 Soprano's showcase
52 "Wings of __" (Husky hit)
54 Spouse of 67 Across
55 Philosophy
57 Coat-of-arms figure
59 Relatives
60 END OF QUIP
66 First offender?
67 Spouse of 54 Across

68 Funny faux pas
69 Article written by Kant
70 Sidle
71 Old __ (Disney dog)

DOWN

1 Paper pitches
2 To and __
3 Wheel part
4 Schubert hymn
5 Southwestern sight
6 Menu listing
7 Mustard greens
8 Sodom escapee
9 King of Siam's favorite word
10 Folksinger Phil
11 Tipple
12 Minimum of a sort
13 Wisenheimer
18 Hit the books
22 "That's what you think!"
23 __ Plaines, IL
24 Timber tool
25 Johnny of *Edward Scissorhands*
27 "I could __ horse!"
28 Eastern European
31 *The Addams Family* dance
33 Deneuve's darling
35 "Weird Al" Yankovic film

37 Sandwich salad
38 Runners carry it
39 No early bird
40 Evildoer
43 Keep out
44 Singer Sumac
45 Raised, as prices
46 Make the grade
47 Frank
48 Evil-minded
49 At any time
50 '50s "Awesome!"
53 Too large
56 Gooey stuff
58 Pump, for one
61 Actor Danson
62 Greet warmly
63 Out of sorts
64 Artichoke heart?
65 Make a blunder

46 ENTOMOLOGY

by Shirley Soloway

ACROSS

1 Toddler perches
5 *Father of the __*
10 Periodic-table stat.
14 Conditioner ingredient
15 Extend a lease
16 Bass instrument
17 Against the rules
19 Start of the show
20 *The Third Man* star
21 Gridiron spheroid
23 Bad marks
24 Objective
26 Marquee word
27 Cheap quarters
30 Cotillion attendee
33 "Battle Hymn of the Republic" writer
36 Small brook
37 "__-Loo-Ra-Loo-Ral"
39 Some exams
41 *Red October*, for one
42 Bulgaria's capital
43 Jai alai basket
44 "Oh"
46 One-stripe GI's
47 Keystone character
48 Oversize dos
51 Home appliance
53 "Open 10 __ 6"
54 Wyo. neighbor
57 Barcelona bucks
60 Copies, in a way
62 Feel sore
63 Tony Randall Broadway role
66 Convinced
67 Beast of Borden
68 Outlaw Younger
69 Stallone et al.
70 Like some jackets
71 Smell __ (be suspicious)

DOWN

1 Knight weapon
2 Unconcerned
3 Annie of *Designing Women*
4 Religious group
5 More like seawater
6 __ room
7 Variety
8 Far-reaching
9 Singer Ruth
10 Sailor's shout
11 Quite miffed
12 Reply to the Little Red Hen
13 Lena of *Havana*
18 Honest-to-goodness
22 Main points
25 Sothern role
27 Fedora fabric
28 Makeup variety
29 Even if
31 Actor Stoltz
32 Farm sounds
33 Debt
34 Treat with milk
35 In a petulant manner
38 Clumsy one's comment
40 Wooden shoe
45 Put out
49 Glossy finish
50 Fashion mag
52 Orchestra section
54 __ it (troublebound)
55 Perry's aide
56 To date
57 Go by
58 Earth sci.
59 Bank ins. initials
61 Killer whale
64 Nimitz's grp.
65 Music marking

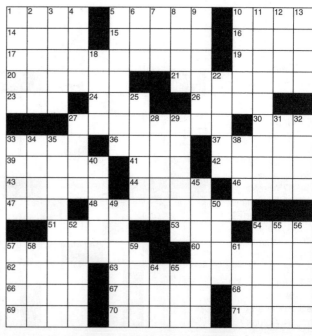

47 ALO-HA

by Donna J. Stone

ACROSS

1 Jockey's prop
5 It may suit you
10 *Hook* pooch
14 Top-notch
15 Horned in
16 Abba of Israel
17 Diamond Head dessert?
19 Cardinal's home
20 Sedan season
21 "It's a Sin to Tell __"
22 Cut canines
24 MacLachlan of *Twin Peaks*
25 __ Fein (Irish political group)
26 Photo tints
29 Robert Taylor film of '51
33 Sourpuss
34 Wreak havoc on
35 Fictional captain
36 Cut __ (dance)
37 Stops trying
38 And more of the same: Abbr.
39 Breakfast bread
40 Exploits
41 Play area?
42 James Galway, e.g.
44 Went by SST
45 Cooper's tool
46 Just adorable
47 Downhill run
50 Sandy stuff
51 Audiophile's purchase
54 Piltdown man was one
55 Swaying aircraft?

58 Tel __
59 Bleaching agent
60 Kenyatta of Kenya
61 Food store
62 Blade type
63 Chilly powder

DOWN

1 Dracula's wrap
2 Defeat decisively
3 *Lean __* ('89 film)
4 Zing
5 Toddler's mishaps
6 Sergeant Bilko
7 Ready to pick
8 Prizm or Storm
9 They may be limited
10 Maui musical?
11 Foster a felon
12 *Bed Riddance* author
13 Kick in
18 Palindromic craft
23 Part of SASE
24 Hawaiian ruler?
25 Fills the bill
26 Boa, but not cobra
27 Robin of '38
28 Pop singer Abdul
29 Peace's partner
30 Coup __
31 Public persona

32 Did cobbling
34 Charlotte __ (dessert)
37 *Jeopardy!*, for example
41 Scrap
43 NFL stats
44 Kitchen appliance
46 Stick one's neck out
47 Large herring
48 Harbor locale
49 Hard rain?
50 Gooey mess
51 Like __ of bricks
52 Short note
53 Freighter front
56 *Raid on Entebbe* weapon
57 Dr. Dentons

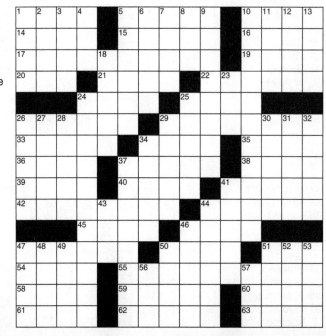

48 THREE IN A ROW

by Eric Albert

ACROSS

1 Short swims
5 "That's awful!"
10 Lab runners
14 *To Live and Die __*
15 All possible
16 Layered stone
17 Give the once-over
18 Lent a hand
19 Roughen, in a way
20 It rains on some parades
22 *New York Enquirer* boss
23 Purpose
24 Look back in anger
25 Jerry of the Chicago 7
26 Whiskey cocktail
28 White water
29 Witch craft
30 Yellow shade
33 Green's opposite
34 Poor taste
37 Bed clothes
40 Catches cold?
41 Cuts close
45 No longer edible
47 Mini-mistake
48 Mutual home
49 Not so happy
52 Oomph
53 Stare slack-jawed
54 Behave oneself
56 Fully grown
57 Mad as a wet hen
58 Solemn appeal
59 Service scores
60 Reviews highly
61 Dog in *Beetle Bailey*
62 "A grand old name"
63 Put into action
64 Persian plaint

DOWN

1 Break in on
2 Canine neighbor
3 Control substance
4 Went underwater
5 Per annum
6 Señora Peron
7 Chest material
8 Party paper
9 Actor Wilfrid __-White
10 Test model
11 Occupy
12 Gold-extraction chemical
13 Cost item
21 I strain?
25 Test result, before curving
27 Go bad
28 *Norma __*
30 Enjoy Sun Valley
31 "__ Reveille" (Kyser tune)
32 Hosp. pros
35 Rascal
36 Theater abbr.
37 Create software
38 Kingston's locale
39 Red catch
42 Make unnecessary
43 Indicate
44 By hook or by crook
46 Fifth-rate
47 Command
49 Detergent ingredient
50 Hit the road
51 Unqualified
54 Grow weary
55 Be vaguely menacing

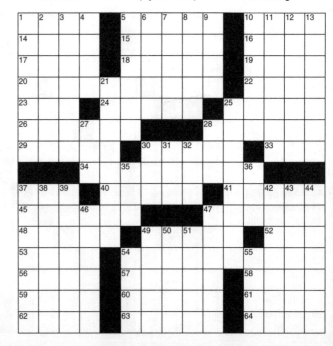

49

SATIRIZATION

by Peter Gordon

ACROSS

1 Half a sawbuck
4 Grad
8 Floor connectors
14 Lennon's lady
15 Ms. Barrett
16 Walk daintily
17 Pi follower
18 Part of MIT
19 Star in Aquila
20 Satire publication
23 She, in Seville
24 __ Alamos, NM
25 Catch flies
29 Most profound
32 Boo-boo
35 Actress Verdon
37 Emend again
38 Cover boy of 20 Across
42 Worshiped
43 A whole bunch
44 Florida county
46 Ships or pots
51 Leave out
52 Mao __-tung
54 Smell __ (be suspicious)
55 Catchphrase of 38 Across
59 Exodus locale
63 Competent
64 Gallaudet U. communication method
65 Contrite one
66 With "up," spill the beans
67 Driving area
68 Crack a cipher
69 Guitar part
70 *Calvin __ Hobbes*

DOWN

1 Put together
2 Gasp or sniff
3 Brain, so to speak
4 Opera highlight
5 Outspread
6 Like some peanuts
7 Passover staple
8 Getz of jazz
9 Word-game piece
10 Prone (to)
11 "Give __ rest!"
12 King, en France
13 Sun. oration
21 Former gas-station freebie
22 Distinctive doctrine
25 Goblet part
26 "If I __ Hammer"
27 Related
28 Lay hold of
30 Wading bird
31 Bjorn Borg is one
33 Actress Cara
34 Grinch creator
36 Court divider
38 Eliot's __ *Bede*
39 Burt's ex-wife
40 Campus club
41 Voting time
42 Latin I word
45 Incoming-plane stat.
47 __ Paulo, Brazil
48 Typo list
49 "The Sea Wolf"
50 Fixed up, as hair
53 Employees
55 Dandelion, e.g.
56 Fabled race loser
57 Otherwise
58 TV's Batman
59 Swell, in slang
60 Hot time in Tours
61 Bashful's brother
62 __-Cone

50 EGOMANIA

by Eric Albert

ACROSS

1 Wasteland
6 Chew the fat
10 Humorist Bombeck
14 Gallic goodbye
15 Praise crazily
16 Sudden ouster
17 I
20 House drawing
21 Rural hotel
22 Awkwardly situated
23 Went down
25 "__ Ideas"
26 Bette role of '90
29 Munch mousily
30 Money player
33 Be ready for
34 Boxer Max
35 Skip
36 I
39 Pound unrelentingly
40 Help in a crime
41 Photo finish
42 Gridiron gains: Abbr.
43 Jacques __ Cousteau
44 Kind of roll
45 Tops and trains
46 Sticking point?
47 Grammatical category
50 Opposite of 51 Across
51 Opposite of 50 Across
55 I
58 Bring home
59 "Has 1001 __"
60 Fighting
61 Change another's mind

62 Catch sight of
63 Choreographer Twyla

DOWN

1 Bend out of shape
2 Admired one
3 Ohio town
4 Place for a good student
5 Donne's "busy old fool"
6 Thick piece
7 Song of praise
8 Gibbon or orangutan
9 *Short Time* star
10 Great acclaim
11 Mouth part
12 Pasteur portrayer
13 High point
18 Hirschfeld's daughter
19 All over
24 Vocal range
25 Maladroit
26 Too sentimental
27 Wool fabric
28 Some peers
29 Strong winds
30 Hatches a scheme
31 Way to go
32 "For sale by __"
34 Toyland visitors
35 Cultural organization
37 Service shade?

38 General Bradley
43 Andrew's dukedom
44 Jackson or Smith
45 Really small
46 First name in flags
47 A long time
48 Pull out a pistol
49 Miles of film
50 __ down (resign)
52 Sioux City's state
53 Stage-door symbol
54 Tombstone lawman
56 Superman's insignia
57 Scoundrel

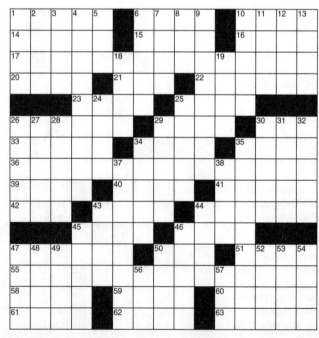

51 BODY FOOD

by Randolph Ross

ACROSS

1 __ a doornail
7 Buck or stag
11 Cheese partner, often
15 Salad ingredient
16 Dirty air
17 Author Calvino
18 *Concentration* conjunction
20 Pastoral god
21 Pub quaff
22 Car-radiator part
25 Give the once-over
26 Sheena's role on *Miami Vice*
27 __ *Like It Hot*
29 Driver's place
31 Brubeck of jazz
32 Partner in crime
33 Addition column
34 Circuit breakers
36 Chan's remark
37 Great deal
38 Vane dir.
39 Trainee
40 "Mein Gott!"
41 It's bagged at the market
44 Brian of rock
45 *Kama* __
48 Tub toy
49 Spaghetti's thinner kin
53 Salad ingredient
54 Minor quarrel
55 Army : private :: navy : __

DOWN

1 Stuffed delicacy
2 Mr. John
3 ". . . carry __ stick"
4 Médico
5 Some time
6 Struck down
7 Diana Ross film of '75
8 *You __ There*
9 Mauna __
10 Matriculants
12 Initials on a post-office poster
13 Animation frame
14 *Napoli* native
15 Nile snake
19 Lets out
21 Scotsman's "sure"
23 Slow down, in mus.
24 __ *Great Pumpkin, Charlie Brown*
25 Come out
26 Arguments against
27 Grassland region
28 Shades of meaning
29 Football great Tarkenton
30 Staff colleague
31 TV role for Dwayne
32 Soda-machine feature
35 Actress __ Park Lincoln
36 Hardwood tree
38 Two-person card game
40 The Ram
41 Puccini opus
42 Gobbled up
43 __ loss for words
46 Channels 14 and up
47 Russian chessmaster
48 Lyman Frank __
50 Cumberland, for one
51 Columnist LeShan
52 Harper Valley org.

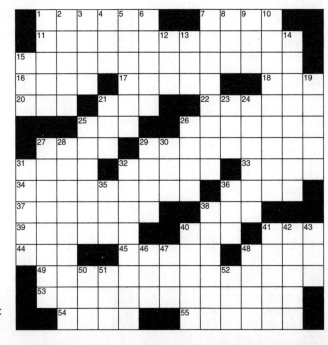

by Fred Piscop

ACROSS

1 This: Sp.
5 Adding devices
10 Burger side dish
14 Dough
15 Turn yellow, perhaps
16 Poi source
17 Loser of '64
20 Palmer, for short
21 UN license plate abbr.
22 Mr. T's former group
23 Word form for "height"
25 Proficient
27 *Mal de __*
30 True to fact
32 Roadster, e.g.
35 Chester __ Arthur
37 %
38 Where it's at
40 Loser of '68
43 Slow tempo
44 *Wheel of Fortune* purchase
45 First-rate
46 Tennis call
47 Hero's lover
50 Word preceding amis
51 Quintessential pirate
52 Rock singer Clapton
54 *Our Miss Brooks* star
57 Stirrup's site
59 __ del Sol
63 Loser of '72
66 Mimicry specialist
67 Ale kin
68 Stage direction
69 Actor Calhoun
70 Green sauce
71 Prepare memos

DOWN

1 Napoleon slept there
2 Fly high
3 Actor Rip
4 Some courtyards
5 Sweater part
6 "Clinton's __" (Erie Canal)
7 Each
8 Last place
9 Sen. Lugar's home
10 Frame of mind
11 Overdue
12 Linoleum measurement
13 Despicable one
18 Belt out
19 Clobber
24 Went gingerly
26 Milder, weatherwise
27 Taj __
28 Get away from
29 African capital
31 __ *Frome*
32 Billiards shot
33 Coeur d'__, ID
34 Point __ National Seashore
36 Electron's charge: Abbr.
39 Half a dance?
41 Making angry
42 Beat another's price
48 "__ Fideles"
49 Edward G. role
51 Irish county
53 Want for oneself
54 Ice-cream ingredient
55 __ *Man* (Estevez film)
56 Person of action
58 Bible book
60 Alluring
61 Fall down, maybe
62 Prefix for date
64 Telepath's power
65 Onetime Pontiac model

53 HAPPY BIRTHDAY

by Mel Rosen

ACROSS

1 Undeniable data
6 George Burns' cigar, e.g.
10 Tag or War
14 Contract negotiator
15 Run easily
16 Track shape
17 Social class
18 '56 hit for 24 Across
20 Zsa Zsa's sister
21 Test a jacket
23 A bit creepy
24 Singer born May 7, 1931
27 Actress Anderson
28 Fire up, enginewise
29 Guide to treasure
32 Without paying attention
36 Scoff at
38 Diving bird
39 __ Abner
41 Payout ratio
42 Picket-sign word
45 Grass-roots candidate
48 Came upon
49 Toys __ (pre-Xmas mecca)
51 "With malice toward __ ..."
52 '54 hit for 24 Across
57 "Cross of Gold" orator
60 Extreme
61 Compass pt.
62 '57 hit for 24 Across

64 French menu
66 Be the boss
67 Antiquing medium
68 All over
69 Antlered animal
70 Salon order
71 Supermarket section

DOWN

1 Gem surface
2 Yucca kin
3 Composer Franck
4 Boulder breaker
5 Western hat
6 Usher's handout
7 Helicopter part
8 Kitchen tool
9 Soup ingredient
10 Errand runner
11 Declare true
12 African nation
13 Vogue rival
19 Superman star
22 Make a scene
25 Actress Verdugo
26 Joined together
29 Skirt length
30 Tots up
31 Pain in the neck
32 Grad
33 __ up (cram)
34 Easily swayed
35 Pup's plaint

37 Logger's contest
40 Capital-gains category
43 Dunne of films
44 Daily grind
46 Below average
47 Loosened
50 Dirty spot
52 High-tech beam
53 Mr. Gantry
54 Rigoletto composer
55 Computer key
56 Like an oboe's sound
57 Polar explorer
58 Cad
59 Christmastime
63 Kindergarten break
65 Santa __, CA

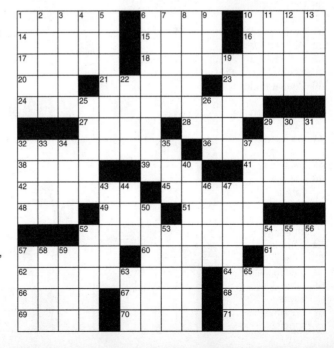

54 LETTER WRITING

by Eric Albert

ACROSS

1 Puzzle fanatic
7 Monster in the closet
14 The fun of it
15 Freezing
16 Greek dessert?
18 Takeoff
19 Dry red wine
20 Numbers game
21 Trigger puller?
22 Patriots' org.
25 Showpieces
26 Party member?
27 Yard event
31 Accomplished
32 *Phaedo* subject
33 Greek challenge?
36 Contractual out
37 Horned hooter
38 Points of view
39 Larry King's locale
40 Charlie Parker's specialty
43 Submissions to eds.
44 Fidel's colleague
45 Deckhand
46 Call it a career
50 Santiago "sir"
51 Greek greeting?
54 Stamps
55 Gets to the bottom line
56 What one wears
57 Gershwin hit song

DOWN

1 "Seward's Folly"
2 Smartly dressed
3 Delaware dynast
4 Snow place like home
5 White-hat wearer
6 One-third tbsp.
7 Onion-topped roll
8 Kareem's college
9 Tackle and such
10 Pinnacle
11 Italy's shape
12 Previously used
13 __ to Billy Joe
17 Sect's symbol
21 Up-to-the-minute
22 Org. founded in '49
23 Make a run for it
24 Guitarist Paul
26 Soprano's note
27 In addition
28 Opera opener
29 No longer a kid
30 Humorist Mort
31 Patsy
32 Haggard romance
33 Give a fling
34 "Uh-oh!"
35 *Kidnapped* monogram
36 Make a run for it
39 Use the molars
40 Tropical tree
41 Filmdom's Lawrence
42 Read carefully
44 Mean and nasty
45 Conductor Zubin
46 Rough file
47 Soul singer James
48 Boris Godunov, e.g.
49 *Bus Stop* writer
50 Put away
51 FDR program
52 Short flight
53 "__ Now or Never"

55 AYE-AYE

by Matt Gaffney

ACROSS

1 Once owned
4 Butter bit
7 Hairstyling goo
10 Garfield's hand
13 GI show sponsor
14 Hard to catch
16 "It must be him, __ shall die"
17 Jack Lord cop series
19 *The A-Team* muscleman
20 Turner's pride
21 10th grader
22 Short drive
23 Takes to the cleaners
26 Ace place?
28 Swab's target
29 Some NHLers
30 Printer's widths
31 __ firma
34 Erich __ (Harry Houdini)
35 Journalist/muckraker
37 Arm of the sea
40 Shades of color
41 *L.A. Law* characters
44 Biblical language
46 Intertwine
48 Taking it easy
49 "Me and Mamie __"
50 Mr. Nastase
51 Former UN member
54 Hoop group: Abbr.
55 Greek letter
56 Resort sport
60 Gentlemen

61 "My pleasure!"
62 *Foucault's Pendulum* author
63 Newsman Donaldson
64 Jazz instrument
65 Convent dweller
66 Swell place?

DOWN

1 "What was that?"
2 Happy __
3 Depressing situations
4 Architect I.M.
5 Hall-of-Fame boxer
6 Boston-area school
7 Say "Uncle!"
8 Nevertheless
9 Sign of summer
10 Vesuvius victim
11 Gets in
12 Oath taker
15 "*Sprechen __ Deutsch?*"
18 Freshly
22 Capriati foe
23 Service charge
24 Romance language
25 Corporate VIP
27 "Ignorance of the __ excuse"
29 Former Utah Senator Jake
32 Coll. mil. grp.
33 Slugger's stat
35 Farr of *M*A*S*H*

36 Anatomical passage
37 *Arabian Nights* rulers
38 Rapidly shrinking body of water
39 Allies' anathema
41 Felt hats
42 With suspicion
43 Yon sloop
45 Large lizard
47 Pasteur portrayer
49 Utah Senator Hatch
52 Mythical river
53 Adjust the clock
56 Has been
57 Dallas inst.
58 Barbie's beau
59 __ long way (last)

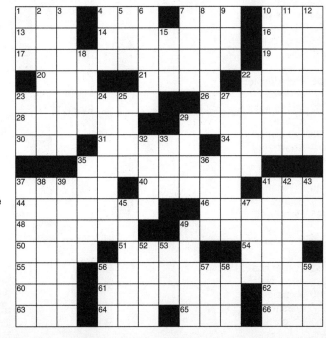

TV ADDRESSES

by Donna J. Stone

ACROSS

1 Phyllis Diller's hubby
5 Soccer great
9 Slow tempo
14 ". . . maids all in __"
15 Wellington's alma mater
16 Burger topping
17 *What's My Line?* host
18 Grade-school gamut
19 Rocket brake
20 The Flintstones' address
23 "Uh-uh"
24 __ culpa
25 Selling point
28 Stead
30 '75 Wimbledon winner
34 Books pro: Abbr.
35 Appear to be
37 Khyber Pass, e.g.
39 The Munsters' address
42 Mom's mission, maybe
43 Pre-owned
44 Short story?
45 Galley directive
46 Perlman of *Cheers*
48 *Peer Gynt* playwright
50 "__ Sera Sera"
51 Old pro
52 The Kramdens' address
60 Message board?
61 Bristol brews

62 Prepare to fly
63 French city
64 Yothers of *Family Ties*
65 Provoked
66 A deadly sin
67 A piece of cake
68 Alternatively

DOWN

1 Rages
2 Smell __ (be suspicious)
3 __ contendere
4 *Car 54, Where Are You?* star
5 Lipstick shade
6 Sundance's sweetie
7 Canadian flier
8 Food processor

9 Liza's half sister
10 From the top
11 Ms. Moreno
12 Like some R-rated movies
13 Yoko __
21 Sends out for food
22 Hors d'__
25 High points
26 Show off
27 Stravinsky's *Le __ du Printemps*
28 Pantyhose part
29 Permeate
30 Cheer rival
31 Thick slices
32 Skater Sonja
33 Keep one's __ (watch)
36 Gridiron ploy
38 Devoted fan

40 Krazy __
41 "The Lady __ Tramp"
47 Greek goddess
49 Wodehouse's Wooster
50 Put the kibosh on
51 Size up
52 Permanent effect?
53 Hawaii's #2 city
54 "Leaving on __ Plane"
55 Literary alias
56 Itches
57 Viscount's better
58 Spouses no more
59 Ebb and flow
60 Hemispheric alliance: Abbr.

HORSING AROUND

by Eric Albert

ACROSS

1 Goldbrick
6 English assignment
11 Jazz session
14 Disturbingly weird
15 In the know
16 Reverent dread
17 START OF A QUIP
19 How some stand
20 Bestselling game
21 Anti-Dracula device
23 "Olé" or "bravo"
24 Stephen King thriller
26 Field hand?
30 Fuse blower
31 Houyhnhnms subject
32 Quid pro quo
33 Mary's boss at WJM
36 MIDDLE OF QUIP
40 Compass pt.
41 No-good sorts
42 $10 gold piece
43 Really excited
45 Soft stroke
46 Mom, so to speak
49 *Rocky III* foe
50 *A Place in the Sun* star
51 Light in the dark
56 Commencement wear
57 END OF QUIP
60 Plate cleaner, often
61 Usher's beat
62 Shoe material
63 Mr. Milland
64 Remote target?
65 Chuck, for one

DOWN

1 Line of clothing?
2 Protagonist
3 Islamic republic
4 Puerto __
5 Don't fret
6 Primeval
7 Move in the breeze
8 Defense-system initials
9 Indiana Jones quest
10 Order response
11 Perry opened it
12 Rise
13 Basement reading
18 Thatcher, e.g.
22 It does a bang-up job
24 Spring events
25 Arizona Indian
26 Computer-storage unit
27 Displays delight
28 What you used to be?
29 Conk on the noggin
30 Nobel was one
32 Spine-tingling
33 Mezzanine section
34 Barn dwellers
35 "Has 1001 __"
37 Tart-tasting
38 Felix's concern
39 Org. founded in 1890
43 Campaign name of '36
44 Moneybags
45 Duster's target
46 Come to mind
47 Wool-coat owner
48 A bit foolish
49 Haystack painter
51 __ bonding
52 Bad spell
53 Fencing need
54 *Betsy's Wedding* director
55 Hardly overbearing
58 Actress Ullmann
59 Road curve

58 PAT ANSWERS

by Mark Diehl

ACROSS
1 Banned chem. sprays
5 PAT
8 Back of the neck
12 PAT of *The Karate Kid*
14 Ostrich kin
15 Alaska's first governor
16 Missing link, maybe
17 DDE's rank
18 Receive an IOU for
19 Home of the NFL's "PATS"
21 Subtraction word
22 Start of spring?
23 Pool gear
24 Give, as odds
26 Soft palates
27 *PAT and Mike* actress
31 __ carotene
34 Boy or girl preceder
36 Home on the range
37 Tennis surface
38 German wine region
40 Ford models
41 Sheeplike
43 Environmental sci.
44 Game-show winnings
45 Pop singer PAT
47 Half of VP
49 Director Craven
50 Dole (out)
51 RR stop
54 College major

57 PAT of *One Day at a Time*
60 "... __ saw Elba"
61 Eur. country
62 "Cut that out!"
63 Deli-counter call
64 King of France
65 Periodic-table components
66 Go out with
67 Cribbage prop
68 Deteriorates

DOWN
1 Chuckleheads
2 Pearson and Barrymore
3 Fourth dimension
4 Political position
5 *The Ballet Class* artist
6 Prayer end
7 Washer load
8 PAT's jeep on *The Roy Rogers Show*
9 *The African Queen* screenwriter
10 0-star reviews
11 Extremities
12 Thick head of hair
13 Bony
20 Chair material
25 Quick to learn
26 PAT Sajak's colleague
27 George I's house
28 Capable of
29 Hire a decorator

30 Chick's home
31 Shapeless mass
32 Roof overhang
33 Dead ringer
35 __ *Tac Dough*
39 Prideful feeling
42 Somme summer
46 B neighbor
48 Hoops position
50 Head honcho
51 March honoree
52 Works hard
53 Tiny workers
54 Patch up
55 Field of expertise
56 Schoolbook
58 Lotion additive
59 __ it (start work)

59 ORDINAL ARRAY

by Wayne R. Williams

ACROSS

1 Old Testament heroine
8 Thespians' union: Abbr.
11 Part of TGIF
14 Raise
15 Treeless tract
17 First followers
19 __ Khayyám
20 Likewise not
21 Rosie O'Neill portrayer
22 Exclude
25 Board member, often
26 Second followers
33 The "al." in "et al."
34 __ Na Na
35 Maiden name indicator
36 Barn bellow
37 Soup sample
39 Get one's goat
41 Zilch
42 Miller or Jillian
43 __ es Salaam
45 Late entertainer MacKenzie
47 Third followers
51 Morning hrs.
52 City on the Po
53 Ease up
56 Sportscaster Scully
57 Right-hand person: Abbr.
61 Fourth followers
65 Desperate
66 Seeing red
67 Draft org.
68 Compass dir.
69 Rental customers

DOWN

1 Display model
2 Jack, of old movies
3 VHS alternative
4 Past the deadline
5 Bleacher cheer
6 One-time connection
7 Red dyes
8 Practice punching
9 Exodus character
10 Doohickey
11 Dies __
12 Conway and Cratchit
13 Matches a bet
16 How cars go up hills
18 A Day at the movies
23 Commits a blunder
24 Moreover
25 Hero's mount
26 Rambling sort
27 Make amends
28 Sandal piece
29 4 on the telephone
30 Like some sanctums
31 Actor Sam
32 Edited out
38 Preceder of excellence
40 Fruit with green pulp
44 10 to 1, e.g.
46 Beethoven pieces
48 Film critic, e.g.
49 Makes corrections to
50 Bridge alternative
53 States further
54 Pix about people
55 Cookie tycoon Wally
56 Room's asset
58 Wise one
59 Trick or game ending
60 Turner and Koppel
62 Boom-bah preceder
63 Chemical suffix
64 Mrs., in Madrid

60 QUITE A CASE!

by Cynthia Lyon

ACROSS

1 Booty
5 Olympian's award
10 Typewriter settings
14 Columbus' home
15 Handy
16 "__ want for Christmas . . ."
17 START OF A QUIP
20 Sphere of influence
21 Party roamers
22 Liked, slangily
24 Prior to
25 PART 2 OF QUIP
33 Eucalyptivore
34 Holds the deed to
35 A question of manners?
36 Senator Hatch
37 Big bankroll
38 Simpson of fashion
40 Peach product
41 Treat meat
42 Slaves away
43 PART 3 OF QUIP
47 Bud's buddy
48 Caviar, essentially
49 Property recipient
54 Loosen, in a way
58 END OF QUIP
61 Start of Caesar's claim
62 Upstanding

63 "__, a thousand times . . ."
64 H.S. exams
65 Sample recordings
66 Hammerhead feature

DOWN

1 Suburban turf
2 Copter's noise
3 Adjutant, e.g.
4 The Naked Maja painter
5 Hawaiian housedress
6 Ordinal suffix
7 Per follower
8 Jai __
9 Kin of Loewe's collaborator
10 Pad
11 Popular houseplant
12 Indistinct sight
13 Occupies an ottoman
18 Hemingway's Santiago
19 Taj Mahal city
23 Mature
25 Flying Down __
26 Ran quickly
27 Harvarder's rival
28 Create bonsai
29 Make beloved
30 __ Finest Hour (Churchill book)
31 Hall decker
32 Rams' ma'ams
33 Sennett squad

38 Show up for
39 "Cock-a-doodle-__!"
41 Made a difference
44 Legal outs
45 Kelly critter
46 Judicial arenas
49 They'll travel anywhere: Abbr.
50 National League park
51 Dismissed
52 Raison d'__
53 Grades K-6
55 Galvanization need
56 Pedestal percher
57 __ colada
59 A soc. sci.
60 AAA job

61 GREEK CLIQUE

by Wayne R. Williams

ACROSS

1 Dispensed
6 Keg feature
9 Campfire remains
14 Stradivari's teacher
15 __ glance (quickly)
16 Fulton's power
17 *Antigone* playwright
19 __ Haute, IN
20 Shoshonean Indian
21 Sha Na Na member, e.g.
23 Suffix for scram
24 It had a part in Exodus
26 Greek comedy writer
28 Pot starter
30 Spread for bread
31 French river
34 Brewery vessels
37 Broadway souvenir
40 Moves emotionally
41 Wedding vow
42 German plane
43 Matching
44 Ink mess
45 Sportscaster Merlin
46 *Typee* sequel
48 In the past
50 *Anabasis* author
54 Bonehead plays
58 Brit. record label

59 One of TV's *Snoop Sisters*
61 __ Tin Tin
62 Delaware senator
64 Plato's student
66 French student
67 "__ been had!"
68 Summon up
69 Union man Chavez
70 Rule: Abbr.
71 More rational

DOWN

1 Conductor Kurt
2 Chew the scenery
3 Used a camcorder
4 Ordinal ending

5 Greek philosopher
6 __ of woe
7 Mr. T's former outfit
8 Old hat
9 From the stars
10 Canonized *femme*: Abbr.
11 Father of History
12 Baseball great Combs
13 Sling mud
18 Political ending
22 Seth's son
25 Riviera resort
27 Snuggling one
29 Satanic
31 Equine beast
32 Call __ day
33 Greek poet
35 Fuss
36 Dorothy's dog

38 Arthur Godfrey's instrument
39 Make illegal
42 Plato's mentor
44 Physicist Niels
47 First game
49 NBA team
50 Three-masted ship
51 Monsieur Zola
52 Radio-studio sign
53 Effrontery
55 Playwright Joe
56 German poet
57 Curl one's lip
60 Victory, in Vienna
63 Spacewalk, initially
65 Caesar's eggs

62 PROCRASTINATORS

by Fred Piscop

ACROSS

1 June honoree
4 Paper packages
9 Not quite right
14 Metal in the rough
15 Glorify
16 Group doctrine
17 Hodges of baseball
18 Procrastinating TV cop?
20 Smooth singer
22 Up (to)
23 Visigoth king
24 Theater letters
26 Lioness in *Born Free*
29 "What's __ for me?"
31 Parapsychology subj.
33 Hereford hotel
34 Reggae relative
36 Iceboat necessity
38 Pluto's path
40 Procrastinating actress?
43 Get rid of the suds
44 "Ciao, baby!"
45 Mediocre grade
46 Late dancer Miller
47 Have to pay
49 Cubic Rubik
51 Gardener's bane
53 Oklahoma town
55 Accomplish, so to speak
59 Evil look
61 Snuggling sorts
63 Procrastinating preacher?
66 Wharton deg.
67 Symbol of leakiness
68 "Taps" instrument
69 Stand __ (don't waver)
70 Lent a hand
71 Sloppy precipitation
72 __ and outs

DOWN

1 Church belief
2 Historian Durant
3 Perry's assistant
4 Come back to
5 Expel, in a way
6 "Up and __!"
7 Heston role
8 Hearst's kidnappers: Abbr.
9 ". . .three men in __"
10 Singer Haggard
11 Like some ink
12 Aegean, e.g.
13 Pigs' digs
19 New Mexico town
21 Three-tone chords
25 Give an account
27 Nasty, as remarks
28 Hill builder
30 Sampled the steak
32 Campy sound effect
34 Porkers
35 Housed a hound
37 Writer Tarbell
39 Pistol property
41 Prefix for natal
42 Suburban event
43 Bitterly cold
48 Getting close
50 Later, maybe
52 Do research
54 Set aside
56 Metronome settings
57 Sort of sprawl
58 H.S. exams
60 *One-__ Jacks* (Brando film)
62 Beat by a whisker
63 Cubs' org.
64 Second-sequel letters
65 Dictionary abbr.

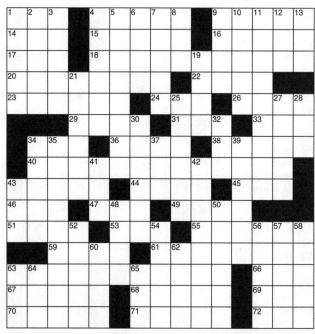

63 CAESAR AT THE MALL

by Eric Albert

ACROSS

1 Spill the beans
5 Western capital
10 Electrically versatile
14 Get up
15 *South Pacific* role
16 Allegro con __
17 Similar (to)
18 Really miffed
19 Not at all shy
20 START OF A QUIP
23 International aid org.
24 Author Umberto
25 Imported auto
27 Actress Taylor
28 Golfer Woosnam
30 Moth's lure
32 Inspire wonder
33 Vaudeville bit
34 Gem-studded headgear
35 MIDDLE OF QUIP
38 Sweet-talk
41 Swiss spot
42 High ball?
45 Count Basie's instrument
46 Rub the wrong way
47 Recurring idea
49 Coffee brewer
50 "Smoking or __?"
52 Dance to rock
53 END OF QUIP
57 Green stone
58 Airport control center
59 *Peter and the Wolf* "duck"
60 Eden's earldom
61 Video-game maker
62 Chimney channel
63 Pesky plant
64 __ around (snoops)
65 Parker who played Boone

DOWN

1 Showy display
2 Car-ad phrase
3 Ludicrous
4 ". . . but it's more important to __"
5 Line on a letter
6 In the thick of
7 "__ Marlene"
8 Late morning
9 Corpsman
10 Golda's colleague
11 What a pryer uses
12 Two-horned thing
13 Not prepaid
21 Neckline shape
22 European capital
26 Unseld of basketball
28 Sparklers
29 In conflict
31 F. Lee's field
33 "Botch __" (Clooney tune)
34 Recipe amt.
35 Debate side
36 Without equal
37 Lodge member
38 PC's "brain"
39 Radio-signal medium
40 Mystery woman
42 Easy to read
43 Threatening
44 *Saturday Night Fever* group
46 Altogether
47 Add icing to
48 Dismount quickly
51 Available in kegs
52 Netman Becker
54 Direct (one's way)
55 Love letters?
56 Roll response
57 Vise part

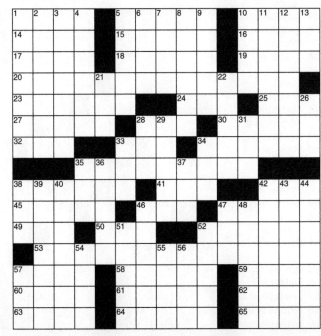

64 TWO THEMES IN ONE

by Alex Vaughn

ACROSS

1 Mrs. David Copperfield
5 Seed source
10 Air pollution
14 Words of worry
15 "With this ring, __ wed"
16 Casino city
17 Riviera resort
18 Wakes up
19 Irritated mood
20 Sweet wine
22 Newspaper notices
24 __-disant (self-styled)
25 Desire deified
27 Republicans' symbol
29 House pet, informally
32 Sufficient space
33 Mss. polishers
34 __ the elbows (shabby)
36 "__ fightin' words!"
39 Canal chamber
41 Riverbank earthworks
43 Fail to include
44 Made a living at
46 Suit component
48 Bikini part
49 Makes a boo-boo
51 Popular stuffed animal
53 Novelty dance
56 Nectar source
57 Make choices
58 Kind of energy
60 Syrian leader
63 Singer Redding
65 "__ Peak or Bust"
67 Elisabeth of *Soapdish*
68 Diet successfully
69 Pizzeria fixtures
70 Irish Republic
71 Part of A.M.
72 Dunaway et al.
73 Tune up for a bout

DOWN

1 Advice, often
2 Glenn's state
3 Smarty
4 What the Tin Man wanted
5 Greek letters
6 Dog in *Beetle Bailey*
7 Smarty's trinket
8 Jeopardy
9 Day starter
10 S.A.T. takers
11 Smarty's attainment
12 Omelet extra
13 "I understand!"
21 It drops from palms
23 Catch sight of
26 Mideast missile
28 Happy sounds
29 Sort of seaweed
30 Loved one
31 "Take __ from me"
35 "A __'clock scholar"
37 "Look at that, Luis!"
38 Have the lead
40 *Show Boat* composer
42 Cut it out
45 Prohibition backers
47 Flushing, NY field
50 *Little __ Horrors*
52 String section
53 "Rah!" relative
54 Author Sinclair
55 Tony of baseball
59 Actor Auberjonois
61 Ambience
62 Whitetail, e.g.
64 Go on dates with
66 Draft org.

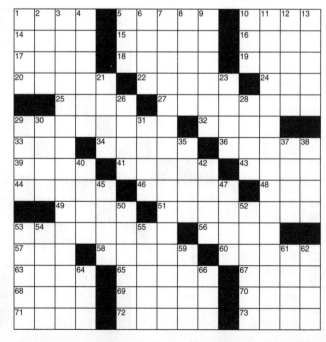

65 SOLVE WITH "EASE"

by Randolph Ross

ACROSS

1 Designer Schiaparelli
5 In the past
8 Army outpost
12 Witches' brew need
13 Quick flash
15 Theater sign
16 Smell __ (be suspicious)
17 *Oklahoma!* aunt
18 Marine life
19 Indicated
21 Not around
23 Overtime cause
24 Calendar col. heading
25 Nutritionist's concern
26 *Joie de vivre*
28 Flown the coop
29 Beatnik's home
32 __ *Under the Elms*
34 Rank too highly
36 Take __ the chin
37 Carousal
39 Western author Wister
40 Romeo's surname
42 Mr. Dangerfield
44 Chang's brother
45 Neighbor to NY
46 Yorkshire river
47 Datum, for short
48 Sapporo sash
49 Vane dir.

52 Hale and hearty
55 Makes do
57 Lendl of tennis
58 Make happy
60 Bar order
61 Acquire
62 Champing at the bit
63 Answering-machine sound
64 Comrade-in-arms
65 Card game
66 Letters near 0

DOWN

1 Pass legislation
2 Poet Jones
3 Jolson's specialty?

4 Envelope abbr.
5 Green Mountain Boys leader
6 __ the lily
7 What *unum* means
8 Cruel sort
9 Wheel shaft
10 Give an autograph
11 Coup d'__
13 Buy a fake beard?
14 Apprentice outlaw?
20 General Bradley
22 Pabst product
25 Swooped down
27 Washer residue
28 Bridge name
29 Tribal emporium?
30 Suit to __

31 Declare untrue
32 Canadian coin
33 Venerable prep school
35 Angling gear
38 Fourth-down play
41 New Testament book
43 Arles assents
47 Phoenix forecast
48 Peripheral
50 Precious gem
51 Organic compound
52 Latvia's capital
53 Face shape
54 It may be posted
55 Long story
56 "It __ laugh"
59 Grad-school major

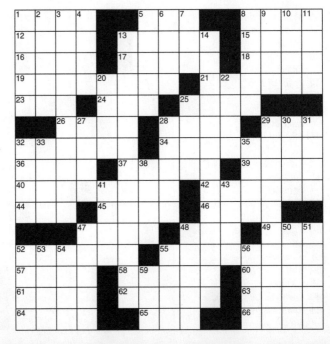

by Donna J. Stone

ACROSS

1 Present day?
5 Vegan's no-no
9 Swab brand
14 Auld lang syne
15 Perry's creator
16 Not turn __ (remain calm)
17 Global band
18 Forgo the fries
19 Conductor's concern
20 START OF AN IRVIN COBB QUIP
23 Drivers' org.
24 Canal zone?
25 Give rise to
28 *Sesame Street* character
30 Goya's *Duchess of* __
34 Cocks and bulls
35 Mob member
37 *The __ the Rose*
39 MIDDLE OF QUIP
42 Joan of Arc, e.g.
43 Haydn epithet
44 *Murder in the Cathedral* monogram
45 Christie concoction
46 Singer James
48 More mirthful
50 Sault __ Marie, MI
51 Fire preceder
52 END OF QUIP
59 Old hat
60 Marina's place
61 Installed, as tile
63 More than enough
64 Roman and Christian
65 Nevada city
66 Gould of *The Prince of Tides*
67 Expected back
68 Single buyer

DOWN

1 Affair of 1798
2 Sky light
3 *New Yorker* cartoonist
4 It takes two
5 Euripides tragedy
6 Buffalo's county
7 Actor Baldwin
8 Restrict Rover
9 Gulf nation
10 In that case
11 Foot of a sort
12 Mammy Yokum prop
13 Sign of stage success
21 Larder
22 Sylvester's snooze
25 Curly's brother
26 Kind of code
27 Houston ballplayer
28 News brief, briefly
29 Tut's turf
30 "What Kind of Fool __?"
31 Koufax, for one
32 Gem State capital
33 In search of
36 *From __ Eternity*
38 Leisurely, to Liszt
40 Conglomerate letters
41 Bond rating
47 Toyota model
49 It's charming
50 TV bishop
51 "__ of robins . . ."
52 *My Friend* __
53 Samples the Chablis
54 Normandy town
55 Made tracks
56 Novelist Hunter
57 Stiff wind
58 Summer-camp activity
59 __ Mahal
62 Giovanni or Johnson

67 J & X

by Eric Albert

ACROSS

1. Not naked
5. Ringlike things
10. Well-protected
14. Actress Turner
15. Wide-awake
16. Decorative molding
17. Rabbi's religion
20. Boyer/Bergman thriller
21. City on the Missouri
22. Large amount
23. Complain constantly
25. Cause to be
29. Raise to the third power
30. Dog doc
33. Allies' foes
34. Muslim palace area
35. Eddie's *Green Acres* costar
36. Close together
40. Shakespeare title word
41. Loudly, in music
42. Goose call
43. Mrs. Turkey
44. Romantic gift
45. Easily broken
47. Drum accompanier
48. Nanki-__ (*The Mikado* role)
49. Elemental
52. Thanksgiving choice
57. Outside the court
60. "Oh, woe!"
61. Old enough
62. Save, as coupons
63. Lane's coworker
64. Played cat-and-mouse (with)
65. *Kiss Me __*

DOWN

1. Stop up
2. *Dr. Zhivago* role
3. Farm workers
4. Writer Roald
5. Wisconsin native
6. Love, to Leilani
7. Teller call
8. Erving's nickname
9. RV center?
10. Make an impression
11. What a diva delivers
12. Perch or piranha
13. Austen novel
18. French river
19. Scale starters
23. Radium researcher
24. Help in a heist
25. Punjab prince
26. Give off
27. *Six Crises* author
28. Franklin invention: Abbr.
29. Hindu stratum
30. Puff adder's poison
31. *Dynasty* star
32. Loquacious
34. Gymnastics device
37. Lesotho's locale
38. Magical sound effect
39. "__ believe in yesterday"
45. Compulsory
46. Thor's foe
47. Leading the line
48. Singer Janis
49. Nestling's nose
50. Wheel joiner
51. Ollie's partner
52. 6/6/44
53. Big name in trucks
54. '40s leading lady Raines
55. Came to earth
56. Hunt and peck
58. Write hurriedly
59. Tabloid topic

68 CAJUN KOOKERY

by David A. Rosen

ACROSS

1 Extra
6 Long rides?
11 Preservative: Abbr.
14 One way to get information
15 Arden of poetry
16 Sleep phenom.
17 Vegetarian TV host?
19 Idle talk
20 Sondheim's __ the Woods
21 Makeup buy
23 Old witches
26 Table listings
27 Bart's dad
28 Debate side
29 Persist suffix
30 Worrier's word
31 Ad __ committee
32 Sketcher's eraser
35 Comparative ending
36 Fraternity parties
38 New Mexican Amerind
39 Excessively ornate
41 Short dog, for short
42 Obscene stuff
43 Hardwood tree
44 German article
45 Buffalo iceman
46 Party stalwart
49 Hardened criminals
50 "__ that remark!"
51 Computer-selection screen
52 Short time?
53 Nutty film critic?
58 __ vivant

59 Kind of jury
60 Wispy clouds
61 George's bill
62 Stunk
63 You __ for It

DOWN

1 Fuss
2 Cartoonist Browne
3 Colonial descendant's grp.
4 May and Stritch
5 It bums you out
6 Jocular Jay
7 Gershwin's Concerto __
8 Young follower
9 Indian, e.g.
10 Dewey, Cheatham & Howe, Esqs.?
11 TV host in the soup?
12 What "you've gotta have"
13 Oscar-awarding org.
18 "__ Impossible" (Como tune)
22 Copper
23 Preside over
24 The old birl game
25 Spicy poet?
26 Concorde compartment
28 Talk fondly
31 Medical insurance grp.
32 Prepare for action
33 Road reversal
34 Parcels (out)
36 Lugs around

37 Uncountable years
40 She-bears: Sp.
42 Asian hunting dogs
44 Big property
45 Roman philosopher
46 Competitive dance
47 Heavenly hunter
48 Against property, in legalese
49 Low land
51 Hand, slangily
54 Diamond __
55 Boat of refuge
56 Prior to
57 Box top

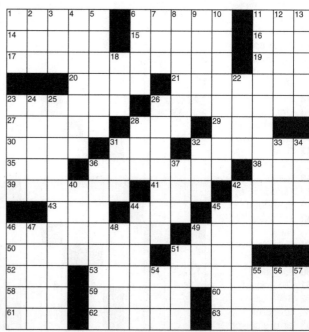

69 FLAG DAY

by Randolph Ross

ACROSS

1 Big parties
6 Quite humid
10 Lose traction
14 Greek : alpha :: Hebrew : __
15 Lotion ingredient
16 French father
17 Gene Krupa portrayer
18 Canadian flag emblem
20 U.S. flag, familiarly
22 Shaker __, OH
23 Enjoy the buffet
24 __ in the Dark
27 Wanders about
29 Signed off on
32 Estranged
34 Two of a kind
35 Soviet flag, familiarly
38 Famous name?
39 Finding offensive
40 Rock star Jon __ Jovi
41 The bottom line
43 Clever ploys
44 Old French coin
45 Lizzie material
46 French flag's colors
55 British flag
56 Got out of bed
57 Composer Rota
58 North-forty unit
59 Terry product
60 Idyllic spot
61 Amaze
62 Water jugs

DOWN

1 Legs, so to speak
2 Touched down
3 Actress Olin
4 Impressionist?
5 Wyoming Indian
6 __ with faint praise
7 "When I was __ . . ."
8 Washing needs
9 Hailed on
10 Get lost
11 Don't give up
12 *Dies* __ (hymn)
13 Dict. entries
19 Important periods
21 Rose-petal oil
24 San Antonio landmark
25 *Lost in Yonkers* writer
26 Clothes lines
27 Citizen __
28 Interjects
29 Chaplin costar in *The Great Dictator*
30 Ceramic ovens
31 Small remnant
32 Ishmael's captain
33 Sea dogs
34 Police stns.
36 Canary's cousin
37 Overrun
41 McCarthy aide
42 Message boards of a sort
44 React to Frankie
45 Subtracted
46 Mystical poem
47 Oklahoma city
48 Sup in style
49 Savoir faire
50 Stocking shade
51 It may be knitted
52 *St. Elmo's Fire* star
53 Spreadsheet worker
54 Snakelike fish

ACROSS

1 Sitting on
5 Rather and Blocker
9 Knitting-book word
13 Bring up
14 Mideast ruler
16 Ersatz butter
17 Powerful shark
18 Famous physicist
19 Ford models
20 Marines' motto
23 __ *Gay* (WWII plane)
24 Antitoxin
25 Indian carving
28 *The Blood on __ Claw* ('71 horror film)
31 Shoreline sight
34 "Zounds!"
36 __ stone (immovable)
37 In the past
38 Andrea __
40 Form prefix
41 Michener bestseller
44 Rigel, for one
45 ". . . __ a man with seven wives"
46 Photo tones
48 Old Mexican civilization
50 Planet's path
52 How others see us
55 Coin phrase
58 Down in the dumps
59 Actress Verdugo
60 Runs in
62 Portrait medium

63 Washday challenge
64 Done with
65 Warts and all
66 JFK landers, once
67 Where Scarlett lived

DOWN

1 Tattoo place
2 Ruffle, as hair
3 "The Old __ Bucket"
4 Engage in hype
5 Clobbered
6 Part of AFT
7 Soft ball brand
8 Some tourney games
9 Sully
10 Threatening words
11 Half the checkers
12 __ Alamos, NM
15 Carnival attractions
21 UN observer grp.
22 Historic times
26 Analyst's concerns
27 *I Remember Mama* mama
29 Midevening
30 Miffed mood
31 Finicky eaters
32 Curved molding
33 Public opinion
35 Gustavo __ Ordaz (former Mexican president)
39 Glassblowers, e.g.
42 Stuffy
43 *Elephant Boy* star
45 "__ tell a lie"
47 Becomes a daddy
49 Big bird
51 Pinball mishaps
53 Tropical fruit
54 Live coal
55 Ivy Leaguers
56 Arthur and Lillie
57 Curriculum section
58 Feathery stole
61 Mrs., in Málaga

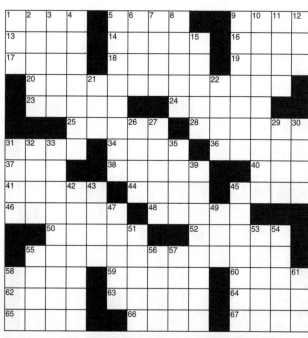

71 GENDER BENDER

by Eric Albert

ACROSS
1 Come to pass
6 Benchley book
10 Fit together nicely
14 WWI battle site
15 Laos' locale
16 Actress Sommer
17 Olfactory input
18 Sash stopper
19 Infernal river
20 Wake-up call?
23 Commands respect
24 Discomfort
25 *L.A. Law* network
28 Baby fox
30 College choice
32 Sounds of surprise
35 "The Last Frontier"
40 Burned up
41 Klutz?
44 God of passion
45 Rhetorical question
46 Compass pt.
47 Just __ in the bucket
49 __ *Dalmatians*
51 Nancy Drew's boyfriend
52 Singer Lennon
57 Find fault
61 Avoiding blame?
64 Bantu language
66 Annul
67 Alpha's opposite

68 A ways away
69 Stage strap
70 Origami need
71 Spanish painter
72 Supplicate
73 Journal note

DOWN
1 Astaire's birthplace
2 Baseball great Rod
3 Witchlike woman
4 Reveal to the world
5 "__ my lips!"
6 Fleece finder
7 Notwithstanding
8 Author Cather
9 Pie-throwing comic
10 "You've Made __ Very Happy"
11 "Rocket Man" singer
12 Aurora locale
13 Bad spell
21 James, for one
22 Rep.'s colleague
26 Light element
27 Posh pancake
29 Oddjob's creator
31 Beast of burden
32 Canoe anagram
33 Moving pack
34 Fairbanks' fighting
36 "__ du lieber!"
37 Reserved

38 Blood relatives
39 Apply oil to
42 Equi- kin
43 From __ Z
48 Nightwear
50 O'Neill's comer
53 Take by force
54 LP holder
55 Kipling's homeland
56 *The __ and the Ecstasy*
58 Well-trained one
59 "Message received"
60 Pole star?
62 Atmosphere
63 U.S.O. stalwart
64 Go off course
65 Strange sighting

WADING GAME

by Trip Payne

ACROSS

1 Donutlike roll
6 Dickens character
9 Battling
14 *Without __* (Caine movie)
15 Vitamin-bottle abbr.
16 More than a nudge
17 START OF A RIDDLE
20 Carson's successor
21 Alamogordo event
22 Car scar
23 Loft bundle
25 "From __ 60 in 8.2 seconds"
27 MIDDLE OF RIDDLE
35 Sports palace
36 Entree "bed"
37 Bro or sis
38 Acorn, e.g.
39 "The Thief of Bad Gags"
41 Water carrier
42 Guinness Book suffix
43 Hydrox rival
44 Gets ready (for)
45 END OF RIDDLE
49 __ Ridge, TN
50 Extinct New Zealand birds
51 Greek vowels
54 Wonderland-cake sign
57 Rock-band gear
61 ANSWER TO RIDDLE
64 Miscalculated
65 Roseanne's TV husband
66 Singer Della
67 Wanton looks
68 Citrus drink
69 Append

DOWN

1 Have a cry
2 Post-workout feeling
3 Hidden valley
4 Foreign debt of a sort
5 Appomattox attendee
6 President __
7 __ fixe
8 Bridge call
9 Blond shade
10 It may be put on
11 Eroded
12 Name that may ring a bell
13 First-of-month payment
18 Actor Robertson
19 Pronto
24 GP's org.
26 Mao __-tung
27 Sahara stopovers
28 Not canned
29 Take care of
30 Mr. Flynn
31 Feel poorly
32 Willow tree
33 Melanie's mama
34 Too large
39 One with lots to sell
40 Sonnet ending
41 Told the future
43 Three __ kind
44 Masters grp.
46 Dorm decor
47 Not susceptible
48 Some votes
51 Daredeviltry name
52 Get bored
53 Cropland measure
55 Leontyne Price role
56 Frog kin
58 Loquacious equine
59 Monterrey money
60 British gun
62 "__ bodkins!"
63 Generation

73 ANIMAL FAMILIES

by Mel Rosen

ACROSS

1 Spanish mark
6 Kennel order
9 Football great Tarkenton
13 *Play It __, Sam*
14 Sapporo sport
15 Captain Kirk's home
16 "Nothing __!"
17 Be a bellyacher
18 Show appreciation
19 Primate family
22 Director Howard
23 Shaving-cream type
24 Barnyard family
32 Misrepresent
33 At hand
34 Say more
36 Seth's son
37 Get duded up
39 As well
40 As well
41 Disorderly conduct
42 Platte or Pecos
43 Desert family
47 Furniture wood
48 Young boy
49 Primate family
58 Insensitive one
59 Book-jacket part
60 Field boss
61 Slots city
62 Christmas trees
63 __ Get Your Gun
64 Churchill successor
65 Porker's pen
66 Sales prospects

DOWN

1 Vocal fanfare
2 "__ a Name" (Croce tune)
3 Hibernation station
4 Flintstones' pet
5 Eat too much
6 Waves at the beach
7 Moslem cleric
8 Long sled
9 Hardly loyal
10 Cast slot
11 Not home
12 Breaks of a sort
14 Tea biscuit
20 Office seeker, for short
21 __-do-well
24 Help in a crime
25 Columbus' hometown
26 Above it all
27 *M*A*S*H* extras
28 __ a customer
29 Legal charge
30 Soothing ointment
31 Collectible car
35 '50s actress Diana
37 Pitcher's coups
38 Korean soldier
39 Draw a bead on
41 *Tobacco __*
42 Profoundly different
44 BBC's headquarters
45 Broadway failures
46 Caboose, e.g.
49 Zoning unit
50 Ran in the wash
51 First-rate
52 Move like a butterfly
53 City SE of Chicago
54 Solitary
55 Turner of Hollywood
56 Battery fluid
57 __ *Having a Baby* ('88 film)

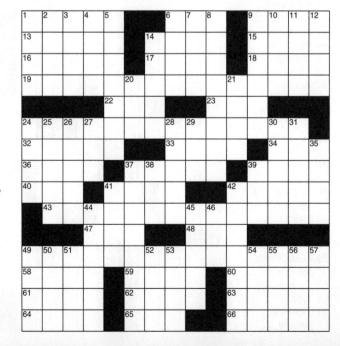

74 *GREEK ALPHABET*

by Fred Piscop

ACROSS
1 Razor brand
5 "Halt!" to a salt
10 Talk like Daffy Duck
14 Icy coating
15 *The __ Kid* (Romero role)
16 Arabian Nights count
17 Alien?
19 Men-only party
20 Sofa fabric
21 Company abbr.
22 Plants a bug
23 Telephone triad
25 Pulsate
27 Fact facer
31 They go for the gold
34 __ ease (antsy)
35 __ pants (women's wear)
38 "The Boy King"
39 Server's rewards
40 Lamb's mom
41 Angelic headgear
42 Mt. St. Helens output
43 *La Belle __* (Jolson show)
45 Kitchen gadget
46 Spiritualist's session
48 Height
50 Tropical fish
52 Profit follower
53 Mackintosh, for one
55 Spider-web type
57 Fertilizer variety

62 Be adjacent to
63 Food preservative?
65 Ade flavoring
66 Occupied
67 Boxer's wear
68 Long-standing argument
69 Port holders
70 Musical work

DOWN
1 Throat-clearing sound
2 "__ the mornin'!"
3 Poorly thought-out
4 *Tosca* tune
5 Squirrel's stash
6 Coq au __
7 Italian wine center
8 Barely sufficient
9 Doors tune of '69
10 Ali KO'd him
11 Computer company?
12 Bathday cake
13 Kiddie-lit trio
18 Sale-ad word
24 Significant __
26 Tire attachment
27 Hayworth and Coolidge
28 Beethoven's *Für __*
29 Bank convenience?
30 __ Cruces, NM
32 Foot-long device
33 *Who's Minding the __?*
36 Reverence

37 Dodger Hall-of-Famer
41 Smash show
43 %
44 Type of dancing
45 Seer's deck
47 Took home
49 Mobile homes
51 Wrestling locale
53 Knee neighbor
54 Theater award
56 Air-cond. units
58 Root for Hawaiians
59 On
60 *Song of India* actor
61 Rainbow segments
64 "Go __ your mother"

75 SHORT WEEKEND

by Eric Albert

ACROSS

1 Big blowout
5 Figurine mineral
9 Poet's feet
14 "Omigosh!"
15 Love, in the flesh
16 Go bad
17 Hood's confessor
19 Jessica or Hope
20 *Anne __ Gables*
21 Say again
23 Pigeon perches
24 X-rated stuff
25 Attack viciously
26 One with examples
27 007's alma mater
28 High point
29 Some Chicago trains
30 Soffit location
32 Old Testament heroine
34 TIROS or Echo
36 Mideast capital
39 Singer Cantrell
40 Batter's need
43 Pedestal occupant
44 Give the nod to
46 Language of India
48 Little: Fr.
49 Barbra's *Funny Girl* costar
50 Timex competitor
51 Crew-team crew
53 Adds oxygen to
54 No longer crisp
55 Breaking apart
57 Mortise filler
58 Winemaking center
59 Lorre film role
60 Outer limits
61 Look to be
62 White Christmas need

DOWN

1 Using the army, maybe
2 Plane part
3 Taps
4 The Munsters' family car
5 *Swan Lake* leaps
6 Make __ for it (flee)
7 Grumpy colleague
8 Kayak builder
9 Land in the sea?
10 On __ with (equal to)
11 Lepidopterist's catch
12 Major-league
13 Woody Allen film of '73
18 Overhauled tire
22 Set the dial to
24 Outstanding
27 *The Three Faces of __*
28 Packed away
31 Comfortable
33 Prestige level
34 Actor Mineo
35 Nonclerical
36 Sharp answer
37 Thought about
38 Butler's question
40 Pride or joy
41 In the habit of
42 Scotland's largest city
45 Jayhawker State
47 Waker-uppers
49 Signs of things to come
50 Turn down the lights
52 Fizz flavoring
53 Start stud
56 Put to work

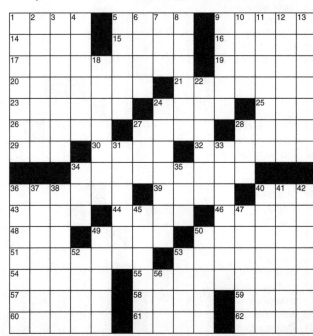

76 ALTERED STATES

by Matt Gaffney

ACROSS

1 __-mo replay
4 Adorns
11 Erving's sobriquet
14 Photo or film
15 Wife-related
16 Wallaby, for short
17 Ted Koppel's network
18 Cotton?
20 Ultimate rewards
22 Acetaminophen alternative
23 Quickness
24 Went quickly
26 Some breads
27 Pennsylvania city
28 Come into one's __
29 Went quickly
31 Oaxaca uncle
32 Proficiency
34 Midmorning
38 "How about a trip to Opryland?"
41 Candidate's concern
42 "The Rain in Spain" is one
43 Ted Turner's pride
44 QB's scores
46 Compete
47 Pound, for one
48 H.S. class
51 Prayer word
53 __ Clara, CA
54 Part of IRS
56 Rhymer's foot
57 Northwestern philanthropist?
60 Actor Wallach
61 Took the gold
62 Pre-tourney activity
63 Salon order
64 Driller's deg.
65 Jailbreaker
66 Give it a whirl

DOWN

1 Long lunch?
2 One of Carnegie's causes
3 They may be special
4 Army horn
5 Ballot marks
6 "Inka Dinka __"
7 Make a mistake
8 Havana export
9 Wilhelm was one
10 Rebuke, so to speak
11 Advise and Consent author
12 The Trials of __ O'Neill
13 Painter Jasper
19 Meredith Baxter __
21 Suffix for Brooklyn
24 Checker's claim to fame
25 Off base, perhaps
28 Gives the thumbs-up
30 __ time (never)
32 Future flower
33 First Red head
35 Plea possibility
36 The Accidental Tourist author
37 Frame of mind
39 Cake spice
40 Ripen
45 Spa features
47 Cong. contributor
48 Large number
49 Salome character
50 Makes level
52 Corpsman
53 NCO, for short
55 Slangy turndown
56 All finished
58 Man-mouse link
59 Short snort

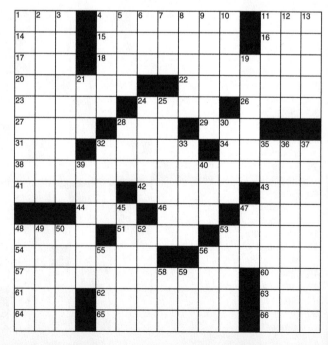

77 HOMOPHONES

by Mark Diehl

ACROSS

1 Equatorial Guinea capital
7 Oolong, e.g.
10 Soak (up)
13 One of the kingdoms
14 Equine entree
15 Big galoot
16 Actress __ Sue Martin
17 Cop, often
19 PARE
21 Goes a round (with)
22 Yen
23 Inventor Rubik
24 Auto pioneer
25 Dull pain
26 12-year-old, for instance
27 Golf prop
28 London neighborhood
29 Partygoers
30 PAIR
32 Austrian composer Oscar
35 __ mater (brain covering)
36 They may be small
39 Attack time
40 Drop suddenly
41 Overcharged
42 Elvis __ Presley
43 Display model
44 Bed material
45 PEAR
48 Tub accessories
49 Bitter feeling
51 Eroded
52 *The Name of the Rose* author
53 *Truth __* (Madonna film)
54 __-Bol (bathroom cleaner)
55 Mail-motto word
56 Drew closer to

DOWN

1 Traveler's aid
2 "__ a day . . ."
3 Citrus drink
4 Mideast rulers
5 Formal dances
6 Norwegian royal name
7 Three times
8 *The Good __*
9 Positive replies
10 Lampoons
11 Ice-hockey situation
12 Folks
17 PÈRE
18 Obliquely positioned
20 *Nouveau __*
21 Guzzler
25 Astronaut's answers
26 Salad base
28 Tart-tasting
29 Robin Williams role of '82
30 Potbelly
31 Bombeck's genre
32 Hebrews' Saturday
33 Like Tallulah's voice
34 Perched
36 Train component
37 Put back
38 Football dist.
40 One with a mortgage
41 Starr character?
43 Northern constellation
44 Raucous sound
46 Seer's discovery
47 Disney film of '82
50 Herring hue

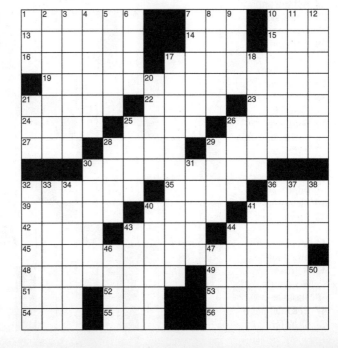

by Eric Albert

ACROSS

1 Reduce drastically
6 Retractor's meal?
10 Samoa studier
14 Author Bret
15 Zero, to Zina Garrison
16 Mrs. Lindbergh
17 Mouth-to-mouth recitation
18 Seth's brother
19 __ St. Vincent Millay
20 START OF A SAMUEL BUTLER QUOTE
22 Pea place
23 Insignificant
24 Bank breaker
25 Devout
27 Act the snoop
28 Road-sign warning
29 Kael the reviewer
31 Make faces
32 Well-defined
33 MIDDLE OF QUOTE
36 Grab greedily
37 CARE package, e.g.
38 Fully attentive
39 "The racer's edge"
40 Flower-to-be
43 Former Met Jones
44 MIT-trained architect
45 Actress Rowlands
46 Tool set
47 END OF QUOTE

50 It's a long story
52 Put in piles
53 Copycat's comment
54 Stir
55 Spread in a tub
56 __ the back (compliment)
57 Emulate Etna
58 He played Klinger
59 Panache

DOWN

1 Creole dish
2 Makeup maker
3 War store
4 Fourteen pounds
5 Man of the hour
6 Button one's lip
7 Spring singer
8 Bread chamber
9 Join metal
10 Fannie __
11 Terminus
12 Tell the world
13 Stubbornly determined
21 Roy's ride
25 Give the lowdown
26 Homeric tale
28 *Macbeth* character
29 Peach center
30 Kind of elephant
31 Actor Sal

32 Press for payment
33 Good ship of song
34 Santa's season
35 Derek and Diddley
36 Small bundles
39 Military zone
40 *Bugsy* star
41 Not at all rad
42 Beginning
44 Kitchen tool
45 High-minded
47 "Time __ the essence"
48 Vincent Lopez's theme
49 Strike callers
51 Black Angus, e.g.

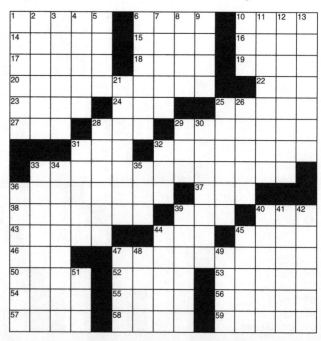

79 BOX OFFICE

by Wayne R. Williams

ACROSS

1 Skin feature
5 Flash of light
10 Aussie birds
14 "Excuse me!"
15 Heart connection
16 __ avis
17 Boxing film of '80
19 Cheese coat
20 Poetry Muse
21 "Old Blood and Guts"
23 Blocker or Rather
24 Narrow cuts
27 On the lookout
30 Boxing film of '49
32 Contend (for)
33 Donut shapes
36 Partnership word
37 School break
39 Rust causer
41 Knight's superior
42 Second showing
43 Chip off the old block
44 Some ships: Abbr.
45 Page-setting job: Abbr.
46 Boxing film of '82
49 Take care of
51 Actor Quinn
52 President pro __
55 Mr. Duck
57 Desire badly
59 Melville novel
61 Boxing film of '37
64 Falling out
65 Freeze, as roads
66 Musical ending
67 Bumbling sorts
68 From Oslo
69 __ over (capsize)

DOWN

1 Cut corners
2 *Pal Joey* writer
3 *King Lear* character
4 Give off
5 One-liner
6 Tennis shot
7 Broke out
8 Finally
9 Beer ingredient
10 Flynn of films
11 Boxing film of '79, with *The*
12 Vase with a base
13 Blue
18 Between-meal food
22 Get narrow
25 Simple shelter
26 "__ It Romantic?"
28 Narrow platform
29 Trial runs
30 Ocean motion
31 Astronomy Muse
33 Law-school course
34 Type of daisy
35 Boxing film of '71
38 __ *fan tutte* (Mozart opera)
40 The Braves' #44
41 *Ben-Hur* costar
43 Racing car, at times
47 Patterned cloth
48 Contents abbr.
50 Horn honks
52 Western resort lake
53 Skirt
54 Olympics prize
56 Related (to)
58 Billiards prop
59 Gold, in Guatemala
60 Actress Farrow
62 Astronaut Grissom
63 Simian

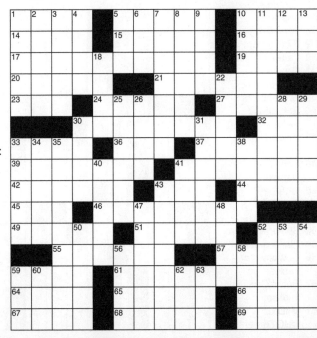

CELEBIRDIES

ACROSS

1 General Alexander et al.
6 NBC drama
11 Magnavox rival
14 African capital
15 Tony of baseball
16 Special-interest grp.
17 *Cheers* star
19 Actor Gazzara
20 Enlistees' food
21 Not appropriate
22 Lab assistant
23 Lost calf
25 TV commercial cry
27 "Do it again!"
30 Not very strong
31 "Go, team!"
32 Giraffe's cousin
35 Yorkshire town
38 "Do __ say . . ."
39 Late-night star
41 Onassis' nickname
42 Spinal parts
44 Something awful
45 "Silent" president
46 Sort of, slangily
48 "You bet!"
50 As a precaution
52 Spelunking fan
54 Plane or pliers
55 Cowboy star Lash
57 *Battle Cry* author
61 Make a misjudgment
62 *The Cosby Show* star
64 Dogpatch's Daisy __
65 Bungling
66 With speed
67 Retirees' agcy.
68 Drills a hole
69 Feathered talkers

DOWN

1 Maltreat
2 Sore spot
3 Cools down
4 Former Connecticut governor
5 Maple goo
6 __ *Doone*
7 Ease one's fears
8 Lacking firmness
9 Hindu incarnation
10 Pale-faced
11 *Lifestyles. . .* host
12 Guiding principle
13 '70s veep
18 "I've got it!"
22 End in __ (be drawn)
24 Pac-Ten team
26 Heat unit
27 Historical periods
28 *Atlantis* group
29 Jazz pianist
30 Old-time interjections
33 Auel heroine
34 Arafat's org.
36 "Phooey!"
37 Farm building
40 The jitters
43 Irani money
47 Part of FDR
49 Doc's brother
50 List parts
51 Dunn and Ephron
52 Decorative paper
53 Anagram of "tunas"
56 Say with certainty
58 Reddish-brown horse
59 Old Peruvian
60 Meets with
62 Poke fun at
63 Popeye verb

81 *LOOKING BACK*

....

by Eric Albert

ACROSS
1 Catch some rays
5 Pasta shape
10 Gymnast Korbut
14 Jazz singer James
15 Woody's *Play It Again, Sam* costar
16 Noble gas
17 He had a hammer
18 Itty-bitty bay
19 Not at all amiable
20 START OF A QUIP
22 Starr of the strips
24 Bryant or Baker
25 Gloria Vanderbilt's logo
27 Ode object
28 Sun __-sen
29 Wild spree
32 Keogh cousin: Abbr.
33 Tire track
34 Knight spot
36 In the know
37 MIDDLE OF QUIP
41 Aware of
42 He made some good points
43 "Gotcha!"
44 Malt drink
46 Can material
47 "__ Love You"
50 Dream acronym
51 Rome conqueror

53 Viscounts' superiors
55 Peke, for one
57 END OF QUIP
60 "Back to you"
61 Passes over
63 Far's partner
64 Give up rights
65 Sandy's owner
66 On a cruise
67 Grasped
68 Calliope et al.
69 Propeller-head

DOWN
1 Double-cross
2 Wisdom personified
3 Restraining order?
4 Gold measure
5 Blue-pencil
6 Occupation

7 Makes a bundle
8 __ *from the Heart*
9 Rec-room fixture
10 A while back
11 *Exodus* author
12 Event of 1849
13 Tempo marking
21 Punjab potentate
23 Cell material: Abbr.
26 Prevail
30 MGM name of the '40s
31 Go predecessor
34 Noah's number
35 Pocket filler?

36 Funny fellow
37 Ecstatic
38 Calgary happening
39 Site of the Tell legend
40 Sank
41 Rowboat device
44 In the past
45 Impasse
47 Kind words
48 Kind of pitch
49 ". . . the witch __"
52 Sunday songs
54 Dam site
56 Kiddie-lit detective
58 Andy's son
59 Brings to bear
62 Burmese statesman

ROACHES!

by Trip Payne

ACROSS

1 Tropical spot
6 Family members
10 Big chunk
14 Hawaiian veranda
15 Organic compound
16 CIA agent, maybe
17 He wrote about a cockroach
19 Official proceedings
20 Squealed
21 Sci-fi vehicle
22 Alpo rival
24 "Till death __ part"
26 Phone patrons
27 His best friend was Cockroach
31 Buffalo NHLer
32 Right-angle shape
33 Court order?
37 Pitch __-hitter
38 Max Roach, for one
42 Theology subj.
43 Pressed the doorbell
45 Mentalist's claim
46 "When the moon hits your eye . . ."
48 Hal Roach sci-fi movie
52 Nelson in the news
55 *Coal Miner's Daughter* subject
56 Mutate, maybe

57 Raft propeller
58 Actress Swenson
62 Use grindstones
63 He wrote about a cockroach
66 Personal quirks
67 Original thought
68 Bizarre
69 Roadside quaffs
70 Costner role
71 Famed physicist

DOWN

1 Landon et al.
2 *Scarlett* estate
3 __ upswing (rising)
4 Sluggishness
5 Columnist Smith
6 Large shark

7 Hard facts
8 __ choy (salad veggie)
9 Like thirst
10 More minuscule
11 Actress Sondra
12 Preacher's spot
13 Knocks on the noggin
18 African antelope
23 Every last bit
25 Place for wood
26 Unexcited
27 Ruler in 1900
28 Mandlikova of tennis
29 Deep black
30 Largo and lento
34 Mill input
35 Eastern European

36 Half of GE
39 Did an angler's job
40 West Point sch.
41 Come down
44 Heathen descriptor
47 Actress Van Vooren
49 Ariz. neighbor
50 Camel cousins
51 Vega's constellation
52 Bombay-born conductor
53 Steer clear of
54 Present time
57 *The Defiant* __
59 Bar food
60 Little lady
61 On the ocean
64 Horace work
65 Deteriorate

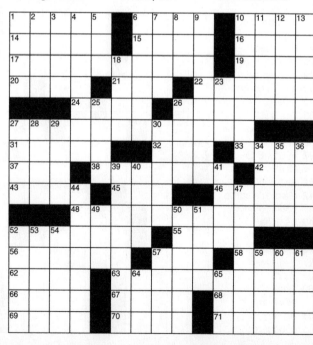

83 ROMAN-TIC MOVIES

by Eric Albert

ACROSS
1 Drum partner
5 Scale a peak
10 Exercise target
14 Laze about
15 Spanish poet
16 *Jungle Book* star
17 Roman-tic movie of '35?
20 Get larger
21 Workshop hardware
22 Hard to solve
23 Christian Science founder
24 Fizz preceder?
25 Baghdad natives
28 Withdraw (from)
29 Pug's punch
32 In progress
33 Letter opener
34 Unadorned
35 Roman-tic movie of '72?
38 Diner sign
39 Paris airport
40 Lab copy
41 Actress Carrie
42 Surrounded by
43 Lacking a key
44 Cut closely
45 Play the horn
46 Achieve through effort
49 Emulate Niobe
50 Swear solemnly
53 Roman-tic movie of '80?
56 Pull apart
57 New Zealand native
58 Brisbane buddy
59 Give the nod to
60 Shirt inserts
61 Novel need

DOWN
1 Diamond damage
2 Tiny bit
3 Fiber source
4 Architectural add-on
5 Makes indistinct
6 On a high plane
7 Pupil's surroundings
8 AT&T competitor
9 Violent reaction
10 Lens setting
11 Café au __
12 Assist in illegality
13 In use
18 Finale
19 Privy to
23 Peter Shaffer play
24 Erle's lawyer
25 *Peer Gynt* playwright
26 Hand off
27 Playing marble
28 Use as a weapon
29 Medea's husband
30 Sports site
31 Cut at an angle
33 *Peanuts*, for one
34 Claus von __
36 Freeze and frieze
37 Inky animals
42 Sills solo
43 *Dynasty* role
44 Tee container
45 *The Champ* Oscar winner
46 '60s hairstyle
47 Hard journey
48 Singer Turner
49 Stallion stopper
50 Small vessel
51 Mr. Preminger
52 Stimulate
54 Tit for __
55 Diminutive demon

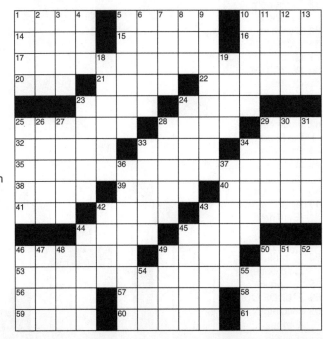

SERVICE CHARGE

by Donna J. Stone

ACROSS

1 Job opening
5 Haarlem export
10 Bogus Bach
13 Coffee-break time
15 Slezak of *One Life to Live*
16 Singer Rawls
17 START OF A QUIP
19 Porter's kin
20 Italian squares
21 In reserve
23 "Later!"
25 English cathedral city
26 Nod or wink
29 Former talk-show host Friedman
31 Jai __
32 Parliament members
33 Ski wood
36 PART 2 OF QUIP
39 PART 3 OF QUIP
41 Lines of thought?
42 It comes from the heart
44 Pack provisions
45 Jewelry material
46 Fly the coop
48 Pyramus' lover
51 "Big Three" site
53 Acid type
54 __ rat (is suspicious)
58 __ spree
59 END OF QUIP
63 Gladiator's item
64 Monteverdi opera
65 Handbag part
66 Spud bud
67 Debra of *Love Me Tender*
68 Head set

DOWN

1 Put one's foot down
2 One of Jacob's sons
3 Recruit-to-be
4 Kilimanjaro's setting
5 Rib
6 Spoon-bender Geller
7 Glowing
8 He was liked in '56
9 Conniption fit
10 Hair braid
11 Sweet, to Solti
12 Pretty peculiar
14 Toyota rival
18 Keen
22 PBS benefactor
24 Troop troupe
25 Word form for "within"
26 Free from danger
27 Bjorn opponent
28 Social clique
30 Whale of a tale
32 Apollo's instrument
33 Dashiell's dog
34 Put an end to
35 Redcoat general
37 Shari Lewis puppet
38 Stud site
40 Magnify
43 Go for it
45 "__ was saying, . . ."
46 Film Tarzan Lincoln
47 Bouillabaisse and burgoo
48 Porterhouse alternative
49 Mead need
50 Fuming
52 __ *in the Dark*
55 Cremona cash, once
56 Feature
57 Snake charmer's crew
60 Keogh kin
61 One of 3M's M's
62 Mini, to McTavish

85 HOLLYWOOD & OVINE

....

by Richard Silvestri

ACROSS

1 Hammett hound
5 Placed on display
10 Open a crack
14 Honest-to-goodness
15 Lake craft
16 Encrypt
17 Sheepish actress?
19 *And __ There Were None*
20 Years and years
21 Got ready for a bout
23 Butler of fiction
26 Put aside
27 Famous family of Virginia
28 Self-image
30 Prepared prunes
33 Pierce portrayer
34 Out-of-the-way
36 Language suffix
37 Easy basket
39 Profit chaser?
40 Dreadlocks wearer
42 Part of NATO
43 Puzzle word
46 Oliver's colleague
47 Abundant supply
49 "__ on a bet!"
50 Young 'uns
51 Alter
53 Late TV exec Arledge
55 Awe-inspiring
57 Feel poorly
58 Kind of exam
59 Sheepish actor?
65 Folklore villain
66 First name in cosmetics
67 Light and graceful
68 Geek
69 Orchestra members
70 Make public

DOWN

1 Hand holder
2 Get an eyeful
3 Put down a road
4 Ms. MacGraw
5 Kid's transport
6 Jessica or Otto
7 Three __ match
8 Mary of comics
9 Proximate
10 On the go
11 Sheepish director?
12 "Zip-__-Doo-Dah"
13 Tear apart
18 Bottom-line gain
22 Make changes
23 Spin a yarn
24 Sheepish actress?
25 Biblical twin
26 "__ to Watch Over Me"
27 Dey-time drama?
29 Grandpa Walton portrayer
31 House and grounds
32 Campus bigwigs
35 Approximately
38 Singer Page
41 In the matter of
44 Lawmaking body
45 Takes steps
48 Soothed
52 Say "Nyah-nyah!"
54 José's hurrah
55 Before you know it
56 Cheer on
57 In the sack
60 Noshed on
61 Make an arrest
62 By means of
63 Make a mistake
64 Ham holder

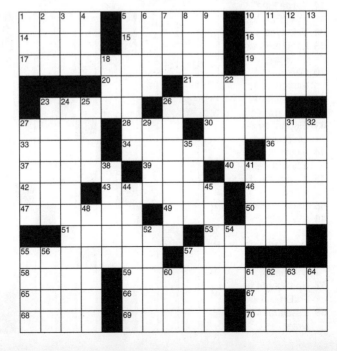

LITERALLY SPEAKING

by Eric Albert

ACROSS

1 Sing the praises of
5 *The Art of Loving* author
10 Coal carrier
14 Moreover
15 Ms. Semple McPherson
16 Palindrome place
17 DE(LOST)ED
20 __ in the Park
21 Spot remover?
22 It flies in fights
23 Hit the mall
24 Narrow waterway
28 Exude odors
29 Hulk Hogan's org.
32 Mail device
33 Mrs. Dithers
34 *Tosca* tune
35 SEN(FLAW)SE
38 Tide type
39 Language expert Chomsky
40 Give a response
41 Sea slitherer
42 Farm dwellers
43 Elephant's counterpart
44 Movie based on a board game
45 It's furry and purry
46 Shoe support
49 SW California city
54 ORDI(NIL)NARY
56 Kandinsky colleague
57 He thought up Friday
58 *Essay on Man* writer

59 Betray boredom
60 Furry swimmer
61 Depict unfairly

DOWN

1 Mary's pet
2 *Et* __ (and others: Lat.)
3 Former UN member
4 Doctor's order
5 Make a spreading search
6 Strictness
7 Leave out
8 What boys will be
9 Mike, to Archie
10 Make possible
11 Rapid pace
12 Double reed
13 Taper off
18 Not as certain
19 Make dinner
23 Blood component
24 Movie part
25 __ *Men and a Baby*
26 Part of RFD
27 On the apex
28 Mel of baseball
29 Inflict
30 Show fear
31 Arbuckle's nickname
33 Big bill
34 Solemn assent
36 Veiled venom
37 Subterranean passage
42 "__ want for Christmas . . ."
43 Comet's colleague
44 Comic Myron
45 Kayak relative
46 Pitch-black
47 Les Paul hit of '50
48 Mixed bag
49 Search (through)
50 Current units
51 Out of control
52 "Uh-uh"
53 Once again
55 Procure

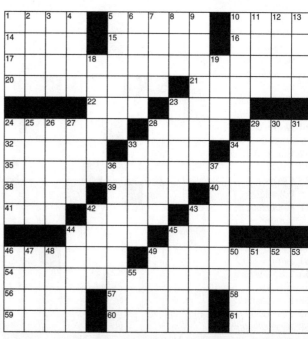

BODY WEAR

by A.J. Santora

ACROSS

1 Abbott or Costello
9 __ Antilles
15 Losing money
16 Natural-gas compound
17 Hoopster's wear
18 Swell, '60s-style
19 Shoebox letters
20 __ Dhabi
21 Little squirt
22 Part of USNA
24 Poet Teasdale
26 Finish-line prop
29 Whole bunch
30 More vigorous
31 Court party
32 XIII quadrupled
34 Beret kin
36 Late author Buscaglia
37 Umps' wear
42 __ Gatos, CA
43 Pittsburgh river
44 Copacabana locale
45 One against
47 Forearm bones
49 All ears
53 Lemon skin
54 Transmission choice
55 Up __ (stuck)
56 Gray work
58 Point (at)
60 Columnist LeShan
61 Literary comparison
63 MPs' wear
65 Kitchen tool
66 Carpenter's creation
67 "Good Night __" (old song)
68 Swore (to)

DOWN

1 Equates
2 Treat glass
3 Load cargo
4 Shoot-breeze link
5 High land
6 King Hussein, e.g.
7 Hairdresser's nightmare?
8 Ames and Jaymes
9 Dancer's wear
10 French infinitive
11 Blows a circuit
12 South America's largest city
13 It may be SWAK
14 Bandleader Alvino
21 Special pleasure
23 Cobbler's piercers
25 Pennsylvania city
27 Social equal
28 An asteroid
30 '60s casual wear
33 "How was __ know?"
35 Fi preceder
37 Thunder sound
38 Sharpen
39 Highly regarded
40 William Bendix TV role
41 Wrongful act
46 Big Ten team
48 Biblical landfall
50 "We __ amused"
51 Hawk
52 Ruffled the hair
55 Walk slowly
57 Gen. Robt. __
59 Fake, for short
61 Scale note
62 Phoneticist's symbols: Abbr.
63 Get __ for effort
64 Satisfied sounds

JOURNALISM 101

by Alex Vaughn

ACROSS

1 Beet variety
6 Some seaweed
11 Ruefully ironic
14 Western show
15 Brings up
16 Farm chopper
17 Classic comedy routine
19 __ Khan
20 Unspecified folks
21 Chicken choice
23 Rented an alley
26 Their work is filling
27 Felt sore
28 Actor with the shortest name
29 Salamander
30 Canonized *femmes*: Abbr.
31 __-Locka, FL
32 Wet Williams
35 Tokyo honorific
36 Besieged one's remark
38 "Xanadu" rock group
39 Dad, so to speak
42 NASA affirmative
43 Southwest predator
44 North Slope quest
45 Back in time
46 Brian of skating
47 Map boundary
50 Makes a face
51 Cube clutcher
52 Pizzeria products
53 Menlo Park monogram
54 Bestselling kids' book
59 Fashioned like
60 Specialized angler
61 "Encore!"
62 Rebellious Turner
63 Lose stiffness
64 Safecrackers, slangily

DOWN

1 Intimidate
2 "That's what you think!"
3 From __ Z
4 Fixes sneaks
5 Spoke monotonously
6 Canine comments
7 Aloha token
8 Small attic
9 Fiery felony
10 Probate concerns
11 Quitter's remark
12 Famous synonymist
13 Long time
18 Actor Beatty
22 Make flour finer
23 __ profundo
24 Based on eight
25 Children's remark
26 Carting cost
28 Speedometer reading: Abbr.
31 Hold the deed to
32 Reaction to a rodent
33 Bugs' pursuer
34 Laughs heartily
37 Pasture plaint
40 After-dinner snack
41 Permissible
43 Give portents of
45 San __, TX
46 Words on an arrow
47 Mighty one of myth
48 Florida city
49 "I didn't know she had it __"
50 Boom-bah preceder
52 Wrongdoer, to cops
55 Antique auto
56 Hang back
57 Appreciate jazz
58 Light-switch positions

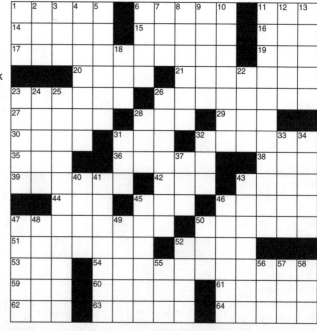

89 ANGLERS

by Randolph Ross

ACROSS
1 Mixologist's milieu
4 Didn't like
9 Bread spread
13 Hwy.
14 Los __, NM
16 Actor Arkin
17 Chapter in history
18 He reached his peak
20 Mrs. Flintstone
22 Mauna __
23 Texas city
27 Shiite belief
32 *The Way We Were* director
34 Dopey's brother
35 Climbing vines
36 Hall-of-Fame pitcher
41 *Do __ Waltz?*
42 Common Market abbr.
43 *Wild Kingdom* host
48 MP's quarries
49 Nineveh native
51 USSR successor
53 "__ Theme" (*Doctor Zhivago* tune)
55 Lincoln's Chief Justice
62 Byron work
63 Part of WATS
64 Ho Chi Minh City, once
65 French diarist
66 Tailless cat
67 Rent out
68 Hood's "heater"

DOWN
1 Cook up
2 Large courtyards
3 Kingdoms
4 Take a chance
5 It may be pale
6 Typewriter setting
7 Down Under bird
8 Small blob
9 Glove-box contents
10 __ Baba
11 Asian ox
12 "__ for the money . . ."
15 Jack of *Barney Miller*
19 Trap, in a way
21 Director Elaine
24 Cree or Crow
25 Most with August birthdays
26 Chinese nuts
28 Chair part
29 Short street
30 Rent-__
31 Ger. currency, till 1999
33 __ *Man!* ('73 film)
36 Tobacco chunk
37 Dynamic start
38 Sky-high
39 __ Kid (Cagney role)
40 Towel word
41 "__ Believer"
44 French philosopher
45 A Mandrell sister
46 Singer Peeples
47 Lamour outfit
50 Gymnast Comaneci
52 Officeholders
54 Mailed away
55 *Cheers* role
56 Southern constellation
57 Author Deighton
58 Factor of makeup
59 Go quickly
60 Khan opener?
61 Morse message

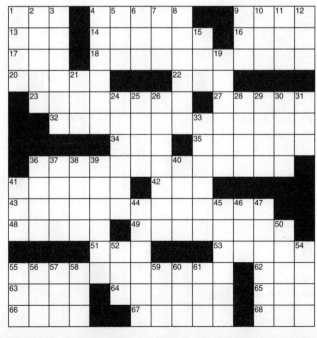

by Eric Albert

ACROSS

1 Spa feature
10 Savalas role
15 Frozen dessert
16 Lloyd Webber hit
17 START OF A DISRAELI QUOTE
18 Delicious
19 List item
20 European airline
21 Get moving
24 *The __ Hawk* (Flynn film)
25 Phone bug
28 "__ heeere!"
29 Meat cut
31 Drink a bit
32 Argentine region
33 MIDDLE OF QUOTE
37 London square
39 Schedule abbr.
42 Darkroom device
43 Abandon
46 Beast of burden
47 Make public
48 Salary standard
49 Sask. neighbor
50 Mr. Goldfinger
51 Comedian Smirnoff
54 END OF QUOTE
58 Legal defense
59 Court addict
60 British diarist
61 Booth and Guiteau

DOWN

1 Put in stitches
2 Bat material
3 Hula strings
4 Four-and-a-half score
5 C-major's analog
6 Pasta shape
7 In pieces
8 Diminutive
9 __ up (in a lather)
10 Bogart thriller
11 Egg cell
12 Kirk, to McCoy
13 Cash device: Abbr.
14 Bandleader Kyser
20 Skewered meat
21 Alts.
22 "__ believe in yesterday"
23 Pregame speech
24 Shankar's instrument
25 Casual shirt
26 "__ was saying, . . ."
27 School grp.
29 DC-10 device
30 Hockey-shutout box score
32 Message unit
34 "The Tears __ Clown"
35 Uncommon sort
36 Hoopster Baylor
37 *Miss Pym Disposes* author
38 Cell molecule
40 Furry scarf
41 Whichever
43 Boat basin
44 Unchanged
45 School break
48 Gets real angry
49 __ Dick
50 Puts fear into
51 Jabber
52 Fermented drink
53 Runner Keino
54 "Let's call __ day"
55 __-Wan Kenobi
56 Sister of a sort
57 Printer's units

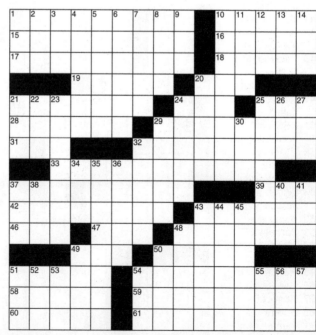

91 MOVIE DIRECTION

by Wayne R. Williams

ACROSS

1 In addition
4 Elevator inventor
8 Poirot, e.g.
14 Coffee server
15 Roof device
16 Country singer Nelson
17 Crouse movie of '77
20 *My Name Is __ Lev*
21 Tip or hip ending
22 Backtalk
23 Diminutive suffix
25 Pants man Strauss
27 *My Three Sons* grandpa
29 Can't stand
31 Wrap up
36 Chemical ending
37 Wear away
39 Haitian rum
40 Kind of triangle
42 Parody writer
44 Spanish hero
45 Train station
47 "The Boy King"
48 Pennsylvania school
50 Legendary tale
51 Shaker __, OH
52 OK Corral lawman
54 Golfer Ballesteros
56 West et al.
60 Poi base
62 Shady spot
65 Finney movie of '84
68 Hereditary
69 *Enterprise* crewman
70 Kitchen topper
71 Hole enlarger
72 *Hook* role
73 The Mormons: Abbr.

DOWN

1 Tubby the __
2 Raw minerals
3 Peck movie of '59
4 Dillon movie of '79
5 Inventor's initials
6 Quaint hotels
7 Reached an agreement
8 Veer
9 __ Abner
10 Wallach and Whitney
11 Arm bone
12 Some football results
13 Dame Myra __
18 Drenched
19 __ Haw
24 Work for
26 Wilding movie of '50
27 Swiss city
28 Ted, to JFK, Jr.
30 __ the line (obeyed)
32 Toy-store magnate Schwarz
33 Sorvino movie of '83
34 West Pt. grad
35 Pub fliers
38 Catch sight of
41 XIII quadrupled
43 Prize monies
46 Josephine was one
49 Tea-party host
53 Bowl cheer
55 Trade-training abbr.
56 *The Ghost and Mrs. __*
57 Charles' sister
58 Author Ferber
59 Cloth line
61 Egg cell
63 Novelist Bagnold
64 Curtain hardware
66 Hwy.
67 Grand __ Opry

92 U-U-U

by Eric Albert

ACROSS

1. Clear tables
4. Wife of Jacob
8. Handy
14. Give __ whirl (try)
15. Egg
16. South American
17. YEW
20. Letter from Paul
21. *Boyz __ Hood*
22. Heart of the matter
23. __ *supra* (see above)
25. A bit immodest
29. For example
30. Mine find
33. Quaid film of '88
34. Sedate
35. The one left standing
37. EWE
41. Safari land
42. "__ River"
43. Goon's gun
44. Crack a code
47. Radio regulators: Abbr.
50. Shapeless mass
52. Speak roughly
53. "Ooh __!"
54. Person with a PC
56. Obsolete eatery
59. YOU
63. Thriller of '60
64. One revolution
65. Yanks' home
66. "__ they run . . ."
67. Perry's creator
68. Cal. page

DOWN

1. Weightlifter's pride
2. Perfect place
3. One's marbles
4. Yuppie abode
5. Mr. Knievel
6. "Till we meet again"
7. Med. ins. co.
8. Irish province
9. Merit-badge holder
10. Old anesthetic
11. Cone producer
12. Burmese statesman
13. Tennis stroke
18. Comedian Kabibble
19. Reverse the effects of
24. Not alfresco
26. Rib relinquisher
27. Rooster's topper
28. Chatter
30. "__ to Be You"
31. Comedienne Charlotte
32. Dazzling display
34. Foul spot
36. Harrison's *Star Wars* role
37. Ground grain
38. Latch __ (get)
39. Bug-zapper ancestor
40. Fuse word
41. Soviet spies
45. Before
46. Actress Irene
47. Known to all
48. Contract part
49. Forty winks
51. Big name in beer
53. Chaney of film
55. London section
57. Caspian Sea feeder
58. Ripped up
59. Second ltr. addendum
60. Vane dir.
61. Ham holder
62. Soap ingredient

93 BRASS TACTICS

by Donna J. Stone

ACROSS

1 Machine parts
5 Sudden spurt
10 King's mad dog
14 Foster a felon
15 F. Scott's spouse
16 Birdsong of basketball
17 Munich mister
18 History homework
19 Computer command
20 START OF A QUOTE BY RICHARD STRAUSS
23 Sushi-bar selection
24 Society-column word
25 Lysol target
28 Wine word
31 __ mater
34 Corn portion
35 Cover stories?
38 Exeter elevator
40 MIDDLE OF QUOTE
43 Nest or burrow
44 Slogan of a sort
45 Symbol of sturdiness
46 Prepare to fly
48 "How was __ know?"
49 Ersatz emerald
51 Under the weather
53 Foreman's forte
54 END OF QUOTE
62 Field of study
63 Excite
64 Euro Disney attraction
65 Spice-rack item
66 Everyday
67 Worshipper's place?
68 Salami shop
69 Sordid
70 Lifesaver flavor

DOWN

1 "All the Way" lyricist
2 Busy as __
3 Mr. Griffin
4 *Julia* actress
5 Conductor George
6 Uruguayan coin
7 To boot
8 Sitting Bull's st.
9 Guatemalan language
10 Singer Elvis
11 Hatch's home
12 Teasing talk
13 Sugar suffix
21 Recovery regimen, for short
22 Scones partner
25 Genesis character
26 Mystical deck
27 Luncheonette lure
28 Exodus locale
29 Roeper's partner
30 The __ Kid (Western hero)
32 Cretan king
33 Black key
36 Dachshundlike
37 Word of salutation
39 Little guy
41 Baja city
42 Errata
47 UN branch
50 In the heavens
52 *Mission: Impossible* actor
53 Singer Smith
54 Perry's victory site
55 Late singer Carter
56 Get up
57 Blue hue
58 Magellan discovery
59 Stereo's ancestor
60 Gouda alternative
61 Unimportant
62 Slap on

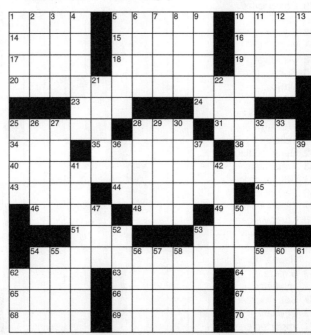

CAPITALISM

by Bob Lubbers

ACROSS

1 Mineo and Maglie
5 Pale-faced
10 Rotisserie need
14 __ happens (incidentally)
15 Banal
16 Mitchell mansion
17 South Korean singers?
19 Algerian port
20 *The Messiah* composer
21 Coming to terms
23 Capri, for one
25 Gets the point
26 Toyland visitors
29 "What's __ Pussycat?"
32 Composers' org.
35 Cookie tycoon Wally
36 Mini-river
38 *Ben-__* (Heston film)
39 __ Jose, CA
40 Plays for time
41 Western Indian
42 Rural lodging
43 Arab rulers
44 Cut short
45 Part of USNA
47 Teacher's deg.
48 Karpov's game
49 Move slowly
51 Diamond Head's home
53 Sinatra specialty
57 Country, to Caesar
61 Imported cheese

62 Italian lovers?
64 Author Morrison
65 Villain's expression
66 Greek letters
67 Sp. miss
68 Group doctrine
69 Budget component

DOWN

1 Miss America wear
2 Taking a cruise
3 Detroit NFLer
4 Bones up on
5 Bikini, for one
6 __ Lanka
7 Derisive sound
8 Suffix for leather
9 Duck dwellings
10 Fur wraps
11 French skydiver's gear?
12 OPEC member
13 Sharp taste
18 Not so much
22 Workhorse groups
24 Main course
26 Washbowl
27 Hotpoint competitor
28 German jet-setter?
30 Slipped up
31 Kook
33 Saturn and Mercury
34 Gets ready, for short

36 Newsman Donaldson
37 DDE opponent in '56
40 Soft minerals
44 Camera part
46 Tiredness cause
48 Number-one son's surname
50 Actor Buchholz
52 In two
53 "Shall we?" response
54 Nasal appraisal
55 Zilch
56 FBI agents
58 Solemn ceremony
59 Optimist's words
60 Exec. aide
63 Shoe width

95 AQUARIANS

by Eric Albert

ACROSS

1 Needed a massage
6 Cutting comment
10 Bush Cabinet member
14 Triangle, e.g.
15 Healing plant
16 Superman's mother
17 Apple implement
18 Frat event
20 *Stand by Me* star
22 Cola cooler
23 Weight
24 Refuser's phrase
28 Won out over
31 Epic '59 film
32 Ms. Lauder
33 Peruvian place
36 Fool's wear
37 Twain portrayer
41 Old hand
43 "My Way" composer
44 Signals for a cab
47 Eagerly accept
50 Small stinger
51 Render illegible
52 Actor O'Shea
55 Glasgow "go"
56 *Sullivan's Travels* actress
60 *Cosmos* author
63 Kidney-related
64 Producer De Laurentiis
65 South African native
66 Commercial manicurist
67 Serb or Croat
68 Building add-ons
69 More self-conscious

DOWN

1 Chalk up (to)
2 Options
3 Tryon novel
4 Fencing need
5 Author Earl __ Biggers
6 Wash down
7 Standoffish
8 He's synonymous with synonyms
9 Noodle, so to speak
10 Harsh horn
11 Stirrup site
12 *The A-Team* heavyweight
13 Fork over
19 Needle dropper
21 Advanced deg.
25 "Hello, Young Lovers" musical
26 Beer holder
27 Physics unit
29 "__ for Two"
30 Snakelike swimmer
31 Bullion shape
33 Mr. Chaney
34 Sort
35 Wall St. employee
38 Boater or skimmer
39 Shout of surprise
40 Boat propeller
41 Nightwear
42 Jamaican export
45 Trickle-out amount
46 NFL player
48 His name may ring a bell
49 Zeus' son
50 Ad follower
52 Industrialist
53 As a total
54 *Peanuts* character
57 Tear down
58 Munitions
59 Rachel's sister
60 LP successors
61 Be under the weather
62 Geneticist's letters

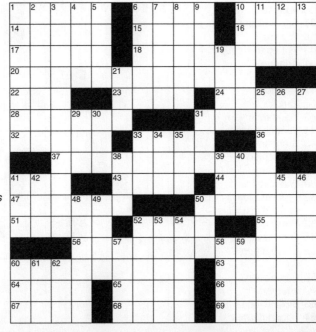

ACROSS

1 Hindu title
4 Scare away
9 Mississippi quartet?
14 Checkers
15 Actor Andrew
16 Mother-of-pearl
17 Military asst.
18 Oscillation anagram
20 Helmsley's namesakes
22 Spherical bodies
23 Garr of *Tootsie*
24 Stevedores' grp.
27 Los __, NM
31 Permutation anagram
34 Giant great
35 Kimono sash
36 Pet-shop buy
37 Ballet wear
38 Pruned
40 Not up to snuff
41 Ariadne's father
42 "__! poor Yorick"
43 Yucatan Indian
44 Feedbag tidbit
45 Stand for
46 Desecration anagram
50 Wild cat
52 __ kwon do (martial art)
53 Puts on TV
54 Grub
56 Close a purse again
58 Percolation anagram
63 Biblical judge
64 Sports figures
65 Benefit
66 Wide width
67 Marriage-vow word
68 Spills the beans
69 Bolshevik

DOWN

1 Mosaic pieces
2 Cash in
3 Procreation anagram
4 Friends of faunae: Abbr.
5 German toast
6 Black gold
7 "Sail __ Ship of State!"
8 Casino game
9 Make possible
10 Spanish beat
11 Part of M.S.
12 Pause fillers
13 Complete collection
19 Fuming
21 Mythical crier et al.
25 Greek satirist
26 Number cruncher
28 Enumeration anagram
29 Director Preminger
30 Erwin and Gilliam
32 Make free (of)
33 One of the Graces
37 Crownlets
38 __ Alto, CA
39 Baldwin or Guinness
41 Shemp's brother
43 Words to live by
46 Not refined
47 Jump the tracks
48 Irish city
49 Sighted
51 Baltic residents
55 Minor fight
57 Building wings
58 Austral. state
59 DDE's arena
60 Propel, in a way
61 "__ been had!"
62 White House nickname

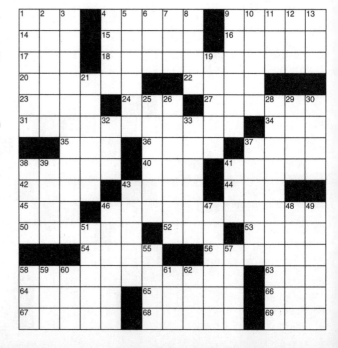

97 THAT'S A WRAP

by Eric Albert

ACROSS

1 Thick rug
5 African tree
11 G&S princess
14 Rail rider
15 Senescence
16 Sort of sauce
17 French revolutionary
19 Fine and dandy
20 Noble principles
21 Marshy area
22 "It's cold!"
23 Like a non-rolling stone?
24 Mah-jongg piece
26 Carson replacement
27 Bouquet
28 Like some hair
29 Slow up
30 __ Hari
31 Winker
32 Space center
36 Song of the south
37 Take to heart
38 Striking object
39 Court jester
40 Chicago NBAer
44 Party cheese
45 Numerical suffix
46 Melville book
47 Be a stool pigeon
48 Lend a hand
49 Footballer/actor Alex
50 __ Dhabi
51 Hot stuff
54 Oil source
55 Put into words
56 Dorothy Gale's dog
57 Wool source
58 Harbor builder
59 Playing-fields place

DOWN

1 Barbie seafood
2 Bad-luck bringer
3 Convent head
4 Use restraint
5 Conks on the noggin
6 Mideast name
7 Coleridge composition
8 Sot
9 Come to terms
10 "I've __ Lonely Too Long"
11 Columbus' queen
12 Simile hardware
13 *Driving Miss Daisy* actor
18 Underhanded
24 "See ya!"
25 Rowena's husband
26 Rude look
28 Texas city
29 Colored cloth
30 Become engaged
31 Risk-taker Knievel
32 She had "It"
33 Native ability
34 Walk the floor
35 One billion years
36 Hold tight
39 Felt hat
40 From memory
41 Eradicate
42 Bring about
43 Instruction unit
45 Church offering
46 License plate
48 Egyptian snakes
49 Athlete's trouble spot
52 Scientist's place
53 WNW opposite

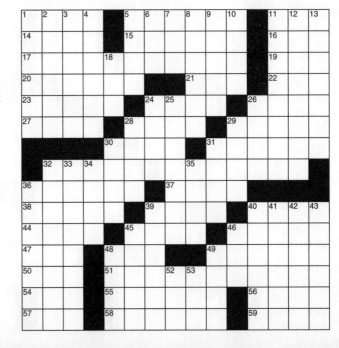

by Matt Gaffney

ACROSS

1 French states
6 Kept a low profile
9 Reference-book name
14 Biblical verb
15 White House nickname
16 Glue variety
17 MARS
19 Quite disgusted
20 Computer command
21 Keats work
22 Asset adjective
25 Kind of beef
29 Road reversal
30 Ogle
32 Where many folks live
33 End-of-day rituals
35 Chapel Hill sch.
36 Passed out
38 Musical taste
40 Gunfight site
42 Ratio phrase
43 Space Needle's city
44 Golf's "Slammer"
45 Camden Yards Players
47 Some Tuscans
48 "For Me and My __"
49 Impromptu outing
51 Chris, to Evonne
54 PLUTO
58 Winter month, in Mexico
59 __ Marie Saint
60 Mrs. Kramden
61 Assad's land
62 "Uh-huh"
63 Religious belief

DOWN

1 Flow out
2 __ Aviv
3 Jack Benny's 39, e.g.
4 Japanese dish
5 Add, perhaps
6 Ms. Jessica
7 "Yeah, sure!"
8 __ Moines, IA
9 Grid judge
10 Unseal, old-style
11 NEPTUNE
12 Spread out
13 Hunted and pecked
18 Silly Caesar
22 Polynesian party
23 "__ skin off my nose!"
24 MERCURY
25 Ranch beasts
26 "Be good __ gone"
27 Look over
28 Rebel Turner
30 Men's shop buys
31 Melodic
34 Exemplar of evil
36 Stable infant
37 Comic Johnson
39 Serling and Stewart
41 Corp. boss
42 How jet-setters travel
44 Singer O'Connor
45 Folklore beasts
46 Pluvial
47 Groan evoker, maybe
49 Baloney, so to speak
50 PDQ
52 *Exodus* character
53 Mauna __
54 *L.A. Law* actress
55 CCLI doubled
56 Lt.-to-be's place
57 The __ State (Idaho)

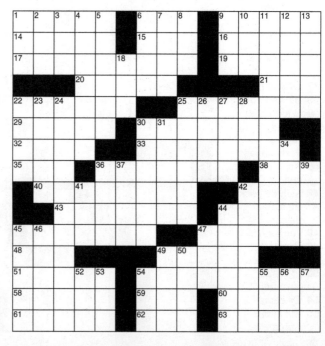

99 WILDE ADVICE

by Wayne R. Williams

ACROSS

1 Columnist Bombeck
5 Sounded shocked
11 Police dept. alert
14 Hood's knife
15 *Taxi* role
16 *Horton Hears a __!* (Seuss book)
17 START OF AN OSCAR WILDE QUOTE
20 Hindu group
21 Simon and Tsongas
22 Jason's objective
25 Position troops
26 Rodeo rope
27 Climb up
30 UFO pilots
31 Of a leg bone
33 Kind of hygiene
37 MIDDLE OF QUOTE
40 Stock order
41 Ukrainian port
42 Fire preceder
43 Hold back
45 National Leaguer
47 Comrades in arms
50 Deep singers
51 Gorby's missus
52 Coral island
54 END OF QUOTE
60 Vane dir.
61 Phoneticist's marking
62 Light gas
63 Sun. homily
64 Brown ermines
65 Watch over

DOWN

1 Cornerstone abbr.
2 Greek P
3 $1,000,000, for short
4 Shorebird
5 Formation flyers
6 Like crazy
7 Rational
8 Bakery buy
9 USN rank
10 Dig out
11 Fifth-rate
12 Sleuth Vance
13 Overbearing
18 Leave empty
19 Peke or pom
22 Guitar ridges
23 Limber
24 Studio support
25 Cold-cut emporia
27 Put up with
28 Trig functions
29 Hamlet contraction
32 Sikorsky and Stravinsky
34 WPA projects
35 Burning
36 Metallic fabrics
38 M. Pascal
39 Incendiary substance
44 Bailiwicks
46 On an angle
47 Van Gogh locale
48 "Jezebel" singer
49 Birdman of Alcatraz, e.g.
50 Good things
52 Taj Mahal site
53 Quick pace
55 Meal ingredient
56 Cpl. or Sgt.
57 Born, in Bordeaux
58 Swindle
59 Last word

ACROSS

1 Author Seton
5 Surfeit
9 Toss out
14 Felt bad about
15 *Goodbye, Columbus* author
16 Library no-no
17 Leading man?
18 At a distance
19 Moving about
20 Supporting a London paper?
23 Charlotte et al.
24 Mr. Guthrie
25 Mail again
28 Snacked on
29 Con game
33 Opening words
34 Make __ (achieve some progress)
36 One-time link
37 Baltimore paper's annual cycle?
40 Botch up
41 Danny and Stubby
42 __ nous
43 Goes to seed
45 Dallas sch.
46 Commencement
47 Cavs or Bucs
49 Gin flavoring
50 Surround a Boston paper?
56 Plotting group
57 Bleachers level
58 Fall birthstone
59 R&B singer Adams
60 "__ Petite" (Jackie Wilson song)
61 Bill-signing needs
62 Reach
63 Talks and talks and talks
64 *The Razor's* __

DOWN

1 A man from Amman
2 Hosiery shade
3 "No problem!"
4 Stage-door Johnnies, e.g.
5 Gave marks
6 Some apartments
7 A Four Corners state
8 Appears menacing
9 Sluggish sort
10 Sagan book
11 Confirmation, for one
12 Yard-sale sign
13 __ annum
21 Northerner of film
22 Italian city
25 Stair part
26 Start of a Spanish year
27 React with surprise
28 It's often bid
30 Untouchables, e.g.
31 Take __ for the worse
32 *Olympia* artist
34 Unevenness
35 Put on __ (act snooty)
38 Kind of congestion
39 Award-show prop
44 Nested layers
46 States of warning
48 Bright display
49 Mindless followers
50 Auto racer Yarborough
51 Phrase of doubt
52 "__ yellow ribbon . . ."
53 Newspaper page
54 Sudden noise
55 Ultimatum word
56 Vital part

101 POSTSCRIPTS

by Randolph Ross

ACROSS

1 Brit's raincoat
4 Complain
8 Nicolas of *Moonstruck*
12 Verdi opera
13 Mild cigar
15 Quite excited
16 Early Beatles song
18 Math. course
19 "__ you so"
20 Boards Amtrak
22 "Sausage" anagram
25 Hard work
26 Biblical song
31 Bottle tops
34 Dessert wedge
35 __ Gay
36 Have a bug
37 You may mind them
40 Come out first
41 First-quality
43 College in NYC
44 On the briny
45 Artful liar
49 Casino implement
50 WWII camps
54 In the cellar
58 Bowling-alley button
59 Auto rod
60 Freud's line
63 *Let's Make a Deal* choice
64 Ancient Aegean region
65 In a snit
66 Wallet fillers
67 Beatty and Buntline
68 Hear a case

DOWN

1 Spritzes
2 Bolivian bye-bye
3 Draft orders
4 20% of MXXV
5 Draft order
6 Mirthful Martha
7 Immediately if not sooner
8 Majorcan language
9 Culture commencer
10 Enter
11 Meringue ingredients
12 Samoan capital
14 __ sorts (peevish)
17 Harem quarters
21 Six Flags attractions
23 Open spaces
24 Director Kazan
27 __ Park, NJ
28 They may be exchanged
29 Nastase of tennis
30 Carvey or Delany
31 Yokum's creator
32 Snobs' put-on
33 Ballet move
37 Step on it
38 Archaeological expeditions
39 Bow out
42 Columbo's cases
44 Minimally
46 Giraffe's cousin
47 Tutoring session
48 Asian apparel
51 Early American tycoon
52 Madison VP
53 Eye problem
54 Pedestal part
55 Former Nebraska senator
56 Spiny houseplant
57 Actress Daly
61 El __ (Spanish hero)
62 Gives birth to

OPINION OPINION

by Eric Albert

ACROSS

1 Get the hang of
7 Like some victories
15 C to C, e.g.
16 Defeat
17 START OF A QUIP
19 Wield an axe
20 No longer new
21 Hoop star Thurmond
22 Razor's asset
24 Addams uncle
26 PART 2 OF QUIP
31 Slalom curve
32 Thwart a thrust
33 Pours down
35 Day-care denizen
36 Bird call
38 '60s hairstyle
42 Western resort
44 League rule
45 Crowded, initially
48 PART 3 OF QUIP
51 Orion's trade
53 Ex-Yugoslav leader
54 Wine region
55 Fly rapidly
57 "__ the ramparts . . ."
60 END OF QUIP
65 Honored one
66 Turns of phrase
67 New one in town
68 Astaire/ Rogers classic

DOWN

1 Sweater muncher
2 Sign of strain
3 Worried state
4 Little bit
5 Night before
6 Safe place
7 Unpartnered
8 Roman poet
9 Gerbil, maybe
10 __ Lanka
11 Holy symbols
12 Chip in
13 Feigns feelings
14 Puts off
18 "Aha!"
22 Swamp dweller
23 Finish with the dishes
24 Wacky Wilson
25 Poet's nighttime
26 Inclined (to)
27 One opposed
28 Biblical boat
29 Sky sign
30 Watering hole
34 Authority
36 *Mermaids* star
37 Opp. of vert.
39 Follies name
40 Controlled
41 Be in the red
43 Friend of Tarzan
44 Drill insert
45 Shoulder garments
46 Head headlong for
47 In a road show
49 Big name in elevators
50 Silly-willy
52 Jeweled headdress
55 Fancy party
56 Lustful look
57 "Oops!"
58 Madame Bovary
59 Take five
61 Col. superior
62 Joplin opus
63 Altar vow
64 Tout's offering

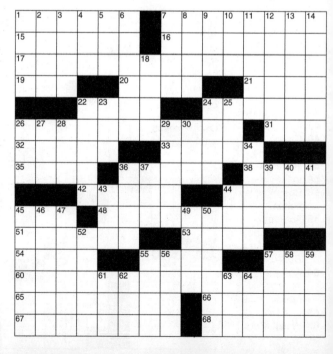

103 ROCK CONCERT

by Bob Lubbers

ACROSS

1 Western actor Jack
5 Makeshift store
10 Straw vote
14 Name for a poodle
15 Japanese-American
16 Part of B&O
17 How geologists take things?
19 Tach readings
20 Noisy napper
21 Park art
23 Ignore the script
26 GI entree
27 Highway hangings
30 John __ Passos
32 Upper crust
35 Refuses to
36 Genderless
38 Mannerless man
39 Vane dir.
40 Protective coats
41 __ out a living
42 Half of CIV
43 Pencil's place
44 Govt. agents
45 Sci-fi weapon
47 Choose: Abbr.
48 Civil-rights leader Medgar
49 Fumble one's speech
51 Lively dances
53 Wealthy woman
56 Don't act up
60 "Nova" anagram
61 Geologist's assay gear?
64 Frying medium
65 What you see
66 Twist out of shape
67 Some brothers
68 Wyoming range
69 Collar insert

DOWN

1 Gees' preceders
2 Elsa's dad
3 Continental prefix
4 Itinerant worker
5 Traffic tie-up
6 Foil material
7 "__ live and breathe!"
8 NBA team
9 Eating plans
10 Mine entrance
11 Geologist's favorite song?
12 Pie ingredient
13 Investor's bane
18 Bright shades
22 Sound-alikes of a sort
24 High standards
25 More daring, like a geologist?
27 "Peachy keen!"
28 Old Aegean region
29 Geologist's encouraging words?
31 Brosnan role
33 Bet acceptor
34 Perfect places
36 Classical prefix
37 Make a mistake
40 Shoulder movement
44 *Maude* and *Rhoda*
46 Four-legged Kenyans
48 TVA power
50 Send simoleons
52 *The Beverly Hillbillies* star
53 Broad valley
54 Roundish shape
55 Frost
57 Get __ on the back
58 Ms. Miles
59 Catch sight of
62 *The __ in the Hat*
63 In olden days

SPORTS CENTER

by S.N.

ACROSS

1 Oil initials
5 __ Hari
9 Drink deeply
14 Canadian prov.
15 *Jeopardy!* name
16 Excessive
17 Klinger portrayer
18 Undaffy
19 Aircraft walkway
20 Comes home, sort of
22 Scout Carson
23 Wedding-column word
24 "If __ a Hammer"
26 Road "beetles"
29 __ *bene*
31 Absolute ruler
32 Schnozz
33 Pirate Hall-of-Famer
36 1980 Wimbledon winner
37 Midwestern hockey team
38 __ *Wonderful Life*
39 Manor master
40 Troubleless
41 Badminton boundary
42 A little change
43 Graceful tree
44 Shake up
45 Antebellum Confederacy
50 Kiddie-lit elephant
53 Hawaiian holiday spot
54 '60s spy airplane
55 Flabbergast
56 RBI, e.g.
57 Charlotte et al.
58 Posh
59 Slangy turndown
60 "__ a Lady" (Jones tune)

DOWN

1 Clumsy folk
2 Urban map
3 Raison d'__
4 CBer's need
5 En __ (as a group)
6 Jai __
7 French Revolution event
8 Tree cutter
9 Dennis of *Innerspace*
10 Single thing
11 Paid notices
12 Spoon or joy ending
13 Professional payment
21 Absorbed, as a school subject
22 Writer Capek and director Reisz
25 Saltlike
26 Not arterial
27 British alemaker
28 Keel-rudderpost connectors
29 Replace an old obligation
30 Orchestral member
31 Have nothing __ (get stuck, detective-wise)
32 Makes alluring
33 Varnish ingredient
34 Penn's partner
35 Mercer and Normand
42 Singer Mariah
43 Mrs. Bunker
44 Dizzy's genre
46 Waikiki feast
47 Western state
48 Bird call
49 Cartwright boy
50 Ingot
51 "What a good boy __"
52 Mr. Masterson
53 College at E. Lansing

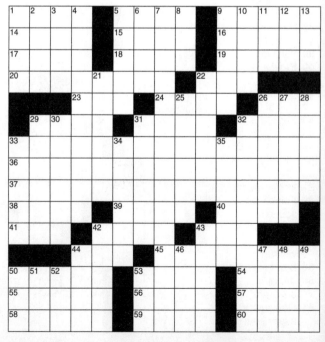

105 AUTO SUGGESTION

by Donna J. Stone

ACROSS

1 Greek-salad ingredient
5 *Soapdish* star
10 __ of the Roses
14 Court-martial candidate
15 *Unsafe at Any Speed* author
16 Seer's sign
17 Floor model
18 Boston Symphony leader
19 Printing process
20 START OF A QUIP
23 Frome of fiction
25 Morse message
26 Show follower
27 Bud's buddy
28 Sound of shock
32 Old saw
34 Poet's foot
36 "OK with me!"
39 MIDDLE OF QUIP
42 Sea World attraction
43 Spitz sounds
46 Gandhi, e.g.
49 Spirited steed
51 Letters of credit?
52 *Wheel of Fortune* buy
53 Erich __ Stroheim
56 Capp character
58 END OF QUIP
63 Dilatorily
64 Philip Nolan's fate
65 Just around the corner
68 *Dukes of Hazzard* deputy
69 Term-paper need
70 The Fatman's friend
71 Bears' lairs
72 First sign
73 *Kismet* setting

DOWN

1 In thing
2 Flock female
3 Barnum attraction
4 Ho "Hi!"
5 Chest gripper
6 Be idle
7 Lupino and Tarbell
8 Small salamanders
9 Thalia's sister
10 Despicable one
11 It multiplies by dividing
12 Tommy of *Lassie*
13 Cop some Z's
21 MIT grad
22 Hayes or Stern
23 Cotton gin name
24 __ T (perfectly)
29 "I've Got __ in Kalamazoo"
30 Pea product
31 Turkish title
33 Action time
35 Melville character
37 Successor
38 Author Ferber
40 "__ Got a Friend"
41 Slickers and such
44 "The Gold Bug" author
45 Big __, CA
46 Rained hard?
47 Crackers
48 Vegas singer
50 Do away with
54 __ a customer
55 *Six Crises* author
57 Dog star
59 Musical Myra
60 Counterchange
61 Björn opponent
62 Splinter group
66 Alias letters
67 Purchase paperwork: Abbr.

by Alex Vaughn

ACROSS

1 Way to address a lady
5 *M*A*S*H* character
10 Exxon's ex-name
14 __ *La Douce*
15 Run off and wed
16 Zhivago's love
17 Mortgage, e.g.
18 Something extra
19 Radiate
20 Joey carrier
23 Bullfight "bravo"
24 Had what __ (measured up)
27 Syrup source
30 Because you were challenged
34 French "one"
35 They kiss
37 Direction, in Durango
38 Neighborhoods
39 Introduction to metrics?
40 Sup at home
41 At __ (wholesale)
42 Visigoths' doing
44 Bard's "before"
45 He really kneads you
46 Actor Beatty
47 *Cheers* star
49 Wine word
51 Matter-of-taste remark
58 Himalayas' home
60 Still in contention
61 Rubik's device
62 Visual signal
63 Sham artist
64 Recline idly
65 Keyed up
66 Makes level
67 Peers at

DOWN

1 Cereal partner
2 Moffo solo
3 Solemn assent
4 Tropical fruit
5 Kind of collision
6 Actor Ray
7 Unprogressive one
8 Each
9 Louvre display
10 Vote in
11 Revered Texan
12 __ Lanka
13 Bran source
21 Spiny houseplants
22 Western Indian
25 Airline-board phrase
26 Wailed
27 Skipped a line
28 __ borealis
29 Ringmaster's word
31 Assumed name
32 They're round and flat
33 Buy a pig in __
36 Rode the bench
37 Lobe's locale
40 Mr. Zimbalist
42 Southwestern capital
43 Dismissals
45 Bird Maoris once hunted
48 Not very secure
50 Repetitive pattern
52 Croat, for one
53 Reebok rival
54 Pizza place?
55 Harbor bobber
56 Well-qualified
57 Solidifies
58 Wide-eyed wonder
59 Imogene's cohort

107 MAP OF THE STARS

by Randolph Ross

ACROSS

1 Former Congressman Aspin
4 __ facto
8 Mr. Waller
12 Clinton's home
14 Touch against
15 *Arsenic and Old Lace* actress
17 "You're __ and don't know it"
18 CIA predecessor
19 *Exodus* hero
21 *Monitor* foe
25 Learner's need
27 Media revenue source
28 Simile center
29 Sushi-bar selections
30 *Cheers* actress
35 *Perry Mason* role
36 *The Big Chill* actress
38 Aid in crime
39 __ for "Apple"
40 Reb inits.
43 All __ (Miller play)
46 Gets rid of
49 Slalom curve
50 Shoe specification
52 Employee's last words
53 Wimbledon winner in '70
58 Golden-__ (senior citizen)
59 Astronomical event
60 One of Jacob's sons
61 Bartlett's abbr.
62 Night spot

DOWN

1 Drank like a cat
2 Scoreboard column
3 Killy, for one
4 Business-letterhead letters
5 Greek letter
6 "My Gal __"
7 Cold capital
8 Like some bottoms
9 Lawyers' org.
10 Sandwich order
11 Germfree
13 Italian wine region
16 Small snake
17 *I __ Fugitive from a Chain Gang*
20 Bitsy preceder
22 Comic actress Gibbs
23 Ore analysis
24 Unwitting dupe
26 Civil War signature
30 __ the city (mayor's bestowal)
31 Sort
32 Let __ (don't touch)
33 Make a clean slate
34 NRC predecessor
35 Equine event
36 Jerry Herman musical
37 Just awful
40 Golf links
41 Was right for
42 Member of 9 Down
44 Silents siren
45 Diver's place
47 "New Look" designer
48 Short news item
51 Author Bombeck
54 Gun the engine
55 Lunch ending
56 As well
57 Where to see Larry King

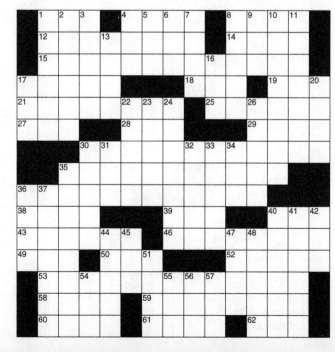

108 HEAVEN FOR BID!

by Donna J. Stone

ACROSS

1 Analyzed sentences
7 Clammy
11 Race downhill
14 Pianist de Larrocha
15 Bridge support
16 Groan producer
17 START OF A QUIP
19 Part of SBLI
20 Robert __ Marley
21 Cleanse
23 *Three Men __ Baby*
26 Admitted, with "up"
29 *Scarface* star
30 Last word in fashion
32 Mythical twin
34 Cartoon cat
35 Boss' note
36 MIDDLE OF QUIP
41 Cut out cake
42 Giggle sound
45 Most promptly
49 Tile game
51 Behold, to Brutus
52 Jeweler's measure
54 As a result
55 Mideast nation
57 Tall story?
59 Dos Passos trilogy
60 END OF QUIP
66 Velvet finish
67 Get-up-and-go
68 Crewel tool
69 Drain-cleaner ingredient
70 D'Artagnan prop
71 Whirled

DOWN

1 Pastoral god
2 Inn quaff
3 *6 Rms, __ Vu*
4 Game plan
5 Irish republic
6 Former *Family Feud* host
7 Armless sofa
8 Justice Fortas
9 Framing need
10 Play thing?
11 Inflationary pattern
12 Martial art
13 Atlas features
18 Periodic-table info: Abbr.
22 Montevideo's loc.
23 Campaign name of '36
24 Dundee denial
25 Punctually
27 ". . . __ saw Elba"
28 St. Paul's feature
31 Ooze
33 March, but not mazurka
35 *The A-Team* star
37 Go for broke
38 Salad cheese
39 Feeling low
40 Restaurateur Toots
43 MIT grad
44 Inflated feeling
45 *Batman Returns*, e.g.
46 *Purple Dust* playwright
47 Gas rating
48 PBS benefactor
49 __ Hari
50 Bring into harmony
53 Alto or bass
56 Tear down
58 Completed the cake
61 Helpful hint
62 *Wheel of Fortune* buy
63 A mean Amin
64 Message to a matador
65 Nancy Drew's boyfriend

109 YES, YES, YES!

by Trip Payne

ACROSS

1 *Casablanca* role
4 Lobster eater's wear
7 Lustrous fabric
13 Pretended to be
16 Geronimo, for one
17 Warn
18 Mine workers
19 Prove false
20 Dry, as wine
22 "This is only __"
23 Haughty one
24 Tissue cell
26 Like some pots
28 Kind of file
32 Hindu chant
35 Males
36 Aware of
37 Does as told
38 Winner's prize
39 Coming next
40 "Whip It" rock group
41 __ and aah
42 __ Creed (religious statement)
43 Rebekah's son
44 Cactus type
46 Not up
48 Mail agcy.
52 Fuel nuggets
55 4/15 org.
56 Floorboard sound
57 Like some inspections
59 Tibetan hideaway
61 Riffled (through)
62 *The Moon and __*
63 Gets narrower
64 Gaming cube
65 Understanding words

DOWN

1 Warms up for a bout
2 Standish stand-in
3 Rumba relative
4 Out of shape
5 Mr. Amin
6 Droopy dog
7 Fish, in a way
8 Bee-related
9 Logically expected event
10 Top level
11 "__ a Lady"
12 Superman's alias
14 Groucho show
15 Ray Charles' commercial backup
21 Social pariah
24 Hunters' org.
25 Offs' opposite
27 __ *gratia artis*
29 Kitty starter
30 British gun
31 Skin feature
32 Manner
33 Burrows and Vigoda
34 St. Petersburg's river
38 Raccoon relative
39 Put on TV
41 CIA forerunner
42 Shrewish type
45 Tacit
47 Nitrate, e.g.
49 "__ evil . . ."
50 Shrivel with heat
51 Some terriers
52 Stable child
53 Draftable person
54 PDQ kin
56 Horn, for one
58 Bradley and McBain
60 1011, to Tacitus

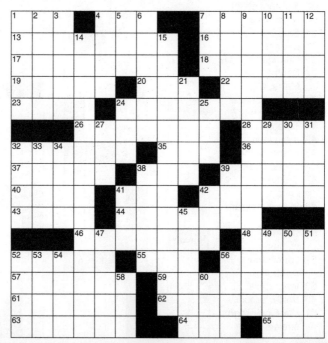

110 SIX FIFTEENS

by Mel Rosen

ACROSS

1 __ Romeo
5 Complete victory
10 Not processed
13 Mother of William and Harry
15 Jeweled headpiece
16 Miss. neighbor
17 Newspaper staffer
20 Speedometer's meas.
21 Make (one's way)
22 Knock for a loop
23 "__ Old Cowhand"
25 Tough test
29 Check total
31 Trumpet effect
32 Sixth sense
35 Sperry's partner
36 Changes shades
37 Sault __ Marie, MI
38 Iowan, for one
43 Half and half?
44 Clapton of rock
45 A big jerk
46 Home, in the phone book
47 Chihuahua child
48 Plumed military hats
50 Dry-cleaning worker
52 Lancastrian symbol
53 Inner drive
55 Prefix for focus
57 Die Fledermaus subject

60 Carpentry contraption
65 Early gardener
66 Pleasure boat
67 Couldn't stand
68 Round Table address
69 Miller rival
70 Evergreen shrubs

DOWN

1 Hockey star Oates
2 Emulate Daffy
3 Dior, for one
4 Wheel of Fortune buy
5 Mr. Musial
6 Department-store staffer
7 Do lunch

8 Poetic preposition
9 Mini-notebook
10 Hiker's risk
11 Manager Felipe
12 Put on notice
14 Dam in Egypt
18 Bivouac quarters
19 "This __ fine how-do-you-do!'"
24 Newsman Roger
26 Beams of light
27 Eat more sensibly
28 Additional
29 Jouster's protection
30 Memorable vessel
33 Office skill, for short
34 Job benefits

39 Carson successor
40 Moran of Happy Days
41 Cellar stock
42 Thick-piled rugs
48 Mex. miss
49 Cheap booze
51 Alert color
53 Puts to work
54 Sitarist Shankar
56 Judges of a sort
58 Once more
59 Koppel and Turner
61 Coll. deg.
62 "Xanadu" group
63 Old card game
64 Loft material

111 WATER MUSIC

by Donna J. Stone

ACROSS

1 British buggy
5 Window sticker
10 Bridge charge
14 Old bird
15 Display conspicuously
16 "__ Around" (Beach Boys tune)
17 College courtyard
18 Wagner's father-in-law
19 Loquacious equine
20 Italian water music?
23 Pine product
24 R-V hookup?
25 Texas state tree
28 "So that's your game!"
31 Tire Town, USA
35 Epoch
36 Cantaloupe's cousin
39 Narrow shoe size
40 French water music?
43 Czech river
44 Singer Brewer
45 Sleeve contents?
46 Ball-bearing attractions?
48 Neighbor of Jord.
49 *Gaslight* star
51 Inept sort
53 Wine and dine
54 Chinese water music?
61 Jupiter's alias
62 Michelangelo subject
63 Hardly hyper
65 Sacred cow
66 Cockamamie
67 Raison d'__
68 Scads
69 Vacuum-tube gas
70 Pants part

DOWN

1 Pronto, initially
2 No gentleman
3 *Queen for __*
4 Pavarotti's birthplace
5 Dutch pottery
6 Way out
7 Old Testament kingdom
8 Cooper's tool
9 Baltic natives
10 Faraway place
11 Mythical monster
12 Lascivious look
13 Inc., in Ireland
21 Light weight
22 "Make __ double!"
25 Señorita's shekels
26 Carve a canyon
27 __ cropper (failed)
28 Grate stuff
29 Like Esau
30 Capp character
32 Settle accounts
33 In reserve
34 *Unsafe at Any Speed* author
37 ABA member
38 Horse cousin
41 Bobby Vinton #1 tune
42 Off-limits
47 Lose energy
50 Lots and lots
52 Recruit's NJ home
53 Valhalla VIP
54 Skywalker's teacher
55 Revlon rival
56 Big name in westerns
57 Writer Hunter
58 Producer De Laurentiis
59 Hung up
60 Pound of poetry
61 Dandy's first name?
64 Even so

112 HIGH HOPES

by Shirley Soloway

ACROSS

1 Get away from
7 Colorful shell
14 Footstool
15 New Jersey river
16 Wishful pursuit
18 Gary and Mary
19 *Dallas* matriarch
20 Ottawa's prov.
21 Sword handle
24 Make a choice
28 Clairvoyant ability
30 Slow mover
32 Caviar
33 Bea of vaudeville
35 *One Day at __*
37 Wishful pursuit
41 O'er opposite
42 Expenditure
43 One-third of MCCIII
44 Blossom holder
45 Art, to Antony
48 Mr. Melville
52 Wedding vows
54 Comic Philips
56 "You __ be congratulated!"
58 Mint jelly
60 Wistful pursuit
65 Large wardrobe
66 Is indicative of
67 Hold back
68 Hams it up

DOWN

1 Fuel gas
2 Gets underway
3 The bottom line
4 Pennsylvania sect
5 Hook's nemesis
6 Liberia's lang.
7 Asian inland sea
8 __ out (uses a chute)
9 *L.A. Law* guy
10 Suit grounds
11 Western Indian
12 Slangy refusal
13 Printer's widths
14 Acapulco octet
17 Payback
22 Punching tools
23 Paper sheets
25 Buffalo's lake
26 Robin Cook book
27 Be abundant
29 Evil scheme
31 Turned gooey
34 Self suffix
35 Tooth pros' grp.
36 "__ Little Tenderness"
37 About 2.5 centimeters
38 Old-time Persian
39 Matched set
40 Brat in *Blondie*
46 Fame
47 Strikes down
49 Feudal estate
50 Bandleader Shaw
51 Gets close to
53 Antidrug advice
55 Folk singer Phil
57 Laces up
59 Flue dust
60 A long way off
61 Raw metal
62 Man behind the catcher
63 Commemorative verse
64 Neither masc. nor neut.

113 SO THEY SAY

by Eric Albert

ACROSS

1 Deep black
4 Leading lady Lamarr
8 Borgnine role
14 *Messiah* is one
16 Tooth covering
17 Pedestrian path
18 Unremarkable
19 HOME
21 Fish eggs
22 When Paris sizzles
23 Glimpse
26 Declare openly
28 British baby buggy
32 Farrow of films
33 Scandinavian city
35 *My Favorite Year* star
37 FAMILIARITY
40 Writer Welty
41 Ms. Sommer
42 Unit of energy
43 Checkup
44 Music symbol
46 Lavish attention (on)
47 Ave. crossers
48 Ram's mate
50 MISS
58 Get back
59 One with a marker
60 Chinese philosopher
61 Hungry for company
62 Oscar-winner as Mrs. Kramer

63 Picnic predators
64 Before marriage

DOWN

1 Kid around
2 Pennsylvania port
3 "Voila!"
4 Bookstore section
5 Clean the boards
6 Pickle flavoring
7 __ Ono
8 Cautionary sign
9 100-buck bill
10 Mata __
11 Clips and shells

12 Incline
13 Building extension
15 Towel material
20 Corp. boss
23 Patter provider
24 Crazy Horse, for one
25 Bamboo bruncher
26 Swiss peak
27 Marks a ballot
28 "El Dorado" writer
29 Cowpuncher competition
30 Make aware of
31 Join forces
33 "__ the ramparts. . ."
34 Get wise
36 Pipe type
38 Piper's son

39 PBJ alternative
45 Leg. title
46 Salami shops
47 Take by force
48 Major happening
49 Walks through water
50 Essential point
51 Composer Stravinsky
52 Recent
53 Pac-10 member
54 Common supplement
55 Kind of collar
56 Dome home zone
57 Kite nemesis
58 *Kidnapped* monogram

114 SECURITY RISK

by Donna J. Stone

ACROSS

1 Dict. abbr.
4 Epsilon follower
8 Coeur d'__, ID
13 Perrins' partner
14 Cheese choice
15 Partonesque
16 START OF A QUIP
19 Calculator ancestor
20 Ale place
21 Sapphire side
22 Make up (for)
24 Citrus cooler
26 Busy as __
27 Napoleon's fate
28 Aftereffect
29 "Cool!" in school
30 Numerical suffix
31 Folklore being
32 MIDDLE OF QUIP
35 Menotti title character
38 Tropical tuber
39 Sine __ non
42 Scads
43 Belgian Congo, today
45 Hair balls?
46 Parker product
47 They may be greased
48 Shearer of *The Red Shoes*
49 '60s dance
51 Short snooze
52 END OF QUIP
55 Take __ at (attempt)
56 Make a buck
57 Vane reading
58 Bedtime reading
59 Eye problem
60 Cherry shade

DOWN

1 Morgiana's master
2 Wrote graffiti
3 Local booster
4 The *Odyssey* character
5 Actor Byrnes
6 Asian philosophy
7 Explosive
8 Superior to
9 Mechanic's job
10 Chef's concentrate
11 Kind of sun
12 Funnyman Philips
17 No longer in style
18 Maureen O'Sullivan role
19 Out of range
22 Skating maneuver
23 Dickens character
25 Go wrong
27 *Sea Hunt* shocker
28 Actor Mineo
30 __ Aviv
31 Exit-ramp word
32 Kid's query
33 Crew-team members
34 Ending for press
35 Audiophile's purchase
36 Cary Grant's '33 co-star
37 Food coloring
39 Malaria medicine
40 Like some movies
41 Urgent letters
43 Ms. Pitts
44 __ *Restaurant*
45 Pain in the neck
47 Reserve
48 Foot wiper
50 Kaiser's counterpart
51 French film
52 Great time, so to speak
53 *Krazy* __
54 Ironic

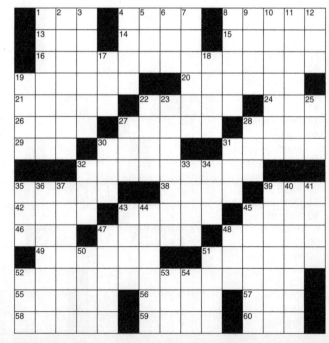

115 *ALPHABETS*

by Lois Sidway

ACROSS

1 Way off
4 Orchestral areas
8 Alabama city
13 "Isn't It a __?" ('32 tune)
14 Conversation filler
15 Burger topping
16 Folklore baddie
17 Blind part
18 Shakespearean forest
19 Key letters
22 Actor's quest
23 __ de corps
27 One: Ger.
28 OR personnel
30 Matador's foe
31 Young hog
34 Message from Morris
36 Top bond rating
37 Behave
40 Vane reading
41 A Kentucky Derby prize
42 Postulate
43 "I've Got __ in Kalamazoo"
45 A Bobbsey twin
46 Evildoing
47 Tell
49 Ruse victims
53 Victory sign, to Morse
56 Where you live
59 Matured
60 __ Camera (basis for Cabaret)
61 Western capital
62 Extra
63 Prepare to swallow
64 San Diego baseballer
65 James Bond's alma mater
66 Holyfield stats

DOWN

1 Night's work for Holyfield
2 Awesome hotel lobbies
3 Deli need
4 Car part
5 Eastern religion
6 Thailand export
7 __ precedent
8 Midday TV fare
9 Filled with delight
10 It may be flipped
11 A Stooge
12 Actress Jillian
13 Ice-cream buys
20 Perry White's occupation
21 They'll buy burritos
24 Interstates
25 OPEC delegate
26 Breakfast order
28 Elevated
29 Gets some z's
31 Sloppy brushstroke
32 Be contingent
33 Peyton Place star
34 Western plateau
35 American elk
38 Musical group
39 Like Teflon
44 Painter's need
46 Depress
48 "__ Kangaroo Down, Sport"
49 Word form for "wing"
50 Spud country
51 Furniture designer
52 Henry Higgins' creator
54 British title
55 "__ the sun in the morning . . ."
56 Cleo's cobra
57 Ewe said it
58 Like Mother Hubbard

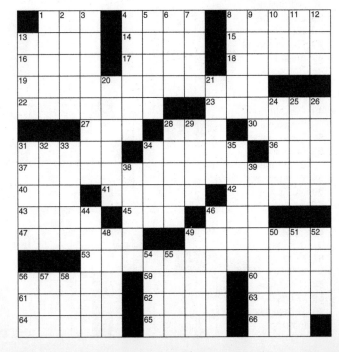

116 BODY SOUNDS

by Fred Piscop

ACROSS

1 __ it up (overacts)
5 Wilma's hubby
9 Birch relative
14 Blind as __
15 Like some hair
16 Superman star
17 Ms. Barrett
18 Krugerrand, for one
19 Like some fences
20 TOE
23 Phonograph needles
24 Form of wrestling
25 Gun grp.
28 Ave. crossings
30 Melee starter
33 "Do __ say . . ."
36 Aid partner
39 Pelvic bone
40 EYE
44 Toyota model
45 Fuss
46 Composer Rorem
47 Plain as day
49 Deviate from the course
52 Temp. unit
53 Bridges or Brummell
56 Well-dressed
60 NOSE
64 Barber's offering
66 __ pas (mistake)
67 Hard to believe
68 Navel type
69 Wings: Lat.
70 Thpeak like thith
71 Spiral-shelled creature
72 Legendary apple splitter
73 Greek H's

DOWN

1 Ethereal instruments
2 More or less
3 Macho
4 Stable units
5 Central points
6 Civil disturbances
7 Root or Yale
8 Blew up
9 Jason's craft
10 __ day (2/29)
11 School kid's punishment
12 Cain raiser
13 Richard Skelton
21 Clever chap
22 Author L. __ Hubbard
26 Meet the old grads
27 Gave guns to
29 __ Jose, CA
31 Org. once led by Bush
32 Under the weather
33 Traveled a curved path
34 Italian wine
35 Join the melting pot
37 Milk component
38 Comedian Philips
41 Suffix with drunk or cow
42 Humorist Bill
43 Mr. Rogers
48 Warriors' org.
50 Part of Q&A
51 Turkey-throat feature
54 Allan-__
55 Business as __
57 Genetic feature
58 Oral Roberts U. site
59 Canine's cries
61 Emulating Lucifer
62 Oddball
63 Rink jump
64 Mama pig
65 "What did you say?"

117 NOTTINGHAM REVISITED

by Randolph Ross

ACROSS

1 Skyline sight
6 Some tires
13 __ *Knowledge* ('71 film)
14 Loathed one
16 Nottingham lithographs?
18 Upswing
19 In the matter of
20 Silvery fish
21 Meet with
23 Repressed, with "up"
25 Gin name
26 Nottingham bride?
31 Had a bite
32 Midmonth day
33 Garry and Melba
37 Make a bad pact
39 Hindu heaven
40 Middle of *Macbeth*
41 "__ Be Cruel"
42 Enthusiasm
43 Nottingham gangsters?
46 TV initials
49 Reliever's stat
50 Big __, CA
51 Separates socks
54 Grande and Bravo
56 Mount Snow machine
59 Nottingham merchant?
62 Popular sitcom
63 Palate projections
64 Introvert's trait
65 Like Mr. Universe

DOWN

1 Calcutta clothing
2 Most prim
3 Destitute
4 Hamelin pest
5 Ms. Lanchester
6 Roof holders
7 *Julius Caesar* character
8 Bit of Morse code
9 Like __ (candidly)
10 "Psst!" elative
11 Flood preventative
12 Common sense
13 EMT training
15 Italian wine region
17 Fish hawk
22 Charlie Sheen's brother
24 Comedian's need
26 One of the Bears
27 Suffix for problem
28 Quick-thinking retorts
29 Oliver and Sheree
30 Cuomo's title: Abbr.
34 Auk feature
35 Oklahoma city
36 Undermines
38 Broadcast medium
39 Preceder of "the above"
41 Goes through mitosis
44 Captains of industry
45 Beat on the track
46 V.I. Lenin's land
47 Cheerful sounds
48 Just-picked
52 Deuce beater
53 Exemplar of grace
55 Urban-renewal target
57 Have __ in (influence)
58 Numbered hwy.
60 *A Chorus Line* number
61 Eggs

by S.N.

ACROSS

1 Wants to know
5 Switch positions
9 Purina rival
13 Dalmatian's name
14 Bowling term
15 *Mommie Dearest* name
16 Walk nervously
17 Reddy to sing?
18 Kick in a chip
19 October activity
22 Once around the track
23 Wilm. is there
24 *Wheel of Fortune* purchase
27 Stinky cigar
30 Thrill
35 Entertainer Falana
37 Acapulco gold
38 Made night noises
39 October activity
42 Oblivious to ethics
43 One __ customer
44 Ltr. enclosure
45 Critic, often
46 Divine food
48 Sun. speech
49 __ de cologne
51 Head stroke
53 October activity
61 Notorious Ugandan
62 __ *for the Misbegotten*
63 PDQ, O.R.-style
65 Retail
66 Set-to
67 Ingrain deeply
68 Quite dark
69 Van __, CA
70 Give's partner

DOWN

1 Nile reptile
2 Minor disagreement
3 *Mayor* author
4 Mill output
5 Phone letters
6 It may be free
7 Elm Street name
8 Good judgment
9 Open a crack
10 Actress Anderson
11 Crown of the head
12 Some bills
14 Lathe, e.g.
20 Had been
21 Hurricane of '85
24 Wedding platform
25 __ *Rae*
26 *The Waste Land* poet
28 Hockey Hall-of-Famer
29 "Ya __ have heart . . ."
31 A whole bunch
32 Opera highlights
33 Suffering stress
34 Gardener's device
36 Suburban square?
38 *Colors* star
40 Black or Valentine
41 Director Howard
46 Waikiki wear
47 Travel grp.
50 Larry Storch's *F Troop* role
52 Rec-room piece
53 Sitarist Shankar
54 Prayer ending
55 Eccentricity
56 May event, familiarly
57 Ride for a kid
58 Colleague of Clark and Jimmy
59 Feminine-name ending
60 Pillage
64 "__ end"

119 REVERSALS

by Wayne R. Williams

ACROSS

1 One-time Wimbledon winner
5 Ecology org.
8 Least risky
14 Faster way
16 Said grace
17 Interrupt
18 Stair elements
19 Furry swimmer
20 Most secret
22 Calendar letters
23 Make a choice
25 Australian area
29 Hot tub
30 Turndown vote
31 Jeff Bridges film of '84
32 $2 exacta, e.g.
33 DDE defeated him
34 Life of Riley
35 Gets tiresome
38 Ornery equine
39 Inferno writer
40 Model Macpherson
41 Friday was one
42 __ Ridge, TN
43 Teddy's niece
45 Coral islet
46 Sphere
49 Withdraw
50 Killer whale
51 Act dovish
52 Cattle food
54 Fur tycoon
56 Musical chords
59 Catch up to
61 Tight spot
62 Corporate buyout
63 Overacts
64 Olsen of vaudeville
65 Makes one

DOWN

1 Classy neckwear
2 Pipe down
3 Devon drink
4 Irish Gaelic
5 Author Umberto
6 Virtuousness
7 Env. abbr.
8 Alfalfa form
9 Manilow's record label
10 Basketball maneuver
11 Look over
12 Sun. homily
13 NFL scores
15 Power seats
21 Charlton role
24 Bit of butter
26 To __ (unanimously)
27 The players
28 Leg flexer
32 Morning meal
33 Egyptian cobra
35 Coach Ewbank
36 Ms. Fitzgerald
37 Sir Guinness
38 Major artery
39 Tot service
41 Soup and salad
42 Long paddle
44 Brain, so to speak
45 Contemporary
46 From C to C
47 Flimflammed
48 Drills, e.g.
53 Arrive at
55 Put away
56 Kin of les and der
57 Hit head-on
58 Prefix for metric
60 __ out a living

120 MUSIC APPRECIATION

by Eric Albert

ACROSS

1 Sop ink
5 FDR topic
9 Film sensitivity
14 Tasty tubers
15 __ California
16 Genghis' gang
17 START OF A QUIP
19 Sigourney Weaver film
20 Flagpole topper
21 PART 2 OF QUIP
23 Expects
25 March ender
26 Messy Madison
29 Nasal-sounding
33 Kid around
36 "Oops!"
38 Napoleon, twice
39 Mideast name
40 PART 3 OF QUIP
42 __-de-sac
43 National Zoo attraction
46 Cry like a baby
47 Computer noise
48 Swallow up
50 Peruvian beast
52 Close with force
54 "__, you fool!"
58 PART 4 OF QUIP
63 Price twice
64 Bouquet
65 END OF QUIP
67 Like a lot
68 Immense volume
69 Enthusiastic
70 Some cookies
71 Turn aside
72 All those in favor

DOWN

1 Two, to Revere
2 Legal drama
3 End-all
4 Prufrock's poet
5 Agents' org.
6 Simplicity
7 Trojan War hero
8 House style
9 Invitation to dance
10 Amendment XXIV subject
11 Canal of song
12 Land west of Nod
13 Auto mark
18 Pups and parrots
22 Take a loss in
24 Flat-bottomed boat
27 *Pequod* skipper
28 Fit for a queen
30 Jet-set resort
31 Stick together
32 Short shout
33 Make fun of
34 Zesty spirit
35 Birds do it
37 Allen Ginsberg opus
41 Strong rebuke
44 Tidying tool
45 Eager to hear
47 Pre-overtime amount
49 Low-tech cooler
51 Spanish surrealist
53 Diamond gloves
55 "Wild and crazy" Martin
56 *West Side Story* song
57 "Dear me!"
58 Falls behind
59 Common diet supplement
60 Convertible, maybe
61 Cranny's colleague
62 Jacks, but not Jills
66 Recently arrived

121 FULL OF BEANS

by Eric Albert

ACROSS

1 Mr. Sharif
5 Persian potentate
9 Kind of orange
14 Raging blaze
16 Tony of baseball
17 '70s auto
18 It "keeps on ticking"
19 Tattletales
20 Ewe's partner
21 To some extent
24 Employment aid
28 Baby Snooks portrayer
29 Papergirl's path
31 Mai __ (cocktail)
32 Paper puzzle
33 Circus shooter
34 Likely (to)
35 *On the Town* lyricist
38 Golfer's goal
40 Jacket parts
41 Guns the engine
44 Corn holder
45 "If __ a Rich Man"
46 Bit of salt
47 Unspecified person
49 Exhaust one's creativity
50 Was in front
51 Entity
53 Highly motivated
56 Knee tendon
60 Monk's cloister
61 Avant-garde composer
62 Minnie of Nashville
63 Dampens
64 Bush's alma mater

DOWN

1 Out of synch
2 "O Sole __"
3 Part of ETA
4 Blushing
5 Be frugal
6 Bumper-sticker word
7 Tatum and Carney
8 Med. ins. plan
9 Prose alert
10 Out on __ (vulnerable)
11 Vitality
12 Actress Arden
13 Over easy
15 Church top
20 Brake parts
21 Computer co.
22 New Deal org.
23 Inca conqueror
24 Tarzan's home
25 Concluded
26 Grab forty winks
27 Radio to assemble
29 Ice-T, e.g.
30 __ *Majesty's Secret Service*
33 Like old bathtubs
36 *Thimble Theater* name
37 *Silver Spoons* star
38 *Treasure Island* character
39 Display delight
42 Taper?
43 Avoiding fame
46 Kicks, in a way
48 Berry tree
49 Takes a flier
51 Unornamented
52 Give out
53 Casual topper
54 Justice Fortas
55 Hoop group: Abbr.
56 Take an axe to
57 Call __ day
58 Nada
59 "That's awesome!"

122 GYM NEIGHBORS

by Wayne R. Williams

ACROSS

1 Puppeteer Lewis
6 Harm, in a way
10 Be up and about
14 More than ready
15 M*A*S*H star
16 Painter Joan
17 Sound of a critic?
19 Erelong
20 Sicilian landmark
21 Superman villain Luthor
22 Burstyn and Barkin
24 Broker's lots
26 Handle capably
27 Sound of an actor?
30 Be sick
33 Lucy's landlady
36 Entreaties
37 Novelist Levin
38 Heavy sound
39 Toothy displays
40 Map out
41 Make leather
42 Got up
43 Emitted beams
44 Army insect
45 Sound of a ballplayer?
47 Out-and-out
49 Prepare
53 Disarm a bull
55 Squeak curer
57 __ podrida
58 Old lament
59 Sound of an actress?
62 Melancholy
63 Nautical adverb
64 Ike's missus
65 Mineo and Maglie
66 Desires
67 Winter gliders

DOWN

1 Ed Norton's workplace
2 Author Bret
3 Booster rocket
4 Brought back
5 Nettle
6 Stable female
7 Jeopardy! name
8 Actress Lupino
9 Portuguese wines
10 T-shirt size
11 Sound of an actress?
12 Tailor's need
13 Howard and Nessen
18 Roy Rogers' real last name
23 Not as many
25 Up to, briefly
26 Hot dog
28 Brouhaha
29 Prime social category
31 "Dies __"
32 Touch down
33 Jazz singer James
34 Comparative word
35 Sound of a Bowery Boy?
39 Smallest city with an NFL team
40 Beethoven's Sixth
42 Mimic
43 Sage of Concord's monogram
46 Eye amorously
48 Fuel-line components
50 Ghostbusters goo
51 Spanish hero
52 Walks off with
53 Pats lightly
54 Joyce of Roc
55 Author Wister
56 March time
60 Bullring cheer
61 Apt. ad abbr.

123 GREEN LIGHT

by Matt Gaffney

ACROSS

1 Act testily
7 Erivan native
15 Bob, but not Joe
16 "Misty" start
17 Open an envelope
18 Captain Stubing's command
19 Guys' dates
20 "Our __ your gain"
22 Met Life's bus.
23 Computer key
25 Storage unit
26 Yon bloke's
28 In __ (disheveled)
30 Inn offerings
35 Summer drink
36 Well-executed
37 Just plain awful
38 Green-light phrase
41 Cookout locales
42 Gator's home, maybe
43 Free (of)
44 Merlin of TV
45 In unison
46 Sea plea
47 Farrow et al.
48 Know-nothing remark
50 Obstinate equine
53 Beer holder
55 Vaccine name
58 Perry victory site
60 Visigoth leader
62 Book's edition
63 Saskatchewan's capital
64 "Diagnose" anagram
65 Donald Sutherland's kid

DOWN

1 The Color Purple character
2 Barrie barker
3 Theater spots
4 Egg on
5 Oklahoma city
6 Ring a bell
7 Green-light phrase
8 They're often ruled
9 Z or M
10 Supplements, with "out"
11 Catch a crook
12 Even odds
13 __ for All Seasons
14 Is left with
21 West Indies belief
24 Aviator of the comics
26 Duck Soup soloist
27 Optimal
29 Kitten's cries
30 Rose up
31 Buckeyes' sch.
32 Filmdom's Zhivago
33 Former Governor Cuomo
34 Snow gliders
37 Actress Cannon
39 Stamping tool
40 Rope feature
45 Musty house's need
47 Madame Curie
49 The way we word
50 Swiss range
51 Lee of cakedom
52 Spud covering
53 "You __ do!"
54 Carefree frolic
56 Reinforce, in a way
57 Former Chrysler category
59 Last part
61 Aiea adornment

124 *"GEEZ!"*

by Fred Piscop

ACROSS

1 Some sandwiches
6 Blue-ribbon event
10 Tijuana cheers
14 __-garde
15 Discourteous
16 Mr. Hackman
17 Rho follower
18 Flash of brilliance
19 Research info
20 Mom's rock-pile admonition?
22 Daredeviltry name
23 Smoke-detector output
24 Mean and nasty
26 Condescended
30 Comb impediment
31 Big apes
32 Application phrase
36 Succotash bean
37 Novelist Rand
38 Sills solo
39 Service holder of a sort
42 *Tobacco Road* family name
44 In this way
45 Simple life
46 It's spotted in the zoo
49 Turin "Ta-ta!"
50 Get an __ effort
51 Antelope city?
57 German capital
58 Forsaken
59 Stan's cohort
60 __-dry (arid)
61 ". . . __ saw Elba"
62 Frosted, in recipes
63 Controversial tree spray
64 "Dagnabbit!"
65 Some votes

DOWN

1 Door fastener
2 Sinful
3 Shankar genre
4 "__ honor, I will do my . . ."
5 Producing plays
6 "__ or foe?"
7 Imported automobiles
8 March 15th, for instance
9 Justifications
10 Angry poet?
11 Go out
12 Go in
13 Mattress name
21 Opposers of 65 Across
25 Beans spiller
26 Knucklehead
27 Buffalo's county
28 __ *Camera* ('55 film)
29 Pesky rebellion leader?
30 __ Clemente, CA
32 Caustic stuff
33 Comic Johnson
34 Appearance
35 Shucker's needs
37 Capp and Capone
40 "*Now* I see!"
41 Stole from
42 Pinocchio, often
43 Save-the-earth science
45 *The __ Winter*
46 __ the Hutt (Lucas character)
47 "__ and his money . . ."
48 "You're __ Hear from Me"
49 Healer
52 Author Ephron
53 *Cosmopolitan* competitor
54 Word of woe
55 Jet-set city
56 Bishops' realms

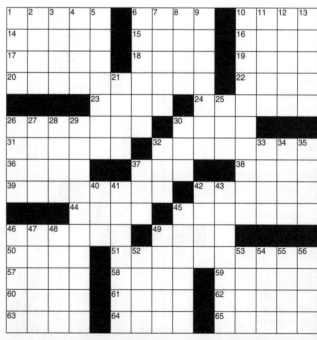

125 PARALLEL BARS

by Eric Albert

ACROSS

1 Turn away
6 *Pygmalion* playwright
10 Camel feature
14 Resort isle
15 Short note
16 Laos' locale
17 BAR
20 *Joy of Cooking* abbr.
21 Guitar kin, for short
22 Clear a channel
23 Southpaw's sobriquet
26 Joyride
27 Red wood
29 Floor covering
30 Block a broadcast
33 High home
34 Actress Delany
35 Brouhaha
36 BAR
39 Director Kazan
40 Wines and dines
41 *Where's __?* ('70 film)
42 Howard of *Happy Days*
43 Big jerk
44 Dressing table
45 Pretentiously picturesque
46 Puts on the payroll
47 Mr. Kosygin
50 Golfer Woosnam
51 *Murphy Brown* network
54 BAR
58 G&S character
59 Walk out
60 *Lost Horizon* director
61 Pipe part
62 Painter Magritte
63 Makes meals

DOWN

1 Large quantity
2 Love god
3 Prince tune of '84
4 Decline
5 Chou En-__
6 Great __ Mountains National Park
7 "I'm present!"
8 Rock-band gear
9 Punny business
10 Safe place
11 Practiced
12 Flash's foe
13 Top of the head
18 Import tax
19 Border lake
24 *All My Children* character
25 Ad word
26 Hole in your head
27 Silly prank
28 Surprised exclamation
29 Something banned
30 *SNL* alumnus
31 Well-practiced
32 Coral-reef denizen
34 Humdinger
35 Kind of steak
37 Unfaithful one
38 On __ with (equal to)
43 Brought up
44 Trattoria offering
45 Universal truth
46 Rapidity
47 Proposes as a price
48 Spoils of war
49 Sommer of *The Prize*
50 "When the moon __ the seventh house . . ."
52 Tree feature
53 Mineral springs
55 Tin Man's tool
56 Radio regulator: Abbr.
57 __ Paulo

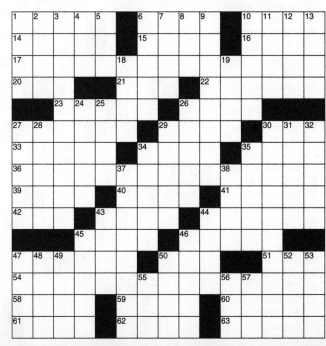

126 *WHAT A DOG!*

by Trip Payne

ACROSS
1 Syrup source
6 Elbow room
11 Walk like pigeons
14 Vermont town
15 Condor's claw
16 Vane abbr.
17 With 62 Across, a 1991 award winner
19 New-style "Swell!"
20 *Hamlet* phrase
21 *Romeo Must __ Album*
23 British maid
26 Award won by 17 Across
29 Garfield's middle name
31 "For shame!"
32 Bits of butter
33 Hexer's belief
35 React to yeast
38 With 53 Across, 26 Across' awarder
42 Wild guess
43 New Orleans school
46 Woodpile spot
50 Zodiac animal
52 Words of consolation
53 See 38 Across
57 Stash away
58 Mysterious knowledge
59 Poi source
61 Viscount's drink
62 See 17 Across
68 UFO pilots
69 "Oh, hush!"
70 Plumber's prop
71 Anonymous Richard
72 Door joint
73 Barely defeated

DOWN
1 Kittenish sound
2 Gray shade
3 "__ Love You" (Beatles tune)
4 Doyle's inspector
5 Montreal player
6 Mason's assistant
7 Handle roughly
8 *Arabian Nights* name
9 W.'s National Security Advisor, familiarly
10 No __ sight
11 Cannon's name
12 *Cat __ Tin Roof*
13 Sprinkles, in a way
18 Head away
22 Seer's sense
23 Cleveland NBAer
24 Showtime rival
25 "Pretty maids all in __ "
27 Of interest to Bartleby
28 Dime-like
30 Rolling stone's lack
34 Mel of baseball
36 Fast flier
37 Needle case
39 Playwright Connelly
40 Norwegian dog
41 Sari wearer
44 Doze (off)
45 Female antelope
46 Hamill or Witt
47 Bit of legalese
48 Box up
49 Genetic letters
51 Change genetically
54 Methuselah's father
55 Hawaiian island
56 Totally outlaw
60 U.S. national flower
63 __ Arbor, MI
64 Smoke, for short
65 Droop down
66 __ out a living
67 Was in first

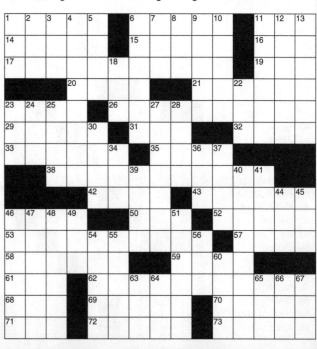

127 THREE OF A KIND

by Matt Gaffney

ACROSS

1 Slows down
8 Slugger's tool . . .
11 . . . and what it's made of
14 Walter Hickel, for one
15 Cornered
17 Versatile one
19 "Who am __ argue?"
20 HS class
21 Franklin et al.
22 Hunters' wear
25 Grazing land
26 Forearm bones
27 Sounds of relief
29 M. Descartes
31 Word before driver or school
34 Campaign staffer
35 Blazed trails
38 Bogie's Oscar film
41 Fore's opposite
42 Show anger
43 Colorado city
44 *Edward Scissorhands* star
45 Lose rigidity
46 Fast car
49 Circle section
52 Women's mag
56 Jai __
57 Grammy winner Irene
59 Nothing at all
60 Lion
65 Scott hero
66 Like some basements
67 Singer Tillis
68 Stylish, '60s-style
69 Goes over

DOWN

1 Indira's son
2 Fill with delight
3 Baja noshes
4 Pose an issue
5 *King Kong* studio
6 Off one's rocker
7 Traffic tie-up
8 Warsaw Pact member
9 Fitting
10 Punish severely
11 Eve or Elizabeth
12 "You look like you've just __ ghost!"
13 *Steppenwolf* writer
16 Casino furniture
18 Be duplicitous
23 Mock fanfare
24 *Amadeus* playwright
26 Not uniform
28 IHOP freebie
30 Ferber and Best
31 El stop: Abbr.
32 Channels 14 and up
33 After taxes
34 Hole in one
35 Author Buscaglia
36 Always, in verse
37 Spiral molecule
39 Had an effect on
40 Sudden impulse
44 Lower oneself
46 Eric B. & __ (rap group)
47 Still in it
48 Ear feature
50 Bowl yell
51 Fancy flapjack
53 Conniver's quest
54 Stirred up
55 Gravity-powered vehicles
58 Trojan War fighter
61 Bit of resistance
62 Egg __ young
63 Chapel Hill sch.
64 Wedding-announcement word

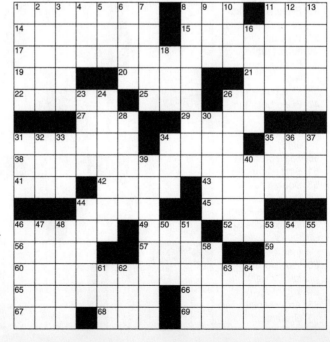

WHERE YOU LIVE

by Cathy Millhauser

ACROSS

1 Bullring cheers
5 Winter weather
9 Something easy
14 Old Testament book
15 Bread spread
16 Sky blue
17 Prefix for social
18 Dressed
19 Broadway awards
20 Cape Canaveral structure
23 High-fashion mag
24 Slippery one
25 Family member
28 Think alike
30 Rank beginner
32 "Snow" veggie
33 Failing totally
37 "Rule Britannia" composer
39 Wee bit
40 Toad feature
41 Does mining work
46 Mr. Lombardo
47 Bring back the line
48 Fictional Jane et al.
50 Tee's preceder
51 Singer Peeples
53 Double curve
54 Beef selections
59 Richard's *Pretty Woman* costar
62 Family member
63 Word form for "thought"
64 Trimming
65 *An American Tail* characters
66 Zilch, to Zapata
67 Bagpipers' wear
68 Fits to __
69 Frenzied

DOWN

1 Evangelist Roberts
2 Moon goddess
3 Caesar said it
4 Black eye
5 Inner-ear part
6 North's nickname
7 Low in fat
8 Sly trick
9 Library fixture
10 Arrow rival
11 Convent dweller
12 Hue's partner
13 Gentlemen
21 Music marking
22 Colony founder
25 Farm storage
26 Mythical flier
27 Rosalynn followed her
28 Hawks' homes
29 Sacred river
31 Ex-GI org.
32 National Leaguer
34 USPS delivery
35 Fall behind
36 Wedding words
38 Immigrant's course: Abbr.
42 Furniture ornaments
43 Getting __ years
44 Bequest receiver
45 Fabric worker
49 Eye feature
52 *Battlestar Galactica* commander
53 Prevention unit
54 Dagger handle
55 Cut it out
56 Gouda alternative
57 Make over
58 Become drenched
59 NYC airport
60 Mentalist Geller
61 __ Abner

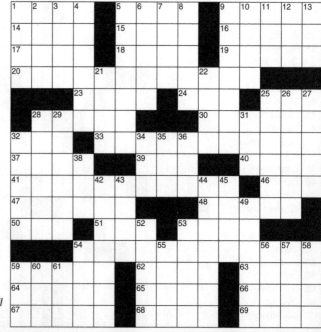

129 SMART QUOTE

by Wayne R. Williams

ACROSS

1 Painter Edgar
6 Kodak spokesperson
11 Geom. shape
14 Antilles isle
15 Jacques, for one
16 She-bear: Sp.
17 START OF A QUOTE
19 Go bad
20 Minimal
21 Treats seawater
23 Odds' colleagues
24 Folklore beasts
27 Mexican city
28 Shingle letters
29 Defense org.
30 Ski spot
31 Fictional exile
32 Calls
33 MIDDLE OF QUOTE
36 Source of quote
37 Inner disposition
38 Societal standards
39 Steamed
40 Writer Sinclair
41 CO clock setting
44 Lunar plain
45 Well-behaved kid
46 Washed-out
47 Profession of 36 Across
49 Cartoonist's need
51 __ Aviv
52 END OF QUOTE
55 Dir. opp. WSW
56 Boredom
57 Biko of South Africa
58 Draft letters
59 Musical notation
60 All in

DOWN

1 Touched lightly
2 Short trip of a sort
3 Some hoopsters
4 __ *Irish Rose*
5 __ serif
6 Wall St. analyst's designation
7 Bobby of hockey
8 Like some rolls
9 Highland hillsides
10 Cravings
11 Brando Oscar role
12 U-235 and U-238
13 Tangled mess
18 Squealer
22 Stands for
25 Rival of Navratilova
26 Became unraveled
29 __ Dame
30 *The Rookie* star
31 "It" is this
32 Released, in a way
33 Brings to life
34 Crusaders' adversaries
35 Makes jump
36 Wee speck
38 Auto stat.
40 Never praised
41 Kitchen tool
42 Record holder
43 Designated
45 Unanimously
46 Singer LaBelle
48 Spud's buds
50 Be idle
53 Destructive one
54 CX

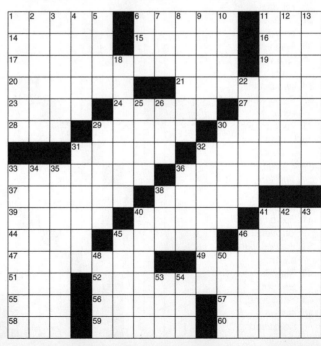

130 THUMB-THING ELSE

by Trip Payne

ACROSS

1 *West Side Story* heroine
6 Skater Thomas
10 "__ she blows!"
14 Man from Muscat
15 Author Hunter
16 Make angry
17 Thumb user
19 __ impasse
20 Supplement, with "out"
21 Frozen rain
22 Draw forth
24 Washington paper
25 Sea foam
26 Wheedle
29 Japanese vehicle
32 Clear the board
33 Asian capital
34 "What's __ name?"
35 Two cubes
36 Reservation symbol
37 Peel an apple
38 Be the interviewer
39 Lauren of *The Love Boat*
40 Birds in formation
41 Fixed leftovers
43 Viewed with alarm
44 Skunks' weapons
45 Smidgens
46 Actress Berenson
48 Arp's genre
49 By way of
52 "__ It Romantic?"
53 Thumb users
56 *Cosby Show* son
57 Flow slowly
58 Actor Lew
59 Geog. region
60 Poor grades
61 Baker's ingredient

DOWN

1 *Utopia* author
2 One way to run
3 Uncontrolled anger
4 Chemical ending
5 Pet-carrier need
6 Accounting entry
7 Mr. Knievel
8 Keep out
9 Room-to-room device
10 Characteristics
11 Thumb user
12 Jai __
13 Dollars for quarters
18 Lessen the load
23 Mischievous god
24 Prepare to be shot
25 Court assessments
26 Fragrant wood
27 Come to mind
28 Thumb user
29 Put a value on
30 Licorice flavor
31 Went down
33 Gordie and Elias
36 Frog or cat, e.g.
37 Black and Baltic
39 New Mexico art colony
40 Vacation motive
42 Journal boss
43 Cliched dog moniker
45 Toyland visitors
46 Catcher's gear
47 Laver contemporary
48 Catch some Z's
49 Actress Miles
50 Makes furious
51 Helper: Abbr.
54 Caviar
55 Caustic solution

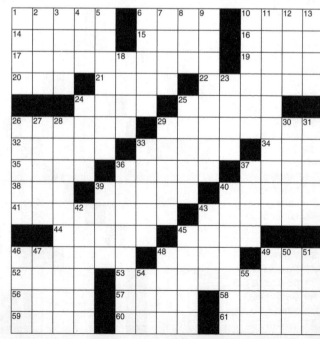

131 DANCE BAND

•••••••••••••••••••••••••••••••••

by Randolph Ross

ACROSS
1 __ Aires
7 "Hey you!"
11 Pa Clampett
14 Tie score
15 Mustang, but not stallion
16 Poker "bullet"
17 Dancing animator?
19 __ de mer
20 Much-loved
21 Final course
23 Purina rival
26 Diet-food phrase
28 Movie pooch
29 Davis of *Thelma & Louise*
31 Thumbs-down vote
32 Wallace and Douglas
33 Witness
35 Second Beatles film
36 AAA suggestion
37 Candy-bar ingredient
39 Man-mouse link
42 Farmer's friend
44 Flower parts
46 Thumper's friend
48 Put a top on
49 Adidas alternatives
50 Nobelist Wiesel
51 Sherlock portrayer
53 Early cartoonist
54 Night light
56 Hideaway
58 Baton Rouge sch.

59 Dancing pollster?
64 __ out a living
65 Rubberneck
66 Tennis great Pancho
67 Watched Junior
68 "The __ the limit!"
69 Folksinger Pete

DOWN
1 Gift feature
2 Actress Merkel
3 Sushi selection
4 Still in progress
5 Eleven: Fr.
6 Family car
7 __ de deux
8 When *60 Minutes* is on
9 Cutlery metal
10 Stocking stuffers
11 Dancing president?
12 Two-handed card game
13 River features
18 Press corps member?
22 Go to sea
23 Ice-cream ingredient
24 Riga resident
25 Dancing colonist?
27 South American capital
30 Computer-data format
32 Breakfast fruit
34 Make leather

35 *Leave __ to Heaven*
38 Down in the dumps
40 Comedienne Charlotte et al.
41 Coll. prof. rank
43 Help do wrong
45 Connection
46 __-lettres
47 "Seward's Folly"
48 Storefront feature
51 Referee's order
52 Windblown soil
55 Coop group
57 Curved molding
60 Scale notes
61 Big galoot
62 Vein contents
63 Something to shoot for

132 INJECTING HUMOR

by Donna J. Stone

ACROSS

1 Lays down the lawn
5 Godunov or Badenov
10 Bassoon kin
14 Throw in the towel
15 On the ball
16 Nice or Newark
17 *The __ Reader* (literary mag)
18 Trooper's tool
19 Auel heroine
20 START OF A QUIP
23 Fathered a foal
24 "__ the Walrus" (Beatles tune)
25 Graduation gear
27 Alts.
28 Swig like a pig
32 Shogun costume
34 Missionary, often
36 Boot out
37 MIDDLE OF QUIP
40 Sailed through
42 Author Smollett
43 Copier supplies
46 Prepare to fly
47 Cover-girl Carol
50 Speedometer abbr.
51 __ jiffy
53 Metal fabrics
55 END OF QUIP
60 Saltwater fish
61 Ryan or Tatum
62 Baltic resident
63 El __, TX
64 Michelangelo masterpiece
65 Heron relative
66 "__ o'clock scholar"
67 Land on the Red Sea
68 Bound bundle

DOWN

1 Wet-sneaker sound
2 Wearing apparel
3 Bistro patrons
4 Canyon of fame
5 Roseanne Arnold, née __
6 Oil of __
7 Overhaul
8 OPEC representative
9 Make tracks
10 Whitish gem
11 Eagle, for one
12 Joan of Arc site
13 SFO stat
21 Adds fringe to
22 Brit. record label
26 Florist's need
29 Dos Passos trilogy
30 Actress Lorna
31 Spec episode
33 Brahman bellows
34 Oriental-art material
35 Marching-band member
37 Egg plant?
38 Pack complement
39 __ Selassie
40 S&L convenience
41 Mimic
44 Free (of)
45 A bit too curious
47 It multiplies by dividing
48 Soup ingredient
49 Fearsome fly
52 *Oklahoma!*'s Ado __
54 Off-the-cuff
56 Knowledgeable about
57 Be abundant
58 Hoopster Archibald
59 Pizzazz
60 Exercise place

133 HUMAN ANIMALS

by Shirley Soloway

ACROSS

1 Western wear
6 Line of poetry
11 Increases
14 Troy lady
15 Artist Matisse
16 Society-page word
17 Overachiever
19 Newsman Rather
20 Small songbird
21 Billboard displays
22 Walk out on
24 Fountain in Rome
26 More prudent
27 Edith, to Archie
30 *I Dream of Jeannie* star
33 Gee's preceder
36 Burmese or Bornean
37 Make a hole __
38 Part of RFD
40 US summer setting
41 Canceled projects
42 Up for __ (available)
43 Standing tall
45 Orly lander, once
46 Mixed bag
47 Highway menace
49 *Max __ Returns* ('83 film)
51 Blue ribbon, e.g.
54 Whirlpool rival
56 Supply troops to
58 Extra
60 Circle segment
61 WWII aviator
64 Recipe phrase
65 Hard to see
66 Lend __ (listen)
67 Drunkard
68 Bandleader Skinnay
69 Hair jobs

DOWN

1 __ out (discipline)
2 *Damn Yankees* tune
3 Inspirational author
4 Hammered, in a way
5 SAT taker
6 Backyard building
7 Afternoon socials
8 Bill to pay: Abbr.
9 Attribution
10 Brings on board
11 Nonfavored ones
12 Nectar source
13 Conveyed
18 Barbara and Conrad
23 "__ evil, hear . . ."
25 Perfume bottles
26 Poster word
28 Biblical judge
29 Port of Iraq
31 Hazzard deputy
32 Robin's roost
33 As a result
34 Roll up
35 Timid soul
37 Being dragged
39 More or less
44 Tennis pro Michael
47 Sleeve style
48 Mischievous girl
50 Faux pas
52 Reviewer Ebert
53 Wild fancy
54 *Serpico* author
55 Mr. Guthrie
56 Skirt length
57 Farm animals
59 Goes awry
62 Chinese principle
63 Dance genre

134 REVERSE ENDINGS

by Wayne R. Williams

ACROSS

1 Tip
5 Circle fully
11 Actress Gardner
14 Software buyer
15 Carolina river
16 Super ___ (Lee Trevino)
17 Crooked heath?
19 "Black gold"
20 Rocking-chair locales
21 Patch a wall
23 Quite perceptive
24 Compass pt.
25 Life preserver?
33 Sour-cream product
36 Author Anita
37 Wed in haste
38 Time to remember
39 Wearing a cloak
41 Use the microwave
42 Light wood
44 Oblique line: Abbr.
45 Chicago trains
46 Where grouches worship?
50 Word after want
51 Battle of the ___
55 Small generator
59 Barrymore and Richie
61 Tuscaloosa's loc.
62 Slots jackpot?
64 Forceful stream
65 Barrymore and Merman
66 Concerning
67 Woodsman's need
68 Usher again
69 Some votes

DOWN

1 *Mea* ___
2 Part of PGA
3 Indian statesman
4 Land areas
5 Dueling sword
6 Beatty et al.
7 Precious stone
8 Wedding vows
9 Start up again
10 Moonstruck
11 Run ___ (lose control)
12 Bridal wear
13 Wheel shaft
18 Close-call comment
22 Amoeba, for one
26 Stevedores' grp.
27 ___ *Cane* ('63 film)
28 Dominant idea
29 Shiite's belief
30 Percolate
31 Milky mineral
32 ___ up (livens)
33 Something owed
34 "Dies ___"
35 Tropical tree
39 Landlubber's woe
40 Psyche part
43 C-___ (cable channel)
47 House and grounds
48 Band member
49 Shorebird
52 Mrs. Helmsley
53 "Battle Hymn" word
54 Senator Kefauver
55 Goya subject
56 *Family Ties* role
57 Entryway
58 Protest-singer Phil
59 Actress Kedrova
60 *Meet Me ___ Louis*
63 Haw preceder

135 COMPOSITION

by Eric Albert

ACROSS

1 Neon, e.g.
8 Avoided the issue
15 Bring up
16 Part at the start
17 START OF A ROSSINI QUOTE
18 Free
19 Handle badly
20 Sounded the horn
21 Falsification
22 I is one
27 Feminine ending
28 PART 2 OF QUOTE
33 Regarded with reverence
34 New York county
35 New York county
38 Gas rating
40 High-school outcast
41 Hardly touch
44 PART 3 OF QUOTE
47 Doctor's charge
50 Got too big for
51 Rule, in India
52 Donnybrook
56 Too big
58 Rice dish
60 END OF QUOTE
62 Nickname of a sort
63 Police ploy
64 Last course
65 Detection devices

DOWN

1 Provide a feast for
2 Outs
3 Casino shows
4 Nights before
5 Careful strategy
6 Munched on
7 Vast expanse
8 FDR program
9 Dudley Moore film
10 Major crime
11 Kind of custard
12 Wait in the shadows
13 Competitive advantage
14 Action
23 Off-color
24 __ Town
25 Vane reading
26 Off-the-wall
29 Riga resident
30 Keogh alternative
31 Beelzebub's business
32 Ball holder
33 Literary alias
35 __ Khan
36 Author Deighton
37 Garden spot
38 "__ from Muskogee"
39 Pfeiffer role
41 S.F. setting
42 Line of thought?: Abbr.
43 Mid.
45 Can't stand
46 Hair quality
47 Raisin center
48 Less trouble
49 Tosses out
52 Ginger's partner
53 Perfect for picking
54 Warts and all
55 Folding beds
57 Elmer's nemesis
59 Mel of Cooperstown
60 6-pt. scores
61 Mine rocks

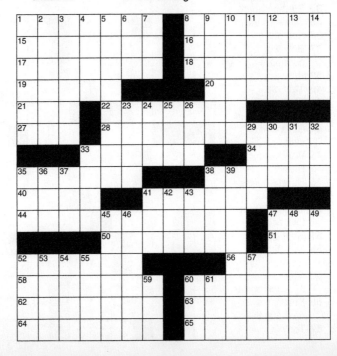

136 GROUNDKEEPERS

by Wayne R. Williams

ACROSS

1 Health resort
4 Hotshot
7 Kind of camera: Abbr.
10 Singer Stafford et al.
13 Steam engine
15 DMV procedure
17 Set up
18 Thankless one
19 Chopin's *chérie*
21 Blood quantity
22 Stitched
23 Teachers' org.
24 Latin 101 verb
25 Hindu mystics
29 Genetic letters
30 Shade source
33 Came to earth
34 Sell out
37 Bossy's comment
38 *Aida* guy
40 That girl
41 Throbs
43 Irrigation need
44 Calls one's own
45 Bandleader Brown
46 Short snooze
48 Forks over
50 Tammy Faye's former grp.
51 Take off
55 Novelist Seton
56 *Steel Magnolias* star
60 Speak hesitatingly
62 Too old
63 Saved, as a mag article
64 Old pro
65 Partnership word
66 Paid notices
67 Compass dir.
68 Mos. and mos.

DOWN

1 Some deer
2 Blender setting
3 Hood's missile
4 Building add-on
5 *Picnic* playwright
6 Ultimate letters
7 Fishing nets
8 Actress Carter
9 Rule: Abbr.
10 *Upstairs, Downstairs* star
11 Caesar's port
12 Doesn't dele
14 Hayloft locales
16 Hooky player
20 Testifier of '91
26 Merchandise
27 "Woe is me!"
28 Ctr.
29 Bowler's button
30 Nero, for one: Abbr.
31 Bud's partner
32 Famous feminist
34 Mrs. Truman
35 Light-dawning cry
36 "Absolutely!"
39 Shemp's brother
42 Turkish staple
46 Is taken aback
47 Burning
48 Rigatoni, e.g.
49 Singer Susan
50 Alias: Abbr.
52 Psychedelic doctor
53 *Pomp and Circumstance* composer
54 Idyllic places
57 Tennis term
58 Actor Montand
59 Honor with a party
61 Extinct bird

137 BODY BEATERS

by Randolph Ross

ACROSS

1 Dieter's entree
6 Ran into
9 Fitting
12 Handsome guy
14 Home to billions
16 Bowl sound
17 Rousing hoedown tune
19 LP filler
20 Sixth sense
21 Tough puzzle
23 Laissez-___
24 "Life Is Just ___ of Cherries"
25 Terrestrial
28 Middle Easterner
29 Comet and friends
32 Salinger girl
35 Current unit
36 Took a rip (at)
38 *Shop ___ You Drop*
39 Disoriented
41 Side dishes
44 Chagall and Antony
47 Code of silence
48 Craze
49 One of the Chipmunks
51 Unfaithful friend
53 Vane dir.
56 Lodge member
57 Funny joke
59 Pub choice
60 Royal address
61 Second banana
62 *Mal de ___*
63 Poker pile
64 John of rock

DOWN

1 Out of danger
2 Fusses
3 Airplane maneuver
4 Hill builder
5 Break up
6 Ike's missus
7 Sports Channel rival
8 Clasp of a sort
9 Threatening one
10 Expert group
11 Hammer wielder
13 Long steps
15 Isle off Venezuela
18 Boathouse hanging
22 Unit of sound
23 Summer appliance
25 Like Sabin's vaccine
26 Verne character
27 Tasty morsel
28 "Small world, ___ it?"
30 Mas that baa
31 Winning streak
33 Oven accessory
34 Designer Schiaparelli
37 Kowtows
40 Scuba gear
42 Bahrain, for one
43 *Tin ___* ('87 film)
45 Takes a chance
46 Siamese attraction
48 *Atlantic City* director
49 Red as ___
50 Butcher's wts.
51 Smile broadly
52 Space starter
53 Dalmatian's name
54 Utah state flower
55 British architect
58 Campaign pro

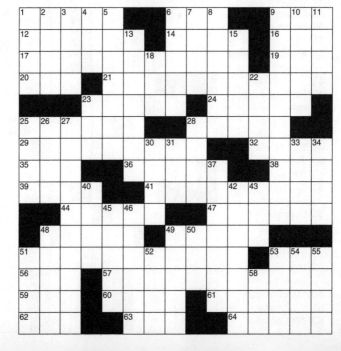

138 MONSTROUS

by Trip Payne

ACROSS
1 Vinegar acid
7 On the __ (fleeing)
10 Eye part
14 Texas city
15 College climber
16 Hockey player's protection
17 European airline
18 Make known
19 Tavern buys
20 Monster you can't fool?
23 Become one
26 Part of TNT
27 Squeaker or squealer
28 High transport
29 Dodger Hershiser
31 Ethereal
33 Church areas
35 Smart aleck
37 Tiny, to Burns
38 Monster's game equipment?
42 __ in "nudnik"
43 Raymond Burr role
45 Dull hues
48 __ uproar
49 Work hard
50 Tiriac of tennis
51 "__ your old man!"
53 Crumpet complement
55 Napoleonic marshal
56 Monstrous novel?
60 Melville opus
61 __ Kapital
62 Wild equine
66 Become winded
67 Sign a contract
68 Soda units
69 Red and Black
70 Both Begleys
71 Go AWOL

DOWN
1 Ms. MacGraw
2 Bandleader Calloway
3 Prior to, in poetry
4 Period of office
5 Dostoyevsky character
6 Where to park your parkas
7 Taleteller
8 Oversized birdcage
9 The Thin Man name
10 __ the crack of dawn
11 Holds dear
12 Channel swimmer
13 Determine worth
21 "Sacred" word form
22 Cossack leader
23 "That's super!"
24 Actor Estrada
25 Lucie's dad
30 Comedian Bruce
32 Kidney enzyme
34 Coors rival
36 '92 Wimbledon winner
37 Absolutely
39 Persona non __
40 Zodiac beast
41 McClurg of movies
44 Bridge expert Culbertson
45 Legs of lamb
46 Dormmate
47 Mother on Bewitched
48 Bali, but not Mali
52 Goody, maybe
54 Palmer, to pals
57 Caldwell et al.
58 Suggests a price
59 Scarfs down
63 "__ whillikers!"
64 Make a miscue
65 Q-U connectors

139 SOMETHING'S BREWING

by Trip Payne

ACROSS

1 A Leno predecessor
5 Picket-line crosser
9 Beef-rating org.
13 Cartoonist Peter
14 There's nothing in it
15 Stuck-up person
16 Reviewer Rex
17 Essayist's alias
18 Practice piece
19 Voice of the teapot in *Beauty and the Beast*
22 Rabbit-sized rodent
23 Publicize loudly
24 Carroll's teapot dweller
29 Buffalo NHLers
33 Overwhelming emotion
34 Gene carriers
35 Van Gogh locale
36 Author Rand
37 Assail
38 WWII contingent
39 I love, to Livy
40 Travel-guide name
41 Teapot Dome figure
44 Freight hauler
45 Utter bomb
49 Tempest in a teapot
53 Two-time Nobelist
54 Assemble a film
55 Caron film
56 Fort Knox bar
57 Dinner bed, often
58 Made a misstatement
59 Former South Yemen capital
60 Spree
61 Foal's father

DOWN

1 Graph lead-in
2 Field of battle
3 "Wall Street Lays __"
4 Copland opus
5 Knife cases
6 Lassie, e.g.
7 *Inter* __ (among other things)
8 Boston's nickname
9 Not schooled
10 Like lime pie
11 Comedian Goodman
12 Feasted on
15 Organic lubricant
20 Guitars' ancestors
21 Miffed
25 *The __ the Jackal*
26 Golden Rule word
27 European valley
28 Guesses: Abbr.
29 "I never __ purple cow"
30 Asian sea
31 Tell all
32 Economic downturn
36 Sometimes-shy person
37 Kind of eclipse
39 Word form for "air"
40 Move to and fro quickly
42 Bowl-O-Rama button
43 Somalia's home
46 Operadom's "Bubbles"
47 IV x XXVII
48 Cargo ship
49 It may be mutual
50 Exhort
51 Singer Adams
52 __-de-camp
53 Espionage grp.

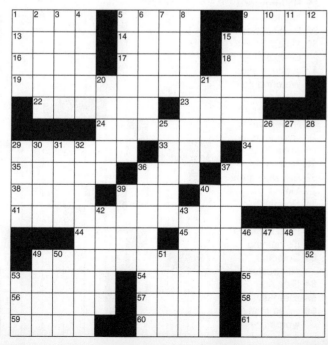

140 TIMELY ADVICE

by Donna J. Stone

ACROSS
1 Coral and Red
5 Discombobulate
10 Church area
14 David's instrument
15 Producer Ponti
16 Thailand neighbor
17 As a result
18 Right: Fr.
19 "__ forgive those . . ."
20 START OF A QUIP
23 Soothes
24 Junior, for one
25 '20s auto
28 Fish-and-chips partner
29 "If I __ Hammer"
33 Telescope view
35 Hairdresser's nightmare
37 Pianist Gilels
38 MIDDLE OF QUIP
42 Jupiter's alias
43 Watering hole
44 Jittery
47 Be important
48 Supermarket-scanner data: Abbr.
51 Teut.
52 Baseball great Mel
54 Dogpatch dweller
56 END OF QUIP
61 It's nothing
63 Coleco competitor
64 Blue hue
65 Eternally
66 __ so many words

67 Wear a long face
68 Florida county
69 Pass a law
70 Sound-stage areas

DOWN
1 Aussie woman
2 Sharp scolding
3 Sock style
4 Spinning-reel part
5 Electrically versatile
6 Theda of the silents
7 Elvis __ Presley
8 Opens an envelope
9 Frank
10 Jai __
11 Deli delicacy
12 Piglet's mom
13 Vane dir.
21 Leading man?
22 Strangers __ Train
26 Leave the stage
27 Thimble Theater name
30 Citrus cooler
31 Air conduit
32 __ Is Born
34 Boxer Spinks
35 TV talker
36 Peace Nobelist Myrdal
38 Lane marker
39 Like some nobility
40 Even so
41 Sheer fear
42 Run for the health of it
45 Came by
46 Natural gas component
48 Inimitable
49 Next-to-last syllable
50 Haunted-house sounds
53 Rocky Mountain range
55 Bill of fashion
57 Knight time
58 Bank deposit?
59 Author Ambler
60 "__ She Sweet?"
61 Last letter in the OED
62 Zsa Zsa's sister

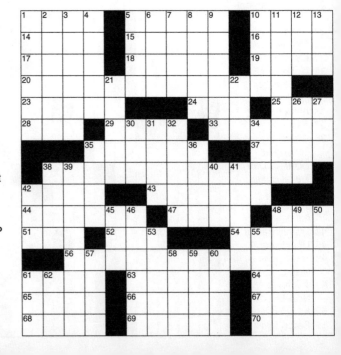

141 STRANGE QUARTERS

by Randolph Ross

ACROSS

1 Havana honcho
7 Tennis pro, often
14 Wind instrument
16 Take a rest
17 Defensive wall
18 Stockpiles
19 Rock stars, to teens
20 *Bolero* composer
22 *Pinta* partner
23 Tiny touches
24 "__ 'em!" (coach's exhortation)
29 Bit of comedy
30 Make repairs to
31 Lead astray
32 Efficiency apartment?
34 High-rise fortune teller?
35 Deluxe aerie?
37 Sandinista leader
38 Some sisters
39 Blushing
42 Rear parts, in anatomy
43 Reagan Secretary of State
44 "__ Ha'i"
45 Shed, in Sheffield
47 Stalagmite fan
48 Winery activity
52 Hard to catch
54 Rashly
55 Troop group
56 Loud speaker
57 Fairly good

DOWN

1 Managing somehow
2 Maine national park
3 Lamour costume
4 Song refrain
5 They'll be darned
6 "Let Me Be the __"
7 Eastern Europeans
8 Precious resource
9 Val Kilmer film of '85
10 "__ bodkins!"
11 Ring stats
12 Lea lady
13 TLC dispensers
15 Willy-nilly
21 In the gut
23 Neural branches
25 Hatred
26 Judy Garland, née __
27 Old French coin
28 President pro __
30 No philanderer
31 It may be on the house
32 Secret messages
33 Soup or salad
34 It holds a qt. of milk
35 *The Bride Came __*
36 Coronado's quest
39 Deep ditch
40 News time
41 Worst-case descriptor
43 More immense
44 Fundamental
46 Aware of
47 Medical discovery
48 "__ the season . . ."
49 Hill builder
50 That girl
51 Summer shade
53 Youngster

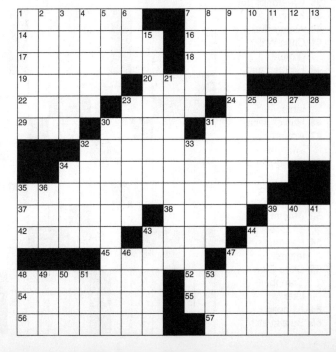

142 CITRUS MUSIC

by Cathy Millhauser

ACROSS

1 Make an exchange
5 Mardi __
9 Bette, in *All About Eve*
14 Prepare __ (the way)
15 Roof runoff
16 Nautical adverb
17 Son of Zeus
18 Dismantle
19 Potter's finish
20 Citric Dylan tune?
23 Mighty peculiar
24 Three, in Capri
25 Goat quote
28 Court cry
31 In
36 Creator of Boy
38 Keep at it
40 Alamo rival
41 Citric Welk group?
44 Reagan and Howard
45 Like Nash's lama
46 Half of deca-
47 Armed swimmers
49 Wonderland bird
51 Averse to mingling
52 African slitherer
54 Rap-sheet letters
56 Citric Glen Campbell tune?
64 All over
65 Be a kvetch
66 Revolution line
68 Word expert Peter Mark __
69 Musical tempo
70 Greek philosopher
71 Make an LP
72 Preeminent
73 Churchill's successor

DOWN

1 Springs are here
2 Nice and friendly
3 State confidently
4 Green sauce
5 Solomon of rhyme
6 Called up
7 Go-fer
8 Quick drink
9 Fridge device
10 *M*A*S*H* nurse
11 Stationery stack
12 Mideast region
13 Soothsayer's sign
21 Find smashing
22 Qum resident
25 Part of MGM
26 Literally, "for this"
27 Catalyst, e.g.
29 Mr. von Furstenberg
30 Marked off, in a way
32 Find awful
33 Bakery hardware
34 Jolly feeling
35 Opinion piece
37 To boot
39 Peace Prize city
42 Humid
43 Piped up
48 Palette set
50 Flue feature
53 Warsaw et al.
55 Make gape
56 Distort
57 Inventor Sikorsky
58 Hockey structure
59 Goes quickly
60 French milk
61 __ La Douce
62 Cut down
63 Mid evening
67 Chip off the old block

143 MONETARY POLICY

by Eric Albert

ACROSS

1 Jezebel's husband
5 Disconcert
10 *Ghost* cast name
14 Lose appeal
15 He-manly
16 Beasts of burden
17 Birthright barterer
18 Dampen with drops
19 __ Hari
20 START OF A QUIP
23 Key of one flat
25 Wedding walkway
26 Of a sense
27 Summon silently
31 Black as night
32 *The Third Man* actor
33 Class-rank stat.
36 Baseball great Speaker
37 MIDDLE OF QUIP
38 Biceps exercise
39 Darling
40 Catch in a lie
41 Frozen raindrops
42 Made a quick note
43 Ms. Gaynor
44 Yellowish brown
47 Bad temper
48 END OF QUIP
53 Spread in a tub
54 Oil source
55 Be stunning
58 Founding father?
59 Ward off
60 First name in fashion
61 Sandbox patron
62 Put to use
63 Criminal crowd

DOWN

1 *The Naked* __
2 Is owner of
3 *Freebie and the Bean* star
4 Toronto team
5 Fossil resin
6 Boxer Max
7 Aussie rock group
8 New York ballpark
9 Bay
10 Field of activity
11 Checkups, for example
12 Oxide component
13 Foolish
21 Encyclopedia bk.
22 Myanmar neighbor
23 Orchestra leader Percy
24 Saki's real name
27 Suit
28 Marry in haste
29 Make murky
30 Iodine source
32 Toad feature
33 OAS member
34 Hold dear
35 Dead tired
38 Sidewalk vendor's offering
40 Corrida cry
42 Robbins of Broadway
43 Speed-limit letters
44 WWII craft
45 Antiquated
46 Piece of luck
47 Refine ore
49 Was dressed in
50 Bend an elbow
51 Pickable
52 Recovered from
56 Buddhist belief
57 Silly Putty holder

144 IN THE MOOD

by Randolph Ross

ACROSS

1 Rummy variety
8 Seed coverings
13 Fellow employee
14 They have brains
15 Cooperating in crime
16 "__ Mountain High Enough"
17 Kennedy matriarch
18 Dali feature
20 Binge
21 Half the world
22 __ *Championship Season*
25 Pitcher feature
28 Seventh-century date
30 Cosmic countenance
35 Judge's shout
36 Spiteful ones
37 Expected
38 Match a raise
39 Informal refusals
40 Gov't purchasing org.
42 Reference-book name
46 Congealment
49 Normandy town
53 "Amen!"
54 Rational thinker
56 "¡__ días!"
57 May birthstones
58 Rose oil
59 Saw again

DOWN

1 Michigan arena
2 Inspires grandly
3 Bit of marginalia
4 Mr. Carney
5 Economize
6 Sax range
7 State one's case
8 Met highlight
9 Southfork, e.g.
10 Wealthy
11 Ball-game summaries
12 __ Paulo, Brazil
13 Sleeper, for one
14 Garfield, but not Roosevelt
19 Stew
20 *A __ Born*
22 Completely
23 Limits risk
24 Home of Iowa State
26 "Excuse me!"
27 Eat one's words
29 Kind of verb: Abbr.
30 Mike or Mary
31 Half the course
32 Trainee
33 Unspecified degree
34 "__ Lisa"
41 Field of battle
43 Texas tackler
44 Folklore being
45 __ on (urged)
47 Big name in fashion
48 UFO crew
49 "Get lost!"
50 Bathroom square
51 *Shane* star
52 Switch settings
53 Entrepreneur's agcy.
55 S&L offering

145 PLAY BALL!

by Eric Albert

ACROSS

1 Indonesian island
5 Decision-making power
10 Finn's floater
14 __ *vincit omnia*
15 Body of soldiers
16 Gardner of mystery
17 Kids' game
20 Compass pt.
21 Sills solo
22 Pick up on
23 Mötley __ (rock group)
24 Fischer's opponent
25 Pack up and leave
28 On __ with (equal to)
29 Blue as the sky
30 Close-fitting
31 Mess-hall meal
35 Woody Allen, in *Bananas*
38 Fuss
39 River Napoleon navigated
40 Par minus two
41 Stare slack-jawed
42 *Mr. Ed* is one
43 Take a wrong turn
47 Renders speechless
48 Assert without proof
49 "Oh!"
50 "Mamma" follower
53 Deteriorating
56 State strongly
57 Full
58 Singer Fitzgerald
59 Sleuth Wolfe
60 Dark hardwood
61 Become lachrymose

DOWN

1 Make fun of
2 Author Kingsley
3 Cast a ballot
4 Circle segment
5 Foment
6 *L.A. Law* lawyer
7 Exercise system
8 Soak (up)
9 Where columns are found
10 Landlord's loot
11 First sign
12 Small bit
13 Easily irritated
18 Did damage to
19 Not far off
23 Composer Gian __ Menotti
24 White of a wave
25 Plumb loco
26 Singer Pinza
27 Signaled an anchor
28 Point of view
30 Cuts quickly
31 Course meeting
32 Lofty
33 Scandinavian city
34 Sigh of relief
36 Kind of
37 River embankments
41 Chevalier musical
42 Like a suit fabric
43 Cartoonist Wilson
44 Martini garnish
45 Make a change
46 Part of MGM
47 Very pale
49 "Take __ the Limit"
50 Track distance
51 Wait at a light
52 Without delay: Abbr.
54 Chew the fat
55 Royal Botanic Gardens site

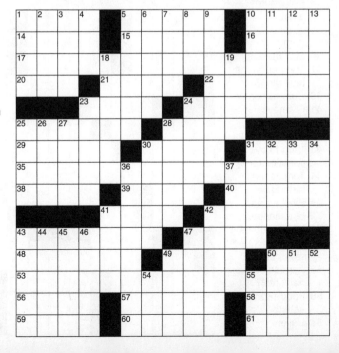

SHELL SHOCK

by Fred Piscop

ACROSS
1 Boxer Max
5 __ to stern
9 Teases
14 Choir member
15 "__ a heart!"
16 Exemplar of perfection
17 Police, slangily
18 Cheater's sleeveful
19 Montreal's subway
20 Newscaster on the half shell?
23 Spot to drive from
24 Long. crosser
25 Lubricate anew
28 Animal-product eschewer
31 *The __ and I*
34 Petroleum giant
35 __-pop (family-owned)
36 Mr. Onassis
37 Trapper on the half shell?
40 Summer drink
41 Overjoys
42 Banana throwaway
43 "And I Love __" (Beatles tune)
44 Tom Jones' birthplace
45 Finches and pheasants
46 Make a dress
47 Wag's wordplay
48 Actress on the half shell?
55 Food-processor setting
56 Sullen

57 Oolong and pekoe
59 Less cordial
60 Lively subjects
61 Admiral Zumwalt
62 Pains in the neck
63 Chess ending
64 Bread and booze

DOWN
1 Word from Scrooge
2 Actor Baldwin
3 Latin list ender
4 Earth's action
5 *Evening __* (sitcom)
6 Sonora snack
7 Neck and neck
8 Arizona city
9 Excellent
10 What "i.e." stands for
11 Turn down
12 Have coming
13 __-mo replay
21 Blanc or Tillis
22 Grassy plains
25 Indian chief
26 Wear away
27 Earthy color
28 Soundtrack component
29 Overact
30 Comic Kaplan's namesakes
31 Buffet patron
32 Conquistador's quality
33 Half the third-graders

35 African nation
38 Ring bearers
39 She never married
45 Kramden's vehicle
46 Sloppy precipitation
47 Prize money
48 *Time* founder
49 Crocus kin
50 __ *Bede* (Eliot novel)
51 Vaudevillian Bayes
52 Jeff's partner
53 Slippery
54 Like some excuses
55 Dickens character
58 Sea plea

147 HOLD THAT TIGER

by Trip Payne

ACROSS

1 Trick takers, often
5 Moves diagonally
9 Where to detrain
14 With the exception of
15 *Mirabella* rival
16 Kind of football
17 No contest, e.g.
18 Circus musician
19 Stuck in the mud
20 Cereal with a tiger mascot
23 Vaudevillian Eddie
24 __ up (be honest)
25 Play for time
28 Go nuts, with "out"
30 Circumference segment
33 Indulging in revelry
34 Roger of *Cheers*
35 *Jacta __ est*
36 Comic strip with a tiger
39 Swiss artist
40 Screenwriter James
41 Computer accessory
42 In the dumps
43 Crop pest
44 Stocked with weapons
45 Cook book
46 Corn or form starter
47 Description of Blake's tiger
53 Perry destination
54 Rocky spot
55 New York college
57 Without company
58 __ *Kleine Nachtmusik*
59 Any thing at all
60 *The Maids* playwright
61 Zipped along
62 Singer James

DOWN

1 Little viper
2 Barn baby
3 For all time
4 Pacino film
5 Like some sauces
6 Nautical adverb
7 Pleased as punch
8 Livestock device
9 Linen fabric
10 Satie and Estrada
11 *Fils'* parent
12 *The Defiant __*
13 Lincoln son
21 Conductor Georg
22 Pet-shop purchase
25 Loots
26 Refrain sounds
27 Was under the weather
28 Room fresheners
29 Richards of tennis
30 Obsolete platter
31 Singer Della
32 Scoped out
35 Goolagong is one
37 Wynonna's mother
38 Muscat fellow
43 Easter finery
45 Poet Hart
46 Egged on
47 Loft cube
48 Fairy-tale word
49 Film worker
50 Poison
51 A lot of fun
52 Cross-shaped fastener
53 Wild tear
56 Airline to Tokyo

148 *HORSING AROUND*

by Karen Hodge

ACROSS

1 Bit of barbecue
4 Author Ferber
8 Carpenter's tool
13 Just standing around
15 Former sr.
16 Take __ (throw the bout)
17 Colt's stable?
19 Carnation containers
20 Beast of Borden
21 Nag's sickness?
23 Attack
25 Bowling surface
26 Ski-resort machine
28 Distinct styles
33 Sound sheepish
36 Hairdo
39 *My Three Sons* role
40 Newlywed horses' dream?
44 Take care of
45 Asian fruits
46 Q-U link
47 Fords of the '50s
49 Sewer line?
52 Seep slowly
55 Con jobs
58 Equine charm?
63 Captures on paper
65 Neighborhoods
66 Mustang menagerie?
68 Oscar de la __
69 Assigned function
70 Admired one
71 Alpine strain
72 Jean Auel character
73 Be a landlord

DOWN

1 Swarming (with)
2 Admired ones
3 Great time
4 Freud's concern
5 Tap one's fingers
6 Kind of congestion
7 Author Rogers St. Johns
8 Pale purple
9 Wax-covered cheese
10 Passport stamp
11 At any time
12 __ majesty (high crime)
14 Mr. Ness
18 Dagwood's neighbor
22 Police-blotter abbr.
24 Nutmeg spice
27 It's over your head
29 Like some vbs.
30 __ about
31 Farrow et al.
32 Shipped off
33 Army outpost
34 Imitated
35 Potent potables
37 "__ Were a Rich Man"
38 Confused states
41 Polished off
42 Movie-hype word
43 Takes off the shelf
48 Soak (up)
50 Current letters
51 Wetlands
53 African equine
54 Jetson kid
56 "__ tov!"
57 Made a vow
58 Grant from Hollywood
59 Hydrox rival
60 Libraries do it
61 *Little Man __* (Foster film)
62 Take it easy
64 Flue grime
67 Teachers' org.

149 ACTING CLASS

by A.J. Santora

ACROSS

1 Women's mag
5 Overcharge
9 General Dayan
14 Witt maneuver
15 *Star Trek* propulsion
17 Betting setting
18 *Death Becomes Her* star
19 Coach Parseghian
20 Electrical units
21 Fencing sword
22 __ a dime
24 Last year's plebe
26 Real-estate abbr.
27 Smarmy to the max
29 Most unhappy
31 Works hard
32 Cashmere kin
35 Moffo of opera
36 Batter of verse
37 "__ a man with . . ."
41 Makes fun of
43 Kroft of *60 Minutes*
44 Chapter XI column
47 Gives in
49 Area code 302: Abbr.
50 Start off
53 Rogers' rope
54 Ed or Nancy of TV
56 Having troubles
58 Dernier __ (latest fashion)
59 *Thelma & Louise* star
61 Green stone
62 Poll subject of '92
63 Mars' alias
64 Percolates
65 Yale students
66 Polite bloke

DOWN

1 Ringling Brothers' home
2 Elbow grease
3 *Havana* star
4 Eb's wife
5 Cosmos' Carl et al.
6 __ close to schedule
7 US booster rocket
8 Buddy
9 Author Rita __ Brown
10 Will-__-wisp
11 Food basic
12 Ax handlers
13 Mariel's grandpa
16 Bungle
20 The enemy
23 *The Greatest Story Ever Told* role
25 __ polloi
28 Govt. agent
30 Mailer's profession
33 East, in Essen
34 "__ real nowhere man"
36 Some teeth
38 Health program
39 *Our Miss Brooks* star
40 Most peevish
42 From __ Z
43 Swindle
44 Old sayings
45 Dionysus' mother
46 Floppy-disk holder
48 Envelope attachments
51 Maternally related
52 Part of USNA
55 Cut quickly
57 Rock legend Hendrix
60 Foolish sort
61 Binge

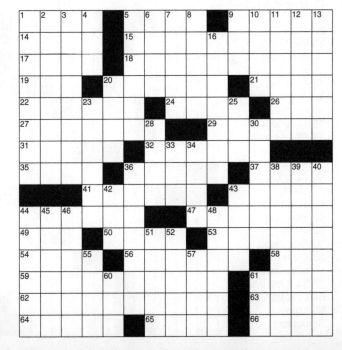

by Randolph Ross

ACROSS

1 Uno follower
4 Scads
8 Engine cos.
11 Additional phones: Abbr.
13 Nintendo forerunner
14 Long journey
15 With *The*, Lee Marvin film of '67
17 Replete (with)
18 Australian city
19 Musical transition
20 Murphy had one
21 Buttons or Barber
22 Certain psychologist
24 ME-to-FL hwy.
25 Hero of the '54 World Series
27 Posted
29 Work on a persistent squeak
30 Hash house
35 Some carolers
36 Letter opener
39 Blues great
45 Animation frame
46 Agitated states
47 Cut (off)
48 Bear: Sp.
49 Björn Borg, e.g.
50 Fertilizer chemicals
52 Moa relative
53 Loaded
55 "The doctor __"
56 Author James et al.
57 Pre- kin
58 Hallow ending
59 Actress Diana
60 Slalom curve

DOWN

1 Joyce hero
2 Enzyme class
3 Spreading around
4 Disagreeing
5 Use a hammock
6 Vein contents
7 Badge material
8 Quite cold
9 Disarm
10 Shooting events
12 "Gateway to the West": Abbr.
13 Parting word
14 Operatic effects
16 Feminist Molly
19 Onetime Amoco rival
22 They may have it
23 De __ (too much)
26 Secret meeting
28 Redeemed
31 Family Ties mom
32 Periodic-table no.
33 In order (to)
34 $C_{10}H_{14}N_2$
37 Takes out, in a way
38 Muddles through puddles
39 Carter secretary of state
40 Not so smart
41 Attracted
42 Exclusive groups
43 David Lee and Philip
44 Like a gymnast
50 Padre or Pirate, for short
51 Southern constellation
53 Mania
54 "__ to Extremes" (Billy Joel tune)

151 TRUE GRID

by Fred Piscop

ACROSS

1 Air conduit
5 Crockett defended it
10 Are: Sp.
14 Job-safety org.
15 Sand bit
16 Time-machine destination
17 Footballer's detention center?
19 "__ first you don't . . ."
20 *The War of the Worlds* visitor
21 Make out
23 Church area
24 Grove
25 Printer's proof
28 Temple quorum
31 Where it's at
34 Melon cover
36 Answer back
37 NOW cause
38 Debate side
39 Mr. Carney
41 Native: Suffix
42 Ice-cream flavor
44 High-flying toy
46 Agitated state
47 Stamp-pad devices
49 TV option
51 Taoism founder
53 Photographer Adams
57 Harsh-tempered
59 Ninepins pin
61 Blubbers
62 Footballer's magazine photo?
64 Turkey __ (dance)
65 Prepare to be knighted
66 Cassini of fashion
67 Aussie rockers
68 Walk heavily
69 French statesman Coty

DOWN

1 Tenet
2 Run-of-the-mill
3 Visual aid
4 Steak order
5 Turkish official
6 Author Hubbard
7 Track-meet org.
8 Botch up
9 Egotistic belief
10 Unisex
11 Footballer's fastener?
12 Ivan, for one
13 Envelope abbr.
18 Grievous
22 Avoid, as an issue
24 __ voyage
26 __ bono (free)
27 Orr's milieu
29 Word form for "height"
30 Nikolai's negative
31 Trucker's wheels
32 Mashie or niblick
33 Footballer's fishing gear?
35 *Star Trek* character
38 Chocolate substitute
40 Confederate
43 Publishing family
45 Freezer product
46 Bought by mail
48 Stays on
50 Hibernation station
52 Skunk's trademark
54 Made off with
55 Novelist Glasgow
56 Narrow shelf
57 Wine region
58 Country humor
59 Watch part
60 Some seaweed
63 Classical beginning

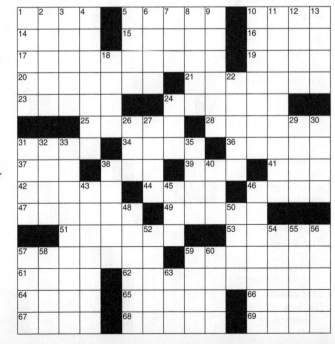

152 FROM THE HORSE'S MOUTH

by Trip Payne

ACROSS

1 Eyeglasses, for short
6 Red-tag event
10 Blue shade
14 Marsh bird
15 Mr. Love?
16 Phoenix team
17 "What's that bird overhead, Tonto?"
19 South American monkey
20 Lots of quires
21 Romania, once
22 Retro singing group
25 Pay attention
26 *Mommie* ___
27 Actor Gerard
28 '60s protest grp.
29 Forgets about
30 Brief beachwear
32 Puts on TV
33 Blackmore character
35 Joyce of *Roc*
38 Secretary's task
40 Spelunking fan
41 Part of MPH
43 Slaloming shape
44 Sign of the future
46 Baal's challenger
48 Some promgoers
49 Magi
50 Temple's trademark
51 Smokes, for short
52 "How was that joke, Gumby?"
57 Tighten ___ belt
58 Supplements, with "out"

59 Pica alternative
60 Subjunctive word
61 TV's Batman
62 Stay a subscriber

DOWN

1 Get the point
2 Faldo's grp.
3 Unit of work
4 Animation art
5 Author Laurence et al.
6 Trig term
7 Bouquet
8 Gehrig and Gossett
9 Atlanta's zone: Abbr.
10 ___ *Is Born*
11 "How fast should I go, Lone Ranger?"
12 Let loose
13 Mongols, e.g.
18 Half-___ over (tipsy)
21 Melting-watch painter
22 Prefix for sweet
23 "What's my mane made of, Roy?"
24 Bohemian
25 Price rise
26 Quaid film of '88
27 Juniper product
30 Cranberry spot
31 "How keen!"

33 Couch potato's dream device
34 Switch positions
36 Microscope part
37 Thou follower
39 Soup ingredient
40 Fridge section
41 Donna of *Angie*
42 Stritch or May
44 Most pristine
45 Sale-ad word
47 Senator Helms
48 Record machines
50 Royal Crown rival
52 Chop down
53 Word a matador adores
54 Relatives
55 Somme time
56 Bow wood

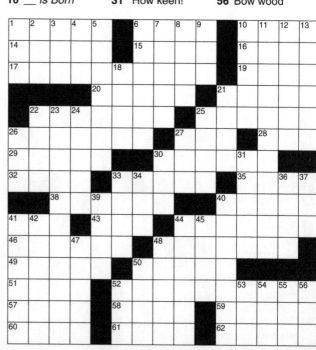

153 NOW HEAR THIS

by Matt Gaffney

ACROSS

1 Explorer Amundsen
6 Applies grease to
11 Some ammo
14 Telecast component
15 "Me, __ I call myself"
16 "*Certainement!*"
17 SOUND SLEEPER
20 Ms. Caldwell
21 Song refrain
22 Seep slowly
23 Larry King's network
24 Sarge's shout
27 *Taxi* star
30 Slobber
33 Glass square
34 America's Cup contender
38 LEAKY TIRE
41 Fan, sometimes
42 August Moon offerings
43 Basketball maneuver
44 Casino naturals
47 Russian refusals
50 Grill's partner
51 Tough spot
54 Thumbprint feature
56 Douglas, e.g.
59 GHOST
63 Be in the red
64 War cry
65 Apartments
66 Old crony
67 Barn adjuncts
68 Electrical device

DOWN

1 Deride
2 Moussaka washdown
3 Pickaxe relative
4 Columnist Smith
5 A whole bunch
6 Take it easy
7 WWII town
8 Gillette invention
9 Cease-fire region: Abbr.
10 "__ you!"
11 Dunderhead
12 Edwin Aldrin
13 Shoe clerk's query
18 Canadian export
19 Religion founder
23 Louder, to Liszt
25 Banned insecticides
26 Messes up
27 Cellar-door attachments
28 Cartographic closeup
29 Archaic verb
31 Merlin of TV
32 Hartman and Kirk
33 Ltr. addenda
35 *For the Boys* grp.
36 Ukr. and Lith., formerly
37 Pompous sort
39 Stick around
40 Store-window word
45 Spain's longest river
46 Grounds for the Victoria Cross
48 __ a kind (poker hand)
49 "Go ahead!"
51 Cartoon coquette
52 Tom Harkin's state
53 "The First __"
55 "Uh-oh" cousin
56 Thwart a plot
57 Tiny amount
58 Promising
60 Athena's symbol
61 "What have we here?"
62 *A Chorus Line* finale

154 SHIP SHAPE

by Shirley Soloway

ACROSS

1 Head over heels
5 Devonshire drinks
9 Flowers-to-be
13 Actor Richard
14 "__ we all?"
15 On a cruise
16 Incline
17 Makes wait, in a way
19 Feeling poorly
20 California county
21 High-school student
23 Modify copy
27 Ginza gelt
28 Dogpatch's Daisy __
30 "__ out? Decide!"
31 Cassette player
34 Army priests
36 *Hawaii Five-O* star
37 More cunning
39 Byron works
40 Seals' singing partner
42 Least lax
44 Guided trip
45 Retirees' org.
46 One's partner
47 On fire
49 Fashion expressions
52 Halogen salts
55 Crude cabin
56 Acknowledging applause
60 Garage job
61 Grand in scale
62 Road reversal
63 Author Wiesel
64 Love too much
65 Gives permission to
66 Iditarod vehicle

DOWN

1 See the light
2 Well-coordinated
3 Typesetter's sheet
4 Strong bug
5 Make __ for it (escape)
6 Baltic resident
7 Give guarantees
8 Put away
9 "Nonsense!"
10 Soldier-show grp.
11 DuPont's HQ
12 Down in the dumps
14 Little or Frye
18 Gymnast Comaneci
20 Some machines do it
22 Necessary
24 "My One __"
25 FDR confidant
26 Boulevard liners
28 CCXXX quintupled
29 *Prelude to __* ('92 film)
31 Close attention, for short
32 Heart line
33 Pothook shape
34 Ante- kin
35 Jet-set plane
38 Frat letter
41 Get into condition
43 "Darn it!"
45 Unruffled
48 Business bigwig
49 Created clothing
50 James Blake's nickname
51 Fine mount
53 Be adjacent to
54 Craggy hills
56 Danson of *Cheers*
57 Overseas addr.
58 Baby beaver
59 Rocks at the bar
60 Bandleader Brown

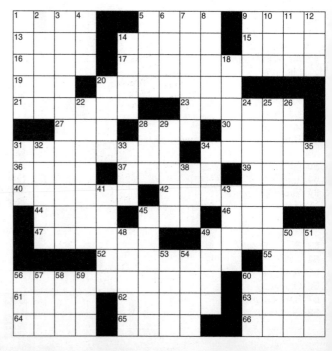

155 TOP BANANAS

by A.J. Santora

ACROSS

1 *Bells __ Ringing*
4 Actress Dalton
8 __ deux
13 Pol. party
14 Silents star
15 Market for goods
16 Rocks with rye
17 Top banana in baseball
19 Top banana in movies
21 Scale notes
22 Overwhelm
23 Dublin distances
25 Fits to __
26 Clumsy one
29 Mrs. Kovacs
31 Acts to excess
34 First woman M.P.
35 Top bananas at concerts
39 *Tugboat __*
40 Went fishing
41 Phaser setting
42 Bishop's domain
43 *Twelve O'Clock High* grp.
47 Stand __ stead
51 Bantu language
53 Religious deg.
54 What top bananas get
57 Top banana in vaudeville
59 Name in UN history
60 Shaw et al.
61 Slightly open
62 Brittany season
63 "__ is human"
64 Singing syllables
65 Bolshevik

DOWN

1 __ dozen (abundant)
2 Say it isn't so
3 Come out
4 Song star Paula
5 Sockless
6 Highland hill
7 Sleepy sign
8 Sound of the West
9 Control-tower staff: Abbr.
10 Scheduling phrase
11 Mockery
12 Airport stats.
15 "You can count __"
18 Seneca's *sum*
20 Chess promotion
24 Leftover
27 "__ way to go!"
28 Flowerless plants
30 Hesitator's syllables
32 Ginnie __
33 Cooking herb
34 Noshed on
35 Barker and Bell
36 Clark Kent or Ratso Rizzo
37 Overwhelm
38 Kind of error
44 "The Duke of Brooklyn"
45 Grown together
46 Tired out
48 Noted Canadian physician
49 Singer Redding
50 Comic actor Aykroyd
52 *Ne plus __*
53 One of those things
55 Genuine
56 __ California
58 Film-set VIP

156 SPECIALIZATIONS

by Randolph Ross

ACROSS

1 Small towns
6 Non-clerical
10 Radar image
14 Biblical patriarch
15 Siam visitor
16 Four-star review
17 Soda-jerk's specialty?
19 Brainstorm
20 Take aback
21 Sought office
22 Marty portrayer
24 Literary initials
26 Cozy
27 Writer's specialty?
33 Path's beginning
34 German article
35 Hang in the balance
37 AP rival
38 Court procedure
41 Golfer's position
42 Full of calories
44 Theater attendee
45 Words to the audience
47 Egyptian's specialty?
50 Lauder rival
51 Female pheasant
52 Fireworks name
55 Be shy
57 Sandy stuff
61 Doozy
62 Tour-guide's specialty?
65 "Pronto!"
66 Sped away
67 Allow to ride
68 Family rooms
69 Chop __
70 Idolize

DOWN

1 Loman's son
2 Voice of America org.
3 Make fun of
4 Newspaper name
5 __-fi
6 Tra trailer
7 Sometime soon
8 "Minuet __"
9 Hot peppers
10 Raise
11 Fill a hold
12 Currier's partner
13 Marsh material
18 Treat with milk
23 Place to be stuck
25 Restaurateur Toots
26 Mexican state
27 Dinner jelly
28 New York city
29 Transcribe again
30 More desperate
31 Archaeological find
32 Bagnold et al.
33 __ Town
36 Actress Wallace Stone
39 Vanity cases
40 Fill
43 Vocal reflexes
46 Got to first base
48 Fox sitcom
49 Guitarist Atkins
52 Bag brand
53 Scheme
54 __ Bator
55 Grimm character
56 Cheese product
58 Mag printing process
59 Fictional aide
60 Tony-winner Daly
63 Chit
64 Slangy suffix

157 TOO WISE FOR YOU

by Shirley Soloway

ACROSS

1 Caesar's sidekick
5 Football play
9 Kind of shark
13 "Famous" cookie maker
14 Picker-upper
15 Moistureless
16 Sour-tasting
17 Wiser, maybe
18 Funny Foxx
19 Dairy-case buy
22 "I've __ up to here!"
23 Bubbled again
27 Anchor's place
30 Slyly disparaging
31 Earring holder
34 Dogpatch patriarch
38 Actor Vigoda
39 Open courtyards
40 Prefix for system
41 Annually
44 Citrus drinks
45 Cosmetics name
46 One with airs
48 Firmly determined
52 Dow Jones component
56 Sunny shade
59 Soft mineral
62 Homeric epic
63 Gymnast Korbut
64 Baseball manager Felipe
65 Clock sounds
66 *Hud* Oscar-winner
67 Become fuzzy
68 Fresh talk
69 Flying piscivore

DOWN

1 Angler's haul
2 Astaire's hometown
3 Prepared apples
4 Straddling
5 Fabric, for short
6 Choice words
7 Prolonged attack
8 Use steel wool
9 Singer Al
10 *People __ Funny*
11 Little goat
12 Out-of-the-ordinary
14 Trifle (with)
20 Hwy.
21 Full of promise
24 Found pleasing
25 Draw out
26 Test recordings
28 Do a vet's job
29 Actress Jurado
31 Paint coat
32 Too heavy
33 Finishes ahead of
35 Judge's intro
36 Zadora et al.
37 Tall story
42 Happen again
43 Eerie Lugosi
44 Colorful shell
47 Miner's find
49 Inventory count
50 Shire of Rocky
51 Ambler and Blore
53 Not as hale
54 Utah city
55 Low-lying land
57 Talks too much
58 PGA distances
59 File-folder feature
60 Winner's take, often
61 Gossett or Gehrig

158 PHYSICAL FORECAST

by Randolph Ross

ACROSS

1 Take notice, maybe
6 Variety-show fare
10 Toy-magnate Schwarz
13 "Take Me __"
14 Braid
15 Matterhorn, e.g.
16 Thinking lucidly
18 Dot on a French map
19 Cools one's heels
20 Slip of a sort
22 Pinpoints
25 Melding game
27 Atlantic islands
28 Get smaller
29 Meted (out)
30 "Entertainment" preceder
31 "When __ door not a door?"
34 Extremities
35 Hot-tempered
36 Oxlike antelopes
37 Society newcomer
38 Rolling, in a way
39 Makes a scene
40 Pop star Richie
42 Et __
43 Wound in a reel
45 Mideast capital
46 Twist of prose
47 Baseball manager Joe
48 It may be spared
49 Kind and generous
55 12/24 or 12/31
56 Clamorous
57 Farm-machine name
58 Actor Beatty
59 Pull (in)
60 Best and Ferber

DOWN

1 Air Force org.
2 Ind. neighbor
3 Lower digit
4 Without warning
5 Like some movies for preteens
6 "Too bad!"
7 No gentleman
8 Overtime reason
9 Patron of Fr.
10 Easily sunburned
11 Parcel out
12 Puccini work
14 Favorites
17 Gets moving
21 Was in charge of
22 Worked on the docks
23 O_3
24 Without remorse
25 Quite careful
26 Bohemian
28 Beach find
30 Installed mosaics
32 *Kama __*
33 Syrian leader
35 Stooge Larry
36 Brought together
38 Crusade, e.g.
39 Mark again
41 Charged atom
42 Relief org.
43 Squad-car feature
44 Make one's case
45 Danish physicist
47 Fed. agent
50 *Bells __ Ringing*
51 *Louis Quatorze* was one
52 First-down yardage
53 Fab competitor
54 __ Moines, IA

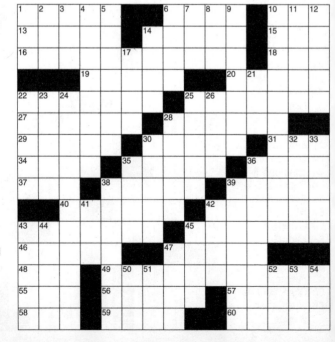

159 KINSHIP

by Cynthia Lyon

ACROSS
1 Art style
5 Put off
10 "What __?"
14 *Lucky Jim* author
15 Toothpicked delicacy
16 Cry of acclaim
17 START OF A QUIP
20 Consoles
21 Coat of arms
22 Joad-family member
23 Went left
26 PART 2 OF QUIP
32 Analyze sentences
33 Skip
34 Spill the beans
36 __-disant
37 Magnani and Moffo
38 Harvarder's rival
39 Austen's Miss Woodhouse
41 Paraphernalia
42 Like __ (50-50)
44 PART 3 OF QUIP
47 Fry's *The __ Not for Burning*
48 Monastery address
49 Arnaz autobio
52 The Syr Darya feeds it
56 END OF QUIP
60 See 8 Down
61 Stable worker
62 Hollywood clashers
63 Baseballer Sandberg
64 Medieval guild
65 Everything else

DOWN
1 Roast table
2 Shot
3 TV knob
4 __ a pig
5 Scale starter
6 Flora in an O'Neill title
7 Little lie
8 One of two raft riders?
9 Pron. type
10 Work on a soundtrack
11 Quitting time for some
12 "A Little Bitty Tear" singer
13 Cutting
18 "__ to bury Caesar . . ."
19 Nation in the Atl.
23 Mass-market books?
24 It's for the birds
25 Long-dist. line
26 *Dixit* lead-in
27 Fashion model Campbell
28 "Donkey Serenade" composer
29 Unfrequented
30 Kate Nelligan film of '85
31 Chic shop
35 Small snack
37 Improved, cheesewise
40 Sinatra tune
42 Kind of comprehension
43 Less
45 Munro's alias
46 "Time will doubt __": Byron
49 Place of worship?
50 Substance
51 Yves St. Laurent's birthplace
52 Bustles
53 Wise one
54 Piccadilly statue
55 A.D.C.
57 I may follow them
58 Refrain fragment
59 Way out there

PUN JABS

by Randolph Ross

ACROSS

1 Call for help
4 NFLer, e.g.
7 Angle measure
13 Daley's city, for short
14 Finish third
15 Third of an inning
16 Squealer
17 Indian children's game?
19 Lunchroom lure
21 Tide type
22 Indian stocking stuffer?
26 Long ago
30 Peter, Paul & Mary's "Day __"
31 Bar furnishing
32 Brutus' breakfast?
35 Important time
36 Fraught with pitfalls
37 Indian lunches?
41 Blackmail, perhaps
42 GM auto
43 Compass pt.
44 Bulls and Bears
45 Ocean floor
48 *Garfield* dog
49 Indian pirate flag?
53 Jeff Bridges' brother
55 Habituate
56 Indian farming?
62 Archaeological expedition
63 Toxic substance
64 Gstaad gear
65 "Wow!"
66 Squirrel, for one
67 Beer barrel
68 Pipe shape

DOWN

1 Beanpole
2 Butler's wife
3 Squash, maybe
4 Greek letter
5 Stewart or Serling
6 Use credit
7 Actress Blakley
8 Forever __ day
9 Tyrannical
10 __ *Dalmatians*
11 Razor-billed bird
12 Ultimate degree
14 Persian potentates
18 Green Gables girl
20 16th-century start
23 I.e., for long
24 Mrs. Dithers
25 *I Married __* ('42 film)
27 Nogales night
28 Elton John pitched them
29 *Family Ties* mom
31 Indian honorific
32 "__ Billie Joe"
33 Overwrought
34 Mongolian range
36 __-four (standard plank)
38 Headquarters
39 Taxing org.
40 "Let's shake on it!"
45 Aretha's realm
46 Eastern Indians
47 Cupid or Quayle
49 Pleasure trip
50 Beauty-pageant VIP
51 The Little Mermaid
52 German philosopher
54 Wharton subj.
56 Fool's mo.
57 Sticky stuff
58 Be free (of)
59 "For shame!"
60 Mini-guitar
61 Apparatus

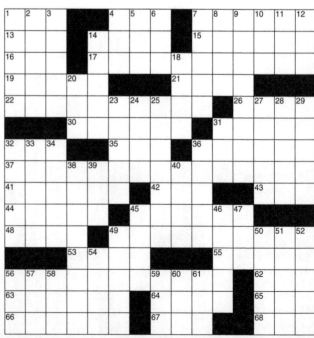

161 DON'T WALK

by Fred Piscop

ACROSS

1 Fuel-gauge reading
6 Got blubbery
10 No Honest Abe
14 Comic Anderson
15 Football's __ Alonzo Stagg
16 "*Der __*" (Adenauer)
17 RUN
20 Not fem.
21 *Days of Heaven* star
22 Like week-old bread
23 Moe's cohort
25 Darning __ (dragonfly)
26 War fleets
29 Sow's mate
30 Play reveille
31 Animation frame
32 __ tai cocktail
35 RUN
40 Radical campus org.
41 Att.'s title
42 Consequently
43 Meets with
45 Ceramic servers
47 Decathlon components
50 Craze
51 Joshua of Broadway
52 Sportscaster Albert
53 Ratio phrase
57 RUN
60 "Waiting for the Robert __"
61 Cher ex
62 Quotable catcher
63 X-ray units
64 Goose kin
65 Shady place

DOWN

1 Jr. high preceder
2 "__ Lisa"
3 Propels a shot
4 Haberdashery buy
5 The Beatles' "__ Blues"
6 '40s baseball brothers
7 Rough stuff
8 Lech Walesa, for one
9 Lao-__
10 Second of two
11 Its hero is Achilles
12 Bikini, e.g.
13 Richards of tennis
18 Taj Mahal site
19 Government workers' org.
24 "Zip-__-Doo-Dah"
25 Vincent Lopez's theme
26 Eyebrow shapes
27 Crucifix
28 "__ the word!"
29 Actor Vereen
31 __ au vin
32 __' War (racehorse)
33 C.P.A.
34 Turner and Pappas
36 Golfer's pocketful
37 Feminine suffix
38 Bangkok resident
39 Mr. Fixit
43 Bags
44 Sicilian spewer
45 Game fish
46 #10's, e.g.
47 Bugs' pursuer
48 "Success!"
49 Urged, with "on"
50 Polynesian peak
52 Persian's plaint
54 Belgradian, for one
55 Poi, essentially
56 General Bradley
58 Cable-network letters
59 Unfilled time-slot abbr.

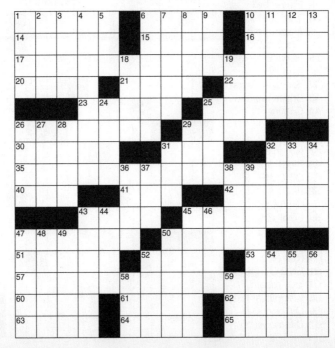

162 FRANKLY SPEAKING

by Cathy Millhauser

ACROSS

1 Hold up
5 PC owner
9 Flavorful
14 Sonic clone
15 __ contendere
16 Madrid museum
17 START OF A QUIP
20 Doc
21 *Quo Vadis?* role
22 Reuben's bread
23 Mag. execs
24 Wartime offense
26 Actress Freeman
27 It gets letters
32 Finished, in a way
35 Hit the bell
38 *The Neverending Story* author
39 PART 2 OF QUIP
42 Yours, in Tours
43 British servant
44 Continent's dividers
45 Big shot
47 Nix, in a way
49 PART 3 OF QUIP
52 PART 4 OF QUIP
55 Fidel's friend
58 Sgts., e.g.
59 Lower (oneself)
61 END OF QUIP
64 '50s record
65 Insignificant
66 Old one: Ger.
67 Did modeling
68 Some votes
69 Hideout

DOWN

1 "__ Be the One"
2 Felt sore
3 Loses one's coat
4 Writer Morrison
5 Awaiting delivery
6 Acapulco warmer
7 Ms. Verdugo
8 Popular posies
9 Folksy instruments
10 Canine comment
11 *Up to __* ('50s game show)
12 For no reason
13 Senate VIP
18 Army creatures?
19 Animal feeder
25 Planet of the Apes, really
26 College major
28 Film studio, for short
29 "A one __ two . . ."
30 Admired one
31 Chippendale quartet
32 Esau's wife
33 Baum barker
34 One of the Ghostbusters
36 "That's it!"
37 Chutzpah
40 Water partner
41 Square one
46 Gave clues
48 *The Courtship of __ Father*
50 Big-headed, sort of
51 Helena's competitor
52 Inventor Nikola
53 West Indies nation
54 ATM key
55 Pork order
56 Nativity-play prop
57 Remnants
60 Ground grain
62 Stamping machine
63 Top at the pool

163 GROWING THINGS

by Wayne R. Williams

ACROSS

1 Magazine layout
7 Tight spots
11 Have more to say
14 *Ruby* star
15 Brainstorm
16 Martial-arts legend
17 At home
18 Gilding material
20 Shop equipment
21 In a careless way
22 Coffee servers
24 Meat dish
26 Sherlock's hat
30 Unite
33 Woody's son
34 Frog kin
35 __ one's time
36 Division word
37 Does paperwork
38 Israeli guns
39 Free-for-all
40 Ripped up
41 Poker pack
42 Craving
43 Electricity sources
46 William or Sean
47 Singer Wooley
48 Mountain lions
51 Greyhound pacer
55 Skier's maneuver
59 Guarantee
60 Feeling blue
61 Son of Isaac
62 Small sofa
63 Word that filers ignore
64 Landlord's due
65 Word form for "intestine"

DOWN

1 Go to sea
2 __ colada
3 Remainder
4 Peace Nobelist of 1912
5 Birch-family trees
6 Alice __ Live Here Anymore
7 Lively dance
8 Fuss and feathers
9 Gibson or Tillis
10 "The Ballad of the Green Berets" singer
11 Emcee Trebek
12 Business arrangement
13 Challenge
19 Belli's field
23 Took a chair
24 Fleming and Hamill
25 Kennedy and Koppel
26 Holstein's home
27 Bert's buddy
28 John of rock
29 French river
30 Dry up
31 Proclamation
32 Class furniture
35 *Buck Privates* co-star
37 English prep school
43 Annoy
44 *Wheel of Fortune* category
45 Use yeast
46 Actress Dawber
48 Attention-getting sound
49 Home of the Jazz
50 Ancient Persian
52 Scottish island
53 *Champagne* bucket
54 *Vincent & __* ('90 film)
56 Put to work
57 Hightailed it
58 Obsessive fan

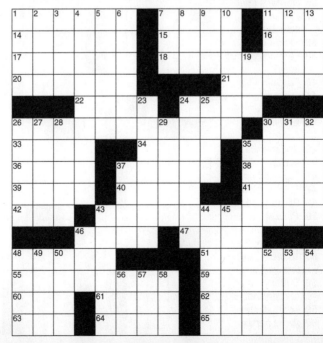

TASTE TEST

by Scott Marley

ACROSS

1 Kind of chop
5 Trucker, often
9 Guff
13 Western show
14 Bank (on)
15 Aware of
16 Cousteau's domain
17 Make eyes at
18 A Four Corners state
19 Saves
21 Reply to *gràzie*
22 Pub order
23 "__ She Sweet?"
24 Keep score, in cribbage
25 Gielgud's title
26 Watering hole
30 Hobo's dinner
33 Night sight
36 Hunter's need
37 Comic Johnson
38 Kilmer classic
39 Feel no __ (be tipsy)
40 Franklin's flier
41 Quick summary
42 Art Deco name
43 Space-race starter
45 Signs off on
47 Shirt or blouse
48 Be audacious
50 *Playbill* paragraph
53 Like some keys
56 To the __ (all the way)
58 Butter alternative
59 Football score
60 *Arroz* partner
61 Move like a hummingbird
62 __ Eleanor Roosevelt
63 Out-and-out
64 Certain Hindu
65 Honey bunch
66 Annoying one

DOWN

1 Union group
2 Designer Simpson
3 Walnut's innards
4 Dwarf tree
5 Promote, in checkers
6 Bible word
7 Jed Clampett's daughter
8 Ham's mate
9 Poor loser's attitude
10 Put into the pot
11 For men only
12 London district
13 Singer Julius La __
20 Landing place
21 According to
24 Globetrotter's need
25 Fondness for desserts
26 La __ Tar Pits
27 Mr. Sharif
28 Drop off
29 Semiautomatic rifle
30 Fifth Avenue store
31 Fall clumsily
32 Caesarean phrase
34 Difficult journey
35 '60s nuclear agcy.
44 Likewise not
46 Maintain the pace
48 Newsperson Sawyer
49 World book
50 Sings like Merman
51 Small bay
52 Telltale sign
53 Mary Quant and colleagues
54 Jai __
55 Schmo
56 Shade of white
57 Instructional method
59 Yak away

165 *PENNY-WISE*

by Donna J. Stone

ACROSS

1 Door part
5 Parish priest
10 Roads scholar?
14 Israeli airline
15 __ Gay
16 At any time
17 Moore of *Mortal Thoughts*
18 Get __ (eliminate)
19 Nelson's river
20 START OF A QUIP
23 Soft metal
24 Spruce up
25 Brainy brats?
30 Offer an opinion
34 '75 Wimbledon winner
35 Tipped off
37 Peanuts character
38 Menlo Park monogram
39 MIDDLE OF QUIP
41 Tom, for one
42 Striped stone
44 Heavy metal instrument
45 Heart's desire
46 Go over again
48 Acts like Attila
50 Cremona cash, once
52 Actor McShane
53 END OF QUIP
61 Intaglio material
62 Cantaloupe or casaba
63 Easy stride
64 Grimm creature
65 Coeur d'__, ID
66 Brainchild
67 Call the shots

68 Filled to the gills
69 __-do-well

DOWN

1 Champions of the Force
2 Pianist Templeton
3 Early sitcom
4 Crepe cousin
5 Betty's rival
6 "What's __ for me?"
7 Musical postscript
8 Overhead
9 Basket fiber
10 Shakespearean subject
11 *Metamorphoses* author
12 Endless band

13 Hydrox rival
21 Relative of -ist
22 In a weird way
25 Saudi Arabia neighbor
26 Grammarian's concern
27 "Do __ a Waltz?"
28 Take the Pledge?
29 Frame
31 Disguised, for short
32 Smooth-spoken
33 Senator Kefauver
36 Skater Thomas
39 "__ to please"
40 Dumped on
43 Wired, in a way

45 Hand-lotion ingredient
47 Some TV shows
49 On the __ (fleeing)
51 Cub Scout leader
53 Gimlet, but not daiquiri
54 *Picnic* playwright
55 Dame Hess
56 "__ a Song Go . . ."
57 Not a soul
58 Centering point
59 Piece of fencing?
60 Century segment

166 SPICE RACK

by Richard Silvestri

ACROSS

1 Young fellow
4 *War Games* group
9 Scored well on an exam
13 On the rocks
15 Puff up
16 Quite positive
17 Procession VIP
19 Place for corn
20 Examined thoroughly
21 Airline-board info: Abbr.
22 Metal sources
23 16 and 21, e.g.
25 Delight in
27 From the heart
31 Iron man?
34 Cove relative
35 Gentleman's gentleman
37 "What Kind of Fool __?"
38 Comment conclusion
39 British diarist
40 Sinful
41 Ariz. neighbor
42 Dropped pop, e.g.
43 Made away with
44 Threatener's words
46 Rankled
48 Anne, to Margaret
50 German coal region
51 Huck's transport
53 Prefix for skeleton
55 Colored slightly
59 Like crazy
60 Dawdle
62 One of the strings
63 Born first
64 Ear part
65 -kin kin
66 Gary Cooper role
67 A fistful of dollars

DOWN

1 Wilted
2 Rent-__
3 Art follower
4 One in want
5 Ending for scram
6 Hard to get
7 Téte-__
8 Makes mad
9 Cucumber-like?
10 Seek through flattery
11 The __-Lackawanna Railroad
12 American Socialist Eugene
14 Candidate, at times
18 Sired
24 Bank client
26 Trifling amount
27 Manilow's instrument
28 Go in
29 Devil's symbol
30 In the __ luxury
32 M. Zola
33 Got one's goat
36 Guitars' ancestors
39 Came before
40 Timeless
42 Compass pt.
43 Sober-minded
45 Chicken or Rich
47 Bacchus' attendants
49 Nolan's fate
51 Enthusiastic review
52 Got down
54 Antiquated "antiquated"
56 Incandescence
57 Island near Corsica
58 Applied henna
61 Held first

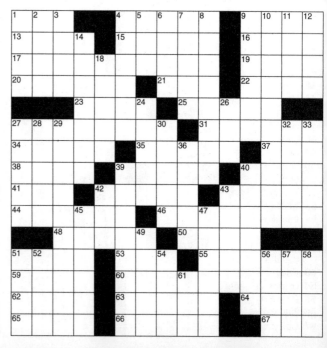

167 THE ELEMENTS

by Wayne R. Williams

ACROSS

1 Canseco or Ferrer
5 Lends a hand
10 NYC cultural attraction
14 Grub
15 Nicholas Gage book
16 From the beginning
17 EARTH
20 Started up: Abbr.
21 Jean Renoir film
22 Tearful woman
26 Emcee's job
30 AIR
34 Board material
35 Classic car
36 Singer Kitt
38 Not fer
39 CIO's partner
40 CCXXV + CCCXXVI
41 Out of sorts
43 Hood's heater
44 Witty remark
46 Dundee of boxing
48 Santa __, CA
49 Up to
51 FIRE
53 Paradisiacal
55 Wish granter
56 French 101. verb
58 "Eye" word form
62 WATER
68 Pitts of comedy
69 Church honoree
70 Highway division
71 Object
72 Turner and Louise
73 Hazzard deputy

DOWN

1 Ballet movement
2 Thole inserts
3 RBI or ERA
4 Juan Carlos' realm
5 *Playboy* nickname
6 "Xanadu" group
7 Superman foe Luthor
8 Nabokov novel
9 Mideast region
10 Hindu sage
11 "Sail __ Ship of State!"
12 Actress Harris
13 Dumbfound
18 Stood for
19 Bancroft or Boleyn
23 Florida city
24 Showing off
25 Erhard's discipline
27 Jamaican music
28 Writer Fallaci
29 Language structure
30 *Violin and Palette* painter
31 Money back
32 Limestone variety
33 Be a bandit
37 William __ White
42 Tanner's need
45 Conifer arbor
47 Band engagement
50 Vilnius' loc.
52 Pester the comic
54 High point
57 Morales of *Bad Boys*
59 __ Bator
60 Late-night name
61 Assayer's material
62 Israeli gun
63 Tended tots
64 Weather-vane dir.
65 Brooch, e.g.
66 Genetic letters
67 Part of TGIF

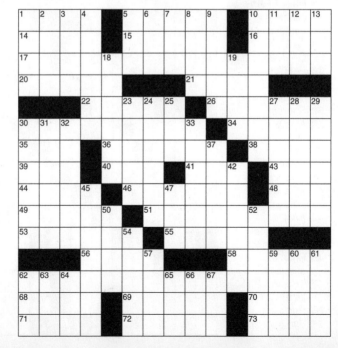

168 MATH ANXIETY

by Randolph Ross

ACROSS
1 Headquarters
6 Most wise
12 Piece of needlework
14 Competed on the Charles
15 Basement entrance
16 Predestines
17 START OF AN OLD JOKE
19 Big Apple initials
20 Dreamer's phenom.
21 Ms. Lupino
24 Arm of the Riviera?
27 Impressionist
29 Signs up
31 __ Palmas
32 Kind of blade
33 Hall-of-Fame pitcher Fingers
34 PART 2 OF JOKE
36 PART 3 OF JOKE
37 Makes up (for)
38 Shortfall
39 Agnew's nickname
40 Contract details
41 Haul away
42 Mamie's predecessor
43 AAA suggestion
44 Taunter's cry
45 Shooter ammo
47 THE PUNCH LINE
53 Pugilist
56 Eye opener?

57 Hôpital resident
58 Soiree time
59 Hollow stones
60 Clear the tape

DOWN
1 Italian port
2 NYSE rival
3 Gives rise to
4 Quarterback John
5 Ocean views
6 Get lost
7 Imported auto
8 Iris' cousin
9 Actor Wallach
10 Sun Yat-__
11 6-pt. plays
12 European airline
13 Scandinavian rug

14 Comparatively steamed
18 Unencumbered
22 Water down
23 Liqueur flavorings
24 Swell up
25 Roof beam
26 Classify
28 Bill-signing souvenir
29 Dallas daddy
30 Tournament placements
32 Arden et al.
33 Open to suggestion
35 Caught in a net
36 Baseball club
38 Bird on a Canadian $1 coin

41 Word of comfort
42 Cereal topper
44 Bakery equipment
46 Fishing specialist
48 Raison d'__
49 Lemony quencher
50 "Oh, what a relief __!"
51 *And Then There Were* __
52 Bit of work
53 Fruit tree
54 Feminine-name ending
55 Onetime sports car

169 HARD TO SWALLOW

by Randolph Ross

ACROSS

1 Knocks for a loop
6 Caesar's 300
9 *King Kong* co-star
13 "It's the end of __!"
14 Parlor, for one
16 Roll-call response
17 Less, in La Paz
18 "__ se habla español"
19 Geometric lines
20 Practiced restraint
23 Lost
27 Shoe holder
30 PC screen
31 Fashionable Drive
32 Tear apart
33 Men and boys
34 Warning signals
35 "Gotcha!"
36 Quilters' convention
37 Middling grade
38 Scale notes
39 Talkative type
41 Talent for music
42 Nastase of tennis
43 Capri and Wight
44 Pod preceder
45 Beatty and Buntline
46 Talked idly
50 Retracted a remark
54 Pasta choice
57 Have __ (know somebody)
58 Actor Patrick
59 Wickedness
60 Stand up to
61 __-car
62 Turns colors
63 Mind-altering drug
64 Wild fancy

DOWN

1 Door frame
2 "Dedicated to the __ Love"
3 Fast time
4 Ran slowly
5 Prokofiev's bird
6 Apple bearer
7 Acts the flirt
8 *The Little Engine That __*
9 A question of motive
10 Reviewer Reed
11 *Diamonds __ Forever*
12 "Without a doubt!"
15 Not at all spicy
21 Artist/illusionist
22 Bizarre
24 Swimmer Gertrude
25 Virgilian epic
26 Plays horseshoes
27 Like *Hamlet*
28 Go over old ground
29 Make possible
34 Letter flourishes
36 Attack on all sides
37 Heel over
40 Moans and groans
41 Immigrants, e.g.
42 Vocalizer
47 Unwilling to listen
48 On key
49 In __ (briefly)
51 Russo of *Lethal Weapon 3*
52 Bank deposit?
53 Verbal attack
54 Londoner's last letter
55 Wall climber
56 Music marking

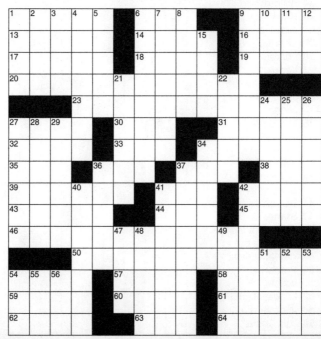

170 PUNCTUATIVE

by Wayne R. Williams

ACROSS

1 From a distance
5 They're serious
11 Package letters, often
14 Painful
15 Bathroom bottle
16 Word form meaning "sharp"
17 Exodus directive
19 Majors or Marvin
20 Lawrence portrayer
21 Department-store section
23 Major annoyance
24 Aftward
25 Nasal expression
27 Sports venues
30 Forceful trends
33 Prefix for while
35 Jenny in *Love Story*
36 Muckraker Tarbell
37 Sleep inducers
40 Research thoroughly
41 Raised trains
42 Starter chips
43 Gear features
45 Disarm a bull
48 Wheat variety
50 Prepares cutlets
52 Mideast liquor
56 In proportion
58 Just about
59 "Eureka!"
60 Gum-related
63 According to
64 Old Testament prophet
65 Urgent
66 Launch counter?
67 French Revolution leader
68 Gets it

DOWN

1 British racecourse
2 Civil War expert Shelby
3 Knight clothes
4 Deep regret
5 Bucks
6 Measuring stick
7 Nav. rank
8 Bearings
9 Write in the margin
10 Gordon or Irish
11 Portico's companion
12 Cart team
13 Re-colors
18 *The Tempest* king
22 High dudgeon
24 Fills with fizz
26 Hold your horses
28 Came down
29 Sound bored
30 In deadlock
31 Running in neutral
32 Driver's display
34 Pipe part
38 Slender cigar
39 Speaker system
44 Quick trips
46 Bobby of hockey
47 Gathered in
49 Robert of *Soap*
51 "Mack the Knife" singer
53 Bandleader Shaw
54 __ Boothe Luce
55 Rote and Rote, Jr.
56 *Hair* producer
57 Big bird
61 Shakespearean contraction
62 "Now I see!"

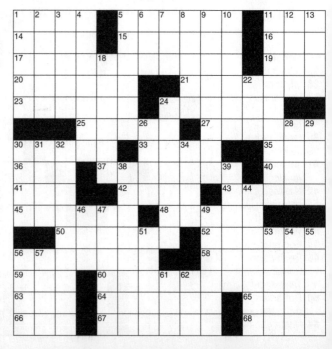

171 SILVER LINING

by Donna J. Stone

ACROSS

1 Pugilistic pokes
5 Grating
10 *Casablanca* setting
14 Square measure
15 Bring bliss to
16 Blind as __
17 Analyze poetry
18 Light beer
19 Run the show
20 START OF A QUIP
23 Adams and McClurg
24 Put in stitches
25 __ *Rosenkavalier*
27 Fam. member
28 Hollywood clashers
32 Hardly hyper
34 Proofer's findings
36 In the know
37 MIDDLE OF QUIP
41 Asian desert
42 Legendary quarterback
43 Verdi opera
46 Moon Mullins' brother
47 Antipollution grp.
50 Bear's lair
51 Peter out
53 Diverse
55 END OF QUIP
60 Gooey stuff
61 Join up
62 Part of Batman's garb
63 Coward of drama
64 *Cheers* chair
65 Nautical adverb
66 Creole veggie
67 Celica model
68 Runners carry it

DOWN

1 Artist Johns
2 Give consent
3 __ '66 (Sergio Mendes group)
4 Have a hunch
5 Dean Martin role
6 Jai __
7 Old clothes
8 Sunflower supports
9 Caduceus carrier
10 "__ Mia" ('65 tune)
11 A dime a dozen
12 Tiny Tim's trademark
13 When Strasbourg sizzles
21 Grenoble's river
22 Flock female
26 Auto acronym
29 Terrier threat
30 Iolani Palace locale
31 Reeked
33 Kennel critters
34 Depraved
35 Reebok rival
37 Seven-pound computer
38 Jacob's partner
39 Ending for prior
40 David's great-grandmother
41 Neptune, but not Earth
44 Kapaa keepsake
45 Preoccupy
47 Sing the praises of
48 Mr. Reese
49 Rattled one's cage
52 Namibia native
54 Pizarro victims
56 Oscar __ Renta
57 Play thing
58 Third-rate
59 __ podrida
60 *Starpeace* artist

172 *HOLLYWOOD REPORTER*

by Wayne R. Williams

ACROSS

1 Sentence break
5 Change for a five
9 Manhandled
14 Rights grp.
15 Storm the comedienne
16 Actor Milo
17 First Henry Aldrich movie
19 Dueling tools
20 Some anchors and stringers
21 Nonviolent protest
23 Babylonia, today
25 Read a poem
28 Rommel et al.
32 Shoshone tribe
34 Profit figure
35 Boorish one
36 Sore spots
37 Bleacher yell
38 Neck and neck
39 Glynnis O'Connor film
40 Stood up
41 Geom. shape
42 Blue shades
43 Sahara mount
44 Function
45 Roll-call call
46 Isn't colorfast
47 Duke of Edinburgh
49 Ms. Teasdale
51 Like a standoff
53 Priest's hat
58 Stone worker
60 Abbott and Costello film
62 Nonsensical
63 Ireland's alias
64 European capital
65 Rose essence
66 Paramount structures
67 Blossom support

DOWN

1 Tony Orlando's backup
2 Charley horse
3 Shredded side dish
4 Crude dwellings
5 Lustful lookers
6 Mrs. Yeltsin
7 Pixie
8 Gets a load of
9 49 Across, e.g.
10 Spicy jelly
11 Van Johnson movie
12 Wide-shoe letters
13 Pub. defenders' foes
18 __ acids
22 Peaceful Greek
24 Gores' predecessors
26 Back-combed
27 Merman and Barrymore
28 Ocular device
29 Fill with joy
30 David Janssen movie
31 Charged atom
33 Kazurinsky and Conway
36 __ *Lap* ('83 film)
39 Bawls
40 Actress Charlotte
42 Stephen King novel
43 Mild cigar
46 Half the honeymooners
48 Hotelier Helmsley
50 Scrub a mission
52 She sheep
54 Genesis name
55 Evaluation
56 Roof piece
57 Energy source
58 *"Mamma __!"*
59 Grasshopper's colleague
61 Hurry up

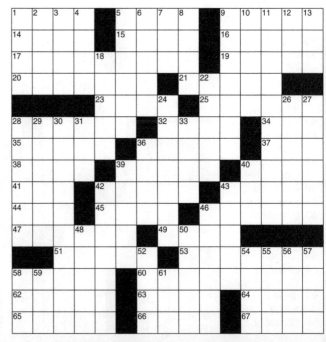

173 HOW CUTE!

by Trip Payne

ACROSS

1 Color Me __ (pop group)
5 Courtly dance
10 Michigan, e.g.
14 BSA part
15 Ms. Trump
16 Yoked team
17 Lopez's theme
18 Asocial one
19 Parker products
20 SPEAKER OF QUOTE
23 Big ape
24 Houston player
28 Dover dish
31 Half-grown herring
33 Baby food
36 START OF A QUOTE
38 "I smell __!"
40 *Gaslight* star
41 Florida's Miami-__ county
42 MIDDLE OF QUOTE
45 British Airways craft
46 Equestrian's cry
47 Fix typos
49 Prized violin
50 Gets warm
54 END OF QUOTE
60 It brings people closer
63 Compel
64 US alliance
65 See 43 Down
66 Electrolysis particle
67 Statuesque model
68 Marquis or viscount
69 Shows team spirit
70 Ltr. enclosure

DOWN

1 *Deliverance* dueler
2 "My Cherie __"
3 Reese of *The Royal Family*
4 Tuckers out
5 Arizona river
6 What Stratford's on
7 Homestead Act offering
8 Unique item
9 Trim, as expenses
10 Hardly close
11 Firefighter's need
12 Barbie's beau
13 Nav. rank
21 They may be colossal
22 Spineless one
25 Bonet and Simpson
26 Bagnold et al.
27 Convened again
29 Earring spots
30 Ham it up
31 Eydie's singing partner
32 Ran on TV
33 Shells or spirals
34 __ *With a View*
35 Turkish title
37 Pinkerton logo
39 Philanderer
43 With 65 Across, Monty Python member
44 Hirschfeld's daughter
48 Pete Sampras' field
51 *Battlestar Galactica* name
52 Moreno and Coolidge
53 *Basic Instinct* star
55 Worshiping place?
56 Words for Nanette
57 Small band
58 Kilt wearer
59 Sawbucks
60 State follower
61 Wordsworth work
62 Flamenco cry

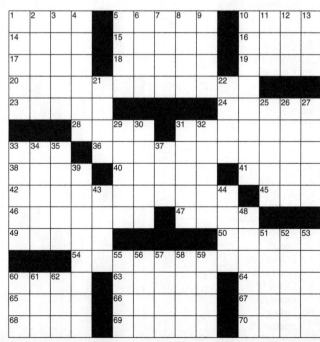

174 WHERE'S MR. LINCOLN?

by Eric Albert

ACROSS

1 Swerve or twist
5 Attorney-__
10 Pillow cover
14 Curb cry
15 Tibetan capital
16 Our Gang dog
17 *Butterfield 8* star
20 Drenched
21 Hardly exciting
22 "Olde" store
23 Highway marker
24 Prepare
25 Virginia, once
28 Babe's bed
29 Holyfield's pride
32 Island greeting
33 Animated character
34 Delany of *China Beach*
35 Filed wrong, maybe
38 Squared away
39 Stand up
40 Director Walsh
41 Above, in verse
42 Cream buy
43 The sky, so to speak
44 Pawn
45 Jupiter's alias
46 Again and yet again
49 FDR's place
50 Shake up
53 Gung-ho expression
56 Finely appointed
57 Packing a rod
58 Barn dance
59 Crude cartel
60 Styne show
61 Brisk

DOWN

1 Lamb dish
2 Green veggie
3 Way to go
4 Expert
5 Hudson River city
6 English homework
7 Past due
8 Timber tree
9 Phone service
10 Secretly observe
11 Samaritan's offering
12 At the zenith
13 Nothing more than
18 Lacking a key
19 Ishmael's boss
23 "Over There" writer
24 Investigate thoroughly
25 Walk-on
26 Green shade
27 Dangerfield persona
28 Run by gravity
29 Informal instrument
30 Better
31 With low spirits
33 Use your noodle
34 Ladd or Lane
36 Bob Barker prop
37 Become broader?
42 Somewhat: Mus.
43 Improv offering
44 Soprano's attainment
45 Is in accord
46 Galley glitch
47 Earring variety
48 Trick
49 Mildly moist
50 Off-road vehicle
51 Declare formally
52 Bank (on)
54 Stab
55 Returns org.

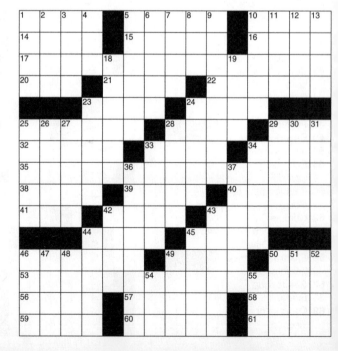

175 INTRODUCTIONS

by Scott Marley

ACROSS

1 Political movement
6 Bar in a car
10 "__ Ha'i"
14 A, as in Athens
15 Like a bishop's move: Abbr.
16 "The doctor __"
17 Classic movie line, supposedly
20 Prefix meaning "outside"
21 Fireplace tool
22 Singer Trini
23 "Get lost!"
24 Qty. of heat
25 Do or sol
27 Have the lead
29 Sound beater?
32 '83 play
36 Soccer target
37 Nightfalls
38 __ upswing (rising)
39 Hit tune of '65
42 *Padre's* sister
43 Contentment
44 Barbershop sound
45 It runs when broken
46 Encouraging remarks
48 Make __ out of (disprove)
51 Earth tremor
53 Armstrong affirmative
56 Cohan tune end
59 To __ (unanimously)
60 *The Wizard __*
61 Gobbled up
62 Outdoor meals, for short
63 Moist, in a way
64 City on the Rhone

DOWN

1 Checked in
2 Actor Karras
3 Till
4 __ Na Na
5 Made of clay
6 *A Bell for __*
7 PED __ (corner sign)
8 Troubadour's repertoire
9 Rational mind
10 Theater name
11 "The earlier, the better!"
12 Occupation
13 Don Juan's mother
18 Gnu home
19 Extreme
23 Copy editor's concern
24 Deep voices
25 Mama Judd
26 Midwest city
27 Set starter
28 Hawaiian idol
29 Mideast region
30 Rascal
31 Lacrosse-team complement
33 "What __!" (bored one's remark)
34 Willie of baseball
35 Beef cuts
36 "Vamoose!"
40 Pola of the silents
41 Pequod survivor
45 Brings home
46 Posh
47 Holmes clue
48 41 Down's captain
49 Helpless one
50 Asian nation
51 Not out
52 Sufficient, in poems
53 Regarding
54 Sign of tomorrow
55 Some dolls
57 George Burns role
58 Scottish river

176 POSSESSIONS

by Wayne R. Williams

ACROSS

1 Fiery crime
6 Actor Erwin
9 French priests
14 Martin's toy
16 Ruth's mother-in-law
17 Edith's dessert
18 Diamond boot
19 Ms. Ono
20 Singing voices
22 Fast food
23 Change color
24 Elements
26 Small band
30 Astrologer Sydney
32 Likes a lot
34 Pearl's family
38 Post-WWII strongman
39 *Jagged Edge* star
41 Bigotry
42 C.P.'s gardening tool
44 Drunk as a skunk
46 High times
47 Mimics
48 Magic word
51 *Nova* network
53 Miami team
54 Moe victim
57 To be, to Marie
61 Org.
63 Margaret's joint
65 Office skill
66 Edwin H.'s wrap
67 Ruhr Valley city
68 Half of *deux*
69 Fly-eating bird

DOWN

1 Drained of color
2 Word form for "current"
3 Water well
4 *Novus ___ seclorum*
5 PM periods
6 Hackneyed
7 Wrongful act
8 As far as
9 *Wheel of Fortune* buy
10 Red's dance
11 ___ acid
12 Chew the scenery
13 Becomes a dad
15 Collar insert
21 Open spots
23 Female rabbit
25 Peeve
26 "Memory" musical
27 Valhalla VIP
28 Lorre role
29 Jerry's pitch
30 Orchestra group
31 Greek M's
33 Training center
35 Welles character
36 Way: Lat.
37 Beatty et al.
40 Either Chaney
43 Tippler
45 Prof.'s aides
48 Look of the moon
49 Takes breaks
50 Does gently
51 Trim a tree
52 West Virginia senator
55 Rights grp.
56 Chestnut horse
57 Ending for opal
58 Spring event
59 Opportune
60 Dueling sword
62 Issue side
64 Recipe meas.

177 ROADSIDE VERSE

by Cathy Millhauser

ACROSS
1 Exile isle
5 Hashhouse spheroid
10 Complaining sort
14 Bartlett or bosc
15 Up __ (stuck)
16 Attract
17 Top of the head
18 Tome home
19 Singer Redding
20 START OF A VERSE
23 5 Across feature
24 Brewer's oven
25 A Bobbsey
26 Retain
27 Dennis' neighbors
31 Make beam
34 Line that isn't there
36 Floral garland
37 PART 2 OF VERSE
41 Director Howard
42 Pot covers
43 Groups of two
44 Necessitates
47 Old oath
48 Genetic material
49 Orion has one
51 Word before sister or story
54 END OF VERSE
59 "__ the mornin'!"
60 Where the blissful walk
61 Livy's love
62 Inventor Sikorsky
63 Handy

64 Slave away
65 A lot
66 Broadway bestowals
67 "Smooth Operator" singer

DOWN
1 __ Lederer (Ann Landers)
2 Spinach descriptor
3 Enjoy the ocean
4 2-D extent
5 South Seas explorer
6 Aramis' colleague
7 Italian city
8 Hard to hold
9 Stain again
10 Troupe group
11 Old Testament name
12 Scotto solo
13 Top-rated
21 Kayak user
22 __ ammoniac (ammonium chloride)
26 Nonprescription: Abbr.
27 Mental faculties
28 Ms. Korbut
29 Requirement
30 Remains idle
31 Rochester's love
32 Doctorow's __ Lake
33 Polly, e.g.
34 Rental name
35 Marked a ballot

38 __ Eve
39 Deles, maybe
40 Comic Louis
45 Shaded spots
46 One-million link
47 Distress signals
49 Conk
50 Post of etiquette
51 Pago Pago's land
52 Egg-shaped
53 Texaco Star Theater star
54 Working hard
55 Order phrase
56 Familiar with
57 Golden Rule word
58 Bartholomew Cubbins' 500

178 A CROSSWORD

by Wayne R. Williams

ACROSS

1 Joke around
5 Fleming and Carney
9 English racecourse
14 Assert positively
15 Stare open-mouthed
16 Take off
17 July 1, in Moose Jaw
19 Tiberius' tongue
20 Not quite right
21 Pencil-box items
23 Take a total
24 Sully
26 Fermi's concern
28 S.A. nation
29 Japanese novelist
33 Trajectories
36 Talked like
38 "Encore presentation"
39 Resting spot
40 *Bolero* composer
42 Scotland __
43 __ *Bulba* (Gogol novel)
45 City on the Arno
46 Deep black
47 George Wallace, for one
49 Cliburn or Morrison
51 Arrived
52 Skycap's tote
56 Actress Arthur
58 Brief bio
61 Coll. basketball tourney
62 Flynn of films
64 Indian chief
66 Board of education?
67 Nordic name
68 Singer Sonny
69 Lab work
70 Gumbo ingredient
71 Album tracks

DOWN

1 Reformer Riis
2 Get around
3 Dispatches
4 La-la lead-in
5 Culture medium
6 Detection device
7 "__ brillig . . ."
8 Actresss Ione
9 Top player
10 __ of Marmara
11 Racing boat
12 *Metamorphoses* author
13 Look after
18 Moose cousin
22 Uncooked
25 Islamic bench
27 Following directions
29 Kline or Costner
30 Fruity quaffs
31 Ottoman
32 *60 Minutes* name
33 Cinema canine
34 Honest-to-goodness
35 Falconlike birds
37 Haydn's nickname
41 South Seas skirt
44 Bakery freebies
48 Debussy's *La* __
50 Teen ending
52 State of India
53 Type of pear
54 James Dean film
55 Cultural spirit
56 Highest-quality
57 Perry's penner
59 Melville novel
60 *Columbo* star
63 Mel of baseball
65 Telephonic 2

179 SING SING

by Trip Payne

ACROSS
1 DeMille production
5 Well-qualified
9 Hoop star Thomas
14 It's undeniable
15 Clothes line?
16 John __ Garner
17 Regrets
18 Barbara Mason tune of '65
20 Actor Wallach
21 "__ Lang Syne"
22 Using chairs
23 Like Poe's stories
25 Small cobras
26 Mr. Wiesel
27 Aid in crime
28 Hitter's stat
31 New World explorer
33 Shutterbug buy
35 Pearl Buck character
36 Sevareid et al.
37 "Dedicated to the __ Love"
38 Beef cut
40 Parachute parts
41 Jimmy's daughter
42 Cool treats
43 Ballet garb
44 Bolger costar
45 Hose material
48 Taxing subject
51 Sisters or mothers
52 Recipe phrase
53 UB40 tune of '88
55 MP's quarry
56 Former Dodge
57 Actress Swenson
58 Back of the neck
59 Library no-no
60 Hideaway
61 Goes blonde

DOWN
1 Zimbalist of *The F.B.I.*
2 Singer Abdul
3 Vanilla Ice tune of '90
4 Dol. parts
5 Guarantee
6 Blues street
7 Alan or Cheryl
8 Dash lengths
9 Kind of interview
10 Long stories
11 "You're soaking __!"
12 Land measure
13 Hung onto
19 Make judgments
21 Slightly
24 Without company
25 How some are taken
27 Wanted-poster word
28 Slade tune of '84
29 Extorted
30 Wading bird
31 Caesar's partner
32 Reunion attendee
33 Less restrained
34 Salvation Army founder
36 Was artistic with acid
39 Popular cat
40 Ornery sort
43 Unmusical quality
44 Bodies of knowledge
45 Molds and mushrooms
46 Take the honey and run
47 *Twice-Told* __
48 OPEC member
49 Rex's sleuth
50 Half of DCCCIV
51 Ricci or Foch
54 Comic Shriner
55 &

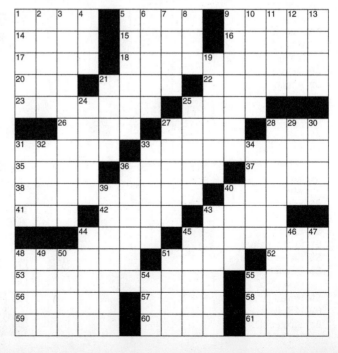

180 STOCK ANSWERS

by Harvey Estes

ACROSS

1 Collins of rock
5 Manner of walking
9 "Excuse me!"
13 Mystical poem
14 Brit's 14 pounds
15 What love may mean
16 Stock company?
18 Miscellany
19 Racy beach?
20 Hollywood hopeful
22 Adored ones
24 Spread in a tub
25 Café cup
28 Soup sample
30 Grump's exclamation
33 *Ordinary People* actor
35 Captures
37 Zsa Zsa's sister
38 Desire deified
39 Apollo 11 module
41 Become boring
42 Damage
43 *M*A*S*H* nurse
44 Sell wholesale
46 Vote in
48 Part of TNT
50 Eat away
51 Porcine meal
53 Entanglement
55 Columbus landfall
58 Hare __
62 U.S.
63 Stock option?
65 Cleo's queendom
66 Musical sounds
67 Peña's passion
68 Well-handled
69 Medium
70 Flintstones' pet

DOWN

1 Stir to action
2 Kona dance
3 Jones' nickname
4 Radicals
5 Makes off with
6 Carload
7 Ultimate aims
8 Spaghetti sauce
9 Portuguese possession
10 Stock exchange?
11 Northeast port
12 Not worth arguing about
14 Word form for "Chinese"
17 Copland ballet score
21 *The Sound of Music* scenery
23 Lounge entertainers
25 Main focus
26 Ear-oriented
27 Stock holder?
29 Chum
31 Flee from
32 Batman's alias
34 S. Dak. neighbor
36 Hyacinth's home
40 SST concern
41 Southern California town
43 Bit of matter
45 Spooky
47 Bordeaux beverage
49 More black
52 Solemn agreements
54 Parentheses' shapes
55 Shortwave, e.g.
56 Gallic girlfriend
57 Smithy's item
59 Sphere starter
60 Inert gas
61 __-American Symphony (Still opus)
64 Wee hour

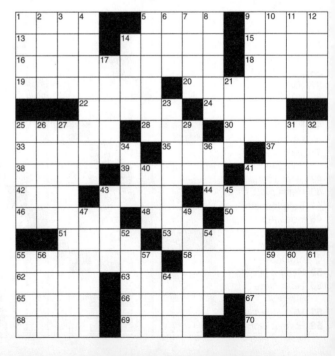

181 ON FOOT

by Shirley Soloway

ACROSS

1 Skim and 1%
6 Balance center
9 Put together
13 TV studio sign
14 Make eyes at
15 Expended
16 Asian evergreen
18 Barnum's singer
19 Author Bagnold
20 Come after
21 A piece of cake
22 Eastern Indians
24 VT clock setting
26 Gun the engine
27 Infused with zeal
32 Photo
35 Utility device
37 Like lettuce
38 Pueblo material
40 Rap-sheet letters
41 Flynn of films
42 Clunky car
43 Streisand co-star in '91
45 Mao __-tung
46 Hitchcock film of '36
48 Election winners
50 Recipe amt.
51 Lack
55 Pear choice
58 Painter Rembrandt
61 Inflight offering
62 Utah resort
63 British collegians
65 Close loudly
66 Kingly address
67 High-ceiling halls
68 Orchestra member
69 WWII region
70 Finishes ahead of

DOWN

1 Heston role
2 Senseless
3 Bandleader Lester
4 Joking sort
5 Sp. lady
6 Swelled heads
7 Felipe of baseball
8 Cash in
9 Driver of a sort
10 Where most people live
11 Family rooms
12 Sea swirl
14 Keeps
17 GI's time off
23 Bonds together
25 They may be vented
27 Tea type
28 River to the Caspian Sea
29 Move quickly
30 Strange sightings
31 Nabors role
32 Good buddies
33 Inspiration
34 Search thoroughly
36 Sharp flavor
39 Marine base
44 Rome's river
47 Place side by side
49 Mideast resident
51 Spiny houseplant
52 Closes in on
53 "Shut up!"
54 Lanchester and Maxwell
55 Big party
56 __ podrida
57 Lead player
59 Leave the stage
60 Continental prefix
64 Bit of hair cream

182 DIAMOND CRIMES

by Randolph Ross

ACROSS

1 June dance
5 Inferior
9 Allan-___
14 Verdi heroine
15 Skating maneuver
16 Mideast desert
17 What the runner did
20 Picketers, perhaps
21 Wipes out
22 Actor Frobe
23 Applications
24 Vegas hotel
26 Guinness Book suffix
27 Agatha's colleague
31 5th-century pope
32 National spirit
34 Poetic adverb
35 What the third-base coach did
38 Pitch ___-hitter
39 Copier chemical
40 Exigencies
41 Laugh heartily
43 Headline of '14
44 Nursery sounds
45 Lends a hand
47 Reagan confidant
48 Harmonize
51 Zeppelin's forte
55 What the slugger did
57 Nosey Parker
58 Fancy wheels
59 S-shaped curve
60 Bullish sound
61 Dance routine
62 Highway

DOWN

1 Written permission
2 Director Martin
3 Skunk's weapon
4 Libeled
5 Sci-fi weapons
6 Put out
7 Short times
8 Thruway warning
9 Conductor Previn
10 Insult
11 Turkish leaders
12 ___ majesty (high crime)
13 Nights before
18 Squeezed by
19 Greek sage
23 Wedding-party member
24 Office worker
25 Say OK to
26 The upper atmosphere
28 Richards of tennis
29 It's on the Aire
30 Messes up
31 Persian potentate
32 Lab burners
33 Daily event
36 Snow form
37 One next door
42 Cosmetics queen
44 Drive-in server
46 Unmoving
47 Casino order
48 Bits of current
49 Chance to play
50 The Andrews Sisters, e.g.
51 Mine entrance
52 Shakespearean villain
53 No contest, perhaps
54 Albertville vehicle
56 Chi-town trains

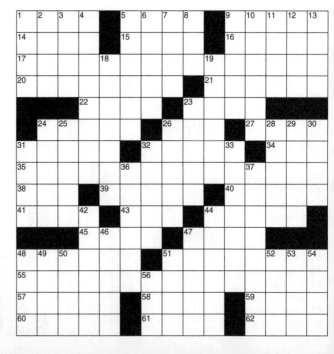

183 FIRST PERSONS

by Wayne R. Williams

ACROSS

1 Union bane
5 Calendar abbr.
9 Tavern orders
14 Unpunctual
15 State with authority
16 Actor Delon
17 Individuals
18 Recent retiree
20 Wedding tradition
22 Harsh-looking
23 In the know
24 Tailor, often
26 Nosed out
28 Roll-call count
30 Speaks grandiloquently
34 Red-headed riot
39 Star's stage
40 Colorado Rockies owner
41 Fellow
42 Chips, at times
43 Seth's son
44 *Kate & Allie* costar
46 Evita's title
49 *Discovery* agcy.
50 Student's souvenirs
53 At the ready
57 Ipanema's locale
60 *North Dallas Forty* star
62 Author Benchley
63 Reagan aide
66 Folk tales
67 Nicholas Gage book
68 Govt. training pgm.
69 Margot role
70 Thickheaded
71 Waste allowance
72 Poetic works

DOWN

1 Indolence
2 Tippy transport
3 Mr. T and crew
4 Miss America of '45
5 Actor Mineo
6 Arden et al.
7 Pro golfer Calvin
8 Group of three
9 One with the funds
10 "Xanadu" rockers
11 For one
12 Edgar ___ Burroughs
13 Crackle's colleague
19 Mythical ship
21 Rains cats and dogs
25 Actress Charlotte
27 *The Purple Rose of Cairo* actor
29 Epic tale
31 Lug around
32 At any time
33 Fresh language
34 Hotshot pilots
35 Nary a one
36 Palindromic time
37 Capek play
38 Hebrew letter
42 Famed fabler
45 Atlas page
47 What Nancy called her hubby
48 Ion source
51 Choose
52 Handle the helm
54 Got up
55 Spooky
56 Prepare for work
57 Musical mouthpiece
58 Not busy
59 Author Wister
61 Spanish direction
64 Officeholders
65 Dig in

184 FARM TEAM

by Wayne R. Williams

ACROSS

1 Take up
6 Antonym: Abbr.
9 Jack the dieter
14 Jason's wife
15 Aussie leaper
16 Dress style
17 British actress Joan
19 Makes a scene
20 Sun. speech
21 Inventor Nikola
22 Pampas backdrop
23 Train unit
24 Diplomacy
26 Really enjoy
29 Like some farm animals
34 Currency-exchange fee
35 Arafat's grp.
36 Switch on
37 Abrasive tool
38 Not as polite
40 To be, in Toulouse
41 One-celled animal
43 Tax agcy.
44 Poverty
45 Very scary
47 Tries out
48 Sothern and Sheridan
49 Track action
50 Let up
53 Little green man
56 Actress MacGraw
59 Sound

60 Hull collection
62 *The Maltese Falcon* actress
63 Greek letter
64 *Cannery Row* star
65 Rock-strewn
66 Cariou of musicals
67 Poke fun at

DOWN

1 Rock-concert gear
2 Remove from text
3 Fragrance
4 Basilica bench
5 Kind of sauce
6 Assns.
7 Sci-fi writer Frederik
8 It may be hot
9 Crusader's opponent
10 British royal house
11 Outer covering
12 Pot starter
13 Hardy heroine
18 Cash ending
23 Joint effort
25 Mimics
26 Fergie's first name
27 Old World lizard
28 Cap part
29 TV actor Gulager
30 *The Age of Bronze* sculptor
31 Merits
32 Long-plumed bird
33 Property records
35 Shrimp kin
39 Unit of work
42 Parched
46 Señora Perón
47 One renting
49 Pa Cartwright
50 Gardner et al.
51 Rope fiber
52 Singing voice
54 Past due
55 Pro boxer Barkley
56 __ breve
57 "Why not?"
58 Comment of clarity
61 Iowa college

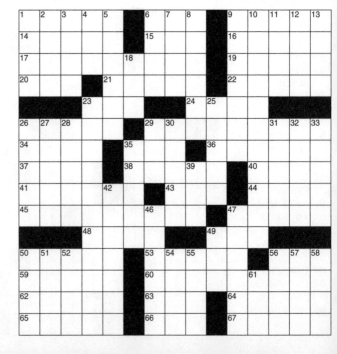

185 ENGLISH MAJORS

by Randolph Ross

ACROSS

1 They're often exchanged
5 __ Raton, FL
9 Asian priest
13 Gulf state
14 Gem weight
15 Riviera seasons
16 Stead
17 Clear as __
18 They fly by night
19 Raven rhymester?
22 Big belly
23 Concert closers
24 Letter getter
29 Negotiations
30 Rhyming wisecracker?
32 Ring result
33 Menlo Park monogram
34 Ms. MacGraw
37 Actress doing screenplays?
43 Minneapolis suburb
45 New hires
46 Salon work
48 Peak
49 Autobiographer president?
54 Disassemble
55 Leans (toward)
56 Given the boot
58 Slay
59 George of *Star Trek*
60 Ship out
61 Nine-digit IDs
62 H H H
63 Extremities

DOWN

1 Actor Kilmer
2 Garfield's canine pal
3 Unwelcome growth
4 Cozy up
5 Rum cake
6 Pitcher Hershiser
7 Spanish street
8 Home of the Hawks
9 Maestro Stokowski
10 Busy
11 Free-for-alls
12 ADCs
14 Egg holder
20 Subtle glow
21 Sen. Helms' state
24 *A-Team* actor
25 NASA assent
26 Bar's beginning
27 In the know about
28 Had in mind
31 Yogi, for one
34 Went to Wendy's
35 *To Kill a Mockingbird* author
36 Auditing org.
37 Dennis' neighbors
38 Monogram part: Abbr.
39 Ms. Fabray
40 '60s dance
41 Something hysterical
42 Synchronous
43 Cultural group
44 __-the-wool
46 Desert Storm targets
47 Tony the Tiger's favorite word
50 "Times of your Life" singer
51 Citrus drinks
52 Draft team
53 Tear apart
57 Tooth pro's deg.

ACROSS

1 Shriver of tennis
4 "Delicious!"
7 Obi-Wan, for one
11 De Niro role
13 Smooth
15 50-year-old
17 Hypnotized
18 Smoke, for short
19 JFK's predecessor
20 Shake, in prescriptions
21 Strength
24 __ majesty (sovereign crime)
25 Wine word
26 Debater of '92
27 Yearned (for)
28 Run-of-the-mill
29 Pizarro victim
30 Southwest city
33 Nutrition stats.
34 Santa __
35 Heartless one
36 Glide on ice
37 B&O stop
40 High point
41 Moriarty's creator
42 K-6
43 Promulgate
44 *Flying Down to* __
45 In unison
46 Onetime NHL team
51 Touch-and-go
52 Leads
53 Sundance's love
54 LAX client
55 Questioning comments

DOWN

1 Dive in
2 Low-pH
3 *Olympia* painter
4 Pronoun with two homonyms
5 Actress Merkel
6 Ryan or Foster
7 Discombobulate
8 Prints, perhaps
9 World's lowest lake
10 Destitute
11 Blue shades
12 O followers
13 Nasty mood
14 Witchlike woman
16 Real, in Regensburg
21 Course listing
22 Basra's land
23 Happy-__
24 *Peanuts* character
26 Budweiser rival
27 Arouse ire
28 Nonchalant
30 TV's Batman
31 Mideast carrier
32 Unit charge
33 Loser's demand
35 Pyrenees resident
36 Any minute now
37 Pushover
38 Group principles
39 In __ (disheveled)
41 Chop up
42 -ish relative
44 Grid official
45 Lend a hand
47 Lea plea
48 UN Day mo.
49 Ducat word
50 Genetic material

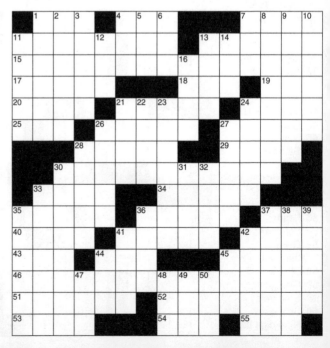

FAMILY TV

by Mark Ryder

ACROSS

1 Extensive
5 Saharan transport
10 PBS science show
14 Come up against
15 "What __ is this": Pepys
16 Actor Bates
17 Classic '50s sitcom
20 Go for it
21 Revealing pictures
22 Score part
23 GI address
24 Yale student
25 '60s Arden sitcom
34 Distorts
35 Sale condition
36 Storm or Gordon
37 The Big Band __
38 Snitch
41 Parts of qts.
42 Exxon's former name
44 __ gin fizz
45 Perturb
47 '70s Natwick detective drama
50 Shipping unit
51 Govt. purchasing org.
52 Closet hangings
54 Singer Cleo
57 P.O. poster people
60 TV psychologist
63 Polynesian carving
64 Kid-lit elephant
65 Mr. Roberts
66 Realtor's sign
67 Chevy __, MD
68 In the past

DOWN

1 Travel, as an aroma
2 Construction piece
3 It may call
4 Ordinal ending
5 Metaphorical temptation
6 "Diana" singer
7 More than a few
8 Personalities' parts
9 Actor Ayres
10 Arrester's activity
11 Tub in the fridge
12 Flower holder
13 Industrious insect
18 __ facto (retroactively)
19 One-person performances
23 Fuse unit
24 To be: Lat.
25 Sing like the birdies sing
26 Irritating
27 Clear a tape
28 *Little Iodine* cartoonist Jimmy
29 Bar legally
30 Irks
31 Boo-boo
32 Take in, e.g.
33 Adam and Rebecca
39 ". . . unto us __ is given"
40 Autumn apple
43 Bonelike
46 School org.
48 A bit too interested
49 Pay no mind to
52 Work for three
53 H-M link
54 Jacob's first wife
55 Eban of Israel
56 Tax-deferred accts.
57 Flowerless plant
58 Bric-a-__
59 Global speck
60 Wino's bane
61 Ont. network
62 "Yoo-__!"

188 PLACE NAMES

by Wayne R. Williams

ACROSS

1 Hostess Perle
6 Homecoming attendees
11 Tie-up
14 Blood of the gods
15 Thurmond and Archibald
16 Shoshonean
17 Actress from Peking?
19 Mauna __
20 Sound a horn
21 Troop's camp
22 Window ledge
23 Tiny amounts
25 Sand bars
27 Kind of assault
30 After-shower powder
31 Hasty flight
32 Word form for "skull"
35 Western lake
38 Composer Khachaturian
40 Iberian river
42 Ship of 1492
43 Columbus' home
45 Uses a fork
47 French article
48 Be up and about
50 Proximate
52 On land
54 Warren Beatty role
55 Lead player
56 Rocky debris
58 False god
62 Comparative ending
63 Film director from Warsaw?
65 "Agnus __"
66 Zoo beast
67 Missouri mountains
68 Sprightly character
69 Stair post
70 *Corrida* beasts

DOWN

1 GM's home
2 Reverberation
3 Kicker's target
4 Asia's Gulf of __
5 Coach Parseghian
6 Playwright from Vientiane?
7 Vesuvian flows
8 Texas sch.
9 Slightest
10 123-45-6789 org.
11 Cook from Santiago?
12 Coral ring
13 What American Plan includes
18 Slow down
22 Large seabird
24 Where some stks. trade
26 Bowler or boater
27 Get tired
28 Few and far between
29 Actor from Muscat?
33 Weirdo
34 Tennis pro from Teheran?
36 Till contents
37 Bridge position
39 It's under the hood
41 Toed the line
44 Make public
46 Blue
49 Do cobbling
51 Nixon pal
52 Stage whisper
53 Girder material
54 Construction machine
57 Hammer part
59 From a distance
60 Bushy do
61 Albanian currency
63 Pig's digs
64 Tiny amount

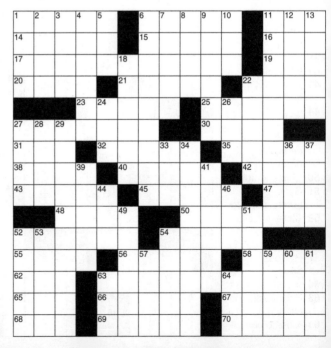

189 BRIGHT SAYING

by Eric Albert

ACROSS

1 *Blondie* boy
5 100 centavos
9 Just for this
14 Slay
15 Declare true
16 *Thelma & Louise* name
17 Lollygag
19 Put up with
20 START OF A QUIP
22 Gathers up grain
23 Be obliged
24 Part of TGIF
27 Carrie Nation, e.g.
28 Overly sentimental
31 Had in mind?
32 Seed or germ
34 Sulu, on *Star Trek*
35 MIDDLE OF QUIP
40 Column order
41 Kind of daisy
42 S&L concern
43 Actress Moorehead
45 Popinjay
48 __-jongg
49 Seaport, for short
50 Troop group
52 END OF QUIP
57 Riyadh resident
59 Judo award
60 *Glengarry Glen Ross* star
61 "Rama __ Ding Dong"
62 Sacred cow
63 Religious devotion
64 Recedes
65 London gallery

DOWN

1 Composer Elgar
2 Do-nothing
3 Lose for a bit
4 Available
5 Forest way
6 Not at all noble
7 18-wheeler
8 Nevada neighbor
9 Playing marble
10 Salami seller
11 Cold capital
12 Sean Lennon's mom
13 Crow cry
18 Start's start
21 Rte.
25 Marky Mark fan
26 Big gulp
28 Speak lovingly
29 Bobby of hockey
30 Party's purpose, perhaps
31 Comedian Stubby
32 Huff
33 Cpl.'s inferior
34 Make an attempt
35 __ *Bede*
36 Caesar's partner
37 Ferdinand was one
38 Cancel suddenly
39 Dos' followers
43 Succor
44 Talk turkey?
45 Peanuts character
46 Wild cat
47 Club-shaped tool
49 Pluvial
50 Boggy ground
51 Moon's track
53 Mark copy
54 Fine steed
55 Pyramid, essentially
56 Christmas-poem beginning
57 Somebody's fool
58 Onassis, informally

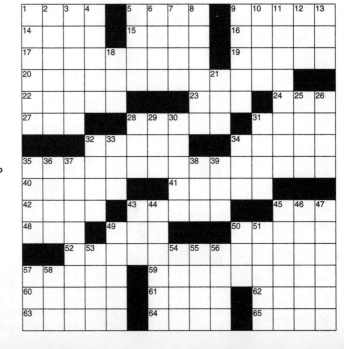

190 VIRTUOUS PEOPLE

by Randolph Ross

ACROSS
1 Sea "king"
5 Goya subject
9 Invites to the penthouse
14 Apollo's mother
15 Get an __ effort
16 Glorify
17 Obsessed by
18 "__ first you don't . . ."
19 Imported auto
20 Virtuous newswoman?
23 Iraqi money
24 "__ live and breathe!"
25 __-cat (winter vehicle)
26 Stanford-Binet scores
29 Point of view
31 Campus mil. grp.
33 Tropical isle
34 Ordinal ending
36 Cardboard creations
38 Virtuous film buddies?
41 Witty exchange
42 Big bird
43 Russian city
44 Sea dogs
46 Carrying a carbine
50 Buddhist sect
51 Military address
52 Have the title
54 Santa __, CA
55 Virtuous Neil Simon character?
58 *Amerika* writer

ACROSS (cont.)
61 La Scala solo
62 Touched down
63 Back way
64 Apply wax to
65 Countdown end
66 Comic-book cries
67 Cast opening?
68 Idyllic place

DOWN
1 Dover attraction
2 Fix a carpenter's mistake
3 Legendary conqueror
4 Italy's shape
5 Milkers of song
6 *An __ to Remember*
7 Shaw title character
8 Creative
9 Opening word
10 Wood choppers
11 Jazz instrument
12 Eskimo knife
13 Gal. parts
21 Mad milliner
22 Concert bonus
26 Piece of poetry
27 Wharf
28 Bro's sib
30 High country
32 More peculiar
33 Conductor Kurt
35 *Panama __* (Merman musical)
37 __ clef (fiction genre)
38 Roll response
39 Ready for retailing
40 Asian region
41 Russell's nickname
45 Church party
47 Posted
48 All-inclusive
49 Wright brothers' hometown
51 Changes another's mind
53 Marine mammal
55 Turn aside
56 Shoe holder
57 Knock down
58 Arthurian knight
59 Hearty brew
60 Mr. Ziegfeld

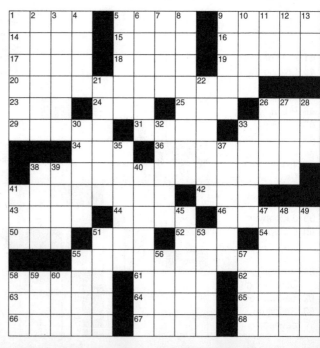

191 BEAUTIFICATION

by Alex Vaughn

ACROSS

1 Sweet side dishes
5 West Point mascot
9 Marsh wader
14 "There oughta be __!"
15 Large land mass
16 Make ecstatic
17 Holding forth on the good old days
20 Hamlet's title
21 Be lacking
22 Try to learn
23 Driving game
25 Blithe romp
27 Faux __
30 Trudge through mud
32 Most achy
36 Hockey great's nickname
38 Taj Mahal site
40 Pound portion
41 Paragons
44 Alaskan art form
45 Pup's protest
46 Breathe quickly
47 Russian plain
49 Scissorhands portrayer
51 Noun suffix
52 Star in Cetus
54 Vaccine pioneer
56 Peak A/C time
59 Dried up
61 Televised ribbings
65 Shea Stadium's locale
68 First name in photography
69 Designer von Furstenberg
70 Jai __
71 Disheveled
72 Didn't hang onto
73 Did hang onto

DOWN

1 Uncouth cry
2 Controversial orchard spray
3 Ankle-length
4 Big Band music
5 Strait man
6 Nimitz's org.
7 Largest shareholder?
8 Three-legged stand
9 Clearance height
10 Building wing
11 Shankar specialty
12 Birdsong of basketball
13 Bottle part
18 Sgts. and cpls.
19 Afternoon events
24 Socked in
26 Big Bertha's maker
27 Those who bug
28 Like __ (fast)
29 Nastiness
31 Midas' quality
33 China's Chou __
34 Part of the Lauder line
35 Short-tempered
37 Early aft.
39 Car bars
42 With a saucy twinkle
43 Plain to see
48 ". . . __ saw Elba"
50 Clear of snow
53 Synthetic fiber
55 Ketchikan craft
56 A remote distance
57 Arm bone
58 Puff of wind
60 Frozen-waffle name
62 Cod alternative
63 Loaded question
64 Playlet
66 In readiness
67 Discouraging words

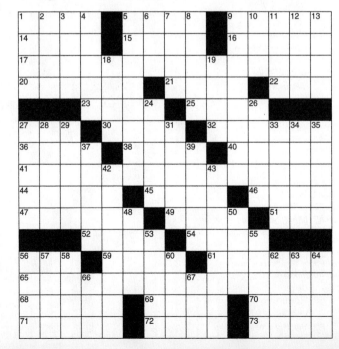

192 FULL SCALE

by Wayne R. Williams

ACROSS

1 More, to Morales
4 Resort activity
8 SMU's home
14 Worshiper of a sort
16 Set properly
17 Sorrowful, in music
18 Gas figure
19 Canine comments
20 Medieval singer
22 Snick-and-__ (old knife)
23 Suffix for pun
25 *In* __ (actually: Lat.)
26 Meal prayer
28 Lasting impression
31 Soggy ground
33 National League park
35 Howard of *GWTW*
39 Wallach or Whitney
40 Tonal qualities
42 Indy Jones' quest
43 Worships
45 Tax-free bond, briefly
46 *Norma* __
47 Ms. Bombeck
49 Lean one
51 Spoiled kid
54 Ore. neighbor
56 Advanced degs.
59 Recurring verses
62 Vault
63 Eurasian language group
64 Tiny Tim's range
68 Tailor's tool
69 Ran
70 Play up
71 Change the decor
72 Wordsworth work

DOWN

1 Exemplar of greed
2 Embellish
3 Vocal exercise
4 Needle-nosed fish
5 Word form for "ear"
6 Guitarist Paul
7 Wharton hero
8 Scot's preposition
9 Eyebrow shapes
10 Pup groups
11 Women's mag
12 Frank and Tyler
13 Inscribed stone
15 The hare, for one
21 4/15 payee
23 Disunion
24 Pour profusely
27 Fall flower
29 Grip tightly
30 Norse pantheon
31 Actress Arthur
32 "__ Hickory" (Jackson)
34 Defensive weapon: Abbr.
36 Slow tempo
37 Novelist Levin
38 __ out a living
41 Actor Tamblyn
44 Make a second swap
48 Grain beard
50 Cop __
51 Grain coverings
52 Find a new tenant
53 Following
55 With regard to
57 Passé
58 China name
60 Feels poorly
61 Sews up
65 Tailless mammal
66 Ran first
67 Sellout sign

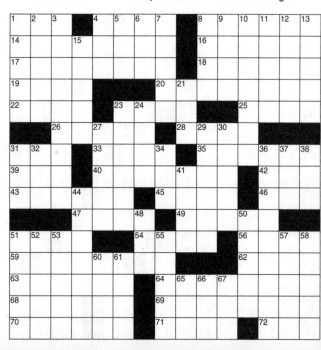

193 SEASONING

by Matt Gaffney

ACROSS
1 LP speed
4 Botch the job
10 Angkor __
13 __ *Girls* (2004 movie)
15 Diner, e.g.
16 Vow words
17 Rock's "Boss"
19 Certain sister
20 National Leaguer
21 In a nifty way
23 Will ritual
28 Suggestion start
29 Moral obligation
32 Salami shop
33 Card game
34 I, as in Innsbruck
35 __ the finish
36 Puttin'-Ritz link
39 Flamenco shout
40 Return
42 A question of method
43 Decathlete Johnson
45 Dealing with a full deck
46 Application
47 Ramsgate refreshment
48 Author Ludwig
49 Mars' alias
50 Woes
52 Passed a law
54 *Le Roi* __ (Louis XIV)
56 Most important
59 Silly Putty holder
60 Queen of disco
66 __ de toilette
67 Sedative
68 Except for
69 One or more
70 Horseshoes shot
71 To catch a thief

DOWN
1 *6 __ Riv Vu*
2 Cartoon skunk Le Pew
3 Engels' colleague
4 Command to Spot
5 __ Cruces, NM
6 Mel of baseball
7 Miniscule
8 Peace goddess
9 Actress Daly
10 Swiss city
11 Grown-up
12 Neil Simon collection
14 Rather cold
18 Swed. neighbor
22 Rachins of *L.A. Law*
24 Garfield's pal
25 Clinton Cabinet member
26 First state, alphabetically
27 Immense
29 Fashion name
30 *Daily Bruin* publisher
31 Lee Majors series
33 Chinese cooker
37 Footwear
38 Wool-coat owners
40 Coll. srs.' test
41 Boston NBAer
44 Alternatively
49 Revolutionary Sam
50 Prediction start
51 Boston's airport
52 Run off, in a way
53 Grounded Aussie
55 Admired one
57 "__ Old Cowhand"
58 Leningrad's river
61 Singer Peeples
62 A Bobbsey
63 Wolfed down
64 Rev.'s address
65 Civil War soldier

194 TREE TOWNS

by Randolph Ross

ACROSS

1 Winds do it
5 Lose buoyancy
9 Fixes the outcome
13 Skywalker's mentor
14 Mötley ___ (rock group)
15 Author Ferber
16 Physical, for one
17 Actress Veronica
19 Business arrangement
20 City near Little Rock
23 Imported auto
25 Hawks' org.
26 Where Sonny Bono was mayor
31 Iron in the rough
32 Trig ratios
33 Author Bombeck
36 Craggy ridges
38 Sault ___ Marie, MI
39 "Phooey!"
40 Perturbed mood
41 Dandelions, e.g.
43 CPR expert
44 2nd largest Hawkeye city
48 Poetic night
49 Postman's path
50 Atomic research center
56 Square measure
57 Actress Braga
58 Stephen King beast
62 Engird

63 Difficult situation
64 Easily bruised items
65 Fill fully
66 Midmonth day
67 Mother and daughter

DOWN

1 Parting word
2 Smoked salmon
3 Harem quarters
4 Bead money
5 Slivovitz or aquavit
6 Dies ___
7 Desensitize
8 Capsize, with "over"

9 Obviously embarrassed
10 Light bulb, symbolically
11 Snarl
12 Breakthrough bacteriologist
18 Inhalers of a sort
21 Treas. Dept. agcy.
22 Football positions: Abbr.
23 Carradine, in *The Ten Commandments*
24 Man of the cloth
26 Garden-store supply
27 Stage platform
28 Prefix for cede

29 "I ___ drink!"
30 Run in
34 Ike's missus
35 "___ boy!"
37 Ship accomodations
41 Magic sticks
42 Big ranches
45 "Agnus ___"
46 Charged atom
47 Coneheads?
50 Shell propellers
51 Scotto solo
52 Reeve role
53 Asian desert
54 Author Bagnold
55 Pitchfork part
59 "That's yucky!"
60 Coffee, so to speak
61 CIA precursor

195

SAY WHAT?

by Shirley Soloway

ACROSS

1 Part of ABM
5 Hoss' big brother
9 Union bane
13 Sea of Tranquillity site
14 Dressed to the __
16 El __, TX
17 Good goose?
19 Chimp snack
20 Greet, in a way
21 Adaptable
23 Inform performers?
26 Type widths
27 Drill sergeant's syllable
30 Vaudevillian Tanguay
31 First shepherd
33 Actor Roberts
35 Falls from grace
37 . . . __ Man, Charlie Brown
40 Wide neckwear
42 Baton Rouge sch.
43 Start of 37 Across
44 Harness horse
45 Feinstein and Clinton: Abbr.
47 Reach across
48 Hebrew month
50 Piece of the action
51 TV's Tarzan
52 Part of PST
54 Veggie buy?
58 Cookery genre
60 Free
64 Bank (on)
65 Doctor duo?
68 Running in neutral
69 Carved stone
70 Considerably
71 Spring times
72 Tributes in verse
73 Sawbucks

DOWN

1 Rock-concert gear
2 Author Ephron
3 Plane, but not train
4 Contribution of ideas
5 Half of LA
6 Prefix for meter
7 Former governor Richards
8 Jason's wife
9 Hot tubs
10 Are forbidden to run off?
11 Gomez Addams portrayer
12 Some pears
15 Nacho topping
18 Eroded
22 No longer a threat
24 Lesser of two __
25 Jose of baseball
27 Bucket of bolts
28 Bear: Lat.
29 Get lucky in one's choice?
32 Self-images
34 Like some dorms
36 First light
38 Kind of exam
39 Say it's false
41 Make an outline
46 Marks of infamy
49 Rubs roughly
52 Curtain fabric
53 Bara of silents
55 "Super!"
56 Two-way preposition
57 Peace Prize sharer
59 Louis and Carrie
61 Floor covering
62 Sacred image
63 Sleek fliers
66 Radical
67 Tabard Inn serving

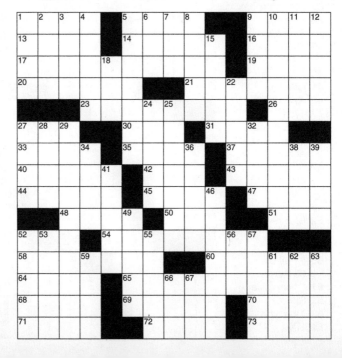

196 FULL DECK

by Matt Gaffney

ACROSS
1 Basic skills
5 Sea World attraction
10 Lounge around
14 Boxing match
15 Fireballer Ryan
16 Muscat's locale
17 Stadium feature
20 Crooner Garfunkel
21 Stretches the truth
22 Flower holders
23 Like Nash's lama
25 Mass response
27 *White Palace* star
31 Legal matter
34 St. __ *Fire*
35 "The King"
36 Actor Wallach
37 Pie __ mode
38 Senator Specter
39 Medication instrn.
40 Actor Beatty
41 Glue guy
42 Astronomer Tycho
44 CBS symbol
45 "Yeah, tell me about it!"
47 Borscht ingredient
48 Jai __
49 Committee type
52 Bluish-white element
54 "Eureka!"
57 #1 hit by 35 Across
61 Choir voice
62 Spree
63 Tide type
64 "*Très __*!"
65 Animal's track
66 Christiania, today

DOWN
1 "Dancing Queen" group
2 Wild hog
3 Specially-designed
4 Sault __ Marie, MI
5 Escargots
6 Duffer's target
7 Start of a Shakespeare title
8 Satire magazine
9 Cycle starter
10 *Death of a Salesman* character
11 Andy's pal
12 Author Grey
13 Wraps up
18 React to a sneeze
19 Declares positively
24 Recent, in combinations
25 Comment upon
26 Chow __
27 Stateswoman Kirkpatrick
28 Kirstie of *Cheers*
29 Give the go-ahead
30 *Manhattan* director
31 Gets back
32 Nobelist Root
33 Half a cassette
38 Soothing plant
41 Escape button
42 Spew smoke, as a volcano
43 GE acquisition
46 Long for
47 Element #5
49 *Moby-Dick* captain
50 Sandwich shop
51 Can't stand
52 Founder of Stoicism
53 *Othello* villain
55 Get better
56 Purina rival
58 Gun pellets
59 Move like lightning
60 Lennon's lady

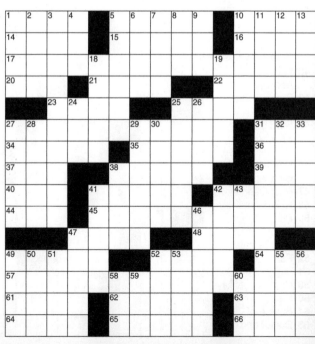

197 NET ANATOMY

by Wayne R. Williams

ACROSS

1 Drops dramatically
6 Eyed lasciviously
11 Lumberjack's tool
14 Stand by
15 Wharton character
16 Coach Parseghian
17 Where the strings are
19 Study
20 *Our Man in Havana* author
21 Capriati's weapon
23 Track figures
24 CO clock setting
26 Garbo and Scacchi
27 Appropriate
28 Game units
29 Lobber's target
34 Follow closely
38 Kukla's friend
39 Evergreen tree
40 Break in the audience
41 St. Paul, once
42 Service error
44 Fail to hit
47 Do-it-yourself purchase
48 Least
51 Cave-dwelling fish
52 View quickly
56 Smashing shot
58 Theatrical group
60 Court divider
61 Hacker's malady
63 Sked abbr.
64 Church feature
65 Ward off
66 Farm enclosure
67 Actress Della
68 Nuisances

DOWN

1 Singer Donna
2 Oscar, e.g.
3 Spiked the punch
4 Is partial to
5 Anna of *Nana*
6 Slightly askew
7 Political payoff
8 Wacky
9 Come forth
10 Namib or Negev
11 Former Egyptian leader
12 Sports venue
13 Magic sticks
18 Musical pace
22 Greek hearth goddess
25 Packs to capacity
27 Perfect service
28 Seles swing
29 Jackson and Derek
30 So. state
31 Actor Gulager
32 "Trees" poet
33 *Blame It on ___*
35 Sun Devils sch.
36 Out of sorts
37 Voided serve
40 Sternward
43 Pinball miscues
45 Beatty/Hoffman movie
46 Founder of *The Tatler*
48 Lisa and others?
49 Navratilova rival
50 Make a second attempt
51 Ferber and Best
52 Figure out
53 Sugar shapes
54 Nautical direction
55 Small salamanders
57 Poker stake
59 Swing a sickle
62 Wrath

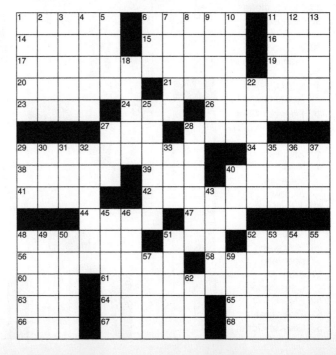

198 BORED GAME

by Donna J. Stone

ACROSS
1 Prudhomme's cuisine
6 Took off
10 Pianist Templeton
14 Bryant or Ekberg
15 Valhalla villain
16 Lower California
17 Valhalla VIP
18 Perfect place
19 Does Little work
20 START OF A QUIP
23 Dug in
25 "For shame!"
26 Like a lummox
27 Rake over the coals
29 English diarist
31 Mosey along
32 Manuscript book
33 Service member?
36 Act like Etna
37 MIDDLE OF QUIP
38 Physicist Niels
39 Take everything
40 __ apso
41 Stimulate
42 New Hampshire campus
43 Job security
44 Right-fielder Tony
46 Halloween decoration
47 Actor Carmichael
48 END OF QUIP
52 Toto's creator
53 Gray or Moran

54 "The Man Without a Country"
57 Grimm creature
58 Bring down the house
59 Grenoble's river
60 Sidereal, e.g.
61 Petty clash?
62 Selling point

DOWN
1 Cornfield cry
2 Pitch __-hitter
3 '40s dance
4 Hatch's home
5 Actress Fabray
6 Sweeney Todd's street
7 City near Stockton
8 Gets by, with "out"

9 Manitoba's capital
10 Puts down
11 Accept eagerly
12 Tape-deck button
13 "The Man in Black"
21 Wish undone
22 Jet-black
23 Discombobulate
24 Conductor's concern
28 Fish-and-chips quaff
29 Self-confidence
30 Author Ferber
32 *The Black Camel* sleuth
33 __ St. Jacques
34 *Star Trek* character

35 Gussy up
37 Play grounds?
38 Coal container
40 Stubbs or Strauss
41 Porky's pal
42 Val of *Thunderheart*
43 Smidgen
44 Inedible orange
45 Singer Branigan
46 "John Brown's Body" poet
48 "__ Named Sue"
49 Rope in
50 Ms. Minnelli
51 It's often total
55 *Hearts __ Wild*
56 Gladiator's item

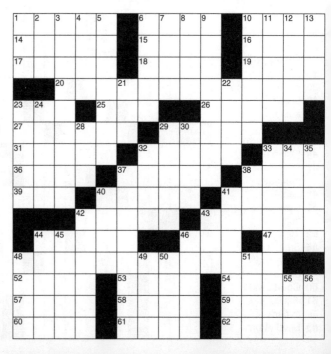

199 VOWEL CLUB

by Shirley Soloway

ACROSS

1 Wilander of tennis
5 Horse's gait
9 Bank grants
14 Touched down
15 Director Clair
16 Nepal's neighbor
17 Individual performance
18 Heron kin
19 Blows a horn
20 PAT
23 Driver's purchase
24 Easy desserts?
25 *Tonight Show* host
27 Marching musicians
30 Soaks up
33 Cell part
34 Word form for "Chinese"
36 Feathered missile
37 Bovine bellow
38 PUT
41 Actor's signal
42 Remnants
44 Uris or Trotsky
45 Take the podium
47 Guinness statistics
49 Calorie counter
50 Tony relative
51 Letter enc.
52 In the past
54 PIT
60 Theodore of *The Defiant Ones*
62 Night light?
63 "I Want __ Happy"
64 Coeur d'__, ID
65 Sleuth Wolfe
66 Actor Richard
67 Uncovered
68 "So be it!"
69 South African currency

DOWN

1 Opposite of fem.
2 Baseball Manager Felipe
3 Lean to one side
4 Bent over
5 Family groups
6 Picture puzzle
7 Step __ (hurry)
8 Try out
9 Petrol measures
10 Mrs. Lennon
11 PET
12 Naldi of the silents
13 Answer back
21 Lets go
22 Funny bone's locale
26 Doze off
27 Hall of __ (sports star)
28 Hole __ (ace)
29 POT
30 Ever's partner
31 He's no gentleman
32 Take the reins
34 Canonized *Mlles.*
35 Wedding words
39 Church official
40 Rock music, to some
43 Show sorrow
46 Come back in
48 Plundered
49 Man-made fabric
51 Gaze steadily
52 Rhyme scheme
53 Southwestern lizard
55 Annapolis inst.
56 Single unit
57 Caesar's garb
58 Abba of Israel
59 Tear apart
61 Chemical ending

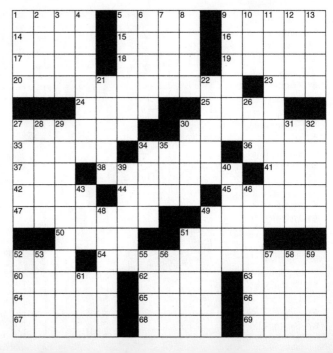

200 BODY LANGUAGE

by Donna J. Stone

ACROSS

1 North Eur. airline
4 Military materials
9 Bosc alternative
14 "Evil Woman" rockers
15 Hazardous gas
16 Circus jugglers
17 *Diamond __*
18 Puppetry?
20 Novelist Binchy
22 Tallow source
23 Descend upon
26 Import tax
30 Oust from office
32 Tire type
34 Drink like a dachshund
36 Calcutta clothes
38 Busybody
39 Montreal player
41 Michelangelo masterpiece
43 Ice-cream ingredient
44 As a companion
46 Tremble
48 Caribou kin
49 Batman and Rin Tin Tin
51 Undercoat
53 Meryl of *Death Becomes Her*
55 Football equipment
58 Spineless
60 Get to
61 Lips?
67 Skater Midori

68 Muscat native
69 Peachy-keen
70 *Wayne's World* word
71 Frawley role
72 Actress Burstyn
73 Sect starter

DOWN

1 Alabama city
2 *America's Most Wanted* info
3 Shoe?
4 Cubbins' creator
5 College bowl roar
6 Big scene
7 Gift wrap items
8 Newfoundland's

nose
9 Auto accessory
10 PBS benefactor
11 Actress Smithers
12 Time-honored
13 Nav. designation
19 Cold feet
21 Allied vehicle
24 Hippety-hop
25 Aziz of Iraq
27 Brainchild
28 Nail polish?
29 *__ Attraction*
31 Traffic jam
33 High old time
34 Rachel's sister
35 Wheel shafts
37 Very simple
40 __ about
42 Related

45 "Holy cow!"
47 "The Sage of Concord"
50 Trickle
52 Shoe width
54 Pamphleteer Thomas
56 Part owner?
57 Gandhi garb
59 Boat bottom
61 She's tops with Pops
62 Doolittle's digs
63 Former Mideast alliance: Abbr.
64 Big bang letters
65 Presidential nickname
66 Sedan season

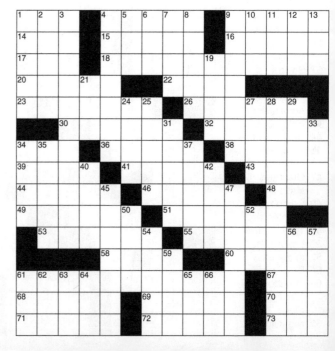

201 *JUMP FOR JOY*

by Cynthia Lyon

ACROSS

1 Drunk, in W.S.'s day
4 Noggin
8 Necklace part
13 New Zealander
14 Casino city
15 Joust weapon
16 START OF A COMMENT
18 Chips in
19 Big step
20 PART 2 OF COMMENT
22 Passover feast
23 "Lest we lose our __": Browning
25 "__ Blu Dipinto di Blu"
26 Wages, old-style
27 Popeye's foe
28 Wallenda's walkway
29 Wind up
30 Little look
31 "Hi, sailor!"
32 PART 3 OF COMMENT
35 Somewhat
37 Pipe problem
38 1955 merger initials
41 Sustenance
42 "__ to the wise . . ."
44 Jazz flutist Herbie
45 The __ Khan
46 Don or John
47 Booty barterer
48 PART 4 OF COMMENT
50 Decreased?
51 "__ an arrow . . ."
52 END OF COMMENT
55 Anti-vampire weapon
56 Bide-__
57 Otherwise
58 Rusty of *Make Room for Daddy*
59 Explosive sound
60 Deli buy

DOWN

1 First-point value, in tennis
2 Gave
3 Was sympathetic
4 Party nosh topping
5 Alway
6 Ques. opposite
7 Sometime in the near future
8 Pole star?
9 Crow's-nest cry
10 The Merchant of Venice
11 Vistas
12 Mortar mate
13 __ Kate
17 Ten-cent profile
21 Yoko
23 Part of G.E.
24 York or Edinburgh
27 Bird's bill, in Brest
28 Hammerstein-Kern song
30 Call's colleague
31 Warbucks henchman, with "The"
32 Part of RSVP
33 Screws up
34 Accomplished
35 Pine Tree State capital
36 Stephanie of *The Colbys*
38 With shrewdness
39 Joss stick
40 Wound up
41 Starve
42 Big fuss
43 Concerto setting
44 "Hey, Look __"
46 Thin side of a weight-loss ad
47 Calendar abbr.
49 Baloney
50 The same
53 Utility bill abbr.
54 Verily

202 ODDBALLS

by Matt Gaffney

ACROSS

1 Hummingbird's home
5 Deli delicacy
8 Kind of point
13 World's fair
14 Be different
15 Video-game name
16 General Custer's nemesis
19 Sylvester, to Tweety Pie
20 Sportscaster Cross
21 What the nose knows
22 On the lookout
24 Rights org.
27 Caustic chemicals
30 Change the decor
31 Actress Garr
32 Swiss miss
33 Broadcast
35 Gymnast Korbut
37 Turn down
38 Golf star
42 Jazz style
43 Catcalls
44 __ of Aquarius
45 Usher's beat
47 Peach feature
49 Cottage or castle
53 Feed the kitty
54 Daddy
55 La Scala locale
56 Highly excited
58 Chum
60 Lyricist Gershwin
61 Pop parodist
66 Botched up
67 Snead stroke
68 Car scar
69 Infield corners
70 Health club
71 Desire deified

DOWN

1 Ambrosia partner
2 Complete a sigh
3 Acted meanly
4 Stocking stuffer?
5 Caterpillars and tadpoles
6 ". . . man __ mouse?"
7 Affair of 1798
8 Saudi king
9 King Ralph star
10 Hod job?
11 __ longa, . . .
12 Stretch the truth
14 TV taper
17 In shape
18 __ Asked for It
23 Sound like Simba
25 Confuse
26 Cheerful song
28 Actress McClurg
29 Early evening
31 Peter, Paul & Mary, e.g.
32 Den __ (Holland's capital)
34 "Let __ Me"
36 Schwarzenegger's birthplace
38 It's hard-pressed for money
39 On the second floor
40 Couch potato's place
41 Radar's drink
42 Ram's remark
46 Stowe villain
48 Viva __! (Quinn flick)
50 Twist or North
51 Dolphin Dan
52 Lays down the law?
54 Green org.
55 "I have a dream" initials
57 Track data
59 Carpenter, e.g.
61 Charlotte's pride
62 Pitcher's stat.
63 CD ancestors
64 "Uh-huh"
65 Keats creation

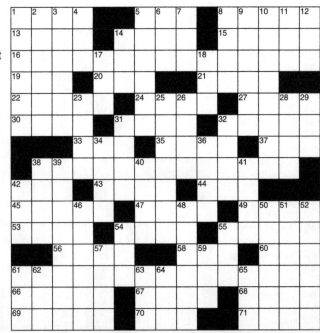

203 RLS REVISITED

by Fred Piscop

ACROSS

1 Forty winks
4 Dauntless
8 *Pomp and Circumstance* composer
13 Wading bird
15 Where most Indians live
16 Stiller's partner
17 Bottle part
18 "That was close!"
19 Jolson's "My __"
20 R.L. Stevenson duo
23 *Victory* __ (TV oldie)
24 __ Alamos, NM
25 Numbers man?
28 Wore
32 On one's __ (alert)
33 SAT takers
36 Ms. St. Vincent Millay
37 Makes little cubes
38 Cartoon magpies
42 Hand-cream additives
43 "__ me in!"
44 Draft agcy.
45 Commiserate with
46 Purchase plan
49 Catchall abbr.
50 Electrified swimmer
51 Fits neatly together
55 Children's game
60 Turning ripe
62 Teed off
63 Kitchen ending
64 Driving area
65 Welles role
66 In the bag
67 April 1 exploder
68 Out of control
69 Singer Benatar

DOWN

1 Turtle type?
2 As red as __
3 Guitar accessories
4 Blubber
5 Industrial-safety grp.
6 Mortgage, e.g.
7 Waste time
8 TV awards
9 Call the shots
10 Fighting roosters
11 Pitcher's asset
12 Actor Bolger
14 Some terriers
21 Boutonniere locales
22 Mason's device
26 Banana throwaways
27 Biblical beasts
29 Pindaric poem
30 Genetic info
31 *Driving Miss Daisy* star
32 Sudden spasm
33 Pentagon, for one
34 Fired up anew
35 Squelching
37 Presidential middle name
39 A or E, but not I
40 Narc's org.
41 Bone of contention?
46 "Light-Horse Harry"
47 "Seward's Folly"
48 *Oui* and *ja*
50 Lawn-trimming gadget
52 Inept opponent
53 Aquarium fish
54 Trapshooting
56 Actress Swenson
57 Social critic Chomsky
58 Bond flick
59 Pocket-protector wearer, maybe
60 Compass drawing
61 Moo goo __ pan

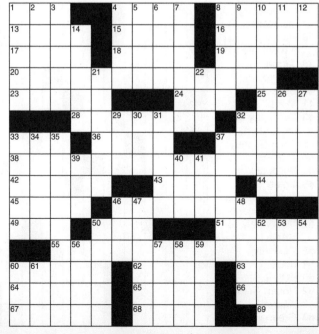

204 FOLLOW THE NUMBERS

by Bob Lubbers

ACROSS

1 Neck and neck
5 Save a bundle
10 Revlon rival
14 Spanish surrealist
15 Jousting weapon
16 Floor model
17 ONE
19 Next in line
20 Nelson Eddy hit
21 Singer Flack
23 __ Plaines, IL
24 Large quantities
25 Disney art
28 TWO
33 Ham's platform?
34 Tizzy
35 Cured a kielbasa
36 Roll with the punches
38 Jacket feature
40 Season
41 Moses' sister
43 Out of the rat race: Abbr.
45 Actor Chaney
46 THREE
48 Bulldogs
49 Color characteristics
50 Hasty escape
52 Moderately, to Mehta
55 Dexterity
59 Mata __
60 FOUR
62 Robert Craig Knievel
63 Green lights
64 *State Fair* state
65 Acts kittenish
66 Accomplished
67 As recently as

DOWN

1 Bahrain bigshot
2 *Ristorante* refresher
3 Swing and Big Band
4 Desert drifters
5 Tillstrom colleague
6 Buck or bull
7 Sajak sale
8 Ironing accident
9 Mexicali misters
10 Stickiness
11 Turn sharply
12 Fail to mention
13 Asta's mistress
18 Tahiti, *par exemple*
22 Grinned from ear to ear
24 Dolls up
25 Charley horse
26 Mrs. Steve Lawrence
27 Get the idea
29 Bobwhite's bill
30 Jolly Roger visage
31 Poet Jones
32 Barbara and Anthony
34 Beat the bronc?
37 Freshwater ducks
39 "__ the ramparts . . ."
42 Guitarist Carlos
44 Most exaggerated
47 Shaped with a hammer
48 Designer Gucci
51 Pershing's grp.
52 "May I get a word in?"
53 Place for pews
54 Actress Barrymore
55 Bandleader Fields
56 Hired hood
57 Beagle bellow
58 Waiter's item
61 Mao __-tung

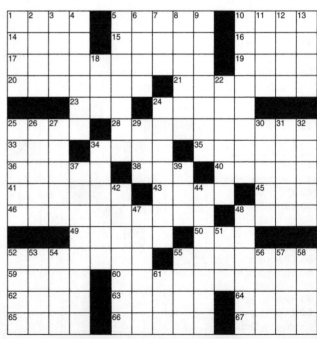

205 HARMONIZATION

by Harvey Estes

ACROSS

1 Starring role
5 Madame Bovary
9 Former Atlanta arena
13 Differential part
14 Give the slip
15 Wreak havoc on
16 Nero's seat
18 "That __ excuse"
19 Ring championship
20 From Valdosta
22 Gentleman of leisure?
24 Smart
25 At __ for words
28 Sports noncombatant
30 Square one
33 Upright: Abbr.
34 Took it easy
36 Gridiron gadget
37 Part of ERA
38 Pull one's leg
39 "Born in the __"
40 Horace's __ Poetica
41 Swell place?
42 Sibling's daughters
44 Huff
45 Nervous about verbs?
47 Rowan or Rather
48 Ore deposits
49 Look intently
51 Strait-laced
53 Frying pans
56 Emulate Arachne
59 Surveyor's item
60 Strumming accessory
63 Actor Guinness
64 Drive up the wall
65 The __ and Future King
66 __ egg (savings stash)
67 Dresden denial
68 Hammer head

DOWN

1 Once around the track
2 Way out
3 Jai __
4 Filling pro
5 The night before Christmas
6 Westminster reject
7 Pixie and Dixie
8 Type of committee
9 The __ of Species
10 Orchestra easel
11 1492 vessel
12 Privy to
14 Cain's victim
17 Auto pioneer
21 Valerie Harper sitcom
23 Wore down
25 "Cut it out, Popeye!"
26 River embankment
27 Sacred music makers
29 Skillful in a language
31 Spooky
32 Exams and quizzes
34 Half of CIV
35 Feminine suffix
38 Prepare to propose
43 Couturier Oleg
44 Bubbly beverage
46 Choose
48 Sleeper or bench-presser
50 King Lear character
52 Out of town
53 Ollie's buddy
54 Leafy green veggie
55 Adjust an Amati
57 Climbing plant
58 __ Homo
61 Heavy weight
62 Barbie's one-time boyfriend

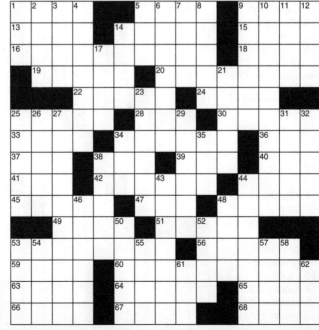

206 TRIPLE PLAY

by Eric Albert

ACROSS

1 Former Iranian ruler
5 Bring up
9 Waste material
14 "Whatever __ Wants"
15 *The Neverending Story* author
16 Sermon subject
17 Round shape
18 Unheeding
19 Give an extension
20 PLAY
23 *A Nightmare on __ Street*
24 No vote
25 Be a barbarian
26 London's __ Gardens
27 Teller's cry
28 Big flap
31 "Later!"
34 Singing mayor of Palm Springs
35 Homeric hero
36 PLAY
39 Ann Landers, for one
40 Fawn's father
41 Actress Sophia
42 Link letters?
43 Gala gathering
44 Continually carp
45 Poppycock
46 Hanks or Cruise
47 Cribwear
50 PLAY
54 Guitarist Eddy
55 Piece of one's mind?
56 Bluish green
57 Highway maneuver
58 Orange outside
59 Missile-crisis name
60 Bearded rock group, except Frank Beard
61 Sews up
62 Hustler Rose

DOWN

1 Be inclined
2 Poor house
3 Eyeopener?
4 One, to two
5 Sketch again
6 Us, according to Pogo
7 Economist Smith
8 Russian who couldn't leave
9 Severe
10 Endorsed item
11 Truckee River city
12 The last word?
13 Praying place
21 Seize an advantage over
22 Ancient German
26 Quick-witted
27 V-shaped cut
28 Open a bit
29 British title
30 Yokemates
31 "__ boy!"
32 Crowing time
33 "__ you not!"
34 Sudden flare-up
35 Fascinated
37 Bring down
38 Memorable building?
43 One prone to sheepless nights?
44 Moving men?
45 What a beatnik beats
46 General direction
47 Irritation
48 Horsed combat
49 Moccasin, e.g.
50 Egyptian port
51 Horse and __
52 Wednesday's warrior
53 Ballfield protector
54 Vietnam War initials

207 POULTRY IN MOTION

by Cathy Millhauser

ACROSS

1 Delhi wrap
5 Montezuma, for one
10 Small bottle
14 Candid
15 Hoosier State flower
16 *The Neverending Story* writer
17 Drink for the newly-hatched?
20 __-Whirl (carnival ride)
21 Initials, perhaps
22 Praying figure
23 Dada founder's family
25 Some temps
26 Hart part
29 Severed trunks
31 Like raunchy roosters?
33 New Haven tree
36 Hertz competitor
37 Bill and coo
38 Bank of Scotland?
39 Made tracks
40 Hens' hot rods?
42 Spectacle
43 Bottom decks
44 Like some garages
47 City in Oklahoma
48 Kind of candle
49 Lay down the lawn
51 Links master Sam
55 What the shapely chick did?
58 Key

59 Mrs. Claus von Bulow
60 Mason's wedge
61 Links gizmos
62 Cropped up
63 '60s sitcom trio

DOWN

1 Out of condition
2 2nd Q. start
3 Rod's partner
4 Places, as fixtures
5 PD alert
6 Goose eggs
7 Pilfered
8 Baseballer Slaughter
9 Charisse of *Silk Stockings*
10 Swerved swiftly
11 Pre-Pizarro Peruvian
12 Hersey town
13 Tough turns in traffic
18 Pants style
19 Lavished attention (on)
24 Make it big
25 Inga of *Benson*
26 At a distance
27 Celestial flash
28 Bed type
29 Salt away
30 *Cat on __ Tin Roof*
32 Well-informed
33 Suffix with switch
34 Finnish northerner
35 Unger upsetter?

38 Chutzpah
40 Barely there
41 Like autumn weather
42 Libra's symbol
44 Planetary path
45 "It's __!" (quitter's comment)
46 Monsieur Zola
47 Heavenly spots
49 Urge on
50 Cry of despair
52 Canyon comeback
53 Comparable
54 Brit. war awards
56 NATO member
57 Reuben ingredient

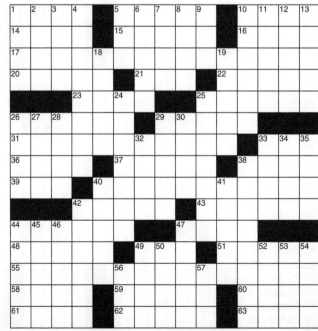

208 STYLISH

by Bob Lubbers

ACROSS

1 __ up
(got in shape)
6 Baby food
9 Winter warmer
14 Battery
terminal
15 Songwriter
Gershwin
16 In need of
a plumber
17 Jocular Jerry
18 Sushi fish
19 Bandleader
Shaw
20 Reduces
expenses
23 Loser to DDE
24 Tiger tracks
25 __ of Capricorn
27 Where Cleo
barged in?
29 Furrier family
32 Mornings: Abbr.
35 *The Wizard
of Oz* actor
38 Winged
walker: Var.
39 Simpletons
41 Snickers
shape
42 Set jewels, e.g.
43 Body beginner
44 Extreme cruelty
46 '60s college org.
47 *The __ House*
(Pfeiffer film)
49 Entre __
(confidentially)
51 Over, in Orvieto
54 Points the finger
58 GI hangout
60 Goofs on stage
62 Wild partying
64 A/C measure
65 Arles aunt
66 Poetic beat
67 Cot or crib

68 Islamic prince
69 Pines (for)
70 Puget, for
one: Abbr.
71 Fashionable
frocks

DOWN

1 Soft minerals
2 Seize an
advantage over
3 CNN transition
phrase
4 "The Wizard of
Menlo Park"
5 Picture
verbally
6 Wharf
7 "__ we all?"
8 Less colorful
9 Joins hands
10 "__ the fields
we go . . ."

11 Underground
passageways
12 *The Grapes of
Wrath* figure
13 Yes votes
21 Norwegian
capital
22 Crowd noise
26 Bit of gossip
28 Exile island
30 Actress
Donna
31 Beer, slangily
32 Ice-cream
ingredient
33 Restaurant
roster
34 Begins a
journey
36 Move (about)
37 "__ go bragh!"
40 Most definitely,
in Durango

42 Attempted
to equal
44 Be a boatman
45 Reacts to
soaps?
48 Draws a
conclusion
50 Deli meat
52 Heavyweight
Tony
53 Frequently
55 Sal of *Exodus*
56 Computer key
57 Crystal
gazers
58 Sch. at West
Point
59 Build on __
(chance a
profit)
61 Animated
Elmer
63 Shoe width

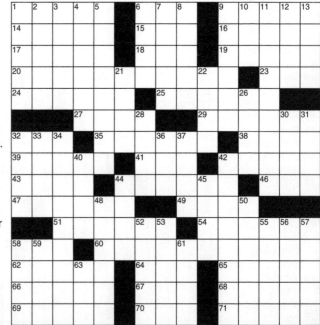

209 PRESS YOUR LUCK

by Richard Silvestri

ACROSS
1 Beer ingredient
5 Training inst.
9 Home or away
13 Operatic solo
14 Polio vaccine pioneer
16 Put on the payroll
17 Press your luck
20 Harshness
21 Run in
22 *You __ There*
23 Pulitzer Prize author James
24 Lodge
28 Kind of hammer
29 Three-time ring champ
32 Hold forth
33 Raft-traveler Heyerdahl
34 Angry state
35 Press your luck
38 Actress Barbara
39 Eight furlongs
40 Something to stake
41 Roulette bet
42 Laze about
43 Major triads, e.g.
44 Takes a chair
45 *Little Red Book* author
46 St. Francis' home
49 Binge
54 Press your luck
56 Suspend
57 Out of the ordinary
58 Fabric fuzz
59 Kitchen end
60 Trophy rooms, perhaps
61 Word of woe

DOWN
1 Spy name
2 God who sounds like a zodiac sign
3 Like a wet noodle
4 Finish line
5 Have great hopes
6 Metz menu
7 "__ Named Sue"
8 Roman 504
9 Soothing word
10 "__ kleine Nachtmusik"
11 Parabolic paths
12 Bump into
15 Falls for lovers
18 Interteam deals
19 Sketched
23 Companionless
24 His name is Mudd
25 Wear down
26 Gorged
27 Pour __ (try extra hard)
28 Prepare champagne
29 Lend __ (listen)
30 Hopping mad
31 List components
33 Coin-flip call
34 Farm structure
36 Rush of feeling
37 No place for Mary's lamb
42 Call a spade a "thpade"
43 Yule tunes
44 Prolonged attack
45 Expert
46 Arthur of tennis
47 Jalousie feature
48 Dispatched
49 Headquarters for Batman and Robin
50 Home of the Bruins
51 Leave port
52 Eleanor Roosevelt's given first name
53 A great deal
55 Affirmative action?

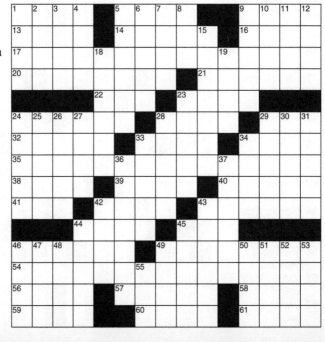

210 MAKING SENSE

by Randolph Ross

ACROSS

1 They're often cast
7 "__ the Beautiful"
14 Giants' home
15 Venezuelan hero
16 Unwelcome comment
18 Start of MGM's motto
19 Like dishwater
20 Happening
21 Currier's partner
23 Red-ink entries
25 Make a comeback
28 Bit of negativity
29 Say please
32 Popeye, e.g.
34 It's often tacky
35 Trial
40 Words of comprehension
41 Head for bed
42 Fathers and grandfathers
43 Princess tester
45 Feral
49 Caliph's kin
51 Eye drop
52 Capital of Tibet
54 Meryl's *Out of Africa* role
57 From __ Z
58 Dial-less devices
61 Increasingly upset
62 Pencil box items
63 Taps out the same message
64 Montana's team, for short

DOWN

1 Deprive
2 Free admissions
3 Summer setting in NY
4 Committed perjury
5 Humdinger
6 Detected a traitor
7 Pecs' partners
8 Additionally
9 NFL side
10 Covers with frost
11 Terrible name
12 Shopper's aid
13 Scroll holder
14 Flight segment
17 Road sign
22 "If You Knew __"
24 Without inspection
26 __ room (family place)
27 Moo goo __ pan
29 He flattened Foreman
30 Eastern riser
31 Beer barrel
33 Acclamation for Escamillo
34 Tony the Tiger's adjective
35 Dandy dude?
36 Exploit
37 Bear's lair
38 Aachen article
39 Pottery or poetry
43 Apply a thumbtack
44 Walking on air
46 More like a junkyard dog
47 Restaurant patrons
48 Refuse
49 "__ *bleu*!"
50 Feel poorly
52 Solitary
53 Warm greetings
55 Foolish date: Abbr.
56 Tatar top man
58 Pine product
59 Hesitator's syllables
60 Sugar suffix

211 MOVING RIGHT ALONG

by Trip Payne

ACROSS

1 Pull into traffic
6 Play with bubble wrap
9 "__ an idea!"
14 *Paper Moon* Oscar winner
15 Aussie critter
16 Not so hot
17 Clamming up
20 Botanist Gray et al.
21 Vain act
22 Literary monogram
23 Former Dodger third-baseman
24 Tailor's measure
28 Quartet
30 Mao __-tung
32 Microscopic helix
33 "Lady Soul"
35 Beans on the bean
37 Disney refrain
40 Settles down
41 Don of *Trading Places*
42 What did ewe say?
43 Drink with bangers
44 Loafer adornment
48 Detergent ingredient
51 Director Howard
52 Vane dir.
53 Brace oneself
56 Gameboy rival
57 Bill Griffith comic strip
61 Worried
62 Huzzah of sorts
63 Imitate a signature
64 Chaplain
65 Take a gander at
66 Also-ran

DOWN

1 *Amadeus* role
2 Send to Elba
3 Big spread
4 Generational problems
5 Yale student
6 Actress Ashcroft
7 Herman Melville novel
8 Fourth-down option
9 "__ the bag!"
10 Gives a hand
11 Word form for "bee"
12 Bigwig, for short
13 The two Begleys
18 Required
19 1813 battle site
23 Singer Irene and family
25 Author Ferber
26 Egyptian symbol
27 Bell and Barker
29 Fascinated
30 School paper
31 The Marquis de __
34 Dabbling duck
35 Cagney role
36 Dedicated poems
37 Strong fervor
38 Author Dinesen
39 Squids' kin
40 Hoop grp.
43 "And that __ hay!"
45 Mocking looks
46 Attract
47 King of the hill
49 Bond-value phrase
50 Philippine island
51 Shankar simoleon
54 Sabot or clog
55 Pretty slippery
56 "Get out!"
57 Laser-beam sound
58 "Make __ double!"
59 __ XING (street sign)
60 Patriots' assn.

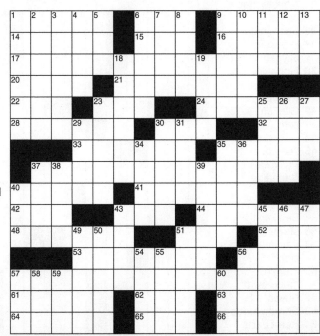

212 FRACTURED FILMS

by Shirley Soloway

ACROSS
1 Hits hard
5 Attired
9 Palm readers
14 Mideast gulf
15 Buddhist bigwig
16 *Dallas* matriarch
17 Singer Julius La __
18 From the top
19 Full of pep
20 James Stewart film
23 Flat hat
24 Journal ending
25 Paint-shop purchases
27 Tilting, to a tar
30 XC
32 "Unforgettable" name
33 Seal group
34 Provide oxygen to
38 Liz Taylor film
42 Winter weasel
43 Gladiator's item
44 __ polloi
45 Tried out
47 Pull away
49 Canadian province
52 Skater Babilonia
53 Mauna __
54 Paul Newman film
60 French menu word
62 Reveal all
63 Dorothy's dog
64 Heart parts
65 Caspian's neighbor
66 Cabell of baseball
67 Pie part
68 Pie apple
69 Actor Auberjonois

DOWN
1 Fishhook feature
2 Bouquet
3 Chihuahua coin
4 Asp and anaconda
5 One beside himself?
6 Volcanic flow
7 Part of USA
8 McGavin of *Kolchak*
9 Brine
10 Building wing
11 Upper crust
12 Adversary
13 Appears to be
21 Superlative suffix
22 Kind of play
26 __ *Breckinridge*
27 Date starter
28 Cowardly Lion portrayer
29 Particular
30 Neither's neighbor
31 "What have __?"
33 Magic word
35 Flu symptom
36 Spinks stats
37 Prepare for the press
39 Wee being
40 Listless
41 Cherry or cranberry
46 Sole sauce
47 Ares' area
48 John of *Hearts Afire*
49 Ocean organisms
50 Unwilling (to)
51 Wilkes-__, PA
52 Tutu fabric
55 Caligula's nephew
56 Chowder ingredient
57 Couldn't be better
58 *Blame __ Rio*
59 The scenter of your face
61 Zip

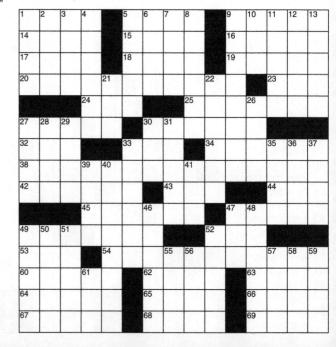

213 BLACK AND WHITE

by Harvey Estes

ACROSS

1 The good old days
5 Indian chief
9 Small cut
13 Regretful one
14 "Never __ moment"
16 Roll-call response
17 Black-and-white snack
19 She sheep
20 Type of pear
21 Trattoria beverage
23 Play by ear
25 Maryland athlete, for short
26 Allstate rival
29 John __ Passos
31 Grammarian's concern
34 Org. leader
35 Social butterflies
37 Pod occupant
38 Computer in *2001*
39 Cutesy suffix
40 Salty spread
41 Sch. subj.
42 British verb suffix
43 Crept slowly
45 Cheese board choice
46 Harass
48 Over there
49 Brainteaser
50 __ instant (at once)
52 Bull Run victor
54 Deli delicacy
57 Carve a canyon
60 Buffalo's water
61 Black-and-white stumper
64 Unskilled laborer
65 Milker's seat
66 Dweeb
67 True grit?
68 Grandson of Adam
69 Blows away

DOWN

1 Paid player
2 Atmosphere
3 Taken in
4 Paris and Priam, for two
5 *Eating __* ('82 film)
6 Hubbub
7 Single file?
8 Ms. MacGraw, et al.
9 Goes off course
10 Black-and-white dailies
11 Brings to a boil?
12 Chilean money
15 Word form for "thin"
18 Musical finale
22 Wear hand-me-downs
24 Foolishness
26 Gardener's bane
27 Blank a tape
28 Early black-and-white medium
30 Cool as a cucumber
32 Bottle dweller
33 More than willing
35 Workweek start: Abbr.
36 Mr. Serling
39 Diva Lorengar
44 End of the world?
45 Joseph of *My Favorite Year*
47 Mean
49 Parisian papa
51 Takes forty winks
53 With __ on (eagerly)
54 Animates, with "up"
55 Geometry calculation
56 Trombone accessory
58 Actress Barrymore
59 Joyce's homeland
62 Beastly place?
63 Driller's deg.

214 GOING UNDER

by Shelley Wolfe

ACROSS
1 Receipt stamp
5 Niches for riches
10 Small pie
14 Aware of the plot
15 Rigg of *The Avengers*
16 Jai __
17 Winter forecast
18 __ *Me* (Tomlin film)
19 King of gorillas
20 Barbera's partner
22 Actress Raines
23 *Picnic* playwright
24 Asian metropolis
26 Horseshoe toss
28 Cancel
31 In competition
33 Came down to earth
34 Have __ in one's bonnet
36 Map collection
40 Long-running sitcom
41 Bayes and Ephron
43 Corned-beef concoction
44 Nasty smile
46 Santa __, CA
47 Spanish direction
48 Greek physician
50 Actress Loren
52 Cavalry advance
55 Lucy's landlady
57 Angelic topper
58 Portable container
60 Grapevine item
64 Not worth __ (valueless)
65 General course
67 Place for pews
68 Send into shock
69 Removed a squeak
70 Pleased
71 Grp. advocating designated drivers
72 River transports
73 Architectural add-ons

DOWN
1 Ritzy
2 *The King and I* character
3 "Blame __ the Bossa Nova"
4 Completely
5 '60s coll. grp.
6 Choreographer Alvin
7 Be overeager
8 Organic compound
9 Pay hike?
10 Getting married, maybe?
11 By the side of
12 Grazing ground
13 Circus cat
21 NASA affirmative
25 Shakespearean actor Edmund
27 __ manner of speaking
28 Merino males
29 High spirits
30 Carpentry grip
32 Affirmative votes
35 Wet blanket
37 Mascara site
38 __ Spumante
39 Mets' playground
42 Waist definer
45 Joplin piece
49 Church reader
51 "__ the ramparts . . ."
52 Yawning gulf
53 "¡ __ mañana!"
54 Audibly
56 Article of faith
59 Soprano's showcase
61 Shopper's paradise
62 Gem shape
63 Beatty/Keaton film
66 Periodontist's deg.

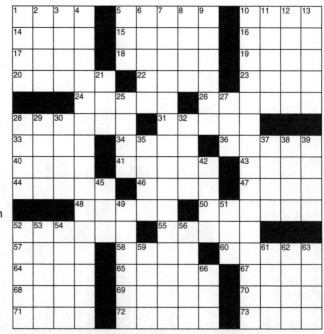

215 FAMOUS FICTION

by Stanley Newman

ACROSS

1 Prerecorded
6 Greetings for the villain
10 Young lady
14 Bart or Ringo
15 General's assistant
16 "__ girl!"
17 Card-game pot
18 Game-show winnings
19 Actress Celeste
20 Alice Walker novel
23 McMahon and Sullivan
24 Metal-laden rock
25 Repress
29 Exact duplicate
31 Superman's insignia
34 Erie or Suez
35 Broad smile
36 __ Hari
37 Lorraine Hansberry play
40 Unintelligent one
41 Takes into custody
42 For days __ (interminably)
43 Missouri city: Abbr.
44 Suburban plot size
45 Kind of photo
46 It's between "fa" and "la"
47 Gloomy
48 Willard Motley novel
56 Printing process, for short
57 Actress Miles
58 Propelled a canoe
60 Concerned with
61 Composer Satie
62 Squawk
63 Chimney dirt
64 Took the bus
65 Off-the-wall

DOWN

1 Sound of reproach
2 Working hard
3 Route
4 Art Deco artist
5 Battery types
6 Fancy dances
7 1 AM, Armywise
8 Stench
9 Crucial tennis situation
10 Olympic skier Phil
11 Surmounting
12 "__ never work!"
13 Knight's counterpart
21 Poem of praise
22 Coffee brewer
25 Lots
26 Fortune-telling card
27 Considering everything
28 __ accompli
29 Native American group
30 Sports statistic
31 Simplifies
32 Bowls over
33 Annie's dog
35 Snarl
36 *Send __ Flowers*
38 Well-to-do
39 Minimize
44 Swell, in space
45 Cheerful
46 Rush off
47 Pipe cleaner?
48 Singer Kristofferson
49 Taboo
50 Maestro Klemperer
51 Pianist Peter
52 Dry as a desert
53 Honolulu's island
54 "It either rains __ pours!"
55 Pay for the use of
59 Actress Susan

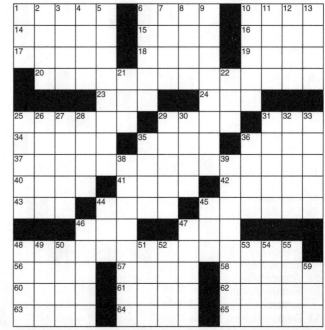

216 GOOD "O" FOLKS

by Randolph Ross

ACROSS

1 Classroom no-no
4 Nonclerical
8 Game participants
13 The Plastic __ Band
14 Easter
15 Hardware item
16 Hugh's constellation?
19 Scroll site
20 Itch
21 Jolie daughter
22 Computer command
23 Anita's dawn?
26 Prayer
29 It's sometimes bitter
30 Take a look at
31 Code-cracking org.
32 Pie nut
34 Impressionist John
35 Peter's hammer holder?
37 "__ home is his castle"
40 Hebrew month
41 Salutation word
44 Meet event
45 They're rated in BTUs
46 Zero
48 Madalyn Murray's coifs?
51 Writer Hart
52 Former Mideast confed.
53 Goof
54 Olive stuffing
57 Elusive, like Ryan?
60 Helping hand
61 Boxer Griffith
62 Sault __ Marie, MI
63 *Rawhide* prop
64 Great dog
65 John Jr.'s uncle

DOWN

1 Todman's partner
2 Removes a checkrein
3 Czech territory
4 Stroller's spot
5 Take __ (try)
6 I, in Essen
7 Montana Indians
8 Reeked
9 __ Saud
10 Made much of
11 Heighten
12 Dropout from the flock
14 __ de deux
17 Bad day for Caesar
18 Leader
24 Practical person
25 Jet black
27 Goes (for)
28 Classical beginning
33 Agreed
34 Pro __ (without fees)
35 "Dedicated to the __ Love"
36 Secret rival
37 Excitement
38 Gospel singer Jackson
39 Mites and ticks
41 Most promptly
42 Establish
43 Did cobbler's work
45 Square measure
47 Ness' crew
49 Copy, for short
50 1992 Olympics site
55 Capri or Man
56 Shemp's sib
58 Footlike part
59 Singer Sumac

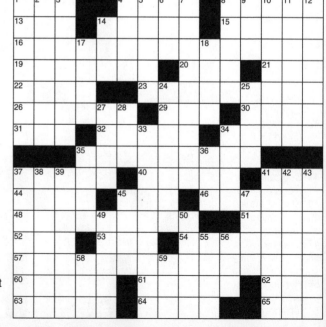

217 PLAYING IT SAFE

by Bob Lubbers

ACROSS

1 Fond du __, Wisconsin
4 En __ (all together)
9 Mexican munchies
14 Comic Kabibble
15 Certain Indo-European
16 Pullman choice
17 Like zeppelins: Abbr.
18 Night scenes
20 *Tosca* tunes
22 Head set?
23 Solidify
26 Global specks
30 Hide oneself
32 Restrict Rover
34 Language suffix
36 Weather outburst
38 Fry lightly
39 Rock star David Lee __
41 *Cheers* chair
43 Give the cold shoulder to
44 Chorale members
46 Poke around
48 Infielder's stats.
49 Noontime nap
51 Perforated screen
53 REM events
55 Curled one's lip
58 Bring up
60 Mosey along
61 Orphan Annie's trademark
67 Slanting: Abbr.
68 Augusta's state
69 Leno or Letterman
70 Whole bunch
71 Fowl family
72 Joyrides
73 Onetime USAir rival

DOWN

1 Fragrant bush
2 Houston player
3 Mail scheme
4 Ilona and Raymond
5 Onassis' nickname
6 Thesaurus offering: Abbr.
7 Wise guy
8 Chou __
9 Scuffles
10 PD alert
11 Tax pro, for short
12 *Star Spangled Banner* preposition
13 Last year's jrs.
19 Prefix for while
21 Turkish title
24 Hts.
25 Acts piratical
27 Sched. guesses
28 Zeus' zapper
29 Arrangement
31 Off target
33 Confederates
34 Historical periods
35 Three-dimensional
37 Secures the ship
40 Argyles and anklets
42 Meat cut
45 Headed the bill
47 Fills the bill
50 Congregation response
52 Moon vehicle
54 Willy Loman's concern
56 Pasta shape
57 Actress Burke
59 Cavort
61 UN post
62 Egypt and Syr., once
63 Book-jacket feature
64 Numero __
65 201, to Tiberius
66 He's a real doll

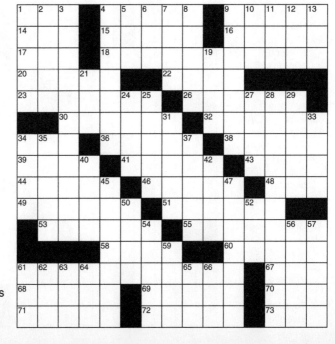

CHILD'S PLAY

by Alice Long

ACROSS

1 Shades worn at the beach?
5 Fleet
10 "__ pinch of salt"
14 Early boatwright
15 Post of propriety
16 *Mission Earth* author Hubbard
17 Toys for foes of child labor?
19 Flying start?
20 Show
21 California volcano
23 Skater Babilonia et al.
24 Piper units
25 Unacquainted with ethics
28 Filer's aid
31 Wheel hub
32 Page number
33 Succor
34 Toys from a watch company?
38 Slip up
39 Seaside swoopers
40 Palo __, CA
41 Steps onto the platform
43 Robert Guillaume sitcom
45 Injures
46 Olympian Spitz
47 Breastbones
49 Unusual distrust
53 Lo-cal's modern adjective
54 Toys for juvenile hall?
56 "Famous" cookie cook
57 Delight
58 He and she
59 Shed tears
60 Former Yugoslavian coin
61 *In* __ (really)

DOWN

1 Square-topped fastener
2 First-quality
3 Polish place
4 Oxford form
5 Give a second sentence to
6 Pile up
7 Illus.
8 Sort
9 Reading disorder
10 Seward setting
11 Toys for girls?
12 Scale start
13 Erelong
18 March Madness org.
22 Part owner?
24 Life line locales
25 Chipped in, so to speak
26 Slalom champ Phil
27 Where a child may exercise control?
28 Musical chimes
29 Stay in place, nautically
30 Pelé's first name
32 Hosts of the '52 Olympics
35 Grasp
36 Made a face
37 Dough, of sorts
42 Least usual
43 Sweeney Todd's occupation
44 Of an historic time
46 Valletta's locale
47 Cabbage dish
48 *Newsweek* competitor
49 Blueprint
50 Protest singer Phil
51 Store on *The Waltons*
52 "__ sow, so . . ."
55 Yale player

219 SOUND OF MUSIC

by Harvey Estes

ACROSS

1 Drinks like a doberman
5 *The Prince of Tides* star
10 __ weevil
14 Singer Guthrie
15 Nebraska city
16 Ma Joad, for one
17 String-section curtsies?
19 Genealogy diagram
20 Montezuma was one
21 Calander. col.
22 Piece of work
23 Phone starter
26 Overhaul
28 Watch stem?
34 Adjectival suffix
35 __ *Abner*
36 *Roots* Emmy winner
37 Casserole cover
38 Criminal
41 Travel org.
42 *Par* __
44 He raved about a raven
45 Hue's partner
46 Heavy metal instrumentalists?
51 Studies
52 Down the drain
53 *Laura* actor Clifton
56 *Hearts __ Wild*
58 Ancient Greek region
62 Blue shade
63 Fishing line?
66 Interlude
67 "__ Be Me"
68 In addition
69 *To __ a Mockingbird*
70 Tickle pink
71 Installs

DOWN

1 Pele output
2 Cal. neighbor
3 Map out
4 Sober
5 *Persona __ grata*
6 Govt. finance org.
7 Vientiane's country
8 Frustrate
9 Egg-roll time
10 Timothy of *The Last Picture Show*
11 Gumbo ingredient
12 Is inexact?
13 Scallion's big brother
18 Decorated the cake
24 Porgy part
25 Indigo plant
27 Twofold
28 Relinquish
29 World's largest democracy
30 Caught some Zs
31 Legislate
32 Moves toward
33 Cafeteria item
34 Middle Eastern airline
38 *Bus Stop* playwright
39 Aim
40 Dynamic start
43 Character
47 Not qualified
48 Where shekels are spent
49 "__ something I said?"
50 Stashes away
53 Pathway
54 Word form for "identical"
55 Male elephant
57 "¿*Cómo __ usted*?"
59 Shade of green
60 Part of MIT
61 Matures, like wine
64 Plop down
65 Sault __ Marie, Ont.

PEOPLE OF HONOR

by Cynthia Lyon

ACROSS

1 Soup server
6 James __ Garfield
11 Cubs' box score letters
14 Serve
15 Rooster Cogburn's portrayer
16 Try (for)
17 Oldies deejay
19 Army grp.
20 Garden bloomer
21 Yule refrain?
23 Checker color
24 Reagan or Colman
25 Has it out
29 Nursery noise
30 Fess Parker role
31 "Use __ My Girl" ('78 song)
32 Go out of control
35 Lummox
36 Winter archer
37 Jackson 5 member
38 Actress Goodman
39 Plow pullers
40 __ Goes to College
41 Mortised
43 Plane place
44 Judgmental criteria
45 Fez's land: Abbr.
46 Tarzan's home
47 San Francisco Bay city
52 Alias abbr.
53 Fictional tec
55 Dopey colleague
56 Frank composition?
57 Quitter's cry
58 "We __ the World"
59 Randi of *CHiPs*
60 Anesthetic

DOWN

1 Code content
2 Declare
3 Mrs. Roy Rogers
4 Long sentence?
5 New Haven symbol
6 Having bristles
7 Mexican region
8 Scandinavian rug
9 Emulated Brokaw
10 Vietnam delta
11 "It's Too Late" singer
12 Note of note
13 "__ be Queen o' the May"
18 Kong's kin
22 Pillbox-hat designer
24 Jerry of the Chicago 7
25 Front four?
26 Chewy candy brand
27 Renowned radio comedy writer
28 Eternal
29 Opened wide
31 Penguins' garb?
33 Chichén __, Mexico
34 Way in
36 __ Otis Skinner
40 Like Bach's works
42 Ohio city . . .
43 . . . and its description?
44 Director George
45 *The Bells of St.* __
46 Actress Pinkett Smith
47 Dijon dad
48 Charley's alter ego?
49 Solidarity's Walesa
50 Market leader
51 Dilly
54 "Mighty __ a Rose"

221 DON'T HOLD YOUR BREATH

by Scott Marley

ACROSS

1 Swindle
5 Tobacco wad
9 Homes for *hombres*
14 First-rate
15 Big wheels?
16 Computer company
17 Unlikely occurrence
20 Deli equipment
21 Get the point
22 Rival of 16 Across
23 Like the Sahara
25 The Emperor's clothes
28 __ au vin
31 Close
33 Actor Mineo et al.
34 Credit slips?
36 The E in QED
38 Yellow stone
41 Unlikely occurrence
44 Emerson opus
45 Muscle quality
46 Venus de Milo's "amputations"
47 __ *Well That Ends Well*
49 Fruit holder
51 Little one
52 Humbleness
55 *Grapes of Wrath* character
57 What's missng?
58 Feel unwell
60 Largest US tribe
64 Unlikely occurrence
68 Eng. Dept. course

69 Mistruths
70 German port
71 A lot
72 Pops
73 Catch sight of

DOWN

1 Band and table
2 Kind of mine
3 Con
4 Hajji's aim
5 Humorous poem of a sort
6 Wasn't it
7 Electrical units
8 Suitor
9 __ in "cat"
10 Police notice, briefly
11 Wet blanket
12 Cover story?
13 Historic march setting

18 Word often embroidered
19 Driver's needs
24 Was audacious, once
26 Proceeds
27 Hilo hello
28 Refer to
29 They accompany aahs
30 Tortilla melt
32 Yucatán yummies
35 Butcher-shop fixture
37 Lone Ranger's companion
39 Magazine's contents
40 Relish
42 Olive's kin
43 Lamblike quality

48 She takes the lead
50 Farrow and Sara
52 Taj __
53 __ *Time* ('70s Broadway show)
54 Give in
56 Suggest, artistically
59 *Star Wars* character
61 Hertz competitor
62 Army vehicle
63 Paris airport
65 Topper
66 Dix and Worth, for short
67 Last letter in London

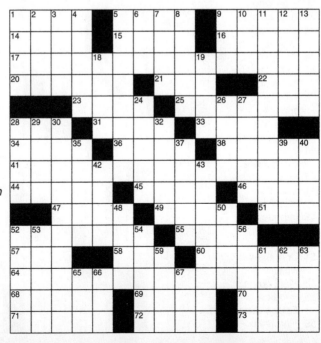

222 APT SNACKS

by Cathy Millhauser

ACROSS

1 Self-confidence
6 Word on a keyboard
11 Pen pal?
14 Wrench type
15 Yankees manager Joe
16 Mine material
17 Sage's snack?
19 Relatives
20 Enjoy the Jacuzzi
21 "Two-by-two" structure
22 Worrell or Hemingway
24 Radiates
26 Use a ewer
27 "Two-__ action!" (movie-ad promise)
30 Pipe type
33 Holy crosses
34 __ about (nearly)
36 Pump, e.g.
37 Ugandan heavyweight
38 Witch's snack?
41 Final finale
42 She liked Ike
44 Clinton or Bush, once
45 Kind of crust
47 Surfer's term
49 Impudent
50 It's spun by mouth
51 Cop-show wailer
53 Plaid fabric
55 __-Alicia of *Falcon Crest*
56 Find fault

60 "Yes," to Yvette
61 Clone's snack?
64 Cheerleader's quality
65 Blake of jazz
66 Triptych images
67 Loop loopers
68 Cut corners
69 Terminal

DOWN

1 Kitten's mitts
2 Mixed bag
3 *Casablanca* role
4 "Love __ not itself to please . . .": Blake
5 Herein, in brief
6 Get down to business
7 Pawns

8 Rub the wrong way
9 Bahamas town
10 Sheer fear
11 Snoop's snack?
12 Author Murdoch
13 Nice chap
18 Sudden attack
24 __ *on the Run* ('90 film)
25 Become engaged
27 Confidence
28 Julie Christie's birthplace
29 Twiggy's snack?
30 __ *de grâce*
31 Moves like molasses
32 Tipsy, maybe
34 The yoke's on them

35 Compass pt.
39 Makes smooth
40 Foolproof
43 Bacteriologist's base
46 Edible floppy disk?
48 Carpentry and printing
49 Strathclyde hillside
51 Salk colleague
52 Narrows
53 Wear a long face
54 *The Mammoth Hunters* writer
57 Perched on
58 Paradise for a pair of dice?
59 "Ahem!"
62 Where: Lat.
63 Executed

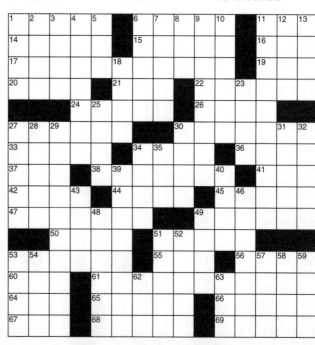

223 INKA DINKA DOO

by Trip Payne

ACROSS

1 Cabbage concoction
5 Beer ingredient
9 TV exec Arledge
14 Peter of reggae
15 Toe the line
16 Lot measures
17 Billy Ray Cyrus tune
20 __ Tse-tung
21 Tennis champ Gibson
22 Forever __ day
23 Gives satisfaction
25 Suspend
27 Actor Alejandro
28 New Mexico resort
30 Have brunch
33 Business attire
36 Mead locale
37 Literary omnibus
38 Children's tune
42 Bosom buddy
43 Textbook headings
44 Frog relative
45 __ Na Na
46 Very dry
47 Laura __ Giacomo
49 Bonkers
51 A jack beats it
55 At __ (differing)
57 Yummy
60 Comic Charlotte
61 Notes in 17 and 38 Across?
64 Rogers' partner
65 Glinda's creator
66 "__ Ideas"
67 Ballads
68 French resort spots
69 "Wild West" showman

DOWN

1 Official seal
2 Townsman
3 ". . . who lived in __"
4 Kid's query
5 Safer of *60 Minutes*
6 Helps a hood
7 Rachel's sister
8 Little one
9 Supportive scream
10 Indian, for one
11 Sweet drink
12 Geeky type
13 Wife in *Bugsy*
18 Really vile
19 Philistines
24 Overly theatrical
26 Quickly, in memos
28 Try a bit
29 Carter and Irving
31 Once again
32 Sour
33 Tries a bit
34 Bountiful setting
35 Hawaiian or Cuban
36 Move a muscle
39 Spree
40 Actually existing: Lat.
41 Rural stopovers
47 Watery fluids
48 Novelist Seton
50 Employing
51 Brimless hat
52 Ragú rival
53 Propelled a shell
54 Short-tempered
55 Lyric poems
56 Robotic rockers
58 Prefix meaning "both"
59 Beaker's kin
62 Draft agcy.
63 Actor Tayback

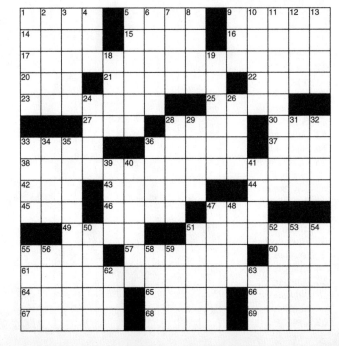

224 BATTLE ORDERS

by Bob Lubbers

ACROSS

1 Sphere starter
5 Some squealers
9 Plant part
13 S. Europeans
15 Court-martial candidate
16 Flying-related
17 Go gaga
19 Hibiscus garlands
20 Argument riposte
21 Diatribes
23 Frost intro
25 Valuable stone
26 Guerrilla Guevara
28 Seasonal gales
33 Trolley sound
35 Lt. Kojak
36 Word of wonder
37 Pawn of a sort
40 Hostile
42 Legendary Giant
43 Get bigger
45 Roof edges
46 One way to pay
50 Lay down the lawn
51 Pie __ mode
52 Raccoon relative
54 Spigots
58 Actress Jackson et al.
62 Defeat
63 Hook and ladder
65 At rest
66 Single quantity
67 Stereo component
68 __ moss
69 Beatty and Buntline
70 Rocker Townshend

DOWN

1 Stereo type?
2 Coup d'__
3 African nation
4 Wasted
5 Designer Picasso
6 __ Jima
7 Part of GI
8 Traveled on snow, in a way
9 Submarine part
10 Prepared to drive
11 Buffalo's county
12 Speedster Stirling
14 Construction area
18 Comic Crosby
22 Darned
24 __ nouveau
26 Bolt material
27 "¡__ mañana!"
29 Half a dance
30 Jazzman Red
31 Gave an Rx
32 Cows and sows
33 Flavor abbr.
34 Group of geese
38 Whale of a time
39 Natl. rights grp.
41 Abating
44 Fem. soldier
47 Gerulaitis gear
48 __ Thesaurus
49 Chip's chum
53 Camper's shelter
54 Wacky Wilson
55 __-de-camp
56 Bruins' sch.
57 __ qua non
59 Eat elegantly
60 Without __ (riskily)
61 Withered
64 Free (of)

225 KNOTS

by Fred Piscop

ACROSS

1 Animated Elmer
5 18-wheeler
9 Rare violin
14 On a cruise
15 Formal dance
16 __ Selassie
17 KNOT
20 Classroom projectile, perhaps
21 From
22 Word form for "outer"
23 Orly lander, once
24 Cheer
26 One of the Lincolns
28 __ Breckinridge
29 Off-the-wall
33 Correo __ (air mail, in España)
36 Restrain
38 Ferrigno and Rawls
39 KNOT
42 Quick snack
43 Daminozide brand
44 Ill-tempered
45 Loud sleepers
47 Clinches
49 Olivier title
50 Wimbledon champ of '75
51 WWII craft
54 Saddler's tool
57 Beam bender
59 "Tell __ It Is"
61 KNOT
64 Kate's partner

65 Numbskull
66 Verne captain
67 Self-evident
68 Collar command
69 Part of NAACP

DOWN

1 Preferences, briefly
2 PC enthusiasts
3 Rid, à la the Pied Piper
4 *Happy* __
5 Not as plump
6 Goof up
7 Form-related
8 Little devils
9 Biblical instrument
10 Actor Hunter
11 Irritate
12 Ex-footballer Karras
13 Floor model
18 "Psst!"
19 Bad to the core
25 Record companies
27 Polk's veep
28 Dashboard display on an MG
29 *A __ Born*
30 Entre __
31 1994 Oscar role for Hanks
32 Catch sight of
33 PD broadcasts
34 Actress Moran
35 Printing process, for short
37 Coach Parseghian

40 Group of monkeys?
41 Sylvester's co-star
46 Actress Brennan
48 Start of a Dick Van Dyke film
50 Tie type
51 Actor's delivery
52 Reads quickly
53 Grand __ National Park
54 PDQ
55 In good health
56 Tra-__
58 Dozes off
60 __ moth
62 Sundial numeral
63 Dock workers' org.

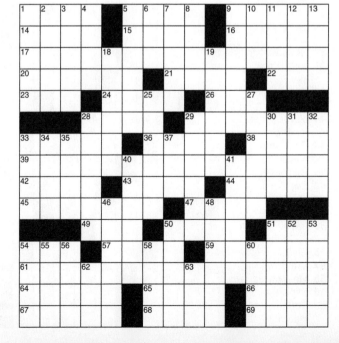

SYMPHONIC VARIATIONS

by Ronnie Allen

ACROSS

1 Carried away
5 Enthusiasm
10 Mr. Addams
14 Baseballer Cabell
15 Go on stage
16 Sacred
17 Penitential period
18 Bogged down
19 Actress Gray
20 Nerd
22 Kitchen ticker
24 Sgt. Bilko, e.g.
25 Stir sir
27 Awakened
29 Got steamy
31 Word form for "stomach"
33 Sternward
34 __ Attraction
36 Less risky
39 Gospel writer
41 "Big Three" site
43 Composer Schifrin
44 Montezuma, for one
46 Eucalyptus eater
48 Bear's lair
49 Set
51 Final syllable
53 "My __ Amour" ('69 tune)
55 Frolic
57 Cut down
58 Messed up
60 Expert
63 Spring bloom
65 1860's Blues
67 French friend
68 Tot's taboo
69 "Me, too!"
70 Al Capone's nemeses
71 Actor Griffith
72 A real knockout
73 __ of Eden

DOWN

1 Moolah
2 From the top
3 Opus for oboe?
4 Stellar
5 Prized person
6 Join forces
7 Follow the fiddler?
8 Abound
9 They may be marching
10 Evita character
11 Trumpeter's trouble spot?
12 Woody Allen film
13 Church council
21 Stk. description
23 Goes bad
26 6/6/44
28 Orenburg's river
29 Mexican peninsula, for short
30 The Wizard __
32 Utah resort
35 Adopt
37 School before jr. high
38 Gossipy Barrett
40 Close by
42 Grad
45 Baby bed
47 Goya's patron
50 Mislead
52 So far
53 Cabinet members?
54 Blue bird
56 Make __ of it
59 "Step __!"
61 Slapstick stock
62 Mobile home
64 Sauce source
66 Hide-hair connector

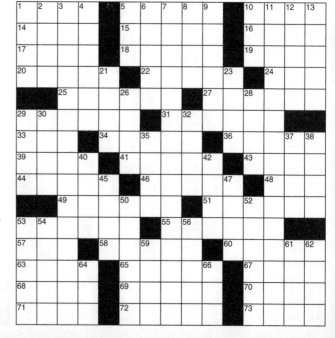

227 DOOR OPENERS

by Harvey Estes

ACROSS
1 The two
5 Czechs and Poles
10 Word form for "Chinese"
14 Cadabra preceder
15 Blender setting
16 Handle
17 Car-door opener
19 "Clinton's Big Ditch"
20 With-it
21 As a result
22 Detective Queen
24 Objective, for one
25 Pants part
26 Struck down
28 Countdown conclusion
32 Passing fancy
33 Fibbed
34 Egg-shaped
35 Saudi, e.g.
36 Head-turner
37 Reebok rival
38 Actress Moore
39 Sign of the future
40 Was certain of
41 Takes to the cleaners
43 Exceed 55 mph
45 Down the line
46 Full of pep
47 Mini-chicken
50 Card game
51 In thing
54 Jai __

55 Door opener of last resort
58 The Flintstones' pet
59 Ancient Aegean region
60 Sandbar
61 Short jacket
62 Lent a hand
63 Defeat

DOWN
1 Big name in baroque
2 Bassoon relative
3 *The Parent* __
4 Fez or fedora
5 Few and far between
6 Thrust
7 Fleece-seeking ship
8 Victory sign
9 Alfresco aria
10 Versatile door opener
11 Concerning
12 Film __
13 Carry out orders
18 Race division
23 Bandleader Brown
24 Locker-door opener
25 Couturier Calvin
26 Virago
27 Gloria Estefan's home
28 Takes the bait
29 Just like ewe
30 Put on an act
31 Took off
32 Crumpled papers
33 Light unit
36 Coffee country
42 Trait transmitter
43 Margarine or marmalade
44 Univ. teacher
46 *Parade* composer
47 Commanded
48 Came down to earth
49 Second starter
50 Provide bread
51 Let go
52 Master hands
53 Dexterous
56 "*Le __ Soleil*"
57 Sphere

228 '92 IN REVIEW

by Matt Gaffney

ACROSS

1 Capital of Iceland
10 "The Lady __ Tramp"
13 Naturalized *señoras*
15 Revolutionary
16 Leno's inheritance in '92
18 Sellout letters
19 Cpl.'s superior
20 Feminine suffix
21 "Open 9 __ 6"
22 Collar a crook
25 Satyric trait
27 Import tax
29 Texas city
31 "I hate to break up __"
32 Senate Minority leader in '92
33 One of 3 in '92
38 Do-nothing
40 Lyricist Gershwin
41 Game of chance
42 Witness' task
45 He makes it all up to you
46 Impart
47 Fools with photos
49 Tolerated
51 Muscovite, e.g.
52 Society-column word
53 Party animal?
54 Actor Morales
56 Coat part
58 Cambridge coll.
59 Midyear getaways
64 Past
65 Raul Julia's birthplace
66 Cozy room
67 One of 3 in '92

DOWN

1 Inform
2 Comedian Philips
3 Japanese cabbage?
4 Mr. Kristofferson
5 Rock lightly
6 "Attention!" in Augsburg
7 Dye container
8 Atlas feature
9 Madeline of *Clue*
10 Familiar fixture
11 Printing stroke
12 __ in sheep's clothing
14 *The Benefactor* author
17 Sneaky sort
22 Rock bottom
23 Dwelling
24 One of 3 in '92
26 "As I __ ..."
28 Lock up again
30 Looked like Lothario?
34 "... __ shall die"
35 Amazing name
36 Gawk
37 Traveler or Trigger
39 Richards and Taylor
43 Makes sense
44 Wheels for kids
48 Drive-in employee
49 Sportscaster Rashad
50 Almond kin
51 Graph opener
55 East Asian river
57 *Mondo Cane* tune
60 Hosp. areas
61 Peace, in Petrozavodsk
62 Author Umberto
63 Drunkard

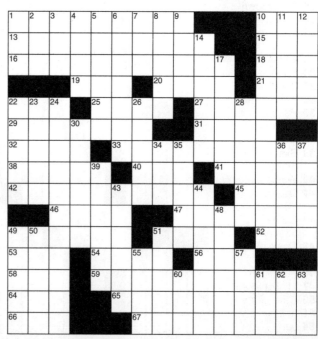

229 PRESLEY PLATTERS

by Randolph Ross

ACROSS

1 Head of France?
5 West Indian
10 Unruly group
13 "Over The Rainbow" composer
14 Cara or Castle
15 Zsa Zsa's sister
16 Presley platter of '56
19 Pragmatic
20 Tony or Edgar
21 Cal. segments
22 Nitrous oxide, e.g.
23 Slim and trim
24 Classic cars
27 Hot time on the Riviera
28 __ Alamos, NM
29 Incapacitate
33 Public disturbance
34 Presley platter of '57
37 Sugar shape
38 Fired up
39 Genetic protein
40 Godfrey's instrument
41 Cat call
44 Take a space
46 HS grp.
49 Fish lightly
51 Baffle
52 Collar makers?
55 Presley platter of '69
57 Before, to Byron
58 Lincoln's in-laws
59 Like some gemstones
60 __ Moines, IA
61 Brewer's ingredient
62 MTV viewer

DOWN

1 Aftershock
2 Go by
3 Garr of *Young Frankenstein*
4 __'acte
5 About
6 They're coded
7 Nonfictional
8 Squid's defense
9 Act appropriately
10 Like gold and silver
11 Caught up to
12 Most worn, as a tire
13 Interrupter's word
17 Hanks film
18 Be behind, in a way
23 Take the reins
25 Garfield's friend
26 Part of RSVP
27 "So what __ is new?"
30 Unsteady
31 Top-notch
32 Hidden microphone
33 Teased
34 Turning point
35 You can count on them
36 Sleep stage
37 Betrayed
40 Full of oneself
42 Danish seaport
43 Leavenworth leader
45 Diamond authority
46 Urges
47 *Who Do You __?*
48 DDE opponent
50 "Hey, you!"
52 Radames' love
53 X-rated material
54 Fork part
56 Speedy Sebastian

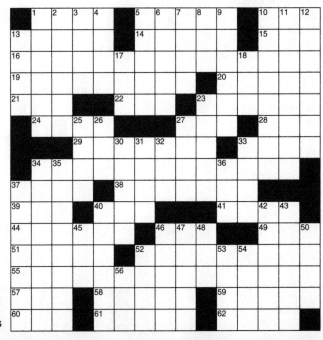

230 CAREER MOVES

by Robert H. Wolfe

ACROSS

1 Guesses: Abbr.
5 Mexican fare
10 Theater man Hart
14 Singer Campbell
15 Conform
16 *Falstaff* feature
17 What gymnasts try to do
20 Warhorses
21 Eastern canal
22 Mayday, to Morse
23 Leander's love
24 Visit abroad
26 *Norma* __
28 Makes calm
32 Nurtured
37 Sp. miss
38 What a mimic tries to leave
42 Disney sci-fi film
43 12:50
44 Handpicks
48 Lemony drink
49 Put in order
51 Meander
55 Clairvoyant's claim
58 Cookware coating
59 Cookware coating
61 What basketball players do on an airplane
64 Unburden
65 "Go fly __!"
66 Arden and Plumb
67 Call it quits
68 Feel
69 Take a break

DOWN

1 Basket filler
2 A deadly sin
3 Snicker sound
4 Scoff
5 Little ones
6 Hoo-ha
7 Underground explorer
8 La Scala offerings
9 Try hard
10 West of Hollywood
11 Mine finds
12 Grain building
13 Get smart
18 Venerated
19 Take notice of
24 Swarm
25 Rodeo rope
27 *Exodus* hero
29 The Magi, e.g.
30 007's school
31 Rational
32 Gym equipment
33 Fairy-tale monster
34 Hammer or hoe
35 Sharpens
36 Govt. division
39 Scan
40 Final point
41 Sound system
45 Soft drink
46 Musical syllables
47 Caress
50 Meese or Booth
52 Propose
53 Survival film of '93
54 Certain spies
55 Supplements, with "out"
56 Usher in?
57 Uruguayan coin
59 Corner
60 *Empty* __
62 Get-up-and-go
63 Half qts.

231 MISSING THE BUSS

by Donna J. Stone

ACROSS

1 Graduation gear
4 Conductor Karl
8 *Ragged Dick* author
13 Half and half?
14 Field of study
15 African capital
16 START OF A COMMENT BY BOB HOPE
19 Filled the bill
20 Strauss stuff
21 Mid-size band
22 Cuttlefish kin
24 Little lie
26 Action figure
27 Prepare home fries
28 Get an __ effort
29 Slap on
30 Sulk
31 Actress Verdugo
32 MIDDLE OF COMMENT
35 Appendix neighbor
38 Singer Simone
39 *La Fanciulla __ West*
42 Not (one), with "a"
43 Mess around
45 Carson's successor
46 Merger inits. of 1955
47 Cassandra, for one
48 Dog star?
49 Religious beads
51 Zone
52 END OF COMMENT
55 He picks pix
56 Author Angelou
57 Center of Shintoism?
58 He had a gilt complex
59 British gun
60 Remnant

DOWN

1 Sandwich locale
2 Flagged
3 Lapwing, for one
4 Smooth-pated
5 Lodestuff
6 Fell
7 Elephant man?
8 Put on
9 Bolger/Haley costar
10 African skyscraper?
11 Agronomist's concern
12 Fracas
17 Hound or hamster
18 Mayberry mite
19 Cream or cola
22 Easy marks
23 Dignified
25 Bikini half
27 Sea plea
28 Wayfarer's whistle wetter
30 Betty Crocker product
31 Century 21 competitor
32 Essential
33 Doorway part
34 Whichever
35 Ltd., stateside
36 *Out of Africa* setting
37 Sank down
39 Regular customer
40 Had a ball
41 Meat cut
43 Dreadful
44 Gaping gorges
45 Consul's assistant
47 Deices, in a way
48 Writer Kaufman
50 Antitoxins
51 Tatum's dad
52 Minify a midi, maybe?
53 Plopped down
54 Pipe cleaner?

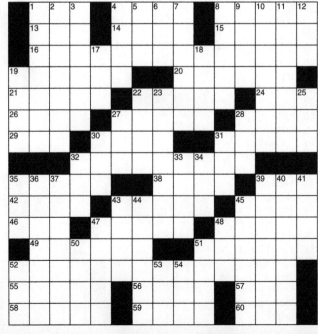

232 NEAR-MISSES

by Karen L. Hodge

ACROSS

1 Crystallize
5 "What __ mind reader?"
9 Strip in the Middle East
13 Jai __
14 Protracted
15 Colonial newsman
16 Not quite a thoroughbred?
18 Dance under a bar
19 Sixth sense
20 ". . .ground, to scratch it with __": Warner
21 Actuaries, e.g.
22 Less-than-perfect aide?
24 Committee
28 Mork's planet
29 Suspect's need
30 Cook book
32 Barely open
36 Below-par postal service?
39 Eager
40 Jury member
41 Edge along
42 South American tuber
43 "Farewell, Fernando!"
44 Game-show also-ran?
51 Elate
52 Not as much
53 Confused feeling
56 Really mad
57 Poorly attended party?
59 Disheartening one?
60 Thai tutor
61 Team mates?
62 Baseballer Slaughter
63 Suds from a bar
64 Brontë's governess

DOWN

1 Shade of green
2 Yalies
3 Light source
4 Recline
5 Hi, in HI
6 Nitwit
7 Atlas closeup
8 Get better in the bottle
9 Southern staple
10 Intended
11 Referee, slangily
12 "Ring around __ . . ."
15 Singer Petula
17 Lincoln's first VP
21 Part of RFD
23 Mr. Simpson
24 Cram
25 Healing plant
26 Shade of green
27 Browning's black
30 Lucid
31 Poem of praise
32 Ardent
33 *Star Wars* knights
34 Folk singer Guthrie
35 Bread and booze
37 Florida attraction
38 "Because __!" (authoritarian response)
42 Hold out
44 Electricity
45 Cook wear
46 Mild cigar
47 March toys
48 Coeur d'__, ID
49 Patriot Silas
50 __ as the eye can see
53 Sly
54 Unusual sort
55 Critic Shalit
57 Bill
58 Unhatched fish

233 COOK'S TOUR

by Cathy Millhauser

ACROSS

1 Stole stuff
5 Gloomy
9 Guitar accessories
14 Gouda alternative
15 Toy brick brand
16 Hokkaido city
17 Zip, to Zapata
18 West Coast sch.
19 Bandleader Prado
20 Bake belongings?
23 TV Tarzan
24 Cardiac exits
25 Take five
27 With 47 Across, massage one's pal?
31 Mine car
34 It may be acute
38 Married Mlles.
39 Painter Magritte
40 Made to yawn
41 Prohibition
42 Banks hold them
43 Fava or lima
44 Mare fare
45 Lightens
46 Palo __, CA
47 See 27 Across
49 Student's ordeal
51 Paul Hogan, for one
56 Old witch
58 Char lollipops?
62 Arm
64 Reagan Cabinet member
65 Teamwork obstacles
66 Charge
67 Keystone site
68 Fade away
69 Brick worker
70 Unsurpassed
71 Stallone et al.

DOWN

1 Brain trust?
2 Spud state
3 The pits
4 Sears competitor
5 It makes bread tough
6 Mr. Walesa
7 Tangelo type
8 Sound of distress
9 Thicket
10 Had, in a way
11 Skin oaks?
12 Turgenev's birthplace
13 Skier Chaffee
21 Played croupier
22 Mardi __
26 Narrow ridge
28 Imprison
29 String king?
30 Packed
32 "Snowbird" singer Murray
33 Army meal
34 Israel's Eban
35 Greeting-card word
36 Shred pieces?
37 Tanglewood town
42 __ Tho (Vietnamese statesman)
44 All __ (Tomlin film)
48 Zero
50 Cottonwood kin
52 Swerves
53 *Love Story* teller
54 Wit with a twist
55 Strauss trio?
56 Skipper's place
57 Blue hue
59 *Pequod* captain
60 Uncommon
61 Unleashes, perhaps
63 "__ to Pieces" ('65 tune)

GEOMETRICAL
by A.J. Santora

ACROSS
1 Stylish
5 *Fame* name
9 Down with, in Dijon
13 Half steps
15 Suppressed
17 Rehab practitioner
18 Sneezing sound
19 Ed Sullivan's network
20 Pop container
22 Vegas game
23 __-Prayer (phone service)
26 Butcher's special
28 Rocket feature
30 Flat-backed fiddles
31 Plying away
32 Surgeon's request
34 Chimney bottom
36 Euphrates people
39 "Che" Guevara
41 Golden Rule word
43 Pulled one's crate?
45 World's largest office building
47 Increased gradually
49 Envelops
50 "He's __ Picker" (Berlin song)
51 Brad tool
52 Antagonist
53 Helicopter part
55 Simultaneously
60 "Comin' __ Wing and a Prayer" ('43 tune)
61 Use logic
62 Prefix for "while"
63 Glaze basis
64 *Cope Book* aunt

DOWN
1 AR zone
2 Scornful sound
3 __ *Mine* (Harrison bio)
4 Prepare to resist
5 Fox reality TV series
6 Sajak sale
7 Damsel's hero
8 Take __ at (try)
9 Al Jolson's given first name
10 Starting-over direction
11 Close behind
12 Part of ASAP
14 *Cigare* filler
16 Alcove
21 __ *Sunday* ('60 film)
23 Genes designer?
24 Speck
25 Sale condition
26 Hundred-dollar bill
27 "To __ little glass of wine . . ."
29 "Song __" (Rimsky-Korsakov)
33 Made footnotes
35 Ins. abbr.
37 Ms. Swenson
38 Check
40 Bee participant
42 Come-__ (lures)
43 Guthrie of theatre
44 Protagoras or Pericles
46 "It takes __ tango"
47 __ *passu* (fairly)
48 Tower over
52 Stop food
54 Scoundrel
56 *Love Story* composer
57 Scand. country
58 __ laude
59 Homeric character

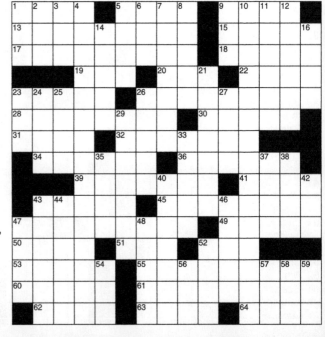

235 NAME THAT TOON

by Matt Gaffney

ACROSS

1 Maltese money
5 Downhill equipment
9 Fuzzy
12 Like Nash's lama
13 Actress Louise
14 Do a double take, perhaps
16 Wascally wabbit . . .
18 . . . and his cwazy enemy
19 Umpire's call
20 Umpire's call
22 Santa __, CA
23 Wallace of *Cujo*
24 Bat wood
27 Danish cheese
29 Candy __ (hospital volunteer)
32 Heat again
33 *Año* opener
34 Farm measure
35 Batty bird
41 World's fair
42 Reeves of *River's Edge*
43 Indirect route
46 Hoards
49 Appalachian range
51 __ *Rosen-kavalier*
52 Tear apart
54 Lean-__ (sheds)
55 Follow closely
57 "__ for yourself!"

59 Author Jong
61 Demented drake
64 Helicopter part
65 Nobelist Wiesel
66 Margarine
67 Hot off the press
68 Level-headed
69 Hard to find

DOWN

1 Like ears
2 Habituates
3 Kick oneself
4 To boot
5 R-V link
6 Relatives
7 Rural hotels
8 Doctor's directive
9 Md. neighbor
10 Simon & Garfunkel hit
11 Reba of country music
14 Superman portrayer
15 Mobile home
17 Intellectual
21 Out of the way
25 Gush forth
26 Man of the hour
28 Problem solver?
30 Hardwood tree
31 Swindles
35 Emmanuel Lewis sitcom
36 Jumbo shrimp, e.g.

37 Like "jumbo" and "shrimp"
38 With 45 Down, scroll site
39 Do the driveway
40 Get-up-and-go
44 Shankar's specialty
45 See 38 Down
47 Actress Andress
48 Two-__ (swimsuit)
50 Teams
53 Tea type
56 Tra-__
58 Foul stench
60 Bull's beloved
62 Shark giveaway
63 Lawyer's charge

236 ALL THAT JAZZ

by Charles E. Gersch

ACROSS
1. Go __ for (defend)
6. Summer cooler
9. Ignoble
13. "Softly, __ dream"
14. New Orleans jazz style
17. New Orleans' nickname
19. Liqueur flavoring
20. Gets to
21. Pro-gun grp.
22. Capillary kin
24. British gun
25. Short drive
27. New Orleans cuisine
30. Adjectival suffix
31. G.B., for one
33. Visionary
37. New Orleans university
39. Bonzo nosh
40. Euripides heroine
42. "For shame!"
43. Fix a fight
44. Raspy
46. Slaps on
47. The A train?
50. Nehru's successor
53. Herr's hearer
54. __ strict line (conform rigidly)
56. Town
58. "__ New Orleans" ('20s tune)
62. Where New Orleans is
63. Eared seal
64. Harbors: Abbr.
65. Stand for
66. Sits down

DOWN
1. Make lace
2. Job-safety org.
3. New Orleans' founder
4. __ régime (pre-1789 French rulers)
5. Ankles
6. They may be clasified
7. More risky
8. Put out
9. Casino actions
10. Chem. compound
11. New Orleans footballer
12. __ nous
15. Squid's weapon
16. Actress Cannon
18. Shelley's sundown
23. Exp. opposite
24. Penn or Young
25. Where it's at
26. Actor Newman
28. Baby blues
29. Security problem
31. Up on
32. Antitoxins
34. New Orleans party time
35. Oklahoma town
36. Joplin pieces
38. Rubdown target
41. Magazine
42. Japanese export
45. Gumshoe Mike
46. Stopped, in the French Quarter
47. Go for strikes
48. Total disorder
49. "Quit babbling!"
51. Book's ID no. of old
52. Royal house
54. Prepare salad
55. WWII news agcy.
57. New Orleans trumpeter
59. E, to Morse
60. Quaker grain
61. Gov. Pataki's concern

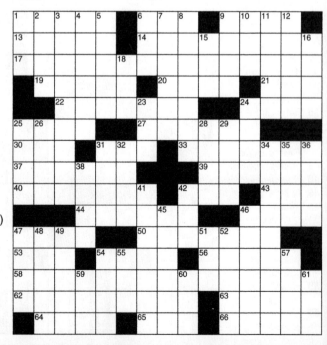

237

QUIET INSIDE!

by Randolph Ross

ACROSS

1 Slightly open
5 Trotter's tootsy
9 Kitchen gadget
14 Mustached modern artist
15 Jai __
16 __ Gay
17 Broadway successes
19 Coach/commentator Hank
20 Lake Michigan city
22 Pro foe
23 *A Touch* __ ('73 film)
26 Big-boy sizes
28 Smoked or salted
29 Mini-mounts
30 Scare up
31 Marks a map
32 Bowler, for one
35 Not as much
36 Makes mulligatawny
37 Thanksgiving abbr.
38 Ski material
39 First-place medals
40 Kid stuff?
41 Tweed type
43 Miss Hannigan's charge
44 "Peace Train" singer
46 Arden and Sherwood
48 Ferrer musical
49 Easton and others

51 Gluck et al.
53 Greasy spoon
57 Canines, e.g.
58 Piedmont province
59 Component
60 Helena's competitor
61 Tsp. or in.
62 __ up (get in shape)

DOWN

1 Pitches
2 Toast topper
3 Pie __ mode
4 Safe
5 Otto and Jessica
6 Grab bags
7 Flicka food
8 Cod catchers
9 __ Plaines, IL
10 Absorption
11 Poultry variety
12 Bring bliss
13 *Ghostbusters* actor Harold
18 Cabbage and lettuce units
21 Family members
23 Central Florida city
24 Pollution
25 Indy gear
27 Jackie, to Roseanne
29 Trudges along
31 Easter dinner, perhaps
33 Look at the books
34 Stand fillers

36 Toe travails
37 Ignores
39 SAT's big brother
40 Purcell of *Real People*
42 Emulate Earhart
44 Roofing material
45 Mah-jongg pieces
46 Roman holiday?
47 "__ Blindness" (Milton work)
50 Life of Riley
52 Yonder yacht
54 Juan's one
55 Transgression
56 When Strasbourg sizzles

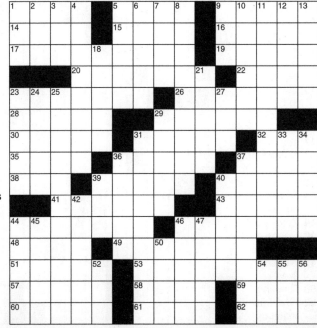

238 THIS BUD'S FOR YOU

by Matt Gaffney

ACROSS

1 Stomach flattener
6 Genetic letters
9 Become engaged
13 Largest artery
14 Sgts. and cpls.
15 Montreal player
16 Lover
18 Don't dele
19 Bronco's lunch
20 "__ Woman" (Reddy hit)
21 Mosque feature
23 Lust after
25 Filmed again
26 Run-of-the-mill
29 Exist
30 __ Solemnis
31 Strong as __
32 *Wayne's World* word
33 Southwestern sight
34 "It Had to Be __"
35 Munich's locale
37 Youngster
40 Nutritional amts.
42 Actor Beatty
43 *Beetle Bailey* bulldog
44 Zeus' shield
46 Coupe grp.?
47 Yes votes
48 Sipped slowly
50 Cunning
52 First Triumvirate member
54 "__ Were a Carpenter"
55 Some ammo
58 Clinton's hometown
59 Idaho-Montana range
62 Store-window sign
63 Sore
64 Confection
65 Musical symbol
66 Turner or Pappas
67 Wing

DOWN

1 Waist band
2 *State Fair* state
3 Deck member
4 Colorado Indian
5 Barbecue area
6 Zenith rival
7 Comic Crosby
8 Bustling
9 Avignon address
10 Pretzel variety
11 Does 85
12 Scones' accompaniment
14 Pulitzer poet Howard
17 Fine cigars
22 Herculean labor site
23 Peepers portrayer
24 Lockjaw
26 For instance
27 Lennon's lady
28 Fox's rationalization
33 Birthing specialist
35 Triangle parts
36 It's the truth
38 Wolfed down
39 John __ Passos
41 Conflict
43 Mighty tree
44 Brokaw or Rather
45 Common Market locale
49 One of the Emirates
51 Around, datewise
53 Under the weather
55 Beethoven's birthplace
56 Portend
57 Charon's river
60 Common article
61 Kurosawa epic

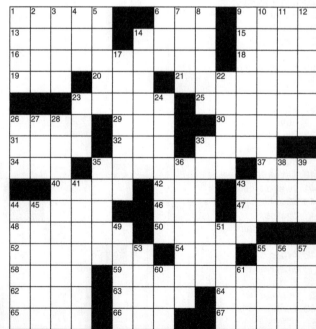

239 FIRST FAMILY

by Trip Payne

ACROSS

1 Indian state
6 Physique, for short
9 Ina of *The Black Orchid*
14 *The Great __ Pepper*
15 Silly Charlotte
16 Singer Turner's autobiography
17 Three-time Masters winner
18 "__ no wonder!"
19 Porous
20 Tenzing Norgay's companion
23 Wild plums
24 All-purpose exclamations
25 Sound sleepers?
28 Maximally
31 Numbers for one
32 Josip Broz
33 Shooter ammo
35 AFC champs from '90 to '93
40 Toper
41 Drug buster
42 Ewes' guys?
43 Slogan
45 Try to hit
48 Actress Taina of *Les Girls*
49 Disdain
50 Thomas Carlyle's sobriquet
55 Miles of jazz
56 Card game
57 Seeps out
59 Ring or rink
60 Plastic __ Band
61 Engine sounds
62 Ulysses Grant's real first name
63 Toothpaste type
64 Collar needs

DOWN

1 "Isn't that cute!" sounds
2 All there
3 Iditarod vehicle
4 Hepburn/Tracy movie
5 The "M" of LEM
6 They're given away
7 "Egad!" and "Zounds!"
8 Lucie's father
9 Thornton of *Hearts Afire*
10 Colonel's command
11 He's fabulous
12 Pitch-black
13 Senate vote
21 Postal Creed word
22 Bingo relative
25 VIP transports
26 Not at all
27 Singer Adams
28 Be out of sorts
29 Water-balloon sound
30 Actress Hopkins
32 *Tic __ Dough*
34 Little helper?
36 Poster pointer
37 Red River city
38 Use a spider
39 Resolves a problem
44 Taylor of *I'll Fly Away*
45 Porpoise pack
46 Weed beater
47 Low decks
49 Teatime treat
50 Gujarat garb
51 Maintain
52 Beat hard
53 Old Testament book
54 Eaglet's home: Var.
55 Morse click
58 Draft agcy.

240 BIRTHRIGHT

by Donna J. Stone

ACROSS
1 Ms. Minnelli
5 Clanton foe
9 Kitchen kingpin
13 Mr. Hershiser
14 Take in, perhaps
15 Vegetate
16 START OF A QUIP
19 Writer Hentoff
20 ". . . __ shall die"
21 Left no stone unturned
22 Places for patches
24 Antiquity, in antiquity
25 Select
28 Fabric ornament
33 Slowly, to Solti
34 *M*A*S*H* star
35 Em or Bee
36 Chemical suffix
37 SPEAKER OF THE QUIP
40 Columbus campus, briefly
41 Hose mishap
43 Thailand neighbor
44 "¿*Cómo está* __?"
46 California city
48 Belong
49 Ending for Capri
50 Warbucks, for one
52 *Marcus Welby, M.D.* actress
56 Patriotic org.
57 Symbol of wisdom

60 END OF QUIP
63 Shoot down
64 Rocket starter
65 *Show Boat* composer
66 Dumb __ ox
67 "Hey, you!"
68 Intaglio material

DOWN
1 Kind of roast
2 Role for Shirley
3 Citrus peel
4 *Freedom Road* star
5 J.R.'s mama
6 Had some hash
7 Confederates
8 Moral laws
9 Mrs. Lyndon Johnson
10 Appointment-book division
11 In addition
12 Hightailed it
14 Come to terms
17 Sarge, e.g.
18 Dict. type
22 Baby beaver
23 Snore
25 Anklet feature
26 Eastern dye
27 *Superfly* star Ron
29 Mrs. Smith's specialty
30 Bartlett bit
31 Big name at Indy
32 Clementi piece
34 Pants part
38 *Moby-Dick,* for instance
39 Permafrost area
42 Todman's partner
45 Deficient
47 ". . . three men in __"
48 Spud state
51 Texas athlete
52 __ *Villa!*
53 Meadow mamas
54 Pro follower
55 Hydrox competitor
57 Writer Wister
58 Guarded
59 Onetime Mercury model
61 Ultimate
62 Bowe stat

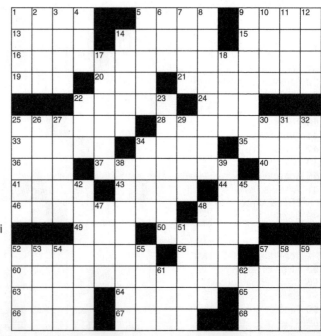

241 *WHERE'S LADY BIRD?*

by Matt Gaffney

ACROSS
1 Amazing act
5 Muffin topping?
9 Schwarzenegger's hometown
13 Tear down
14 Dizzying designs
16 Seize the day
17 Part of QED
18 The winter's tail?
19 Unlocked
20 Top fashion model
23 "__ is me!"
24 Word on a dime
25 Hot topic
27 Humiliate
29 Fond du __, WI
31 Oolong, e.g.
32 __ *Can* (Sammy Davis book)
33 Corinth's country
36 GA's zone
37 *The Golden Girls* actress
40 Clear (of)
43 Emulate Fred Noonan
44 Pieces' partners
48 Be in debt
49 Mousse alternative
50 Delaware senator
51 Clavell's __ *House*
53 Grass à la mowed?
55 Oops!
56 West Virginia senator

61 One of the Jacksons
62 Celebrity bash
63 Joyce's land
64 Sherman Hemsley sitcom
65 Shampoo-bottle word
66 Nicholas or Ivan
67 Ezio Pinza, for one
68 Shifty glance
69 Chicks' moms

DOWN
1 Express road
2 Stud site
3 Showy shrubs
4 Head of France?
5 __ *Holiday*

6 Quickly
7 Irving hero
8 Keystone's place
9 Sheen
10 Clever comeback
11 Boulevards
12 Buddhist movement
15 Useful article
21 Curly poker?
22 Houston coll.
26 Feast on fries
28 Bro or sis
29 Riga resident
30 Flu symptom
33 Donated
34 Staircase part
35 History division
38 Gung-ho

39 Baseball stat.
40 Director Howard
41 WWII locale
42 Lincoln-Douglas encounters
45 Put on a pedestal
46 Mideast capital
47 Noisy nappers
50 "See ya!"
52 City on the Rhone
53 *Steppenwolf* author
54 In search of
57 Hockey legend Bobby
58 Wind
59 *Citizen* __
60 Mr. Walesa
61 Filing aid

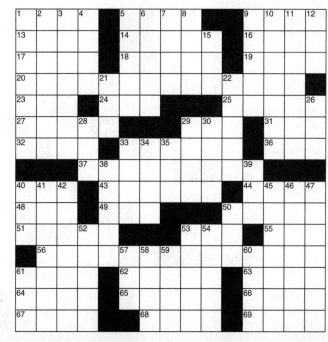

242 GEOLOGIZING

by A.J. Santora

ACROSS
1 Coal container
4 Ailing, perhaps
8 Exercise target
12 "It's __-win situation!"
13 Tower town
15 Melodious McEntire
16 Geometry suffix
17 California course
19 New Hampshire's nickname
21 Monastery heads
22 "I never saw __ cow . . ."
26 __ Happy (Elvis film)
27 Driller's deg.?
29 Decrease?
30 Dulles abbr.
31 Mouthy Martha
33 Impassioned
35 Like some jeans
38 Inner self
40 Show
41 "This __ test"
44 Pumice source
45 Hearty bread
46 Luke's book
47 "Diddle Diddle Dumpling" footwear
50 From the heart?
52 Carole King song
55 Bakery favorites
58 Deli choice

59 *Rigoletto* rendition
60 Lineal start
61 Kapaa keepsake
62 Peterman
63 Boggy stuff
64 Computer key: Abbr.

DOWN
1 Impediments
2 Like *Galileo*
3 Emollient
4 Fosters a felon
5 Woods dweller?
6 Abates
7 Mouth features?
8 Something for nothing
9 Actress Thompson
10 Easy as __

11 Crank's comment
14 *Quantum* __
17 Cherry center
18 A/C measure
20 See 24 Down
23 Easily forecast
24 With 20 Down, Cambodian leader
25 Otolaryngologist's field: Abbr.
27 Tint
28 Truman opponent
31 *Palais* personage
32 Tiny toiler
33 Nile reptile
34 Letter from Athens
36 Refuse repository

37 Medieval weapon
38 Exit letters
39 Critic's god?
42 Puts down
43 Epicure's antithesis
45 Porter
46 Eyebrow shape
48 Holbrook or Roach
49 Utah city
50 Make the grade
51 Certifies
53 Rank high
54 Gumbo thickener
55 New Jersey cape
56 Live
57 Equipment

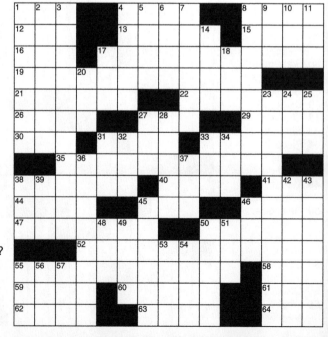

243 SOUNDS OF THE CITIES

by Bob Carroll

ACROSS

1 Reply to the Little Red Hen
5 Iraqi port
10 Study hard
14 Gemayel of Lebanon
15 Functioned
16 __-my-thumb
17 Inventor visibly aged?
19 Brainstorm
20 Not as far
21 Make out
23 Snare
24 Diogenes, for one
25 Had a meeting
28 "There __ crooked man . . ."
30 Looks daggers
34 Very French?
36 Yrs. and yrs.
38 October 31 option
39 Em, to Dorothy
40 *Songs in the __ Life* (Stevie Wonder album)
42 Bananas
43 Speaker's request
45 Barbie or Ken
46 Nev. neighbor
47 They buy hot stuff
49 Roulette bet
51 *The Ghost and __ Muir*
52 Handles
54 Bite a bit
56 "__ Fire" (Doors hit)
59 Gas rating
62 Singer Pinza
63 Thorn in the Enlightened One's side?
66 Standard
67 NYC neighborhood
68 __ *Called Horse*
69 Unemployed
70 Fix the brakes
71 Yahoo

DOWN

1 Arrest
2 Straw in the wind
3 Word-game piece
4 Altar acquisition
5 Sans saddle
6 Rent-__
7 Grunter's grounds
8 Sounding like an oboe
9 Calculating
10 Truckload of Diors?
11 Took a trolley
12 Impressionist
13 Horror-film sound effect
18 Shot up
22 Delta stuff
24 Grand and Bryce
25 Crook
26 As __ (usually)
27 Mortise's mate
29 Origin
31 Get guns again
32 Rarin' to go
33 Forest males
35 Cattle ranch?
37 Unaccompanied
41 Pulled back
44 Flat rate?
48 Grave
50 Ms. Moreno
53 __ of (through)
55 Kind of cross
56 Director Riefenstahl
57 Sportswear maker
58 Beatles tune of '65
59 "How __ coincidence!"
60 *Nautilus* skipper
61 Jacob's twin
64 Pickpocket
65 It's a real blast

NO END IN SIGHT

by Alice Long

ACROSS

1 Terrible time?
5 B-vitamin acid
10 Smoker and diner
14 Act the drifter
15 __ ten (rating scale)
16 Touched down
17 Stretch
18 Indian, e.g.
19 Refute
20 Cause for a draw at the board
23 S-shaped molding
24 Bolt down
25 Inches along
28 Medic
33 "__ quack, there . . ."
34 *Planet of the Apes* setting
35 Tin Woodsman prop
36 Staple of melodramas
39 Confessional confession
40 Film-set shots
41 Divided, in a way
42 Commit arson
44 Plague
45 Grid position
46 Membrane opening
47 Long, long time
54 Retreat
55 *Home* __
56 Trig term
57 Doing nothing
58 Hourly charges
59 Microwave, for one
60 Gusto
61 Prepared to be knighted
62 Brokaw's beat

DOWN

1 Drainpipe part
2 Sported
3 "Moon __ Miami"
4 Strong nation, nautically
5 Author Shelby and family
6 Perfectly timed
7 Mr. Iacocca
8 Type type, for short
9 Orchestral offerings
10 Plebes, e.g.
11 Evelyn's brother
12 Ice Capades workplace
13 Boar-ed room?
21 Sweetbrier
22 Helter-skelter
25 Topic of 20 Across
26 Fix a cravat
27 "__ we all?"
28 Phoebe of *Gremlins*
29 Hockey's Bobby et al.
30 __ Carta
31 Wheel shafts
32 Essentials
34 Actress Sommer
37 Early animal, alphabetically
38 "Just 'cause I felt like it!"
43 Black weasel
44 "No, really!"
46 Game-show group
47 Wash out
48 Canvas cover?
49 Oomph
50 Learning method
51 Seedy joint
52 From the top
53 Itches
54 Designer Claiborne

245 OPTICAL ALLUSIONS

by Cathy Millhauser

ACROSS

1 Bow or Barton
6 Rigatoni kin
10 Toody and Muldoon
14 Actor Warren
15 __ impulse (spontaneously)
16 Field of study
17 Putting tattersall on a tote?
20 Sandwich cookie
21 Compete
22 Chula __, CA
23 Pakistan neighbor
25 Hot chamber
27 Making lines on a perch?
33 Honored with a party
34 Trace
35 "Am I right?"
36 Sailed through
37 Genesis disaster
39 Analyze poetry
40 Pine product
41 Rosenberg of *Civil Wars*
42 In pieces
43 Adding polka dots to slips?
47 Can't stand
48 Evasive phrase
49 Mystery award
52 Rhoda's mom
53 George or Victoria
57 Depicting drapery?
61 Scrutinize
62 Bar order

63 Dome home
64 "Good grief!"
65 Cryptographer's concern
66 Nuisances

DOWN

1 Ms. Chanel
2 He had a mane role
3 To __ (precisely)
4 Drew back
5 Say please
6 City-planner's concern
7 *Bus Stop* playwright
8 Way, out East?
9 Bedding setting
10 Betting setting
11 Shakespeare's spheres
12 __ moss
13 It's a long story
18 Director Reitman
19 Turn inside out
24 Free (of)
25 Columbus' milieu
26 Peddle
27 News in a nutshell
28 In __ (unborn)
29 Flip-flop
30 Prize of a guy
31 Burns a bit
32 It may be pitched
33 Antoine Domino
37 Dart about
38 Cugat ex

39 Summer food problem
41 Coleco competitor
42 Graphic stuff?
44 Became friendlier
45 Wear well
46 Sound like Simba
49 On __ (tense)
50 Wet blanket
51 Mideast strip
52 Topped a cake
54 Troubles
55 Long-hair hassle
56 Those, in Toledo
58 *SNL* network
59 Prizm or Storm
60 Prepare to pour

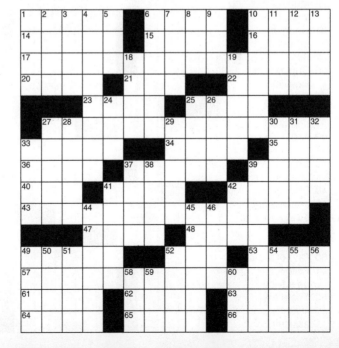

246 ROMANESQUE

by Trip Payne

ACROSS

1 Viking name
5 Reduced
10 Early TV comedy
14 Hawaiian seaport
15 Steal the spotlight, maybe
16 "Look __ this way . . ."
17 After-school treat
18 *Roots* role
19 Tahoe town
20 54
23 News detector?
24 Davis of *Evening Shade*
25 Common expression
28 Muffin ingredient
31 Chariot terminus
32 30
36 Captain Hook's sidekick
37 Sprang up
38 Amneris' opera
42 1101
45 __ Altos, CA
48 Snake charmer's crew
49 Election or anniversary
50 Tilting, to a tar
52 "*Dies* __"
54 1009
60 One of a pair
61 Follow, as advice
62 The mad scientist's assistant

64 Suit to __
65 __ Ste. Marie, Ontario
66 Agatha's colleague
67 Popularity-contest loser
68 Ship crew
69 The mind's I?

DOWN

1 Melodramatic cry
2 Currency introduced by Charlemagne
3 Actor Baldwin
4 Paper feature
5 Lap dogs
6 Tickle one's fancy
7 Guidry and Santo

8 Caesar said it
9 Wheel partner
10 Schoolhouse employees
11 Relaxed, in the army
12 She's a Pearl
13 Repentant one
21 "Arrivederci, __"
22 Jennifer on *WKRP*
25 Taggers
26 Turn down
27 Pushcart purchase
28 Big helps
29 Hinge
30 Blows away
33 Saturn and Mercury
34 Lose one's footing
35 Green qualities

39 "__ got it!"
40 Actor Castellaneta
41 Supermodel Carol
43 Popular hors d'oeuvre
44 Parent
45 Sheriff or deputy
46 Ester type
47 *My __ Eileen*
51 Silver or Scout
52 "__ you so!"
53 Carries on
55 Hasty
56 Mar. Madness sponsor
57 Phaser setting
58 Grimm creature
59 Gunsel's gal
63 Foul caller

247 SOUNDALIKES

by Matt Gaffney

ACROSS

1 West Indian
6 Spout forth
10 Cheer competitor
14 *Home __*
15 ME-FL highway
16 Opponent
17 Enjoys Emerson
18 Make bread?
19 Slugger Musial
20 Make peace
23 Mil. schl.
24 Singer Davis
25 That woman
26 *Peter Pan* author
32 Descendant
35 Secretaries set them
36 Employ
37 Be bent upon
38 Rivers and Baez
40 German Buick
41 Gore and Yankovic
42 Do Europe
43 Poker stakes
44 Bakery favorite
48 Thompson of *Back to the Future*
49 Musical ability
50 Cpl.'s superior
53 Lyndon Johnson opponent
58 Rigatoni relative
59 Countess' husband
60 Basketball venue

61 Scott Turow book
62 Away from the wind
63 Long for
64 Canoeist's pitfall
65 Clasped
66 Silly Soupy

DOWN

1 __-load (gorge on pasta)
2 Alaska native
3 Emulates Leo
4 The __ 500
5 Ring holder
6 *Never on Sunday* setting
7 Hatch's home
8 Antitoxins
9 Drop clues
10 Major appliance
11 Barge in
12 Pronto, to Ben Casey
13 Relatives
21 He acts badly
22 Mr. Addams
26 Tiny bit
27 He put the beat in the Beatles
28 Isle of __
29 Gun pellets
30 "Understood!"
31 Slippery swimmers
32 Ear cleaner
33 Ring up
34 Added fireproofing
38 Average guy

39 __ *Miss Brooks*
40 Individual
42 Ski lift
43 Frequency band
45 In a macabre manner
46 Hollered
47 Paw part
50 Incredible bargain
51 Category
52 Prefix for port
53 Tie up
54 "She Loves You" refrain
55 Strong wind
56 Hurler Hershiser
57 __ code
58 Akins or Caldwell

ACROSS

1 Respectful address
5 Clump of dirt
9 Actor Sebastian
14 Host
15 Bear or Berra
16 *Nixon in China*, e.g.
17 *The __ Hunter*
18 Baby whale
19 Talk out of
20 Friday's creator
23 Tilling tool
24 Big scene
25 Ontario's neighbor
27 Shark attack
33 Tavern
34 Eye drop?
35 Angel on high
38 Rivals of LeSabres
40 Music measure
42 Skin moisturizer
43 *The __ Balloon* (David Niven book)
46 Some apples
49 Shoe part
50 Make a mistake
53 Celt
54 Half and half?
55 Southern constellation
58 Certain ads
64 Russian city
66 Golda of Israel
67 Actress Verdon
68 Dumbstruck
69 Pay one's share, with "up"
70 Sphere starter
71 Bacchic attendant
72 Lobe probe?
73 Stumble

DOWN

1 Parents' org.
2 General location
3 "You said it!"
4 Innumerable
5 Weather phenomenon
6 Burden
7 Give the eye
8 Stand apart
9 Cough suppressant
10 Act like Cheetah?
11 One of the March girls
12 Sandwich cookie
13 Grocer's measure
21 Rephrase, perhaps
22 Galena and bauxite
26 Poet Pound
27 Flick
28 Word form for "within"
29 At the __ one's rope
30 Chew the fat
31 Chassis
32 "Big Three" site
36 Shooting match?
37 Achilles' weak spot
39 Close-fitting
41 *Willard* extra
44 Buck
45 First shepherd
47 Led the meeting
48 Egotist's darling
51 Peruvian pack animals
52 Affliction
55 You love, to Livy
56 Latvia's capital
57 Med-school subj.
59 Transmitted
60 In __ (as originally positioned)
61 Water jug
62 Actress Moore
63 Small cut
65 Bond, for one

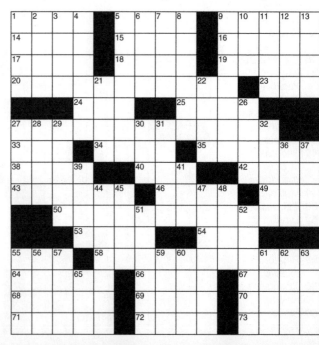

249 PUZZLED STATES

by Randolph Ross

ACROSS

1 Put on
5 Music to Shankar's ears
9 Offended
13 *Bat Masterson* prop
14 Peter Wimsey's school
15 Carroll critters
16 Fixes a fight
17 Wolsey's successor
18 Some spreads
19 Tulsa housewife?
22 Outstanding
23 *Exodus* protagonist
24 Hera's home
27 W or S?
29 For some time
32 Classical beginning
33 Davis' org.
34 Catches flies
35 Wd. of request
36 Member of Kareem's team
38 Geom. figure
39 "Xanadu" group
40 Goes to pieces
41 Fayetteville ten?
45 Moral law
46 Leb. neighbor
47 William, to Charles
50 Syracuse symphony?
53 "Give it __!"
55 Reebok rival
56 Side
57 "Achy Breaky Heart" singer
58 Atlantic isl.
59 Chip in
60 Fastener
61 Elevator units
62 Stocking stuffers?

DOWN

1 Young haddock
2 Terse verse
3 Point of view
4 Southwestern sight
5 Sorrow
6 Very, very, very small
7 Skirt shaper
8 Wild flowers
9 Sober as a judge
10 Stuffs a suitcase
11 Wolverine automaker
12 Slalom shape
15 Asian metropolis
20 Calls a cab
21 Plus
25 Not yet firm
26 Alpha and beta
27 Removable top
28 Using little power
29 Broadway org.
30 Helicopter noise
31 Attentive ones
35 Nonphysical
36 Filthy __
37 Genesis craft
39 Catch a glimpse of
40 Packs of pecks
42 High two-pair
43 Small salamanders
44 Argue
47 Pool person
48 Get on a soapbox
49 Identifies
51 Costa __
52 Photo finish?
53 Essen expletive
54 Scandinavian rug

250 NATIVE INTELLIGENCE

by Randolph Ross

ACROSS
1 BLT spread
5 Emulated Arachne
9 Candied, as fruits
14 Decrease?
15 SSS classification
16 Worked up
17 Entre __ ('83 film)
18 Horse course
19 Tolerate
20 Disney duck
22 In stitches?
24 Moving vehicle?
25 Crest competitor
27 Woodworking tools
29 Rooftop toppers
32 Rhoda character
33 Grant or Gehrig
34 Fool
35 Zero in on
39 Lie in wait
41 Moxie
43 Waiter's item
44 Similarly
46 Space starter
48 Sixth sense
49 "__ Hear a Waltz?"
50 Cut short
52 __ of Alcatraz
56 Stylish neckwear
57 Benz chaser
58 Don Juan's mom
60 "Return to __" (Elvis tune)
63 Make true
65 Arabian channel
67 Actress Thompson
68 Richards of tennis
69 Literary pseudonym
70 Textbook heading
71 Condition
72 Director David
73 "Why don't we?"

DOWN
1 Babysit
2 Buck ender
3 Progressive thinker
4 Discounted
5 Unemotional type
6 Out __ limb
7 Doberman docs
8 Greases the wheels
9 Alhambra's locale
10 Women's __
11 Survival film of '93
12 Closet material
13 Anthony and Barbara
21 Beam bender
23 Kahlua cocktail
26 Russell role
28 Split hairs?
29 "__ Want for Christmas"
30 It's often modified
31 Nursery-rhyme dieter
36 Working dog
37 Orient
38 Italics or agate
40 Choreographer Michael
42 Actress Miles
45 Convention winner
47 Way back when
51 Embassy official
52 Wall Street pessimists
53 Small bay
54 Isabella or Ena
55 Stair post
59 Middleweight champ Tony
61 Correct copy
62 Peanuts expletive
64 Understand
66 Cir. bisector

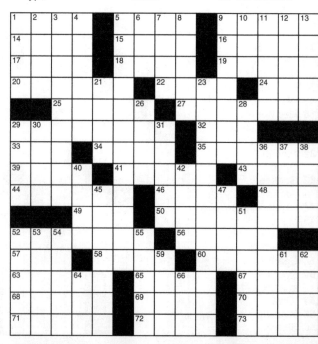

251 *I STRAINS*

by S.E. Booker

ACROSS
1 Urban fleet
5 Have in mind
9 Raise the price
14 Stage telephone, e.g.
15 __ mater
16 Sheepish?
17 "I __": Popeye
19 Tattooed lady of song
20 Sacked out
21 Ground grain
23 __ a Wonderful Life
24 Encouraging word
25 Aimless
27 Bound by contract
31 Lumberjack
34 FDR measure
35 Outdoorsy
37 Actor Waggoner
38 Surrendered
40 Author Levin
41 "__ brillig . . ."
42 Supplemented, with "out"
43 Tumbledown
46 Garfunkel or Fleming
47 Makeshift shelter
49 "Black" and "white"
51 Movie mogul Zanuck
53 Bemoan
54 Make public
56 *My Life as* __
57 Cornered
60 Work a mill, maybe
62 *I* __ : Paar
65 Picture
66 Ohio lake
67 Go for
68 Less feral
69 Toboggan
70 Strong as __

DOWN
1 Spring summer?
2 Munitions
3 Orange or Sugar
4 Globe
5 Poet Arnold
6 Actor Wallach
7 "I __": Madonna
8 Appointed
9 Mess (up)
10 It goes up walls
11 "I __": Sinatra
12 Kind of pricing
13 Soup starters
18 Separated
22 Like __ of sunshine
26 Pool-table top
27 Well-behaved kid
28 *Golden Hind* skipper
29 "I __": King
30 Dog on *Topper*
32 Eye opener?
33 Retreats
36 Rhett's last word
39 Author Ferber
43 Assembly-line inventor
44 Rambled about
45 "I Want __ Want Me"
48 Stock market participant
50 Cosmic cloud
52 Harnesses
54 Keep __ (persevere)
55 *My Friend* __
58 Has __ with (knows well)
59 Mrs. Lennon
61 Generation
63 Fade out
64 Country singer Ritter

252 WHAT'S IN A NAME?

by Eric Albert

ACROSS

1 Unruly bunch
4 Pinza, for one
8 "The Scourge of God"
14 Easy to love
16 It should be looked into
17 Kitchen covering
18 Tearjerkers?
19 What "Emily" means
21 Neon or nitrogen
22 Supply weapons to
23 Purple shade
26 Stone film
28 Characters in *Antigone*
33 Blonde shade
34 Female rabbit
35 Excess formality
36 What "Robert" means
40 Western capital
41 First mate?
42 *A Raisin in the Sun* star
43 *As You Like It* locale
44 *Oklahoma!* baddie
45 Egg container
46 Pussy-cat's companion, in verse
48 Watchdog org.
50 What "Amanda" means
58 Luau site
59 Luau interrupter?
60 Makes nervous
61 Visionary view
62 Mason's assistant
63 Quiz
64 Cyclone center

DOWN

1 French Sudan, today
2 Thor's boss
3 Become buddies
4 Model airplane material
5 Helps on a heist
6 Play legato
7 Rig
8 __-*propre*
9 Pot maker
10 Crowd?
11 Geritol ingredient
12 Solitary
13 __ *longa, vita brevis*
15 Blusher kin
20 Acorn, in time
23 Turkish official
24 Leading man?
25 "The French Chef"
26 Revive
27 Not as many
29 Bumbler
30 Line of business
31 High points
32 Piece of paper
34 Heredity letters
35 Sault __ Marie, MI
37 Born
38 Very quickly
39 College climber
44 Houseguest?
45 Ship-related
47 Bridge ancestor
48 Chimney channels
49 He played Mr. Chips
50 Mickey's creator
51 Man __ (thoroughbred)
52 Partly pink
53 Fail to mention
54 Wash out
55 Mr. Nastase
56 Prying
57 Ready and willing
58 Owns

NAMESAKES

by Fred Piscop

ACROSS

1 Attempt
5 Early man
9 Hold out
14 Soccer great
15 Lincoln or Ford
16 Physicist Enrico
17 Sect's symbol
18 __ Scott Decision
19 Jung friend
20 Freddie and __ ('60s rockers)
23 Heart of Houston?
24 Long, long time
25 Appropriate
27 Bend, in a way
31 Powerful
34 "That's __, folks!"
35 Distributed
38 Flight segment
39 Flutter
41 One Stooge
42 Author Ferber
43 Course ender
45 Beethoven wrote one
48 Some MIT grads
49 Adriatic peninsula
51 Takes off the rough edges
53 Brazilian dance
55 "Slippery when __"
56 Tiny circle
58 Child star Freddie
64 Hacienda material
66 Othello, for one
67 Trim
68 Dumb move
69 Paper page
70 Egyptian goddess
71 Stretches
72 Ruby and garnet
73 No. cruncher

DOWN

1 Rotisserie part
2 Part of RIT
3 Medicinal plant
4 Toot
5 Rhythmic flow
6 Vibes
7 Bit of gossip
8 Junction points
9 Compensates for
10 Not "agin"
11 Skelton's "Freddie the __"
12 Ostrich cousins
13 Disencumbers
21 __ to Rio
22 NFL positions
26 Commedia dell'__
27 Kiddie-music singer
28 Immigration island, once
29 Bedrock's Fred
30 __'shanter
32 Forty-__ (prospector)
33 Astroturf alternative
36 Chop off
37 __ off (sore)
40 Mitchell homestead
44 Loosens (up)
46 Edits, maybe
47 Explorer Tasman
50 With 56 Down, "Honeymoon" preceder
52 No man's land?
54 Knight wear
56 See 50 Down
57 Stench
59 Hit the bottle
60 Did garden work
61 Not fem.
62 Colorful Viking?
63 Greeley's direction
65 Ms. Arthur

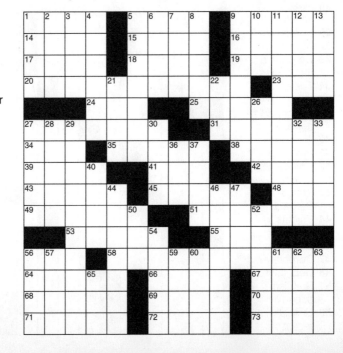

254 *HORSE SENSE*

by Eric Albert

ACROSS
1 Austen offering
5 It often has one line
9 Score symbol
14 Out of gas
15 Doing business
16 Popeye's girlfriend
17 April, 1961 fiasco
19 Put the check in the mail
20 Response evoker
21 Mangle a message
22 Dandy dude?
23 Feel the heat
24 One way to park
28 Roads scholar?
29 Spree
32 At rest
33 He knew all the Angles
34 Fuss
35 Southern city
39 *Rescue 911* network
40 13 witches
41 Profound
42 Drill sergeant's shout
43 Actress Barbara
44 Phidias product
46 *Misery* star
47 Corporate VIP
48 Debt fluid
51 Spanish dance
56 Upscale region
57 Chili ingredient, perhaps
58 Hall-of-Famer Lombardi
59 Not quite closed
60 Elwes of *The Princess Bride*
61 Stand in good __ (be useful)
62 Like a fox
63 "Babe" rockers

DOWN
1 Declines
2 Potatoes' partner
3 Polite request
4 Bit of the universe
5 Rag man
6 Poppy product
7 Barroom barrels
8 Navy rank: Abbr.
9 Very cheaply
10 Salesperson
11 An arm or a leg
12 Satan's bag
13 Throw a party for
18 Japan's peak peak
21 Hungarian leading lady
23 Confine
24 White wood
25 Brick base
26 Hold tight
27 Barbie's beau
28 Refuge
29 Jackson or Leigh
30 "*Au revoir!*"
31 Flip
33 *The __ Percent Solution*
36 Wreck location
37 Famous film maker
38 Author Tarbell
44 Watch
45 "What __?"
46 About that time
47 Ear feature
48 Acts racy?
49 Leave the stage
50 Sci-fi classic
51 Pacific island group
52 Basics
53 Pinlike?
54 Coleman or Cooper
55 Semiprecious stone
57 Dog's dog

255 HEAD START

by Donna J. Stone

ACROSS

1 Pugilistic pokes
5 Huff and puff
9 "__ Excited" (Pointer Sisters hit)
13 Perched on
14 In all respects
15 "Cheerio!"
16 Fountain order
17 Brought to ruin
18 Kaiser's counterpart
19 START OF A DEFINITION
22 European capital
23 Winter malady
24 Looking for, in the personals
26 Metric start
27 Rat pack?
31 Interference
33 Run the show
35 Valhalla villain
36 SUBJECT OF DEFINITION
40 Zilch, to Zina
41 Earl Grey's place
42 Astoria's locale
45 "Confound it!"
46 Scorpius' neighbor
49 Keatsian crock
50 Baby beaver
52 Saint-Saëns trio?
54 END OF DEFINITION
59 Out of town
60 Run a risk
61 First victim
62 Common possessive
63 Cockamamie
64 Prego competitor
65 "Zip-__-Doo-Dah"
66 Mobile home
67 Prepare cherries

DOWN

1 Derek of *I, Claudius*
2 Makes up (for)
3 Fandango kin
4 Give rise to
5 Weaponry
6 Nurse's helper
7 Packing a wallop
8 Powers a trike
9 Poison ivy symptom
10 Bar-mitzvah blessing
11 Astral
12 Propel a shell
14 Quid pro __
20 Bittern relative
21 "For shame!"
25 601, to Tiberius
28 "__ Gotta Be Me"
29 Coming up
30 Midas' sin
32 Got off
33 Diver Louganis
34 So. state
36 Used the library
37 Kitchen gear
38 "__ Lazy River"
39 Pole star?
40 Bud's buddy
43 Endorses
44 Dumb ox
46 Blind __
47 Weasel out
48 Sanctuary
51 Cawdor big shot
53 Boom and gaff
55 AMEX rival
56 *Love Me Tender* star
57 Canadian coin
58 Vein contents
59 "Gotcha!"

256 CUTTING EDGE

by Randolph Ross

ACROSS
1 Sorcerer
6 Put up with
11 Deli meat
14 Nicholas Gage book
15 Lyons lid
16 Turkish VIP
17 Hugh Beaumont role
19 Pine product
20 Acted surreptitiously
21 Crossworder's need
23 John Ritter's dad
24 Playwright's ms.
26 Reaction to bad news
27 Light beer
30 Streaky
32 Roman author
33 Arm holder
34 Onetime United rival
37 Actress Ullmann
38 Helicopter
39 Sharp projection
40 Lemon cooler
41 Hatted Hedda
42 Top-notch
43 Evening galas
45 Bumpkins
46 Ballpark figs.
48 Mr. and McMahon
49 Help a waiter
50 Porpoise pack
52 Pawn
56 Lower digit
57 Sgt. Pepper bandleader
60 Century 21 competitor
61 "You're All __ to Get By"
62 "To __ human"
63 Reviewer Reed
64 Wired
65 Take care of

DOWN
1 Kitten cries
2 Actor Rachins
3 *Power* star
4 Like some memos
5 In worse health
6 Undercover?
7 Maude portrayer
8 Sportscaster Cross
9 Spiritual tune of '17
10 Raison d'__
11 Malicious attack
12 A second time
13 Mrs. Donahue
18 Archvillain Luthor
22 *Wayne's World* word
24 Russian grasslands
25 Fancy flapjacks
27 Notorious Montez
28 Psyched up
29 Fires
30 Obliquely positioned
31 __ Lingus
33 Coast
35 Peter out
36 Stone and Golden
38 The Windy City, for short
42 Spartan
44 Barcelona bear
45 Makes haste
46 Organic compound
47 20
49 Diddley and Derek
51 Newspaper notice
52 London park
53 Alpine river
54 Pluck
55 Sinclair rival, once
58 Dawson or Deighton
59 Guitarist Paul

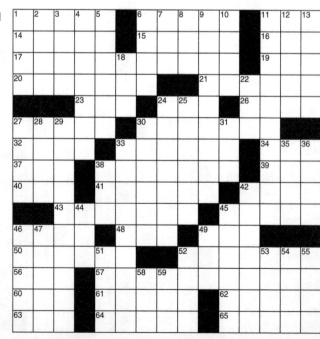

257 *E.T.*

by Dean Niles

ACROSS

1 '70s hairdo
5 IBM products
8 Like some rocks
13 Barcelona bull
14 Aim
15 Woody Allen film of '90
16 Spirited steed
17 Poet Wilcox
18 Tijuana tykes
19 Early E.T. hit
22 Stimpy's pal
23 Seeded bread
24 Sheer fear
28 Knucklehead
31 Interstate, e.g.
35 Playwright Oscar
36 Formal agreement
38 Slugger's stat
39 E.T., in full
43 Took command
44 One of the Strausses
45 Nary a soul
46 Strong alkalis
48 Violin part
50 Dead duck
51 Catch some rays
53 Shocker for Cousteau
55 One of E.T.'s exes
63 *Taras Bulba* author
64 Cartoonist Peter
65 Skye of *Say Anything*
66 Full of energy
67 Lament
68 Urgent appeal
69 They're easy to see through
70 Pipe type
71 Astrology-hotline worker?

DOWN

1 Loony Laurel
2 Israeli dance
3 Smell __ (be suspicious)
4 Asian desert
5 Where to spend a zloty
6 "__ Me Irresponsible"
7 Eastern European
8 Virile
9 Stone or Reed
10 Trig term
11 James Herriot, for one
12 "Certainly!"
14 Actor Hackman
20 Trying experience
21 Standing tall
24 Reside
25 Bendix role
26 Slur over
27 Cooper's tool
29 Eye-related
30 Oom-__
32 Acrylic fabric
33 Have __ to pick
34 More urgent
37 Hair hassle
40 Classic comedian
41 First lady?
42 "__-hoo!"
47 Made an effort
49 Ear part
52 Van Gogh locale
54 Short jacket
55 Actress Albright
56 Opposed to, in Dogpatch
57 Improvise, in a way
58 Russian city
59 Puppy bites
60 Filet fish
61 On bended __ (begging)
62 Sidereal or solar
63 Opening

258 PRODUCTIONS

by Matt Gaffney

ACROSS
1 Cooler company
9 "Over There" composer
14 Darwin site
15 "Oh, give me __ . . ."
16 Grocery-store option
17 Societal values
18 Gardner et al.
19 Make up
21 Aardvark's prey
22 Monthly expense
23 Mus. medium
24 Heaps
26 Refrain starter
27 Impair
29 Caesar and Vicious
32 Swell place?
35 808, for Hawaii
37 Patient person's motto
41 Song dedicatee, with "the"
42 3 times, to a pharmacist
43 Feminine suffix
44 Part of USAR
45 Gibson or Harris
48 Mr. Eban
50 Churchill's "so few"
53 Soft-drink choice
54 Squealer
56 "__ day's work"
58 Sophoclean tragedy
59 Von Bülow portrayer
61 Drive up the wall
63 Go along
64 Wheeling sight
65 Misplaces
66 Church points

DOWN
1 More debonair
2 *Nación* east of Portugal
3 Eniwetok event
4 Terrier threat
5 Beyond zealous
6 __-dale
7 Bully's motto
8 Manuscript enc.
9 Bedouin's transport
10 "What have we here?"
11 Alger and Nelson
12 Mass word
13 Fit together
14 In pieces
20 Least common
25 Wilde card?
28 It may follow you
30 Banned pesticide
31 "I told you so!"
32 Pitcher Dave
33 Elver's elder
34 Lacking principles
36 Blow away
37 Garden tool
38 Actress Jillian
39 NHLers from Ottawa
40 Madison or Fifth: Abbr.
45 California desert
46 Makes merry
47 Less severe
49 Supports
51 Dickinson of *Police Woman*
52 __ Islands (Danish possession)
53 Nitpick
54 Irani money
55 Craft of myth
57 Vientiane's land
60 Born: Fr.
62 Poet/painter Jean

259 SHOOT THE WORKS

by Fred Piscop

ACROSS

1 Part of CPA
5 Adam's little brother
9 Disconcert
14 Starch source
15 Hercules' love
16 Muscovite moolah
17 READY
20 Hold __ (corner)
21 Mac
22 Palmer's pocketful
23 TV scanning lines
26 Ruminate
28 Sky stalker
30 Import duty
34 M*A*S*H extras
37 Bullring cheers
39 Actor Murphy
40 AIM
44 Substitute
45 Minn. neighbor
46 Inc., in Ipswich
47 Tankard material
49 Take the reins
52 Collar type
54 Graceland and Tara
58 9 inches
61 Miss Piggy's pronoun
63 Field worker
64 FIRE
68 Furry fisher
69 __-Ball (arcade game)
70 Caligula's nephew
71 Garden intruders
72 Jane __
73 Turned right

DOWN

1 Financial phrase
2 Magna __
3 Baby beds
4 Missile from the audience, perhaps
5 Evaded the seeker
6 Punch line?
7 Neatnik's nemesis
8 __ cholesterol
9 Rainbow shape
10 Go for some brownie points
11 Irish Rose lover
12 Wild plum
13 Party animals?
18 Viewer
19 Border on
24 Free-for-all
25 Athenian statesman
27 __ Basin (German region)
29 Revenge of the __
31 Rocker Billy
32 Ali weapon
33 Chicken chow
34 Reagan role
35 Concerning
36 Put away
38 Outpouring
41 Spread out
42 Da opposite
43 Luau instruments
48 Easy win
50 Handy bit of Lat.
51 Running amok
53 Ear pollution?
55 Wigwam kin
56 __ nous (confidentially)
57 Put up with
58 Tell's partner
59 Fancy appetizer
60 Prefix for diluvian
62 Black
65 Horace's __ Poetica
66 Plunk preceder
67 "Now __ here!"

260

W

by Randolph Ross

ACROSS

1 Piglet's creator
6 Mexican region
10 Singer Zadora
13 "She's __" (Lesley Gore tune)
14 Snug as __ . . .
15 Moses or Peter
16 Tubby's pal
18 Dentist's order
19 Coach Ewbank
20 Maestro Toscanini
22 Bother
25 Honshu seaport
28 Fuel-gauge reading
29 Man or stallion
31 Advent
33 Cannon shot
35 With 30 Down, Yorkshire breed
38 Tulsa coll.
39 Extreme
41 Clothe, with "up"
42 Went back to the drawing board
44 Living-room piece
46 Cordial flavoring
48 Chemise or tent
49 Intrinsically
51 Wet blanket
53 Prefix for "while"
54 __ form (unusually good)
56 Any day now
58 Catch in the act
59 Peace Nobelist
65 Oklahoma tribe
66 Cheeseboard choice
67 Imbibes excessively
68 Thrice: Pharm.
69 __ packing (dismiss)
70 Derogatory

DOWN

1 __ de mer
2 "__ Ruled the World"
3 Sodom escapee
4 Ailing
5 *Mirabella* rival
6 Stallone role
7 __ Dhabi
8 Cal. page
9 Juan's water
10 Luau appetizers
11 Like some gases
12 Pester
15 Blew one's top
17 Cartoon cry
21 Enjoyed a party
22 Support
23 Put on a pedestal
24 South African fighter
26 Pigtail stylist
27 Author Ambler
30 See 35 Across
32 Eaker and Levin
34 Blabs away
36 Windblown soil
37 Discharge
40 House paper
43 Discounted
45 Delaware River city
47 Destroyed, as hope
49 Champagne grape
50 Related to Mom
52 Sticky stuff
55 Dwindles
57 Goes (for)
60 High dudgeon
61 Moral wrong
62 AP competitor
63 Actor Danson
64 Apply

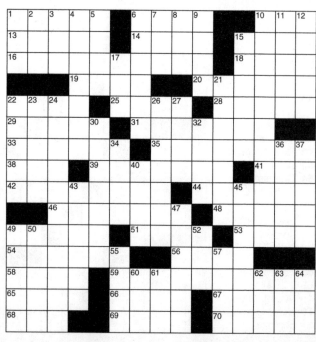

261 SHOWS WITHIN SHOWS

by Trip Payne

ACROSS

1 Petty clash
5 A, in Arabic
9 He had a gilt complex
14 Cabbagelike veggie
15 Mediocre
16 Shelved for now
17 Loy costar
18 Big sport?
19 Extend, in a way
20 Play-within-a-play in *Hamlet*
23 Teacup part
24 Vociferate
25 Ring master?
29 "Boy, that's something!"
30 Scarfs down
31 Enzyme ending
32 Dallas County city
35 Naysayer, e.g.
36 Farm animals
37 Film-within-a-film in *The Bodyguard*
40 __ Bator
41 Shoshoneans
42 *A Lesson from __*
43 Loser to DDE
44 Old ending
45 Home terminals, for short
46 Visionary
48 "Wow, look at that!"
49 Tack on
52 TV-show-within-a-TV-show in *Newhart*
55 Holiday song
58 Stout relatives
59 Raggedy
60 To no __ (useless)
61 Austin or Copley
62 Perry victory site
63 Wedding performers
64 Socks
65 Family rooms

DOWN

1 Execute axels
2 Turkish title
3 Let out, maybe
4 Gilbert & Sullivan, e.g.
5 Confirm
6 Really bad
7 "Oh, woe __!"
8 Tootsy soaks
9 Marshy ground
10 Klutzy
11 Awful noise
12 __ bandage
13 Stitch up
21 Vast quantity
22 Fix a shoelace
26 Chutney ingredient
27 __ *World Turns*
28 Settles down
29 Federal agts.
30 Log
32 Platoon subdivision
33 Swiss mathematician
34 Pad's paper?
35 Upshot
36 Feels troubled
38 Exterior
39 "*Stille __*"
44 Odors
45 *Happy Days* character
47 Steer clear of
48 They're inimitable
49 Love to pieces
50 "Splish Splash" singer
51 Units of force
53 Pat on the buns?
54 Was behind, in a way
55 Hack
56 Video award
57 Took off

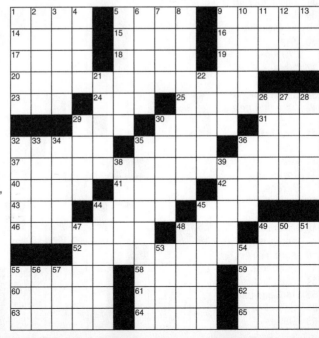

262 THERMOMETRY

by Shirley Soloway

ACROSS

1 Imported cheese
5 Hoax
9 Graceful bird
13 Melodious McEntire
14 Watering holes
16 Bed of roses
17 Frosted
18 TV commercial, e.g.
19 Genealogist's output
20 No consolation
23 Damage
24 Holliman or Scruggs
25 Stitch over
27 Talk like Daffy Duck
29 Trick ending
31 Tilted, to a tar
34 Italian noblewoman
36 *The __ Kid* ('79 film)
37 "How adorable!"
38 Stage whisper
40 Luke and Leia's friend
41 Novelist Marcel
44 Peacefully
47 Prince of Darkness
48 Diet component
49 Medicine measure
50 More ironic
52 Discharge
54 Silly Lillie
56 Remains calm
61 Kind of sax
63 Gaiters
64 Hawaiian port
65 Toboggan
66 __-ski party
67 Verve
68 *From __ to Eternity*
69 Whirlpool
70 "Auld Lang __"

DOWN

1 Author Ambler
2 Art __
3 First herdsman
4 Least rational
5 Lethargy
6 Like a paper tiger
7 From
8 *Cats* tune
9 Solidify
10 Greeting-card message
11 On a whale watch, perhaps
12 __-do-well
15 Achy
21 Drac's wrap
22 Russian autocrat
26 Ransom __ Olds
27 "Too-Ra-__ . . ."
28 Having difficulties
30 Mikhail's missus
32 It'll give you a weigh
33 Cereal-eating tiger
34 Cagney and Lacey
35 Grabbed a chair
36 __-de-lance (viper)
39 Loathed
42 Mideast inits.
43 Trim, in a way
45 Trim, in another way
46 Degrees
48 Ice-cream concoction
51 *Born Free* lioness
53 Gold of *Benson*
54 Gala event
55 *Vogue* competitor
57 Dry-goods measure
58 Fawning
59 *The Good Earth* heroine
60 Isolated
62 Pindaric poem

263 GRIDIRON ACTION

by Harvey Estes

ACROSS
1 Shed tears
5 Church service
9 Socks
13 Part of OAS
14 *Wait __ Dark* ('67 film)
16 Grandpa McCoy
17 Sack
18 Fright site?
19 Piece of cake
20 Control closely
23 Payable
24 AAA offering
25 Tallahassee coll.
28 Mesmerize
31 Hogan dweller
36 Prince Charles' sister
38 Hatch's home
40 Wyoming range
41 Party hearty
44 Runs without moving
45 Dudley Do-Right's darling
46 Be important
47 __ Pieces (ET's munchies)
49 Constructed a cobweb
51 Yellowstone hrs.
52 Plutarch character
54 Birthstone, e.g.
56 Seder
63 A shake in the grass?
64 Old hat
65 Shipshape
67 Gulf state
68 Eastern Europeans
69 Ghost or golf
70 Fade away
71 Apt. bldg. worker
72 Sign of the future

DOWN
1 Female flier
2 Mideast monarch
3 Condor country
4 In thing
5 Summon
6 Contra- kin
7 Dateless deer?
8 Use cross hairs
9 Corned-beef concoction
10 Prefix meaning "all"
11 Bathday cake
12 Eerie insight
15 Reveal
21 Holidayless mo.
22 Lawn-mower path
25 Muslim mendicant
26 Mean
27 Ben or Sam
29 "Blame __ the Bossa Nova"
30 You can see through them
32 Swerve
33 Peppard series, with "*The*"
34 Shakes up
35 Kickoff
37 Gets by, with "out"
39 Beatles flick
42 PC enthusiasts
43 Bowe bout
48 Has a ball at the mall
50 Born
53 Racetracks, e.g.
55 Chutney fruit
56 Cougar
57 Thicke or Alda
58 All there
59 Jacob's twin
60 Invitation letters
61 Lino of clothing?
62 Hardly feral
63 Interrogative adverb
66 Jack's predecessor

264 PAST MASTER

by Donna J. Stone

ACROSS

1 Chan portrayer
6 Tach meas.
9 *All My Children* siren
14 Sleep disorder
15 Sundial numeral
16 *The Champ* director
17 START OF A QUIP
20 Utter
21 Way off base?
22 From __ Z
23 Billing area?
25 Wang Lung's wife
26 One of the Cleavers
29 Gone
31 Benz chaser
32 Dos Passos trilogy
34 Pusan people
38 SPEAKER OF QUIP
40 MIDDLE OF QUIP
41 Muscle type
43 Speedy solution?
44 Nephrologists' org.
45 Least eminent
47 Out of control
48 Author Grey
51 Medieval legal code
54 Fortas or Vigoda
55 Town meetings
56 Fuming
59 END OF QUIP

63 Lorre or Lupus
64 Luau instrument
65 Lummoxlike
66 Cropped up
67 Seer's gift
68 Raleigh's rival

DOWN

1 "Uh-uh!"
2 Talks just like
3 Monogram pt.
4 Tahini base
5 "¡__ la vista!"
6 Ipanema's locale
7 Rice dishes
8 Wednesday
9 First name in stunts
10 Fix a fight
11 Standard
12 Terra __
13 Punishable pyrotechnics
18 Above, to Arnold
19 Country dance
24 Sine __ non
25 Up-front
26 Be a wise guy
27 Bring to ruin
28 Tailed amphibian
30 *Battle Cry* author
32 "Render __ Caesar . . ."
33 Wales peak
35 *Divine Comedy* figure
36 Megalomaniacal captain

37 Sitting Bull's st.
39 Key signature?
42 State one's case anew
43 Had a bite
46 Has a bite
47 Comes around
48 Mothers of Invention founder
49 More competent
50 Peachy-keen
52 Be inexact
53 __ Triomphe
55 Hot stuff
57 Some bills
58 Irish tongue
60 "Be my guest!"
61 With-it
62 Gender

265 SEASON'S GREETINGS

by Eric Albert

ACROSS

1 Fancy flapjack
6 Fill with fear
11 Unfriendly
14 Backpack wearer
15 *The Threepenny Opera* star
16 Blue Eagle agcy.
17 Albino rock star
19 Tuck's mate
20 After-school treat
21 City sound
22 Actress Turner
25 Sundae topper
27 On vacation
28 Enlists
29 Tibetan ox
30 Blank
34 School org.
37 Mine find
38 Cartridge holder
39 5.5 yards
40 Arrange type
41 Pasta description
42 Soreness?
43 Call opener
45 Lead-pipe cinch
46 Crooked
48 Bitter brawl
52 Float on the breeze
53 *Green Eggs and Ham* character
54 Frank's ex
55 "Bad Girls" singer
60 Brooks or Blanc

61 Guatemalan good-bye
62 Permission
63 Out of sorts
64 Broods
65 Tire part

DOWN

1 *Evita* role
2 Disencumber
3 Med. test
4 '50s "Awesome!"
5 Robin of 1938
6 Peas-in-a-poddish?
7 October Revolution name
8 Put a penny in the pot
9 Livestock feed
10 Render imperfect
11 Mattress type
12 Court official
13 Like a lapdog
18 Great grief
21 Hogan of golf
22 Sends to slumberland
23 In the know
24 Serve a prison sentence
25 Woo
26 "Another card!"
28 Soprano Sutherland
30 Rhubarb unit
31 Ornamental shrub
32 Loosen a fastener
33 Driving need

35 Pentateuch
36 Very skilled
44 Put away
45 Almost boil
46 Turbaned teacher
47 Orange variety
48 Light boat
49 Put together
50 "__ the season . . ."
51 Service error
53 Use scissors
55 Lassie's mother
56 *Deep Space Nine* character
57 Rita __ Brown
58 Zsa Zsa's sister
59 Blushing

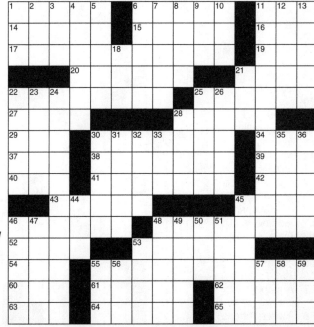

266 FACTOR-IZATION

by Matt Gaffney

ACROSS

1 Utah senator
6 Karate wear
10 Hwy.
13 Heart parts
14 Late chef Child
15 Witch's curse
16 Gable role
18 Bonanza material
19 Baseballer Dykstra
20 Like some nuts
21 Bank org.
22 Pass catchers
24 Flour variety
25 South Korean city
26 *The __ of Casterbridge*
28 Eyes lasciviously
30 Border
32 Formal agreement
33 Rage
34 Bill Clinton was one
38 Even if, informally
39 In __ (positioned)
40 Lennon's lady
41 Pop poets
43 *Wheel of Fortune* host
47 Jessye Norman's forte
48 Mineral spring
51 Bedtime, in ads
52 Sonja Henie's birthplace
53 Miser
56 Game pieces
57 "Annabel Lee" author
58 *Cheers* actress

60 Sullivan and O'Neill
61 Role for 58 Across
62 Gem State capital
63 Function prefix
64 Olympic hawk
65 Fortify

DOWN

1 Manhattan district
2 Parthenon dedicatee
3 In
4 Pasadena coll.
5 Beaver and bowler
6 Montana city
7 Model Macpherson
8 Rearranged the facts?
9 __ *Baby* (Morrison novel)
10 Zimbabwe, formerly
11 *Tootsie* star
12 Carry out
14 Caesar's month
17 Tight spot?
21 Remote
23 Manhattan district
25 Wyoming peaks
27 Big part of the Bible?
28 Fond du __, WI
29 Sonic rebound
31 Eshkol's successor

32 Paterno sch.
34 Musical genre
35 Lost
36 Ave. crossers
37 Bank's offering
38 Flocked together
42 Paid player
44 Comic Walker
45 Relaxed
46 Husky home
48 Circus barkers?
49 Daddy
50 Go __ (flip out)
53 Burn a bit
54 Roll-call reply
55 Spheres
58 JVC competitor
59 Fate

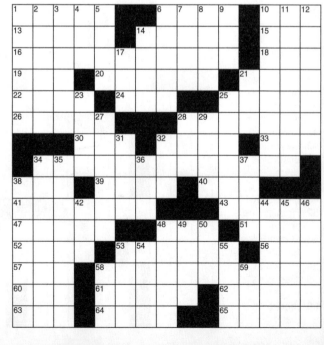

267 SOUND ARGUMENTS

by Karen L. Hodge

ACROSS
1 Mass place
6 Until now
11 Boxing blow
14 Hex
15 Japanese board game
16 NATO member
17 Where to file armor suits?
19 Ctr.
20 Pure Sir in answer to 51A
21 Go by
23 Categorize
24 PA 76, I-80, etc.
25 Fresh words
27 Will be: Sp.
29 Lock part
33 Sad, to Simone
35 Author Hunter
38 King of Broadway
39 Suit spec.
40 Litigation capital?
42 Personal opinion
43 Show to a seat
44 Exam for HS jrs.
45 Room to maneuver
47 Maximum
49 Sleeper, maybe
51 Business-letter word
52 Working
55 Put into effect
57 *Moby-Dick* ship
60 West and Keaton
62 Discharge
63 Result of religious conviction?
66 Architect I.M.
67 Head: Lat.

68 "I fear'd __ might anger thee": Shak.
69 Pressure unit: Abbr.
70 At __ for words
71 Oldtime auto

DOWN
1 Exclamation of disgust
2 Breath holder
3 Case losers' sounds?
4 Smooth __
5 Detox center's objective
6 "On __ of one to ten . . ."
7 Booted?
8 One of the "Three Little Words"
9 Plume source
10 *Wheel of Fortune* category
11 Checkers move
12 Defects and all
13 Commanded
18 The Minotaur's downfall
22 Ski wood
24 Mr. Shankar
25 Play the uke
26 "You __ beautiful to me"
28 Right-hand page
30 Affirmative testifier?
31 Term of endearment
32 Stratagems
34 1/48 c.
36 Home of the Braves

37 TV comedian Louis
41 Sunrise spot
46 Houdini specialties
48 Greek cross
50 Scrumptious spreads
53 Puccini masterwork
54 Perfect
56 Abundant
57 Shakespeare producer
58 Sonny and Cher, e.g.
59 Big boat, initially
60 AC power units
61 Fill up
64 Nav. rank
65 CII minus XLIII

268 *FLIGHT FORMATION*

by Sally R. Stein

ACROSS
1 Chicago jetport
6 Air traveler's bane
10 '60s TV talker
14 Lint collector
15 Ending for attend
16 Flying prefix
17 "Anything goes!"
20 Tobacco oven
21 Chowed down
22 New York city
23 Fairy-tale meanie
25 Mr. Lugosi
27 Doubled up
30 American and rivals
34 Accountant, at times
35 Hold back
36 Suffix for verb
37 Executive's takeover insurance
41 Before
42 Some seafood
43 Like freeways
44 Early NASA rocket
47 Big Big Band name
48 No-no negative
49 Bugs Bunny's pursuer
50 In any way
53 Retainer
54 French silk
58 Sign of safety
62 Stravinsky's The __ of Spring
63 Hawaiian strings
64 "Deutschland Über __"
65 Stinky

66 Pinball problem
67 Texas shrine

DOWN
1 Aware of
2 Some laughter
3 City rtes.
4 Made over
5 Fraternal member
6 Haste result
7 Pay to play
8 "__ bin ein Berliner"
9 Hole start
10 Potent potable
11 Do followers
12 Newsman Sevareid
13 Beard, once of ITT

18 It's behind the house
19 Calm down
24 Actor Richard
25 Catafalques
26 Columnist Bombeck
27 It beeps
28 Like a lot
29 Wasn't busy
30 "Thereby hangs __"
31 Any old things
32 Cosmetician Lauder
33 Less then luxurious
35 Exhausted
38 Light gas
39 Schlemiel
40 Persuasion to purchase

45 Shook out from the shaker
46 Word-game piece
47 Four-handed piano piece
49 Quite a meal
50 Natural hairdo
51 Follow
52 Italian wine region
53 Sense
55 __ podrida
56 Particular
57 "Tiger in your tank" company
59 Weirdo
60 Enjoy Aspen
61 Call of the mild?

269 FILMS OF THE MONTH

by Trip Payne

ACROSS

1 Easy dessert?
4 Bundy and Hirt
7 Suit badly
14 Ali Kafi's land
16 Acura model
17 Eye-related
18 On the way out
19 French menu word
20 *A Passage to India* subject
22 Look at again
23 Clockmaker Thomas et al.
25 Stew server
28 Long-term goal
30 Indeed
31 Like cavern walls
35 Rodeo animal
38 Threshold
39 Soothing substance
40 Popular solecism
41 James Dean type
43 Luke's teacher
44 Zip along
45 Boathouse item
46 Egg-roll time
48 Runners carry it
49 __ Lanka
50 ___-Star Pictures
51 Lineup
54 Photographer Adams
58 Fiesta Bowl city
61 Krueger's street
63 Put together
64 Supervised
67 Trattoria treat
69 Armed force
70 Calendar period
71 *Being There* star
72 Singer Ritter
73 Draft agcy.

DOWN

1 White-spotted rodents
2 "__ the Nightlife" ('78 song)
3 Snowy bird
4 Modern art?
5 Leg-puller
6 Dresden diet dish
7 Wire gauge
8 Chemical ending
9 Look too long
10 Burt Lancaster film of '64
11 Sponsorship
12 Ocean flier
13 Sorcerer
15 Joan Plowright film of '92
21 Bette Davis film of '48
24 Bracketed word
26 Come unglued
27 Shoelace hole
29 Down in the dumps
32 Oodles
33 Pie à la __
34 Compote component
35 Cell blocks?
36 Mideastern bread
37 Long ago
42 Bring home
47 Sportsman Parseghian
52 Beau __
53 Hand out
55 Wise guys
56 *Dame __ Hollywood*
57 Onetime women's magazine
58 He-cats
59 *Howards End* role
60 Pell-__
62 Lion's pride
65 Strain
66 *How the West __ Won*
68 Dr. Ruth's field

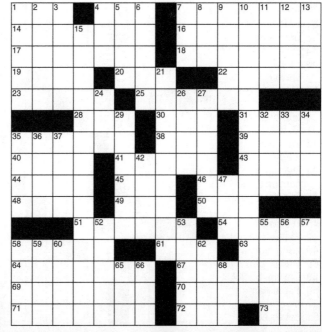

270 NOT SO HOT

by Eric Albert

ACROSS

1 Rocker Jett
5 It comes from the heart
10 Harass a pledge
14 Skilled
15 Navigation danger
16 Execute
17 Dispassionate?
20 Tumbler turner
21 Enterprising captain?
22 "Relax, soldier!"
23 Galileo's birthplace
24 Mast or boom
25 Upward slope
28 "Oops!"
29 Service member?
32 Shy
33 Bates or King
34 Bond foe
35 Just out?
38 Seasons firewood
39 Bladed poles
40 Teases unmercifully
41 Mint
42 Whale of a tale
43 Diet-ad caption
44 Summer-camp activity
45 Dexterous
46 Peace of mind
49 Long story
50 Hen or pen
53 Capote book?
56 Papal name
57 It's often delivered
58 Improve oneself, in a way
59 Singer Adams
60 Asparagus helping
61 Alluring

DOWN

1 Trunk tool
2 Bassoon cousin
3 Sheedy of *Only the Lonely*
4 Composer Rorem
5 Pitch in
6 Butler's bride
7 Symbol of steadfastness
8 Kind of cross
9 Robert De Niro role
10 *The Gulf Stream* artist
11 Israel's Eban
12 Sleepers catch them
13 Rochester's love
18 Resembling
19 Bountiful setting
23 Salon offerings
24 Persian rulers
25 It's near Lake Nasser
26 Put on
27 Hall-of-Fame hitter Rod
28 *Ne plus __*
29 Philosophy
30 Racing surname
31 Oater extras
33 *__ in the Crowd*
34 Tenor
36 One way to play
37 Factory-assembled
42 French river
43 Alms requester
44 Neigh sayer?
45 *Who's the Boss?* star
46 Ready to eat
47 Geraint's lady
48 "Rats!" in Rahr
49 Economy, for one
50 Tender
51 Piltdown man, e.g.
52 Uptight
54 Vim and vigor
55 Barbell letters

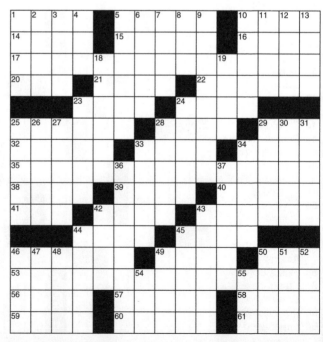

271 PARDON MY FRENCH

by Trip Payne

ACROSS

1 Thornburgh's predecessor
6 Isfahan's locale
10 Criticize harshly
14 At full speed
15 Wine's aroma
16 Spelling of *90210*
17 1958 shocker
20 Catch sight of
21 Finish second
22 Clear a video
23 Little legume
25 Victor
26 Inauguration highlight
32 Toymaking tycoon?
33 *Common Sense* writer
34 Raven relative
37 Leaps
38 Walked in the woods
39 Loft cube
40 "So there!"
41 Dead duck
42 Buffalo coat?
43 Stubborn sorts
45 Doug of the Pirates
48 Inclined
49 *College Bowl* host Robert
50 Debtors' letters
53 Mosque official
57 Promise to never use again
60 Dress style
61 Cold capital (Home of the Edward Munch Museum)
62 Hitching place?
63 *Harper's Bazaar* artist
64 Kiwis' kin
65 Plowmaker John

DOWN

1 Its punch is spiked
2 Green-egg layers
3 Tombstone figure
4 His rock kept rolling
5 Chemical suffix
6 Scoop, for short
7 Deteriorates
8 '68 US Open champ
9 Society-page word
10 Shandy's creator
11 Theatrical salesman
12 Got up
13 He gets down to work
18 Viking name
19 Clear the frost
24 Dawn goddess
25 Reset a watch
26 Folksinger Phil
27 Lotion additive
28 Finish-line marker
29 Have thoughts
30 Charlatan
31 Passionate
34 They hold the mayo
35 Actress Sommer
36 Drinks from bags
38 Skein sound
39 Paris fortress
41 Actress Garson
42 Baby basenji
43 Like some spheroids
44 Event, in El Salvador
45 Tivoli's Villa __
46 Less polished
47 "You __ serious!"
50 Then
51 *Man __ Mancha*
52 Tabloid topics
54 Tiny thing
55 Out of range
56 Only
58 ___-pah-pah
59 "Cool!"

FASTENATION

by Bob Lubbers

ACROSS

1 *Betsy's Wedding* director
5 Till
9 Jack and jenny
14 Debt security
15 Architect Saarinen
16 Buck or Bailey
17 Mainer, e.g.
19 Webber's partner
20 SNAP
22 Shadowy site
23 Encouraging word
24 Museum pieces
26 Rep. or dep.
29 Bulldogs
32 PDQ relative
33 Cuts across
36 Actor Stu
39 Puerto __
40 Dirties
42 __ up (judge)
43 Bracelet site
45 Elementary particles
47 Tra-__
49 Antitoxins
50 Oral examiner: Abbr.
51 Jacks, often
54 Part of Q&A
56 __-jongg
57 TAPE
63 Dumbstruck
65 Microwave, for one
66 Swamp stalker
67 State strongly
68 Wedding cake layer
69 __ Ababa
70 __ souci (carefree)
71 Dutch portrait painter

DOWN

1 Baldwin of *Prelude to a Kiss*
2 Truth twister
3 Lucie's dad
4 Fidgety
5 Sheet fabrics
6 Carson's successor
7 Hydrox competitor
8 Inner mechanism
9 Quiet
10 Coral or Red
11 TACK
12 Bert's pal
13 Husky loads
18 Duel tools
21 "Make __ double!"
25 Foot bones
26 Gillette product
27 Beam broadly
28 NAIL
30 Religious image
31 Pigs' digs
34 Pitcher Ryan
35 Swing around
37 Shirt brand
38 Nitti's nemesis
41 Certain airmen
44 Casino naturals
46 Carries on
48 Fly trajectory
51 Nebraska city
52 Called for
53 Girls of Guat.
55 Reaped row
58 Hindu deity
59 Portent
60 Reebok rival
61 Sprightly dance
62 Drops the ball
64 Hilo dish

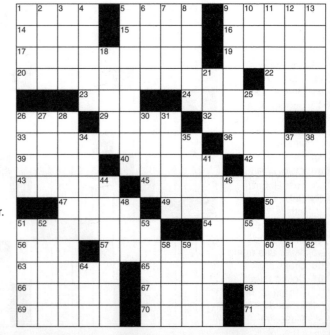

273 AROUND THE ZODIAC

by Bob Carroll

ACROSS

1 Jai __
5 Like some statistics
10 Fells
14 Smith and Fleming
15 Hole __
16 __ the crack of dawn
17 American League team?
20 Minutiae
21 Speed demon
22 Turf
23 Make money
25 Sports conference
29 O'Hara estate
30 Silvery-gray
33 From the top
34 Attack
35 __ and Sympathy
36 Exaggerates?
40 Word form for "same"
41 Green-card holder
42 Light rain
43 They're out of this world
44 Far from swarthy
45 Robbins hit
47 Author Shere
48 So. state
49 Tonto's horse
52 The bridge on the river Kwai
56 Yuppie nosh?
60 From a distance
61 Expect
62 Catches forty winks
63 Count (on)
64 Reed and Harrison
65 "The __ the limit!"

DOWN

1 Crest competitor
2 Put down
3 Archer or Jackson
4 Ain't right?
5 Foresight
6 __ Chicago ('38 film)
7 They toddle
8 Santa __, CA
9 Journey part
10 Person
11 Grand-scale tale
12 Decline
13 Tend the sauce
18 Facility
19 Book boo-boos
23 Ingested
24 Smell __ (suspect)
25 Enjoy the beach
26 __ water (troublebound)
27 Lysol target
28 Brace
29 Mini-guffaw
30 Open courtyards
31 Dr. for children
32 Must
34 Steps in a field
37 Elk
38 Chair piece
39 Plate cleaner?
45 Chooses
46 Cowboy actor LaRue
47 Get the lead out
48 Palmer, to pals
49 Indelible impression
50 Bagdad __
51 October birthstone
52 Recordings, MTV-style
53 Sawbucks
54 Security problem
55 Notice
57 Elevator unit
58 Attribute
59 Tee preceder

274 DIGITAL READOUT

by Shirley Soloway

ACROSS

1 Ann __, MI
6 Kett of the comics
10 Cpl.'s subordinates
14 Former NYC mayor
15 Nadirs
16 Daytime drama
17 Best and Ferber
18 Small cut
19 __ *La Douce*
20 Piano-key count
23 Actor Danson
24 Drivers' org.
25 Sock style
27 Billboard displays
30 Light preceder
32 Crazy as __
33 Greek island
35 Retirement age for some
39 Mountain refuge
40 Lon of Cambodia
41 Comparison: Abbr.
42 Blackjack
45 Complete a salad
46 Not in any way
47 Dallas coll.
49 *The Crying Game* star
50 __ of (eliminate)
52 The whole lot
54 TV Tarzan
55 Convenience chain
62 Throw lightly
64 Easter bloom
65 Dodge
66 Mayberry youngster
67 Author Hunter
68 Transmits
69 Coming up
70 Depend (on)
71 Low cards

DOWN

1 Have __ in one's bonnet
2 "Handy" product-name prefix
3 Explosive sound
4 Nebraska city
5 Say it again
6 Otherwise
7 Singer Tennille
8 Branch bit
9 Paving material
10 Chi follower
11 Certain prospector
12 Moroccan mount
13 Hammett detective
21 Deviate
22 Hector's home
26 Succeed
27 Part of CPA
28 Close the curtains
29 Year of the spirit
31 "The time __"
32 Wheel shafts
34 Domingo, for one
36 Charged atom
37 Bud holder
38 *Born Free* lioness
43 "__ Magic Moment"
44 Vocal mountaineer
45 Least stimulating
48 West of Hollywood
50 Make progress
51 Wed in haste
53 Move with a fulcrum
56 "__ la France!"
57 Mideast airline
58 Manhattan, for short
59 Windmill part
60 Whirlpool
61 "Untouchable" Eliot
63 Make waves?

275 BEANS

by Fred Piscop

ACROSS

1 Seeing red
6 "__ me up, Scotty"
10 Sported
14 Coeur d'__, ID
15 __-Seltzer
16 "Zip-__-Doo-Dah"
17 WAX
20 Certain ammo
21 Berry bushes
22 Stand for
23 Manage somehow
24 __ plexus
27 It's usually four
29 Get one's goat
33 Ever and __
34 River feature
36 GP grp.
37 KIDNEY
40 LAX abbr.
41 Nutritional need
42 Forget
43 Boom type
45 Cal. page
46 Celts
47 "Make my day," e.g.
49 Drunk follower
50 Clock again
53 Chewy confection
57 GREEN
60 Datum
61 Dairy-case item
62 Old toothpaste
63 __ d'oeuvres
64 Flair
65 To be: Sp.

DOWN

1 Big dog
2 "__ a Song Go Out . . ."
3 Swerve
4 Type of medicine
5 Plane spray
6 Actor Max
7 New Haven hardwoods
8 Rap-sheet abbr.
9 San __, CA
10 Prison honcho
11 Garfield's pal
12 Bring up
13 Snaky fish
18 Dachshund doc
19 Ciudad Juarez neighbor
23 Ebert or Roper
24 Presses, as flowers
25 __ a customer
26 Navigational device
27 3/17 event
28 Rapidly
30 "__ with a spoon!"
31 High-tech memo
32 Goes ballistic
34 Box-score abbr.
35 Scout group
38 Pitch tents
39 Glove-box contents
44 Numskulls
46 "Say good night, __"
48 Cultivate again
49 Onassis' nickname
50 Get cracking
51 Word form for "within"
52 Ivan, e.g.
53 Gov't workers' org.
54 Like __ of bricks
55 French state
56 Actress Olin
58 Out of sorts
59 Colonial descendants org.

276 SMALL-TIME

by Bob Carroll

ACROSS

1 Factory teeth
5 Jet set?
9 Orlando's backup
13 Beef cut
14 Throw in the towel
15 De Klerk's predecessor
16 Small-time poet?
18 A trip around the world
19 Catty?
20 Give off
22 Whopper concocter
24 Heroic romance
25 Heel
28 Prone to bumbling
31 Awaken
33 Hard work
34 Painting medium
38 "My Way" composer
39 Treacherous
40 Zion National Park state
41 Suds
42 "Up and __!"
43 Audience cheer
44 Come before
47 Patsy
48 A Musketeer
50 "Ooh __!"
52 Editor Fadiman
54 Easily solved
58 More qualified
59 Small-time race?
62 Donnybrook
63 Right-hand person
64 Caspian Sea, technically
65 Unwanted guest, e.g.
66 Canned
67 Spud buds

DOWN

1 Staff member?
2 Move like molasses
3 Young woman
4 Slow one
5 Rat
6 Star of the day
7 Start of a game?
8 Occupational suffix
9 Small-time actress?
10 Up
11 E.B. or Betty
12 Hoopster Archibald
15 Presages
17 In reserve
21 Light on one's feet
23 Take turns
25 Kvetch
26 Top-rated
27 British nobleman
29 Parceled (out)
30 Dreadful
32 Small-time actress?
35 "Take __ a compliment!"
36 Barbecue rocks
37 Have a ball at the mall
39 DeLuise film
43 Misrepresent
45 __ Dame
46 Experienced
48 The Zoo Story author
49 Dough drawers
51 Generous
52 A summer place
53 Sports org.
55 Beseech
56 Cotton to
57 They left the union
60 Reject
61 William Wordsworth work

277 JEWELRY STORE

by Harvey Estes

ACROSS

1 Confederate president
6 *Li'l Abner* cartoonist
10 Crane or Cummings
13 Author Jong
14 See eye to eye
16 Broad st.
17 Site for scouring
19 Affirmative vote
20 Not on the sched.
21 Actor Pickens
22 Oak nut
24 Wd. part
25 Pool tool
26 Hazardous gas
28 Evidence of angst
32 Porpoise pack
35 East, in Essen
36 Make a knot
37 Some roasts
38 Article written by Pascal
39 Shoe material
41 "__ hands on deck!"
42 *Wheel of Fortune* purchase
43 Hoopster Michael
44 Prison paraphernalia
48 European capital
49 Inclined
50 Audiophile's purchase
53 "Later!" in Lyon
55 Hindu avatar
57 "*O Sole __*"
58 *Diamond __*
59 Kegler's targets
63 Buddy
64 Expect
65 Egg containers
66 Like a fox
67 AMEX rival
68 Old hat

DOWN

1 Obligations
2 Sheik site
3 Essential
4 I, in Augsburg
5 Posed for pics
6 Wired
7 Cultural start
8 Yellow flower
9 Cross product
10 Stabbed in combat
11 Above
12 Hit the batter
15 "Good heavens!"
18 Nothing special
23 Grass eater
25 Corp. kingpins
27 Sternward
28 "__ voyage!"
29 Part of SST
30 Verdi opera
31 MTV viewer
32 Thick slice
33 Fountain order
34 Jed Clampett, e.g.
38 Now happening
39 "__ would seem"
40 Keatsian crock
42 Landers or Jillian
43 *Shogun* setting
45 Director Spike
46 Caribbean island
47 Berber, for one
50 Out of kilter
51 Coins
52 Oater group
53 Hannibal's route
54 Face
56 Baba and MacGraw
60 Hold the deed
61 Economist's abbr.
62 Chick chaser

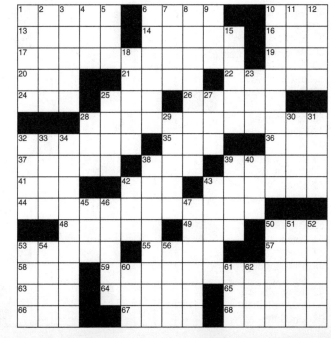

278 TONY WINNERS

by Rich Smreker

ACROSS

1 Jupiter's neighbor
5 Seaside sidler
9 Steep slope
14 "The wolf __ the door"
15 Word form for "blood"
16 Puzzle with pictures
17 Tony-winning musical of '84
20 Be in a bee
21 Canadian tribe
22 For fear that
23 Spoils
25 Prego competitor
27 Lays down the lawn
30 Tony-winning play of '70
35 __-Magnon
36 Soprano Te Kanawa
37 In short supply
38 Arrested
40 '60s campus org.
42 Susan Lucci role
43 AA offshoot
45 Galley features
47 Tom or tabby
48 Tony-winning play of '88
50 Seas, in Sedan
51 '75 Wimbledon winner
52 Dynamic start
54 "Back in the __"
57 Kicked oneself
59 Minneapolis suburb
63 Tony-winning musical of '60
66 Uncanny
67 Author Bagnold
68 Teddy trim
69 Opera prop
70 Ramon's room
71 Peepers

DOWN

1 Wire measures
2 PDQ relative
3 Burn up the road
4 Stable compartments
5 Señor Guevara
6 Nuclear devices
7 Manchurian river
8 They take seconds
9 Sign of success
10 Kind of phone
11 Skilled
12 French streets
13 Attention-getter
18 Day-__ pigment
19 Bold acts
24 Oriental sash
26 Stares open-mouthed
27 "Get lost!"
28 Toothbrush brand
29 Danube, in Dresden
31 Get __ (throw out)
32 Streisand played her . . .
33 . . . and then won this
34 Abbey Theatre director
36 Trunk features
39 Decorating technique
41 Dressing part
44 Outmoded jacket
46 "Comin' Thro' the __"
49 What an alumnus does
50 Spacecraft segment
53 Sleep stage
54 Western Indians
55 Limelites leader
56 Withered
58 __ May Oliver
60 Ray Charles' "What'd __?"
61 Congenial
62 Tennis points
64 Poetic word
65 US govt. agency

279 KNIT WIT

by Shirley Soloway

ACROSS

1 Hammer part
5 __ breve
9 Tall story?
13 Apple variety
14 Peach products
15 Burr or Copland
16 START OF A QUIP
18 Watching machine?
19 Al __ (firm)
20 Defer
22 Casserole cover
23 PART 2 OF QUIP
29 Spanish queen
30 Cockney endearment
31 Actor Borgnine
32 Emulates Ice-T
35 Reach
36 Nest-egg abbr.
39 PART 3 OF QUIP
41 Smash letters
42 Alabama city
44 Peau de __
45 Michael of *Broken Arrow*
47 151, to Tacitus
49 Loser's locale
52 PART 4 OF QUIP
55 Fictional collie
56 Bow or Barton
57 Fuming
59 Moll Flanders' creator
62 END OF QUIP
65 Fall birthstones
66 Key
67 Out of shape
68 Not so hot
69 Tetra type
70 Comic Johnson

DOWN

1 Hold tenderly
2 Chinese menu staple
3 Plummer or Blake
4 Took off
5 Chest pounder
6 Golfer's concern
7 Resulted in
8 Syrian leader
9 Penny Marshall role
10 Hosp. areas
11 Antagonist
12 Cable channel
15 On the loose
17 *The Subject Was Roses* actress
21 "See ya!"
24 Spiritual guide
25 Some tracks
26 New Jersey athletes
27 Kaiser's counterpart
28 Director Preminger
33 Arafat's grp.
34 1991 Wimbledon winner
36 "__ Her Again" ('66 hit)
37 First female Attorney General
38 To boot
39 Releases conditionally
40 Port preceder
43 __ X
46 Actress Gardner
48 Horus' mom
49 Cain, for one
50 Crystal-clear
51 "__ Fideles"
53 Comic Stu
54 Move up
58 Melodious McEntire
59 Chemical company
60 MPG monitor
61 Out of reach
63 Mr. Ziegfeld, familiarly
64 Browning's bedtime?

280 FOWL PLAY

by Bob Lubbers

ACROSS
1 Radioer's word
6 Quickly, in memos
10 Some NCOs
14 "Farewell!"
15 "__ Don't Preach" ('86 tune)
16 Third-rate
17 Kind of withdrawal
19 New Rochelle college
20 Pacino and Gore
21 Account entries
23 Actress Ursula
27 Fireman's need
28 __ de Cologne
29 New Jersey's capital
32 Cop grp.
35 Side dishes
37 Roger Rabbit, e.g.
38 HS subject
39 __-Seltzer
40 Gem
41 Pianist Gilels
42 Make tracks
43 Coop group
44 Syrup source
45 East ender?
46 Napoleon's birthplace
48 Author Deighton
49 Lab lackey
51 Fellers?
53 Agreeable sort
57 Undivided
58 Play quoits
59 Back away
64 Wipe off the map
65 Biblical preposition
66 Museum piece
67 Fit to __
68 __ the line (obeyed)
69 Kitchen wrap

DOWN
1 Fem. soldier
2 Wedding words
3 __ Abner
4 Chest material
5 Current connectors
6 Cal. page
7 Benefit
8 Top
9 Place for street talk?
10 Turns around
11 Sign of a chill
12 Muscle quality
13 Niñas' moms, for short
18 Georgia was once part of it
22 Years on end
23 Add fizz to
24 Carpenter, frequently
25 Avoid commitment
26 Hunting dog
30 High times?
31 Adenoid neighbor
33 Water heater
34 Steve and Ethan
36 Talent for music
38 Actress Arthur
40 Quick way home
44 Fridge-door doodads
46 Take in
47 Make a fricassee
50 Beau __
52 Salami type
53 Gillette product
54 Chimney lining
55 Cry of dread
56 Formality
60 Parcel letters
61 Hockey great Bobby
62 "Born in the __"
63 Heavy weight

281 SLIPPERS

by Dean Niles

ACROSS

1 Actress Russell
5 Biological body
9 Might
14 Dodger Hershiser
15 Caspian feeder
16 Likeness
17 "Gracious!"
18 Transmit a signal
19 Nixon Defense Secretary
20 Sarandon film
23 Bandleader Brown
24 Get a load of
25 Sports org.
27 Yellow-flowered plant
33 Mil. address
34 Ms. Parks
35 Run off the tracks
38 Meter maid of song
40 Galahad or Gawain
42 *The Sun __ Rises*
43 Weakness
46 Feudal domain
49 Certain sib
50 Legendary hustler
53 Pillow cover
54 Strain
55 Draft agcy.
58 Work need
64 Blush
66 "Waiting for the Robert __"
67 Worthless
68 Convenient excuse
69 Bring up
70 Stuff
71 Mail money
72 Painful
73 They act badly

DOWN

1 "Uptown Girl" singer
2 Mythical vessel
3 Around the corner
4 Primogenitary
5 Arctic adjective
6 Sandwich cookie
7 *Serpico* author
8 Nut tree
9 Hamlet
10 "__ Believer" ('66 tune)
11 Author Godwin
12 Frightening fellow
13 Bolsheviks
21 __-do-well
22 Sealed the deal
26 Taj Mahal site
27 Actress Theda
28 __ *Smoke* ('78 film)
29 Aleut carving
30 Palm Sunday beast
31 Innocents
32 Hot stuff
36 "__ something I said?"
37 It's often total
39 Author Kingsley
41 Copacabana city
44 Come into
45 Simile kin: Abbr.
47 Bric-a-brac stand
48 County event
51 Smoldering remains
52 "Pardon my __"
55 Trauma aftermath
56 Food fish
57 Willowy
59 Toast topper
60 Put on
61 A certain something
62 Bridge bid
63 *Desire Under the __*
65 Kimono accessory

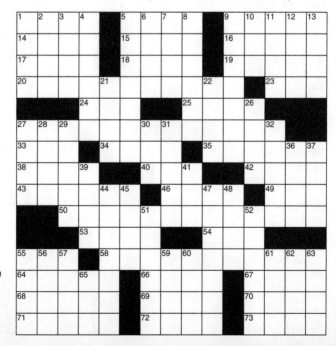

282 NOSING AROUND

by S.E. Booker

ACROSS
1 Nag
5 Quarterback Starr
9 Cryptography work
14 Latin love
15 At a distance
16 Ms. Winfrey
17 __ stick
18 Allegro con __
19 Bushed
20 START OF A QUOTE
23 Goes astray
24 Actress Meyers
25 Casual shirt
26 Busybody
31 Artificial waterway
34 Cold-storage candidates
35 Chow
36 __ Bravo
37 SPEAKER OF QUOTE
40 Tina's ex
41 Cain raiser
43 Elizabethan epithet
44 Less refined
46 Big beast
48 Actor Chaney
49 Scandinavian rug
50 Tennis type
54 END OF QUOTE
58 Comb contents
59 Total
60 Tubby's tootsie
61 Bizarre
62 Take it easy
63 Qum's country
64 Out-and-out
65 Liquidate
66 Suffragette Carrie

DOWN
1 "The __ Crusader" (Batman)
2 Get __ on (begin)
3 Maris or Moore
4 Proportionately
5 Drivel
6 Bushy hair styles
7 Sudden attack
8 Paris' home
9 Chicken
10 Employment opportunity
11 "Fiddlesticks!"
12 Some pitchers have them
13 Withdrawn
21 Give in
22 It may be belted
26 Put the kibosh on
27 Coffeemakers
28 Exodus author
29 Use the microwave
30 Driver with a handle
31 Bellyache
32 Office assistant
33 Wordy Webster
34 Worry
38 Axis sub
39 Treasury certificate
42 Business-section fodder
45 Heavenly
47 "You can't pull the wool over __!"
48 Jazzman Hampton
50 To this day
51 Singer Branigan
52 Publicity
53 Beat the Clock action
54 Do Europe
55 Aware of
56 Author Murdoch
57 In the flesh?
58 Monopolize

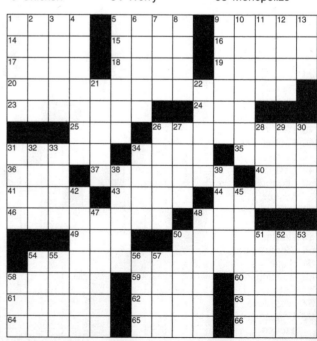

283 GOING BATTY

● ●

by Matt Gaffney

ACROSS
1 Imitate
4 Use scissors
8 Good-natured humor
14 Shark giveaway
15 Charlie's fourth
16 Sarge's "Relax!"
17 *Interview with a Vampire* author
19 Eden, e.g.
20 Bram Stoker character
22 Geraint's lady
23 Un- relative
24 "Now I see"
27 __ Paulo, Brazil
30 Score a four, perhaps
33 Atom part
38 Eyeopener?
39 Vampire-movie spoof
42 Cake topper
43 Annoyed
44 Heiden and Witt
47 Inlet
48 Sundown, to Shelley
49 "The Lady __ Tramp"
51 Now, to Cicero
55 Vampire's homeland
60 Actress Hemingway
63 Overhauled Lugosi's role?
64 Degree
65 Short jacket
66 Water cooler?

67 Takes care of
68 Fake knockout
69 Profit preceder

DOWN
1 __ in the Crowd
2 Western tree
3 Extreme boredom
4 Categorize
5 Why the bar patron wasn't served
6 Enl.
7 Hymn of praise
8 __ Beach, CA
9 Handy bit of Latin
10 Actress Miles
11 Year in Augustus' reign
12 Mao __-tung

13 Ginza gelt
18 Wrap up
21 Capt.'s subordinate
24 Price-tag words
25 Author Bret
26 Dangerous partner
27 Plan part
28 Comic Carney
29 Campy exclamation
31 Actress Bates
32 German river
33 "Für __"
34 Actress Sondra
35 French spa
36 Canadian coin
37 Bird beak
40 Lowe or Reiner
41 Police hdqrs.

45 Theater district
46 Form 1040 entry: Abbr.
50 __ as a beet
51 *Platoon* setting
52 Remove a brooch
53 Heir, maybe
54 Junior officer
55 Connections
56 Some income
57 Tibetan beast
58 Ukrainian city
59 Wind monitor
60 "__ amis"
61 Viking weapon
62 AAA offering

VERBAL ADVANTAGE

by Donna J. Stone

ACROSS

1 Blow for a bounder
5 Of interest to Nelson
10 Prepare potatoes
14 Plumb crazy
15 Nitrous __
16 Marine leader?
17 Lea ladies
18 Lots of paper
19 Psychology pioneer
20 START OF A QUIP
23 African land
24 Shirt style
25 Recline
27 List-ending abbr.
28 Angler's danglers
32 Ethnic
34 Joked around
36 Just
37 MIDDLE OF QUIP
40 Confront
42 Neck of the woods
43 Fantastic
46 Spits, e.g.
47 Fashion model Carol
50 Sgt. or cpl.
51 Buck's beloved
53 Furniture designer Charles
55 END OF QUIP
60 Jubilee
61 Out of gas
62 Smell __ (be suspicious)
63 "I'm working __"
64 __ Gay
65 Intervals
66 Emulate Whistler
67 Actor Quaid
68 Gen. Robert __

DOWN

1 Tawdry type
2 Like some yogurt
3 Vinegary
4 Tough nut to crack
5 *A Doll's House* heroine
6 Skating jump
7 Pharmacy bottle
8 Come clean
9 __ Antilles
10 Goya subject
11 Hooked
12 Old timer?
13 Crone
21 Bridge term
22 Main
26 TV Tarzan
29 Recipe word
30 Sacred cow
31 Operatic hero, often
33 Transformer part
34 Patella's place
35 Art __
37 Puzzle variety
38 Beyond balmy
39 FTD pitchman
40 Lots of laughs
41 Antediluvian
44 Nabokov heroine
45 Hang around
47 Lacking standards
48 Delaware tribesman
49 Fearsome fly
52 Minneapolis suburb
54 Saw
56 Clockmaker Thomas
57 Jeff Bridges film of '82
58 Stayed put
59 *Queen for __*
60 Competitor

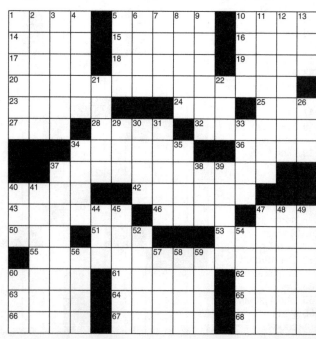

285 ZIP!

by Trip Payne

ACROSS
1 Stimulate
5 Wander about
9 Large tangelos
14 Inauguration highlight
15 Get off the stage
16 Unskilled workers
17 Long-tailed flier
18 Force
19 Barbaric sort (see 3 Down)
20 Shakespearean comedy
23 Put an edge on
24 Directional suffix
25 Lava rock
28 Relating to dinner
33 Magician's phrase
35 Narcs' grp.
36 Turn on, in a way
37 Holm of *Chariots of Fire*
38 Gawain and Guinness
39 Bowler, for one
40 "Piece of cake!"
44 Losers
46 Hams it up
47 Kennel feature
48 "__ See Clearly Now"
49 Sartre treatise
55 Judean king
56 Director Joel
57 Hit the ground
59 "Dash __!"
60 Devour Dickens
61 Mideast strip
62 Helena's rival
63 Corner shapes
64 Looked at

DOWN
1 Chinese vessel
2 Actor Corey
3 (With 19 Across) Caesar's recrimination
4 Wallace Beery movie
5 Biting insects
6 Chemical compound
7 Asti product
8 Sundance's sweetie
9 Raised on high
10 Reading or writing
11 Lummox
12 Excited by
13 Vane dir.
21 Sacred
22 Mathers' role, for short
25 South African statesman
26 Hearing-related
27 Roasting rods
28 Still-life subjects
29 Director Clair
30 __ savant
31 Eagle's base
32 Shoemaking tools
34 Legal claim
38 Hard time?
40 Small roller
41 Dangle
42 Sale goods, often
43 Muscat's land
45 Brightly-colored bird
48 Standard
49 Puts up
50 Roman auxiliary?
51 Farmland unit
52 Playwright Coward
53 Do in
54 Scope
55 Hurry along
58 Small amount

286 *GROCERY JINGLES*

ACROSS
1 Time periods
5 Southern deseeders
9 Wielded
14 Barn adjunct
15 Flawlessly
16 M. Matisse
17 Chocoholic's nosh
20 Bewildered
21 Revlon rival
22 "Be my guest!"
23 __ facto
26 "Has __ uses"
28 Salad veggie
32 "Confound it!"
36 Boxing legend
37 Songstress James
38 TV tec Remington
40 Confess
42 They run east-west in NYC
44 Producer Spelling
45 Way out
47 Go on the road
49 Linking word
50 Cloth worker
51 Fast-food fare
54 Fit
56 Deutschland denial
57 X
60 Auditioner's goal
62 Ms. Comaneci
66 Junk-food treat
70 Concede
71 Eye amorously
72 Skin-cream additive

73 Chick talk
74 Poverty
75 Strong cravings

DOWN
1 "¿Cómo __ usted?"
2 Laugh-a-minute
3 Shakespeare title start
4 Sun: Fr.
5 Sports car, for short
6 Debtor's letters
7 Launch org.
8 Wonder or Nicks
9 Record player
10 Composer Delibes
11 Deep black
12 Ontario's neighbor
13 Conks out
18 Takes place
19 Beer brand
24 Salon request
25 Goes for
27 Brainstorm
28 Worked the hay
29 Gray matter?
30 Petrol unit
31 Singer LaBelle
33 Showed again
34 "Take Me __"
35 Takes care of
39 Prefeathering preparation?

41 "__ perfumed sea": Poe
43 Any day now
46 One's performances?
48 Article in *Le Monde*?
52 Golfer Byron
53 "Rome wasn't built __"
55 Makes tea
57 Bloke
58 *A __ in the Head*
59 Man, e.g.
61 Advantage
63 Ford's running mate
64 Privy to
65 Census data
67 Outdo
68 __ de France
69 Actor Beatty

287 MAKERS

by Harvey Estes

ACROSS
1 Fence piece
5 Dove for the base
9 Halloween mo.
12 Spirited steed
13 Make amends
14 Terrible name?
15 Storage bin
16 Old geezers
17 Moment of truth
18 They make money
21 Change clothes?
22 Damage
23 Sajak or Trebek
25 Jamie __ Curtis
26 Frost-covered
28 Davis' dom.
30 *One Day __ Time*
31 Costa del __
32 Piggie
33 Sagan's subj.
34 They make time
39 Former Atlanta arena
40 Scale notes
41 Zag's counterpart
42 Roman deck count?
43 Wapner's field
44 Tyrannosaurus chaser
45 Paw part
48 Broadway org.
50 Payable
52 Kukla's colleague
54 They make tracks
57 Benedict of *The A-Team*
58 Homeric epic
59 Not feral
60 Forever
61 Make a call
62 PC enthusiast
63 Printer's measures
64 Deadly septet
65 Shut up

DOWN
1 Computer language
2 Camden yards player
3 Greet the general
4 Porterhouse alternative
5 ". . . a dark and __ night"
6 Bath accessory
7 PA system
8 Lucy's love
9 Cloudy
10 CD alternative
11 Big-bang letters
13 Old hand
14 News bit
19 Some combos
20 Bath brew
24 Head set?
27 Santa __, CA
29 Take captive
31 __ Lanka
32 Montana stats.
33 Holidayless mo.
34 Hernando's "Hi!"
35 Oversight
36 Heraldic creatures
37 Capital of India
38 *Six Crises* author
43 Hosp. employee
44 Lear's daughter et al.
45 Tickle pink
46 Pilots
47 Leave flat
49 Arctic birds
51 Accord
53 Ease off
55 Short swims
56 Chemical suffix
57 Wallace of *E.T.*

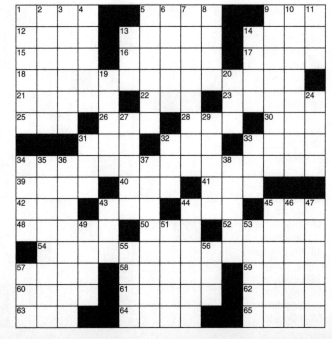

288 SOUND BITES

by Bob Lubbers

ACROSS

1 Big-eyed Betty
5 Butte kin
9 James Herriot, e.g.
13 Eugene O'Neill's daughter
14 Hokkaido city
16 Forehead-slapping words
17 Worker bees?
19 Blubber
20 Appeared to be
21 Knee-slappers
23 Lake tribe
25 Swing a sickle
26 Peanut man
29 Clinton's first Treasury Secretary
32 Sentry's cry
33 Insurance workers
35 Kyser or Starr
36 Gardner et al.
37 Cul-de-__
38 London gallery
39 Sun. talk
40 Astoria's locale
43 Simone's state
44 January stoats
46 They're attractive
48 Algonquian language
49 Ledger entry
50 Little Dipper twinkler
53 Wild ass
57 __ for one's money
58 Toad's drink?
60 Shoestring
61 Cellular salutation
62 Installed tile
63 Lodge brothers
64 Eastern European
65 *Odyssey* characters?

DOWN

1 Ducks a jab
2 Seep slowly
3 Eleven, at the Elysée
4 Remittances
5 Less even-tempered
6 JFK info
7 Shoves off
8 Zone
9 "Who cares?"
10 Tight chick?
11 Unique individual
12 Shirts and sweaters
15 Loan "shark, e.g.
18 Parks or Convy
22 Army VIPs
24 Gets the lead out
26 Moon state
27 Tennis great Rod
28 Rooster rouser?
29 Suit
30 Make anxious
31 Rostov refusals
34 Running game
38 Arm of the sea?
40 Washington bills
41 Outline more sharply
42 *Lolita* author
45 Castle and Cara
47 Ms. Lollobrigida
49 Full of whimsy
50 Uncolorful
51 Test type
52 Ornery Olympian
54 Nanny or billy
55 Literary pseudonym
56 Geom. measures
59 Pie __ mode

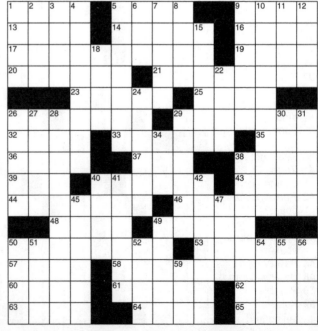

289 SPREADING OUT

by Dean Niles

ACROSS

1 Arm or leg
5 *Suspect* star
9 Open country
13 What a nose knows
14 Wash
15 Frozen over
16 Sociable starling
17 Region
18 Pull together
19 LaBelle tune
22 Sweet potatoes
23 Binds the hay
24 El __ (Heston role)
27 Graphics-software acronym
30 Doll up
32 Scale notes
33 Half an island
37 Restricted lands
41 Pizazz
42 Caviar
43 Roentgen's discovery
44 Common speech
47 Mil. boat
48 High-tech missives
51 Stomping ground
53 Gregory Hines musical
58 Beat around the bush
59 Goals
60 Fail to mention
62 More distant
63 Genuine
64 Cameo, for one
65 Lead player
66 Green Gables girl
67 Historic Scott

DOWN

1 Actor Herbert
2 Pastoral poem
3 __ Lisa
4 Reagan press secretary
5 Unpleasantly moist
6 Pick on
7 At all times
8 Enlarge a hole
9 On the take
10 Leave out
11 Some beers
12 SHAEF commander
15 *The __ Archipelago*
20 Signs of boredom
21 Bottomless pit
24 Espresso spot
25 Matinée figure
26 Mrs. David Copperfield
28 Like some sale mdse.
29 Tiny
31 Stimpy's pal
33 "I'm freezing!"
34 Like Humpty Dumpty
35 Fernando and Alvino
36 Office helper: Abbr.
38 In reality
39 Campaigner
40 Put out
44 More repulsive
45 Cossack chief
46 Go at each other
48 Kick out
49 Radio and TV
50 *Ragged Dick* author
52 Sea arm
54 Poet Teasdale
55 Legal claim
56 Love, to Livy
57 Relay length
58 That guy's
61 Newsman Koppel

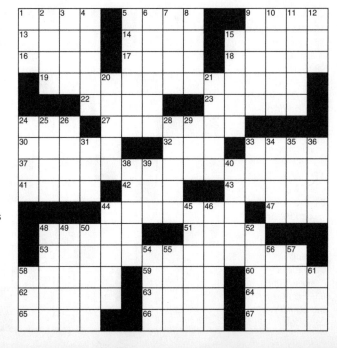

290 SEZ WHO?

by S.E. Booker

ACROSS

1 Tractor-trailer
5 Spruce up
10 Bang the door
14 Satan's specialty
15 "__ cock-horse . . ."
16 __ 18 (Uris novel)
17 "Politics is applesauce"
19 Nays' opposite
20 Colorado Indian
21 "__ deal!"
22 Songbird
24 Show off
26 Former Yemeni capital
27 "I got a million of 'em!"
33 Tableland
36 Western show
37 Wildcat strike?
38 Special edition
40 Greek letters
41 Squiffed
43 Make like
44 Patton portrayer
46 Pot filler?
47 "So long until tomorrow"
51 Downing St. address
52 Horrified
56 Scattered about
59 Singer Vannelli
61 Schmooze
62 Gardener, often

63 "I want to be alone"
66 Designer Cassini
67 City in Italy
68 Noticed
69 Sea swirl
70 Upright
71 At this point

DOWN

1 Conclude
2 Señora Perón
3 Roger Bannister, for one
4 Out of sorts
5 Short term for short-term
6 Fixes
7 Mental picture

8 Debussy's sea
9 Delinquent
10 Fig type
11 Stead
12 "Woe is me!"
13 Prepare potatoes
18 "__, Pagliaccio . . ."
23 Biblical king
25 Open a little
26 Supplements
28 Peter Lorre role
29 Kid
30 "Fish" or "fowl"
31 Cast
32 Actress Sommer
33 Ground grain

34 World's fair
35 Brood (over)
39 "On __ Boat to China"
42 Hasty
45 Hold tight
48 Get-up-and-go
49 ". . . pronounce you __ wife"
50 Psyched up
53 Come to terms
54 Cavalry weapon
55 Beef cut
56 It's left half the time
57 Snitched
58 Bamboo, essentially
59 *Breathless* star
60 Pack __ (finish)
64 Jog
65 Ski material

291 WHAT'S NEWS

by Matt Gaffney

ACROSS

1 Sicilian rumbler
5 __-fi
8 Party wear, perhaps
13 Continue
14 Like old knives
15 Giraffe cousin
16 Schwarzenegger's birthplace
17 Fall birthstone
18 Liverpudlians, e.g.
19 Start of a headline cited by Jay Leno
22 Threaten
23 __ *Rosenkavalier*
26 Bat material
29 Monk houses
30 Epoch
31 Shocking affairs
33 Turning point
35 Witch work
36 __ *résistance*
38 Slip of the tongue
39 Traded barbs
40 Defendants: Lat.
41 Seat cover?
43 Lith., formerly
44 Montana stats
45 Lens shapes
47 End of headline
51 Paperboy's path
53 Actor Stoltz
54 Don __ (legendary lover)
56 Nimbi
57 Color lightly
58 Where many people live
59 Strength
60 Sink down
61 Iodine source

DOWN

1 Tomorrow's turtle
2 Legal wrong
3 Wordy Webster
4 WWII site
5 In a wonderful way
6 Conflicts
7 "Tell me about it!"
8 "Ain't Too Proud __" ('66 tune)
9 Gumbo thickener
10 US track star
11 Likely (to)
12 Bro's sib
14 Frozen treat
20 Tax cheat
21 Heavy wts.
24 Wears away
25 Not for kids
26 Own
27 Made a point
28 Keystone State capital
32 Cpl., e.g.
33 Marine bird
34 Cover the cupcakes
36 Decorator's task
37 Not quite right
39 Oktoberfest area
41 Follow closely
42 Small bays
45 Cardinal point?
46 White's colleague
48 Bountiful setting
49 Clever ploy
50 Letters
51 Pound a portcullis
52 Yves' assent
55 Forty winks

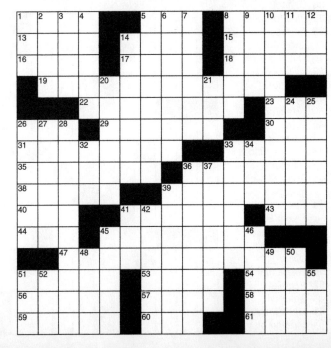

ACROSS
1 Ethereal instrument
5 Almost never
9 Specialist
14 Bridge support
15 Lament
16 Garlic section
17 Disinterested proponents
20 "Maria __" ('41 tune)
21 Deceive
22 Dash lengths
23 No. cruncher
25 Discovered
27 Venezuelan attraction
31 Landon et al.
35 "Inka Dinka __"
36 District
37 Play for time
38 Actress Rita and family
40 Tallinn's land
42 __ of itself (per se)
43 On the safe side
44 Turner network
45 ". . . a __'clock scholar"
46 Popular hors d'oeuvre
49 Tea of Flying Blind
51 Mr. Ziegfeld
52 Dogpatch's Daisy __
55 Like a foal
57 Novelist Shaw
61 1993 Tony-winning play

64 Barrel part
65 Writer Ephron
66 Jet-black
67 Auto type
68 Extremities
69 Robin Williams film

DOWN
1 Sock away
2 First victim
3 Four-star review
4 "Purple Rain" man
5 Approves
6 Actress Patricia
7 French diacritical mark
8 Cover up
9 Singer Marilyn

10 Pie __ mode
11 Go to the polls
12 Tied
13 Nitti's nemesis
18 Reindeer country
19 Baseball's Ed and Mel
24 Bushy do
26 26-nation grp.
27 Let in or let on
28 Nary a soul
29 Tennis star Ivanisevic
30 DDE's rival
32 Joust weapon
33 Brief indulgence
34 Street talk
37 Kind of marble

39 Chemical compound
40 Actor Wallach
41 Ego
43 Papal city, once
46 They spawn fawns
47 Locomotive
48 Dickens' Little __
50 Actress Barkin
52 Church service
53 Pot starter
54 "My word!"
56 Linear measure
58 Port authority?
59 Very unpleasant
60 Opposing votes
62 __ Marie Saint
63 Bell and Kettle

293 CRAZY

by S.E. Booker

ACROSS

1 Bivouac
5 Blew away
9 Tease
13 Colossal commotion
14 In the flesh
15 Together, to Toscanini
16 Cookie favorites
17 Cool it
18 Position
19 Director Reitman
20 Crazy
22 House party?
24 Leander's love
25 Cafeteria burden
27 Kind of comedy
32 Crazy
36 Hue and cry
37 Doozie
38 Course requirement?
40 Traffic sound
41 Taken __ (startled)
43 Crazy
46 Namby-pamby
49 Frame of mind
50 Terrible times?
52 Be that as it may
56 Crazy
61 "Give __ little earth for charity": Shak.
62 It grows on you
63 Ballerina Pavlova
64 Hopeless case
65 Creole veggie
66 Goes bad
67 Improve
68 Dickensian clerk
69 Hit a fly
70 Mrs. Truman

DOWN

1 Tricky pitch
2 Geometry calculations
3 Crazy
4 Seven, on a telephone
5 To boot
6 Oz heavy
7 Conjures up
8 Cut out
9 "Ta-__-Boom De-Ay"
10 Eliot's Bede
11 Western Indian
12 *Wizard of Oz* role
13 Fencing weapon
20 Overpack
21 Haunted-house sound
23 Mork's home planet
26 Big mouth
28 Crazy
29 God, to de Gaulle
30 Exploits
31 Le Pew of cartoons
32 Close noisily
33 Tubby, for one
34 "There oughta be __!"
35 Smidgen
39 Zombie ingredient
42 __ and kin
44 Object
45 Sweetie
47 Promises
48 "__, brown cow?"
51 Nick name?
53 Grape expectations?
54 Prayer finales
55 Back grounds?
56 "Oops!"
57 Phony
58 Red menace
59 Rope in
60 Stand up
64 Chatter

294 TRAVELER'S CHECK

by Donna J. Stone

ACROSS

1 Actor __ Cobb
5 Havana, for one
10 Bible book
14 *M*A*S*H* star
15 Out of the way
16 Crooner Jerry
17 Scheme
18 Like some jackets
19 Turgenev Museum site
20 START OF A QUIP BY HENNY YOUNGMAN
23 Machine part
24 Mitchell homestead
25 Conduit
30 Hook's mate
34 Beyond help
35 Zhivago's love
37 Linen fabric
38 __ Mahal
39 MIDDLE OF QUIP
41 Makes one's mark
42 1970 World's Fair site
44 Brace
45 Movie theater
46 Italian port
48 Tie
50 Present, in the future
52 Corporate VIP
53 END OF QUIP
60 Burn remedy
61 Opera cheer
62 *The King and I* setting
64 Director Peter

65 More competent
66 __ Taft Benson
67 Costner role of '87
68 Savanna sounds
69 He's abominable

DOWN

1 Drink like a dachshund
2 Actress Raines
3 Dutch treat
4 Czech composer
5 *I, Claudius* character
6 Horus' mom
7 Ms. Lollobrigida
8 Proficient
9 Phone button
10 Guacamole base
11 Full-grown filly
12 Toast topper
13 Egotist's darling
21 Seal school
22 Ovid's Muse
25 *The Maltese Falcon* star
26 Resembling
27 Free, in a way
28 *Li'l Abner* creator
29 Riser's relative
31 D.D. Emmett tune
32 Ms. Verdugo
33 Adjust a watch
36 Auto-racer Luyendyk

39 One of the Philippines
40 Plow pullers
43 Smoked fish
45 Fastidious
47 Meteorology line
49 Dolores __ Rio
51 Jet starter
53 *Housesitter* star
54 Gen. Robert __
55 Superman's sweetie
56 Extravaganza
57 At any time
58 __ up (evaluate)
59 Trenchant
63 Actress Zetterling

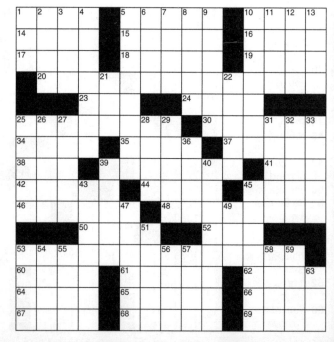

295 THE OTHER CLINTON

by Dean Niles

ACROSS

1 Lip lash?
5 Common contraction
8 Actress Harris
11 1492 caravel
12 Pants part
14 Mah-jongg piece
15 Eskimo kin
16 Official records
17 "__ Rock" ('66 song)
18 Eastwood's *Rawhide* role
20 Feds
21 Pilaf ingredient
22 Informal wear
24 Slip away
28 Southern Butler
30 Actress Miles
31 Director Adrian
33 Golfer Palmer
37 Invite along
39 Seasoned stews
41 Shakes off
42 Nicholas or Alexander
44 Painter Mondrian
45 Equip again
47 "__ in St. Louis, Louis"
49 Walk like a giant
52 Shortly
54 Urge on
55 Eastwood Oscar-winner

61 Eat up
62 Dexterous
63 Literary device
64 Declare positively
65 Prophet
66 Without guile
67 "Sure!"
68 ETO commander
69 Whirlpool

DOWN

1 Storage tower
2 From the top
3 Earring type
4 Old goats?
5 Author Asimov
6 Reading desk
7 Tardy
8 Florida's __-Dade County
9 Glue guy
10 Inclined
11 Golf guideline
13 Try a mouthful
14 Eastwood thriller
19 Traffic sign
23 Without a date
24 Depraved
25 Carson sucessor
26 Circle segments
27 Eastwood western
29 Mrs. Zeus
32 Tibetan Frosty?
34 Night: Fr.
35 Bit of news
36 Punta del __
38 Hand-me-down
40 Knight wear
43 Filled positions
46 Vendettas
48 Auto need
49 Spread out
50 Valuable collection
51 Emulates Sinbad
53 __ Dame
56 Require
57 Son of Enoch
58 Not valid
59 A deadly sin
60 Comic Louis

KNOCK THREE TIMES

by Eric Albert

ACROSS

1 Omit
5 Wing it
10 Racquetball target
14 Novelist Rice
15 Refuse
16 Mitch Miller's instrument
17 KNOCK
20 Meadow muncher
21 Singer Redding
22 Michael Jackson hit
23 Forked out
24 Getz of jazz
25 Two on the aisle, e.g.
28 Tater
29 Ave. crossers
32 Diminish
33 Stigmatize socially
34 Oil cartel
35 KNOCK
38 Clownish
39 Pool accessory
40 Barkin or Burstyn
41 Put away
42 Opus
43 Slender and sleek
44 Headed for the bottom
45 Niger's neighbor
46 Classical hunk
49 Coasted
50 Male swan
53 KNOCK
56 Big boss
57 Actress Keaton
58 Catch forty winks
59 Unload
60 Fiery fragment
61 Swerve

DOWN

1 All there
2 Grasped
3 *Picnic* playwright
4 Schoolboy's shot
5 Already
6 Michelangelo subject
7 Caustic substances
8 Entrepreneur's mag
9 TV, slangily
10 ___ of the Year
11 Help on a heist
12 Ms. Anderson
13 Riga resident
18 Precisely
19 Samoa studier
23 Bag holder?
24 Pluck
25 Tony of TV
26 Wolf-pack member
27 *What's It All About?* author
28 Peanuts or popcorn
29 Small fall
30 Principle
31 Play part
33 Carroll creature
34 Eyed amorously
36 Role for Burr
37 Silver State
42 Ragamuffin
43 Black eye
44 Act surly
45 Genetic duplicate
46 Bow lines?
47 Bewilderment
48 Black or white gem
49 Dagger thrust
50 Prepare pasta
51 Emulate the Blob
52 Make tea
54 Actor Alastair
55 Driller's deg.

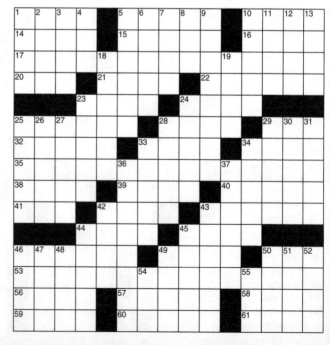

297 SHORT AND SWEET

by Penny A. Roman

ACROSS

1 Fisherman
7 Cream measure
11 Babble on
14 Leatherneck
15 Man __ (racehorse)
16 Call __ day
17 Actress Blake
18 START OF A WINNIE THE POOH QUOTE
20 Yellow slippers?
22 *Carmen* setting
23 Actress West
25 "A" in Arabic
27 Churchman
28 PART 2 OF QUOTE
32 Attempts
33 Gray, in Grenoble
34 Channel designation
37 Skein sound
38 PART 3 OF QUOTE
40 Draft status
41 Vane dir.
42 Visionary
43 Sandbar
44 PART 4 OF QUOTE
47 Sign of balance?
50 Peeved
51 Salon stuff
52 How land is measured
55 Gettysburg victor
57 END OF QUOTE
59 Some arcade machines
62 Benz chaser
63 Journalist Jacob
64 Roman philosopher
65 Blazed the trail
66 Matchmakers?
67 Worn down

DOWN

1 Orthopedists' org.
2 *Platoon* setting
3 Rumor mill
4 Bank holdup?
5 Wins over
6 "Are you sure?"
7 Luau staple
8 "__ only kidding!"
9 Identify
10 Sees the world
11 Triangular sign
12 __ of Two Cities
13 Kitchen gadget
19 Ill temper
21 Part of RSVP
23 Closet pests
24 '60s hairstyles
26 Operatic barber et al.
29 Word to a mouse
30 Part of TNT
31 Canterbury can
34 Mixed up
35 Exhilarating
36 Two-faced
38 Night spot
39 Kin, for short
40 Palindromic shout
42 They trap
43 Something to slip on
44 Paris sight
45 __ de plume
46 1972-80 Broadway hit
47 Defame
48 Hole __ (ace)
49 With __ breath
53 Albany-to-Buffalo canal
54 Struck, once
56 "Book 'em, __!"
58 Slalom maneuver
60 Diamonds, slangily
61 Down

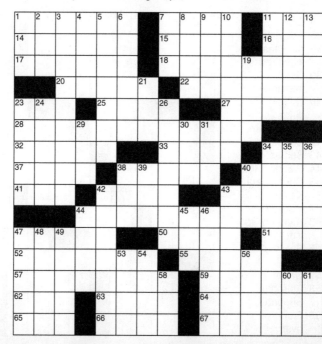

298 SOB STORIES

by Dean Niles

ACROSS

1 Cast off
5 Cuckoo
9 Hiding place
14 Actor Waggoner
15 At rest
16 Curly coifs
17 Church recess
18 German valley
19 Burdens
20 Riverbank tree
23 Mini, to MacTavish
24 Vent
27 Wander off
30 Arm: Fr.
32 Compass pt.
33 Greenish blue
34 Side
35 Adoption org.
36 Miracles tune, with "The"
39 October implement
40 Tabloid fliers
41 Texas town
42 Consumed
43 Self-satisfied
44 Slugger Rod
45 Country star Kathy
47 PC linkup
48 Stephen Rea film
55 Ran the show
57 Orient
58 Astronaut Shepard
59 French river
60 Model Macpherson
61 Frying need
62 Prepared to be shot
63 Mailer's The __ Park
64 Proposes

DOWN

1 Cabbage concoction
2 PR job
3 Otherwise
4 Full of meaning
5 Big name in entertainment
6 Saw
7 Diamond defect
8 Actress Garr
9 Roughened skin
10 In progress
11 Cellar substitute
12 Brick carrier
13 Curvy letter
21 "__ the Line" (Cash tune)
22 Full of rich soil
25 Real-estate account
26 Moore opener
27 Planes
28 Range toppers
29 Soapbox derby, e.g.
30 Obfuscate
31 Merino males
34 Soybean product
35 Scorch
36 Mine car
37 Poisonous plant
38 Pluck
43 Removed the pits
44 Easy pace
46 Comforting word
47 Cotton thread
49 Actor Oliver
50 New Haven campus
51 Wing-ding
52 "Oh, woe!"
53 A+ or C-
54 Some footballers
55 Tear
56 Troop troupe

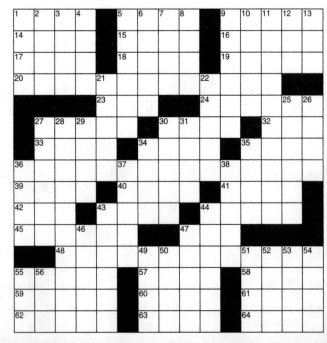

299 KITCHEN STARS

by Bob Lubbers

ACROSS

1 Mil. decorations
5 Took care of
10 Army vehicle
14 Range Indian
15 Once more
16 Coax
17 Melodious McEntire
18 Fuming
19 Tetra type
20 Flip singer?
23 Self-assurance
24 TV Tarzan
25 Pasture sound
28 Stand for
29 Overshoe
32 Boxer's helper
34 County Kerry port
36 Biblical preposition
37 Cheesy star?
40 Sign of sainthood
42 Nile god
43 Avoids capture
46 "¿Cómo __ usted?"
47 PD alert
50 "__ Willie Winkie"
51 Sarnoff's org.
53 *Roma's* land
55 Drippy actress?
58 Proficient
61 Dwight's opponent
62 Major-__ (headwaiter)
63 Jogger's gait
64 Corpsman
65 Terrible name?
66 Facility
67 Saw wood
68 Some bills

DOWN

1 Fin type
2 Russian plain
3 Blue hue
4 "From __ shining . . ."
5 Tub toy
6 Taj turf
7 WWII aux.
8 Deed
9 Ryan and Tatum
10 Refuse
11 Prior to, to Prior
12 Identity
13 Cob's mate
21 Eclipse shadow
22 Bread or booze
25 Singer Sonny
26 Hill dweller
27 Flap
30 Dairy-case purchase
31 Short
33 Den denizens
34 Walked
35 Sponsorship
37 It's often tacky
38 Cunning
39 *Bonanza* prop
40 Fell
41 Porter's kin
44 Century 21 competitor
45 Hightails it
47 Nook
48 Simple Simon's acquaintance
49 Twirlers' tools
52 *As You Like It* setting
54 Check the books
55 Jubilee
56 Actor Ray
57 Noodle topping?
58 Dug in
59 Bikini half
60 __ Alamos, NM

300 ANANGRAMS

by Randolph Ross

ACROSS

1 Jai __
5 NYC div.
9 Date with a dr.
13 Darling, e.g.
16 Rajah lead-in
17 Apt anagram of 13 Across
18 Goofs
19 Highlands tongue
20 Singer Janis
22 __ in "elephant"
23 No gentlemen
26 Smears
28 *A Chorus Line* number
29 Ration
32 A Rose by another name
33 Tone __ (rap singer)
34 She took a shine to shoes
37 Satisfied sounds
38 Francis and Dahl
40 Courses
43 Bern's river
44 Void
46 "The Racer's Edge"
47 Author Hubbard
49 Locality
50 Sundial numeral
51 Least taxing
54 "__ It Romantic?"
55 Erie hrs.
56 ABA title
57 Morse bits
60 Reformer Jacob
62 Penalty
67 Sgts. and cpls.
68 Apt anagram of 62 Across
69 Lab burner
70 Actress Moore
71 Scale starters

DOWN

1 Had a pizza
2 Author Deighton
3 Plus
4 Sorbonne concepts
5 Chilly sounds
6 "This round is __!"
7 Silly Charlotte
8 __ *vincit amor*
9 "Botch- __" ('52 song)
10 Prose symbol
11 Apt anagram of 10 Down
12 *Pravda* source
14 Musical knack
15 Latin abbr.
21 Tuck's mate
23 Fountain order
24 Apt anagram of 25 Down
25 Formal statement
26 Brooks or Blanc
27 Machine part
29 Noisy racket
30 Augury
31 __ majesty
35 Steep
36 Kin of pre-
39 Divine archer
41 Japanese export
42 Rotisserie rod
45 Gangster's gun
48 Never, in Nuremberg
52 Network founded in 1979
53 Cuttlefish kin
54 "My name __" ("I'm ruined")
55 Sea eagle
57 *Carpe* __
58 __ spumante
59 LBJ's VP
61 Pub. pension payer
63 Vane dir.
64 Comedian Philips
65 "Car Talk" network
66 "Waste Land" poet's monogram

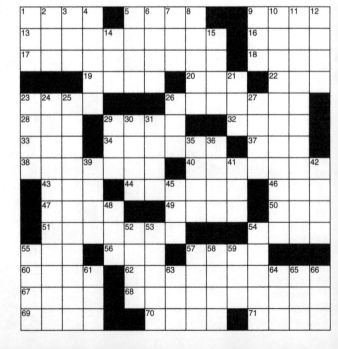

301 BIG STAR

by Dean Niles

ACROSS

1 Scale notes
4 Knife handle
8 *West Side Story* song
13 Mandela org.
14 Competes
15 Kate Nelligan film
16 See 43 Down
19 Strong-arm
20 Actor Morales
21 Navy rival
22 Maynard's good buddy
25 Sail site
29 Actress Remick
30 Of interest to Lord Nelson
31 Nile feature
32 Bathroom worker
33 __ *Mame*
34 BIG STAR FILM
37 Witches
38 Items in the fire
39 Holstein homes
40 New Hampshire campus
41 "Gotcha!"
44 "Auld Lang __"
45 Verbose
46 Controversial tree spray
47 Peasant fellow
49 Cotton fabric
51 BIG STAR FILM
55 Inch along
56 Distant start
57 Hair goo

58 Don one's duds
59 Mgr.'s helper
60 "Kookie" Byrnes

DOWN

1 Alfalfa or Buckwheat
2 "Play it again, Sam!"
3 Plot
4 Blueprint inits.
5 Some terriers
6 Hakim's hat
7 Poetic monogram
8 Thornburgh's predecessor
9 Pond organism

10 Disciplines
11 Chemical suffix
12 Televise
17 Bitingly funny
18 Mr. Simon
23 Finished
24 More daft, in Devonshire
26 Sax type
27 Prod to activity
28 __ kwon do
30 Evenings, on marquees
31 Guitarist Eddy
32 Crockett country
33 Unsigned
34 Shallow server

35 Beeper
36 Provoked thoroughly
37 Dan Rather's network
40 Catholic fraternal org.
41 Assert
42 Pilose
43 WITH 16 ACROSS, BIG STAR
45 Envelops
46 Sturdy wood
48 Summers on the Seine
50 Platoon, e.g.
51 Math. term
52 Flight stat.
53 Afternoon drink
54 Mensa measurements

302

NAME THAT TUNE

by Trip Payne

ACROSS

1 Pit for a pump
5 Not quite straight
9 "Beat it!"
14 Draftable
15 Comic Kaplan
16 Basketball venue
17 Da-da-da-DUM . . .
20 Ms. Lauder
21 Favorable opinion
22 Settle a deal
23 Grew tiresome
25 Storm warnings
29 Sluggish
31 TV Tarzan
32 Smeltery stuff
33 Cracker shape
36 Mock
37 DUM-da-DUM-DUM . . .
41 French designer
42 Navy rank
43 Actress Gardner
44 Period
46 Funds a college
50 Chanter's word
52 __ serif
54 By way of
55 Burger topping
57 Hot spots
59 DUM-DUM-da-DUM . . .
63 "__ mud in your eye!"
64 Sporting blade
65 Birth of a notion?
66 Put out
67 Gobi-like
68 Snooping about

DOWN

1 "Amen!"
2 Cultural agcy.
3 Convention-goer
4 Popular hors d'oeuvre
5 In the past
6 Two-time Grand Slam winner
7 Too heavy
8 __ up (confined)
9 Without harm
10 Felony, e.g.
11 Ring judge
12 Farm animal
13 __-jongg
18 Conforming (to)
19 Circus barker
24 Valhalla VIP
26 Wander about
27 Quiz option
28 Dr. Ruth's specialty
30 Carson's predecessor
31 *Lohengrin* heroine
34 Big flattop?
35 Noshed on
36 Ward (off)
37 Prima donna
38 Horse color
39 Ness and company
40 Horse-drawn cab
41 Holder, like Boulder
44 Actor Borgnine
45 Sudden assault
47 Lay it on
48 Draws back
49 Glide easily
51 Lighthouse or minaret
52 Marsh bird
53 *Roots* Emmy winner
56 Dedicatory verses
58 Prone to preening
59 Popular article
60 Spell
61 Before, to Byron
62 "Well, I'll be!"

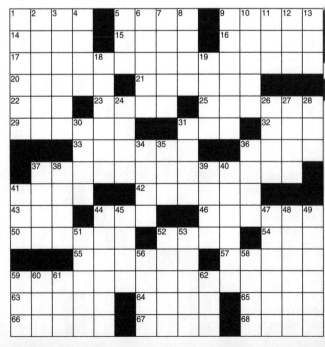

OLD JOKE

by Matt Gaffney

ACROSS

1 Cherbourg crony
4 Darling dog
8 Ohio town
13 Also-__ (losers)
15 WWII alliance
16 Boost in bucks
17 START OF A QUIP
20 Kids
21 Selfsame
22 The Lion in summer
23 Ipanema's locale
24 Base stuff?
25 Dos Passos trilogy
26 PART 2 OF QUIP
30 Cry of discovery
31 Cryptic org.
32 Sword part
35 Molly Brown's boat
38 *Vogue* concern
41 Competition
42 Austrian ice
43 Broadway sign
44 PART 3 OF QUIP
49 Good times
51 Be important
52 Stout relative
53 Architectural addition
54 Zenith
55 Record player
58 END OF QUIP
61 King Gillette invention
62 It's found in the middle of KP

63 __ Can (Davis book)
64 Repose
65 Co. compensation program
66 "HELP!"

DOWN

1 Host
2 It's sometimes held
3 Really tick off
4 Casual refusals
5 Medieval weapon
6 Ultimate state
7 Resources
8 Roentgen's discovery
9 Musical acumen
10 Physicist Bohr
11 "__ bad moon rising . . ."
12 Flying start?
14 Subbed
18 Odin's son
19 Zodiac animal
24 Platter
25 Bountiful setting
26 ". . . __ the whole thing!"
27 Switchblade
28 Verse lead-in
29 Hesitation sounds
33 Wharf sights
34 Sped
36 Picnic intruders
37 Ultimate degree
38 Colonial flute
39 "Just __ suspected!"
40 Data: Abbr.
42 Looks up to
45 Roguish
46 Hot stuff
47 Warsaw Pact adversary
48 Gray matter?
49 Arm bones
50 Square
53 Masterson colleague
54 Farm measure
55 Sow chow
56 Exxon's ex-name
57 Singer Redding
59 Early 1990s Fox sitcom
60 Lennon's lady

304

SNACK PACK

by Randolph Ross

ACROSS

1 Mutt's pal
5 Petal oil
10 Horseplay?
14 Russian river
15 Doorbell
16 Black stone
17 Milano moola, once
18 Actress Shire
19 Chop __
20 Hacker snack?
23 Jazz form
24 Very popular
25 Parabolic
28 Atlas abbr.
31 Sweeping
35 __ canto
36 Scholar snack?
39 Trebek or Karras
41 Leading
42 *The __ of the Rose*
43 Crook snack?
46 Crash site?
47 Supernumerary
48 Grant or Meriwether
49 Newspaper notices
51 Barcelona bear
53 Elevator unit
54 Carpenter snacks?
61 Bear or Berra
62 Bring up
63 Desert Storm locale
65 Actor Arkin
66 Chemical compound

67 Dachshund's dad
68 Heartstring sound
69 Porterhouse, e.g.
70 "By Jove!"

DOWN

1 Madyear page
2 Author Ambler
3 Old card game
4 Burned dinner?
5 Misbehave
6 One of those things
7 Mah-jongg piece
8 Mideast royalty

9 Get to
10 Atomic antiparticle
11 "Movin' __" (*The Jeffersons* theme)
12 Caustic chemicals
13 Lumbering
21 Places for peas
22 Rail rider
25 Put down
26 Take five
27 Chin feature
28 Taj __
29 Unlucky *numero*
30 Back financially
32 Giraffe cousin
33 Set as a goal
34 Heroic feats

37 Disfigure
38 B train?
40 Office activity
44 Hernando's house
45 Chestnut horse
50 Hurt
52 Mean ones
53 One who deals in stock
54 Day starter?
55 Actor Richard
56 Hops heater
57 Nick at __ (rerun airer)
58 Cruising
59 Math course
60 Poet Teasdale
61 Red Sox great, for short
64 Proof letters

305 MANE EVENT

by Penny A. Roman

ACROSS

1. "__ Not There" ('64 tune)
5. Shacks
9. Start the slaw
14. Give a hoot
15. Organic compound
16. __ Selassie
17. B __ "boy"
18. Brunei's locale
19. "Live Free __" (NH's motto)
20. Possessed hairpiece?
23. Cartoonist Silverstein
24. Building wings
25. Nightclub bit
28. Curled one's lip
30. Bottle top
33. Flapjack chain
35. Curve in a ship's plank
36. Lady of Spain
38. Loverboy
40. Japanese export
42. Kwai, for one
43. Nerds
45. Baseball stat
47. Shut in
48. CIA's predecessor
49. En __ (chess maneuver)
52. Charles or Conniff
53. Misplaced
54. Knock off
56. *Hair* practice?
62. Caribbean nation
63. Similar
64. Fearful words
65. Wide neckwear
66. Marshes
67. Active sort
68. "This __ for the books!"
69. Lip
70. In stitches?

DOWN

1. "Get lost!"
2. Jumble
3. Buffalo's lake
4. Malls
5. "My goodness!"
6. Yapping away
7. Hard work
8. Actor Christian
9. Take upon oneself
10. Angelic instruments
11. Harass
12. Nobelist Wiesel
13. Billy __ Williams
21. Interrogative exclamations
22. Bullring cheers
25. __-surface (missile route)
26. Chinese canines
27. Big books
29. Witnesses
30. Vegetation, often
31. Fight site
32. Bash
34. For each
37. Little bite
39. Stem, to stern
41. Embarrassing
44. Mouth off
46. Earnest
50. Attack from above
51. "__ Skylark" (Shelley ode)
53. Admit
55. Urges
56. Source for Pravda
57. Puerto __
58. Managed, with "out"
59. Loafer, e.g.
60. Once again
61. Desolate
62. "Bali __"

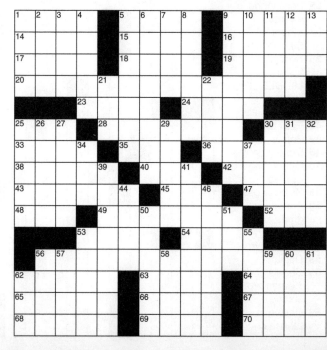

306 GETTING TO WORK

by Matt Gaffney

ACROSS

1 Peters out
5 "Coffee, __ milk?"
10 Side
14 John Irving character
15 Troublemaker
16 "Eat your carrots __ dessert!"
17 START OF A QUIP BY GEORGE WILL
20 In the bag
21 Arts' partner
22 Entryway
24 Gabor et al.
25 Wilde, for one
28 Cut of bacon
30 Puts up
34 Trams transport it
35 Philosopher's inventory?
37 Singer Sedaka
38 Hoot and holler
40 MIDDLE OF QUIP
41 See socially
42 Pack away
43 Pop in
45 Despondent
46 Opera singer Stratas
48 Place to play
50 Annapolis grad.
51 Literary pseudonym
53 Denials
55 *Snows of Kilimanjaro*'s setting
59 California athletes

63 END OF QUIP
65 In the distance
66 Try to be safe?
67 Spread-out
68 Stoolies
69 Presidential nickname
70 Beef dish

DOWN

1 Basket fillers
2 Unadorned
3 Cauldron contents
4 Shell out
5 Libyan city
6 Dawn goddess
7 "Rock of __"
8 Prevention dose
9 Brings back
10 Actor/director Robert
11 Mr. Sevareid
12 Pay to play
13 __ scale (mineral hardness measurement)
18 Pairs
19 Time for a revolution
23 Spokes
25 Defeat decisively
26 Fuming
27 Operatic hero, often
29 Golfer King
31 Stop
32 Real big guy
33 Goes downhill

36 Laotian native
39 Splinter remover
43 Least humble
44 Streetcar
47 Eastern European
49 Do business
52 Supermarket pathway
54 Turns aside
55 Kaiser's counterpart
56 __ Romeo (auto)
57 Shipshape
58 Dry-as-dust
60 Revise a manuscript
61 Uncouth
62 Act like Etna
64 Unmatched

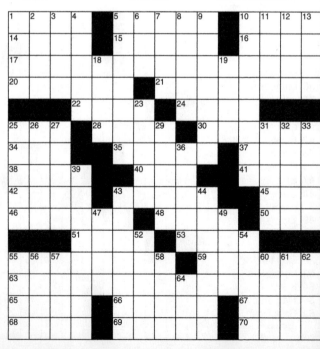

307 CRAFTY

....

by Bob Lubbers

ACROSS
1 Medal metal
5 Made a footnote
10 Top guns
14 Woodwind instrument
15 Do dais duty
16 Taxi tab
17 Wabash feeder
19 Scurry about
20 Game fish
21 Prepares a pump
23 Beer mug
24 Bring up
25 Kitchen worker
31 Bible book
34 Abound
35 Lamb product
36 Dem.'s opponent
37 Word form for "split"
39 Adjective suffix
40 Thoughts
43 "Cheerio!"
44 Be a brat
45 One-man rule
48 Ski lift
49 Set __ for (try to trick)
52 Chosen field
55 Agricultural land
57 Where buns bake
58 Like some tapes
61 Lemon skin
62 Lofty spaces
63 Hornet house
64 Citrus drinks
65 Takes off
66 Nor. neighbor

DOWN
1 *I've __ a Secret*
2 Newspaper pieces
3 '50s pitcher Eddie
4 Push in
5 Tropical treats
6 Mideast power
7 Soaks up rays
8 WWII arena
9 More profound
10 Declares
11 Cool-headed
12 Part of HOMES
13 Prepares the table
18 Homeric
22 Merry Martha
24 Sends cash
26 Church reader
27 Composer Franz
28 Land east of the Urals
29 Fleming and McShane
30 Turns blue
31 Parched
32 Word form for "center"
33 Crude cartel
38 Babe Didrikson __
41 Is present
42 Kemo __
44 Sports injuries
46 Podiatric adjective
47 Particular
50 Former VP
51 "__ porridge hot . . ."
52 Mrs. Dithers
53 Eager
54 Actress Russo
55 Start of a spell
56 Cut coupons
59 Singer Lemper
60 Inc., in Ipswich

308 KITCHEN SET

by Trip Payne

ACROSS

1 Rhône feeder
6 Prudish person
10 Imitated
14 Singing chipmunk
15 Atmosphere
16 Greek philosopher
17 *Peter's Friends* actor
19 The gamut
20 Layer of eggs
21 A, in Arabic
22 In a feeble way
24 __ *and Old Lace*
26 Chair man
27 GE company
28 "__ Bill the Sailor"
31 It'll give you a weigh
34 Shimon of Israel
35 Away from home
36 Cryptogram
37 Shred cheese
38 Dorothy's dog
39 Drillers' org.
40 Golf clubs
41 Memento
42 Singer Elliot
44 "That's it!"
45 __ de Chine
46 Leaving the stage
50 Thelma's friend
52 Thin
53 Director Spike
54 Teacup handles

55 "I Feel Good" singer
58 To be, in Tours
59 Revlon rival
60 Flood barrier
61 *Wide Sargasso Sea* author
62 Biblical trio
63 Roeper's partner

DOWN

1 Figure skater Cohen
2 Change
3 Hot spots
4 Tuck's mate
5 Add value
6 Hysteria
7 Fancy collar
8 Kind of verb: Abbr.

9 French capital's nickname
10 Showy shrub
11 *Beyond the Fringe* star
12 Chemical compound
13 Half asleep
18 Director Kazan
23 Sothern and Jillian
25 Perry's creator
26 Hauls
28 Casserole components
29 Stringed instrument
30 Harrow's rival
31 Racket
32 Musical ending
33 Onetime MTV host

34 Novel medium
37 Toast spread
38 Perfectly
40 Covers cupcakes
41 Sewing item
43 Comes up
44 Imaginary line
46 Nicholas Gage book
47 "__ a Parade"
48 Less established
49 *The Maids* playwright
50 Suggestive look
51 Vow
52 Urban problem
56 Gardner of *Mogambo*
57 Dixie fighter

309 JAM SESSION

by Cox & Rathvon

ACROSS

1 Snack spot
5 Before
10 Exemplar of redness
14 Cadabra preceder
15 Taco topping
16 Like a blue moon
17 Ballerina's support
18 START OF A QUIP
20 Depose
21 Poetic pugilist
22 Trellis climbers
23 PART 2 OF QUIP
27 St. Paul's architect
28 Chocolate Town, USA
32 Blueprints
34 Cookbook direction
36 Before
37 Hamelin pest
38 PART 3 OF QUIP
41 Chicken __ king
42 Grand __ Opry
43 Flying grp.
44 Following
46 Vast holdings
49 Angers
50 PART 4 OF QUIP
54 Rouen's river
57 Gone by
58 Tonsorial request
60 END OF QUIP
63 Back from work
64 Not apt to bite
65 Was slimy
66 Gets by, with "out"
67 Sirius, e.g.
68 Borg or Bergman
69 Garnet and ruby

DOWN

1 Roman orator
2 Approximately
3 Trout's milieu
4 Part of EST
5 As right __
6 Plant stem
7 Borden bovine
8 Barbecue remains
9 Lah-di-__
10 UCLA squad
11 Deserve
12 Canal, lake, or city
13 Roman Polanski film
19 Ended
24 Try out
25 Smell
26 Word form for "sun"
29 Summertime health hazard
30 Della's creator
31 Once around the sun
32 Univ. staffer
33 Composer Schifrin
34 Swiss city
35 "Son __ Preacher Man" ('68 tune)
39 __ tight ship
40 Patio server
45 It tickles
47 Metal worker
48 Hand-me-down
49 Tristan's love
51 Corn color
52 Looked like Lothario
53 Intended
54 Fleet on the ground
55 French state
56 __ *Fugitive from a Chain Gang*
59 Military meal
61 Call for help
62 Drag

310 CALIFORNIANS

by Harvey Estes

ACROSS

1 Caprice
5 "My Heart Skipped __" ('89 tune)
10 Mighty trees
14 Scottish isle
15 Skedaddle
16 Sneaker or sandal
17 Soybean product
18 Like *The Twilight Zone*
19 Knowledge
20 Skelton character
23 Mideast desert
24 Eye problem
25 Oil-can letters
26 Arrange type
27 __ out (removed)
30 Ram's ma'am
31 Finale
32 Botches up
34 Bark sharply
36 CT summer hours
38 Bugs Bunny adversary
42 Revolutionary
43 Griddle
44 Statue stone
47 Smidgen
50 Pen point
52 Bad deal
54 Stolen
55 *You __ There*
56 Head the cast
58 Oxygen isotope
60 Computer-game name
64 Kandinsky colleague
65 "Peter, Peter, Pumpkin-__"
66 Sitarist Shankar
68 *Born Free* lioness
69 *Ghostbusters* goo
70 "Chestnuts roasting __ open fire"
71 Actress Cannon
72 Put up with
73 Harmony

DOWN

1 Cleverness
2 Muncie resident
3 Troop group
4 __ Loa
5 Away from the wind
6 Keg contents
7 Makes a buck
8 Fly a fighter
9 Really small
10 Christiania, today
11 "My kingdom for __!"
12 Seoul man
13 Gardened
21 Get even with
22 Titles
23 Compass pt.
28 Viewer
29 Hoover or Grand Coulee
33 Bart, to Homer
35 Card dot
37 __ Mahal
39 Have a hunch
40 Playground game
41 Furniture wood
45 "Mellow Yellow" fellow
46 When the French fry
47 Raised, as prices
48 By word of mouth
49 Mother of Calcutta
51 Lava rock
53 Hawaiian side dish
57 2 to 1, e.g.
59 WWII planes
61 Nasty
62 Verne captain
63 __ Scott Decision
67 Business abbr.

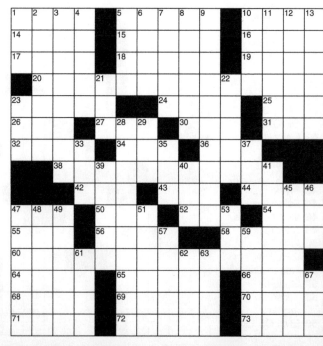

311 *SMARTY PANTS*

by Randolph Ross

ACROSS

1 Nutritionist Davis
7 Rich soil
11 Turkish dignitary
14 Sell to consumers
15 Oklahoma city
16 Let go
17 Beach pants
19 Family members
20 Farm building
21 Actor Tamblyn
22 It's a cinch
23 __ for Sergeants
26 Supporter of the arts?
27 Outdoorsmen's pants
31 Sound of surprise
32 Rest rm.
33 Baltimore athlete
37 Alfresco
39 Meara's partner
40 __ of Innocence (Wharton novel)
41 Apply
42 Bear's lair
43 Girls' pants
47 Cuttlefish cousin
50 Taken care of
51 Cheese chunk
52 "__ she blows!"
53 Algeciras aunts
57 Joplin composition
58 Mod pants
61 Presidential nickname
62 Smell __ (be suspicious)
63 "We __ amused"
64 T-shirt size: Abbr.
65 Active
66 Potters, at times

DOWN

1 Circle sections
2 Knish noshery
3 And so on . . .
4 Mr. Cranston
5 Eye cover
6 Yalie
7 Protein source
8 "Just __!" ("In a moment!")
9 Melodies
10 Hosp. personnel
11 Prepares potatoes
12 Napoleon's fate
13 Streisand role
18 Mourn
22 Pesto ingredient
24 In debt
25 Bartered
26 Most chilling
27 Funny fellow
28 "No dice!"
29 Distinction
30 Summer feature
34 Ye __ Booke Shoppe
35 Lascivious look
36 Marine flappers
38 Tasty
39 Exceptionally good
44 Building stone
45 Fidelity, to Macbeth
46 Not as bland
47 Theater drop
48 Tremble
49 Egged on
52 Univ. of Md. player
54 Actress Skye
55 __ patriae
56 Former JFK jets
58 __-relief
59 Fathead
60 Pod preceder

312 ARRESTED DEVELOPMENT

by D.J. Stone

ACROSS
1 Mighty mite
5 Search for prey
10 Not quite shut
14 All-night dance party
15 Correspondence
16 Bone-dry
17 Bend
18 Foreword
19 No gentleman
20 START OF A HENNY YOUNGMAN QUIP
23 No gentleman
24 Steep
25 Level off
30 Hackney's home
34 Fictional sleuth
35 __ *kleine Nachtmusik*
37 Polk's predecessor
38 Baby bark
39 MIDDLE OF QUIP
41 Actor Tognazzi
42 Jazzman Louis
44 Bjorn opponent
45 Nail type
46 Lodger
48 Cute as a button
50 Lobe probe?
52 Bleak critique
53 END OF QUIP
60 D-Day site
61 Rosey of football
62 Borrow permanently
64 Winglike

65 Touch up
66 Articulated
67 __ a soul (no one)
68 Pub game
69 *The Mikado* character

DOWN
1 Pound plaint
2 Lauder powder
3 Finished
4 Hailing from Hermosillo
5 Nun's kneeler
6 Durban dough
7 Conductor Klemperer
8 On edge
9 Sets free
10 Spittoon

11 Army vehicle
12 Geometry calculation
13 Bank (on)
21 Bad beginning
22 Well-dressed
25 Tut's turf
26 Ream component
27 Remove a brooch
28 Rigatoni relative
29 __ *Gay*
31 Brief ad
32 On the up and up
33 Carve a canyon
36 Writer Bagnold
39 Namibia native

40 Dotted lions?
43 Stonework
45 Asian capital
47 Pulled (on)
49 Writer Santha Rama __
51 Word form for "skin"
53 "Not if __ help it!"
54 Presidential pooch
55 Calendar period
56 Story
57 Coin in Bermuda
58 Superman's lunch?
59 Furniture wood
63 Mideast grp.

313 NUMBER, PLEASE

by Dean Niles

ACROSS

1 Stands up
6 *Moby-Dick* captain
10 Run away
14 Numskull
15 Red herring
16 Hops dryer
17 Contiguous-state count
19 "Do __ others . . ."
20 Before, to Byron
21 Swit sitcom
22 Prison boss
24 Balky
26 Genie's gift
27 Shoebox letters
28 Brown-bag alternative
32 Piano size
35 Recreational racecar
36 __ contendere
37 Take five
38 Antique
39 Spot of liquor
40 "Zounds!" or "Egad!"
41 Rat, to a cat
42 *The __ Bunch*
43 More rad
45 Stain
46 Western coll.
47 Hags
51 Title for Men: Abbr.
54 Word form for "half"
55 Dance, in France
56 Official records

57 Emergency number
60 Avoid
61 Sufficient, slangily
62 Actor Murphy
63 One of Taylor's exes
64 Dustcloths
65 Hearty meal

DOWN

1 Long-term inmate
2 Love a lot
3 Fathers
4 Little guy
5 Frustrated
6 Come up
7 Actor O'Brian
8 Fire aftermath
9 Caught in the middle
10 Exclusive social set
11 Bring the plane in
12 Punta del __
13 007's school
18 Roof edge
23 Lang. for Marlee Matlin
25 Bill with Salmon P. Chase
26 Prolix
28 Farm machine
29 Author Ephron
30 Outfitted
31 Cozy: Var.
32 Sailor's quaff
33 __ *Window*

34 In the matter of
35 Asian nation
41 Light beer
42 Credits in articles
44 Rec-room item
45 Floor model
47 Complaints
48 Where you live
49 Frenzy
50 Glossy
51 Rigging support
52 Talk back?
53 Earring type
54 Cozy
58 One __ million
59 SC summer setting

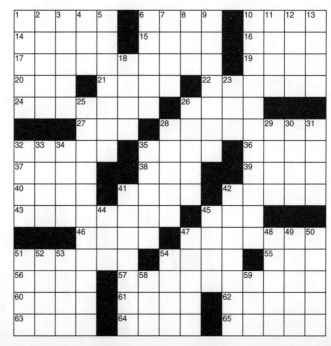

314 BIG SHOTS

by Trip Payne

ACROSS

1 Assessment: Abbr.
5 Enjoy the buffet
10 General Bradley
14 First name in tennis
15 Cover story?
16 Congenial
17 Citation abbreviation
18 "__ Macabre"
19 Paradise
20 He played Frank CANNON
23 One-person performances?
24 Writer Kaufman
25 Exhausted
28 In medias __
30 Guinness Book ending
32 Prior to, to Prior
33 The CANNONball Run actor
38 Hook's mate
39 Reed instrument
40 How fish are packed
41 Crew member
42 Rain buckets
43 CANNONball Express engineer
45 Alf and Mork, for short
46 Toothpaste type
47 __ Lingus
48 Fishes for
50 Prof.'s aides
53 Hold-up man?
57 Dyan CANNON movie
60 Classical figure?
62 Ask for a steak
63 North Indian city
64 Dry-as-dust
65 Rock singer __ Marie
66 Swerve
67 Truckle to
68 Car bomb?
69 Gaelic

DOWN

1 Thinks (over)
2 2:1, e.g.
3 Everything included
4 Hard assignment
5 Actress Thompson
6 Gentle as __
7 Baseballer Coleman
8 Become outdated
9 Zip, to Zola
10 The Main Event actor
11 Intermediary
12 Expert
13 Cartoon chihuahua
21 Psychiatrist's response
22 Squealer
26 Cara of Fame
27 Must-haves
29 Part of life?
31 "Later!"
33 Blockheads
34 Amin's predecessor
35 Jerry's place
36 Still the same
37 Sue Grafton's __ for Innocent
38 Radio type
44 Playwright Anouilh
46 Govt. purchasing org.
49 Green shade
51 Llama's peaks
52 Part of an act
54 Pub order
55 Buenos __
56 Blank look
58 Decide
59 Russian sea
60 Linking words?
61 Do film-editing work

315 CHASED LADIES?

by Cox & Rathvon

ACROSS

1 Cut a little
5 Saharan mount
10 Gear tooth
13 Cuckoo
14 Left the sack
15 Waste
16 Perched on
17 "Whole __ Love" ('70 tune)
18 Level
19 Lombardi or Edwards
21 START OF A QUOTE
23 Gold, to Cortez
25 Attack
26 PART 2 OF QUOTE
30 Human beings
34 Smooths
36 It has its ups and downs
37 Pine tree
38 PART 3 OF QUOTE
40 Bonanza material
41 Proven reliable
45 Contempt
49 Cap and dolman
51 PART 4 OF QUOTE
52 A lot
54 Links goal
55 END OF QUOTE
59 Pundit
63 Ill-boding
64 Chopper
66 Western team?
67 Jejune
68 "__ you" (radioman's reply)
69 Give temporarily
70 Tex-__ (southwestern cuisine)
71 Dweebs
72 Santa's route?

DOWN

1 Eastern European
2 Reply to the Little Red Hen
3 Byzantine art form
4 Theater fare
5 Presidential nickname
6 ". . . maids all in __"
7 Closet pests
8 Prize
9 Humble sheds
10 Happy as a __
11 Seep
12 Dancer Verdon
15 Agnes Grey author
20 Passion deified
22 Sported
24 Lennon's love
26 Presents
27 Projecting window
28 Further downhill
29 Bubble maker
31 "With __ in My Heart"
32 Pine tree
33 Treacly
35 Danson of Cheers
39 Electron's chg.
42 Gave a giggle
43 For all time
44 "__ Venice" (Mann novella)
46 Dandy
47 Nest eggs
48 '80s Borgnine series
50 Globe
53 Ed Norton's workplace
55 Early apple eater
56 Passion
57 Cereal brand
58 Samoa studier
60 Skating jump
61 Dish list
62 "Massa's __ Cold, Cold Ground"
65 Sts.

ACROSS

1 State positively
5 Former mach 1 breakers
9 Worn-out
13 Magic charm
14 Rice dish
15 Royal sport
16 Drained
17 Take __ for the worse
18 German auto
19 Catchall abbr.
20 At a disadvantage
22 Tot's toys
24 Capp and Capone
25 "__ a Rebel" ('62 tune)
26 Had significance
31 __ *homo*
34 Hiding place
35 Peyton's quarterback brother
36 Path to power
40 Overly
41 No longer fresh
42 Pupil's place
43 Fondness
45 '88 Dennis Quaid film
47 Moon lander
48 Endocrine output
52 Suspect
57 Party to NAFTA
58 Ukraine capital
59 Colorado brewery
60 Judd Hirsch sitcom
61 Palindromic women's magazine
62 Lose one's tail?
63 Closed
64 Witnessed
65 __ City, Florida
66 Quarterback option

DOWN

1 Cautionary color
2 West African river
3 Kick out
4 Stewart or Laver
5 Locations
6 Aspersion
7 *Scarlett* setting
8 Catch some rays
9 Thinly scattered
10 Psychiatrist's slot
11 Antique adjective
12 Drudgery
14 Finishes the road
20 Tijuana tribute
21 Let out, perhaps
23 Lieutenant Kojak
26 Dull finish
27 Dull pain
28 Philosopher Descartes
29 Fraternal group
30 Record
31 Singer James
32 Ax stroke
33 Jockey's item
34 Voucher
37 Complete
38 Made a face
39 __ Clayton Powell
44 Football team
45 Soak
46 California base
48 Gang of Goths
49 Cornhusker state city
50 Heart of the matter
51 Theater signs
52 Hawaiian strings
53 Longest river
54 Strike out
55 Fountain order
56 Noisy
60 1/3 tbsp.

317

WHOMEVER

by Matt Gaffney

ACROSS

1 Mensa stats
4 Multimedia corp.
7 __-down (topsy-turvy)
13 Pecan or cashew
14 __ one's toes (stay alert)
15 Infernal
16 By means of
17 *Cuatro y cuatro*
18 Gawky guy?
19 "To Whom __:"
22 Spanish stores
23 New Mexico neighbor
27 Sicilian rumbler
28 Sea dog
30 Olympic hawk
31 Bread or booze
34 Blemish
37 Freudian concepts
38 "With whom __?"
41 Tiffany treasure
43 Soccer great
44 "I told you so!"
45 Melville work
47 Wolfed down
49 Much of Mongolia
53 Thornton Wilder classic
56 Trumpet call
59 *For Whom __*
61 Bring to a boil?
64 Term of address
65 Got together
66 '50s music style
67 Evergreen tree
68 Exist
69 Some chords
70 Broadway sign
71 Alphabet sequence

DOWN

1 Be hospitable
2 "Stop that!"
3 Flower part
4 Hajj destination
5 Share a dais
6 Ever and __
7 Indy winner Al
8 Lab dish
9 Poem part
10 Her, in Hamburg
11 Barely passable grade
12 Go astray
14 William of *Hopalong Cassidy*
20 Cost __ and a leg
21 *Cheers* role
24 Not a dup.
25 Composer Rorem
26 Donkey
29 Red as __
32 Baby bark
33 Language suffix
35 Endorses
36 Men's accessory
38 Cupid
39 Backup
40 South American river
41 Sticky stuff
42 Australian bird
46 Ontario city
48 Rich pastry
50 Texas tycoon
51 Jacket type
52 Shoe part
54 George Burns film
55 Cries
57 Latin American plain
58 "Ma! (He's Making Eyes __)"
60 Realms: Abbr.
61 Erie hrs. in Aug.
62 Postman's Creed word
63 French king

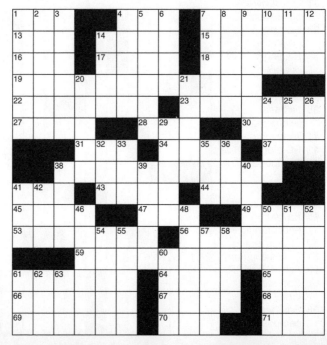

318 PARENTAL RESORT

by Donna J. Stone

ACROSS

1 Silences
5 Unit of loudness
9 "You can __ horse to . . ."
14 Gillette product
15 Campus court
16 Drive forward
17 Attempt
18 New Agey magazine
19 Second to none
20 START OF A QUIP
23 Actor Maximilian
24 __ Alamos, NM
25 Purrfect pet?
27 Hen or pen
28 Lowliest cadets
31 __ de vivre
32 Mr. Koppel
33 Nautical beginning?
34 Singing cowboy
35 MIDDLE OF QUIP
38 Fictional swordsman
41 Teddy trim
42 PD alert
45 Composer Satie
46 Setup
48 Cornhusker st.
49 Be overly encouraging?
50 Smash letters
51 Ty Cobb's team
53 END OF QUIP
57 Capone's crony
58 Southern campus
59 Gobble (down)
61 Nip
62 Pulmonary organ
63 Place for a patch
64 DeMille of dance
65 Dates
66 Risqué

DOWN

1 Helium or hydrogen
2 Lawyer's case?
3 Drew an equation
4 Dark color
5 Cried like a baby
6 Inning components
7 Half an Orkan phrase
8 Swimmer Gertrude
9 Filches
10 Kuwaiti ruler
11 It's often in a jam
12 Hit rock bottom
13 Cockpit fig.
21 Marty Robbins hit
22 Dawn goddess
23 Fast way to the UK, once
26 *The Daughter of Time* author
29 Be human?
30 Cooks in a cauldron
31 Hooch holder
34 Listless
35 Rub the wrong way
36 Napa Valley vessel
37 Bar tool
38 Asian sect
39 Holding forth
40 '60s affirmation
42 Sea animal
43 Confuse
44 Air gun ammo
46 __ Lanka
47 Tyrolean tunes
50 Short shows
52 Stares stupidly
54 To be, in Toulouse
55 Turn about
56 Actor Franchot
57 Cryptic org.
60 Tina of *Mean Girls*

319 *M*A*S*H NOTES*

by Matt Gaffney

ACROSS

1 Iron fishhook
5 Emulate Mahre
8 "So what __ is new?"
12 Divvy up
14 Vandyke site
15 Journalist Jacob
16 Reserve
17 Hockey player Gordie
18 Little devils
19 *M*A*S*H* surgeon
22 Some bills
23 Dispensed the deck
25 Purcell and Miles
29 Usual: Abbr.
30 Cross letters
32 Keep __ (persist)
33 ". . . who lived in __"
35 "Golly!"
36 *M*A*S*H* nurse
40 __ nutshell
41 L.A. athlete
42 "Let __!" ("Who cares?")
43 Impact sound
44 Taxing org.
45 Smart ones, to Wilhelm
47 Dietetic, in ads
49 Naturalist Fossey
51 *M*A*S*H* clerk
57 Mideast canal
59 Marx or Malden
60 Mikhail's missus
61 Actress Bancroft

62 Devil's thing
63 Available
64 Golf club
65 Certain sib
66 Theater constructions

DOWN

1 Wound
2 Utah resort
3 Ebb's partner
4 Service member?
5 Has a ball at the mall
6 Fuzzy fruit
7 Beatles song from *Help!*
8 Author Jong
9 Spots for stars
10 Use a straw
11 Snaky letter
13 Canines and molars
14 Joan of *Twin Peaks*
20 *Si* or *oui*
21 Drive away
24 __ of Innocence ('93 film)
25 Master, in Madras
26 Like Schönberg's music
27 *West Side Story* star
28 Part of A&P
29 Norse god
31 Man of La Mancha
33 Inquires

34 Cow or sow
37 Homeric epic
38 Shares, with "in"
39 Sundial numeral
45 Kids' card game
46 *Año* opener
48 Stunned
49 Actress Day
50 "__ be seeing you!"
52 Sitarist Shankar
53 Smith and Fleming
54 See 47 Across
55 GRE relative
56 Spitz sounds
57 Carpenter's tool
58 Juan's "one"

320 FARM STAND

by Shirley Soloway

ACROSS

1 Doggie delights
6 Word of woe
10 IL hours
13 Deal maker
14 Petunia part
16 Canoeing need
17 CORN
19 Actress Merkel
20 Montana's capital
21 Hypersensitivity
23 Frolic
25 __ Now (Murrow show)
26 Red and Coral
29 CABBAGE, with 47 Across
31 Mil. awards
34 SASE, e.g.
35 Combustible heap
36 Train station
37 __ Dame
39 Murals or mobiles
41 Cropped up
42 Sailing vessel
43 Heavenly bodies
45 AAA offering
46 Lady's man?
47 See 29 Across
49 Movie great
50 Pedro's pots
52 Kitchen addition?
54 Bravery
56 Youth lodging
60 Pacino and Smith
61 PEA
64 Carnival city
65 Uptight
66 At full speed
67 Cross product
68 Action time
69 Artist Matisse

DOWN

1 Tub ritual
2 Grimm creature
3 Diamond or Simon
4 Logs
5 Pool hustler?
6 GI's address
7 Apollo vehicle
8 Colonel's command
9 "Ballad of the Green Berets" singer
10 SQUASH
11 Vocalized
12 Cafeteria carrier
15 Actor Waggoner
18 Amusingly pass
22 Duck down
24 Legal starter
26 Have a hunch
27 Col. Tibbets' mom
28 BEAN
30 Argentine dictator
32 __ Rica
33 Take the reins
35 Zest
36 __ Rheingold
38 Moneybags in "Nancy"
40 Shady character?
44 "Down __ Riverside"
47 Fixed spuds
48 Donny or Marie
49 Tahini base
51 Shopping aid
53 Hebrew scroll
54 David's instrument
55 Nobelist Wiesel
57 Gov. employee
58 Kuwaiti leader
59 Anderson of *Nurses*
62 She-bear: Sp.
63 Mystery writer Josephine

321 FUNNY CARS

by Robin & Norman Landis

ACROSS

1 Write quickly
4 Melville monomaniac
8 Little ones
12 One on a coin?
14 Floor covering, in Falmouth
15 Caribbean country
17 Frank place
18 Song-and-dance vehicle?
20 Seer
22 The good earth
23 __ US Pat. Off.
24 Prefix for "plunk"
25 Stick together
27 Plane engines
31 Electrical unit
32 "What __ mind reader?"
33 Water works?
37 Page number?
38 Rajput wraps
39 Be bold
40 À la *Swann's Way*
42 Religious image: Var.
43 Expeditious
44 Poseidon's prop
47 Ad-lib comedy
49 Self-esteem
50 "No, __ thousand times no!"
51 Smack in the mouth?
54 Lamebrain
58 Little Red Corvette?
61 Mrs. Copperfield
62 __ Martin (007's auto)
63 Author Wiesel
64 Certain spiritual leader
65 To be, to Tiberius
66 Yodelers' perches
67 Spearheaded

DOWN

1 Martial art
2 Lollapalooza
3 Toltec city
4 Francis __ Sinatra
5 Go quickly
6 Landers and Sheridan
7 Galoot
8 "Praise __ and Pass the Ammunition"
9 Boathouse item
10 Wedding dessert
11 Navigate
13 Rockmobile?
16 *Bus Stop* playwright
19 British priests
21 David __ Roth
26 Buffalo Bob's vehicle?
27 Talk hoarsely
28 *Omnia vincit __*
29 Walk-ons
30 Solemn
31 Pass out
34 Special time
35 Disney sci-fi film
36 Posted
38 *All in the Family* surname
41 '74 World's Fair site
45 Colors over
46 "Where Do __?" (*Hair* tune)
47 Actress Swenson
48 Bullwinkle, for one
52 Mets' stadium
53 Peddle
55 Hoodwink
56 Egg on
57 Stated
59 Derek and Diddley
60 Hotshot

322 GLOBAL LETTUCE

by Harvey Estes

ACROSS

1 Poet Teasdale
5 White House pooch
9 To __ (unanimously)
13 US leader
14 Kind of heating
15 Govern
16 Dramatic beginning?
17 Game site
18 Brink
19 Money for Maoists?
22 Velvet finish
23 Bandleader Brown
24 Seize power illegally
26 Clog clearer
28 Legal wrongs
32 Word on a pump
33 Center prefix
35 Corporate VIP
36 Act like an ass?
37 L'Euro?
40 The Kingston __
42 Scoundrel
43 Canadian prov.
44 Musical note
45 Meadow munchers
47 Windy City airport
51 Self-confidence
53 Pussycat companion, in verse
55 Ovine whine
56 Low pay in Madrid?
61 Have a go __ (try)
62 It has strings attached
63 Punta del __
64 Director Clair
65 Commercial constructor
66 Hot spot?
67 Walked
68 __-do-well
69 March 15th, for one

DOWN

1 __-out (dazed)
2 Hood or Tell
3 Eye liner?
4 V __ "Victor"
5 Arden or Sherwood
6 Actor Guinness
7 Turner or Wood
8 Damascus dude
9 Fields of study
10 Fender
11 North African nation
12 Born
14 Manuscript enc.
20 Wed secretly
21 Clear tables
25 Be nosy
27 Evil emperor
29 Earth tone
30 CSA soldier
31 Barcelona bull
34 Move very slowly
36 Soap setting?
37 Man from Manila
38 Actor's signal
39 __ Gay (WWII plane)
40 Kitchen meas.
41 Farm alarm?
45 PAC-money recipient
46 Tulip tree
48 Mistreated
49 Baby's toy
50 Atelier items
52 Stuffed
54 Withdraw
57 Terrible tsar
58 Play favorites
59 Diamond place
60 Nostalgic soda name
61 College major

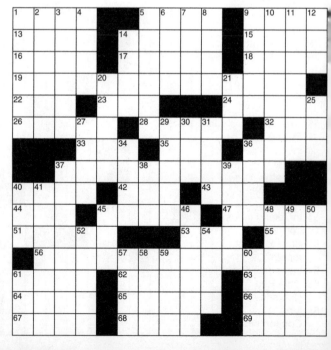

323 AIRPORT COUNTERS

by Randolph Ross

ACROSS

1 Use a crowbar
4 Strong
10 Clock face
14 Chinese philosophy
15 Slit in the sod
16 "Understood"
17 Presidential number-crunchers
20 SSS classification
21 Flight of steps
22 Geog. abbr.
23 "On __ Day"
26 Pay proportionately
28 Something to remember
31 Malicious type
32 Isr. neighbor
33 Monogram pts.
35 Miss Trueheart
36 One million cycles per second
39 Not that great
42 Bristles
43 Ex of Frank
46 Happenings
49 Uncommon sort
51 Excessive bureaucracy
53 Burstyn and Barkin
54 Pitching stat.
55 Moves about at a party
58 Fairy tale opener
59 Cardinal or Padre
63 Sedan seasons
64 Nudges
65 Med. specialty
66 Start over
67 Avers
68 Blvd. crossers

DOWN

1 WWII craft
2 Vulgar
3 Alpine singer
4 Numbered hwy.
5 Crumb
6 River bottoms
7 Textbook heading
8 Throw away
9 Belonging to others
10 Bit of code
11 Quarantine
12 Fills with bubbles
13 Flatt and Pearson
18 Mother of the Titans
19 Cut short
24 "It's a Sin to Tell __"
25 Called up
27 "Puttin' on the __"
29 Farrow and Sara
30 Else
34 __ precedent
36 __ Blanc
37 Undercooked
38 Blue hue
39 More peaceful
40 Celebrated Thanksgiving?
41 Calmed
43 Boulevards
44 *Irises* signature
45 States
47 __-shanter
48 Backbones
50 Sleep like __
52 Put on a pedestal
56 Italian isle
57 Pay-phone feature
60 Bar opener
61 Lea lady
62 Long-eared equine

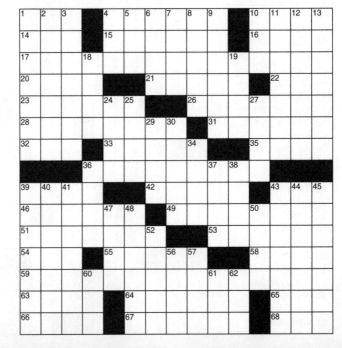

324 KEEP OUT

....

by Matt Gaffney

ACROSS

1 Japanese emperors
8 Sherwood maid
14 Southwesterner
16 __ knife (hobby tool)
17 Rocky Mountain state
18 Turned away
19 Broadcast
20 Big landholder?
22 Never, in Nuremberg
23 Heavenly
25 __ Gigio
29 Minor difficulty
31 Printing measures
32 Mideast gulf
33 __ bell (is familiar)
35 Scandinavian toast
36 KEEP OUT!
40 Boston airport
41 *Watership Down* home
42 Second-hand
43 Metric wts.
44 African tree
48 __ bad example
49 Egyptian leader
51 Baseball stat.
52 Mensa taboo
53 Foreign flier
54 __ on thick (exaggerates)
58 Pain in the neck
61 Consecrate
62 Quit trying
63 Like an oak
64 Moisture

DOWN

1 French wines
2 Unexpected
3 Proper order
4 Black Sea arm
5 Rimsky-Korsakov's *Le Coq __*
6 Out __ limb
7 Egyptian leader
8 Olympic awards
9 Some lines
10 Sought office
11 It's here in France
12 Supped
13 Gesture of approval
15 KEEP OUT!
21 Actress Hedy
23 Like a bee
24 Mailed out
25 __ prisoners (behave aggressively)
26 Bouquet
27 Lawn fertilizer
28 Just
30 Denver suburb
34 Showy trinket
35 Simple weapon
36 Fringe benefit
37 Deep pink
38 "__ Around" ('64 tune)
39 Kill __ killed
43 Like some problems
45 Heathcliff's creator
46 Basic calculator
47 Weightlifter's pride
50 __ Valley, CA
52 "The Swedish Nightingale"
53 Conrad of *Diff'rent Strokes*
54 __ Cruces, NM
55 Aardvark tidbit
56 Second person
57 General's address
59 __ *Got a Secret*
60 Arrange type

325 CLERK WORK

by Randolph Ross

ACROSS

1 Carroll girl
6 Dad's lad
9 Zuider Zee sight
13 *Peter and the Wolf* bird
14 Cad
16 Step __ (hurry)
17 What legal secretaries keep?
20 Overwhelmed by
21 Bo and John
22 President pro __
23 Sell chances
26 Halfhearted welcome at a TV station?
32 Scents
35 Bits of time
36 "King of the Road"
37 American elk
39 Usher
41 Part of HOMES
42 Backtalk
46 Related to mom
47 The sound of many secretaries?
50 Without a key
51 Disfigure
54 Corrida creature
58 Newborn
61 Bad-mouth the boss' visitors?
64 Levin and Gershwin
65 Perry's creator
66 Musical of "Tomorrow"
67 Acerbic
68 Lettuce layer
69 Do a double-take

DOWN

1 Comparative to a fiddle
2 Cleo or Frankie
3 Muslim religion
4 Masticate
5 Smooth the way
6 Rams' horns
7 "__ the fields we go . . ."
8 Buntline or Beatty
9 Entryway
10 Memo words
11 Shot to the shins
12 Parisian's seasons
15 Without a cover
18 Carter's predecessor
19 Cheney, informally
24 Cost
25 TV regulators
26 Prickly plant
27 Newfoundland clock setting: Abbr.
28 Sandal type
29 *State Fair* state
30 News notice
31 Zilch
32 Has obligations
33 Move like a mouse
34 Mayberry boy
38 U-238, e.g.
40 Egg maker
43 From __ Z
44 Thesaurus wd.
45 Stretched over
48 Legendary lawman
49 "__ a Song Go . . ."
51 Exodus food
52 Room at the top
53 Bowler's button
54 Touch up a text
55 Cremona cash, once
56 Russian despot
57 Kiln
59 Actor Sharif
60 Hawaiian goose
62 Celestial body
63 __ du Diable

326 SILENT FEATURE

by Richard Silvestri

ACROSS

1 Willing
5 Croc's cousin
10 Run the stereo
14 Over again
15 Creighton University site
16 Protuberance
17 Scenter of your face?
18 Conditions
19 Humorist Bombeck
20 Contorting
22 Gardener, at times
24 Wrapped up
26 Hints for the future
27 Lively dance
31 Layers
33 "__ for your thoughts?"
35 Sun. talk
36 Buster Brown's dog
40 Signifies
42 Clear-cut
44 Ground cover of a sort
45 Pioneered
47 Esoteric
48 Like some tiles
51 Germany's Pittsburgh
52 Type type
55 Mrs. Gorbachev
57 Give an account
59 Memory aid
64 Marsh bird
65 Sierra __
67 Enthusiastic review
68 Not quite round
69 Formed a fillet
70 Congregational comeback
71 Cincinnati sluggers
72 __ as dust
73 "__ we forget"

DOWN

1 The Jets, e.g.
2 In a bit
3 Butte kin
4 Washstand item
5 Entered
6 Puts right
7 Clay pigeons
8 Resistance unit
9 Kind of file
10 Branch of physics
11 Greene or Michaels
12 Commercial creators
13 *Two __ Before the Mast*
21 Inclined
23 Get moldy
25 *Scott* v. *Sanford* (1857 decision)
27 Writing tablets
28 Amenable (to)
29 Funnyman Jay
30 Smart alecks
32 Region
34 Shout
37 Lupino and Tarbell
38 Splicer's material
39 Macmillan's predecessor
41 Burn
43 Defeat decisively
46 Ring rock
49 Bottom line
50 Banquet meal
52 Glitch
53 Be off
54 Greek epic
56 Run-down
58 Mediterranean isle
60 Articulated
61 June, April, or August
62 Currier's partner
63 Coin
66 Dawn goddess

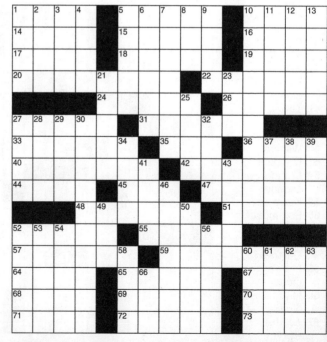

327 FOOD FOR THOUGHT

by Eric Albert

ACROSS

1 Fling
5 Bottom of the barrel
10 Stick in the mud
14 Prime the pot
15 Hit the high points
16 From the top
17 Tragic monarch
18 Stronghold on high
19 Abide
20 START OF A QUIP
23 Asimov genre
24 Salt element
27 List ender
28 *Reversal of Fortune* star
33 Rub clean
34 Bach composition
36 Couturier Cassini
37 MIDDLE OF QUIP
39 Borodin prince
41 "__ you do!"
42 Philanthropist
44 After-school treats
45 Spoil
48 Speak frankly
50 Archie's better half
52 END OF QUIP
57 Oil cartel
59 Serenity
60 Sour substance
61 Genuine
62 Bit-part performer
63 Melody
64 *Casablanca* setting
65 Quite dear
66 Pianist Myra

DOWN

1 *Honor Thy Father* author
2 Like a play without intermission
3 Interference
4 Letter line
5 Pass slowly
6 Stagger
7 Neutral tone
8 Dieter's dread
9 Set of requirements
10 Clumsy
11 Approves, in a way
12 Gun
13 Woolly female
21 Pigeonhole
22 Garden tool
25 Exploit
26 Ryan or Tilly
29 Author Anita
30 Monteverdi character
31 *60 Minutes* correspondent
32 Upper crust
34 Record
35 Be a parrot
37 Unmusical
38 Relaxed
39 Altar answer
40 Republicans, collectively
43 Jog along
45 Error
46 Guitarist Chet
47 Aegean isle
49 Organ pieces
51 __ *Valley Days*
53 On deck
54 Door to a garden
55 *God's Little __*
56 Spring
57 Hobbit foe
58 Princess perturber

328 TAILOR-MADE

by Randolph Ross

ACROSS

1 Have to have
5 O'Hara estate
9 Sonora snacks
14 Comic Johnson
15 Wedding vows
16 Absurd
17 Made amends
20 And others
21 Poetic contraction
22 Kiln
23 Country stopovers
25 Actor Mineo
27 Was apathetic
34 Zodiac sign
35 Prima __
36 Canon camera model
38 Prejudice
39 "Get __!" (remark to a snoop)
40 Small cut
41 Form of ID
42 Stone monument
43 "Some of __ Days"
44 Hesitated
47 Travel org.
48 Prepared to drive
49 Beer
52 __ Paulo, Brazil
55 Villainous looks
59 Insisted
62 Come to terms
63 Entryway
64 Aural
65 High-strung
66 Posted
67 Stadium fillers

DOWN

1 Back of the neck
2 Part of QED
3 Kett of the comics
4 Says no
5 Evening the score
6 Contribute (to)
7 Learning method
8 Tennis great Arthur
9 __ Pan Alley
10 Namibia neighbor
11 Hernando's house
12 Responsibility
13 Opening mo. in HS, usually
18 Allusions
19 Crackers
24 Moved stealthily
26 Nabokov heroine
27 Light touches
28 Like the Blarney Stone
29 Actress Keaton
30 "Look at this!"
31 __ terrible
32 Extend a subscription
33 Dissonance
37 Floored it
39 Relaxed
40 __ meaning (nuances)
42 Little, in Edinburgh
43 "And __ wrote . . ."
45 Hoi polloi
46 Wasteland
49 Petty clash
50 Press
51 Laura or Bruce
53 Totals up
54 Oklahoma tribe
56 "¿Cómo __ usted?"
57 Wreak havoc upon
58 Short times, for short
60 Look at
61 Sweetie

329 AFTER THE COLON

by Trip Payne

ACROSS

1 Library sound
5 "With __ in My Heart"
10 Geometry calculation
14 Capable of
15 Flight part
16 Flight parts
17 *Daily Planet* name
18 Brief argument
19 Labels
20 Subtitle of Thoreau's *Walden*
23 Actress Barkin
24 Part of EST
25 "Eureka!"
27 Mao __-tung
28 Raised cattle
32 Busy place
34 Illinois city
36 __ *Well That Ends Well*
37 Subtitle of Kazantzakis' *The Odyssey*
41 Shepard or King
42 Show to the door
43 Chose one's phrasing
46 *Hawaii Five-O* role
47 Zombie base
50 Rent out
51 Quarterback's resource
53 Kid a bit
55 Subtitle of Richardson's *Pamela*
60 Stoic Greek philosopher
61 Newspaper type
62 *The Egg* __
63 Bellicose deity
64 Schoolroom spinner
65 __ precedent
66 Look deeply
67 __ Park, CO
68 Matchmaker from Olympus

DOWN

1 Young hen
2 Booty
3 Put a lid on
4 "We're Off __ the Wizard"
5 Part of NAACP
6 Galley word
7 Inauguration highlight
8 Informal evenings?
9 Development
10 Choir member
11 Clearly written
12 Off-white
13 Simpleton
21 Sleeping
22 *Deep Space Nine* character
26 Show stoppers?
29 Caviar source
30 Miscalculates
31 Feasted
33 Tightly drawn
34 Swimming hole
35 Cruising, perhaps
37 Skin softener
38 *L.A. Law* actor
39 Long, long time
40 Necessary amount
41 Leatherworking tool
44 Wolf down
45 Menial worker
47 Comic Gilda
48 Familiar with
49 *In __ res*
52 Times at the table
54 Rub out
56 Shade of red
57 Run amok
58 Czech river
59 Exes' followers
60 Turn sharply

330 PARADOX

by Shirley Soloway

ACROSS
1 Part of EMT
5 Melville captain
9 Gray matter
14 Place for pews
15 Roy's missus
16 Mikhail's missus
17 Historic Scott
18 Dross
19 First name in daytime talk
20 Singer K.T.
22 Author Angelou
24 START OF A QUERY
31 Roget wd.
32 1970s TV monogram
33 Get up
34 Does road work
37 In accord
38 MIDDLE OF QUERY
43 Deli draw
44 Ballerina's supports
45 Offshoots
47 Took nourishment
49 VMI or UCLA
52 END OF QUERY
56 Ontario native
57 Animated
58 Hearty entrée
62 Praise highly
65 Privy to
66 In the know
67 "Now __ me down . . ."
68 Indian tourist city
69 Prepared an apple
70 Kitchen addition?
71 Grounded fleet

DOWN
1 Bestows
2 Like the Everglades
3 Actress Keyes
4 Made over
5 Pitches
6 Holbrook or Linden
7 Texas landmark
8 Started
9 NYC thoroughfare
10 Talk to the music
11 Ventilate
12 "Rose __ rose . . ."
13 Slangy negative
21 __ de plume
23 Affirmative vote
25 James or Place
26 Hurt
27 Pro __ (proportionately)
28 Sacred image: var.
29 Sell
30 Chem. suffix
35 '30s movie studio
36 Make a vow
38 Whale of a tale?
39 Black, to Chirac
40 Out of control
41 Lost control
42 Piedmont city
43 Bit part in Shakespeare?
46 HS student
48 Space walk: Abbr.
49 Playground favorites
50 Prance about
51 Laughing carnivores
53 High home
54 Gave out cards
55 Inventor Howe
58 Cul-de-__
59 Deuce
60 Musical sensitivity
61 Anagram of 60 Down
63 Napa vessel
64 Spud bud

331 OUT OF CONTROL

by Manny Nosowsky

ACROSS

1 Speculation
5 Sounds of wonder
9 Curly coifs
14 Lay __ thick
15 Med. sch. subj.
16 Duplicity
17 Lose control
20 Bring bliss to
21 Rabbit kin
22 2004 presidential candidiate
23 Bring on board
25 Greek Cupid
27 Lose control
31 Spanish article
34 October stone
35 Winter bug
36 Downright
38 Lévesque or Clair
39 Damascus' state
42 Advantage
43 Take hold of
45 __ and outs
46 Deli side dish
47 Cheer for a team
48 Lose control
52 Garfield's pal
53 Lee or Teasdale
54 16th-c. queen
57 "Darn!"
59 Nebraska city
63 Lose control
66 Sheeplike
67 Basso Pinza
68 Supreme Court count
69 Tendon
70 Fax, perhaps
71 License plates

DOWN

1 Teeming
2 "__ never work!"
3 Kind of bean
4 Lumber flaws
5 Lout
6 Covertly
7 It's a laugh
8 Sound investment?
9 Palindromic potentate
10 Endows
11 Take public transportation
12 __ podrida
13 Noticed
18 Sinn __ (Irish political group)
19 Mister, in Munich
24 Ring judges
26 Approvals
27 Gershwin character
28 *Tosca*, for example
29 Philippine island
30 Radium researcher
31 Punch server
32 Bach's instrument
33 Distorts
37 One of two Bible portions
40 Washday challenge
41 Home to over two billion
44 The third degree?
49 General assistant?
50 Parts of poems
51 Stepped on
52 Ecology concern
54 Identities
55 First name in jeans
56 Put __ writing
58 Wood trimmer
60 *La Traviata* highlight
61 Suspended
62 Does impressions
64 Fresh from the store
65 Signal assent

332 NON-NOBELISTS

by Matt Gaffney

ACROSS

1 Auction action
4 From A __
7 Kitchen wear
12 Skater Thomas
13 Golfer Ballesteros
14 Augusta's state
15 Poker pair
16 Augury
17 Lobbied for
18 Non-Nobelist for literature
21 Ransom __ Olds
22 Madison or Fifth: Abbr.
23 Disparages testimony
27 Skier Phil
29 Offspring
31 Low digit?
32 Admitting, with "up"
34 James Dean classic
36 Non-Nobelist for peace
39 2004 World Series champs, slangily
40 Backbone-related
41 Zsa Zsa's sister
42 Aegean island
43 Garbo or Nobel
46 Send home, in a way
49 Lamb's mom
50 "__-Gadda-Da-Vida"
52 Non-Nobelist for physics
56 Desert flora
59 Ex-UN member
60 Closed
61 Sigourney Weaver film

62 Women
63 Race parts
64 Trumpet sound
65 Witch's curse
66 Bat wood

DOWN

1 Deprive of wind
2 Michener opus
3 Platter
4 Arizona State site
5 Ended
6 Founder of Stoicism
7 Bring a smile to
8 Second section
9 Fix the outcome
10 Undivided
11 Nancy Drew's boyfriend
12 Knight's counterpart

13 In the black
19 Canal blocker?
20 Poetic vase
24 2002 Olympics site
25 Author Morrison
26 Arrange type
28 Santa sounds
29 Breaks under pressure
30 Today, in Turin
33 "__ Excited" (Pointer Sisters tune)
34 Tackled a bone
35 Comic Eric
36 Maneuver a bishop
37 PDQ relative
38 Jeopardy! questions

39 Place to plant
42 "Am __ understand . . ."
44 Restaurant offerings
45 "No more!"
47 Playful animal
48 North Sea feeder
49 English county
51 Unpopular picnickers
53 Husky command
54 '75 Wimbledon champ
55 __ de Pascua (Easter Island)
56 Hack
57 Every single one
58 Spy grp.

333 OUT OF OFFICE

by Tony Stone

ACROSS
1 Navigator need
4 Rough it
8 Star flower
13 Fancy horseplay?
14 Puccini piece
15 Resort lake
16 *Exodus* author
17 Camera's eye
18 Forebodings
19 Trivia buffs?
22 Bones' partner
23 Roof extension
24 US union
27 *Sí* or *oui*
28 Dadaism founder
31 Cape Verde cash
33 Tiny animals
36 Dry as dust
37 Halloween need?
41 Aware of
42 Greek sea god
43 Spirited session?
45 Jillian or Sothern
46 No. cruncher
49 Sea dog
50 Popular snack cookie
53 Guide down the aisle
55 Slovenly soothsayers?
59 Self-move firm
61 Walked all over
62 Architect Saarinen

63 Ms. Q?
64 Relaxation
65 "Unto us __ is given"
66 Make changes to
67 Does and ewes
68 Fam. member

DOWN
1 It may get a boost
2 __ *Restaurant*
3 Stations sentries
4 Unruffled
5 Space
6 Pie filling
7 High-muck-a-muck
8 Expiates
9 Identical
10 Synonym sources
11 Long time
12 Scale notes
13 Swollen
20 SeaWorld whale
21 "Nobody Knows de Trouble __"
25 Bank agcy.
26 Big vein
29 Babes in motion
30 Jury member
32 NBA team from Ohio
33 "This weighs __!"
34 Street salutation
35 Hammett hound
37 Outlay
38 Draft status
39 Look to heaven?
40 Accumulate
44 Lost ardor
46 Omelet filling
47 Rolls fuel
48 Bad lighting?
51 Senator Kefauver
52 Talk tycoon
54 Start gathering wool
56 Destroy
57 Deep pink
58 Poems of praise
59 UN member
60 Buzz

334 HUE DOWNS ETC.

by Shirley Soloway

ACROSS

1 PD alerts
5 Speak ill of
10 Farm measure
14 Token taker
15 Took a chance
16 Lean-to
17 Mandlikova of tennis
18 Demeanors
19 __ colada
20 GREEN __
23 Fluffy canine, for short
24 Chad, e.g.
25 Sampras shots
27 Join forces
30 Supreme Court member since 1990
33 Tranquil
36 Egotist's love
38 Emporium
39 British beer
40 Lab worker
42 Spy org.
43 Earl Hines' nickname
45 Largest amount
46 Slate, for short
47 Chemical compounds
49 Radiate
51 Part of CEO
52 Very best
56 That woman
58 YELLOW __
62 Ye __ Gift Shoppe
64 Norman Vincent __
65 __ rug (dance)
66 Vivacity
67 James and Kett
68 Month between Shevat and Nisan
69 Sunbeams
70 Mine duct
71 DC figures

DOWN

1 Pale-faced
2 Important person, in urban slang
3 Lisa of *The Cosby Show*
4 Arena
5 Warn
6 Barbara or Conrad
7 Greek war god
8 Transmitted
9 Ford follies
10 Poisonous reptile
11 BLUE __
12 Casino city
13 Dutch cheese
21 Calendar abbr.
22 Birds do it
26 However
28 Really rain
29 *St. __ Fire*
31 Pennsylvania port
32 Peruse the news
33 Eatery
34 "How awful!"
35 RED __
37 Throw out a line
40 Considerate one
41 Most rigid
44 Jinx
46 New York Indians
48 Extents
50 Coll. hoop contest
53 Give off
54 Evil one
55 Peter and Nicholas
56 Gardener, at times
57 Actress Raines
59 Adam's third son
60 "I could __ horse!"
61 Norwegian king
63 Naval off.

335 TRICK-STERS

by Cathy Millhauser

ACROSS

1 Union bane
5 Irish county
10 Canadian Indian
14 English composer
15 Spiral
16 Unctuous
17 BOO-STER?
19 Snoot
20 Nile feature
21 HAM-STER?
23 Record protector
25 Clear a tape
26 Caligula's nephew
28 Spread out
32 Terre Haute coll.
35 Seated Beatle
38 Locust, e.g.
39 SHY-STER?
43 Rumple
44 Shroud site
45 Approvals
46 Race between poles
49 Word form for "within"
51 Humble
54 Burns a bit
58 LOB-STER?
62 Movies' Superman
63 Alligator label
64 OY-STER?
66 Joyce's homeland
67 Emulate Bryan
68 Yearn
69 Den din
70 The Gondoliers character
71 Overdue

DOWN

1 Bits of time, so to speak
2 Catch holder
3 Secret motive
4 Shellacked
5 Wrigley Field box score letters
6 Opposite of dextro-
7 Animated
8 Stand for a soprano
9 Supernumeraries
10 Musical composition
11 Run wild
12 Additional
13 Ogler
18 Watering hole
22 Egyptian snake
24 Estrada of CHiPs
27 "Step __!"
29 Woody's boy
30 Work period
31 "Why don't we?"
32 Tenets
33 Synagogue
34 Heavenly bear
36 Dik-dik's cousin
37 Baddie
40 NHL player
41 French wines
42 Jawaharlal's daughter
47 Kimono sash
48 Animal on the gridiron
50 The Hairy Ape playwright
52 Future fern
53 Aunt __ Cope Book
55 Columbus's birthplace
56 Olympic contest
57 Coat material
58 Bleacher feature
59 Pinza of South Pacific
60 Writer Ephron
61 Makes a choice
65 Meadow

336 FOWL-MOUTHED

by Donna J. Stone

ACROSS

1 Stayed put
5 Heston role
10 Actress Chase
14 Pinza of the Met
15 Sierra __
16 Slave
17 *Alice's Restaurant* name
18 THE WORD DEFINED
20 Retreat
21 Elsa's mistress
22 Fermented tea
23 Actress Stapleton
25 Black plus white
26 Place for a blade
29 Linen in the beginnin'?
30 Dawber of *My Sister Sam*
33 Fate
34 Job opening
35 Mrs. Zeus
36 START OF A DEFINITION
39 Red ink
40 Skirt shaper
41 Pipe cleaner?
42 Mislead
43 Dame Hess
44 Wine home
45 Clean a counter
46 Sheet of stamps
47 Unmitigated
50 DC bigwig
51 Call it a day
55 END OF DEFINITION

57 Provo's home
58 Safe place?
59 Well's partner
60 *Bus Stop* playwright
61 Man from Mayberry
62 Artist's subjects
63 Light gas

DOWN

1 Get better
2 Pound of poetry
3 Caron role
4 Entryway features
5 Biblical prophet
6 Bucket of bolts
7 Clone
8 Chemical suffix
9 Pretty up
10 Land of lasagna
11 Timber wolf
12 Potter's need
13 Shake __ (hurry)
19 Wheedle
24 Handy bit of Latin
25 Library fixture
26 Cranium
27 Asian capital
28 Rub out
29 Plant life
30 Pansy part
31 Fight site
32 Estate house
34 Salt away
35 Comic character

37 Tut or Mubarak
38 Temptation location
43 Ho Chi __
44 Jet-set site
45 Off-the-wall
46 Get one's goat
47 "Waterloo" group
48 Nolan of baseball
49 *The Fountainhead* author
50 Lose control
52 Magazine subtitled "A different read on life"
53 *Othello* heavy
54 Not now
56 Actor Gulager

337 BRACE YOURSELF

by Dean Niles

ACROSS

1 Triumphant cries
5 Latin parent
10 Prepare potatoes
14 Hamlet
15 *M* man
16 The younger Guthrie
17 Good match
19 Journalist Jacob
20 Full-blown
21 "__ Up Before You Go-Go" ('84 tune)
23 Jury member
25 Insignificant quantities
26 Historic period
29 Southeast Asian
30 Sufficient, poetically
31 Kind of game
33 Leaves
37 Marsh plant
38 "__ Rock" ('66 song)
39 '92 Disney film
43 Computer peripheral
46 Movie theater
47 Sleep stage
48 Conclude
49 Ode division
52 Strikebreaker
54 "Born in __" ('84 song)
55 Selfishness
59 Masterson colleague
60 Stand-in
64 Close examination: Abbr.
65 Fuming
66 Ger.
67 Biblical graffito
68 Mans the bar
69 Fr. holy women

DOWN

1 "__ boy!"
2 Wolf wail
3 Way off base?
4 Be nosy
5 Tableland
6 NASA affirmative
7 Angle starter
8 Seabird
9 Claret, e.g.
10 Samuel Clemens
11 Sharon of Israel
12 *Ghostbusters* goo
13 Wets (down)
18 Gas and coal
22 On
24 Computer acronym
25 Koppel or Kennedy
26 Bible book
27 Stagger about
28 Neck of the woods
32 Simon play, with *The*
34 Assess
35 Govt. agents
36 Gemstone
40 Short swims
41 Occupy
42 Formerly known as
43 Number 7 on a telephone
44 Falls back
45 Adult insect
49 Cook veggies
50 Macbeth's title
51 Showed again
53 Matches
56 Cynical rejoinder
57 Swing around
58 Shea men
61 Mine find
62 Mr. Quayle
63 Since 1/1, to a CPA

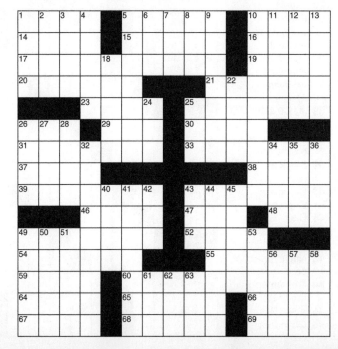

338 JUST ADD WATER

by Eric Albert

ACROSS
1 Green stone
5 Journalist Joseph
10 Handle Bazookas?
14 Evangelist Roberts
15 Longest French river
16 Solemn assurance
17 JUST ADD WATER
20 Tee preceder
21 Tyler's successor
22 Kobe robe
23 Piece
24 Postwar alliance
25 Pooh's pal
28 Die
29 *Dallas* network
32 Culinary by-product
33 Green Hornet's assistant
34 Baldwin of *Malice*
35 JUST ADD WATER
38 Their jobs are on the line
39 Black as night
40 Composer Copland
41 Deli preference
42 Hill dwellers
43 Ninja Turtle, for one
44 Trek among the trees
45 Actor Richard
46 Obscures
49 Cabbage cousin
50 Actor Vigoda
53 JUST ADD WATER
56 Singer Guthrie
57 Like Yale's walls
58 Union Jack, for one
59 __ *Gynt*
60 Easy mark
61 Big bash

DOWN
1 San __, CA
2 Large boats
3 Honoree's platform
4 North Pole worker
5 Total
6 Lazes about
7 Under the weather
8 Great Bruin
9 Baby game
10 Women's mag
11 Angel topper
12 Thames town
13 Owl howl
18 Show up
19 Locale
23 *Stand and Deliver* star
24 Missing marbles
25 Sulky horse
26 Dramatic device
27 Tevye's wife
28 Wine vats
29 Bow or Barton
30 "Don't __ it!"
31 Bouquet
33 Kunta of *Roots*
34 Hard stone
36 Firing notice
37 Hardy's other half
42 Hired helper
43 Tune
44 Indulge
45 Opens wide
46 Applaud
47 Group knowledge
48 Stare at
49 Craft a cardigan
50 Proficient
51 Cop's route
52 Border
54 Eggs
55 Deviating from

339 SAFARI SIGHTS

by Bob Lubbers

ACROSS

1 Dreary
5 Get better
9 Music org.
14 Double agent
15 *Casablanca* character
16 Yale yell
17 Pith helmets?
19 Singer Skinnay
20 Truth
22 Curved molding
23 Bring from overseas
26 Pink tones
28 Actor O'Shea
29 Boom-bah preceder
32 Rich soil
33 "What's in __?"
35 Hang around
37 Little devil
40 Damp
41 Plastic __ Band
42 *L.A. Law* character
44 9-digit ID
45 Sword handles
47 "Jezebel" singer
48 Devour Dickens
50 Blonde shade
52 Regretful one
53 Prime-time choice
56 Los __, NM
58 Sgt. Friday's employer
59 Tropical malady
62 Meat jelly
64 Kenyan claret?

68 Martin or Lawrence
69 Hawaiian city
70 Religious image
71 "... after they've seen __"
72 One-pot dinner
73 Ago, to Burns

DOWN

1 Auto bur.
2 Caviar
3 One's partner
4 Realtor's concern
5 Drummer's cymbals
6 Mideast airline
7 __ spumante
8 Holds up
9 Fortas or Burrows
10 California city
11 Home with a river view?
12 Foreign
13 Matador maneuvers
18 Painter Gerard __ Borch
21 Southern address?
23 Muslim leaders
24 Underworld judge
25 Serengeti singer?
27 True-blue
30 Object of worship
31 Yearly visitor
34 Fictional Frome
36 Setback
38 *Exodus* actor
39 Looks intently
43 Unique character
46 The same as before
49 Salad ingredient
51 '30s film vamp
53 Anklet feature
54 "¡__ mañana!"
55 Wood strips
57 Fracture facts
60 Café au __
61 Skilled
63 Passing grade
65 Frosty
66 __ sequitur
67 Vane letters

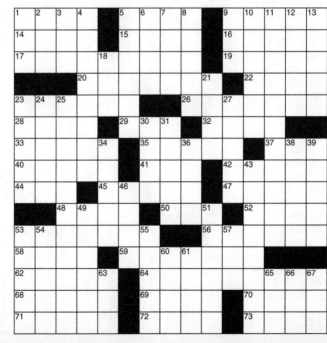

340 FOUR DOWN

by Dean Niles

ACROSS
1 Atlas material
5 Third Greek letter
10 Con game
14 First shepherd
15 Sky hunter
16 Mountain lion
17 Bring up
18 Full of sediment
19 Mine extracts
20 Blah, blah, blah . . .
21 DOWN
23 Chicago Bears coach George
25 Tackled the trail
26 Signal once more
28 Verdon and Stefani
30 Feverish feelings
31 Subatomic particle
32 Indicate approval
35 Steady stare
36 Eccentric
37 Body, in biology
38 Cabinetmaker's tool
39 Cease, to a sailor
40 __ on (fussed over)
41 Gray poem
42 Reno business
43 Engine
45 Wading bird
46 DOWN
49 Writing tablet
52 "Hi-__, Hi-Lo"

53 On the lookout
54 Dog-food name
55 Actor Baldwin
56 Have a feeling
57 Folk singer Joan
58 Combats
59 Passover meal
60 *Jane __*

DOWN
1 Full-grown filly
2 Help a hood
3 DOWN
4 Type of camera: Abbr.
5 Attend unaccompanied
6 Opera highlights
7 Pepper holder
8 Lorre role
9 No place in particular
10 Scares
11 Nobelist Marie
12 Make a change
13 Sail support
21 "Woe is me!"
22 In the __ (healthy)
24 Sheltered, at sea
26 Indian music
27 Old-fashioned oath
28 Having moxie
29 Imperfection
31 Marsh, for short
32 DOWN
33 Harbinger

34 Column part
36 Cloverleaf feature
37 Mediocre
39 Matty or Felipe
40 Pub projectile
41 Moral principles
42 Middle
43 __ letter (use the post office)
44 Famous Canadian physician
45 Pinto or palomino
46 Talon
47 Run away
48 Tear apart
50 Mimic
51 Snooze
54 Presidential nickname

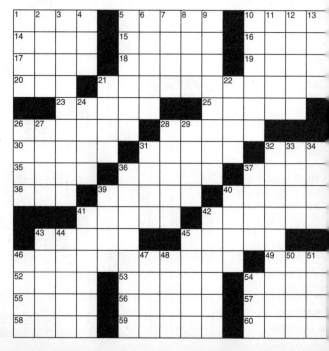

341 INDEPENDENT LADIES

by Matt Gaffney

ACROSS
1 Epic stories
6 Walled city
13 Senator Lott
14 Senate topic
15 Act one?
17 Longfellow subject
18 Cross product
19 "It's a Sin __ a Lie"
21 City on the Rhône
22 Smack
24 Lemieux's grp.
25 Pug or peke
27 Star Wars abbr.
28 Asleep on the job
30 Used to be
33 Jonas Savimbi, e.g.
35 Singer Bonnie
37 Independent ladies of TV
40 Zinc __ (skin protector)
41 Pulled a scam
42 Affirmative answer
43 Furrier family
45 NFL div.
47 And so on: Abbr.
48 Actress Hagen
49 Bridge coup
51 Get better
54 Dried fruit
57 Undivided
58 Some numbers
60 Noted naturalist
62 Domino's delivery
63 Good, to Garcia

64 Cold spells
65 Scatter

DOWN
1 Telegram interruptions
2 Van Cleef's partner
3 *A League of Their Own* actress
4 Landers or Sothern
5 Editor's order
6 Throw in the clink
7 Honors
8 Born yesterday
9 *The Name of the Rose* setting
10 Paris or Hoboken
11 Hostess snack cake
12 __ even keel
14 Independent ladies of film
16 "Da Doo __" ('63 tune)
20 Liberals
23 Longed (for)
26 *Hamlet* character
29 Some ads
30 Roadside blossom
31 Had for dessert
32 Pig pad
34 Like Gatsby
36 Bailiwicks
37 Actress Myrna

38 Timber tool
39 "What __" (Ditto)
44 Rasp
46 Feline nemesis
47 Role for Audrey
50 "Nothing can stop __!"
51 Kachina craftsman
52 Bana of "Troy"
53 Woodworking tool
55 MacGraw and Baba
56 Collars a crook
59 Coax and coax
61 Groove

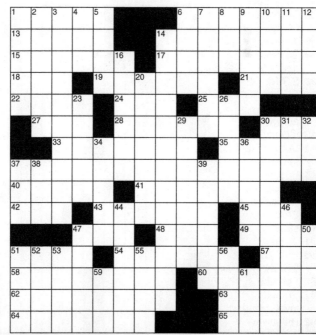

342 BEDSIDE MANNER

by Donna J. Stone

ACROSS

1 __ Krishna
5 Ran, as dyes
9 Bates' bailiwick
14 Churchill's successor
15 Key signature?
16 Duck
17 Singer Falana
18 Elvis' daughter
19 Statement entry
20 SUBJECT OF DEFINITION
23 Bell ringer
24 Dick Tracy's girlfriend
25 Coffee break
28 "Old Blood and Guts"
32 Boxer Jake La __
36 Killer whale
38 Strong desire
39 START OF DEFINITION
42 Pasteur portrayer
43 Identify
44 "And Jill came tumbling __"
45 Sudden emotions
47 Lily locale
49 Stocking stuffers
51 __ pie
56 END OF DEFINITION
60 Perhaps
61 Show favoritism (for)
62 Hideaway
63 Little women
64 Mystery man?
65 Comic Johnson
66 Winter weather
67 Forest fauna
68 Ginger cookie

DOWN

1 Pitches in
2 Really like
3 Let up
4 Legislate
5 Column credit
6 Secular
7 Actress Lanchester
8 Dispensed
9 A Gorgon
10 Cram
11 Can openers
12 Singer Adams
13 "__ bygones be bygones"
21 Bar mitzvah reading
22 High kingdom
26 Couch
27 Walk heavily
29 Run lightly
30 Grimm creature
31 Within earshot
32 Some PTA members
33 "Movin' __" (*The Jeffersons* theme)
34 Narrow shoe size
35 Like some watchbands
37 Role for Liz
40 Beginning
41 Peace Nobelist of '78
46 Annoy
48 Less messy
50 Tatter
52 Marner of fiction
53 Hunger (for)
54 Singer Bryant
55 Throat bug
56 Howl
57 Thornfield governess
58 The old days
59 Rod
60 Booker T. and the __

343 FOOD INDIGO

by Dean Niles

ACROSS

1 Two tuba toots
7 Chore
10 Lose tension
13 Curly or Moe
14 Physically sound
15 Zero
16 Tea man
17 Broad sts.
18 He stung like a bee
19 Greek mountain
20 Music category
22 Nourished
23 Choreographer Tharp
25 Piano piece
27 Vietnamese capital
30 Major mess
33 Puts into office
35 Partially existent
39 Bibl. book
40 Socrates' student
42 Revolve
43 Where one stands
45 Took the measure of
47 Locker-room hangings
49 Uprisings
50 Romantic expedition
53 Grammarian's concern
55 Keats' container
56 Classical hunk
59 Equal
63 Turkish title
64 Drug buster
65 High-class hound
67 Wine word
68 Move slowly
69 Got a look at
70 Adherent suffix
71 Rebel grp.
72 Settled down

DOWN

1 Cold capital
2 Elevator man
3 Swabs
4 Blue snack
5 Past
6 Funny Youngman
7 Al Hirt tune
8 Couturier Cassini
9 Ask on bended knee
10 Complete botch
11 Felt unwell
12 Sail along
14 Blue drink
21 Subordinate Claus?
24 Wilde was one
26 Blue candy
27 Dickensian clerk
28 Not to mention
29 Clears
31 Social worker?
32 Highlander
34 Quick trip
36 Vehicle
37 Waste allowance
38 Wraps up
41 Singer Rawls
44 "Best Picture" of 1997
46 Work unit
48 Govt. assistance
50 Resembling, at first
51 Prods along
52 Put into law
54 Ski spot
57 Rather and Quayle
58 Bo Derek film
60 Modify text
61 "Waiting for the Robert __"
62 Comic Foxx
66 Sweet suffix

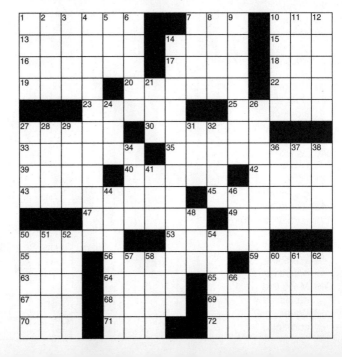

344 MOVIE TITLES

by Manny Nosowsky

ACROSS
1 Sarcastic salutation
7 Takes off
14 Congenital
15 Beg
16 MacLaine film
18 Crack up
19 __-pocus
20 "Jingle Bells" preposition
21 Knight time?
22 Napoleon's troops
23 Monogram ltr.
24 Undivided
25 Lingerie items
26 Solemn peal
27 Hwys.
28 Phnom __
29 Steed seat
30 Milan money, at one time
31 Peppy
32 Not in class
35 Put-on
36 Scepter's sidekick
39 Electronics device
40 Tara resident
41 PBS benefactor
42 "Rabbi Ben __" (Browning work)
43 Spare spot
44 Went like hotcakes
45 Move like molasses
46 Water pipe contents
47 Aries month
48 Tati film
51 Murmuring
52 Rise and shine
53 Unbeatable foes
54 Assembly instruction

DOWN
1 Hardest substance
2 Toughs it out
3 Humiliate
4 Tiber town
5 Outrage
6 Vote into the Hall of Fame
7 Low cards
8 Come after
9 School grps.
10 Some collectibles
11 Did planning-commission work
12 Get sick
13 Surprise
16 Daley in Chicago, e.g.
17 Pizazz
22 Tip off
23 Place to race
25 Book binding
26 Destiny
29 Initiate ignition
30 Castor's mother
31 Enlist the unwilling
32 NBA coach Rick
33 Really weird
34 Cereal grass
35 Cold-shoulders
36 Not in stock
37 Plymouth model
38 Not well
40 Speechifies
43 Paddle pin
44 Director Lee
46 Some sandwiches
47 Word of woe
49 Take advantage of
50 Have property

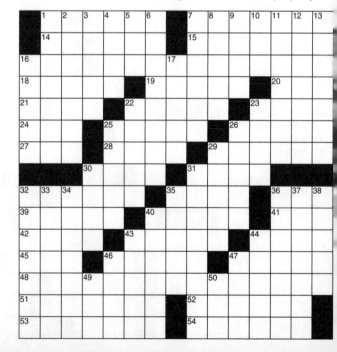

345 *EGO TRIP*

by Bob Lubbers

ACROSS

1 *Cheers* order
5 Foxy
8 Make a choice
14 Stamped over
16 Asian ass
17 Self-defense testifier?
18 Oblique maneuvers
19 Barracks assignments
20 Make a match
21 Do a Little bit
22 One of the Great ones?
23 Greek vowels
25 Worker's ID
26 Classic cars
27 Remnant
28 Runs second
30 Subjective lady?
32 Himalayan people
34 A mean Amin
37 Conscience?
39 Onetime Atl. crosser
40 Under __ (tranquilized)
42 Photographer's abbr.
44 Long-eared leapers
45 Some ships: Abbr.
47 "__ a Song Go ..."
51 John __ Passos
52 Durango dough
53 Prefix for "drama"
54 Mountain peak
55 __ Moines, IA
56 Actor Rod
59 "__ Through the Tulips"
61 Self-awareness?
62 Kind of play
63 Sporty Chevy
64 Read carefully
65 Craving
66 Supreme leader?

DOWN

1 Corruptive one
2 Fix a lamp
3 Actor Estevez
4 Dull
5 Dele's opposite
6 __ Antilles
7 Football stats.
8 Medicine measures
9 Oklahoma town
10 Dishonorable sort
11 Mirrors?
12 Profundity
13 Gaelic
15 Compass dir.
20 Carried on
24 Room renters
25 Mercury's sun
27 He loved Lucy
28 Suburbanite's obsession
29 Between game and match
31 Pelts
33 Poet's family
34 Sort of: Suff.
35 Due date
36 Self-promoter?
38 Waters down
41 Loser to DDE
43 One that restrains
46 __ Lee Browne
48 Smooth, to Solti
49 Votes in
50 Rich cakes
52 Golfer Calvin
54 At the summit
55 Physicians, for short
57 Actor Rip
58 Part of SASE
60 Frat letter
61 Frosty

346 SOLVE FOR X

by Fred Piscop

ACROSS

1 Musical chord
6 Atkins diet no-no
10 Guitar device
14 Esther of *Good Times*
15 Controversial tree spray
16 Arabian sultanate
17 X
20 Develop slowly
21 Hon
22 Involved with
24 Making a racket
25 Richardson novel
29 Globetrotter Meadowlark
32 2001, for one
33 Lifting device
34 __ Lanka
37 X
41 __ *Life to Live*
42 Norse pantheon
43 Sty cry
44 Old-fashioned footwear
45 Fish-eating hawk
47 Mutual of __ insurance
50 "__ Enchanted Evening"
52 Former NFL commissioner
55 Jay and the Americans tune
60 X
62 __ *of Eden*
63 Currency replaced in 2002
64 Bamboo eater
65 Horse-drawn cart
66 Former Senator Simpson
67 Moral infrastructure

DOWN

1 Math subject
2 Macbeth or Mork
3 Woes
4 Came down
5 Report fully
6 Proofer's mark
7 Pie __ mode
8 Squealers
9 Make beer
10 Inducement
11 Valuable violin
12 *Is __ Burning?*
13 Musically correct
18 Sicilian peak
19 Latino lady
23 Southern school, familiarly
25 Word form for "fire"
26 A long, long time
27 Russell role
28 Pitcher's stat.
30 "Be it __ so humble . . ."
31 Mal de __
33 Satyric trait
34 Recipe instruction
35 M. Descartes
36 Very dark
38 Incendiary substance
39 Teachers' org.
40 Chop off
44 Like some rock formations
45 General Bradley
46 Mexican shawl
47 Rounded
48 Tooth type
49 California town
51 Most of the world
53 "Whatever __ Wants"
54 Wicked
56 Rat-__ (drum sound)
57 Ho Chi __
58 __-European
59 Turkish rulers
61 Lyricist Gershwin

347 MR. SUSPENSE

by Matt Gaffney

ACROSS

1 Film by 35 Across
7 Film by 35 Across
15 Approximately
16 "See ya!" in Sapporo
17 __ scales (influence)
18 Sets up
19 Summer quencher
20 Dinner course
22 Emulates Ross
23 Journalist Jacob
24 A little too suggestive?
25 Gouge the gullible
28 It falls in fall
30 *Star Wars* princess
31 Coll. cadets
32 G-men
35 Master of suspense
40 Deli order
41 Tear up the track
42 __-de-camp
43 Squeakers
44 Pint-size
47 Portuguese protectorate
50 Pay-stub abbr.
51 Footnote abbr.
52 More courageous
54 Where blokes get news
57 Film by 35 Across
59 Gather together
61 Man on *M*A*S*H*

62 Colonel's command
63 Picked
64 Film by 35 Across

DOWN

1 __ Hari
2 Like a desert
3 Film by 35 Across
4 Pecan or cashew
5 Be part of
6 Ideal
7 Nicholas and Alexander
8 Rabbit relative
9 Brontë heroine
10 Sort of snake
11 __ Court (British legal societies)
12 Rants and raves
13 Ms. Barrymore et al.
14 Fresh
21 Suit accompaniment
24 P.D.Q. __
25 Collaosed
26 Pickpocket
27 Musical ability
28 Place to park
29 Footnote abbr.
30 Chem room
31 Edge
32 Nip in the bud
33 A follower?
34 '50s nickname
36 Bass Pinza
37 Bashful's colleague

38 Garden tool
39 Purrer
43 Dorothy of *Peyton Place*
44 Actress Ullmann
45 Martian feature
46 Seer's cards
47 Arizona sights
48 __ *of Two Cities*
49 Conspiracy
50 Capacitance unit
52 Slug
53 Discourteous
54 Bric-a-__
55 Big party
56 *The People's Choice* basset
58 Tic-__-toe
60 Spanish king

348 CAPITAL PUN-ISHMENT

by Trip Payne

ACROSS

1 Long gone
5 Non-elite types?
10 Reverberate
14 Hankering
15 Stupefy
16 Wet forecast
17 Reverse, e.g.
18 Croc kin
19 Russian-born artist
20 Italian hotel feature?
23 Masticates
25 Comes back
28 French leeches?
31 *M*A*S*H* country
32 Part of NAACP
33 Young fella
34 Individual
35 Band instrument
36 Flowers' home
37 Plump
41 Because
42 Swedish rock group
46 Enthusiast
47 Chow from 31 Across?
49 In a singular way
51 "__ Romance" (Kern tune)
52 Irish backgammon equipment?
55 Bread spread
57 Slogan specialist
58 "__ la vie"
61 Actress Anderson
62 Annoy
63 Office hangings?
64 Computer input
65 Marine raptors
66 Rapid City's st.

DOWN

1 Porky or Petunia
2 Did lunch
3 Trick-or-treaters, perhaps
4 Add something extra
5 Patti of music
6 "__ corny as Kansas . . ."
7 Provided the banquet
8 Possession of Portugal
9 Start a match
10 Muscle that raises
11 Vocations
12 Top-10 song
13 Wee hour
21 Bks.-to-be
22 Signed a contract
23 April 15 VIP
24 Possesses
26 Old-time auto
27 __ Angelo, TX
29 "Now __ me . . ."
30 Put a strain on
34 Cuzco's country
35 Bush
36 Show disapproval
37 Winter bug
38 Nol of Cambodia
39 Clear
40 Big Californian
41 Nobelist Richard
42 Influences
43 Gem State cap.
44 __ vivant
45 *Fables in Slang* author
47 Curving fastball
48 Dr. Frankenstein's workplace
50 Cheer
53 Beer buy
54 French article
55 Antique
56 Mauna __
59 Vast expanse
60 "Naughty, naughty!"

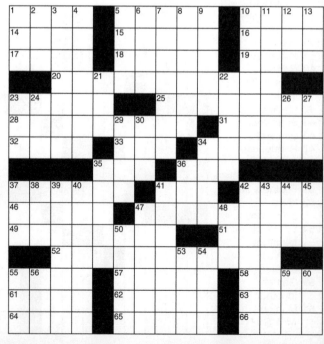

349 FINAL THREESOME

by Dean Niles

ACROSS
1 Newts
5 Pull a con
9 Indian chief
14 "It's a Sin to Tell __"
15 Sign of sanctity
16 Send packing
17 Stuff to the gills
18 __ instant (at once)
19 *Dancer at the Bar* artist
20 Reproductive material
23 Foot part
24 Take advantage of
25 Robert Edward __
26 Tijuana cheer
29 Start
31 Gleamed faintly
34 Home: Abbr.
36 Track alternative
37 State of confusion
38 Buried-treasure direction
42 Love god
43 Wine cooler?
44 "Poppycock!"
45 Aquatic sport
48 Workaholic sort
52 Get a load of
53 CT hours
54 Vietnamese New Year
56 Nav. rank
57 Take a nap
60 Idiosyncrasy
64 Rubs the wrong way
65 __ terrier
66 Correspondence
67 Like autumn leaves
68 Legs, so to speak
69 Attack
70 Musical Myra
71 Fr. holy women

DOWN
1 "__ Be Hard" ('69 song)
2 Perfume bottle
3 Church offerings
4 Crystal gazer
5 Wedges
6 Kayak cousins
7 "Oh dear!"
8 *2001*... stone
9 Use a coupon
10 Bunyan's tool
11 Sprightly dance
12 __ carte
13 "__ So Fine" ('63 tune)
21 Peripheral
22 Dues payer
26 Popular cookie
27 For fear that
28 Asner and Wynn
30 Clean the blackboard
32 Monopoly prop
33 Meaningless
35 __ grade (goes from 1st to 3rd)
38 Medical photo
39 Tiny bit
40 From Edinburgh
41 __ voce (softly)
42 Flock female
46 Calculate
47 Outsiders
49 Observe on the sly
50 Pepsin, e.g.
51 Take the measure of
55 Some curves
58 Algonquian language
59 E-mail contents
60 P-T link
61 Dubai's loc.
62 *Addams Family* cousin
63 __ *Bravo* ('59 film)

350 TINTED TUNES

by Bob Lubbers

ACROSS

1 Sloop feature
5 Matinee __
9 Fit for a king
14 Sapporo sport
15 Completed
16 Actress Verdugo
17 Dorsey tune
19 Narratives
20 Unfair treatment
21 __ Paulo, Brazil
23 Nav. concern
24 Specks of land
26 Chopper blades
28 Common contraction
31 Fatty substance
33 "__ You Lonesome Tonight?"
34 Strauss opera
37 Facilitate a felony
40 Bottom of the barrel
42 California county
43 Very serious
44 Seal
45 Expressed a view
47 __ Tin Tin
48 Read the paper
50 *As You Like It* setting
52 Coincidences
54 Rooms at the Ritz
57 __ Lingus
58 Teachers'. gp.
60 Church spire
64 Called strikes
66 Irving Berlin tune of '27
68 Nick of *Cape Fear*
69 Actor Neeson
70 Greek letters
71 Curl one's lip
72 Snaky fish
73 Architectural detail

DOWN

1 Ch. title
2 Atmosphere
3 Fish-eating duck
4 Wheel adjustments
5 Paragon
6 Moriarty's creator
7 Single
8 Minus
9 Update the factory
10 Pay ending
11 Top-10 tune of '61
12 Keep __ to the ground
13 Endures
18 Robin roosts
22 Ms. Francis
25 Tales
27 Despicable one
28 Arrest
29 General vicinity
30 Bing Crosby tune
32 Obote's foe
35 "Are you a man or __?"
36 Drinks like a Doberman
38 New York county
39 Ark. neighbor
41 Go after
46 Palm produce
49 Provide
51 Smelled strongly
52 Rural deities
53 Crummy car
55 Run-of-the-mill
56 "Ten __ or less"
59 Can-do
61 Bread with a pocket
62 Call the shots
63 Exxon's ex-name
65 When Strasbourg sizzles
67 Fib

351 FORGET IT!

by Donna J. Stone

ACROSS
1 Olympic VIP
5 __ buddies
10 Scoundrels
14 *Lohengrin* soprano
15 It multiplies by dividing
16 "__ forgive those . . ."
17 Carol word
18 Column style
19 Analyze poetry
20 START OF A QUOTE BY RITA MAE BROWN
23 Biscayne Bay city
26 Offspring
27 Compass pt.
28 Ms. Huston
32 Ocean's motions
34 Dwight, on campaign buttons
35 Bulwark
38 MIDDLE OF QUOTE
42 Like a woodie
43 Inoperative
46 Stops trying
49 Like some ink
52 Checkout scanning no.
53 Indian export
56 Hand out
57 END OF QUOTE
62 Japanese city
63 Donated
64 Tourists' neckwear
68 Friars, e.g.
69 Actor's rep
70 Forearm bone
71 Duck soup
72 Sonata movement
73 Mouthy miss

DOWN
1 Asian sect
2 *Xanadu* rockers
3 Exploit
4 Strauss opera
5 Commanded
6 Melville work
7 Manor worker
8 Parting words
9 Virile
10 Cooper's concern
11 Rise
12 Actor Hickman
13 Has a hunch
21 Zip
22 __ nous
23 *Printemps* month
24 Sign
25 "Leaving on __ Plane"
29 Turkey neighbor
30 Topographic feature
31 Plenty of
33 __ a Living
36 "Bon voyage" site
37 *A Man __ Woman*
39 Make a choice
40 "¡__ luego!"
41 Whimpers
44 Popular vaccine
45 Professional charge
46 Marmalade fruit
47 Former New Jersey campus
48 Aviation pioneer?
50 Salutation word
51 Sanctuary
54 Mystery award
55 Chihuahua chum
58 Treat like a tot
59 Tied
60 Repair
61 Aware of
65 Elm City collegian
66 Rural hotel
67 Jazz combo instrument

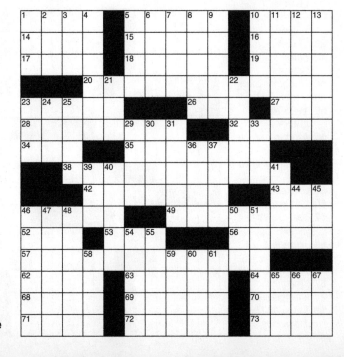

352 EYE TEST

by Dean Niles

ACROSS

1 __ Here to Eternity
5 Flat boats
10 "Dear me!"
14 Take a risk
15 "That's __" (Dean Martin tune)
16 Civil wrong
17 Prayer conclusion
18 Georgia city
19 Centers
20 Winnie the __
22 Rolaids rival
23 Okla. neighbor
24 90210 star
28 Pipe dregs
31 Eats lavishly
32 "Both Sides Now" composer
37 Lush
38 Cartoonist Wilson
39 Flub it
42 Nurses actress
46 Prefix for path
49 Some Arabs
50 1993 Nobel author
55 Atomic-particle suffix
56 Reptilian word form
57 Strikebreaker
60 Carry around
62 Van Gogh locale
64 Trumpeter Al
66 Wrathful feelings
67 New Hampshire city
68 Falco of The Sopranos
69 Backtalk
70 Our Miss Brooks star
71 Wise guy

DOWN

1 Regulatory agcy.
2 Kind of incline
3 Nabisco nibble
4 Amahl and the Night Visitors composer
5 Zodiac animal
6 Stradivari's teacher
7 Point of attention
8 Step on
9 Feel vibes
10 Part of NATO
11 __ on (visit)
12 Esoteric
13 Bee barbs
21 Actress Celeste
25 Sit on the throne
26 The "bad" cholesterol: Abbr.
27 __ Abner
28 Spinners of a sort
29 Tic-tac-toe win
30 Cable network
33 Skater Babilonia
34 Half a ballroom dance
35 Solo of Star Wars
36 "The __ near"
39 Atty.'s title
40 Louis XVI, e.g.
41 Med. staffers
42 Oahu welcome
43 __-pah band
44 Love god
45 Western spreads
46 Ear trouble
47 Mexican state
48 Govt. debt securities
51 Japanese metropolis
52 Less common
53 "If I __ the World"
54 Cara of Fame
58 Verdi heroine
59 Sea cell
61 Curvy letter
63 Sun Yat-__
65 Links platform

353 IN THE RED

by Randolph Ross

ACROSS

1 Flower supports
6 Duck
11 Last section of the OED
14 Prevent legally
15 Runner-up
16 Wood chopper
17 Major no-no
19 Breadbasket st.
20 Forest peaks
21 Bounce
23 Actor Roger
24 Church feature
26 Hester wore one
31 Junks, e.g.
32 Circle of light
33 Social Register word
35 Chip in
36 Confidence
38 Gray's subj.
39 __ *Tac Dough*
40 Uniformed group
41 Free as __
42 Spring bloomer in DC
46 Butters
47 Noun ending
48 Houston or Austin
51 Meant
55 Flub one
56 Alabama's nickname
59 *Lunes* or *martes*
60 Bizarre
61 Mortise attachment
62 Wild blue yonder
63 Bridges
64 Sordid

DOWN

1 Religious group
2 Peter or Alexander
3 Raison d'__
4 Serve as emcee
5 Nasty ones
6 Go by
7 Tennessee footballers
8 Long-eared equine
9 "*Agnus* __"
10 Guevara's real first name
11 Western name
12 Corporate VIP
13 Red ink
18 A Christmas carol
22 Lear product
24 Word of woe
25 Throw stones at
26 Boom variety
27 Stumbling block
28 Seek a ride
29 Composer Morricone
30 Provide with new weapons
31 Mr. Masterson
34 Airport abbr.
36 Time in office
37 Sunbeams
38 Truant
40 Hypnotic states
41 Flight paths
43 Chapter in history
44 Frame inserts
45 Aware of
48 Danson and Weems
49 Actor Estrada
50 Picture of health?
51 "__ the Mood for Love"
52 Actress Merrill
53 Esau's alias
54 Disavow
57 Agent
58 Keogh cousin

354 MASTER QUOTE

by William Lutwiniak

ACROSS

1 Cookie king Wally
5 Acts sullen
10 Dumbo's wings
14 Low blow
15 Disoriented
16 Squad ldrs.
17 START OF A QUOTE
20 Break
21 British insurers, for short
22 Frankfurt's river
23 Flick
24 Moved rudely
27 PART 2 OF QUOTE
31 Pluto's domain
32 Estonians, e.g.
34 Period
35 Continually
36 With 49 Across, source of quote
37 Principal
38 Summer sign
39 They may be counted
40 Founded
41 Likes a lot
43 Dillon portrayer
44 PART 3 OF QUOTE
45 "Too bad!"
46 Dissident Sakharov
49 See 36 Across
53 END OF QUOTE

56 "Vengeance is __ ..."
57 Blue shade
58 1/16 ounce
59 Downhill racer
60 Ayn and Sally
61 Hardens

DOWN

1 Yonder
2 Song from *Mondo Cane*
3 Scoreboard info
4 Sort of sweater
5 Touched on the head
6 Supplementary
7 Function
8 Part of AT&T
9 Chew out
10 Bury
11 Sore
12 Way to travel
13 *Aerospatiale* products
18 Flanks
19 Fitzgerald et al.
23 Saws down
24 Book support
25 "__ nice day!"
26 Classical theater
28 Realty deal
29 Eastern Indians
30 __ *of Iwo Jima*
32 Opera voice
33 Actor Vigoda
36 Man of verse
37 Sloping roofs
39 Some Japanese-Americans
40 Moss leaf
42 Prepared hair
43 '86 sci-fi sequel
45 Plant pest
46 Jacket parts
47 Simon or Diamond
48 *Moonrise* actor Clark
50 In the bag
51 Sports datum
52 Certain meter reading
54 JFK datum
55 Prepare leather

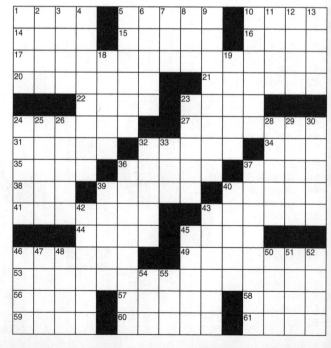

355 BREAKFAST MENU

by Dean Niles

ACROSS

1 Texas city
5 __ *Entertainment!*
10 Small bog
14 Name that may ring a bell
15 Send a check
16 Unusual: Scot.
17 Jacks, for one
18 Love, to Luigi
19 Basics
20 Foundation of a sort
23 Azure, in Apulia
25 Oscar-winner Kingsley
26 Tightly packed
27 "__ luck!"
29 Ballet barre
32 Andrea __ Sarto
33 Vicinity
34 '50s car feature
37 English essayist
42 "*From the __ the Moon*"
43 Elite or pica
44 Mil. address
47 __ dixit
48 Extra
49 Center of power
51 Mideast federation: Abbr.
53 WWII agency
54 Klutz
59 "Do __ once!" ("Hurry!")
60 Actor Delon
61 Currency since 1999
64 Actress Campbell
65 People: Sp.
66 Green land
67 European river
68 Ltr. enclosures
69 Holiday

DOWN

1 Roguish wit
2 Ms. Gardner
3 Apple, for one
4 Draft rating
5 Vestige
6 Musclebound guy
7 Frenzied
8 Wear out
9 Pipe part
10 Fault phenomenon
11 Relax
12 Point a finger at
13 Music genre
21 Hoop grp.
22 Wing it, in a way
23 Gil __ (Le Sage hero)
24 Singer of *Fame*
28 Bank feature
29 Nouveau __
30 Set down
31 In that case
34 Canvas covering
35 Colony residents
36 Postwar alliance
38 Poker move
39 Attention-getter
40 Magnum __
41 Untouchables name
44 One without melanin
45 Acted sullenly
46 Musical interval
48 Bonnet buzzer
50 Out-and-out
51 Draw together
52 Actress Moorehead
55 Joplin pieces
56 Dog bane
57 Fleming and Smith
58 Hazard to navigation
62 Slow down: Mus.
63 Number or pronoun

356 JOLLY OLD ENGLAND

by Matt Gaffney

ACROSS

1 Poetic contraction
4 Flowerless plants
9 __ Clemente
12 Hay portion
14 Ridiculous
15 L.A. thoroughfare
16 "Tower Bridge Ahead"?
19 Diner offerings
20 Escape capture
21 NASA name
22 Big __ outdoors
24 Stubborn sorts
27 Skier's transport
28 Sternward
31 Most populous continent
32 Diviner's decks
34 Draw
35 Chaucer works?
38 Kept out of sight
39 He doesn't buy it
40 Spender, for one
41 Important period
42 Industrial containers
43 Word on a nickel
44 Upper-crust
46 P __ "pneumonia"
48 Enjoy
50 Providence neighbor
54 Lord Nelson?
57 Nonstandard contraction
58 Lot fillers
59 Structural suffix
60 Unseen substance
61 Kilimanjaro like
62 Rug rat

DOWN

1 Recipe amt.
2 Greet with pomp
3 Ms. Korbut
4 Tootled, perhaps
5 __ nous
6 Encouraging sounds
7 Vane dir.
8 Match part
9 Tryout of a sort
10 Passed easily
11 Winning margin
13 Beg
15 Become cloying
17 Singer Redding
18 Name in the news
22 "Plato is __": Nietzsche
23 Nymph chaser
24 Papier-__
25 Delta rival
26 Krystle Carrington portrayer
27 Bridge support
29 __ mignon
30 Battery components
32 Unexpected pleasure
33 Ease off
36 __ Madigan
37 Starts speaking candidly
43 Fifi's five
45 Artist's quarters
46 Street-sign shape
47 Fresh
48 Frat party
49 Puccini piece
50 Roman orator
51 Arcade infraction
52 Double Stuf, for one
53 Barber's call
55 Scale notes
56 Starter's need

357

ON TV

by S.E. Booker

ACROSS
1 Dampen a stamp
5 Rendezvous
10 In vogue
14 Will-__-wisp
15 Uproar
16 __ Hashanah
17 Toe the line
18 With 62 Across, Billy Wilder quote on TV
20 Most advanced
22 ". . . __ singing birds": Johnson
23 That is, for long
25 Tour de force
26 Brooch
28 Head set?
30 Unwelcome winds
34 UK part
35 Clumsy one
37 Pleasure boat
38 Runner, maybe
39 Writer Jones
41 Deli bread
42 Early infatuation
45 Eighth word of "The Star Spangled Banner"
47 Trucking unit
48 Sewed an edge
50 __ colada
51 Newman/Neal film
52 __ impasse
54 Jazzman Blake
56 "Guaranteed!"
59 California's motto

62 See 18 Across
65 Have __ for (crave)
66 "Ma! (He's making eyes __)"
67 Stared at
68 __ off (angry)
69 The best
70 "__ Fools Fall in Love?"
71 Make out

DOWN
1 Cuckoo bird?
2 "Let __" (Beatles tune)
3 With 31 Down, Frank Lloyd Wright quote on TV
4 __ up (tense)
5 "__, folks!"
6 Decay
7 "That hurts!"
8 Grain bundle
9 Made suede
10 *City Slickers* star
11 Cowboy Gibson
12 "There __ little enemy": Franklin
13 Pot holder
19 Rips apart
21 Go for
24 Aligned
26 Freshwater fish
27 Toughen
29 Handbag holder
31 See 3 Down
32 "Happy Birthday __"

33 Use up
36 Campy exclamation
40 Sly hint
43 Breaks
44 Excited
46 Actor in *The Jungle Book*
49 Scopes' defender
53 Stable sound
55 Furious
56 Italian auto
57 Aware of
58 Sgt. Preston's group
60 Don't give up
61 *60 Minutes* name
63 Wily
64 Multi-vol. lexicon

358 SCORE KEEPING

by Dean Niles

ACROSS

1 Famous feminist
5 City rides
9 Trimmed the lawn
14 Magical syllables
15 On the main
16 Spring up
17 See 51 Across
18 Small brook
19 Former senator Helms
20 Diver's locale
22 Gave the willies to
24 Attention-getter
25 Expose
26 Genesis craft
29 Sills song
31 Brought down
36 German engraver
38 Bad-check marking
40 St. Theresa of __
41 Knock for __ (stun)
42 Cruet contents
43 Fix a street
44 Sean and William
45 Vitamin stat.
46 Savage
47 Hardly high-class
49 Sicilian spouter
51 With 17 Across, temp phrase
52 Poet's contraction
54 Glacial mass
56 Mexico neighbor
60 Art style
64 Hold firmly
65 Word of praise
67 Buffalo's county
68 Distress signal
69 Actress Sommer
70 Work alone
71 Tijuana title
72 Pit or stone
73 Reception interference

DOWN

1 Anti-DWI org.
2 Tony's cousin
3 Shoe stretcher
4 Buccaneer's home
5 Calling
6 Turkey's area
7 __ canto (singing style)
8 Nacho dip
9 Shaw play
10 Sweet treat
11 Fab rival
12 To be, to Ovid
13 Boy Scout act
21 Marksman
23 Ms. Zadora
26 Adjust to conditions
27 Foot-long device
28 Swedish money
30 Stage digression
32 Declare positively
33 Gym exercise
34 Overjoy
35 Brave one
37 Long times
39 Busted
48 Hankering
50 Had to have
53 Goes ape
55 *Cagney & Lacey* star
56 Poodle plaints
57 Stir up
58 A Karamazov
59 Goose egg
61 Wrinkle remover
62 Storage place
63 Catty remark
66 Corrida cry

359 PIOUS PEOPLE

by Matt Gaffney

ACROSS
1 Riga residents
6 Toreador's "Bravo!"
9 Beer ingredient
13 Awesome hotel lobbies
14 Kook
15 Bring out dinner
16 Pious silents star?
19 Pious toon?
20 Under the weather
21 "__ was saying . . ."
22 Anytown, USA address
26 Cereal grain
28 Bring to naught
29 Act as facilitator
35 Stuck-up ones
37 This very minute
38 Newsperson Shriver
39 Galileo gadget
41 Sean Connery, e.g.
42 Grassy field
43 Mansion's grounds
45 Uncommon sense
47 Thirst
51 Pious novelist?
55 Reggie Jackson's pious nickname?
58 *My Fair Lady* character

59 Beatnik's interjection
60 Hair, in Hamburg
61 René's head
62 Hog's home
63 Went astray

DOWN
1 Fond du __, WI
2 Ordinal ending
3 Missile's path: Abbr.
4 Akron product
5 Spicy dips
6 Roger of NBC News
7 Soaps star Susan
8 Revolutionary Allen
9 Thin, crispy bread
10 Some Semites
11 XXIX doubled
12 Midmorning
15 Fitness center
17 "Not from where __!"
18 Inert gas
22 Is forced to
23 Novelist Rice
24 Admired person
25 Award since 1901
27 USN officer
29 Yoko __
30 Mini-explosion
31 Ram's mate
32 Killer whale
33 Hilarious person

34 Quench completely
36 Vane dir.
40 West Pointer
43 Julia Roberts' brother
44 Boil with anger
45 Monsieur Zola
46 Trash-collecting dept.
48 Moppets' schools: Abbr.
49 Dieter of rhyme
50 Literary device
52 Beauregard's grp.
53 Fly high
54 Ski-lift type
55 Ran into
56 Before
57 Spectrum part

360 TOEING THE MARK?

by A.J. Santora

ACROSS

1 Inhabitants: Suff.
5 Some chops
9 Boastful boxer
12 START OF A QUOTE
15 MIDDLE OF QUOTE
16 END OF QUOTE
17 Thompson of *Family*
18 Tom's mate
19 Sleep __ (decide later)
20 Incompetents
21 Mythical nymphs
23 Ventilated thoroughly
26 Massive
27 Vowel rhyme
28 Massachusetts motto word
29 *Casino* __
30 Make a blouse
31 Swizzle
33 Plays the ponies
35 Ecol. agcy.
38 Lauder et al.
40 Chervil or chive
44 Source of quote
46 Pin type
47 Forgiveness
48 A Finger Lake
49 Ancient serf
50 German coal area
52 Kiddie __ (*Jeopardy!* category)
53 Word form for "thought"
54 Magic words
57 Squirrel nosh
58 Harbor barrier
59 Some AMA members
60 Part of CBS
61 Polaroid part

DOWN

1 __ numbers (rounded)
2 Asian capital
3 They do their level best
4 Lincoln or Kennedy: Abbr.
5 Sundial numeral
6 Rapture
7 Half a Heyerdahl title
8 Computer perch, perhaps
9 Fabled warriors
10 Irma's epithet
11 Fretting
13 __ Island Red
14 Berry and Kercheval
17 Scotch partner
20 *Reader's Encyclopedia* compiler
22 Long time
24 Señora Perón
25 Actor's résumé
27 Cardiologist's adjective
29 Gotten up
32 Doctrine
34 Holmes' "One-Hoss __"
35 Piece of artwork
36 Stacked high
37 Little chimps
39 *Champs* __
41 Take after
42 What you eat
43 Straw hats
45 Melville novel
46 Rod of baseball
48 Heavy barrel
51 Med. subj.
54 Dict. abbr.
55 Use a crowbar
56 __ ammoniac

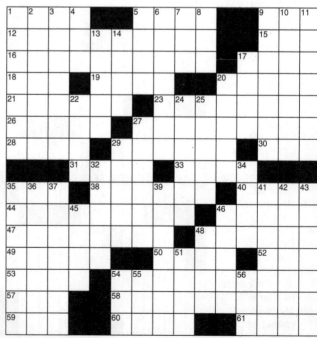

361 OPPOSITES

by Wayne R. Williams

ACROSS

1 Tot holder
5 Fancy
9 Russian range
14 Protagonist
15 Lamb's pen name
16 Flyer
17 Lawyer's cinch
20 Mount for Moses
21 Non-believer
22 U-turn from WSW
23 Witty reply
27 Scottish loch
29 Like Abner
30 More tense
35 Posed questions
37 Medieval-romance figure
38 Leaning
41 Explosive letters
43 Magic sticks
44 Dwarfed tree
46 Gray and Moran
48 Necessitate
49 Take first
50 Fish choice
54 Excuses
57 Holiday concoction
58 Flamenco accompaniment
62 John Jacob or Mary
64 Quite plainly
68 Tizzies
69 Dueling tool
70 Ed or Nancy
71 Actor Davis
72 Drenches
73 Makes one

DOWN

1 Picked
2 Yearn after
3 Cara and Papas
4 __ fide
5 Coop up
6 Antique
7 Boom-bah beginning
8 Lots of laughs
9 With 36 Down, Sandy Dennis movie
10 Texas university
11 Jai __
12 Setback
13 Editor's instruction
18 One of the four elements
19 Express vocally
24 Type
25 Painter Mondrian
26 Yesterday's papers
28 Latin beat
31 See-through material
32 Writer Fleming
33 *Howards* __
34 Sts.
36 See 9 Down
38 Presidential nickname
39 Heavy weight
40 Bank pymt.
42 Small combo
45 Of the intestine
47 Rural stopover
51 Punctual
52 Took spoils
53 Way out
55 To one side
56 Old saying
58 Japanese soup
59 Sothern and Sheridan
60 Slugger's stats
61 Word form for "height"
63 Major Barbara's creator
65 *The Naked* __
66 Profit
67 __ Moines

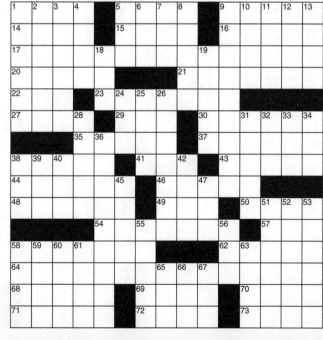

362 ITALIAN TOUR

by Randolph Ross

ACROSS

1 Teacher's deg.
5 King of the hill
10 Goof
13 Orbit point
15 Actress Anouk
16 Alumni newsletter word
17 Italian eateries?
19 Surcharge
20 Italian utility?
22 "Moonlight" music
23 Cuts in two
25 List extending abbrs.
26 DDS group
28 Make a sharp turn
29 Mao __-tung
30 Prince Charles' game
32 Pumpkin relatives
34 Italian soul singer?
36 Agree (to)
39 Sermon topics
40 Reagan DOD project
43 Boxing venue
44 Sam on *Cheers*
45 Alda's TV costar
46 Expurgate
49 Most ready for picking
51 Italian bug catcher?
54 Apiece
55 Italian sweet stuff?
57 *People __ Funny*

58 They're coded
59 "The best is __ come"
60 Dr. Leary's drug
61 Doesn't hide
62 Deer

DOWN

1 Cartographer's product
2 Taps
3 Main meaning
4 Ross and Rigg
5 Relief org.
6 San Juan or Blueberry
7 Microscopic sight
8 Grenoble gratitude
9 Annoyers
10 Temptress
11 Did a double take
12 Reviewer Reed
14 Apt name for a Dalmatian
18 Top bond rating
21 Variety show
22 Go down
24 Next yr.'s alums
26 Norton nemesis
27 Search for water
30 Barrie character
31 Table scrap
32 Canasta cousin
33 Tie breakers: Abbr.
34 Opened
35 Went underground
36 Parabolic path
37 Bilko portrayer
38 Looked villainous
40 Testify under oath
41 Question the truth of
42 Cousin of the Addamses
44 Plains dwelling
45 More agile
47 Simone and Foch
48 Rumor result, maybe
49 Singer Cooder et al.
50 Teeny-weeny
52 Complaints
53 More, to Browning
54 Buddy
56 Battery abbr.

363 TABLE MANNERS

by Donna J. Stone

ACROSS

1 Drug buster
5 *Rich Man, Poor Man* author
9 Kitchen kingpin
13 Geometry calculation
14 Seated Beatle
15 Hartman or Bonet
16 Beethoven's birthplace
17 __ Selassie
18 Jai __
19 START OF A QUIP BY HENNY YOUNGMAN
22 Ryan's *Love Story* costar
23 Short play
24 Like wreaths and pumpkins
29 Thickset
33 Current measurements
34 Gen. Robt. __
36 Col. Tibbets' mother
37 Compete
38 MIDDLE OF QUIP
40 Litter sound
41 Bring bliss to
43 Pony
44 Cry over cards?
45 Illinois city
47 Reno residents
49 Dull
51 Ivy Leaguer
52 END OF QUIP
59 Home of Columbus
60 Transmission parts
61 Soho streetcar
63 *The Egg* __
64 Remove a Reebok
65 Othello's foe
66 Disposition
67 It may come from Montana
68 Role for Liz

DOWN

1 Catch a crook
2 Graceland name
3 Monsieur Clair
4 Look for votes
5 Wild guess
6 It grows on you
7 Van Gogh locale
8 Inflicts
9 Moore of *The Lone Ranger*
10 Hawaiian city
11 Genesis redhead
12 Evenhanded
14 Fez wearer
20 "Evil Woman" rockers
21 Check cheat
24 Reserved, as a seat
25 Author Zola
26 "Silent upon __ in Darien": Keats
27 Baldwin of *Malice*
28 Pick up
00 It may give you pause
31 Comic Robert
32 Tedium symptoms
35 Singer Adams
38 Last name in law
39 Heads
42 Gossipy paper
44 Not too bright
46 Outstanding
48 Smith and Yankovic
50 Serengeti scavenger
52 Wander
53 "What have I done?"
54 Fashionable resort
55 Feedbag contents
56 *Battle Cry* author
57 Orenburg's river
58 Kid at court
62 Bossy remark?

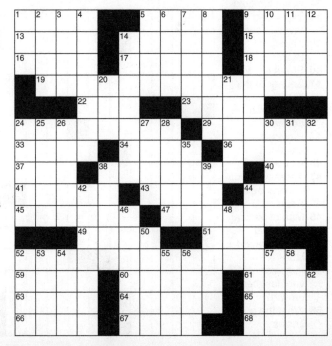

364 DOUBLE TAKES

by Randolph Ross

ACROSS

1 A Baldwin
5 Mommy's mate
10 Frisbee, e.g.
14 *De* __ (afresh)
15 Peruvian peaks
16 Famous next-to-last words
17 Gift for a Texan with a swelled head?
20 In moderation
21 Sinatra CD
22 Genealogical construction
23 Beseeched
25 Like cows in India
28 Escaped a debt, with "out"
32 Hosiery shade
33 Small pies
34 Acapulco gold
35 Expanded Vivaldi opus?
39 Knight or Baxter
40 Street show
41 Sooner of the '30s
42 Dashboard device
44 Provides shelter
46 All over
47 Attorney general before Reno
48 Man of Muscat
51 Proverbial place for hard labor
55 Indicator of very fast beard growth?
58 What the nose knows
59 Bring to mind
60 Dried up
61 Many, many years
62 Limey's pal
63 Clothes lines

DOWN

1 Unwelcome picnic guests
2 *Wayne's World* costar Rob
3 Tied
4 Draw a conclusion
5 Sleep sofa
6 Point of view
7 WWII turning point
8 __ Rio, TX
9 Fashion monogram
10 Strip
11 Spillane's __ *Jury*
12 RBI or ERA
13 Budget reductions
18 Become bored
19 Black Sea city
23 Intrinsically
24 Past the deadline
25 Fracas
26 Felt sore
27 Words to live by
28 Irrigate
29 Appearances
30 Bert's friend
31 Medicinal allocations
33 Tossed
36 Peaceful
37 Concert proceeds
38 Moonshiner's concoction
43 Estates
44 WWII admiral
45 *Vanity Fair* journalist Maureen
47 Scott : slavery :: __ : affirmative action
48 Midwestern tribesman
49 Beatles' "Love __"
50 Shortly
51 Highlander
52 __ *fixe*
53 *Cheers* character
54 Woolly female
56 Moon lander
57 Cato's eggs

SMOKE DETECTORS

by Cathy Millhauser

ACROSS

1 Traversed the Tiber
5 Caesar's partner
9 Berry of *Jungle Fever*
14 "Eek!"
15 They give a hoot
16 Euclidean statement
17 Sneezing attack?
19 Tarantula toxin
20 Pablo's pal
21 Zilch
23 Dos Passos trilogy
24 Some Czechs' smellers?
28 Sha Na Na member
32 Odin's offspring
33 Mare fare
34 Sgt., e.g.
36 Forbidden
40 Nosy pair on TV?
44 Actor Davis
45 License plate
46 SSS status
47 Absorbs, with "up"
50 With caution
52 Bee's beezer?
56 Yoko ___
57 Thicke of *Growing Pains*
58 Dame Edith
63 Corday's victim
65 "Congrats" to Schnozzola?
68 Soul
69 "... ___ saw Elba"
70 Carryall
71 Windshield attachment
72 Ooze (out)
73 Portent

DOWN

1 Love seat partner
2 Impulse
3 Part of ABM
4 Synthesizer inventor
5 Corn holder
6 Keep one's balance?
7 Horseshoe game sound
8 Invite for a date
9 Indigents
10 *Wizard of Oz* prop
11 *Peanuts* kid
12 Relaxed, so to speak
13 Actresses Samms and Thompson
18 Dandies
22 Bible bk.
25 Casino city
26 Sunoco rival
27 Cicero, notably
28 "Jump," in computerese
29 Bowl cheers
30 Hot times in Toulouse
31 St. Francis' birthplace
35 Former New York Giants star
37 Proclivity
38 Pitcher Hershiser
39 Key opener?
41 Post-delivery
42 Swedish car
43 Spherical home: Var.
48 Bakker's TV club
49 Embarrasses
51 Jamesian journalist Leon
52 Lapp, for one
53 Fatuous
54 Antiseptic acid
55 Harden
59 Nix
60 Enrico Fermi's concern
61 Short letter
62 Cinematographer Nykvist
64 Doc bloc
66 Alphabetic ultimate
67 Nil

366 CANINE QUEST

by Matt Gaffney

ACROSS
1 Chan phrase
5 It may be grand
9 Loser of '17
13 Angry mood
15 Toledo's water
16 Mrs. Chaplin
17 START OF A QUIP
20 Health club
21 With 30 Down, Porter tune
22 Minimal money
23 New Orleans NBAers
25 Ski-lift type
27 Pitcher part
28 Early VP
29 Ore. neighbor
32 Nag
34 Sports palaces
36 ". . . __ iron bars a cage"
37 PART 2 OF QUIP
40 Bustle
41 Trail users
42 Takes home
43 Bran variety
44 Small songbird
45 Knight title
46 Asian beasts
47 Gorbachev's successor
51 Berth place
53 Lug around
54 As well
55 PART 3 OF QUIP
59 Like crazy
60 Soothing plant
61 Matt's *Today* cohost
62 Farmer's place
63 China buys
64 END OF QUIP

DOWN
1 Prone to imitation
2 Zoo favorite
3 Calculator button
4 No longer stylish
5 Kids
6 *Trinity* author
7 Nautical gear
8 Ginza gelt
9 Rapunzel's home
10 Augsburg offspring
11 Working without __ (acting riskily)
12 Sprinted
14 Swiss mathematician
18 Favorite
19 Egyptian amulet
24 Midday breaks
25 Home style
26 Sea cells
28 German region
29 Coast-to-coast road
30 See 21 Across
31 Part of BA
32 Borgia's "bye"
33 *M*A*S*H* star
34 Smug expression
35 Little shavers
38 Impede a plan
39 Troop group
45 Glossy
46 Barbra role
47 Team frames
48 Ordinal ending
49 Ancient Greek region
50 Eminent
51 Mucho money
52 Object of adulation
53 Harness race
55 Dear old one?
56 Used to be
57 Grand __ Opry
58 Sleeper, e.g.

367 OUT OF THE WOODS

by Dean Niles

ACROSS

1 Mild cigar
6 Lip
10 Moves it
14 *King Lear* daughter
15 On the sheltered side
16 Egyptian cross
17 Nitrogen compound
18 Hit the ground
19 Words of comprehension
20 Resign under fire
23 Sault __ Marie, Ont.
24 Vows
25 Of hearing
29 Snug
30 Track alternative
32 __ mode (stylish)
33 Juan Carlos' land
36 Fido fluff
37 The nights before
38 Long John Silver saying
41 Slender bristle
42 Lion's lair
43 Humble dwelling
44 Where *Lost* is found
45 Submissions to eds.
46 Family group
47 Popular search engine
49 Winter woe
51 Bishop's domain
54 College expense, often

57 Spill the beans
60 Grade option
61 Ike's rival
62 Sitarist Shankar
63 Caesarean phrase
64 Last but not __
65 Aid a felon
66 Gangbuster Eliot
67 Fills a hold

DOWN

1 Bird's crops
2 Paul of *Melvin and Howard*
3 Nimble-footed
4 Station
5 Corresponding completely
6 It should be first
7 First Hebrew letter
8 Betrays the cause
9 Ward of *Sisters*
10 Japanese verse form
11 Election victors
12 __ out (supplement)
13 __ *Stoops to Conquer*
21 Ponds and bunkers
22 Apprehend
26 Shiny black
27 On one's toes
28 Cattle catcher
29 Vena __ (blood line)
31 Sang, in a way
33 Paine piece

34 Solomon's queenly visitor
35 Slope
36 Marshy area
37 Abba of Israel
39 Barracks buddy
40 Spaghetti may support it
45 Cow comment
46 2000 event
48 Sphere of influence
50 Endures
51 Side dish
52 Remove
53 Bleeps out
55 Straightforward
56 Music halls
57 Swimsuit top
58 Guinea-pig place
59 Wide rd.

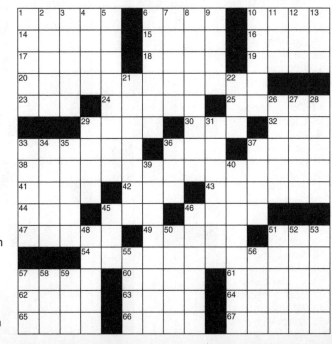

368 BOXING LEGENDS

by Fred Piscop

ACROSS

1 Little brother, perhaps
5 Dizzying designs
10 Bonkers
14 Apropos of
15 Bandleader Shaw
16 __ about (circa)
17 Boxing legend?
19 Sleuth Wolfe
20 Sprite competitor
21 Pushed through the crowd
23 Put into action
24 Peculiarity
25 Extra goods
28 Mix up
32 *Critique of Pure Reason* writer
36 Motorists' org.
37 Haifa's locale
38 Actor Beery
39 Be frugal
41 Reo maker
42 __ straight (poker hand)
44 *Tic __ Dough*
45 Leaner's locale
46 Fluff up
47 South African politico P.W.
49 Muffed grounder, e.g.
51 Poolroom props
56 __ surfing (tube-watcher's activity)
59 Take back
61 Monetary unit for 47 Across
62 Boxing legend?
64 '84 Nobelist
65 Snack with milk
66 *Momma* cartoonist Lazarus
67 "Your __ is showing!"
68 Kemo Sabe's buddy
69 Thermometer type

DOWN

1 VCR button
2 Antique auto
3 Comic Martin
4 Copier additive
5 Honolulu's island
6 Stage gizmo
7 From __ Z
8 __ Island (NYC penitentiary)
9 Inventor Nikola
10 Boxing legend?
11 Turn over __ leaf
12 Driver's exhortation
13 Stepped on
18 Aware of
22 Prejudice
24 Arnold was one
26 Place for posies
27 Scarf down
29 Spanish surrealist
30 Digital displays
31 *Born Free* lioness
32 Heal, as bones
33 Tops
34 Shuttle grp.
35 Boxing legend?
37 Seven-year phenomenon
40 Rebellious Turner
43 Bruce or Laura
47 Ravel composition
48 St. Louis sight
50 Transplant
52 Santa Anna took it
53 Highland Games missile
54 *To __ Mockingbird*
55 Limburger property
56 PC screens
57 Drive a semi
58 Opposed to
59 Civil disturbance
60 Former Sinclair competitor
63 Stimpy's pal

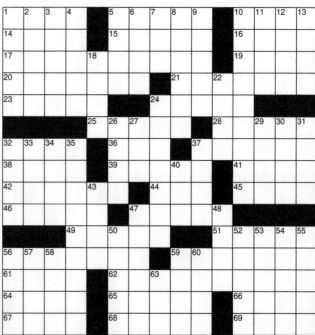

369 UP, UP AND AWAY

by Donna J. Stone

ACROSS

1 Used a playground piece
5 Ballerina Shearer
10 Grouch
14 Positions
15 Rock singer John
16 *Les Misérables*
17 Washington bills
18 Brick man
19 Making a crossing
20 START OF A COMMENT
23 Wind, essentially
24 Identical
25 Early epic
30 Responsible
34 Actor O'Neal
35 Improves, perhaps
37 Lox smith?
38 Summer setting in Conn.
39 MIDDLE OF COMMENT
41 Zsa Zsa's sister
42 Author Jong
44 Spanish painter
45 Makes out
46 Piano piece
48 Take up with an old flame?
50 Prepares leather
52 Yalie
53 END OF COMMENT
61 The O'Hara estate
62 Opening remark?
63 Scat singer Fitzgerald
64 Milky gem
65 Deep-seated hate
66 Actor Cobb
67 Cher film of '85
68 Golf club
69 Lodging option

DOWN

1 Uncultured one
2 Actress Anderson
3 It keeps things cool
4 That haughty feeling
5 Common D.C. sight
6 Norwegian king
7 __ *Wonderful Life*
8 Housetops
9 Temper, as metal
10 French castle
11 Parcel marking
12 *The Morning Watch* author
13 Big pig
21 Part of RSVP
22 Friend, in Florence
25 Locusts, e.g.
26 Water power, for short
27 Like some kitchens
28 Beside oneself
29 Ornamentation
31 Engender
32 Carpenter's tool
33 Wipe out
36 Terrier type
39 __ *Attraction* ('87 film)
40 Net
43 Backstage passage
45 With nastiness
47 Be that as it may
49 Tact ending
51 Ingmar Bergman, for one
53 Bit of matter
54 Wine region
55 Eventful periods
56 "Put __ on it!"
57 Funny money
58 Mr. Kadiddlehopper
59 Sir Guinness
60 Indian chief

370 SIX PIX

by Wayne R. Williams

ACROSS

1 Ms. Midler
6 Pluto's tail?
10 School grps.
14 Actor Hawke
15 Top-notch
16 Cry of distress
17 Marvin/March pic
20 Diligent insect
21 Supplemented, with "out"
22 Poolside place
23 Pen dwellers
25 Programmer's instruction
27 Old French coin
28 Pollution patrol grp.
30 Hacienda hats
34 Author Glasgow
36 Welfare
37 Opp. of SSW
38 Hamilton/Saint James pic
42 Whopper
43 Columnist Herb
44 Male voice
45 Alaskan harbor
48 *The Ice Storm* director Lee
49 Solo of *Star Wars*
50 Fireside yarn
52 Verbal skirmish
55 Get on
57 Printer's measure
59 Señor's cheer

60 Turner/Gavin pic
64 Folktales
65 High beginner?
66 Kidney enzyme
67 Defeat
68 Malt-ed beverage?
69 *them* author

DOWN

1 Greek letters
2 Word form for "race"
3 Ron Moody pic
4 Skater Babilonia
5 Noun ending
6 Brief appearances
7 Hope/Crosby pic
8 Actress Sheridan
9 Gumshoe
10 Pulpy refuse
11 MacLaine/ Bancroft pic
12 Against
13 London area
18 Heart chart
19 Light work at the Met
24 *Pursuit of the Graf __*
26 Barbra's *Funny Girl* costar
29 Big snake
31 Lib. collection
32 Not fooled by
33 Prognosticator
34 Scatter Fitzgerald

35 Cut of meat
39 Black goo
40 Accomplishment
41 Uncle __ (rice brand)
46 Bret and others
47 *Sense and Sensibility* heroine
51 *Focault's Pendulum* author
53 Film remade in 2004
54 The green years
55 Check
56 *Typee* sequel
58 '60s do
61 Slot filler
62 Bar rocks
63 Meadow

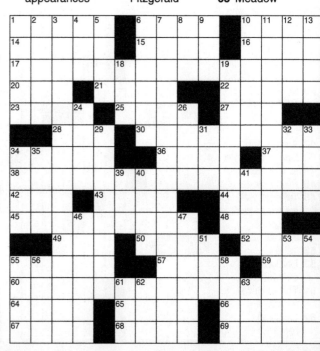

371 ONE-TRACK MIND

. . . .

by Donna J. Stone

ACROSS
1 Moonshine ingredient
5 __ Spumante
9 Throws in the towel
14 At rest
15 Rich soil
16 Lobbies for
17 Sophoclean tragedy
18 Fall rudely
19 *Roots* Emmy winner
20 START OF A DEFINITION OF A BORE
23 "The Enlightened One"
24 Bit of Morse code
25 PC key
27 "__ you sure?"
28 Marsh birds
31 Folk singer Suzanne
32 Upcoming grad.
33 Celebratory suffix
34 Got one's feet wet
35 MIDDLE OF DEFINITION
38 Places for ports
41 Stewpot
42 Giant legend
45 Outer limits
46 Knight wear
48 Born yesterday
49 Bonanza material
50 __ Saud
51 Leisurely, to Liszt
53 END OF DEFINITION

57 Decent
58 Jai __
59 Elitist
61 Actress Verdugo
62 Poker-player's phrase
63 __ Taft Benson
64 Eleanor's uncle
65 Rambling
66 Hold up

DOWN
1 Actress Sara
2 Break up
3 Defame
4 Put the whammy on
5 Collected letters?
6 Go it alone
7 Kit Carson House site
8 Get in the way of
9 Peck part
10 Heavenly bear
11 Set afire
12 Adolescent
13 Ukr., formerly
21 Soupçons
22 Carol word
23 __-relief
26 Spoiled
29 Adjective suffix
30 *Cheers* chair
31 Napa vessel
34 "__ Say" ('59 tune)
35 Endorses
36 Einstein's birthplace
37 Lambent
38 __-Magnon
39 Igloo feature
40 Finger-painted
42 Crisp fabric
43 They'll keep you in stitches
44 Low card
46 *Six Feet Under* network
47 Have as a consequence
50 Furniture detail
52 Photographer Adams
54 Hourglass contents
55 Admiral Zumwalt
56 Eaves' drops?
57 Came upon
60 Halloween decoration

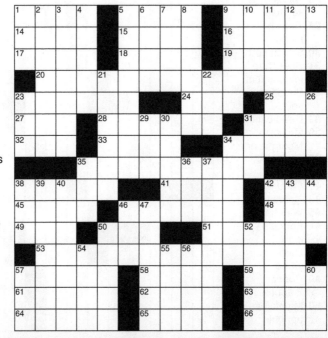

372 INTERSECTION

by Bill Swain

ACROSS

1 Operatic voices
7 Economist Milton
15 Makes fit
16 Find and carry back
17 King of the Franks
18 Dashboard gauge
19 Dollar : penny :: ruble : __
20 DXXV quadrupled
21 Liqueur flavor
22 Seed: Prefix
23 One-time connection
24 Brains behind a UFO
25 Use a keyhole
28 Turkish money
30 Consumed
31 Speech impediment
32 Buddhist sect
33 Dead-center
39 Musician Montgomery
40 __ O'Neill Chaplin
41 Cultural org.
42 __-ski
45 With hatred
47 Kanga's kid
48 Card game
49 Runner Zatopek
50 Maintained uprights
53 __ Always Fair Weather
54 Noted violin maker
55 Circumlocutory
57 Typewriter roller
58 Plot outline
59 Worked over
60 E-mail predecessor
61 Brings to bear

DOWN

1 Spot for a car critic
2 Medical practitioner
3 Way station
4 Forbidding
5 Composer Satie
6 Draft letters
7 Cap-à-pie
8 Railway worker
9 "Am __ understand . . ."
10 Columnist Bombeck
11 __ Bien Phu
12 Occupation
13 Zoroastrian sacred texts
14 Sea nymph
20 Wetland
26 Turns on a pivot
27 Hip pad
28 Gypsy Love composer
29 Chemical suffix
32 Greek philosopher
34 Have debts
35 Cream-filled pastries
36 Disney employee
37 Opposing stubbornly
38 Exit words
42 41 Across beneficiary
43 Swoop down
44 Short poem
45 Keys music?
46 Started again from scratch
51 __ kleine Nachtmusik
52 Bummer
54 Mr. Trebek
56 Drop the ball, perhaps
57 __-game show

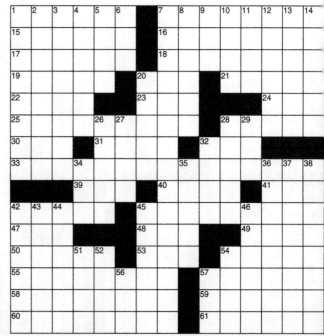

373 CHIEF LOCATIONS

by Randolph Ross

ACROSS

1 Clothier Strauss
5 VIP's vehicles
10 Four-legged omnivore
14 Kitchen warmer
15 Vacuous
16 Prefix meaning "all"
17 Apple source
20 Tycoon's digs
21 Eight-legged creature
22 Be in store
24 French pronoun
25 Midwest capital
31 Quay
33 Raison __
34 __ kwon do
35 Bricklaying equipment
36 Stores (away)
37 Papered place
38 Wrath
39 Actor Delon
40 Superman's birth name
41 Robert James Waller locale
44 Actor Torn
45 German admiral
46 Cure
51 Rug source
55 Spot off Manhattan
57 Jackson or Tyler
58 *Middlemarch* author
59 First name in gymnastics
60 Acts the mendicant
61 Like bamboo
62 "Sure!"

DOWN

1 Rob of *The West Wing*
2 Perón and Gabor
3 Suit's third piece
4 Breathing aids
5 *In the __ Fire* (Eastwood film)
6 Gerundial ending
7 First name in spydom
8 __ about (approximately)
9 State pair
10 Like certain arches
11 Gulf sultanate
12 Con
13 Laced
18 Knock __! (stop)
19 Tea cake
23 Middle of the road
25 Blasé
26 Archaeological find
27 Pool members
28 NATO member
29 Chaucerian chapter
30 Let off steam
31 Caprice
32 Circle dance
36 Simulated page turn
37 Downfall
39 In private
40 Some joints
42 Spring bloomers
43 Snobbish
46 Riyadh resident
47 __ But the Brave
48 Chinese society
49 Conference opener
50 Nobelist Wiesel
52 Vaccine name
53 Actress Swenson
54 __ at the Races
56 Horror director Browning

374 WINDOW DRESSING

by Dean Niles

ACROSS
1 Indian prince
6 Child or Beard
10 Mo. for many Virgos
14 Scarlett or John
15 Members list
16 Mag for *filles*
17 Jolson staple
18 Parkay is one
19 Economist Greenspan
20 Flow away
21 Mood
24 Eskimo neighbor
26 Ups the bet
27 Go through again
29 Trombone part
31 Slack-jawed
32 Church cry
33 Big bird
37 Adjective for the 1890s
38 Court conclusions
41 Bobby of hockey
42 Cheese choice
44 Postwar alliance
45 NC-17 moviegoer
47 Large tangelos
49 Prizes
50 Forty winks
53 Goodman's genre
54 '60s singing family
57 Corp. takeover
60 James __ Jones
61 Ticket punishment

62 Fancy headdress
64 Mrs. Lou Grant
65 Push
66 Map feature
67 Comedienne Charlotte et al.
68 Onion kin
69 Throws out a line

DOWN
1 Colosseum city
2 Melville monomaniac
3 Creole dish
4 Shirt part
5 Sneezin' reason
6 Certain Slav
7 Actress Celeste
8 Robt. __

9 Tile, perhaps
10 More sleazy
11 Immigrants' island
12 Wood shaver
13 Leans (toward)
22 Wish undone
23 Hula hoops, e.g.
25 Bottle edge
27 High dudgeon
28 Old oath
29 Former *L.A. Law* actor
30 Late-night name
32 Jai __
34 Sand container
35 Perry's creator
36 __ and Entertainment Network

39 Forbidden, in a way
40 Cruel
43 Pecs and abs
46 Put on
48 Pontiac model
49 Shoemaker's tool
50 Use the rudder
51 "If __ Hammer"
52 Supernatural
53 Glossy
55 Father
56 *Picnic* playwright
58 Writer Harte
59 Cookie ingredients
63 Once __ blue moon

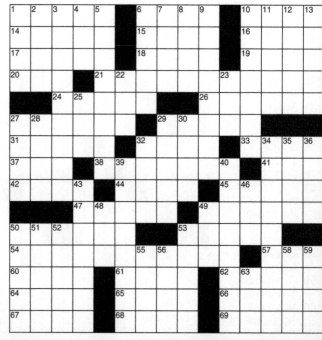

375 STAR-CROSSED

by Wayne R. Williams

ACROSS

1 Declare untrue
5 Rudiments
9 Brazilian dance
14 Verdi number
15 Patsy
16 Two-toed sloths
17 *Bang the Drum Slowly* star
20 Ice cream server
21 Remove from text
22 Inhabitant of: Suff.
23 Easy gait
25 Woodstock, e.g.
28 Compass pt.
30 Egyptian deity
32 Less than chipper
33 Samuel's teacher
34 Literary leader
35 Hawaiian hardwood
38 *Time After Time* star
42 Eskimotel?
43 Single thing
44 Author Rita __ Brown
45 4/15 addressee
46 Make amends
47 Bus. abbr.
48 Forcefully effective
51 Ollie's partner
53 Resistance unit
54 Arthur of the courts
56 *Enigma Variations* composer
59 *Black Like Me* star
63 Festoon
64 Model Macpherson
65 Cager Archibald
66 *"A votre __ !"*
67 Roy Rogers' real surname
68 Ogled

DOWN

1 They'll hold water
2 Ambler or Blore
3 *The Seven Percent Solution* costar
4 Loudmouthed lummox
5 Mature
6 Blacker type
7 *Death of a Salesman* star
8 Creeper's stem
9 __ generis
10 Santa __, CA
11 *Manhattan* star
12 Projects forward
13 So far
18 Hardy horse
19 __ room
24 Actor Jannings
26 About .6 of a mile
27 Took off
28 Partial prefix
29 Smelting residue
31 May honoree
36 __ Bator
37 Composer Wilder
39 Taro tuber
40 Work with a soloist: Abbr.
41 Iniquity sites
46 Stadium pathways
48 Dickens' Spenlow et al.
49 Mary's friend from New York
50 Inventor's initials
52 Unchallenged
55 Slippery
57 Pot starter
58 Marsh growth
60 TV part
61 *A Chorus Line* tune
62 Opie's aunt

376 PEOPLE FOOD

by Randolph Ross

ACROSS

1 Dull-colored
5 Not glossy
10 Spielberg blockbuster
14 General's staffer
15 Young Jetson
16 __ Bator
17 Beef entrée
19 Flood wall
20 Painter Matisse
21 Pourer's problem
23 Actress Hagen
25 Hot times in Le Havre
26 Pass catcher
27 French dessert
32 Snitch
33 Upswing
34 Author Silverstein
38 Guild member
40 Shows up
43 Heavy hammer
44 Petri dish contents
45 Inlet
46 Breakfast entrée
51 ASAP
54 Grub
55 Yale student
56 Cats and dogs
59 Atlas feature
63 Drop
64 Popular dessert
66 Head: Fr.
67 Prufrock's creator
68 Crowd sound
69 Nasal input
70 Fender flaws
71 Posted

DOWN

1 Élan
2 Ceremony
3 Arabia's Gulf of __
4 Endure
5 Club __ (vacation destination)
6 MacGraw and Baba
7 Circus swinger
8 Marquee word
9 Button hole
10 Karate cousin
11 Kicking partner
12 Rouse
13 Bergen voice
18 Check tamperers
22 D-Day craft
24 Home to billions
27 Study all night
28 __ avis
29 Caesarean phrase
30 Cmdr.'s org.
31 Compass pt.
35 Mata __
36 Author Ambler
37 Would-be atty.'s exam
39 Tact suffix
40 Epoch
41 Sheet of stamps
42 Main-event opener
44 Vote "present"
47 "Wow!"
48 Having spaces
49 Addison's colleague
50 Restaurant patrons
51 Passport requirement
52 Like the Capitol
53 South American capital
57 -arian relative
58 Highlander
60 Gin flavoring
61 Abba of Israel
62 Sour-tasting
65 Alts.

377 THE HARD STUFF

by Dean Niles

ACROSS

1 Ballet leap
5 Medieval Danish king
9 It may waft
14 Gung-ho
15 Easy gait
16 Pickle palaces
17 Little thing
18 Part of
19 Unwelcome wind
20 Hide-and-seek cousin
23 "Big Blue"
24 Poetic dusk
25 Beelike
29 Fix, as in memory
32 "I __ Little Prayer"
36 Jumper's cord
38 "If __ a Hammer"
40 __ generis
41 Out-of-the-mainstream music
44 Vane dir.
45 Test type
46 Show
47 Roll-call response
49 "Excuse me!"
51 Most of the earth
52 Turkey part
54 Hosp. area
56 Crisp greens
64 Pushy move
65 Glide along
66 __ Minor
67 He cares too much
68 __ Cong
69 "Shall we?" answer
70 Tuckered out
71 Specific advantage
72 Canadian Indian

DOWN

1 Window side
2 Bringing trouble
3 South American monkey
4 First home
5 Scale the ladder
6 Generic
7 Once __ a time
8 Sawbucks
9 Mix up
10 Summer features
11 Norwegian king
12 Offend
13 Nova Scotia clock setting: Abbr.
21 Moola
22 Act well
25 Make blush
26 Beat
27 Part of ICBM
28 Era
30 Front-page feature
31 NL or AL city
33 United
34 Southwestern plant
35 Crooner Clay
37 Infuriate
39 Pious
42 Sound of satisfaction
43 Mr. Ocasek
48 *Ocean's* __
50 Surroundings
53 *Sun-Times* critic
55 Tristan and Iseult, e.g.
56 Flapjack franchise
57 Sheep shelter
58 "Let's hear from you"
59 *Passages* author Sheehy
60 Skin powder
61 Manipulative one
62 Quote
63 Make less difficult
64 '60s campus org.

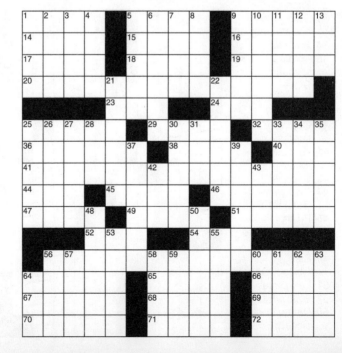

378 CLEANED OUT

by Donna J. Stone

ACROSS

1 Lay an egg
5 Fearless Fosdick's creator
9 Parachute landing
13 Satan's bag
14 Jazzman Chick
15 Architect Saarinen
16 *Symphonie Espagnole* composer
17 Alliance
18 Wolf gang?
19 START OF A QUIP
22 Weimaraner's warning
23 Utters
24 Pass on
29 Bites
33 Give __ for one's money
34 *Hud* star
36 Actress Verdugo
37 Stole
38 Lesser Antilles isle
40 Capt.'s superior
41 '52 button name
43 Chopped
44 Go against Galahad
45 Prompt
47 *Agnes of God* actress
49 San __ Obispo, CA
51 Long time
52 END OF QUIP
60 Not quite closed
61 Accomplished, old-style
62 Spoken
63 Casino city
64 Great Lake natives
65 Bring down the house
66 WWII gun
67 Place a patch
68 Place for a patch

DOWN

1 Composer Bartók
2 Ellipse
3 Grain processor
4 Amazon weapon
5 Bean on the bean
6 Sills solo
7 Menial laborers
8 Black-and-white beasts
9 Coup d'état
10 Swing a sickle
11 Largest dolphin
12 Hardly hurried
14 Jelly fruit
20 Trams transport it
21 One of the Baby Bells
24 Kiddie-lit pachyderm
25 Carve a canyon
26 Misgiving
27 Part of MIT
28 Sultan's pride
30 Philanthropist Rhodes
31 Hillock
32 Like anchovies
35 Rob of *Masquerade*
38 Hole in your head
39 Absorbs
42 Wing thing
44 Tole
46 Highfalutin' headgear
48 Low digit
50 British county
52 Damages
53 "Leaving on __ Plane"
54 Carol of *Taxi*
55 Valhalla VIP
56 Hand-me-down
57 OPEC member
58 Shake up
59 Gen. Robert __

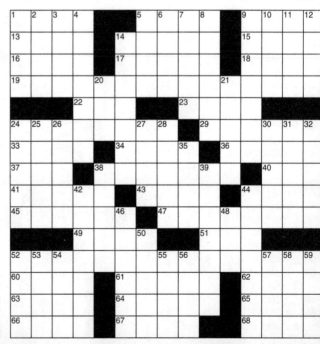

379 A CROSSWORD

by Bill Swain

ACROSS

1 Tin Pan Alley org.
6 Can openers
10 Plays a part
14 Hood of *Our Gang*
15 Shakespearean plaint
16 "__ was no lady . . ."
17 Holy table
18 Winning quarterback in Super Bowl I
20 Grandmothers
22 Athens rival
23 "There oughta be __!"
26 *Raiders of the Lost* __
27 Baseballer Tony
28 "Nearer, My God to Thee" writer
32 Promgoers, in short
33 Rio de la __ (Argentine river)
34 Iron hook
37 Inhaler's target
40 Brilliant beetle
43 German river
44 Indian melodies
46 Author's output, briefly
49 "Teach Your Children" singer
53 Dismay
56 The old college cry
57 Sp. gal
58 Unwelcome winds
60 Grind teeth
62 *Broca's Brain* author
64 Gulf Coast city
68 Aleutian island
69 Black-tie bash
70 Composer Berg
71 "Hey, you!"
72 Asian nursemaid
73 Peter and Ivan

DOWN

1 City in Oklahoma
2 Mineo or Maglie
3 Computer screen: Abbr.
4 *Way of Zen* author
5 Chute starter
6 Knight coat
7 Baked state?
8 Watering hole
9 Concorde fleet
10 Perfume from roses
11 Talismans
12 Fish sauce
13 Fake jewelry
19 Reducing club
21 Flight grp.
23 African snake
24 Song syllables
25 Coach Parseghian et al.
29 Some laughs
30 British autos
31 Kangaroo pouch
35 Cultivate
36 Dutch artist
38 *Cosmo*, e.g.
39 Schedule notation
41 Thickering agent
42 Rope fiber
45 __ Na Na
46 Zany
47 Dieters of rhyme
48 Radioman's nickname
50 Asian stork
51 Actress Daryl
52 Triumphant cry
54 Black key
55 Mil. officers
59 *The Forsyte* __
61 Sports figure
63 Actress Rita
65 Finance deg.
66 Duffer's goal
67 Ques. response

380 B CAREFUL

by R.A. Sefick

ACROSS

1 Porky Pig, actually
5 Item from the horse's mouth?
8 Turkish title
11 Politico Abzug
12 One, in Avignon
13 Better than
15 Catcher cited in Bartlett's
17 Henry __ Lodge
18 Painting the town
19 Some cars
20 In addition
21 Didn't __ eye (took it calmly)
22 Chicago lines
23 Marketing software
26 Break out the books
29 Sissy talk?
30 Sweetums
31 "__ happen to you if you're young at heart"
32 Ventilate
33 Some DC buildings
36 Pinza, for one
38 Power-cell type
39 Seafarer
40 Bear homes
41 Crabby?
45 Good for crops
47 Telly
48 Trite
49 Tropical flora
50 Four seasons, e.g.
51 NYC subway line
52 Suffer an ailment
53 His: Fr.
54 Seeded privilege
55 Vegas figures

DOWN

1 End of "The Purple Cow"
2 Korbut et al.
3 Wouldn't take the blame
4 In a wild way
5 Small towns
6 As to
7 Social drink
8 "The __ Honeymoon"
9 Lose it
10 Outfit that chimes in
11 Invitation advisory
13 Perfume-factory ingredient
14 Aliens: Abbr.
16 Chemical endings
19 Smooth fabric
21 Rum cakes
23 Perilous
24 39 Down and related subjs.
25 Eliel's architect son
26 Queens stadium
27 Pyramid, essentially
28 Throw off
29 Sw?zzles
31 Rhône tributary
34 Moors' drums
35 "__ Nacht"
36 Baseballer Bonilla, for short
37 Touched up against
39 Rock study: Abbr.
41 *The Prince of Tides* actor
42 Like the tabloids
43 Rudolf and I.W.
44 Virginia dance
45 E-Z formula
46 Bright spots
47 __ the hatchet
49 Tot's coverup

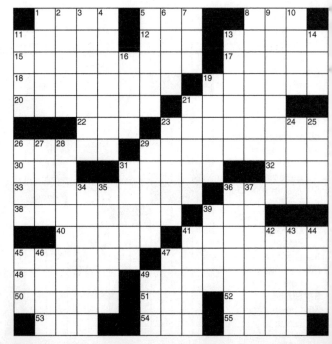

381 NEAR-MISS FILMS

by Wayne R. Williams

ACROSS

1 Fluttery fliers
6 Photographer's request
11 Kipling book
14 Actor Hawke
15 Some down
16 Eddie Cantor's wife
17 Elvis Presley's dog?
20 Ump's cohort
21 Thorny shrub
22 *Pravda* source
23 __ Roberts U.
25 Wacky Wilson
27 Fits of pique
30 Drunkard
32 Psyche components
34 Art school subj.
35 Cast
38 Jolly laugh
40 Coll. exam
41 Teamster candidates?
44 Japanese honorific
45 Actress McClurg
46 Is frugal
47 Work units
49 Weapons
51 Healthy spot
52 Infield covers
54 Popular pet name
56 Cartoon mail-order company
59 *My Favorite __*
61 Costa __
63 Pioneer director Browning
64 Unidentified female jogger?
68 Nabokov novel
69 Humiliate
70 Wear away
71 Place of confinement
72 Nerve-racking
73 Baseball's "Big Poison"

DOWN

1 French subway
2 Tryon novel, with *The*
3 Runner with a grudge?
4 "Eureka!"
5 Fargo forecast
6 Doddering
7 Dark queen?
8 Wedding vow
9 Remaining
10 *Aunt __ Cope Book*
11 Smooching manual?
12 Infamous Amin
13 Scottish-name prefix
18 TV band
19 Annapolis sch.
24 Takings
26 Milne bear
28 Card with a message
29 British guns
31 Yule buy
33 Females
35 Selling feature
36 Bow of the silents
37 Soft drink
39 Inning divisions
42 Evergreens
43 Palm thatch
48 *The Pursuit of the Graf __*
50 Evening gathering
53 Former Middle East leader
55 Fort Worth sch.
57 World according to Pierre
58 Gardening tool
60 Playwright David
62 Once again
64 Spring runner
65 Poetic piece
66 Game piece
67 Gun-owners' lobby

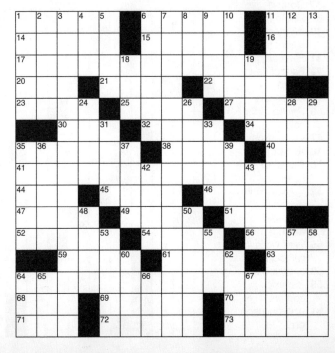

by Bob Lubbers

ACROSS

1 Conference site
6 WWII soldier
10 __ de deux
13 __ Rogers St. Johns
14 Yippie Hoffman
16 Feeling of anger
17 TRAFFIC
19 A fifth of MV
20 "__ pig's eye!"
21 Latin I word
22 Kesey or Olin
23 Box with a bow
27 Fugue intro
29 Smoked salmon
30 Project part
32 Ooze
33 Tyrannical Ugandan
35 Coup d'__
37 Photo finish?
40 Western alliance
41 Flies alone
43 Faucet flaw
44 Drum accessory
46 Receptionist call
47 Fill to excess
48 Ayn or Sally
50 Barrel of laughs
52 "__ was only a bird . . ."
53 Oak-leaf arrangement
56 Well-worn witticisms
58 Lady lobster
59 Summer coolers
61 Anti-pollution grp.
62 Like steak tartare
63 PEDESTRIAN
68 "This __ stickup!"
69 Lake Indians
70 Martinelli and Lanchester
71 Pen type
72 Holy *femmes*, for short
73 Speaks hoarsely

DOWN

1 Owned
2 "__ to Billy Joe"
3 Crumpet partner
4 Island for immigrants
5 Cleo and Frankie
6 Bank roll?
7 Incantation start
8 Like __ on a log
9 Burns props
10 POLICE
11 Traveled a curved path
12 It has two banks in Paris
15 High regard
18 Seaport on the Loire
23 Schemes
24 "The noblest __ of them all"
25 TAXI
26 Wyoming range
28 Goes first
31 Not as colorful
34 Bayes and Charles
36 Poisonous
38 Church contribution
39 Parrying pieces
42 Filched
45 Use allure
49 Interior settings
51 Mrs. Gore
53 Sportscaster Schenkel
54 Smallest amount
55 Mail a payment
57 Lovely lily
60 Hook's mate
64 CIA predecessor
65 Utter fool
66 Spending limit
67 Snaky letter

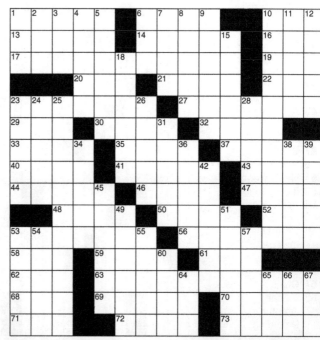

383 REAL ESTATERS

by Wayne R. Williams

ACROSS

1 Legendary tales
6 Bias
11 Brief rest
14 Put into effect
15 Older companion?
16 Japanese sash
17 John or David
18 *A Shropshire Lad* poet
20 Mortise insertions
22 Wrathful
23 Spanish Mrs.
25 Smeltery pile
26 Lived (at)
28 Ado Annie portrayer
31 Model Kim
32 Printer's measures
33 Paradise
37 Responds to leavening
38 Top off
39 Stone marker
40 Tours summers
41 Golf score
42 Eucalyptus eaters
43 Earl Scruggs' partner
45 Dickers
49 Morse signal
50 Scale notes
51 Sci-fi thriller
52 Singer MacKenzie
54 French mathematician
57 Last inning, usually
60 Switch positions
61 Network honcho Arledge
62 Add data
63 Born, in Bordeaux
64 Moved little by little
65 College bigwigs

DOWN

1 Stitch
2 Santa __ winds
3 *Honor Thy Father* author
4 Teen trauma
5 Narrowing, in anatomy
6 Foster river
7 *sex, __, and videotape*
8 Cigar end
9 Modern prefix
10 Established fact
11 Wanderer
12 Let up
13 Yearned (for)
19 __ Lanka
21 Table scraps
23 Frighten
24 Started the fire again
26 Spree
27 High RRs
29 Former wives
30 Courage
33 Lat. list-ender
34 Oscar of fashion
35 Overjoy
36 Branch headquarters?
38 Mama __ Elliot
39 Mollified
41 For each
42 Singer Kristofferson
43 Poe's lady
44 Worked on a manuscript
45 Omelet ingredient
46 Partnerless
47 Washer cycle
48 Turner or Williams
52 Kind of therapy
53 Merchandise offering
55 Distance measure
56 Gear tooth
58 Midmorning
59 Many min.

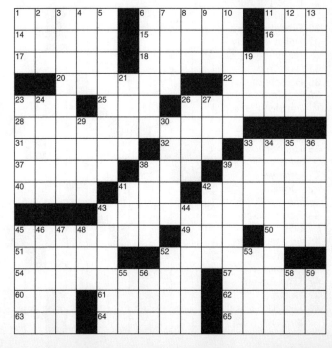

384 TEAM PLAYERS

by Manny Nosowsky

ACROSS

1 Pint in a pub
4 Choose
7 Angry state
14 Webster's offering
16 It may be pernicious: Var.
17 Concerns of 31 Across and 18 Down
19 Prepares for a new start
20 Pennsylvania city
21 Squealer
22 Red Sox old-timer Bobby
23 Cries of disapproval
24 Sagacious
25 Call a halt to
26 Abilene buddy
27 Eggs' partner
28 Banjo sound
30 President Ford
31 Half a comedy team
33 "I do," e.g.
35 Borscht basics
36 " __ for the sky!"
37 __-all (panacea)
38 Uncommon sense
41 Otherwise
42 "Comin' __ the Rye"
43 Screen image unit
45 Fall-sem. start
46 O'Casey or Penn
47 "The Raven" woman
48 Like 31 Across' persona

51 More sallow-looking
52 In mid-bombast, maybe
53 Fancy premises
54 Pot company?
55 Bee chaser

DOWN

1 Refer (to)
2 Pressure
3 Oozed out
4 Earth color
5 Luau side dishes
6 Channel now called Spike TV
7 Cannon clearer
8 *Henry & June* character
9 Ending for check or play
10 Favorite
11 Part of AFL
12 It's a jewel
13 Area north of the Thames
15 Lab assistant name
18 Half a comedy team
23 __-Sadr
24 Merchandise
26 Rate of speed
27 Asteroid's region
28 Do tec work
29 Take a bath
30 Merriment
31 __ straws (makes a futile try)
32 Dynamic beginning
33 Take for granted
34 Author Hanff et al.
37 Meeting heads
38 Strikingly unusual
39 At peace
40 Promise
42 Bit of silly laughter
43 A real nut
44 __ the finish
46 "__ it out!" ("Say it!")
47 Change at Aukara
49 Slangy suffix
50 Go one better

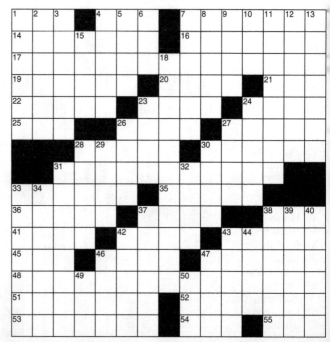

385 INSTRUMENTALS

by Wayne R. Williams

ACROSS

1 *Paper Lion* star
5 Chatter
10 Hurok et al.
14 Stable tyke
15 Location of gutters
16 Say uncle
17 *Deuce Coupe* choreographer
19 Do-others separator
20 Change a title
21 *Sliver* author Levin
22 Word form for "height"
23 Stage classification
24 Rock-and-roll pioneer
26 Ornamental button
28 Mr. Baba
29 Stitch
32 Slot fillers
35 Follow as a consequence
39 1973-76 U.S. Open runner-up
43 Tippy boat
44 Old Testament book
45 Soft, wet ground
46 FDR's Blue Eagle org.
48 Creative drives
51 Infielder-turned-sportscaster
56 Patron saint of France
60 Wheel spindle
61 Cut the grass
62 Eclipse sight
63 Painter Mondrian
64 Famous muckraker
66 Author Ferber
67 Pluck
68 French islands
69 Close up
70 Collect bit by bit
71 Fictional terrier

DOWN

1 Broadcast talent org.
2 Downgrade
3 Singer Taylor __
4 Sherman and others
5 *Our Gang* dog
6 Team support
7 Benefit
8 __ incognita
9 Iberian *nación*
10 __ off (battling)
11 Light weight
12 Petrol unit
13 Tolerated
18 *Amo, amas*, __
24 Proverb
25 Minute circus star
27 Shoshonean
29 Wine description
30 __ Marie Saint
31 Took first
33 Singer Scaggs
34 Philosopher Kierkegaard
36 Blake Edwards movie
37 One, to Juan
38 Fabergé collectible
40 Carbon, e.g.
41 Claudius' nephew
42 Response time
47 Setting a timer
49 Olfactory trigger
50 Slavic land
51 Pokes fun
52 Zinc __ ointment
53 Actress Verdugo
54 Mathematician Kurt
55 In the know
57 Coward and Harrison
58 Estuary
59 Latin beat
62 Columnist Herb
65 Dam-building grp.

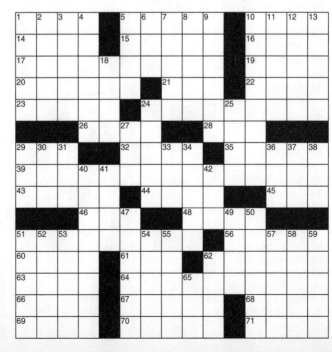

386 SYNTHETICS

by Cathy Millhauser

ACROSS

1 Mrs. Warren's creator
5 More than passed
9 Curtain fabric
14 Singer of films
15 Conn of *Benson*
16 Island off Venizuela
17 Fritzi, to Nancy
18 Mayberry's sot
19 Symbol
20 BANLON
23 Don Juan's mother
24 Manet medium
25 Weekend wear
28 Down __ (Maine)
30 Greek peak
34 LL.B. holder
35 Museum vessels . . .
37 . . . and their openings
39 RAYON
42 Jeweler's measures
43 "Stop that!"
44 Compass pt.
45 Short cut
46 Macmillan's predecessor
48 Horse opera
50 Annapolis sch.
52 Sponges (up)
54 GORE-TEX
60 Basso Ezio
61 Joint effort?
62 Craze

63 *The Wind in the Willows* character
64 Otherwise
65 Neural transmitter
66 Oar pin
67 Batik artist, e.g.
68 Fuzz problem

DOWN

1 Rebuff
2 Appointed time
3 Florence's river
4 Contained by
5 Southwestern dwelling
6 Taxpayers
7 Word on some PC menus
8 Does the hustle
9 Birth-related
10 Settles
11 Zap in the microwave
12 Follow
13 Bert Bobbsey's twin
21 Dis
22 *Pelican Brief* character
25 One-eyed twosome
26 Allen of Vermont
27 Video-game name
29 "By the way" line
31 Play Scrooge
32 Shed light on?
33 *Roots* Emmy-winner
36 Feel bitter about
38 Squid kin
40 Long-locked lady
41 Tomfoolery
47 Applied plaster
49 Like a diamond in the sky
51 Make start
53 Law partner
54 Stem center
55 Proverbial preposition
56 Count (on)
57 Prepare to take off
58 *Ghostbusters* good guy
59 Flat charge?
60 Soup vessel

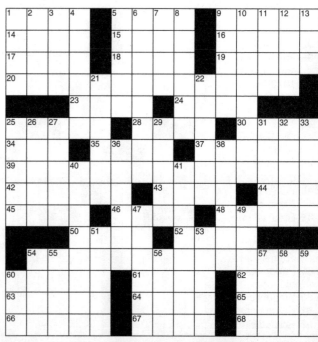

387 SHORT SPELLS

by Richard Silvestri

ACROSS

1 Ambassador's title?
5 Marine creature?
10 Simple treatise?
14 Commuter line
15 Colorful horses
16 Just around the corner
17 Actress __ May Wong
18 Attack
19 Withstand
20 Alumnus memento
22 Iago's wife
24 Lodge members
25 __ moss
26 Small sofa
29 Well-acquainted
33 That girl
34 Men and women
36 Exile isle
37 Between __ and a hard place
39 Plant tub
40 "__ a Grecian Urn"
41 Actress Kedrova
42 Strictness of a sort
44 Harbor helper
45 Revealing
47 Greek goddess
49 Zhivago's love
50 Utah's state flower
51 Wisdom personified
54 "The Lost Continent"
58 Lend an ear
59 Wooden pin
61 Minor weakness
62 Genesis name
63 *A Night at the __*
64 Fencing piece
65 Uninhabited tent?
66 Advantageous-ness?
67 Bad news at the dentist?

DOWN

1 Picture of health?
2 Stroller's site
3 Designer Ricci
4 Red wine
5 Dishonest
6 Taboos
7 Disguise
8 Plane hdg.
9 Prizes
10 Authorized
11 Passion
12 Munro's pseudonym
13 Surface measurement
21 Gloomy
23 __ tai (rum drink)
25 Singer Page
26 Commandment verb
27 Spine-tingling
28 Billy Goats Gruff adversary
29 Warning light
30 "__ Song Go Out of My Heart"
31 Circa
32 Versatility
35 Palate part
38 Telephoned
40 Greek letter
42 Self-contradiction
43 Trounce
46 Shade of brown
48 Outwardly round
50 Inflexible
51 "Excuse me!"
52 Trial
53 Pressure
54 Intimidated
55 Waiter's rewards
56 Topped the cake
57 Go after
60 Top, to bottom: Abbr.

388 PASSION PLAY

by Dean Niles

ACROSS

1 "Hey, you!"
5 Corn color
10 Secluded hollow
14 Slow payer's risk
15 Intentional fire
16 Wander about
17 Sacred image
18 Stirs up
19 *Messiah* section
20 Pontiac model
21 Betray a secret
23 Din
25 "__ you kidding?"
26 Code of silence
28 Spielberg title word
33 Lanai
34 Trio x 3
35 Cow comment
36 __ Minor
37 Very cold
38 Bad reviews
39 Bandleader Brown
40 Gave out hands
41 Implied
42 Pleasing proportion
44 Winter wraps
45 NATO cousin
46 Indian princess
47 Short musket
52 Slugger's stat
55 Completely absorbed
56 Lodes
57 Look listlessly
58 Pay one's share
59 Foy family father
60 Convivial
61 British slammer
62 Interminably
63 Some snakes

DOWN

1 Fussy sort
2 Religious faction
3 "Collie model" is one
4 Whole bunch
5 Actress Berenson
6 Came up
7 Fertility goddess
8 Dreyfus defender
9 Captured
10 Rubs the wrong way
11 Folktales
12 "See no __ ..."
13 Actress Patricia
21 __ and kin
22 "Dagnabbit!"
24 Killer whale
26 Iridescent stones
27 Saunter
28 Adjective for Roger
29 Constituent part
30 Moola
31 Aegean area
32 Amounts to
34 Close
37 Has one's revenge
38 Cut back
40 __ *Poet's Society*
41 Catches rays
43 Talk-show host Williams
44 Left in the dust
46 Arrest
47 Talk big
48 Screen Turner
49 As far as
50 Make over
51 Wait a while
53 Old toon Betty
54 Roadhouses
57 Grad. degree

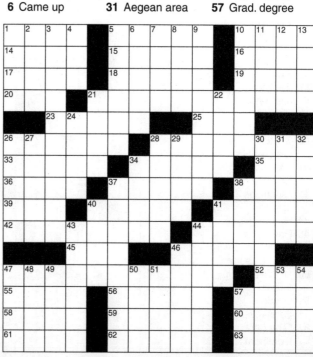

389 SOUNDS LIKE IT

by Shirley Soloway

ACROSS

1 Green stroke
5 Knowledgeable
10 Proclivity
14 Orem's state
15 Actress Shire
16 Medicinal plant
17 Instruct an office worker?
19 Gets off one's feet
20 Mr. Agnew
21 Printer's mark
22 Classify
23 Paramedic: Abbr.
25 Performs in school
27 Do a little retail business?
32 Clamor
33 GI hangout
34 Wed in haste
36 Perry's right hand
40 Corner sign
42 Beneficial beam
44 Garage item
45 Mamas' mates
47 Day in Hollywood
49 Claire or Balin
50 Brit. military branch
52 Taunt a transgression?
54 Brings to mind
58 Attila, e.g.
59 *Duck Soup* prop
60 Elevator man
63 Untied
67 Oklahoma native
68 Select an Easter bloom?
70 Collision result
71 Thread holder
72 In the vicinity
73 Zeus' colleague
74 Streisand film
75 Large volume

DOWN

1 Stock options
2 Lone Star sch.
3 Anklebones
4 *And __ Stood with My Piccolo* (Willson book)
5 Pig's digs
6 Glove compartment items
7 Came down to earth
8 Day starter
9 Created lace
10 Fisherman's catch?
11 Writer T.S.
12 __ Dame
13 Finals
18 Ballet step
24 Statuesque
26 El __ (Heston role)
27 Tooth point
28 *¿Cómo __ usted?*
29 Chicago's business area
30 Kermit's kin
31 __ Downs
35 Saarinen of architecture
37 __ *& Clark*
38 Burt's ex
39 King of comedy
41 Two goldfish?
43 Wealthy
46 Pitcher Maglie
48 Row, in a way
51 Story-time rabbit
53 Consecrate
54 Valerie Harper role
55 Buffet lover
56 Hag
57 Lead singer of R.E.M.
61 Revered object
62 Aberdeen native
64 Toast topper
65 Close with force
66 O'Casey's land
69 Everything

390 BATTLE OF THE SEXES

by A.J. Santora

ACROSS

1 Stratagems
6 Dollops
10 What RNs give
13 Practice piece
14 Birthright seller
15 Small chuckle
16 Tom of *The Dukes of Hazzard*
17 Vermont tree
18 Mezzo-soprano Stignani
19 Killer __ (computer technology)
20 With caution
21 Easter entrée
22 Outbreak
24 Writer Jong
25 Singer Tennille
26 With 42 Across, a Cervantes quote
28 "__ home right now, so when you hear the tone . . ."
30 *Pacem in __*
31 Most boring
32 Fuse unit
34 Snacked
35 Tiny metric meas.
36 Word of assent
37 Paucity
39 "__ in trying!"
41 School team
42 See 26 Across
45 Cash-filled conveniences
46 Singer LaBelle
48 Small bit
49 Omar Sharif role in a '69 film
50 Shatner's *T.J. Hooker* costar
51 Eur. land
52 Poe's time of day
53 Either *Paper Moon* star
54 Keep an __ (watch)
56 "Mona Lisa" singer
57 RBI, for one
58 Threshold
59 NFL scores
60 Existence: Lat.
61 Soothed

DOWN

1 Heat over
2 Literally, "not a place"
3 High cost of leaving?
4 Writer LeShan
5 Ready to go
6 Darlings
7 Clear jelly
8 Wifely attachment?
9 Chop __
10 Kramden saga
11 Like Danny Thomas
12 The Curies, for two
17 *My Little __* (old sitcom)
20 Show who's boss?
23 Trevi coin count
25 10-__ odds
27 Aroused to anger
29 Bach's instrument
32 Nearby
33 Archie's son-in-law
35 *The Producers* star
38 Motor homes, for short
39 Silents' film
40 "*Vive le __!*"
43 Underling
44 Part of ERA
47 Fields of expertise
50 Medicinal amount
54 First mate?
55 "Verily!"

391 IN THE DRINK

by Bob Lubbers

ACROSS

1 __ 1 (the speed of sound)
5 Canadian Indian
9 Cellist Casals
14 Medicinal plant
15 Circle dance
16 Vane pointer
17 Seacoast
19 Performer's platform
20 Yalta conferee
21 The mater tongue?
23 James or Jimmy
26 Give the business to
29 Shakespeare's Moor
32 Actor Dan
33 Primp plumage
34 One who stares
36 "That __ no lady, that . . ."
37 Abel's dad
38 Laotian's neighbors
39 Having smarts
40 Agt.
41 Old dashboard features
42 Road repair markers
43 Washed away
45 Jostled
47 Manorial property
48 Embattled European
49 Set the stage with props
51 Gone aloft
56 Exhibited
58 U. of West Florida home
61 Post payment
62 Novelist Leon
63 __ Well That Ends Well
64 Actress Papas
65 What's My Line? host
66 Ararat visitor

DOWN

1 Door accessories
2 Landed
3 Musical epilogue
4 Obedience school command
5 Last name in perfumes
6 Balderdash
7 Before, to Moore
8 Basketballer Monroe
9 Muni role
10 More showy
11 Battle site of 1777
12 Ship's diary
13 Run a tab
18 Add a lane
22 South American mountain chain
24 Hilo hail
25 Arizona town
27 Rented
28 Takes the heat off
29 Marching __ (walking papers)
30 Harding administration scandal
31 Blouse border
33 "Gay" city
35 Cotton thread
38 Cinematic princedom?
39 "Oh, boy!"
41 Cold War respite
42 Hooded snake
44 Galápagos visitor
46 Loud and shrill
50 KP peelable
52 __ Get It for You Wholesale
53 Aviate alone
54 First name in scat
55 Last name in light verse
56 __ Lanka
57 Not him
59 Memorable period
60 Zilch

392 FILM OFFSPRING

by Wayne R. Williams

ACROSS

1 Highlands hat
4 Let in
9 Howled
14 Be penitent
15 Type of linen
16 "Be-Bop-__" ('56 tune)
17 Curtis film of '66
20 Tropical tree
21 '60s protest grp.
22 Dress styles
23 Western Samoa capital
25 Small songbird
26 Ape film of '98
32 Felt (for)
33 Mars' equivalent
34 Caviar
35 Epochs
36 He's treating
38 Give as an example
39 Onetime JFK plane
40 Front of the calf
41 See-through
42 Eddie Murphy film of '86
46 Alien crafts
47 Dash
48 Ariel, e.g.
51 Bishopric
52 Beef-rating org.
56 Bob Hope film of '51
59 Gobbled up
60 Acid in apples
61 Eur. land
62 Lock of hair
63 Contract details
64 Pokey

DOWN

1 Hidden snag
2 Faint glow
3 Blackbird
4 Jeep, e.g.: Abbr.
5 "Nobody __ Better"
6 Noon
7 French specks of land
8 Painter Gerard __ Borch
9 F. Lee and Pearl
10 Unpigmented
11 Chinese currency
12 German river
13 __ Inn (hotel chain)
18 Mental pictures
19 Life's work
24 Advanced deg.
25 Sported
26 Wetlands
27 Hot under the collar
28 Mansfield or Meadows
29 An archangel
30 Well-known
31 Actor Will
32 "__ la vie!"
36 Plant tissue
37 Helps out
38 "Hang in there!"
40 Thaws out
41 __ Na Na
43 Sneaky ways
44 Goad
45 Religious figure
48 Editor's directive
49 __ Lap (horse film)
50 Neural network
51 Crisp cookie
53 Pass over
54 Desperate
55 Arabian seaport
57 Mantras
58 Lt.-to-be's sch.

393 WORDS AT PLAY

by Randolph Ross

ACROSS

1 GI hangouts
5 Fastener
9 Drum's partner
13 Summer weasel
14 Approve
15 Clark's coworker
16 Where to take a sports suit?
19 __ the Head (Sinatra film)
20 Musical talent
21 Dining area
24 Shimon of Israel
28 Wimbledon gala?
32 Office sub
33 Compound word?
34 Not clerical
36 Little legume
37 Tach reading
38 Nested
41 __ Lingus
42 Lowe or Reiner
43 Walked over
44 Hideaways
46 Dot in the sea
48 Links lessons?
51 He went to town
53 Despot
54 Something to chew on
56 Not at all
60 Fielding gem?
65 Done
66 Reagan secretary of state
67 Pub contest
68 Turns the ship
69 Wheel connector
70 Hot times in Le Havre

DOWN

1 Jazz's home
2 Mediocre
3 West Coast city
4 Having the most nerve
5 Pal around
6 Wanted-poster initials
7 The Godfather role
8 Nabors role
9 Broccoli cluster
10 Chit
11 Douglas' tree
12 Guinness Book suffix
13 Govt. agcy. for retailers
17 Muscular spasms
18 Put the lid on
22 With reason
23 Style
25 Fix
26 Arab princes
27 Thinly populated
28 Burning hot
29 Tell all
30 Like Jack of nursery rhymes
31 Ignited
35 Row of columns
39 Bit of work
40 Play the horn
45 Restaurant of yore
47 Gardening tools
49 Site often raided
50 "How __ Be Sure?"
52 Hero
55 Rajah starter
57 Donned
58 Army insects
59 NFL gain
60 Tarzan's kid
61 Frank's ex
62 Suture
63 Careless
64 __ Abner

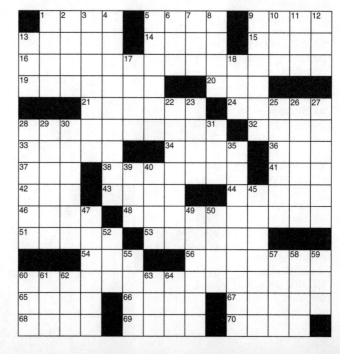

394 WORLD SERIES

by Robert H. Wolfe

ACROSS

1 Tanning lotion ingredient
5 Computer corrupter
10 Tale
14 Like 2 or 20
15 Banal
16 Slangy suffix
17 Baked clay vessels
20 Like some equations
21 Water pitcher
22 Teeny
23 More, to some
24 Competition sites
26 Getz's instrument
28 Yearn for
31 Feeling disgust
36 Do woodwork
38 Gulf of Lions port
42 Wildly
43 Mollycoddles
44 Blender settings
48 __ Boot ('81 German film)
49 Window treatments
51 PGA props
55 Drunkard
58 Snarl
59 Processed grain
61 In the manner of a nabob
64 Altar activity
65 Slalom curves
66 Sermon
67 __ Show of Shows
68 Feats
69 Caesar's being

DOWN

1 Role for Rigg
2 Use
3 Swiss capital
4 Pot builders
5 Contender
6 Place to stop
7 Less cooked
8 Not at all impressed
9 Quiet
10 Mouth, or mouth off
11 In __ (lined up)
12 Memorization method
13 Winning margin
18 Bother
19 Historical periods
24 Skating move
25 Strong fiber
27 He had a divine right
29 Signalled, in a way
30 Noun ending
31 Doctors' grp.
32 Dawber and Shriver
33 Type of plane, for short
34 Questioned
35 551, to Ovid
37 __ Moines, IA
39 Means justifiers?
40 Prescription agcy.
41 Rural
45 Therefore
46 Did the reel
47 Few and far between
50 Rub out
52 Make happy
53 Fitzgerald and Raines
54 Peddles
55 Nimble-footed
56 Mishmash
57 Ballet wear
59 Feel the loss of
60 Actor Dick Van __
62 Numerical word form
63 Danson or Kennedy

395 OLYMPIC GAMES

by Walter Williams

ACROSS

1 Practice punching
5 Mr. Bumppo
10 Took a chair
13 Bean curd
14 Painter's pigment
15 Art __
16 Thicke or Cranston
17 Lose deliberately
18 "__ each life . . ."
19 Unable to decide
20 Morris' musing
21 VHS adjunct
22 Charlie Weaver's Mount __
24 Losers' consolation phrase
26 Actress Massey
29 Board a rush-hour subway
30 Filament element
32 Dressed for the Forum
36 Landed
37 Actress Samantha
39 "__ Excited" ('84 tune)
40 Metropolis menace Lex
42 Railroader
44 Rare __ (metallic elements)
46 Hearty brew
47 The cost of leaving
49 Toy merchant __ Schwarz
50 Singer Joplin
51 Second son
53 Sitcom radio station
57 Strong bugs
58 Avoid capture
59 Butter alternative
60 *Coma* author
61 Contradict
62 Hitchcock's __ *Window*
63 Barbie's ex
64 Slugs
65 Continued

DOWN

1 RBI, e.g.
2 Horse play?
3 A long ways off
4 Cliché, Olympics event?
5 "It's __ cup of tea"
6 Sore spot
7 Cliché, Olympics event?
8 Gardener's tool
9 Tree for bows
10 Have a feeling
11 Played a part
12 Whistle sound
15 Cliché, Olympics event?
21 The Stooges, e.g.
23 German article
25 Tropical fish
26 Like *this*: Abbr.
27 Doozy
28 "Put a lid __!"
29 Wooden pin
31 __ firma
33 Arsenal stock
34 Isaac's eldest
35 Word of warning
38 __ *Gratia Artis* (MGM motto)
41 Bumblers
43 "This __ test"
45 Irish city
47 Lake boat
48 Sultry singer Susan
49 Skedaddles
50 Mr. Palance
52 Computer command
54 Swiss abstract painter
55 Gather up grain
56 Freighter's destination
58 Fade away

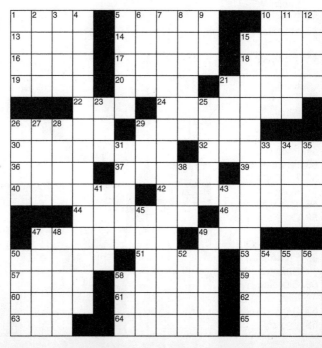

396 RUG PLUG

by Donna J. Stone

ACROSS

1 English county
6 *Fanny* author
10 Improvise, in a way
14 Call up
15 Bass Pinza
16 Singer Redding
17 START OF A QUIP
19 Musical pause
20 The Friendly Ghost
21 Vasco __
23 Esau's wife
25 Sorts
27 Assail
28 Stands for
30 Fossey's friend
32 *Printemps* follower
33 Jazzman Louis
34 Exist
35 MIDDLE OF QUIP
41 Tree tool
42 Long Island town
45 Theorem initials
48 Pipe cleaner
49 Wave, for one
51 Pool
53 Fountain order
55 *Fort Apache* actor
56 This way
58 On the way up
60 Decline
61 END OF QUIP
65 *Three Men __ Baby*
66 Cleveland's lake
67 Drink slowly
68 __-poly

69 "The Swedish Nightingale"
70 Beast of Borden

DOWN

1 Morning moisture
2 Actress Le Gallienne
3 Hot-tempered
4 Eller's musical
5 Catches cod
6 Rocks for rings
7 Missouri's __ Mountains
8 Zilch
9 Sourdough's quest
10 Beat into shape
11 Colonel's command
12 Destiny
13 Graceland, e.g.
18 Mayberry moppet
22 Beame or Burrows
23 Payroll management corp.
24 German article
26 Agra attire
29 Pine product
31 Barnyard enclosure
34 Dealt with dessert
36 Cough up the cash
37 Small businessman?
38 *M*A*S*H* extras
39 Constantinople, currently

40 Mays and Mantle
43 Author Levin
44 By means of
45 Faraway object
46 California town
47 Alpine outfit
48 Brown or Crane
49 Moved with grace
50 Orient
52 Hungarian wine
54 Senator Hatch
57 Cartoonist Silverstein
59 Skye of *Say Anything . . .*
62 Jackie's second
63 "__ live and breathe!"
64 Placekicker's prop

397 AIRMEN

by Dean Niles

ACROSS
1 React to a compliment
5 Farmland units
10 Work on the salad
14 Armbone
15 "Ta da!"
16 "__ us a child is born . . ."
17 Jeremy Irons film
19 Hold back
20 Fight
21 Chef's secret
23 *Norma* __
25 Hits on the noggin
26 Gene Barry series
33 Dismount
34 Carry around
35 Cook's meas.
38 Hecht and Franklin
39 Show (in)
41 Char
42 Bunyan's tool
43 Collar holder
44 Stone or Bronze?
46 Military comic strip
48 Delicious, e.g.
51 Fish-fetcher
52 Taylor film
56 "__ *mañana*!"
61 Aquarium
62 *Saturday Night Fever* group
64 In the old days
65 Exalted
66 Kind of incline
67 Blvds.
68 Blackbird: Var.
69 Mont Blanc range

DOWN
1 Brooklyn Dodgers, in cartoons
2 North Sea feeder
3 ". . . some kind of __?"
4 Actor Dillon
5 "__ *Maria*"
6 Girdle kin
7 Teeming
8 Jazz great's first name
9 States
10 Arouse
11 __ a million
12 Reek
13 Porter products
18 Synagogue scroll
22 Clarinet's cousin
24 Showing shrewdness
26 Rum cake
27 Host Trebek
28 Fork part
29 Booker T. & the __
30 It's a gas
31 __ v. *Wade*
32 Disco light
35 Freshwater duck
36 Wise guy
37 Sitting duck
40 Watched the tot
41 "Star Wars": Abbr.
43 Ooze
45 Shaping machine
46 Jolly good fellows
47 Make possible
48 Equity member
49 Manufacturing place
50 Change for 46 Down
53 __ time (never)
54 "__ Swell"
55 Confederates
57 Taj Mahal site
58 Close up
59 Part-timer
60 Some snakes
63 Slippery one

398 EQUAL SIDES

by Wayne R. Williams

ACROSS
1 Color-changing lizard
6 Folklore being
11 Mule of song
14 ___ lazuli
15 Mother-of-pearl
16 Status ___
17 Megahit
19 Main *número*
20 One who pillages
21 Knight or Williams
22 Night flyers
23 Update, as a factory
25 Madame Curie
26 Provençal love song
30 ___ Dawn Chong
31 Lurch and swerve
32 Wild times
34 Song stylist
36 Fabric
38 Grossly wicked
41 *From Here to Eternity* costar
43 Ring in the ocean
44 Marine raptor
46 Historic period
48 Stick it out
49 Removes rind
50 Get the ball rolling
52 Wallach and Whitney
53 ___ Baba
54 Good, farmlandwise

59 Anaïs the diarist
60 Freezer adjunct
62 Chang's twin
63 Ships' lengths
64 Battery terminal
65 Scale notes
66 Senator Kefauver
67 Acted as a tug

DOWN
1 Priests' garments
2 Festive
3 Putative Bible bk.
4 Mr. Jagger
5 Interviewer
6 African antelope
7 More down-and-dirty
8 Band of a sort
9 Classic sitcom
10 Command conclusion
11 Calculator key
12 Family member
13 Untie
18 Rabbit's title
22 Sea north of Norway
24 Aspect
25 Current craze
26 Well-honed skill
27 Invent facts
28 Bed parts
29 Dresses
31 Miler Sebastian
33 Reciprocals of cosecants
35 Role for Leigh
37 Deposit
39 Form ending
40 Crafty
42 Measuring scale
44 First game
45 Salty
47 Saudi, e.g.
50 Icy rain
51 Cover the tab
53 Old pros
55 ___ cost (free)
56 Forehead
57 Take on cargo
58 Ogled
60 "I Like ___"
61 Amer. ship designation

399 ANIMAL HOUSING

by Bob Lubbers

ACROSS

1 Social stratum
6 Pass twice
11 __ Mahal
14 Motorist's maneuver
15 Cover story?
16 Wedding words
17 Turned (away)
18 Photographic technique
20 NESTS
22 Rock producer Brian
23 Comedienne Charlotte
24 Pool pro
28 *Ste. Jeanne __*
30 Man from Qum
34 Green guarder
35 That girl
37 Adds more mist
39 BURROWS
42 Justice's domain?
43 Merry month
44 Flask
45 "Big Three" site
47 Some projectiles: Abbr.
51 Alan and Robert
53 Slippery swimmer
55 Road-map org.
56 HIVES
61 Hash houses
64 How Lindy flew
65 Utter fool
66 Exploding stars
67 Silver seeker
68 Erté's bag
69 Fatigued
70 Corp. helpers

DOWN

1 Swore at
2 Savvy goddess
3 Swain
4 Very, in Versailles
5 Biblical witch town
6 Rural pet, perhaps
7 Director Kazan
8 Branch
9 Genesis name
10 Pier posts
11 Helpful hint
12 Billboards, e.g.
13 Palooka
19 Casino glassware
21 Tee vista
25 Part of UAR
26 Comedienne Martha
27 Mess-hall workers: Abbr.
29 Padre
31 The Little Mermaid
32 Electron's chg.
33 Melville narrator
36 Pinkerton logo
38 Bake-sale org.
39 Marlo's mister
40 Principal role
41 Magnavox rival
42 Water-power agcy.
46 China group
48 Copland and Nevelle
49 Attractive object
50 Football great Gale
52 British guns
54 Wool-coat owner
57 Soybeans or celery
58 Busy place
59 Have a little lamb
60 Yale team
61 Feathery stole
62 Pitcher part
63 Sternward

400 MATCHING MONOGRAMS

by Randolph Ross

ACROSS
1 Short summary
6 Petri dish contents
10 Surrounded by
14 Bakery attraction
15 Toad feature
16 Spike the punch
17 *Ulysses* author
19 College exam
20 Went to Wendy's
21 Shoe bottoms
22 Bracelet site
23 "This early?"
25 Driver's lic. and dogtag
26 Archie's pal
33 Spartan slave
36 Icelandic works
37 Logger's tool
38 *Exodus* protagonist
39 Some haircuts
40 Watch junior
41 Narc's org.
42 Terra __
43 Vegetarian taboo
45 Cowboys' former coach
48 Bar opener
49 Start a paragraph
53 Poetic preposition
56 Harsh Athenian
59 Card game
60 Bee home
61 "Shoeless" ballplayer
63 Where some worship from
64 Armbone
65 Jungle vine

66 Till slot
67 Bucks, e.g.
68 Ford flop

DOWN
1 Punjab princes
2 Poetry muse
3 Arrives
4 Soul: Fr.
5 Faint
6 Off base?
7 Soulful Marvin
8 Circle sections
9 AAA suggestion
10 Ballerina Alicia
11 Grade
12 Myth ending
13 Take out of print?
18 Author of *Fear of Flying*
22 Pts. of speech
24 Iberian eye
25 Lupino and Tarbell
27 *Leave __ Heaven*
28 Archie's mate
29 TV commercial maker
30 Apollo initials
31 Sixplex sign
32 Match divisions
33 Pilgrimage to Mecca
34 ". . . __ saw Elba"
35 Actor Neeson
39 WWII name
42 Sporelike cell
43 Erstwhile reading aid
44 Last word at the movies
46 Social gatherings
47 Director Vittorio De __
50 Lanchester and Schiaparelli
51 Not a soul
52 Related to sound quality
53 Just one of those things
54 "Take my __, please!"
55 Lendl of tennis
56 Viagara pitchman
57 Actor Auberjonois
58 Slightly open
61 *Oklahoma!* baddie
62 Josh

 # ANSWERS

1

```
  SNIP AMMO   LEA
COATOFPAINT  INS
CITYSLICKER  QTS
SLO SEN ERASURE
    SEDGE   HOES
GOOP    PASTURES
YELLOWJACKET
PRAIRIE  TINTERS
   CAPEHATTERAS
REVELERS    RANT
AUER     THATS
TRESSES AMA EVA
SOR TRAILBLAZER
OPE PLASTICWRAP
NED  ERRS  SEAL
```

2

```
HALT MARLO  HAIL
OMOO IVIED  UGLY
RABBIDAVIDSMALL
ADOANNIE  SPARSE
     GAIL MOON
STRONG  TENUOUS
AAA  HARA  SITKA
SPIRITUALMEDIUM
EISEN DISC   CLI
 READMIT CREAKS
    LIAT CAIN
MALIGN  WORLDWAR
PRISONERATLARGE
AINT ERICH  LAUD
ADDS RATTY  LYES
```

3

```
HEM  BLOBS  SOCK
AXY  AIMEE  ALAI
HEM  BRAGA  NERD
ACAREERISAJOB
    MER  NOLO
WIMSUIT  NOSHOW
ODY  TRIO  SEINE
RE  THATHAS  VEE
EACH QUIP  BEAK
ASHES  SOPHISTS
   ASTI  RAG
GONEONTOOLONG
ROT  IGETA  TARA
AZE  CONIC  EVAN
BEY  STASH  DEFY
```

4

```
APORT LIMB  FEW
RARER IDOL ONIN
CREPE ALLI USDA
HILLSTREETBLUES
   ASH  SHUBERT
ABLY IOC  ERA
IRA CELLO SLIME
ROCKOFGIBRALTAR
SWEAR AMOUR  SRI
 RNS BEN TAKE
EAGLETS   OER
THEMARCHOFDIMES
CENA IRON IVORY
HAIR POLL TITAN
DIX  EDDY HASTE
```

5

```
ARTEMIS  DELIVER
DUEDATE  ORINOCO
ARTICLE  WINSLOW
MARCELMARCEAU
SLAT  CYAN   NBC
    ACDC   ETAL
ESQ CHROME  NERO
MAUREENMCGOVERN
IVAN TOPMAN  RYE
TOSS    AIDE
SRI FRAN    OCHS
  MARILYNMONROE
PRORATA AIRTIME
ABDOMEN STEAMER
LIONESS HELPERS
```

6

```
LANT STOWS  TAT
ONOR THROW  HRS
ROSE OUIJA  ERE
WINESBURGOH HAT
     TETS  IRONS
METTLE   PLATTE
MAHRE  CASUITE
REI WAIST  ILLS
 TXVILLE SONIA
PINION  MESHED
ROWEL    RHEA
DA  LIFEONTHEMS
IL  EDIES TOQUE
NT  YEAST LOUSE
EZ  SATES EDITS
```

7

```
POKES BUMP  EZRA
AGILE AREA  GIAN
CLEVELANDBRONZE
ELIDE SILO   CON
    SEXY CONCORD
PEG RIOTS   DAR
ATOP CUR WORSTS
ARLO AROMA  TWIT
REDIAL LOY  SITE
 FLU FLOWS MOP
STRUDEL  DATA
IOO IMAS  RADII
TINCOMMANDMENTS
ALTO ABLE  PACES
REST SETA  SLAMS
```

8

```
JAKE ISLES  COPS
AVIV CHANT  CROP
POTEMKINVILLAGE
EWE OINK  LIELOW
    SMEE JEFF
ZITHER BITE  DOT
ASWAN WELT  SABU
PAINTTHETOWNRED
PACK AIRS  RATSO
ACE SPRY  CIPHER
    BYES TATS
APPEND OUCH  FEE
PRINCEOFTHECITY
EAST CHLOE  AJAR
XMAS KMART  PILE
```

9

```
MOAB .CAM. SABER
APPLETREE. OCOME
ZEITGEIST. SHOAL
UNA. GABORS. ETNA
MERV. SPOOL. CAT
ARYANS. PLACATE
. .MORSEL. GAMED
ESPRITDECORPS.
ALTER. VOXPOP
HOUDINI. ONALOG
END. SANDS. LORI
AGES. SCOTIA. SIM
DANTE. ELANVITAL
OTTER. NECTARINE
FESTA. TSK. ANAT
```

10

```
GAGE. SEDER. OGRE
IRON. AMILE. FRAT
LAUD. FICKLEFETA
ABDICATE. ABYSS
.AVER. SABRE
ALGERIA. MANACLE
PERSE. PLUS. THEM
AMI. SPOILED. EVE
COED. AGEE. ELDER
ENFORCE. TEPIDLY
.PETER. COMA
EERIE. ESOTERIC
BRIEFORALL. ABBA
BITS. CURIE. DOLT
SCAT. TEMPS. EXES
```

11

```
LIONS. AJAR. FILE
ENVOI. DOPE. ODOF
SCALEDMTEVEREST
SALARIES. INMATE
.RAN. GETA
CLEAN. TOWELOFF
SOUL. AUGER. PIE
WORKINGFORSCALE
UKE. TORTS. ELMS
MESDAMES. GROSS
.ALIE. ZOE
DOWNIN. MOLLUSKS
ONASCALEOFITOIC
NYRO. TEAM. CALLA
OXEN. EELS. SHOOK
```

12

```
DECIMAL. ETC. SHE
IRONAGE. TWO. TEX
MADAMEX. TIN. RAP
.MAN. HANGFIVE
DAZE. TAO. BOOKER
OPART. RUDE. RENT
GENIE. CREDIT
EXECS. ALF. SYNCH
.ATONAL. OMAHA
OLEO. BASE. FITIN
BARNES. TAB. NECK
STHELENS. LOU
EVA. FRY. RAGTIME
SIR. IVE. AILERON
SAD. NET. DRESSED
```

13

```
ASP. CREDO. ASSAY
PCS. HOLED. SPIRE
SAYHEYKID. TAXIS
EMCEE. MERIDA
SPHERE. RAMONA
.DIA. ENS. YMA
TEAFORTWO. AWED
ACLU. PIOUS. BANE
ROLL. CUTANDRUN
ANT. STN. MOO
HARRAD. EDMOND
HEROIC. DETOO
DAWES. TOPTENHIT
INANE. ONAIR. ESE
MAYAS. ETTAS. RED
```

14

```
PLUS. TRIKE. MOAN
RUTH. RIDES. ULNA
OMAR. ICANTSTAND
SPHINXES. IHAVEA
.MEIR. GMAN
PEOPLE. QUANTITY
EXCEL. JUNTA. GEO
PIER. MEONE. MENU
ULA. FORTY. ROTOR
PENALIZE. WHOARE
.EASY. HEED
GOESIT. SITARIST
INTOLERANT. IDLY
STOP. NUDGE. NEON
TONS. SNEER. GABE
```

15

```
ACTOR. MAME. AFRO
CHILI. INON. VAIN
KINDOFKNOT. ALLY
ELECTRA. NRA. SEX
REDHEAD. BADGE
.ARNO. ENMASSE
CAPP. FACETTED
ORE. ABDOMEN. EEG
MUTINEER. SPRY
ANTITAX. HEBE
.INERT. ARALSEA
ORC. DAR. TALLEST
ROOM. BOATSBERTH
FLAB. LURE. ORFEO
FETA. ESTD. ASSES
```

16

```
AMFM. MEESE. CHAP
POOR. ALIAS. RABE
OPUS. SIGNS. ELLA
PER. WASHY. SAFER
.STEAD. TOOKTO
.ELGART. KIEFER
WEEMS. AIRED. FOO
ARNO. NIMOY. BONN
RIP. JONES. SOUSA
MCLAIN. SECTOR
.UPBEAT. RENDS
HASTE. SHEEP. OCT
ANTE. HORAS. CZAR
IKES. INERT. PELE
RANT. TEENS. ANDY
```

17

```
BLIMP. AROSE. BOP
BERYL. NICKS. OWE
STEWARDSHIP. INK
.OZARKS. CLEO
SOCRATES. COHERE
PLOD. SAVER
IDO. HIPBONE. MSG
EEK. ECUADOR. AHA
SRI. MIGRANT. KEW
SCANS. REEK
OBLONG. BAYBERRY
XRAY. HERALD
BIN. TOASTMASTER
ODD. ARLES. KOALA
WES. BETTY. EXXON
```

18

```
ERMA. DEAR. AKEEM
ROAD. ELBA. MCRAE
RTJOHNSON. SKATE
SEALEVEL. ATIT
.PRE. TREASONS
DDSHARP. ELLE
EINE. ENFLEMING
LOU. ANAIS. GOO
LNBURSTYN. CORN
.BETA. EDGORME
GAYBLADE. ELI
RAIL. LICENSEE
AREAS. BBDANIELS
POLKA. ROLL. NASA
ENDED. OWES. GRAU
```

19

```
WASPS. PSST. TBSP
EXTRA. HOWE. ALAI
BLUEMONDAY. KULP
BEDS. MOAN. PEEVE
.SLAM. DELIVER
ROBBER. SIMONE
IGLOO. AVID. LYE
FLUX. AFTER. EVEL
FEE. OBIE. BLEAK
HONORS. TEETHE
SHALLWE. BANG
HOWDY. PALL. ABUT
EVAH. BLUECANARY
LEIA. BUNS. SCRIP
FLIT. SGTS. PERSE
```

20

```
CATO. BALSA. TRAY
LORD. ALIEN. HERE
ENID. MISTS. EATS
MEGJOBETHORAMY
.OBI. NIL
ADOBE. ASA. MAMA
SIS. SORTIE. MASH
HASPERMISSIONTO
ELIA. KELLER. OHO
SECT. DEE. AIRED
.KOD. ANN
QUITEDIGNIFIED
AUNT. VOTED. ULNA
MIDI. IRENE. LION
ITON. LAMAS. LESS
```

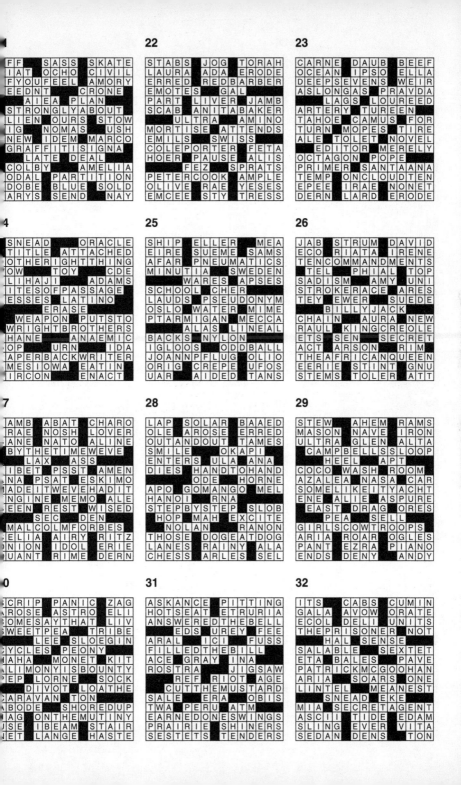

22

```
STABS JOG TORAH
LAURA ADA ERODE
ERRED REDBARBER
EMOTES   GAL
PART LIVER JAMB
SCAB ANITABAKER
  ULTRA  AMINO
MORTISE ATTENDS
EMILS  SWISS
COLEPORTER FETA
HOER PAUSE ALIS
  FEZ  SPRATS
PETERCOOK AMPLE
OLIVE RAE YESES
EMCEE STY TRESS
```

23

```
CARNE DAUB BEEF
OCEAN IPSO ELLA
DEEPSEVENS WEIR
ASLONGAS PRAVDA
  LAGS LOUREED
ARTERY TUREEN
TAHOE CAMUS FOR
TURN MOPES TIRE
ALE TOLET NOVEL
  EDITOR MERELY
OCTAGON POPE
PRIMER SANTAANA
TEMP ONCLOUDTEN
EPEE IRAE NONET
DERN LARD ERODE
```

24

```
SNEAD  ORACLE
TITLE ATTACHED
OTHERIGHTTHING
OW TOY CDE
LIHAJI  ADAMS
ITESOFPASSAGE
ESSES LATINO
  ERASE
WEAPON PUTSTO
WRIGHTBROTHERS
HANE  ANAEMIC
OP URN IDA
APERBACKWRITER
MESIOWA EATIN
IRCON ENACT
```

25

```
SHIP ELLER MEA
EIRE SUEME SAMS
AFAR PNEUMATICS
MINUTIA  SWEDEN
  WARES APSES
SCHOOL CHER
LAUDS PSEUDONYM
OSLO WATER MIME
PTARMIGAN MECCA
  ALAS LINEAL
BACKS NYLON
IGLOOS ODDBALL
JOANNPFLUG OLIO
ORIG CREPE UFOS
UAR AIDED TANS
```

26

```
JAB STRUM DAVID
ECO RIATA IRENE
TENCOMMANDMENTS
TEL PHIAL TOP
SADISM AMY UNI
STROKERACE ARES
TEY EWER SUEDE
  BILLYJACK
CHAIN AURA NEW
RAUL KINGCREOLE
ETS SEN SECRET
ACT ARSON RIM
THEAFRICANQUEEN
EERIE STINT GNU
STEMS TOLER ATT
```

27

```
AMB ABAT CHARO
RAE NOSH LOVER
ANE NATO ALINE
BYTHETIMEWEVE
  LAX ASS
IBET PSST AMEN
NA PSAT ESKIMO
ADEITWEVEHADIT
NGINE MEMO ALE
EEN REST WISED
  SEC DEN
MALCOLMFORBES
ELIA AIRY RITZ
NION IDOL ERIE
QUANT RIME DERN
```

28

```
LAP SOLAR BAAED
OLE AROSE ERRED
OUTANDOUT TAMES
SMILE  OKAPI
ENTERS ULA ANA
DIES HANDTOHAND
  ODE HORNE
APO GOMANGO MEL
HANOI  RNA
STEPBYSTEP SLOB
HOP MAH EXCITE
  NOLAN RANON
THOSE DOGEATDOG
LANES RAINY ALA
CHESS ARLES SEL
```

29

```
STEW AHEM RAMS
MASON NAVE IRON
ULTRA GLEN ALTA
CAMPBELLSSLOOP
  HEEL APT
COCO WASH ROOM
AZALEA NASA CAR
SOMELIKEITYACHT
ENE ALIE ASPURE
EAST DRAG ORES
  PEA SELL
GIRLSCOWTROOPS
ARIA ROAR OGLES
PANT EZRA PIANO
ENDS DENY ANDY
```

30

```
SCRIP PANIC ZAG
ROSE ASTRO ELI
SOMESAYTHAT LIV
SWEETPEA TRIBE
  LEE SLOEGIN
CYCLES PEONY
AHA MONET KIT
ALIMONYISBOUNTY
EP LORNE SOCK
DIVOT LOATHE
CARAVAN TON
ABODE  SHOREDUP
AG ONTHEMUTINY
USE IBEAM STAIR
ET LANGE HASTE
```

31

```
ASKANCE PITTING
HOTSEAT ETRURIA
ANSWEREDTHEBELL
  EDS UREY FEE
ARAL ICI FUSS
FILLEDTHEBILL
ACE GRAY INA
ROSTRA JIGSAW
  REF RIOT AGE
CUTTHEMUSTARD
SALE ERA OBIS
TWA PERU ATM
EARNEDONESWINGS
PRAIRIE SHINERS
SESTETS TENDERS
```

32

```
ITS CABS CUMIN
GALA AVOW ORATE
ECOL DELI UNITS
THEPRISONER NOT
  HAL SENSE
SALABLE  SEXTET
ETA BALES PAVE
PATRICKMCGOOHAN
ARIA SOARS ONE
LINTEL MEANEST
  SNEAD EKE
MIA SECRETAGENT
ASCII TIDE EDAM
SLING EVER VITA
SEDAN DENS TON
```

33

```
TIM LEAKY YAPS
ONE ARNIE PEDRO
ACC TAINT ENJOY
SUCCESSDIDNT
TRAINEE UNLESS
    CTR BREA MAP
SODA SPOILMEIVE
CLODS AXL ELLEN
ALWAYSBEEN VEST
LIE NEAR AMI
YELLOW ACERBIC
  INSUFFERABLE
QUAKY TITLE ALA
EFREM ADOLL LBS
DOTS HONEY LEE
```

34

```
PERSE SWAM BINS
ALOHA CRUE AVON
UMBER HORN TAVI
LOSING NOTE NAP
   KILOGRAMCAKE
CHASTEN ALMA
OAR ACE ASLIP
GRAVEMETERSHIFT
SPLIT ATE EAU
   AHAB CHIANTI
TENLITERHATS
ORA CREE BASSET
PODS ATOM SOLAR
ADEN ILIE CROCE
ZERO NELL ATTHE
```

35

```
AMONG VIOLENCE
RENEE CANNONEER
CLEVELANDINDIAN
HTS ZIRCON ELSE
    TEMPE BASES
REFEREE IGOR
URAL NADIA EKE
HOMEOFTHEBRAVES
ROE BURSA WEEP
    WIRY LOVERLY
BABAS PIKES
IBAR TARSAL SMU
KANSASCITYCHIEF
ESCALATES RODEO
SHOWERED ODETS
```

36

```
MACE LASSO SCOT
AMOS ACTOR CALE
LENT SCUBADIVER
INCAS BLOSSOM
    RTE GUESTS
STEELBAND ODDS
LOT ERIC ISRAEL
ATE CELLIST LMA
BALATA EDNA TUT
SLYE BALTIMORE
   REDONE RAN
WHOOPED SIGMA
HERBALISTS SAIL
AMBI TEASE INRE
MISC ASPEN EGOS
```

37

```
AMS SILAS FACES
LAP ATIME OMEGA
AGE MAKEAFOOLOF
MING LENTIL TSE
OCTOPI DOAS
    PLATE TRADER
RAE ANODE UNITE
ARROYOS MISDEAL
SNERT SMITH SLY
HEIGHT ITSIN
    EARL ANIMAL
MAE FRIEND LAZE
ALLFOOLSDAY MUD
POLLO ETATS ARG
STEAL YOKEL SEE
```

38

```
SHEM ABORT SKAT
PUPA LONER LUNE
ELIS ARENA IRON
WASHINGTONADAMS
   OILS WISP LIE
MODEL FOR ESTER
FRI NOT PAT
ABCDEFGHIJKLMN
   AXL RMS AN
HASNT PEP FINE
IRA RISE EDGE
JANUARYFEBRUARY
ABIT ICONS ATIE
CITE SHUTE NEON
KAYS HERON ARTS
```

39

```
ATLAS JAB LAMA
SWIPE BOIL IGOR
POKER ANDA VAIN
   EXPERIENCEISA
ABA EDS CHINTZ
GORING ASHEN
GOODTEACHER FOP
INCA LAA LARA
EEK BUTSHESENDS
   CANOE RIOTED
MOGULS AER ARE
ENORMOUSBILLS
LEAF URAL OUTDO
DUPE NILE ILIAD
SPEW DST NACRE
```

40

```
SELF CREW SCOTT
ETUI ZITI HAZER
ACRE AVON EBONY
THESTRANGER NOS
    TAIL ALPERT
HEART METOO
TUX ZEAL CLARA
WEIRDALYANKOVIC
OSTEO LONI ODE
EGGAR CLAWS
CUCKOO SKIP
AVA ODDSANDENDS
TUNED IOTA MORE
CLIVE SLIM ANEW
HATER CONE NODS
```

41

```
SCOLD RAFT BUS
TAPER ELIA ENT
DEREKJACOBI AIR
ANON DANE NATE
TOBEHOOPER CREW
    DOA SPAT
PEA RHONE RAHAL
URN RUBYDEE UTE
BANJO SCARF REX
   BARN LAS
LADY EUBIEBLAKE
IDAS ENOS AMEN
NEV EDWARDALBEE
ELI VEER ATOLL
DES ADDS DAMES
```

42

```
RAJAH FAZE DEJA
ONICE EXAM ONES
NEVERKEEPUPWITH
AWE RIBS ANGLE
    PILL WISEMAN
THEJONESESDRAG
WURST TREES
ODE SPREE FAT
    TIARA MELBA
THEMDOWNTOYOUR
CHEEPED IONE
ORATE TASK OFF
LEVELITSCHEAPER
OWER THAI ELATE
RADS TURN SPLAT
```

43

```
ACHE SMEAR ABEL
BLUR HEADY NERO
BUSINESSSECTION
REHEARSE BLONDE
    PRY GRANGER
POPFLY KEEN
AGREE TINA SKEW
CROSSWORDSWITH
KEPT WISE PATTI
   BASK MAKEUP
RADIANT SOW
ADONIS STUNTMAN
FORGOODNESSSAKE
TRIO NOONE AMIS
SECT GABOR RANT
```

44

```
ASAP MEETS PAST
LOGE ALLAH INKY
BLUEONBLUE SNIP
SOANDSOS DOCILE
    DEW PEELS
AVAIL ASHES
BOBBYVINTON MAR
CLEM INNER GABE
STD ROSESARERED
   PHLOX HEXED
IDAHO BRO
REPAST PRANCERS
ALPS BLUEVELVET
TALE SERVE EELY
EYED POLED ONYX
```

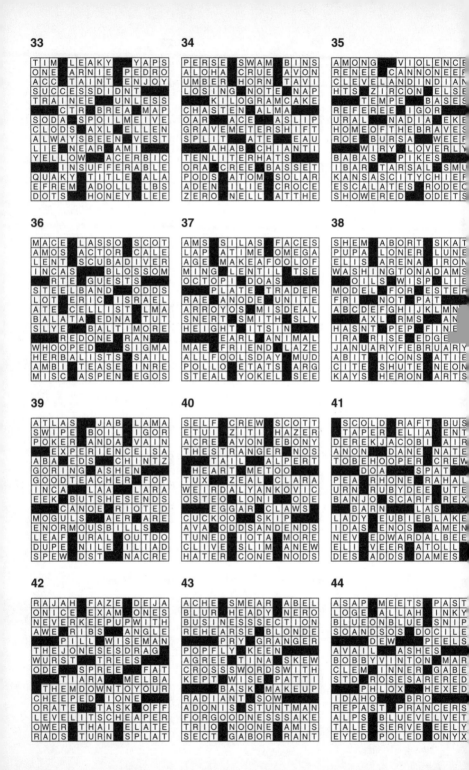

45

```
FRAME   CLEO  IQS
RIVEN   ROTC  MUM
OMESTRETCH    BOA
    MARES   SHIRR
ADA EASES   ABUT
XERTED  ALCHEMY
EPIA    UTAH
  PANTSHAVENO
    GULF  RIGBY
AWBONE  EPIGRAM
RIA ADOVE   HERA
REDO    BEAST
KIN OTHERCHOICE
VE  ZEUS  HOWLER
ER  EDGE  YELLER
```

46

```
LAPS  BRIDE  ATNO
ALOE  RELET  VIOL
NOTCRICKET   ACTI
COTTEN   PIGSKIN
EFS AIM    NITE
   FLEABAGS  DEB
HOWE RILL   TOORA
ORALS SUB   SOFIA
CESTA ISEE   PFCS
KOP  BEEHIVES
   IRON  TIL  IDA
PESETAS   CLONES
ACHE  MBUTTERFLY
SOLD  ELSIE   COLE
SLYS  LINED   ARAT
```

47

```
CROP  SERGE   NANA
AONE  PRIED   EBAN
PUMPKINPOI   NEST
ETE ALIE   TEETHE
   KYLE   SINN
SEPIAS   QUOVADIS
CRANK  RUIN   NEMO
ARUG  QUITS   ETAL
ROLL  USES   STAGE
FLAUTIST   JETTED
    ADZE   CUTE
SCHUSS  GRIT   AMP
HOAX  HULACOPTER
AVIV  OZONE   JOMO
DELI  WIPER   SNOW
```

48

```
IPS  YECCH   MICE
NLA  EVERY   ONYX
SCAN AIDED   CHAP
TICKERTAPE   KANE
ISE  GLARE  RUBIN
ROBROY    RAPIDS
BROOM STRAW   TEE
   TACKINESS
JS  NAILS   CROPS
RANCID    BOOBOO
OMAHA BLUER   VIM
APE  TOETHELINE
RIPE  IRATE   OATH
ACES  RAVES   OTTO
ARY  EXERT   MEOW
```

49

```
FIN  ALUM   STAIRS
ONO  RONA   TIPTOE
RHO  INST   ALTAIR
  MADMAGAZINE
ELLA  LOS    SHAG
DEEPEST   MISTAKE
   GWEN   REEDIT
  ALFREDENEUMAN
ADORED    TONS
MANATEE   VESSELS
OMIT  TSE    ARAT
   WHATMEWORRY
REDSEA  ABLE   ASL
ATONER  FESS   TEE
DECODE  FRET   AND
```

50

```
WILDS   CHAT   ERMA
ADIEU   HYPE   COUP
ROMANNUMERALONE
PLAN  INN   INAFIX
    SANK   IGET
STELLA  GNAW   PRO
AWAIT   BAER   BLOW
PERSONALPRONOUN
PELT  ABET   MATTE
YDS  YVES   KAISER
    TOYS   BARB
ADVERB  SET    RISE
GREEKLETTERIOTA
EARN  USES   ATWAR
SWAY  ESPY   THARP
```

51

```
DEADAS    MALE
ELBOWMACARONI
ARTICHOKEHEART
SMOG  ITALO   OAR
PAN ALE    GRILLE
   EYE   CAITLIN
SOME  FRONTSEAT
DAVE  CRONY  TENS
OVERLOADS   AHSO
BARGAIN    ESE
INTERN  ACH   TEA
NO  SUTRA   BOAT
ANGELHAIRPASTA
HEADOFLETTUCE
SPAT    SEAMAN
```

52

```
ESTA  ABACI   SLAW
LOOT  RIPEN   TARO
BARRYMGOLDWATER
ARNIE DPL   ATEAM
   ALTI   ABLE
MER  LITERAL  CAR
ALAN  PCT   LOCALE
HUBERTHHUMPHREY
ADAGIO  ANI   AONE
LET LEANDER   MES
   KIDD   ERIC
ARDEN EAR   COSTA
GEORGESMCGOVERN
APER  STOUT   EXIT
RORY  PESTO   TYPE
```

53

```
FACTS   PROP   GAME
AGENT   LOPE   OVAL
CASTE  ATEARFELL
EVA TRYON   EERIE
  TERESABREWER
LONI  REV    MAP
ABSENTLY   DERIDE
LOON  LIL    ODDS
UNFAIR   POPULIST
MET  RUS    NONE
  LETMEGOLOVER
BRYAN   ULTRA   ENE
YOUSENDME   CARTE
RULE  AGER   ENDED
DEER  PERM   DAIRY
```

54

```
ADDICT    BUGABOO
LAUGHS    ICECOLD
APPLEPIALAMODE
SPOOF   CLARET
KENO  ROY    NFL
ART HEN   TAGSALE
   DID   SOCRATES
TOUGHRHOTOHOE
LOOPHOLE    OWL
ASPECTS  CNN   BOP
MSS  CHE    MATE
   RETIRE   SENOR
WHATSNUWITHYOU
POSTAGE    TOTALS
APPAREL    SWANEE
```

55

```
HAD PAT  GEL  PAW
USO ELUSIVE   ORI
HAWAIIFIVEO   MRT
CNN  TEEN   SPIN
FLEECES   SLEEVE
EARWAX   GOALIES
EMS TERRA   WEISS
   JACOBRIIS
CANAL TINTS   DAS
ARAMAIC   ENMESH
LAZING   OROURKE
ILIE USSR   NBA
PSI WATERSKIING
HES ANYTIME   ECO
SAM SAX  NUN  SEA
```

56

```
FANG  PELE   LARGO
AROW  ETON   ONION
DALY  ATOZ   RETRO
STONECANYONWAY
    NAH   MEA
ASSET  LIEU   ASHE
CPA SEEM   VALLEY
MOCKINGBIRDLANE
ERRAND  USED   BIO
STET  RHEA   IBSEN
    QUE   ACE
CHAUNCEYSTREET
OUIJA  ALES   TAXI
ARLES  TINA   IRED
SLOTH  EASY   ELSE
```

57

```
SHIRK ESSAY JAM
EERIE AWARE AWE
ARACETRACKS PAT
MONOPOLY STAKE
   CRY THINNER
BATBOY SHORT
YAHOO SWAP LOU
THEPLACEWINDOWS
ESE CADS EAGLE
  AFIRE CARESS
OLDLADY MRT
CLIFT MOONBEAM
CAP CLEANPEOPLE
UMP AISLE SUEDE
RAY TVSET STEAK
```

58

```
DDTS DAB NAPE
MORITA EMU EGAN
APEMAN GEN LEND
NEWENGLAND LESS
ESS CUES LAY
   VELA HEPBURN
BETA ATTA TEPEE
LAWN RHINE LTDS
OVINE ECOL LOOT
BENATAR VICE
  WES METE STA
MATH HARRINGTON
EREI ALB STOPIT
NEXT ROI METALS
DATE PEG ROTS
```

59

```
DEBORAH SAG ITS
ELEVATE PRAIRIE
MATEHANDAIDNAME
OMAR NOR GLESS
   DEBAR CEO
NATURESIGHTWIND
OTHERS SHA NEE
MOO SIP IRK NIL
ANN DAR GISELE
DEGREERATEWORLD
AMS TURIN
ABATE VIN ASST
DIMENSIONESTATE
DOORDIE ENRAGED
SSS SSW LEASERS
```

60

```
SWAG MEDAL TABS
OHIO UTILE ALLI
DIDYOUHEARABOUT
REALM MINGLERS
   DUG ERE
THEMURDERATTHE
KOALA OWNS HOW
ORRIN WAD ADELE
PIE CURE TOILS
SODAPOPFACTORY
  LOU ROE
ASSIGNEE UNZIP
THEBOTTLERDIDIT
VENI ERECT NONO
SATS DEMOS CLAW
```

61

```
METED TAP ASHES
AMATI ATA STEAM
SOPHOCLES TERRE
UTE GREASER OLA
REDSEA MENANDER
   ANTE OLEO
AISNE VATS STUB
STIRS IDO STUKA
SAME BLOT OLSEN
  OMOO ONCE
XENOPHON ERRORS
EMI ERNESTA RIN
BIDEN ARISTOTLE
ELEVE IVE EVOKE
CESAR REG SANER
```

62

```
DAD REAMS AMISS
ORE EXTOL TENET
GIL JOESATURDAY
MELTORME ABLE
ALARIC SRO ELSA
   INIT ESP INN
SKA SAIL ORBIT
WEDNESDAYWELD
RINSE TATA CEE
ANN OWE ERNO
WEED ADA DOITUP
  LEER NESTLERS
BILLYMONDAY MBA
SIEVE BUGLE PAT
AIDED SLEET INS
```

63

```
BLAB SALEM ACDC
RISE EMILE BRIO
AKIN RILED BOLD
VENIVIDIVISAWE
UNICEF ECO BMW
RENEE IAN FLAME
AWE ACT TIARAS
   CAMEWESAW
CAJOLE ALP LOB
PIANO IRK THEME
URN NON BOOGIE
WEWENTSHOPPING
JADE TOWER OBOE
AVON ATARI FLUE
WEED POKES FESS
```

64

```
DORA POPPY SMOG
OHOH ITHEE RENO
NICE STIRS SNIT
TOKAY OBITS SOI
   EROS ELEPHANT
KITTYCAT ROOM
EDS OUTAT THEMS
LOCK DIKES OMIT
PLIED PANTS BRA
ERRS POOHBEAR
BUNNYHOP PEAR
OPT SOLAR ASSAD
OTIS PIKES SHUE
LOSE OVENS EIRE
ANTE FAYES SPAR
```

65

```
ELSA AGO BASE
NEWT GLINT EXIT
ARAT ELLER ALGA
CONNOTED ABSENT
TIE MON DIET
   ELAN GONE PAD
DESIRE OVERRATE
ITON SPREE OWEN
MONTAGUE RODNEY
ENG CONN OUSE
   STAT OBI ESE
ROBUST SUBSISTS
IVAN ELATE SHOT
GAIN EAGER TONE
ALLY WAR OPER
```

66

```
XMAS MEAT QTIPS
YORE ERLE AHAIR
ZONE DIET TEMPO
NOSPEECHCANBE
   AAA EAR
SPAWN BERT ALBA
HES THUG NAMEOF
ENTIRELYBADIFIT
MARTYR PAPA TSE
PLOT ETTA GAYER
   STE AIM
ISSHORTENOUGH
TRITE COVE LAID
AMPLE ERAS ELKO
JASON LENT TEEN
```

67

```
CLAD BANDS SAFE
LANA ALERT TRIM
ORTHODOXJUDAISM
GASLIGHT OMAHA
   SEA CARP
RENDER CUBE VET
AXIS HAREM EVA
JUXTAPOSITIONAL
ADO FORTE HONK
HEN ROSE FLIMSY
   FIFE POO
BASIC DARKMEAT
EXTRAJUDICIALLY
ALAS OFAGE CLIP
KENT TOYED KATE
```

68

```
ADDED LIMOS BHA
DIALO ENOCH REM
OKRAWINFREY YAP
   INTO MASCARA
CRONES CONTENTS
HOMER CON ENT
ALAS HOC ARTGUM
IER SMOKERS UTE
ROCOCO POM SMUT
ASH EIN SABRE
LOYALIST FELONS
IRESENT MENU
MIN PRALINEKAEL
BON PETIT CIRRI
ONE SMELT ASKED
```

69

```
ALAS DAMP  SKID
LEPH ALOE  PERE
INEO MAPLELEAF
TARSANDSTRIPES
    HTS    EAT
ASHOT GADS  OKD
LIENATED   PAIR
AMMERANDSICKLE
MOS   RESENTING
ON COST  RUSES
   SOU  TIN
EDWHITEANDBLUE
NIONJACK  AROSE
INO  ACRE  TOWEL
DEN  STUN  EWERS
```

70

```
ATOP  DANS   PURL
REAR  EMEER  OLEO
MAKO  FERMI  LTDS
SEMPERFIDELIS
ENOLA    SERUM
   TOTEM  SATANS
COVE EGAD  SETIN
AGO  DORIA   UNI
TEXAS STAR  IMET
SEPIAS   AZTEC
  ORBIT   IMAGE
EPLURIBUSUNUM
BLUE ELENA  NABS
OILS STAIN  OVER
ASIS SSTS   TARA
```

71

```
OCCUR  JAWS   MESH
MARNE  ASIA   ELKE
AROMA  SILL   STYX
HENADOODLEDOO
AWES  UNEASE  NBC
   KIT    MAJOR
OHS  ALASKA  SORE
COWINACHINASHOP
EROS WHYNOT  NNE
ADROP     IOI
NED  JULIAN  CARP
  PASSINGTHEDOE
ZULU UNDO   OMEGA
AFAR REIN   PAPER
GOYA PRAY   ENTRY
```

72

```
AGEL  PIP   ATWAR
CLUE  RDA   SHOVE
HEREDOESAHERON
ENO  ATEST   DENT
   BALE   OTO
FSOMEMEANSGOTO
RENA  RICE   SIB
EED  BERLE  PIPE
ST   OREO   PREPS
HOPFORLINGERIE
OAK   MOOS
TAS  EATME  AMPS
ICTORIOUSEGRET
RRED  DAN   REESE
EERS  ADE   ADDON
```

73

```
TILDE   SIT   FRAN
AGAIN  SUMO  IOWA
DOING  CRAB  CLAP
ATROOPOFMONKEYS
    RON    GEL
AGAGGLEOFGEESE
BELIE  NEAR   ADD
ENOS  PREEN  ALSO
TOO  RIOT   RIVER
AFLOCKOFCAMELS
   OAK    LAD
ABANDOFGORILLAS
CLOD  FLAP  COACH
RENO  FIRS  ANNIE
EDEN  STY   LEADS
```

74

```
ATRA  AVAST   LISP
HOAR  CISCO   IOOI
EPSILONTAU   STAG
MOHAIR  INC  TAPS
   MNO    THROB
REALIST   MINERS
ILLAT  HAREM  TUT
TIPS   EWE   HALO
ASH  PAREE  TIMER
SEANCE   STATURE
   TETNA  EEN
COAT  ORB  POTASH
ABUT  BETAETATAU
LIME  INUSE  ROBE
FEUD  CASKS  OPUS
```

75

```
ASH  JADE   IAMBS
IPE  EROS   SPOIL
RIARTUCK   LANGE
OFGREEN  ITERATE
OOSTS SMUT   RIP
ITER ETON   ACME
LS  EAVE  ESTHER
    SATELLITE
IYADH LANA   EGG
DOL  OKAY  TAMIL
EU   OMAR  BULOVA
OARSMEN   AERATES
STALE  SUNDERING
ENON  ASTI   MOTO
DGES  SEEM   SNOW
```

76

```
SLO  BEDECKS   DRJ
PIC  UXORIAL   ROO
ABC  GEORGIABUSH
GRAILS   ASPIRIN
HASTE TORE   RYES
ERIE OWN    RAN
TIO  SKILL  TENAM
TENNESSEEANYONE
ISSUE TANGO   CNN
   TDS  VIE  POET
CHEM AMEN  SANTA
REVENUE   DACTYL
OREGONDONOR  ELI
WON  PAIRING  SET
DDS  ESCAPEE  TRY
```

77

```
MALABO    TEA   SOP
ANIMAL    HAY   APE
PAMELA  ARRESTER
PEELFRUITSKINS
SPARS  ITCH   ERNO
OLDS  ACHE   TWEEN
TEE  SOHO  GUESTS
    POKERHAND
STRAUS  DURA   FRY
HHOUR DUMP   BLED
ARON  DEMO  BRASS
BOSCORBARTLETT
BATHMATS   RANCOR
ATE  ECO   ORDARE
TYD  NOR   NEARED
```

78

```
SLASH  CROW   MEAD
HARTE  LOVE   ANNE
RUMOR  ABEL   EDNA
DONOTMIND    POD
MERE  RUN   PIOUS
RY  DIP   PAULINE
MUG   DISTINCT
LYINGBUTIHATE
OUNCEON    AID
LLEARS STP   BUD
LEON  PEI   GENA
KIT   INACCURACY
EPIC  SORT  METOO
ODO  OLEO   PATON
SPEW  FARR   STYLE
```

79

```
PORE  GLEAM   EMUS
AHEM  AORTA   RARA
RAGINGBULL   RIND
ERATO    PATTON
DAN  SLITS  ALERT
   THESETUP  VIE
TORI  AND   RECESS
OXIDANT  BARONET
REPEAT  SON   STRS
TYP  ROCKYIII
SEETO AIDAN   TEM
  DONALD   CRAVE
OMOO  KIDGALAHAD
RIFT  ICEUP   CODA
OAFS  NORSE   KEEL
```

80

```
HAIGS  LALAW   RCA
ACCRA  OLIVA   ORG
RHEAPERLMAN   BEN
MESS  UNAPT  AIDE
   STRAY  ACTNOW
ENCORE    FRAIL
RAH  OKAPI  LEEDS
ASI  JAYLENO   ARI
SACRA  LOSER   CAL
   KINDA  RIGHTO
INCASE   CAVER
TOOL  LARUE   URIS
ERR  RAVENSYMONE
MAE  INEPT   APACE
SSA  BORES  MYNAS
```

81

```
BASK ELBOW OLGA
ETTA DIANE NEON
THOR INLET COLD
REPARTEE BRENDA
ANITA SWAN URN
YAT JAG IRA RUT
TAVERN WISE
ISWHATYOUWISH
ONTO SEURAT
AHA ALE TIN PSI
REM GOTH EARLS
LAPDOG YOUDSAID
OVER JUMPS WIDE
CEDE ANNIE ASEA
KNEW MUSES NERD
```

82

```
ATOLL SIBS SLAB
LANAI ENOL MOLE
FRANZKAFKA ACTA
SANG UFO KALKAN
USDO CALLERS
THEOHUXTABLE
SABRE ELL RISE
ANO DRUMMER REL
RANG ESP AMORE
ONEMILLIONBC
MANDELA LYNN
EVOLVE OAR INGA
HONE DONMARQUIS
TICS IDEA OUTRE
ADES NESS TESLA
```

83

```
FIFE CLIMB FLA
LOLL LORCA SAB
ATALEOFIICITIE
WAX NUTS KNOTT
EDDY PLOP
IRAQIS WEAN JA
BEGUN SIRS BAR
SLAUGHTERHOUSE
EATS ORLY CLONE
NYE AMID ATONAL
CROP BLOW
ATTAIN WEEP VO
FRIDAYTHEXIIITH
REND MAORI MATE
OKAY STAYS PLO
```

84

```
SLOT TULIP PDQ
TENAM ERIKA LOU
EVENAWAITER ALE
PIAZZAS ONICE
ADIEU EXETER
SIGNAL SONYA
ALAI LORDS ASH
FINALLY COMESTO
EEG AORTA STOW
AMBER ESCAPE
THISBE YALTA
BORIC SMELLSA
ONA HIMWHOWAITS
NET ORFEO STRAP
EYE PAGET EARS
```

85

```
ASTA SHOWN AJAR
REAL CANOE CODE
MERINOHARA THEN
EON TRAINED
RHETT SHELVE
LEES EGO STEWED
ALDA REMOTE ESE
LAYUP EER RASTA
ATL ACROSS STAN
WEALTH NOT TOTS
MUTATE ROONE
SUBLIME AIL
ORAL BAABDENVER
OGRE ESTEE AIRY
NERD REEDS BARE
```

86

```
LAUD FROMM SCO
ALSO AIMEE ELB
MISSINGINACTION
BAREFOOT TOUPEE
FUR SHOP
STRAIT REEK WW
CHUTE CORA ARI
ERRORINJUDGMENT
NEAP NOAM REACT
EEL ANTS DONKEY
CLUE CAT
INSOLE SANTAAN
NOTHINGINCOMMON
KLEE DEFOE POPE
YAWN OTTER SKE
```

87

```
LASTNAME LESSER
INTHERED ETHANE
KNEEPADS GROOVY
EEE ABU TWERP
NAVAL SARA TAPE
SLEW HALER SUER
LII TAMS LEO
CHESTPROTECTORS
LOS OHIO RIO
ANTI ULNAS EARLS
PEEL GEAR ATREE
ELEGY AIM EDA
SIMILE ARMBANDS
OPENER NAILHOLE
LADIES ATTESTED
```

88

```
CHARD ALGAE WRY
OATER REARS HOE
WHOSONFIRST AGA
ONES ROASTER
BOWLED DENTISTS
ACHED MRT EFT
STES OPA ESTHER
SAN WHYME ELO
OLDMAN AOK PUMA
OIL AGO ORSER
TOWNLINE SNEERS
ICETONG PIES
TAE WHERESWALDO
ALA EELER AGAIN
NAT DROOP YEGGS
```

89

```
BAR HATED MAYC
RTE ALAMOS ALAN
ERA ZEBULONPIKE
WILMA LOA
AMARILLO ISLAM
SYDNEYPOLLACK
DOC LIANAS
CATFISHHUNTER
IHEARA EEC
MARLINPERKINS
AWOLS ASSYRIAN
CIS LARAS
SALMONCHASE ODE
AREA SAIGON NIN
MANX LEASE GAT
```

90

```
SAUNABATH KOJAK
ESKIMOPIE EVITA
WHENIWANT YUMMY
ENTRY KLM
HOPTOIT SEA TAP
THEYRE RIBROAST
SIP PATAGONIA
TOREADABOOK
TRAFALGAR TBA
ENLARGER MAROON
YAK AIR BASEPAY
MAN AURIC
YAKOV IWRITEONE
ALIBI TENNISBUM
PEPYS ASSASSINS
```

91

```
TOO OTIS SLEUTH
URN VANE WILLIE
BETWEENTHELINES
ASHER STER SASS
ETTE LEVI
BUB HATE ENFOLD
ANE ERODE TAFIA
SCALENE SPOOFER
ELCID DEPOT TUT
LEHIGH MYTH HTS
EARP SEVE
MAES TARO BOWER
UNDERTHEVOLCANO
INNATE SULU LID
REAMER SMEE LDS
```

92

```
BUS LEAH USEFUL
ITA OVUM LATINC
CONIFEROUSSHRUB
EPISTLE NTHE
PITH VIDE RACY
SAY IRONORE DOA
STAID CHAMP
MOTHEROFALAMB
KENYA OLMAN
GAT DECRYPT FCC
BLOB RASP LALA
USER AUTOMAT
PERSONALPRONOUN
PSYCHO YEAR USA
SEEHOW ERLE SEP
```

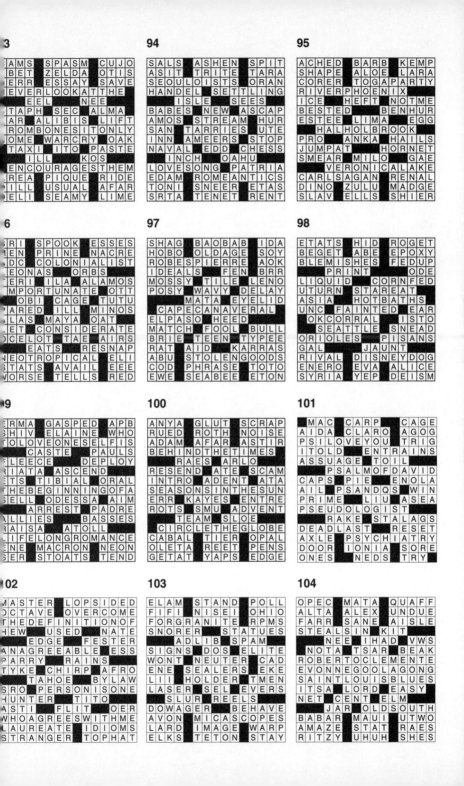

93

```
AMS SPASM CUJO
BET ZELDA OTIS
ERR ESSAY SAVE
EVERLOOKATTHE
      EEL   NEE
TAPH SEC  ALMA
AR ALIBIS  LIFT
ROMBONESITONLY
OME WARCRY  OAK
TAXI ITO  PASTE
ILL        KOS
ENCOURAGESTHEM
REA PIQUE  RIDE
ILL USUAL  AFAR
ELI SEAMY  LIME
```

94

```
SALS ASHEN  SPIT
ASIT TRITE  TARA
SEOULOISTS  ORAN
HANDEL SETTLING
     ISLE  SEES
BABES NEW  ASCAP
AMOS STREAM  HUR
SAN TARRIES  UTE
INN AMEERS  STOP
NAVAL EDD  CHESS
    INCH  OAHU
LOVESONG PATRIA
EDAM ROMEANTICS
TONI SNEER  ETAS
SRTA TENET  RENT
```

95

```
ACHED BARB  KEMP
SHAPE ALOE  LARA
CORER TOGAPARTY
RIVERPHOENIX
ICE  HEFT  NOTME
BESTED  BENHUR
ESTEE LIMA  EGG
HALHOLBROOK
PRO ANKA  HAILS
JUMPAT  HORNET
SMEAR MILO  GAE
VERONICALAKE
CARLSAGAN  RENAL
DINO ZULU  MADGE
SLAV ELLS  SHIER
```

96

```
RI SPOOK  ESSES
EN PRINE  NACRE
DC COLONIALIST
EONAS    ORBS
ERI ILA  ALAMOS
MPORTUNATE  OTT
OBI CAGE  TUTU
ARED ILL  MINOS
LAS MAYA  OAT
ET CONSIDERATE
OCELOT TAE  AIRS
EATS    RESNAP
NEOTROPICAL  ELI
STATS AVAIL  EEE
ORSE TELLS  RED
```

97

```
SHAG BAOBAB  IDA
HOBO OLDAGE  SOY
ROBESPIERRE  AOK
IDEALS FEN  BRR
MOSSY TILE  LENO
POSY WAVY  DELAY
    MATA  EYELID
CAPECANAVERAL
ELPASO  HEED
MATCH FOOL  BULL
BRIE TEEN  TYPEE
RAT AID  KARRAS
ABU STOLENGOODS
COD PHRASE  TOTO
EWE SEABEE  ETON
```

98

```
ETATS HID  ROGET
BEGET ABE  EPOXY
BLEMISHES  FEDUP
PRINT    ODE
LIQUID  CORNFED
UTURN STAREAT
ASIA  HOTBATHS
UNC FAINTED  EAR
OKCORRAL  ISTO
SEATTLE  SNEAD
ORIOLES  PISANS
GAL  JAUNT
RIVAL DISNEYDOG
ENERO EVA  ALICE
SYRIA YEP  DEISM
```

99

```
RMA GASPED  APB
SHIV ELAINE  WHO
OLOVEONESELFIS
CASTE    PAULS
FLEECE  DEPLOY
RIATA  ASCEND
TS TIBIAL  ORAL
HEBEGINNINGOFA
ELL ODESSA  AIM
ARREST  PADRE
LLIES    BASSES
RAISA  ATOLL
LIFELONGROMANCE
ENE MACRON  NEON
SER STOATS  TEND
```

100

```
ANYA GLUT  SCRAP
RUED ROTH  NOISE
ADAM AFAR  ASTIR
BEHINDTHETIMES
    RAES  ARLO
RESEND ATE  SCAM
INTRO ADENT  ATA
SEASONSINTHESUN
ERR KAYES  ENTRE
ROTS SMU  ADVENT
    TEAM  SLOE
CIRCLETHEGLOBE
CABAL TIER  OPAL
OLETA REET  PENS
GETAT YAPS  EDGE
```

101

```
MAC CARP  CAGE
AIDA CLARO  AGOG
PSILOVEYOU  TRIG
ITOLD  ENTRAINS
ASSUAGE  TOIL
PSALMOFDAVID
CAPS PIE  ENOLA
AIL PSANDQS  WIN
PRIME LIU  ASEA
PSEUDOLOGIST
RAKE  STALAGS
DEADLAST  RESET
AXLE PSYCHIATRY
DOOR IONIA  SORE
ONES NEDS  TRY
```

102

```
MASTER LOPSIDED
OCTAVE OVERCOME
THEDEFINITIONOF
HEW USED  NATE
EDGE  FESTER
ANAGREEABLE  ESS
PARRY  RAINS
TYKE CHIRP  AFRO
TAHOE  BYLAW
SRO PERSONISONE
HUNTER  TITO
ASTI FLIT  OER
WHOAGREESWITHME
LAUREATE IDIOMS
STRANGER TOPHAT
```

103

```
ELAM STAND  POLL
FIFI NISEI  OHIO
FORGRANITE  RPMS
SNORER  STATUES
ADLIB  SPAM
SIGNS DOS  ELITE
WONT NEUTER  CAD
ENE SEALERS  EKE
LII HOLDER  TMEN
LASER SEL  EVERS
SLUR  REELS
DOWAGER  BEHAVE
AVON MICASCOPES
LARD IMAGE  WARP
ELKS TETON  STAY
```

104

```
OPEC MATA  QUAFF
ALTA ALEX  UNDUE
FARR SANE  AISLE
STEALSIN  KIT
NEE IHAD  VWS
NOTA TSAR  BEAK
ROBERTOCLEMENTE
EVONNEGOOLAGONG
SAINTLOUISBLUES
ITSA LORD  EASY
NET CENT  ELM
JAR  OLDSOUTH
BABAR MAUI  UTWO
AMAZE STAT  RAES
RITZY UHUH  SHES
```

105

```
F E T A   K L I N E   W A R S
A W O L   N A D E R   O M E N
D E M O   O Z A W A   R O T O
      T H E B E S T T I M E T O
E T H A N   S O S     B I Z
L O U   G A S P     A D A G E
I A M B   G O A H E A D
    B U Y A U S E D C A R
      D O L P H I N   Y A P S
H I N D U   A R A B   I O U
A N E   V O N     A B N E R
I S W H E N I T I S N E W
L A T E   E X I L E   N E A R
E N O S   T O P I C   J A K E
D E N S   O N S E T   I R A Q
```

106

```
M A A M   R A D A R   E S S O
I R M A   E L O P E   L A R A
L I E N   A D D O N   E M I T
K A N G A R O O P O U C H
      O L E     I T T O O K
S A P   O N A D A R E   U N E
P U R S E D L I P S   E S T E
A R E A S   I S O   E A T I N
C O S T   S A C K O F R O M E
E R E   M A S S E U R   N E D
D A N S O N     S E C
    T H A T S N O T M Y B A G
A S I A   A L I V E   C U B E
W I N K   F A K E R   L O L L
E D G Y   E V E N S   E Y E S
```

107

```
L E S   I P S O   F A T S
A R K A N S A S   A B U T
P R I S C I L L A L A N E
A P O E T   O S S   A R
M E R R I M A C   P E R M I T
A D S   A S A   E E L S
    K I R S T I E A L L E Y
D E L L A S T R E E T
M A R Y K A Y P L A C E
A B E T   A I S   C S
M Y S O N S   W E E D S O U T
E S S   E E E   I Q U I T
M A R G A R E T C O U R T
A G E R   M O O N R I S E
L E V I   A N O N   B E D
```

108

```
P A R S E D   D A M P   S K I
A L I C I A   I B A R   P U N
N E V E R W A V E T O   I N S
    N E S T A   P U R G E
A N D A   O W N E D   R A F T
L A U R E N T   R O M U L U S
F E L I X   M E M O
    Y O U R F R I E N D S
      D I E T   T E H E E
S O O N E S T   M A H J O N G
E C C E   K A R A T   E R G O
Q A T A R   A T T I C
U S A   A T A N A U C T I O N
E E N   Z I N G   N E E D L E
L Y E   E P E E   E D D I E D
```

109

```
S A M   B I B   D A M A S K
P L A Y E D A T   A P A C H E
A D M O N I S H   P I T M E N
R E B U T   S E C   A T E S T
S N O B   N E U R O N E
    E A R T H E N   R A S P
M A N T R A   H E S   O N T O
O B E Y S   C U P   A F T E R
D E V O   O O H   N I C E N E
E S A U   S A G U A R O
    R E S T I N G   U S P S
C O A L S   I R S   C R E A K
O N S I T E   L A M A S E R Y
L E A F E D   S I X P E N C E
T A P E R S   D I E   O H S
```

110

```
A L F A   S W E E P   R A W
D I A N A   T I A R A   A L A
A S S I S T A N T E D I T O R
M P H   W E N D     S T U N
    I M A N   O R D E A L
A M O U N T   W A I L   E S P
R A N D   D Y E S   S T E
M I D D L E W E S T E R N E R
O N E   E R I C   Y A N K
R E S   N I N O   S H A K O S
    I R O N E R   R O S E
U R G E     A U T O   B A T
S A N D B E L T M A C H I N E
E V E   S L O O P   H A T E D
S I R   C O O R S   Y E W S
```

111

```
P R A M   D E C A L   T O L L
D O D O   E X U D E   I G E T
Q U A D   L I S Z T   M R E D
E Y E O F T H E T I B E R
      N U T     S T U
P E C A N   A H A   A K R O N
E R A   C A S A B A   T E N A
S O M M E T H I N S T U P I D
O D E R   T E R E S A   A C E
S E A L S   S Y R   B O Y E R
      O A F     W O O
Y A N G T Z E D O O D L E
J O V E   D A V I D   L A Z Y
I D O L   I N A N E   E T R E
M A N Y   X E N O N   S E A T
```

112

```
E S C A P E   A B A L O N E
O T T O M A N   R A R I T A N
C H A S I N G R A I N B O W S
H A R T S   E L L I E
O N T   H A F T   S E L E C T
E S P   W O R M     R O E
    L I L L I E   A T I M E
I M P O S S I B L E D R E A M
N E A T H   O U T L A Y
C D I     S T E M   A R S
H E R M A N   I D O S   E M O
    A R E T O   A S P I C
F O U N T A I N O F Y O U T H
A R M O I R E   D E N O T E S
R E P R E S S   E M O T E S
```

113

```
J E T   H E D Y   M C H A L E
O R A T O R I O   E N A M E L
S I D E W A L K   N O R M A L
H E A R T S L O C A T I O N
      R O E     E T E
E S P Y   A V O W   P R A M
M I A   O S L O   O T O O L E
C O N T E M P T B R E E D E R
E U D O R A   E L K E   E R G
E X A M   R E S T   D O T E
      S T S   E W E
M I L E E Q U I V A L E N T
R E G A I N   C R E D I T O R
L A O T Z U   L O N E S O M E
S T R E E P   A N T S   N E E
```

114

```
A D J   Z E T A   A L E N E
L E A   E D A M   B U X O M
I F Y O U D O A J O B T O O
A B A C U S   T A V E R N
F A C E T   A T O N E   A D E
A B E E   E X I L E   S C A R
R A D   T E E N   S A T Y R
    W E L L Y O U L L
A M A H L   T A R O   Q U A
M A N Y   Z A I R E   B U N S
P E N   P A L M S   M O I R A
    W A T U S I   C A T N A P
G E T S T U C K W I T H I T
A S T A B   E A R N   E N E
S T O R Y   S T Y E   R E D
```

115

```
F A R   P I T S   S E L M A
P I T Y   I S E E   O N I O N
O G R E   S L A T   A R D E N
P H I B E T A K A P P A
S T A R D O M   E S P R I T
    E I N   R N S   T O R O
S H O A T   M I A O W   A A S
M I N D O N E S P S A N D Q S
E N E   R O S E S   P O S I T
A G A L   N A N   S I N
R E L A T E   P A T S I E S
    D I T D I T D I T D A H
A B O D E   A G E D   I A M A
S A L E M   M O R E   C H E W
P A D R E   E T O N   K O S
```

116

```
H A M S   F R E D   A L D E R
A B A T   O I L Y   R E E V E
R O N A   C O I N   G A T E D
P U L L W I T H A R O P E
S T Y L I   S U M O   N R A
    S T S     I N C I T E R
A S I   A B E T   I L I U M
R O M A N N U M E R A L O N E
C A M R Y   T O D O   N E D
E V I D E N T   Y A W
D E G   B E A U   N A T T Y
    R E G A R D S A S T R U E
S H A V E   F A U X   T A L L
O U T I E   A L A E   L I S P
W H E L K   T E L L   E T A S
```

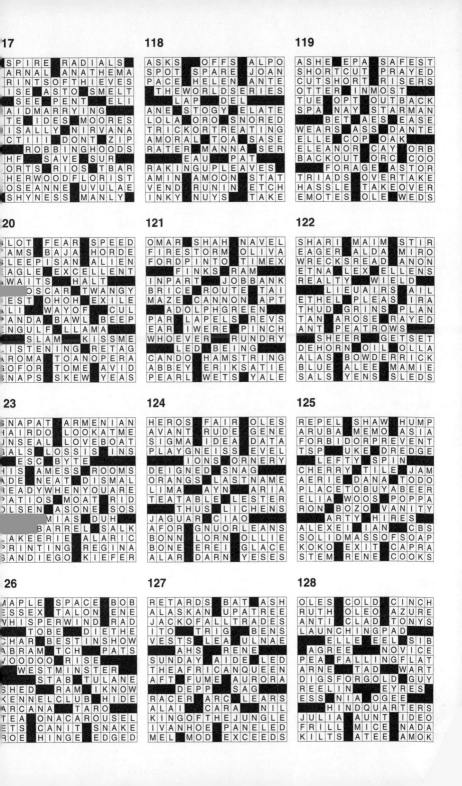

117

```
SPIRE  RADIALS
ARNAL  ANATHEMA
RINTSOFTHIEVES
ISE ASTO  SMELT
SEE  PENT  ELI
AIDMARRYING
TE IDES MOORES
ISALLY NIRVANA
CTIII DONT ZIP
ROBBINGHOODS
HF SAVE  SUR
ORTS RIOS TBAR
HERWOODFLORIST
OSEANNE UVULAE
SHYNESS  MANLY
```

118

```
ASKS  OFFS  ALPO
SPOT SPARE JOAN
PACE HELEN ANTE
THEWORLDSERIES
LAP  DEL
ANE STOGY ELATE
LOLA ORO SNORED
TRICKORTREATING
AMORAL TOA SASE
RATER MANNA SER
EAU  PAT
RAKINGUPLEAVES
AMIN AMOON STAT
VEND RUNIN ETCH
INKY NUYS  TAKE
```

119

```
ASHE EPA SAFEST
SHORTCUT PRAYED
CUTSHORT RISERS
OTTER  INMOST
TUE OPT OUTBACK
SPA NAY STARMAN
BET AES EASE
WEARS ASS DANTE
ELLE COP OAK
ELEANOR CAY ORB
BACKOUT ORC COO
FORAGE ASTOR
TRIADS OVERTAKE
HASSLE TAKEOVER
EMOTES OLE WEDS
```

120

```
LOT FEAR SPEED
AMS BAJA HORDE
LEEPISAN ALIEN
EAGLE EXCELLENT
AWAITS  HALT
OSCAR TWANGY
EST OHOH EXILE
LI WAYOF CUL
ANDA BAWL BEEP
NGULF LLAMA
SLAM KISSME
ISTENING RETAG
AROMA TOANOPERA
OFOR TOME AVID
NAPS SKEW YEAS
```

121

```
OMAR SHAH NAVEL
FIRESTORM OLIVA
FORDPINTO TIMEX
FINKS RAM
INPART JOBBANK
BRICE ROUTE TAI
MAZE CANNON APT
ADOLPHGREEN
PAR LAPELS REVS
EAR IWERE PINCH
WHOEVER RUNDRY
LED BEING
CANDO HAMSTRING
ABBEY ERIKSATIE
PEARL WETS YALE
```

122

```
SHARI MAIM STIR
EAGER ALDA MIRO
WRECKSREAD ANON
ETNA LEX ELLENS
REALTY WIELD
LIEUAIRS AIL
ETHEL PLEAS IRA
THUD GRINS PLAN
TAN AROSE RAYED
ANT PEATROWS
SHEER GETSET
DEHORN OIL OLLA
ALAS BOWDERRICK
BLUE ALEE MAMIE
SALS YENS SLEDS
```

123

```
NAPAT ARMENIAN
HAIRDO LOOKATME
UNSEAL LOVEBOAT
ALS LOSSIS INS
ESC BYTE
HIS AMESS ROOMS
ADE NEAT DISMAL
READYWHENYOUARE
ATIOS MOAT RID
LSEN ASONE SOS
MIAS DUH
BARREL SALK
AKEERIE ALARIC
RINTING REGINA
ANDIEGO KIEFER
```

124

```
HEROS FAIR OLES
AVANT RUDE GENE
SIGMA IDEA DATA
PLAYGNEISS EVEL
IONS ORNERY
DEIGNED SNAG
ORANGS LASTNAME
LIMA AYN ARIA
TEATABLE LESTER
THUS LICHENS
JAGUAR CIAO
AFOR GNUORLEANS
BONN LORN OLLIE
BONE EREI GLACE
ALAR DARN YESES
```

125

```
REPEL SHAW HUMP
ARUBA MEMO ASIA
FORBIDORPREVENT
TSP UKE DREDGE
LEFTY SPIN
CHERRY TILE JAM
AERIE DANA TODO
PLACETOBUYABEER
ELIA WOOS POPPA
RON BOZO VANITY
ARTY HIRES
ALEXEI IAN CBS
SOLIDMASSOFSOAP
KOKO EXIT CAPRA
STEM RENE COOKS
```

126

```
MAPLE SPACE BOB
ESSEX TALON ENE
WHISPERWIND RAD
TOBE DIETHE
CHAR BESTINSHOW
ABRAM TCH PATS
VOODOO RISE
WESTMINSTER
STAB TULANE
SHED RAM IKNOW
KENNELCLUB HIDE
ARCANA TARO
TEA ONACAROUSEL
ETS CANIT SNAKE
ROE HINGE EDGED
```

127

```
RETARDS BAT ASH
ALASKAN UPATREE
JACKOFALLTRADES
ITO TRIG BENS
VESTS LEA ULNAE
AHS RENE
SUNDAY AIDE LED
THEAFRICANQUEEN
AFT FUME AURORA
DEPP SAG
RACER ARC LEARS
ALAI CARA NIL
KINGOFTHEJUNGLE
IVANHOE PANELED
MEL MOD EXCEEDS
```

128

```
OLES COLD CINCH
RUTH OLEO AZURE
ANTI CLAD TONYS
LAUNCHINGPAD
ELLE EEL SIB
AGREE NOVICE
PEA FALLINGFLAT
ARNE TAD WART
DIGSFORGOLD GUY
REELIN EYRES
ESS NIA OGEE
HINDQUARTERS
JULIA AUNT IDEO
FRILL MICE NADA
KILTS ATEE AMOK
```

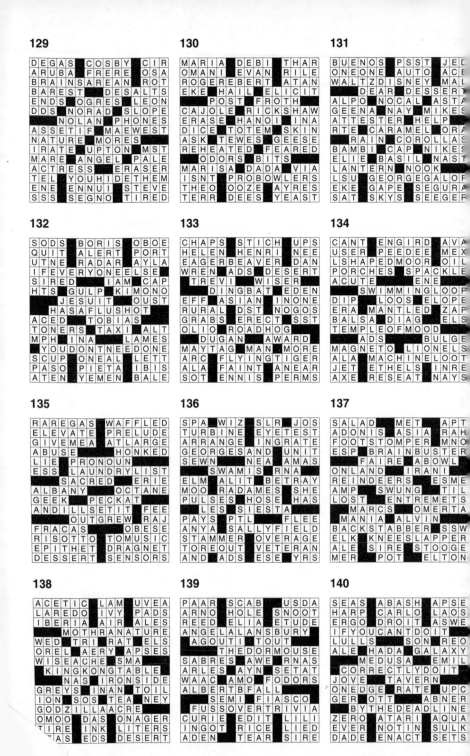

129

```
D E G A S   C O S B Y   C I R
A R U B A   F R E R E   O S A
B R A I N S A R E A N   R O T
B A R E S T     D E S A L T S
E N D S   O G R E S   L E O N
D D S   N O R A D   S L O P E
    N O L A N   P H O N E S
A S S E T I F   M A E W E S T
N A T U R E   M O R E S
I R A T E   U P T O N   M S T
M A R E   A N G E L   P A L E
A C T R E S S     E R A S E R
T E L   Y O U H I D E T H E M
E N E   E N N U I   S T E V E
S S S   S E G N O   T I R E D
```

130

```
M A R I A   D E B I   T H A R
O M A N I   E V A N   R I L E
R O G E R E B E R T   A T A N
E K E   H A I L   E L I C I T
    P O S T   F R O T H
C A J O L E   R I C K S H A W
E R A S E   H A N O I   I N A
D I C E   T O T E M   S K I N
A S K   T E W E S   G E E S E
R E H E A T E D   F E A R E D
    O D O R S   B I T S
M A R I S A   D A D A   V I A
I S N T   P R O B O W L E R S
T H E O   O O Z E   A Y R E S
T E R R   D E E S   Y E A S T
```

131

```
B U E N O S   P S S T   J E ?
O N E O N E   A U T O   A C E
W A L T Z D I S N E Y   M A L
    D E A R   D E S S E R ?
A L P O   N O C A L   A S T ?
G E E N A   N A Y   M I K E S
A T T E S T E R   H E L P
R T E   C A R A M E L   O R A
    R A I N   C O R O L L A S
B A M B I   C A P   N I K E ?
E L I E   B A S I L   N A S ?
L A N T E R N   N O O K
L S U   G E O R G E G A L O ?
E K E   G A P E   S E G U R ?
S A T   S K Y S   S E E G E ?
```

132

```
S O D S   B O R I S   O B O E
Q U I T   A L E R T   P O R T
U T N E   R A D A R   A Y L A
I F E V E R Y O N E E L S E
S I R E D   I A M   C A P
H T S   G U L P   K I M O N O
    J E S U I T   O U S T
    H A S A F L U S H O T
A C E D   T O B I A S
T O N E R S   T A X I   A L T
M P H   I N A   L A M E S
    Y O U D O N T N E E D M E
S C U P   O N E A L   L E T T
P A S O   P I E T A   I B I S
A T E N   Y E M E N   B A L E
```

133

```
C H A P S   S T I C H   U P S
H E L E N   H E N R I   N E E
E A G E R B E A V E R   D A N
W R E N   A D S   D E S E R T
    T R E V I   W I S E R
    D I N G B A T   E D E N
E F F   A S I A N   I N O N E
R U R A L   D S T   N O G O S
G R A B S   E R E C T   S S T
O L I O   R O A D H O G
    D U G A N   A W A R D
M A Y T A G   M A N   M O R E
A R C   F L Y I N G T I G E R
A L A   F A I N T   A N E A R
S O T   E N N I S   P E R M S
```

134

```
C A N T   E N G I R D   A V A
U S E R   P E E D E E   M E X
L S H A P E D M O O R   O I L
P O R C H E S   S P A C K L E
A C U T E     E N E
    S W I M M I N G L O O P
D I P   L O O S   E L O P E
E R A   M A N T L E D   Z A P
B A L S A   D I A G   E L S
T E M P L E O F M O O D
    A D S   B U L G E
M A G N E T O   L I O N E L S
A L A   M A C H I N E L O O T
J E T   E T H E L S   I N R E
A X E   R E S E A T   N A Y S
```

135

```
R A R E G A S   W A F F L E D
E L E V A T E   P R E L U D E
G I V E M E A   A T L A R G E
A B U S E     H O N K E D
L I E   P R O N O U N
E S S   L A U N D R Y L I S T
    S A C R E D   E R I E
A L B A N Y     O C T A N E
G E E K   P E C K A T
A N D I L L S E T I T   F E E
    O U T G R E W   R A J
F R A C A S     O B E S E
R I S O T T O   T O M U S I C
E P I T H E T   D R A G N E T
D E S S E R T   S E N S O R S
```

136

```
S P A   W I Z   S L R   J O S
T U R B I N E   E Y E T E S T
A R R A N G E   I N G R A T E
G E O R G E S A N D   U N I T
S E W N   N E A   A M A S
    S W A M I S   R N A
E L M   A L I T   B E T R A Y
M O O   R A D A M E S   S H E
P U L S E S   H O S E   H A S
    L E S   S I E S T A
P A Y S   P T L   F L E E
A N Y A   S A L L Y F I E L D
S T A M M E R   O V E R A G E
T O R E O U T   V E T E R A N
A N D   A D S   E S E   Y R S
```

137

```
S A L A D   M E T   A P T
A D O N I S   A S I A   R A H
F O O T S T O M P E R   M N O
E S P   B R A I N B U S T E R
    F A I R E   A B O W L
O N L A N D   I R A N I
R E I N D E E R S   E S M E
A M P   S W U N G   T I L
L O S T   E N T R E M E T S
    M A R C S   O M E R T A
M A N I A   A L V I N
B A C K S T A B B E R   S S W
E L K   K N E E S L A P P E R
A L E   S I R E   S T O O G E
M E R   P O T   E L T O N
```

138

```
A C E T I C   L A M   U V E A
L A R E D O   I V Y   P A D S
I B E R I A   A I R   A L E S
    M O T H R A N A T U R E
W E D   T R I   R A T   E L S
O R E L   A E R Y   A P S E S
W I S E A C H E   S M A
    K I N G K O N G T A B L E
    N A S   I R O N S I D E
G R E Y S   I N A N   T O I L
I O N   S O S   T E A   N E Y
G O D Z I L L A A C R E
O M O O   D A S   O N A G E R
T I R E   I N K   L I T E R S
? A S   E D S   D E S E R T
```

139

```
P A A R   S C A B   U S D A
A R N O   H O L E   S N O O T
R E E D   E L I A   E T U D E
A N G E L A L A N S B U R Y
    A G O U T I   T O U T
    T H E D O R M O U S E
S A B R E S   A W E   R N A S
A R L E S   A Y N   S E T A T
W A A C   A M O   F O D O R S
A L B E R T B F A L L
    S E M I   F I A S C O
F U S S O V E R T R I V I A
C U R I E   E D I T   L I L I
I N G O T   R I C E   L I E D
A D E N   T E A R   S I R E
```

140

```
S E A S   A B A S H   A P S E
H A R P   C A R L O   L A O S
E R G O   D R O I T   A S W E
I F Y O U C A N T D O I T
L U L L S     S O N   R E O
A L E   H A D A   G A L A X Y
    M E D U S A   E M I L
C O R R E C T L Y D O I T
J O V E     T A V E R N
O N E D G E   R A T E   U P C
G E R   O T T     A B N E R
    B Y T H E D E A D L I N E
Z E R O   A T A R I   A Q U A
E V E R   N O T I N   S U L K
D A D E   E N A C T   S E T S
```

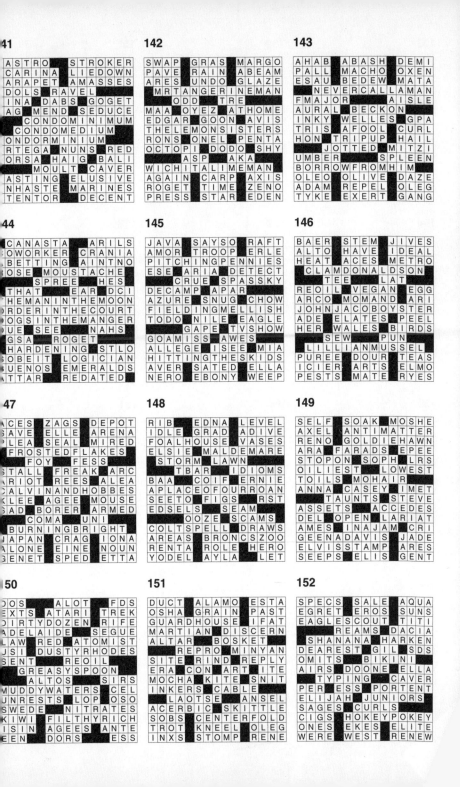

141

```
ASTRO   STROKER
CARINA  LIEDOWN
ARAPET  AMASSES
DOLS  RAVEL
INA  DABS  GOGET
AG  MEND  SEDUCE
  CONDOMINIMUM
  CONDOMEDIUM
  ONDORMINIUM
RTEGA  NUNS  RED
ORSA  HAIG  BALI
  MOULT  CAVER
ASTING  ELUSIVE
NHASTE  MARINES
TENTOR  DECENT
```

142

```
SWAP  GRAS  MARGO
PAVE  RAIN  ABEAM
ARES  UNDO  GLAZE
 MRTANGERINEMAN
     ODD  TRE
MAA  OYEZ  ATHOME
EDGAR  GOON  AVIS
THELEMONSISTERS
RONS  ONEL  PENTA
OCTOPI  DODO  SHY
    ASP  AKA
 WICHITALIMEMAN
AGAIN  CARP  AXIS
ROGET  TIME  ZENO
PRESS  STAR  EDEN
```

143

```
AHAB  ABASH  DEMI
PALL  MACHO  OXEN
ESAU  BEDEW  MATA
  NEVERCALLAMAN
FMAJOR    AISLE
AURAL  BECKON
INKY  WELLES  GPA
TRIS  AFOOL  CURL
HON  TRIPUP  HAIL
  JOTTED  MITZI
UMBER   SPLEEN
BORROWFROMHIM
OLEO  OLIVE  DAZE
ADAM  REPEL  OLEG
TYKE  EXERT  GANG
```

144

```
CANASTA   ARILS
OWORKER  CRANIA
BETTING  AINTNO
OSE  MOUSTACHE
    SPREE  HES
THAT  EAR  DCI
HEMANINTHEMOON
RDERINTHECOURT
OGSINTHEMANGER
UE  SEE  NAHS
GSA  ROGET
HARDENING  STLO
OBEIT  LOGICIAN
UENOS  EMERALDS
TTAR  REDATED
```

145

```
JAVA  SAYSO  RAFT
AMOR  TROOP  ERLE
PITCHINGPENNIES
ESE  ARIA  DETECT
  CRUE  SPASSKY
DECAMP  APAR
AZURE  SNUG  CHOW
FIELDINGMELLISH
TODO  NILE  EAGLE
GAPE  TVSHOW
GOAMISS  AWES
ALLEGE  ISEE  MIA
HITTINGTHESKIDS
AVER  SATED  ELLA
NERO  EBONY  WEEP
```

146

```
BAER  STEM  JIVES
ALTO  HAVE  IDEAL
HEAT  ACES  METRO
  CLAMDONALDSON
     TEE  LAT
REOIL  VEGAN  EGG
ARCO  MOMAND  ARI
JOHNJACOBOYSTER
ADE  ELATES  PEEL
HER  WALES  BIRDS
   SEW  PUN
  LILLIANMUSSEL
PUREE  DOUR  TEAS
ICIER  ARTS  ELMO
PESTS  MATE  RYES
```

147

```
ACES  ZAGS  DEPOT
SAVE  ELLE  ARENA
PLEA  SEAL  MIRED
FROSTEDFLAKES
   FOY  FESS
STALL  FREAK  ARC
RIOT  REES  ALEA
CALVINANDHOBBES
KLEE  AGEE  MOUSE
SAD  BORER  ARMED
   COMA  UNI
  BURNINGBRIGHT
JAPAN  CRAG  IONA
ALONE  EINE  NOUN
BENET  SPED  ETTA
```

148

```
RIB  EDNA  LEVEL
IDLE  GRAD  ADIVE
FOALHOUSE  VASES
ELSIE  MALDEMARE
  STORM  LAWN
    TBAR  IDIOMS
BAA  COIF  ERNIE
APLACEOFOURROAN
SEETO  FIGS  RST
EDSELS  SEAM
   OOZE  SCAMS
COLTSPELL  DRAWS
AREAS  BRONCSZOO
RENTA  ROLE  HERO
YODEL  AYLA  LET
```

149

```
SELF  SOAK  MOSHE
AXEL  ANTIMATTER
RENO  GOLDIEHAWN
ARA  FARADS  EPEE
STOPON  SOPH  LRS
OILIEST  LOWEST
TOILS  MOHAIR
ANNA  CASEY  IMET
  TAUNTS  STEVE
ASSETS  ACCEDES
DEL  OPEN  LARIAT
AMES  INAJAM  CRI
GEENADAVIS  JADE
ELVISSTAMP  ARES
SEEPS  ELIS  GENT
```

150

```
DOS   ALOT  FDS
EXTS  ATARI  TREK
DIRTYDOZEN  RIFE
ADELAIDE  SEGUE
LAW  RED  ATOMIST
JSI  DUSTYRHODES
SENT  REOIL
  GREASYSPOON
  ALTOS  SIRS
MUDDYWATERS  CEL
UNRESTS  LOP  OSO
SWEDE  NITRATES
KIWI  FILTHYRICH
ISIN  AGEES  ANTE
EEN  DORS  ESS
```

151

```
DUCT  ALAMO  ESTA
OSHA  GRAIN  PAST
GUARDHOUSE  IFAT
MARTIAN  DISCERN
ALTAR  BOSKET
  REPRO  MINYAN
SITE  RIND  REPLY
ERA  CON  ART  ITE
MOCHA  KITE  SNIT
INKERS  CABLE
  LAOTSE  ANSEL
ACERBIC  SKITTLE
SOBS  CENTERFOLD
TROT  KNEEL  OLEG
INXS  STOMP  RENE
```

152

```
SPECS  SALE  AQUA
EGRET  EROS  SUNS
EAGLESCOUT  TITI
   REAMS  DACIA
SHANANA  HARKEN
DEAREST  GIL  SDS
OMITS  BIKINI
AIRS  DOONE  ELLA
  TYPING  CAVER
PER  ESS  PORTENT
ELIJAH  JUNIORS
SAGES  CURLS
CIGS  HOKEYPOKEY
ONES  EKES  ELITE
WERE  WEST  RENEW
```

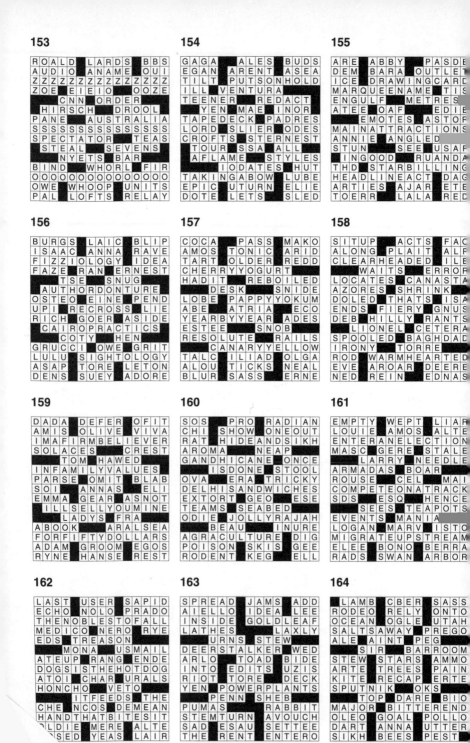

153

R	O	A	L	D		L	A	R	D	S		B	B	S
A	U	D	I	O		A	N	A	M	E		O	U	I
Z	Z	Z	Z	Z	Z	Z	Z	Z	Z	Z	Z	Z	Z	Z
Z	O	E		E	I	E	I	O		O	O	Z	E	
			C	N	N		O	R	D	E	R			
	H	I	R	S	C	H			D	R	O	O	L	
P	A	N	E			A	U	S	T	R	A	L	I	A
S	S	S	S	S	S	S	S	S	S	S	S	S	S	S
S	P	E	C	T	A	T	O	R			T	E	A	S
	S	T	E	A	L			S	E	V	E	N	S	
			N	Y	E	T	S		B	A	R			
B	I	N	D			W	H	O	R	L		F	I	R
O	O	O	O	O	O	O	O	O	O	O	O	O	O	O
O	W	E		W	H	O	O	P		U	N	I	T	S
P	A	L		L	O	F	T	S		R	E	L	A	Y

154

G	A	G	A		A	L	E	S		B	U	D	S
E	G	A	N		A	R	E	N	T		A	S	E	A
T	I	L	T		P	U	T	S	O	N	H	O	L	D
I	L	L		V	E	N	T	U	R	A				
T	E	E	N	E	R			R	E	D	A	C	T	
			Y	E	N		M	A	E		I	N	O	R
T	A	P	E	D	E	C	K			P	A	D	R	E	S
L	O	R	D		S	L	I	E	R		O	D	E	S
C	R	O	F	T	S		S	T	E	R	N	E	S	T
	T	O	U	R		S	S	A		A	L	L		
	A	F	L	A	M	E		S	T	Y	L	E	S	
			I	O	D	A	T	E	S			H	U	T
T	A	K	I	N	G	A	B	O	W		L	U	B	E
E	P	I	C		U	T	U	R	N		E	L	I	E
D	O	T	E		L	E	T	S			S	L	E	D

155

A	R	E		A	B	B	Y			P	A	S	D	E
D	E	M		B	A	R	A		O	U	T	L	E	T
I	C	E		D	R	A	W	I	N	G	C	A	R	D
M	A	R	Q	U	E	E	N	A	M	E		T	I	S
E	N	G	U	L	F			M	E	T	R	E	S	
A	T	E	E		O	A	F			E	D	I	E	
			E	M	O	T	E	S		A	S	T	O	F
M	A	I	N	A	T	T	R	A	C	T	I	O	N	S
A	N	N	I	E		A	N	G	L	E	D			
S	T	U	N			S	E	E		U	S	A	F	
	I	N	G	O	O	D		R	U	A	N	D	A	
T	H	D		S	T	A	R	B	I	L	L	I	N	G
H	E	A	D	L	I	N	E	A	C	T		D	A	G
A	R	T	I	E	S		A	J	A	R		E	T	E
T	O	E	R	R		L	A	L	A			R	E	D

156

B	U	R	G	S		L	A	I	C		B	L	I	P
I	S	A	A	C		A	N	N	A		R	A	V	E
F	I	Z	Z	I	O	L	O	G	Y		I	D	E	A
F	A	Z	E		R	A	N		E	R	N	E	S	T
			T	S	E			S	N	U	G			
	A	U	T	H	O	R	D	O	N	T	U	R	E	
O	S	T	E	O		E	I	N	E		P	E	N	D
U	P	I		R	E	C	R	O	S	S		L	I	E
R	I	C	H		G	O	E	R		A	S	I	D	E
	C	A	I	R	O	P	R	A	C	T	I	C	S	
			C	O	T	Y		H	E	N				
G	R	U	C	C	I		O	W	E		G	R	I	T
L	U	L	U		S	I	G	H	T	O	L	O	G	Y
A	S	A	P		T	O	R	E		L	E	T	O	N
D	E	N	S		S	U	E	Y		A	D	O	R	E

157

C	O	C	A		P	A	S	S		M	A	K	O
A	M	O	S		T	O	N	I	C		A	R	I	D
T	A	R	T		O	L	D	E	R		R	E	D	D
C	H	E	R	R	Y	Y	O	G	U	R	T			
H	A	D	I	T			R	E	B	O	I	L	E	D
			D	E	S	K			S	N	I	D	E	
L	O	B	E		P	A	P	P	Y	Y	O	K	U	M
A	B	E		A	T	R	I	A			E	C	O	
Y	E	A	R	B	Y	Y	E	A	R		A	D	E	S
E	S	T	E	E			S	N	O	B				
R	E	S	O	L	U	T	E		R	A	I	L	S	
			C	A	N	A	R	Y	Y	E	L	L	O	W
T	A	L	C		I	L	I	A	D		O	L	G	A
A	L	O	U		T	I	C	K	S		N	E	A	L
B	L	U	R		S	A	S	S			E	R	N	E

158

S	I	T	U	P		A	C	T	S		F	A	C
A	L	O	N	G		P	L	A	I	T		A	L	F
C	L	E	A	R	H	E	A	D	E	D		I	L	E
			W	A	I	T	S			E	R	R	O	R
L	O	C	A	T	E	S		C	A	N	A	S	T	A
A	Z	O	R	E	S		S	H	R	I	N	K		
D	O	L	E	D		T	H	A	T	S		I	S	A
E	N	D	S		F	I	E	R	Y		G	N	U	S
D	E	B		H	I	L	L	Y		R	A	N	T	S
		L	I	O	N	E	L		C	E	T	E	R	A
S	P	O	O	L	E	D		B	A	G	H	D	A	D
I	R	O	N	Y			T	O	R	R	E			
R	O	D		W	A	R	M	H	E	A	R	T	E	D
E	V	E		A	R	O	A	R		D	E	E	R	E
N	E	D		R	E	I	N		E	D	N	A	S	

159

D	A	D	A		D	E	F	E	R		O	F	I	T
A	M	I	S		O	L	I	V	E		V	I	V	A
I	M	A	F	I	R	M	B	E	L	I	E	V	E	R
S	O	L	A	C	E	S			C	R	E	S	T	
			T	O	M		H	A	W	E	D			
I	N	F	A	M	I	L	Y	V	A	L	U	E	S	
P	A	R	S	E		O	M	I	T		B	L	A	B
S	O	I		A	N	N	A	S			E	L	I	
E	M	M	A		G	E	A	R		A	S	N	O	T
I	L	L	S	E	L	L	Y	O	U	M	I	N	E	
			L	A	D	Y	S		F	R	A			
A	B	O	O	K			A	R	A	L	S	E	A	
F	O	R	F	I	F	T	Y	D	O	L	L	A	R	S
A	D	A	M		G	R	O	O	M		E	G	O	S
R	Y	N	E		H	A	N	S	E			R	E	S	T

160

S	O	S		P	R	O		R	A	D	I	A	N
C	H	I		S	H	O	W		O	N	E	O	U	T
R	A	T		H	I	D	E	A	N	D	S	I	K	H
A	R	O	M	A			N	E	A	P				
G	A	N	D	H	I	C	A	N	E		O	N	C	E
			I	S	D	O	N	E		S	T	O	O	L
O	V	A		E	R	A		T	R	I	C	K	Y	
D	E	L	H	I	S	A	N	D	W	I	C	H	E	S
E	X	T	O	R	T		G	E	O			E	S	E
	T	E	A	M	S		S	E	A	B	E	D		
O	D	I	E		J	O	L	L	Y	R	A	J	A	H
			B	E	A	U			I	N	U	R	E	
A	G	R	A	C	U	L	T	U	R	E		D	I	G
P	O	I	S	O	N		S	K	I	S		G	E	E
R	O	D	E	N	T		K	E	G			E	L	L

161

E	M	P	T	Y		W	E	P	T		L	I	A	R
L	O	U	I	E		A	M	O	S		A	L	T	E
E	N	T	E	R	A	N	E	L	E	C	T	I	O	N
M	A	S	C		G	E	R	E		S	T	A	L	E
			L	A	R	R	Y		N	E	E	D	L	E
A	R	M	A	D	A	S		B	O	A	R			
R	O	U	S	E		C	E	L			M	A	I	
C	O	M	P	E	T	E	O	N	A	T	R	A	C	K
	S	D	S		E	S	Q		H	E	N	C	E	
			S	E	E	S		T	E	A	P	O	T	S
E	V	E	N	T	S		M	A	N	I	A			
L	O	G	A	N		M	A	R	V		I	S	T	O
M	I	G	R	A	T	E	U	P	S	T	R	E	A	M
E	L	E	E		B	O	N	O		B	E	R	R	A
R	A	D	S		S	W	A	N		A	R	B	O	R

162

L	A	S	T		U	S	E	R		S	A	P	I	D
E	C	H	O		N	O	L	O		P	R	A	D	O
T	H	E	N	O	B	L	E	S	T	O	F	A	L	L
M	E	D	I	C	O		N	E	R	O		R	Y	E
E	D	S		T	R	E	A	S	O	N				
			M	O	N	A			U	S	M	A	I	L
A	T	E	U	P		R	A	N	G		E	N	D	E
D	O	G	S	I	S	T	H	E	H	O	T	D	O	G
A	T	O	I		C	H	A	R		U	R	A	L	S
H	O	N	C	H	O			V	E	T	O			
			I	T	F	E	E	D	S		T	H	E	
C	H	E		N	C	O	S		D	E	M	E	A	N
H	A	N	D	T	H	A	T	B	I	T	E	S	I	T
O	L	D	I	E		M	E	R	E		A	L	T	E
S	E	D		Y	E	A	S			L	A	I	R	

163

S	P	R	E	A	D		J	A	M	S		A	D	D
A	I	E	L	L	O		I	D	E	A		L	E	E
I	N	S	I	D	E		G	O	L	D	L	E	A	F
L	A	T	H	E	S				L	A	X	L	Y	
			U	R	N	S		S	T	E	W			
D	E	E	R	S	T	A	L	K	E	R		W	E	D
A	R	L	O			T	O	A	D		B	I	D	E
I	N	T	O		E	D	I	T	S		U	Z	I	S
R	I	O	T		T	O	R	E			D	E	C	K
Y	E	N		P	O	W	E	R	P	L	A	N	T	S
			P	E	N	N			S	H	E	B		
P	U	M	A	S				R	A	B	B	I	T	
S	T	E	M	T	U	R	N		A	V	O	U	C	H
S	A	D		E	S	A	U			S	E	T	T	E	E
T	H	E		R	E	N	T		E	N	T	E	R	O

164

	L	A	M	B		C	B	E	R		S	A	S	S
R	O	D	E	O		R	E	L	Y		O	N	T	O
O	C	E	A	N		O	G	L	E		U	T	A	H
S	A	L	T	S	A	W	A	Y		P	R	E	G	O
A	L	E		A	I	N	T			P	E	G		
			S	I	R			B	A	R	R	O	O	M
S	T	E	W		S	T	A	R	S		A	M	M	O
A	R	T	E			T	R	E	E	S		P	A	I	N
K	I	T	E		R	E	C	A	P			E	R	T	E
S	P	U	T	N	I	K			O	K	S			
			T	O	P		D	A	R	E		B	I	O
M	A	J	O	R		B	I	T	T	E	R	E	N	D
O	L	E	O		G	O	A	L			P	O	L	L	O
D	A	R	T		A	N	N	A			U	T	T	E	R
S	I	K	H		B	E	E	S			P	E	S	T

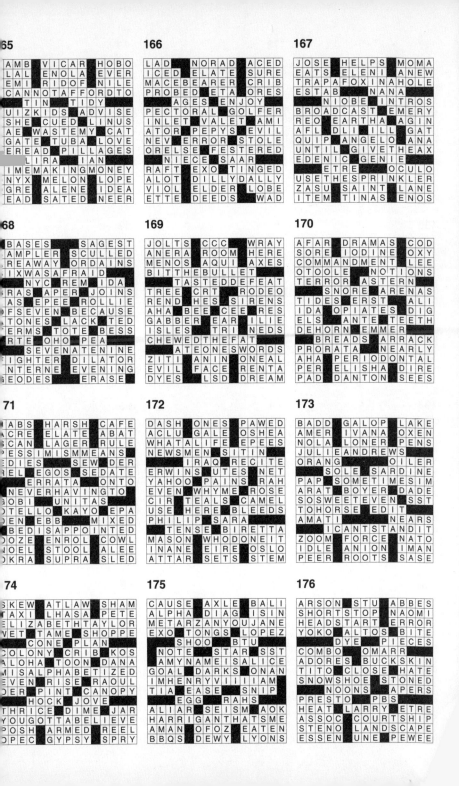

165

```
A M B . V I C A R . H O B O
L A L . E N O L A . E V E R
E M I . R I D O F . N I L E
C A N N O T A F F O R D T O .
. T I N . . . T I D Y . . .
U I Z K I D S . A D V I S E
S H E . C U E D . L I N U S
A E . W A S T E M Y . C A T
G A T E . T U B A . L O V E
E R E A D . P I L L A G E S
. . . L I R A . I A N . . .
I M E M A K I N G M O N E Y
N Y X . M E L O N . L O P E
G R E . A L E N E . I D E A
E A D . S A T E D . N E E R
```

166

```
L A D . N O R A D . A C E D
I C E D . E L A T E . S U R E
M A C E B E A R E R . C R I B
P R O B E D . E T A . O R E S
. . . A G E S . E N J O Y .
P E C T O R A L . G O L F E R
I N L E T . V A L E T . A M I
A T O R . P E P Y S . E V I L
N E V . E R R O R . S T O L E
O R E L S E . F E S T E R E D
. N I E C E . S A A R . . .
R A F T . E X O . T I N G E D
A L O T . D I L L Y D A L L Y
V I O L . E L D E R . L O B E
E T T E . D E E D S . W A D
```

167

```
J O S E . H E L P S . M O M A
E A T S . E L E N I . A N E W
T R A P A F O X I N A H O L E
E S T A B . . N A N A . . .
. . . N I O B E . I N T R O S
B R O A D C A S T . E M E R Y
R E O . E A R T H A . A G I N
A F L . D L I . I L L . G A T
Q U I P . A N G E L O . A N A
U N T I L . G I V E T H E A X
E D E N I C . G E N I E . . .
. . . E T R E . . O C U L O
U S E T H E S P R I N K L E R
Z A S U . S A I N T . L A N E
I T E M . T I N A S . E N O S
```

168

```
. B A S E S . . S A G E S T
. A M P L E R . S C U L L E D
. R E A W A Y . O R D A I N S
. I X W A S A F R A I D . . .
. N Y C . R E M . I D A . . .
. R A S . A P E R . J O I N S
. A S . E P E E . R O L L I E
. F S E V E N . B E C A U S E
. T O N E S . L A C K . T E D
. E R M S . T O T E . B E S S
. R T E . O H O . P E A . . .
. . . S E V E N A T E N I N E
. I G H T E R . D I L A T O R
. N T E R N E . E V E N I N G
. E O D E S . . . E R A S E
```

169

```
J O L T S . C C C . W R A Y
A N E R A . R O O M . H E R E
M E N O S . A Q U I . A X E S
B I T T H E B U L L E T . . .
. . . T A S T E D D E F E A T
T R E E . C R T . R O D E O
R E N D . H E S . S I R E N S
A H A . B E E . C E E . R E S
G A B B E R . E A R . I L I E
I S L E S . T R I . N E D S
C H E W E D T H E F A T . . .
. . . A T E O N E S W O R D S
Z I T I . A N I N . O N E A L
E V I L . F A C E . R E N T A
D Y E S . L S D . D R E A M
```

170

```
A F A R . D R A M A S . C O D
S O R E . I O D I N E . O X Y
C O M M A N D M E N T . L E E
O T O O L E . N O T I O N S
T E R R O R . A S T E R N .
. . . S N O R E . A R E N A S
T I D E S . E R S T . A L I
I D A . O P I A T E S . D I G
E L S . A N T E . T E E T H
D E H O R N . E M M E R . . .
. . B R E A D S . A R R A C K
P R O R A T A . N E A R L Y
A H A . P E R I O D O N T A L
P E R . E L I S H A . D I R E
P A D . D A N T O N . S E E S
```

171

```
. A B S . H A R S H . C A F E
. C R E . E L A T E . A B A T
. C A N . L A G E R . R U L E
. E S S I M I S M M E A N S
. D I E S . . S E W . D E R .
. E L . E G O S . S E D A T E
. . E R R A T A . . O N T O .
. N E V E R H A V I N G T O
. O B I . . U N I T A S . . .
. T E L L O . K A Y O . E P A
. E N . E B B . M I X E D . .
. B E D I S A P P O I N T E D
. O Z E . E N R O L . C O W L
. O E L . S T O O L . A L E E
. K R A . S U P R A . S L E D
```

172

```
D A S H . O N E S . P A W E D
A C L U . G A L E . O S H E A
W H A T A L I F E . E P E E S
N E W S M E N . S I T I N . .
. . . I R A Q . R E C I T E
E R W I N S . U T E S . N E T
Y A H O O . P A I N S . R A H
E V E N . W H Y M E . R O S E
C I R . T E A L S . C A M E L
U S E . H E R E . B L E E D S
P H I L I P . S A R A . . .
. . . T E N S E . B I R E T T A
M A S O N . W H O D O N E I T
I N A N E . E I R E . O S L O
A T T A R . S E T S . S T E M
```

173

```
B A D D . G A L O P . L A K E
A M E R . I V A N A . O X E N
N O L A . L O N E R . P E N S
J U L I E A N D R E W S . . .
O R A N G . . . . . O I L E R
. . . S O L E . S A R D I N E
P A P . S O M E T I M E S I M
A R A T . B O Y E R . D A D E
S O S W E E T E V E N . S S T
T O H O R S E . E D I T . . .
A M A T I . . . . N E A R S
. . I C A N T S T A N D I T
Z O O M . F O R C E . N A T O
I D L E . A N I O N . I M A N
P E E R . R O O T S . S A S E
```

174

```
S K E W . A T L A W . S H A M
A X I . L H A S A . P E T E
E L I Z A B E T H T A Y L O R
V E T . T A M E . S H O P P E
. C O N E . . P L A N . . .
C O L O N Y . C R I B . K O S
A L O H A . T O O N . D A N A
M I S A L P H A B E T I Z E D
E V E N . R I S E . R A O U L
D E R . P I N T . C A N O P Y
. . . H O C K . J O V E . . .
T H R I C E . D I M E . J A R
Y O U G O T T A B E L I E V E
P O S H . A R M E D . R E E L
O P E C . G Y P S Y . S P R Y
```

175

```
C A U S E . A X L E . B A L I
A L P H A . D I A G . I S I N
M E T A R Z A N Y O U J A N E
E X O . T O N G S . L O P E Z
. . . S H O O . . B T U . . .
N O T E . . S T A R . S S T
A M Y N A M E I S A L I C E
G O A L . D A R K S . O N A N
I M H E N R Y V I I I I A M
T I A . E A S E . S N I P . .
. . E G G . . R A H S . . .
A L I A R . S E I S M . A O K
H A R R I G A N T H A T S M E
A M A N . O F O Z . E A T E N
B B Q S . D E W Y . L Y O N S
```

176

```
A R S O N . S T U . A B B E S
S H O R T S T O P . N A O M I
H E A D S T A R T . E R R O R
Y O K O . A L T O S . B I T E
. . . D Y E . . P I E C E S
C O M B O . . O M A R R . . .
A D O R E S . B U C K S K I N
T I T O . C L O S E . H A T E
S N O W S H O E . S T O N E D
. . . N O O N S . A P E R S
P R E S T O . . P B S . . .
H E A T . L A R R Y . E T R E
A S S O C . C O U R T S H I P
S T E N O . L A N D S C A P E
E S S E N . U N E . P E W E E
```

177

```
E L B A   T A T E R   C R A B
P E A R   A T R E E   L U R E
P A T E   S H E L F   O T I S
I F H A R M O N Y I S W H A T
E Y E   O A S T   N A N
      O W N   W I L S O N S
E L A T E   A X I S   L E I
Y O U C R A V E T H E N G E T
R O N   L I D S   D Y A D S
E N T A I L S   F I E
      R N A   B E L T   S O B
A T U B A B U R M A S H A V E
T O P O   O N A I R   A M O R
I G O R   U T I L E   T O I L
T O N S   T O N Y S   S A D E
```

178

```
J E S T   A R T S   A S C O T
A V E R   G A W K   L E A V E
C A N A D A D A Y   L A T I N
O D D   E R A S E R S   A D D
B E S M E A R   A T O M
      A R G   K A W A B A T A
A R C S   A P E D   R E R U N
S E A T   R A V E L   Y A R D
T A R A S   P I S A   I N K Y
A L A B A M A N   V A N
      C A M E   B A G G A G E
B E A   P R O F I L E   N I T
E R R O L   M A H A R A J A H
S L A T E   O L A V   B O N O
T E S T S   O K R A   C U T S
```

179

```
E P I C   A B L E   I S I A H
F A C T   S E A M   N A N C E
R U E S   S A D S A D G I R L
E L I   A U L D   S E A T E D
M A C A B R E   A S P S
      E L I E   A B E T   R B I
C A B O T   F L A S H B U L B
O L A N   E R I C S   O N E I
C U B E S T E A K   C O R D S
A M Y   I C E S   T U T U
      L A H R   F I S H N E T
I N C O M E   N U N S   A L A
R E D R E D W I N E   A W O L
A R I E S   I N G A   N A P E
N O I S E   L A I R   D Y E S
```

180

```
P H I L   S T E P   A H E M
R U N E   S T O N E   Z E R O
O L D F R I E N D S   O L I O
D A Y T O N A   S T A R L E T
I D O L S   O L E O
T A S S E   S I P   P S H A W
H U T T O N   N A B S   E V A
E R O S   E A G L E   C L O Y
M A R   A B L E   D E A L I N
E L E C T   T R I   E R O D E
S L O P   S N A R L
B A H A M A S   K R I S H N A
A M E R   C H O I C E B E E F
N I L E   T O N E S   A M O R
D E F T   S E E R   D I N O
```

181

```
M I L K S   E A R   M A D E
O N A I R   O G L E   U S E D
S A N D A L W O O D   L I N D
E N I D   E N S U E   E A S Y
S E N E C A S   E S T
      R E V   P U M P E D U P
P I C   M E T E R   L E A F Y
A D O B E   A K A   E R R O L
L E M O N   N O L T E   T S E
S A B O T A G E   I N S
      T S P   A B S E N C E
B O S C   P E A L E   M E A L
A L T A   O X F O R D I A N S
S L A M   S I R E   A T R I A
H A R P   E T O   B E S T S
```

182

```
P R O M   L E S S   A D A L E
A I D A   A X E L   N E G E V
S T O L E S E C O N D B A S E
S T R I K E R S   E R A S E S
      G E R T   U S E S
S A N D S   E S T   E R L E
S T L E O   E T H O S   E E R
H E L D U P T H E R U N N E R
A N O   T O N E R   N E E D S
H O W L   W A R   C R I E S
      A I D S   H A I G
A T T U N E   A I R S H I P S
M U R D E R E D T H E B A L L
P R I E R   L I M O   O G E E
S N O R T   S T E P   R O A D
```

183

```
S C A B   S E P T   B E E R S
L A T E   A V E R   A L A I N
O N E S   L E E I A C O C C A
T O A S T   S T A R K   H E P
H E M M E R   E D G E D
      Y E A S   O R A T E S
A N N E M E A R A   N O V A
C O O R S   G U Y   A N T E S
E N O S   A R I M E Y E R S
S E N O R A   N A S A
      N O T E S   P O I S E D
R I O   N O L T E   P E T E R
E D W I N M E E S E   L O R E
E L E N I   C E T A   L O I S
D E N S E   T R E T   O D E S
```

184

```
A D O P T   O P P   S P R A T
M E D E A   R O O   A L I N E
P L O W R I G H T   R A N T S
S E R   T E S L A   A N D E S
      C A R   T A C T
S A V O R   C R O P E A R E D
A G I O   P L O   E N G A G E
R A S P   R U D E R   E T R E
A M O E B A   I R S   N E E D
H A R R O W I N G   T E S T S
      A N N S   B E T
A B A T E   A L I E N   A L I
V A L I D   B A R N A C L E S
A S T O R   E T A   N O L T E
S T O N Y   L E N   T E A S E
```

185

```
V O W S   B O C A   L A M A
A D E N   C A R A T   E T E S
L I E U   A B E L L   O W L S
E D G A R A L L A N P O E T
      G U T   E N C O R E S
M A I L R O O M   T A L K S
R O S E A N N E B A R D
T K O   T A E   A L I
      W I N O N A W R I T E R
E D I N A   T R A I N E E S
S T Y L I N G   T O P
C H E S T E R A A U T H O R
U N D O   T E N D S   A X E D
D O I N   T A K E I   S E N D
S S N S   E T A S   E N D S
```

186

```
  P A M   Y U M     J E D I
A L C A P O N E   S H A V E N
Q U I N Q U A G E N A R I A N
U N D E R   C I G   D D E
A G I T   M I G H T   L E S E
S E C   P E R O T   P I N E D
      B A N A L   I N C A
    A L B U Q U E R Q U E
      R D A S   C L A U S
B E A S T   S K A T E   S T A
A C M E   D O Y L E   E L E M
S O W   R I O   A S O N E
Q U E B E C N O R D I Q U E S
N S A F E   C O N D U C T S
  A     T W A   E H S
```

187

```
W I D E   C A M E L   N O V A
A B U T   A N A G E   A L A N
F A T H E R K N O W S B E S T
T R Y   X R A Y S   O B O E
      A P O   E L I
T H E M O T H E R S I N L A W
W A R P S   A S I S   G A L E
E R A   T A T T L E R   P T S
E S S O   S L O E   U P S E T
T H E S N O O P S I S T E R S
      T O N   G S A
T I E S   L A I N E   F B I
D R J O Y C E B R O T H E R S
T I K I   B A B A R   O R A L
S O L D   C H A S E   O N C E
```

188

```
M E S T A   A L U M S   J A M
I C H O R   N A T E S   U T E
C H I N A R I V E R A   L O A
H O N K   E T A P E   S I L L
      I O T A S   S H O A L S
F R O N T A L   T A L C
L A M   C R A N I   T A H O E
A R A M   D O U R O   N I N A
G E N O A   S T A B S   L E S
S T I R   N E A R E S T
A S H O R E   C L Y D E
S T A R   S C R E E   B A A L
I E R   P O L A N D J O F F E
D E I   E L A N D   O Z A R K
E L F   N E W E L   T O R O S
```

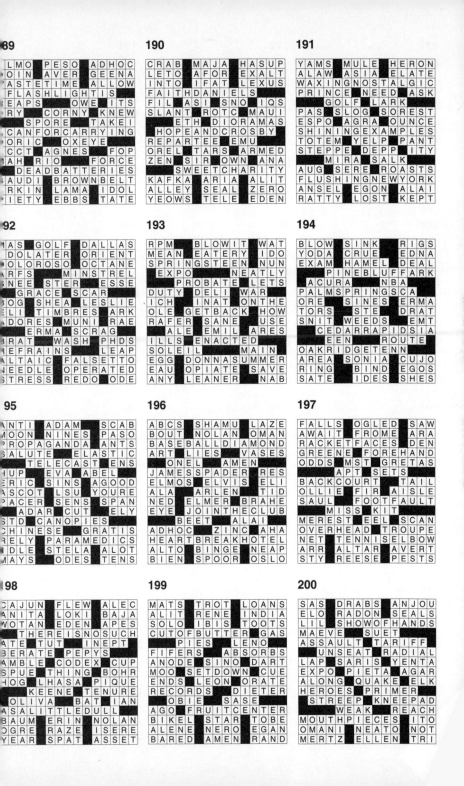

189

```
L M O   P E S O   A D H O C
O I N   A V E R   G E E N A
A S T E T I M E   A L L O W
F L A S H L I G H T I S
E A P S     O W E     I T S
R Y     C O R N Y   K N E W
  S P O R E     T A K E I
C A N F O R C A R R Y I N G
O R I C     O X E Y E
C C T   A G N E S     F O P
A H   R I O     F O R C E
D E A D B A T T E R I E S
A U D I   B R O W N B E L T
R K I N   L A M A   I D O L
I E T Y   E B B S   T A T E
```

190

```
C R A B   M A J A   H A S U P
L E T O   A F O R   E X A L T
I N T O   I F A T   L E X U S
F A I T H D A N I E L S
F I L   A S I   S N O   I Q S
S L A N T   R O T C   M A U I
      E T H   D I O R A M A S
H O P E A N D C R O S B Y
R E P A R T E E   E M U
O R E L   T A R S   A R M E D
Z E N   S I R   O W N   A N A
  S W E E T C H A R I T Y
K A F K A   A R I A   A L I T
A L L E Y   S E A L   Z E R O
Y E O W S   T E L E   E D E N
```

191

```
Y A M S   M U L E   H E R O N
A L A W   A S I A   E L A T E
W A X I N G N O S T A L G I C
P R I N C E   N E E D   A S K
      G O L F   L A R K
P A S   S L O G   S O R E S T
E S P O   A G R A   O U N C E
S H I N I N G E X A M P L E S
T O T E M   Y E L P   P A N T
S T E P P E   D E P P   I T Y
      M I R A   S A L K
A U G   S E R E   R O A S T S
F L U S H I N G N E W Y O R K
A N S E L   E G O N   A L A I
R A T T Y   L O S T   K E P T
```

192

```
M A S   G O L F   D A L L A S
D O L A T E R   O R I E N T
O L O R O S O   O C T A N E
R F S     M I N S T R E L
N E E   S T E R   E S S E
  G R A C E   S C A R
O G   S H E A   L E S L I E
L I   T I M B R E S   A R K
D O R E S   M U N I   R A E
  E R M A   S C R A G
R A T   W A S H   P H D S
R E F R A I N S   L E A P
A L T A I C   F A L S E T T O
N E E D L E   O P E R A T E D
S T R E S S   R E D O   O D E
```

193

```
R P M   B L O W I T   W A T
M E A N   E A T E R Y   I D O
S P R I N G S T E E N   N U N
E X P O     N E A T L Y
  P R O B A T E   L E T S
D U T Y   D E L I   W A R
I C H   I N A T   O N T H E
O L E   G E T B A C K   H O W
R A F E R   S A N E   U S E
A L E   E M I L   A R E S
I L L S   E N A C T E D
S O L E I L   M A I N
E G G   D O N N A S U M M E R
E A U   O P I A T E   S A V E
A N Y   L E A N E R   N A B
```

194

```
B L O W   S I N K   R I G S
Y O D A   C R U E   E D N A
E X A M   H A M E L   D E A L
  P I N E B L U F F A R K
A C U R A     N B A
P A L M S P R I N G S C A
O R E   S I N E S   E R M A
T O R S   S T E   D R A T
S N I T   W E E D S   E M T
C E D A R R A P I D S I A
    E E N   R O U T E
O A K R I D G E T E N N
A R E A   S O N I A   C U J O
R I N G   B I N D   E G O S
S A T E   I D E S   S H E S
```

195

```
A N T I   A D A M   S C A B
M O O N   N I N E S   P A S O
P R O P A G A N D A   A N T S
S A L U T E   E L A S T I C
  T E L E C A S T   E N S
H U P   E V A   A B E L
E R I C   S I N S   A G O O D
A S C O T   L S U   Y O U R E
P A C E R   S E N S   S P A N
  A D A R   C U T   E L Y
S T D   C A N O P I E S
C H I N E S E   G R A T I S
R E L Y   P A R A M E D I C S
D L E   S T E L A   A L O T
M A Y S   O D E S   T E N S
```

196

```
A B C S   S H A M U   L A Z E
B O U T   N O L A N   O M A N
B A S E B A L L D I A M O N D
A R T   L I E S   V A S E S
    O N E L   A M E N
J A M E S S P A D E R   R E S
E L M O S   E L V I S   E L I
A L A   A R L E N   T I D
N E D   E L M E R   B R A H E
E Y E   J O I N T H E C L U B
    B E E T   A L A I
A D H O C   Z I N C   A H A
H E A R T B R E A K H O T E L
A L T O   B I N G E   N E A P
B I E N   S P O O R   O S L O
```

197

```
F A L L S   O G L E D   S A W
A W A I T   F R O M E   A R A
R A C K E T F A C E S   D E N
G R E E N E   F O R E H A N D
O D D S   M S T   G R E T A S
    A P T   S E T S
B A C K C O U R T   T A I L
O L L I E   F I R   A I S L E
S A U L   F O O T F A U L T
    M I S S   K I T
M E R E S T   E E L   S C A N
O V E R H E A D   T R O U P E
N E T   T E N N I S E L B O W
A R R   A L T A R   A V E R T
S T Y   R E E S E   P E S T S
```

198

```
C A J U N   F L E W   A L E C
A N I T A   L O K I   B A J A
W O T A N   E D E N   A P E S
  T H E R E I S N O S U C H
A T E   T U T   I N E P T
B E R A T E   P E P Y S
A M B L E   C O D E X   C U P
S P U E   T H I N G   B O H R
H O G   L H A S A   P I Q U E
  K E E N E   T E N U R E
O L I V A   B A T   I A N
A S A L I T T L E D U L L
B A U M   E R I N   N O L A N
O G R E   R A Z E   I S E R E
Y E A R   S P A T   A S S E T
```

199

```
M A T S   T R O T   L O A N S
A L I T   R E N E   I N D I A
S O L O   I B I S   T O O T S
C U T O F B U T T E R   G A S
    P I E S   L E N O
F I F E R S   A B S O R B S
A N O D E   S I N O   D A R T
M O O   S E T D O W N   C U E
E N D S   L E O N   O R A T E
R E C O R D S   D I E T E R
    O B I E   S A S E
A G O   F R U I T C E N T E R
B I K E L   S T A R   T O B E
A L E N E   N E R O   E G A N
B A R E D   A M E N   R A N D
```

200

```
S A S   D R A B S   A N J O U
E L O   R A D O N   S E A L S
L I L   S H O W O F H A N D S
M A E V E   S U E T
A S S A U L T   T A R I F F
  U N S E A T   R A D I A L
L A P   S A R I S   Y E N T A
E X P O   P I E T A   A G A R
A L O N G   Q U A K E   E L K
H E R O E S   P R I M E R
  S T R E E P   K N E E P A D
    W E A K   R E A C H
M O U T H P I E C E S   I T O
O M A N I   N E A T O   N O T
M E R T Z   E L L E N   T R I
```

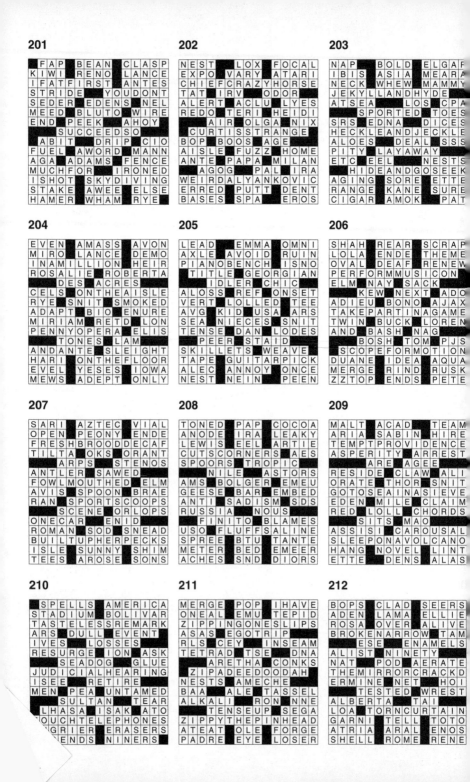

201

```
 F A P   B E A N   C L A S P
K I W I   R E N O   L A N C E
I F A T F I R S T   A N T E S
S T R I D E     Y O U D O N T
S E D E R   E D E N S   N E L
M E E D   B L U T O   W I R E
E N D   P E E K   A H O Y
    S U C C E E D S O
A B I T   D R I P   C I O
F U E L   A W O R D   M A N N
A G A   A D A M S   F E N C E
M U C H F O R     I R O N E D
I S H O T   S K Y D I V I N G
S T A K E   A W E E   E L S E
H A M E R   W H A M   R Y E
```

202

```
N E S T   L O X   F O C A L
E X P O   V A R Y   A T A R I
C H I E F C R A Z Y H O R S E
T A T   I R V   O D O R
A L E R T   A C L U   L Y E S
R E D O   T E R I   H E I D I
    A I R   O L G A   N I X
  C U R T I S S T R A N G E
B O P   B O O S   A G E
A I S L E   F U Z Z   H O M E
A N T E   P A P A   M I L A N
A G O G   P A L   I R A
W E I R D A L Y A N K O V I C
E R R E D   P U T T   D E N T
B A S E S   S P A   E R O S
```

203

```
N A P   B O L D   E L G A R
I B I S   A S I A   M E A R A
N E C K   W H E W   M A M M Y
J E K Y L L A N D H Y D E
A T S E A   L O S   C P A
    S P O R T E D   T O E S
S R S   E D N A   D I C E S
H E C K L E A N D J E C K L E
A L O E S   D E A L   S S S
P I T Y   L A Y A W A Y
E T C   E E L   N E S T S
  H I D E A N D G O S E E K
A G I N G   S O R E   E T T E
R A N G E   K A N E   S U R E
C I G A R   A M O K   P A T
```

204

```
E V E N   A M A S S   A V O N
M I R O   L A N C E   D E M O
I N A M I L L I O N   H E I R
R O S A L I E   R O B E R T A
      D E S   A C R E S
C E L S   O N T H E A I S L E
R Y E   S N I T   S M O K E D
A D A P T   B I O   E N U R E
M I R I A M   R E T D   L O N
P E N N Y O P E R A   E L I S
    T O N E S   L A M
A N D A N T E   S L E I G H T
H A R I   O N T H E F L O O R
E V E L   Y E S E S   I O W A
M E W S   A D E P T   O N L Y
```

205

```
L E A D   E M M A   O M N I
A X L E   A V O I D   R U I N
P I A N O B E N C H   I S N O
  T I T L E   G E O R G I A N
    I D L E R   C H I C
A L O S S   R E F   O N S E T
V E R T   L O L L E D   T E E
A V G   K I D   U S A   A R S
S E A   N I E C E S   S N I T
T E N S E   D A N   L O D E S
    P E E R   S T A I D
S K I L L E T S   W E A V E
T A P E   G U I T A R P I C K
A L E C   A N N O Y   O N C E
N E S T   N E I N   P E E N
```

206

```
S H A H   R E A R   S C R A P
L O L A   E N D E   T H E M E
O V A L   D E A F   R E N E W
P E R F O R M M U S I C O N
E L M   N A Y   S A C K
    K E W   N E X T   A D O
A D I E U   B O N O   A J A X
T A K E P A R T I N A G A M E
T W I N   B U C K   L O R E N
A N D   B A S H   N A G
  B O S H   T O M   P J S
S C O P E F O R M O T I O N
D U A N E   I D E A   A Q U A
M E R G E   R I N D   R U S K
Z Z T O P   E N D S   P E T E
```

207

```
S A R I   A Z T E C   V I A L
O P E N   P E O N Y   E N D E
F R E S H B R O O D D E C A F
T I L T A   O K S   O R A N T
    A R P S   S T E N O S
A N T L E R   S A W E D
F O W L M O U T H E D   E L M
A V I S   S P O O N   B R A E
R A N   S P O R T S C O O P S
    S C E N E   O R L O P S
O N E C A R   E N I D
R O M A N   S O D   S N E A D
B U I L T U P H E R P E C K S
I S L E   S U N N Y   S H I M
T E E S   A R O S E   S O N S
```

208

```
T O N E D   P A P   C O C O A
A N O D E   I R A   L E A K Y
L E W I S   E E L   A R T I E
C U T S C O R N E R S   A E S
S P O O R S   T R O P I C
    N I L E   A S T O R S
A M S   B O L G E R   E M E U
G E E S E   B A R   E M B E D
A N T I   S A D I S M   S D S
R U S S I A   N O U S
    F I N I T O   B L A M E S
U S O   F L U F F S A L I N E
S P R E E   B T U   T A N T E
M E T E R   B E D   E M E E R
A C H E S   S N D   D I O R S
```

209

```
M A L T   A C A D   T E A M
A R I A   S A B I N   H I R E
T E M P T P R O V I D E N C E
A S P E R I T Y   A R R E S T
      A R E   A G E E
R E S I D E   C L A W   A L I
O R A T E   T H O R   S N I T
G O T O S E A I N A S I E V E
E D E N   M I L E   C L A I M
R E D   L O L L   C H O R D S
    S I T S   M A O
A S S I S I   C A R O U S A L
S L E E P O N A V O L C A N O
H A N G   N O V E L   L I N T
E T T E   D E N S   A L A S
```

210

```
  S P E L L S   A M E R I C A
S T A D I U M   B O L I V A R
T A S T E L E S S R E M A R K
A R S   D U L L   E V E N T
I V E S   L O S S E S
R E S U R G E   I O N   A S K
    S E A D O G   G L U E
J U D I C I A L H E A R I N G
I S E E   R E T I R E
M E N   P E A   U N T A M E D
  S U L T A N   T E A R
L H A S A   I S A K   A T O
T O U C H T E L E P H O N E S
  G R I E R   E R A S E R S
  E N D S   N I N E R S
```

211

```
M E R G E   P O P   I H A V E
O N E A L   E M U   T E P I D
Z I P P I N G O N E S L I P S
A S A S   E G O T R I P
R L S   C E Y   I N S E A M
T E T R A D   T S E   D N A
  A R E T H A   C O N K S
  Z I P A D E E D O O D A H
N E S T S   A M E C H E
B A A   A L E   T A S S E L
A L K A L I   R O N   N N E
    T E N S E U P   S E G A
Z I P P Y T H E P I N H E A D
A T E A T   O L E   F O R G E
P A D R E   E Y E   L O S E R
```

212

```
B O P S   C L A D   S E E R S
A D E N   L A M A   E L L I E
R O S A   O V E R   A L I V E
B R O K E N A R R O W   T A M
    E S E   E N A M E L S
A L I S T   N I N E T Y
N A T   P O D   A E R A T E
T H E M I R R O R C R A C K D
E R M I N E   N E T   H O I
    T E S T E D   W R E S T
A L B E R T A   T A I
L O A   T O R N C U R T A I N
G A R N I   T E L L   T O T O
A T R I A   A R A L   E N O S
S H E L L   R O M E   R E N E
```

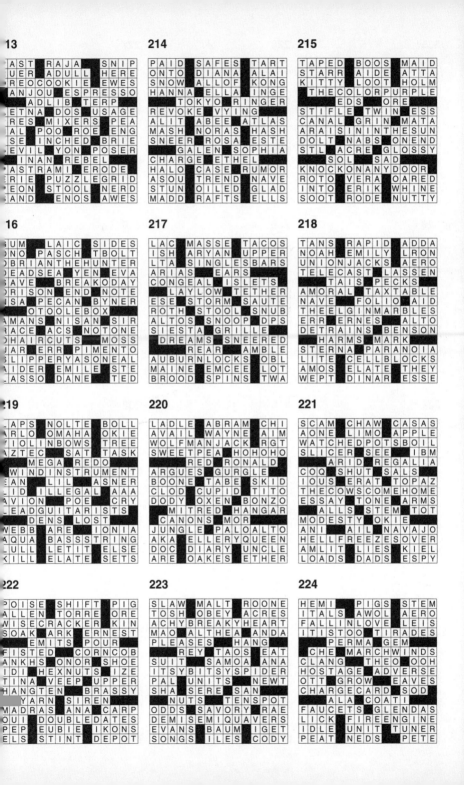

13

```
A S T   R A J A     S N I P
U E R   A D U L L   H E R E
R E O C O O K I E   E W E S
A N J O U   E S P R E S S O
  A D L I B     T E R P
E T N A   D O S   U S A G E
R E S   M I X E R S   P E A
A L   P O O   R O E   E N G
S E   I N C H E D   B R I E
E V I L   Y O N   P O S E R
  I N A N   R E B E L
A S T R A M I   E R O D E
R I E   P U Z Z L E G R I D
E O N   S T O O L   N E R D
A N D   E N O S   A W E S
```

214

```
P A I D   S A F E S   T A R T
O N T O   D I A N A   A L A I
S N O W   A L L O F   K O N G
H A N N A   E L L A   I N G E
    T O K Y O   R I N G E R
R E V O K E     V Y I N G
A L I T   A B E E   A T L A S
M A S H   N O R A S   H A S H
S N E E R   R O S A   E S T E
  G A L E N   S O P H I A
C H A R G E     E T H E L
H A L O   C A S E   R U M O R
A S O U   T R E N D   N A V E
S T U N   O I L E D   G L A D
M A D D   R A F T S   E L L S
```

215

```
T A P E D   B O O S   M A I D
S T A R R   A I D E   A T T A
K I T T Y   L O O T   H O L M
T H E C O L O R P U R P L E
      E D S       O R E
S T I F L E   T W I N   E S S
C A N A L   G R I N   M A T A
A R A I S I N I N T H E S U N
D O L T   N A B S   O N E N D
S T L   A C R E   G L O S S Y
    S O L       S A D
K N O C K O N A N Y D O O R
R O T O   V E R A   O A R E D
I N T O   E R I K   W H I N E
S O O T   R O D E   N U T T Y
```

16

```
U M   L A I C   S I D E S
N O   P A S C H   T B O L T
B R I A N T H E H U N T E R
D E A D S E A   Y E N   E V A
A V E   B R E A K O D A Y
R I S O N   E N D   N O T E
S A   P E C A N   B Y N E R
  O T O O L E B O X
A M A N S   N I S A N   S I R
R A C E   A C S   N O T O N E
H A I R C U T S   M O S S
J A R   E R R   P I M E N T O
S L I P P E R Y A S O N E A L
A I D E R   E M I L E   S T E
L A S S O   D A N E   T E D
```

217

```
L A C   M A S S E   T A C O S
I S H   A R Y A N   U P P E R
L T A   S I N G L E S B A R S
A R I A S     E A R S
C O N G E A L   I S L E T S
  L A Y L O W   T E T H E R
E S E   S T O R M   S A U T E
R O T H   S T O O L   S N U B
A L T O S   S N O O P   D P S
S I E S T A   G R I L L E
D R E A M S   S N E E R E D
    R E A R   A M B L E
A U B U R N L O C K S   O B L
M A I N E   E M C E E   L O T
B R O O D   S P I N S   T W A
```

218

```
T A N S   R A P I D   A D D A
N O A H   E M I L Y   L R O N
U N I O N J A C K S   A E R O
T E L E C A S T   L A S S E N
    T A I S   P E C K S
A M O R A L   T A X T A B L E
N A V E   F O L I O   A I D
T H E E L G I N M A R B L E S
E R R   E R N E S   A L T O
D E T R A I N S   B E N S O N
  H A R M S   M A R K
S T E R N A   P A R A N O I A
L I T E   C E L L B L O C K S
A M O S   E L A T E   T H E Y
W E P T   D I N A R   E S S E
```

219

```
A P S   N O L T E   B O L L
A R L O   O M A H A   O K I E
V I O L I N B O W S   T R E E
A Z T E C   S A T   T A S K
  M E G A   R E D O
W I N D I N S T R U M E N T
E A N   L I L   A S N E R
I D   I L L E G A L   A A A
A V I O N   P O E   C R Y
L E A D G U I T A R I S T S
  D E N S   L O S T
W E B B   A R E   I O N I A
A Q U A   B A S S S T R I N G
L U L L   L E T I T   E L S E
K I L L   E L A T E   S E T S
```

220

```
L A D L E   A B R A M   C H I
A V A I L   W A Y N E   A I M
W O L F M A N J A C K   R G T
S W E E T P E A   H O H O H O
    R E D   R O N A L D
A R G U E S   G U R G L E
B O O N E   T A B E   S K I D
C L O D   C U P I D   T I T O
D O D Y   O X E N   B O N Z O
  M I T R E D   H A N G A R
C A N O N S   M O R
J U N G L E   P A L O A L T O
A K A   E L L E R Y Q U E E N
D O C   D I A R Y   U N C L E
A R E   O A K E S   E T H E R
```

221

```
S C A M   C H A W   C A S A S
A O N E   L I M O   A P P L E
W A T C H E D P O T S B O I L
S L I C E R   S E E   I B M
    A R I D   R E G A L I A
C O Q   S H U T   S A L S
I O U S   E R A T   T O P A Z
T H E C O W S C O M E H O M E
E S S A Y   T O N E   A R M S
  A L L S   S T E M   T O T
M O D E S T Y   O K I E
A N I   A I L   N A V A J O
H E L L F R E E Z E S O V E R
A M L I T   L I E S   K I E L
L O A D S   D A D S   E S P Y
```

222

```
P O I S E   S H I F T   P I G
A L L E N   T O R R E   O R E
W I S E C R A C K E R   K I N
S O A K   A R K   E R N E S T
  E M I T S   P O U R
F I S T E D   C O R N C O B
A N K H S   O N O R   S H O E
I D I   H E X N U T S   I Z E
T I N A   V E E P   U P P E R
H A N G T E N   B R A S S Y
  Y A R N   S I R E N
M A D R A S   A N A   C A R P
O U I   D O U B L E D A T E S
P E P   E U B I E   I K O N S
E L S   S T I N T   D E P O T
```

223

```
S L A W   M A L T   R O O N E
T O S H   O B E Y   A C R E S
A C H Y B R E A K Y H E A R T
M A O   A L T H E A   A N D A
P L E A S E S   H A N G
    R E Y   T A O S   E A T
S U I T   S A M O A   A N A
I T S Y B I T S Y S P I D E R
P A L   U N I T S   N E W T
S H A   S E R E   S A N
  N U T S   T E N S P O T
O D D S   S A V O R Y   R A E
D E M I S E M I Q U A V E R S
E V A N S   B A U M   I G E T
S O N G S   I L E S   C O D Y
```

224

```
H E M I   P I G S   S T E M
I T A L S   A W O L   A E R O
F A L L I N L O V E   L E I S
I T I S T O O   T I R A D E S
    P E R M A   G E M
C H E   M A R C H W I N D S
C L A N G   T H E O   O O H
H O S T A G E   A D V E R S E
O T T   G R O W   E A V E S
C H A R G E C A R D   S O D
    A L A   C O A T I
F A U C E T S   G L E N D A S
L I C K   F I R E E N G I N E
I D L E   U N I T   T U N E R
P E A T   N E D S   P E T E
```

225

```
FUDD . SEMI . STRAD
ASEA . PROM . HAILE
VERYHARDPROBLEM
ERASER . ASOF . EXO
SST . YELL . TAD . .
. MYRA . STRANGE
AEREO . BATE . LOUS
PROTUBERANTLUMP
BITE . ALAR . WASPY
SNORERS . ICES . .
. . SIR . ASHE . LST
AWL . LENS . ITLIKE
SEAVELOCITYUNIT
ALLIE . DOLT . NEMO
PLAIN . STAY . ASSN
```

226

```
GAGA . GUSTO . CHAS
ENOS . ENTER . HOLY
LENT . MIRED . ERIN
TWERP . TIMER . NCO
. . WARDEN . ROUSED
BOILED . GASTRO . .
AFT . FATAL . SAFER
JOHN . YALTA . LALO
AZTEC . KOALA . DEN
. . HARDEN . ULTIMA
CHERIE . GAMBOL . .
HEW . BLOWN . ADEPT
IRIS . UNION . AMIE
NONO . DITTO . TMEN
ANDY . ETHER . EAST
```

227

```
BOTH . SLAVS . SINC
ABRA . PUREE . KNOB
COATHANGER . ERIE
HEP . ERGO . ELLERY
. . . CASE . KNEE . .
SMOTE . BLASTOFF
WHIM . LIED . OVAL
ARAB . CUTIE . NIKE
DEMI . OMEN . KNEW
SWINDLES . SPEED
. . ANON . SPRY . .
BANTAM . FARO . FAD
ALAI . BRUTEFORCE
DINO . IONIA . REEF
ETON . AIDED . BEST
```

228

```
REYKJAVIK . . ISA
AMERICANAS . NEW
TONIGHTSHOW . SRO
. SGT . ENNE . TIL
NAB . LUST . TARIFF
ABILENE . ASET . .
DOLE . GEORGEBUSH
IDLER . IRA . LOTTO
RECREATING . LIAR
. LEND . DOCTORS
ABIDED . MICA . NEE
HEN . ESAI . ARM . .
MIT . SUMMERHOMES
AGO . PUERTORICO
DEN . ROSSPEROT
```

229

```
. TETE . CARIB . MOB
ARLEN . IRENE . EVA
HEARTBREAKHOTEL
EMPIRICAL . AWARD
MOS . GAS . SVELTE
REOS . ETE . LOS
. . DISABLE . RIOT
JAILHOUSEROCK
CUBE . ANGERED . .
RNA . UKE . MEOW
OCCUPY . PTA . DAP
STUMP . ARRESTERS
SUSPICIOUSMINDS
ERE . TODDS . UNSET
DES . YEAST . TEEN
```

230

```
ESTS . TACOS . MOSS
GLEN . ADAPT . ARIA
GOHEADOVERHEELS
STEEDS . ERIE . SOS
. . HERO . TRAVEL
. . RAE . SEDATES
MOTHERED . SRTA
AGOODIMPRESSION
TRON . TENTOONE
SELECTS . ADE . .
. SORTED . ROAM
ESP . LARD . TEFLON
KEEPALOWPROFILE
EASE . AKITE . EVES
STOP . SENSE . REST
```

231

```
CAP . BOHM . ALGER
ALL . AREA . CAIRO
PEOPLEWHOTHROW
SERVED . OPERAS
OCTET . SQUID . FIB
DOER . SAUTE . AFOR
ADD . MOPE . ELENA
. . KISSESARE . .
INDEX . NINA . DEL
NARY . DALLY . LENO
CIO . SIBYL . BENJI
ROSARY . REGION
HOPELESSLYLAZY
EBERT . MAYA . TEE
MIDAS . STEN . END
```

232

```
JELL . AMIA . GAZA
ALAI . LONG . CRIER
DIMEHORSE . LIMBO
ESP . AHOE . RATERS
. . MANTHURSDAY
PANEL . ORK . .
ALIBI . COMA . AJAR
COLONELDELIVERY
KEEN . PEER . SIDLE
. . OCA . ADIOS
JACKFORADAY
UPLIFT . LESS . FOG
IRATE . TEAFORONE
CORER . ANNA . OXEN
ENOS . BEER . EYRE
```

233

```
MINK . GLUM . CAPOS
EDAM . LEGO . OTARU
NADA . UCLA . PEREZ
SHIRRTHINGS . ELY
AORTAE . REST . .
. . KNEADA . TRAM
ANGLE . MMES . RENE
BORED . BAN . LIENS
BEAN . OATS . EASES
ALTO . FRIEND . .
. EXAM . AUSSIE
HAG . SEARSUCKERS
EQUIP . HAIG . EGOS
LUNGE . ARCH . WANE
MASON . BEST . SLYS
```

234

```
CHIC . CARA . ABAS
SEMITONES . SATON
THERAPIST . ACHOO
. CBS . CAN . KENO
DIALA . CUBESTEAK
NOSECONE . VIOLS
ATIT . FORCEPS . .
ASHPIT . IRAQIS
. . ERNESTO . UNTO
TOWED . PENTAGON
PYRAMIDED . WRAPS
ARAG . AWL . FOE
ROTOR . ALLATONCE
INONA . REASONOUT
ERST . FRIT . ERMA
```

235

```
LIRA . SKIS . DIM
ONEL . TINA . REACT
BUGSBUNNY . ELMER
ERROR . SAFE . ANA
DEE . ASH . HAVARTI
. STRIPER . REBOIL
. . ENERO . ACRE
WOODYWOODPECKER
EXPO . KEANU . .
BYPASS . SAVESUP
SMOKIES . DER . RIP
TOS . TAIL . GOSEE
ERICA . DAFFYDUCK
ROTOR . ELIE . OLEO
NEW . SANE . RARE
```

236

```
TOBAT . ADE . BASE
ASINA . DIXIELAND
THECRESCENTCITY
ANISE . IRKS . NRA
. VEINLET . STEN
SPIN . CREOLE . .
IAL . ISL . DREAMER
TULANE . BANANA
ELECTRA . TSK . RIG
. HOARSE . ADDS
BCDE . SHASTRI
OHR . TOEA . BURGH
WAYDOWNYONDERIN
LOUISIANA . OTARY
. SPTS . LET . RESTS
```

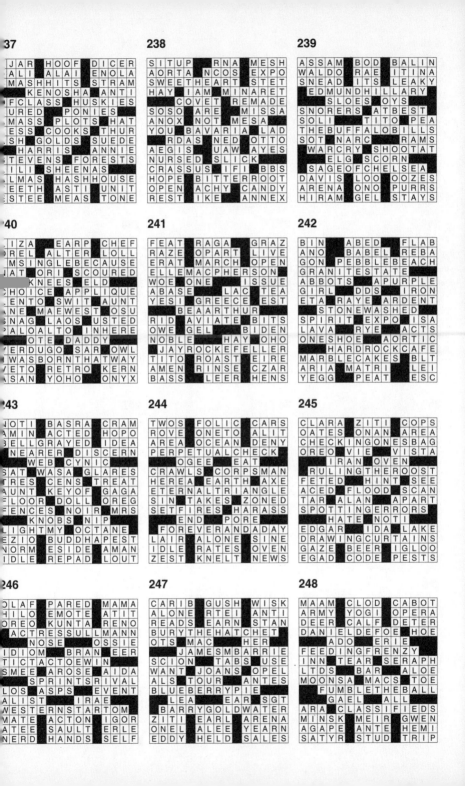

237

```
J A R   H O O F   D I C E R
A L I   A L A I   E N O L A
M A S H H I T S   S T R A M
  K E N O S H A   A N T I
F C L A S S   H U S K I E S
U R E D   P O N I E S
M A S S   P L O T S   H A T
E S S   C O O K S   T H U R
S H   G O L D S   S U E D E
  H A R R I S   A N N I E
T E V E N S   F O R E S T S
I L I   S H E E N A S
L M A S   H A S H H O U S E
E E T H   A S T I   U N I T
S T E E   M E A S   T O N E
```

238

```
S I T U P   R N A   M E S H
A O R T A   N C O S   E X P O
S W E E T H E A R T   S T E T
H A Y   I A M   M I N A R E T
    C O V E T   R E M A D E
S O S O   A R E   M I S S A
A N O X   N O T   M E S A
Y O U   B A V A R I A   L A D
  R D A S   N E D   O T T O
A E G I S   U A W   A Y E S
N U R S E D   S L I C K
C R A S S U S   I F I   B B S
H O P E   B I T T E R R O O T
O P E N   A C H Y   C A N D Y
R E S T   I K E   A N N E X
```

239

```
A S S A M   B O D   B A L I N
W A L D O   R A E   I T I N A
S N E A D   I T S   L E A K Y
  E D M U N D H I L L A R Y
    S L O E S   O Y S
S N O R E R S   A T B E S T
S O L I   T I T O   P E A
T H E B U F F A L O B I L L S
S O T   N A R C   R A M S
W A R C R Y   S H O O T A T
    E L G   S C O R N
  S A G E O F C H E L S E A
D A V I S   L O O   O O Z E S
A R E N A   O N O   P U R R S
H I R A M   G E L   S T A Y S
```

240

```
I Z A   E A R P   C H E F
R E L   A L T E R   L O L L
M S I N G L E B E C A U S E
A T   O R I   S C O U R E D
  K N E E S   E L D
H O I C E   A P P L I Q U E
E N T O   S W I T   A U N T
N E   M A E W E S T   O S U
N A G   L A O S   U S T E D
A L O A L T O   I N H E R E
  O D E   D A D D Y
E R D U G O   S A R   O W L
W A S B O R N T H A T W A Y
V E T O   R E T R O   K E R N
A S A N   Y O H O   O N Y X
```

241

```
F E A T   R A G A   G R A Z
R A Z E   O P A R T   L I V E
E R A T   M A R C H   O P E N
E L L E M A C P H E R S O N
W O E   O N E   I S S U E
A B A S E   L A C   T E A
Y E S I   G R E E C E   E S T
      B E A A R T H U R
R I D   A V I A T E   B I T S
O W E   G E L   B I D E N
N O B L E   H A Y   O H O
J A Y R O C K E F E L L E R
T I T O   R O A S T   E I R E
A M E N   R I N S E   C Z A R
B A S S   L E E R   H E N S
```

242

```
B I N   A B E D   F L A B
A N O   B A B E L   R E B A
G O N   P E B B L E B E A C H
G R A N I T E S T A T E
A B B O T S   A P U R P L E
G I R L   D D S   I R O N
E T A   R A Y E   A R D E N T
    S T O N E W A S H E D
S P I R I T   E X P O   I S A
L A V A   R Y E   A C T S
O N E S H O E   A O R T I C
  H A R D R O C K C A F E
M A R B L E C A K E S   B L T
A R I A   M A T R I   L E I
Y E G G   P E A T   E S C
```

243

```
O T I   B A S R A   C R A M
A M I N   A C T E D   H O P O
B E L L G R A Y E D   I D E A
N E A R E R   D I S C E R N
    W E B   C Y N I C
S A T   W A S A   G L A R E S
T R E S   C E N S   T R E A T
A U N T   K E Y O F   G A G A
F L O O R   D O L L   O R E G
F E N C E S   N O I R   M R S
    K N O B S   N I P
L I G H T M Y   O C T A N E
E Z I O   B U D D H A P E S T
N O R M   E S I D E   A M A N
I D L E   R E P A D   L O U T
```

244

```
T W O S   F O L I C   C A R S
R O V E   O N E T O   A L I T
A R E A   O C E A N   D E N Y
P E R P E T U A L C H E C K
    O G E E   E A T
C R A W L S   C O R P S M A N
H E R E A   E A R T H   A X E
E T E R N A L T R I A N G L E
S I N   T A K E S   Z O N E D
S E T F I R E S   H A R A S S
      E N D   P O R E
F O R E V E R A N D A D A Y
L A I R   A L O N E   S I N E
I D L E   R A T E S   O V E N
Z E S T   K N E L T   N E W S
```

245

```
C L A R A   Z I T I   C O P S
O A T E S   O N A N   A R E A
C H E C K I N G O N E S B A G
O R E O   V I E   V I S T A
    I R A N   O V E N
R U L I N G T H E R O O S T
F E T E D   H I N T   S E E
A C E D   F L O O D   S C A N
T A R   A L A N   A P A R T
S P O T T I N G E R R O R S
    H A T E   N O T I
E D G A R   I D A   L A K E
D R A W I N G C U R T A I N S
G A Z E   B E E R   I G L O O
E G A D   C O D E   P E S T S
```

246

```
O L A F   P A R E D   M A M A
H I L O   E M O T E   A T I T
O R E O   K U N T A   R E N O
A C T R E S S U L L M A N N
    N O S E   O S S I E
I D I O M   B R A N   E E R
T I C T A C T O E W I N
S M E E   A R O S E   A I D A
S P R I N T S R I V A L
L O S   A S P S   E V E N T
A L I S T   I R A E
W E S T E R N S T A R T O M
M A T E   A C T O N   I G O R
A T E E   S A U L T   E R L E
N E R D   H A N D S   S E L F
```

247

```
C A R I B   G U S H   W I S K
A L O N E   R T E I   A N T I
R E A D S   E A R N   S T A N
B U R Y T H E H A T C H E T
O T S   M A C   H E R
  J A M E S M B A R R I E
S C I O N   T A B S   U S E
W A N T   J O A N S   O P E L
A L S   T O U R   A N T E S
B L U E B E R R Y P I E
  L E A   E A R   S G T
B A R R Y G O L D W A T E R
Z I T I   E A R L   A R E N A
O N E L   A L E E   Y E A R N
E D D Y   H E L D   S A L E S
```

248

```
M A A M   C L O D   C A B O T
A R M Y   Y O G I   O P E R A
D E E R   C A L F   D E T E R
D A N I E L D E F O E   H O E
      A D O   E R I E
F E E D I N G F R E N Z Y
I N N   T E A R   S E R A P H
L T D S   B A R   A L O E
M O O N S A   M A C S   T O E
F U M B L E T H E B A L L
      G A E L   A L L
A R A   C L A S S I F I E D S
M I N S K   M E I R   G W E N
A G A P E   A N T E   H E M I
S A T Y R   S T U D   T R I P
```

249

```
SHAM RAGA   SORE
CANE ETON   TOVES
RIGS MORE   OLEOS
OKLAHOMEMAKER
DUE  ARI OLYMPUS
   WISCONSONANT
AWHILE NEO   CSA
SHAGS  PLS LAKER
CIR  ELO BURSTS
ARKANSAWBUCK
PRECEPT ISR  SON
 NEWYORCHESTRA
AREST NIKE  TEAM
CYRUS ICEL  ANTE
HASP  CARS  TOES
```

250

```
MAYO  WOVE  GLACE
IRON  ONEA  RILED
NOUS  OATS  ABIDE
DONALD  SEWN  VAN
   GLEEM  SHAPERS
ANTENNAS   IDA
LOU  SIMP  TARGET
LURK  NERVE  TRAY
INKIND  AERO  ESP
 DOI  TRUNGATE
BIRDMAN  ASCOT
ENE  INEZ  SENDER
ALIGN  WADI  SADA
RENEE  ELIA  UNIT
STATE  LEAN  LETS
```

251

```
CABS  MEAN  BIDUF
PROP  ALMA  OVINE
AMWHATIAM   LYDIA
 SLEPT  MEAL  ITS
   RAH  ADRIFT
ADHERENT   AXEMAN
NRA  TWEEDY  LYLE
GAVE  IRA   TWAS
EKED  FLIMSY  ART
LEANTO   ANTONYMS
 DARRYL  RUE
AIR  ADOG  ATBAY
TREAD  KIDYOUNOT
IMAGE  ERIE  LIKE
TAMER  SLED  ANOX
```

252

```
MOB  BASS  ATTILA
ADORABLE  MIRROR
LINOLEUM  ONIONS
INDUSTRIOUSONE
   GAS   ARM
PUCE  JFK  IOTAS
ASH   DOE  STARCH
SHININGWITHFAME
HELENA  EVE   DEE
ARDEN  FRY   NEST
   OWL  FDA
WORTHYOFLOVING
HAWAII  MAUNALOA
ALARMS  IDEALISM
STREET  TEST  EYE
```

253

```
STAB  CAIN  OFFER
PELE  AUTO  FERMI
ICON  DRED  FREUD
THEDREAMERS  ESS
 EON   STEAL
REFRACT  STRONG
ALL  DEALT  STAIR
FLIT  MOE   EDNA
FINAL  OPERA  EES
ISTRIA  DEBURRS
 SAMBA   WET
DOT  BARTHOLOMEW
ADOBE  MOOR  PARE
BONER  OPED  ISIS
AREAS  REDS  ACCT
```

254

```
EMMA  JOKE  FCLEF
BEAT  OPEN  OLIVE
BAYOFPIGS   REMIT
STIMULUS   GARBLE
 JIM   BASK
BACKIN  HOBO  JAG
IDLE   SAXON  ADO
ROANOKEVIRGINIA
CBS   COVEN  DEEP
HEP  EDEN  STATUE
 CAAN  CEO
REDINK   FANDANGO
EXURB  PINTOBEAN
VINCE  AJAR  CARY
STEAD  WILY  STYX
```

255

```
JABS   GASP   IMSO
ATOP  QUITE  TATA
COLA  UNDID  CZAR
ONEWHOSEFATHER
BERNE   FLU   LLD
ISO  RING  STATIC
 GOVERN   LOKI
 BORNEXECUTIVE
LOVE  TEAPOT
OREGON  DRAT  ARA
URN  KIT   ESSES
 OWNSTHECOMPANY
AWAY  WAGER  ABEL
HERS  INANE  RAGU
ADEE  TENT   STEM
```

256

```
MAGUS  ABIDE  HAM
ELENI  BERET  AGA
WARDCLEAVER  TAR
SNEAKED   PENCIL
 TEX  SCR  OHNO
LAGER  STRIATE
OVID  SLEEVE  TWA
LIV  CHOPPER  JAG
ADE  HOPPER  AONE
 SOIREES  RUBES
ESTS  EDS  BUS
SCHOOL   HOSTAGE
TOE  BILLYSHEARS
ERA  INEED  ERRIS
REX  TENSE  SEETO
```

257

```
SHAG   PCS  MOSSY
TORO  GOAL  ALICE
ARAB  ELLA  NINOS
NATIONALVELVET
   REN   RYE
DREAD  DOPE  ROAD
WILDE   PACT  RBI
ELIZABETHTAYLOR
LED  LEVI  NOONE
LYES  NECK  GONER
 TAN   EEL
LARRYFORTENSKY
GOGOL  ARNO  IONE
ALIVE  KEEN  PLEA
PANES  ELL   SEER
```

258

```
 SEAGRAMS  COHAN
AUSTRALIA  AHOME
PAPERBAGS  MORES
AVAS  INHERE  ANT
RENT  DAT  ALOT
TRA   MAR  SIDS
 SEA  AREACODE
HASTEMAKESWASTE
ONEILOVE  TER
ENNE  RES   MEL
 ABBA  RAF  COLA
RAT  ALLINA  AJAX
IRONS  AGGRAVATE
AGREE  OHIORIVER
LOSES  STEEPLES
```

259

```
ACCT  HOSS  ABASH
TARO  IOLE  RUBLE
PRIMEDFORACTION
ATBAY  BUB  TEES
RASTERS  MUSE
 ORION  TARIFF
GIS  OLES  AUDIE
INTENTORPURPOSE
PROXY  NDAK  LTD
PEWTER  STEER
 ETON  ESTATES
SPAN  MOI  AGENT
HANDAPINKSLIPTO
OTTER  SKEE  NERO
WEEDS  EYRE  GEED
```

260

```
MILNE  BAJA   PIA
AFOOL  ABUG  GUNN
LITTLELULU  OPEN
 WEEB   ARTURO
FAZE  KOBE  EMPTY
ADULT  ARRIVAL
VOLLEY  AIREDALE
ORU  RADICAL  TOG
REWORKED  SETTEE
 ANISEED  DRESS
PERSE  DRAG  ERST
INRARE   SOON
NAIL  BISHOPTUTU
OTOE  BRIE  TOPES
TER  SEND  SNIDE
```

261

```
PAT   ALIF   MIDAS
ALE   SOSO   ONICE
STA   SUMO   RENEW
HEMOUSETRAP
AR  CRY   BESTMAN
   GEE  EATS   ASE
ELMA  ANTI   ANTS
UEENOFTHENIGHT
LAN   UTES   ALOES
ES   STER  PCS
REAMER   OOH   ADD
   VERMONTTODAY
AROL   ALES   WORN
VAIL   TERI   ERIE
ANDS   HOSE   DENS
```

262

```
EDAM   SHAM   SWAN
REBA  OASES  EASE
ICED  PROMO  TREE
COLDCOMFORT  MAR
      EARL  RESEW
LISP  ERY   ALIST
CONTESSA   FRISCO
OOH   ASIDE   HAN
PROUST   SERENELY
SATAN  FAT   DOSE
WRIER   EMIT
BEA  PLAYSITCOOL
ALTO  SPATS  HILO
SLED  APRES  ELAN
HERE   EDDY   SYNE
```

263

```
WEPT   MASS   HOSE
AMER  UNTIL  AMOS
FIRE  STAGE  SNAP
  RUNATIGHTSHIP
      DUE   TOW
FSU  GRIP  NAVAJO
ANNE  UTAH  TETON
KICKUPONESHEELS
IDLES  NELL  RATE
REESES  SPUN  MST
      RHO   GEM
  PASSOVERFEAST
HULA  PASSE  NEAT
OMAN  SLAVS  GAME
WANE   SUPT   OMEN
```

264

```
AISH   RPM   ERICA
PNEA   III   VIDOR
EISSOOLDHEGETS
STATE  AWOL   ATO
MARQUEE    OLAN
UNE    USEDUP
NE  USA  KOREANS
DWYNN    WINDED
OTATOR   ANS   AMA
   LOWEST   AMOK
ANE   DANELAW
BE   FORA   IRATE
LAYINGCHECKERS
ETER   UKE   DENSE
ROSE   ESP   ESSEX
```

265

```
CREPE  ALARM   ICY
HIKER  LENYA   NRA
EDGARWINTER   NIP
   COOKIE   BEEP
KATHLEEN   CHERRY
AWAY      JOINS
YAK  SHUTOUT  PTA
ORE  TONEARM  ROD
SET  ALDENTE  IRE
   HELLO     SNAP
SNEAKY   CATFIGHT
WAFT   SAMIAM
AVA  DONNASUMMER
MEL   ADIOS  LEAVE
ILL   MOPES  TREAD
```

266

```
HATCH   BELT   RTE
ATRIA  JULIA   HEX
RHETTBUTLER   ORE
LEN  SALTED  FDIC
ENDS   RYE  TAEGU
MAYOR    LEERSAT
   HEM  PACT  IRE
  RHODESSCHOLAR
THO   SITU   ONO
RAPPERS    SAJAK
OPERA   SPA   NITE
OSLO  CHEAPO  MEN
POE  RHEAPERLMAN
EDS  CARLA  BOISE
DYS   ARES   STEEL
```

267

```
LTAR   ASYET   JAB
URSE   SHOGI   USA
NIGHTCOURT   MID
GALAHAD   ELAPSE
  LABEL   RTES
ASS   SERA   HASP
RISTE  EVAN   YUL
EG   SUECITY   EGO
SH   PSAT   LEEWAY
OST    SOFA   SIRS
   ATIT   ENACT
EQUOD   BATMANS
XE  SECTSAPPEAL
EI   CAPUT  LESTI
SI   ALOSS   ESSEX
```

268

```
OHARE  WAIT  MRED
NAVEL  ANCE  AERI
THESKYSTHELIMIT
OAST   ATE  UTICA
   OGRE   BELA
PAIRED  AIRLINES
ADDER  STEM   OSE
GOLDENPARACHUTE
ERE   EELS  LANED
REDSTONE  DORSEY
   AINT  FUDD
ATALL   FEE  SOIE
FASTENSEATBELTS
RITE  UKES  ALLES
OLID  TILT  ALAMO
```

269

```
PIE  ALS  MISSEEM
ALGERIA  INTEGRA
CORNEAL  LEAVING
AVEC  RAJ   RESEE
SETHS    TUREEN
   AIM  NAY  DAMP
BRONCO  EVE  ALOE
AINT  REBEL  YODA
RACE   OAR  EASTER
SLED   SRI   TRI
   AGENDA  ANSEL
TEMPE   ELM  MADE
OVERSAW  LASAGNA
MILITIA  ONEYEAR
SELLERS  TEX  SSS
```

270

```
JOAN   AORTA  HAZE
ABLE   SHOAL  OBEY
COLDASACUCUMBER
KEY   KIRK  ATEASE
   PISA   SPAR
ASCENT  UHOH   CUP
START  ALAN  DRNO
WARMOFFTHEPRESS
AGES   OARS  RIDES
HEW   ORCA  BEFORE
   HIKE   DEFT
REPOSE  SAGA   SHE
INFREEZINGBLOOD
IUS   PIZZA  BRAG
DIE   SPEAR  SEXY
```

271

```
MEESE  IRAN  SLAM
AMAIN  NOSE  TORI
CURSEOFTHEDEMON
ESPY  LOSE  ERASE
   PEA    WINNER
OATHOFOFFICE
CLAUS  PAINE  JET
HOPS  HIKED  BALE
SEE  GONER  PARKA
   ORNERYCUSSES
DRABEK    APT
EARLE  IOUS  IMAM
SWEAROFFFORLIFE
TENT  OSLO  ALTAR
ERTE  MOAS  DEERE
```

272

```
ALDA  PLOW  ASSES
LIEN  EERO  PEARL
EASTERNER  PAINE
CRISPCOOKIE  LID
   YEA   STATUES
AGT   ELIS   ASAP
TRANSECTS  ERWIN
RICO  SOILS  SIZE
ANKLE  NEUTRINOS
LALA   SERA   DDS
OPENERS    ANS
MAH  VCRSOFTWARE
AGAPE  TIMESAVER
HERON  AVER  TIER
ADDIS  SANS  HALS
```

273

```
ALAI  VITAL  HEWS
IANS  INONE  UPAT
MINNESOTAGEMINI
 DETAILS  RACER
   SOD  EARN
BIGTEN  TARA  ASH
ANEW  SETAT  TEA
THROWSTHETAURUS
HOM  ALIEN  MIST
ETS  PALE  ELPASO
   HITE  ALA
SCOUT  TRESTLE
CAPRICORNCHEESE
AFAR  AWAIT  NAPS
RELY  REXES  SKYS
```

274

```
ARBOR  ETTA  PFCS
BEAME  LOWS  SOAP
EDNAS  SNIP  IRMA
EIGHTYEIGHT  TED
   AAA  ARGYLE
ADS  TWI  ALOON
CRETE  SIXTYFIVE
CAVE  NOL  ANAL
TWENTYONE  DRESS
NOHOW  SMU  REA
GETRID  ALL
ELY  SEVENELEVEN
TOSS  LILY  EVADE
OPIE  EVAN  SENDS
NEXT  RELY  TREYS
```

275

```
LIVID  BEAM  WORE
ALENE  ALKA  ADEE
BEEHIVEMATERIAL
TRACERS  ELDERS
   LET  COPE
SOLAR  PAR  ANGER
ANON  RAPIDS  AMA
VERTEBRATEORGAN
ETA  NIACIN  OMIT
SONIC  DEC  GAELS
   DARE  ARD
RETIME  CARAMEL
UNSOPHISTICATED
STAT  OLEO  IPANA
HORS  ELAN  ESTAB
```

276

```
COGS  SSTS  DAWN
LOIN  QUIT  BOTHA
EZRAOUNCE  ORBIT
FELINE  RADIATE
  LIAR  GESTE
CAD  CLODDISH
ROUSE  TOIL  OILS
ANKA  FALSE  UTAH
BEER  ATEM  BRAVO
ANTEDATE  SAP
ATHOS  LALA
CLIFTON  SIMPLE
ABLER  CNOTEPRIX
MELEE  AIDE  LAKE
PEST  AXED  EYES
```

277

```
DAVIS  CAPP  BOB
ERICA  AGREE  AVE
BATHTUBRING  YEA
TBA  SLIM  ACORN
SYL  CUE  RADON
  BEADSOFSWEAT
SCHOOL  OST  TIE
LOINS  UNE  SUEDE
ALL  ANI  JORDAN
BALLANDCHAIN
BERNE  APT  AMP
ADIEU  RAMA  MIO
LIL  BOWLINGPINS
PAL  AWAIT  NESTS
SLY  NYSE  PASSE
```

278

```
MARS  CRAB  SCARP
ISAT  HEMO  REBUS
LACAGEAUXFOLLES
SPELL  CREE  LEST
  LOOT  RAGU
SODS  BORSTALBOY
CRO  KIRI  SPARSE
RANIN  SDS  ERICA
ALANON  OARS  CAT
MBUTTERFLY  MERS
ASHE  AERO
USSR  RUED  EDINA
THESOUNDOFMUSIC
EERIE  ENID  LACE
SPEAR  SALA  EYES
```

279

```
CLAW  ALLA  LOFT
ROME  PIES  AARON
AMANNEEDS  TVSET
DENTE  TABLE
LID  AGOODYARNTO
ENA  LUV  ERNEST
  RAPS  GETAT
IRA  PULLTHE  SRO
SELMA  SOIE
ANSARA  CLI  SPA
WOOLOVERHIS  LAD
CLARA  IRATE
DEFOE  WIFESEYES
OPALS  ISLE  BENT
WARM  NEON  ARTE
```

280

```
WILCO  ASAP  SGTS
ADIEU  PAPA  POOR
COLDTURKEY  IONA
ALS  EXPENSES
ANDRESS  HOSE
EAU  TRENTON  PBA
RICES  TOON  BIOL
ALKA  STONE  EMIL
TEAR  HENS  MAPLE
ERN  CORSICA  LEN
IGOR  LOGGERS
ASSENTOR  ONE
TOSS  CHICKENOUT
ROUT  UNTO  TORSO
ATEE  TOED  SARAN
```

281

```
JANE  SOMA  VIGOR
OREL  URAL  IMAGE
EGAD  BEAM  LAIRD
LORENZOSOIL  LES
  SEE  NCAA
BUTTERANDEGGS
APO  ROSA  DERAIL
RITA  SIR  ALSO
ANEMIA  FIEF  SIS
MINNESOTAFATS
SHAM  AIR
SSS  ELBOWGREASE
COLOR  ELEE  NULL
ALIBI  REAR  CRAM
REMIT  SORE  HAMS
```

282

```
CARP  BART  CODES
AMOR  AFAR  OPRAH
POGO  BRIO  WEARY
EVERYBODYWANTS
DERAILS  ARI
TEE  QUIDNUNC
CANAL  FURS  GRUB
RIO  DURANTE  IKE
ADAM  BESS  BASER
BEHEMOTH  LON
RYA  SINGLES
TOGETINTODEACT
HONEY  RUIN  LULU
OUTRE  IDLE  IRAN
GROSS  SELL  CATT
```

283

```
APE  SNIP  LEVITY
FIN  OONA  ATEASE
ANNERICE  GARDEN
COUNTDRACULA
ENID  NON  AHA
  SAO  MAKEPAR
ELECTRON  ALARM
LOVEATFIRSTBITE
ICING  BOTHERED
SKATERS  BAY
EEN  ISA  NUNC
TRANSYLVANIA
MARIEL  REVAMPED
EXTENT  ETON  ICE
SEESTO  DIVE  NET
```

284

```
SLAP  NAVAL  MASH
LOCO  OXIDE  AQUA
EWES  REAMS  JUNG
AFTERALLISSAID
ZAIRE  TEE  LIE
ETC  BAIT  RACIAL
KIDDED  ONLY
ANDDONEMORE
FACE  LOCALE
UNREAL  RODS  ALT
NCO  DOE  EAMES
ISSAIDTHANDONE
FETE  TIRED  ARAT
ONIT  ENOLA  GAPS
ETCH  RANDY  ELEE
```

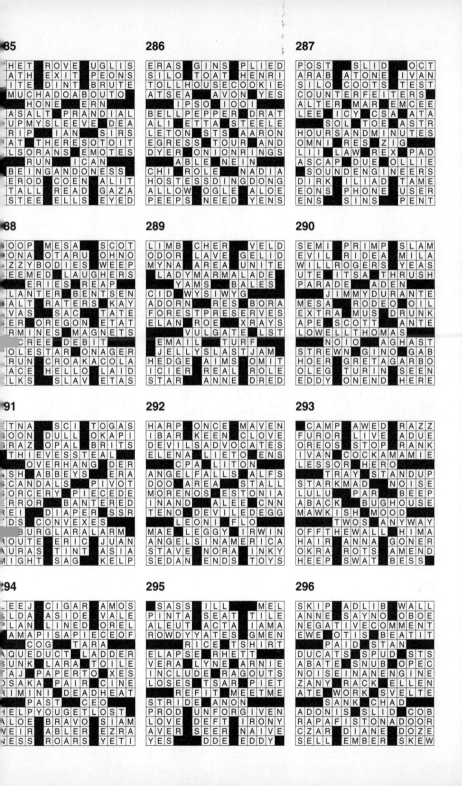

285

```
HET  ROVE  UGLIS
ATH  EXIT  PEONS
ITE  DINT  BRUTE
MUCHADOABOUTO
   HONE  ERN
ASALT  PRANDIAL
UPMYSLEEVE  DEA
RIP  IAN  SIRS
AT  THERESOTOIT
LSORANS  EMOTES
   RUN  ICAN
BEINGANDONESS
EROD  COEN  ALIT
TALL  READ  GAZA
STEE  ELLS  EYED
```

286

```
ERAS  GINS  PLIED
SILO  TOAT  HENRI
TOLLHOUSECOOKIE
ATSEA  AVON  YES
    IPSO  IOOI
BELLPEPPER  DRAT
ALI  ETTA  STEELE
LETON  STS  AARON
EGRESS  TOUR  AND
DYER  ONIONRINGS
    ABLE  NEIN
CHI  ROLE  NADIA
HOSTESSDINGDONG
ALLOW  OGLE  ALOE
PEEPS  NEED  YENS
```

287

```
POST  SLID    OCT
ARAB  ATONE  IVAN
SILO  COOTS  TEST
COUNTERFEITERS
ALTER  MAR  EMCEE
LEE  ICY  CSA  ATA
   SOL  TOE  ASTR
HOURSANDMINUTES
OMNI  RES  ZIG
LII  LAW  REX  PAD
ASCAP  DUE  OLLIE
SOUNDENGINEERS
DIRK  ILIAD  TAME
EONS  PHONE  USER
ENS  SINS  PENT
```

288

```
OOP  MESA  SCOT
ONA  OTARU  OHNO
ZZYBODIES  WEEP
EEMED  LAUGHERS
   ERIES  REAP
LANTER  BENTSEN
ALT  RATERS  KAY
VAS  SAC  TATE
ER  OREGON  ETAT
RMINES  MAGNETS
CREE  DEBIT
OLESTAR  ONAGER
RUN  CROAKACOLA
ACE  HELLO  LAID
LKS  SLAV  ETAS
```

289

```
LIMB  CHER  VELD
ODOR  LAVE  GELID
MYNA  AREA  UNITE
LADYMARMALADE
   YAMS  BALES
CID  WYSIWYG
ADORN  RES  BORA
FORESTPRESERVES
ELAN  ROE  XRAYS
VULGATE  LST
EMAIL  TURF
JELLYSLASTJAM
HEDGE  AIMS  OMIT
ICIER  REAL  ROLE
STAR  ANNE  DRED
```

290

```
SEMI  PRIMP  SLAM
EVIL  RIDEA  MILA
WILLROGERS  YEAS
UTE  ITSA  THRUSH
PARADE  ADEN
JIMMYDURANTE
MESA  RODEO  OIL
EXTRA  MUS  DRUNK
APE  SCOTT  ANTE
LOWELLTHOMAS
   NOIO  AGHAST
STREWN  GINO  GAB
HOER  GRETAGARBO
OLEG  TURIN  SEEN
EDDY  ONEND  HERE
```

291

```
TNA  SCI  TOGAS
OON  DULL  OKAPI
RAZ  OPAL  BRITS
THIEVESSTEAL
OVERHANG  DER
SH  ABBEYS  ERA
CANDALS  PIVOT
ORCERY  PIECEDE
RROR  BANTERED
EI  DIAPER  SSR
DS  CONVEXES
BURGLARALARM
ROUTE  ERIC  JUAN
AURAS  TINT  ASIA
MIGHT  SAG  KELP
```

292

```
HARP  ONCE  MAVEN
IBAR  KEEN  CLOVE
DEVILSADVOCATES
ELENA  LIETO  ENS
   CPA  LITON
ANGELFALLS  ALFS
DOO  AREA  STALL
MORENOS  ESTONIA
INAND  ALEE  CNN
TENO  DEVILEDEGG
   LEONI  FLO
MAE  LEGGY  IRWIN
ANGELSINAMERICA
STAVE  NORA  INKY
SEDAN  ENDS  TOYS
```

293

```
CAMP  AWED  RAZZ
FUROR  LIVE  ADUE
OREOS  STOP  RANK
IVAN  COCKAMAMIE
LESSOR  HERO
TRAY  STANDUP
STARKMAD  NOISE
LULU  PAR  BEEP
ABACK  BUGHOUSE
MAWKISH  MOOD
TWOS  ANYWAY
OFFTHEWALL  HIMA
HAIR  ANNA  GONER
OKRA  ROTS  AMEND
HEEP  SWAT  BESS
```

294

```
EEJ  CIGAR  AMOS
LDA  ASIDE  VALE
PLAN  LINED  OREL
AMAPISAPIECEOF
   COG  TARA
AQUEDUCT  LADDER
SUNK  LARA  TOILE
TAJ  PAPERTO  XES
OSAKA  PAIR  CINE
RIMINI  DEADHEAT
PAST  CEO
HELPYOUGETLOST
ALOE  BRAVO  SIAM
VEIR  ABLER  EZRA
NESS  ROARS  YETI
```

295

```
SASS  ILL  MEL
PINTA  SEAT  TILE
ALEUT  ACTA  IAMA
ROWDYYATES  GMEN
   RICE  TSHIRT
ELAPSE  RHETT
VERA  LYNE  ARNIE
INCLUDE  RAGOUTS
LOSES  TSAR  PIET
REFIT  MEETME
STRIDE  ANON
PROD  UNFORGIVEN
LOVE  DEFT  IRONY
AVER  SEER  NAIVE
YES  DDE  EDDY
```

296

```
SKIP  ADLIB  WALL
ANNE  SAYNO  OBOE
NEGATIVECOMMENT
EWE  OTIS  BEATIT
   PAID  STAN
DUCATS  SPUD  STS
ABATE  SNUB  OPEC
NOISEINANENGINE
ZANY  RACK  ELLEN
ATE  WORK  SVELTE
SANK  CHAD
ADONIS  SLID  COB
RAPAFISTONADOOR
CZAR  DIANE  DOZE
SELL  EMBER  SKEW
```

297

```
ANGLER PINT YAP
MARINE OWAR ITA
AMANDA IAMABEAR
   PEELS SEVILLE
MAE ALIF ELDER
OFVERYLITTLE
TRIES GRIS UHF
HONK BRAIN ONEA
SSE SEER SHOAL
ANDLONGWORDS
LIBRA SORE DYE
INACRES MEADE
BOTHERME ATARIS
ENE RIIS SENECA
LED SETS ERODED
```

298

```
SHED DAFT CACHE
LYLE IDLE AFROS
APSE SAAR LOADS
WEEPINGWILLOW
   WEE OUTLET
STRAY BRAS SSW
TEAL TEAM SPCA
TRACKSOFMYTEARS
RAKE UFOS WACO
ATE SMUG CAREW
MATTEA LAN
THECRYINGGAME
RULED EAST ALAN
ISERE ELLE LARD
POSED DEER ASKS
```

299

```
DSCS SAWTO JEEP
OTOE AGAIN URGE
REBA IRATE NEON
SPATULACLARK
APLOMB ELY BAA
LET BOOT SECOND
   TRALEE UNTO
GRATERGARBO
HALO OSIRIS
ELUDES ESTA APE
WEE RCA ITALIA
FARRAHFAUCET
ABLE ADLAI DOMC
TROT MEDIC IVAN
EASE SNORE TENS
```

300

```
ALAI BORO APPT
TENDERNAME MAHA
ENDEARMENT ERRS
   ERSE IAN EAS
CADS MALIGNS
ONE DOLE PETE
LOC IMELDA AHS
ARLENES ENTREES
AAR NEGATE STP
LRON AREA III
EASIEST ISNT
EDT ESQ DAHS
RIIS PUNISHMENT
NCOS NINETHUMPS
ETNA DEMI DORE
```

301

```
RES HAFT MARIA
ANC VIES ELENI
SCHWARZENEGGER
COERCE ESAI
ARMY DOBIE MAST
LEE NAVAL DELTA
TILER AUNTIE
THETERMINATOR
CRONES IRONS
BARNS KEENE AHA
SYNE WORDY ALAR
SERF MUSLIN
LASTACTIONHERO
CREEP EQUI GEL
DRESS ASST EDD
```

302

```
SUMP ALOP SCRAM
ONEA GABE ARENA
BEETHOVENSFIFTH
ESTEE ESTEEM
ICE WORE ALERTS
TORPID ELY ORE
ANIMAL FAUX
DRAGNETSTHEME
DIOR SEAMAN
AVA ERA ENDOWS
MANTRA SANS VIA
ONIONS OVENS
THEWEDDINGMARCH
HERES EPEE IDEA
EXERT SERE NOSY
```

303

```
AMI NANA XENIA
RANS AXIS RAISE
MYFATHERSCAREER
YOUTHS VERY LEO
RIO DATA USA
ISINRUINSBUT
AHA NSA HAFT
TITANIC FASHION
EVENT EIS SRO
THATSFINEHES
UPS RATE ALE
ELL ACME STEREO
ANARCHAEOLOGIST
RAZOR LMNO YESI
PEACE ESOP SOS
```

304

```
JEFF ATTAR POLO
URAL CHIME ONYX
LIRA TALIA SUEY
COMPUTERCHIPS
BOP HOT
ARCED MTS BROAD
BEL SMARTCOOKIE
ALEX AHEAD NAME
SAFECRACKER PAD
EXTRA LEE OBITS
OSO CAR
HEXAGONALNUTS
YOGI RAISE IRAQ
ALAN ESTER SIRE
ZING STEAK EGAD
```

305

```
SHES HUTS SHRED
CARE ENOL HAILE
ASIN ASIA ORDIE
THEDEVILTOUPEE
SHEL ELLS
ACT SNEERED CAP
IHOP SNY SENORA
ROMEO TEA RIVER
TWERPS RBI PENT
OSS PASSANT RAY
LOST STOP
TRESSREHEARSAL
HAITI AKIN OHNO
ASCOT FENS DOER
ISONE EDGE SEWN
```

306

```
EBBS TEAOR TEAM
GARP ROGUE ORNO
GREEDISENVYWITH
SEWNUP SCIENCES
DOOR EVAS
WIT SLAB ERECTS
ORE IDEAS NEIL
RANT ITS DATE
STOW VISIT SAD
TERESA YARD ENS
ELIA NOES
TANZANIA LAKERS
SLEEVESROLLEDUP
AFAR SLIDE WIDE
RATS TEDDY STEW
```

307

```
GOLD CITED ACES
OBOE ORATE FARE
TIPPECANOE FLIT
TARPONS PRIMES
STEIN REAR
SCULLERYMAID
AMOS TEEM ESSAY
REP SCHIZ INE
IDEAS TATA SASS
DICTATORSHIP
TBAR ATRAP
CAREER ACREAGE
OVEN SUBLIMINAL
RIND ATRIA NEST
ADES LEAPS SWED
```

308

```
SAONE PRIG APED
ALVIN AURA ZENO
STEPHENFRY ATOZ
HEN ALIF PALELY
ARSENIC CANER
RCA BARNACLE
SCALE PERES OUST
CODE GRATE TOTO
ADA IRONS TOKEN
MAMACASS AHA
CREPE EXITING
LOUISE SLIM LEE
EARS JAMESBROWN
ETRE AVON LEVEE
RHYS MAGI EBERT
```

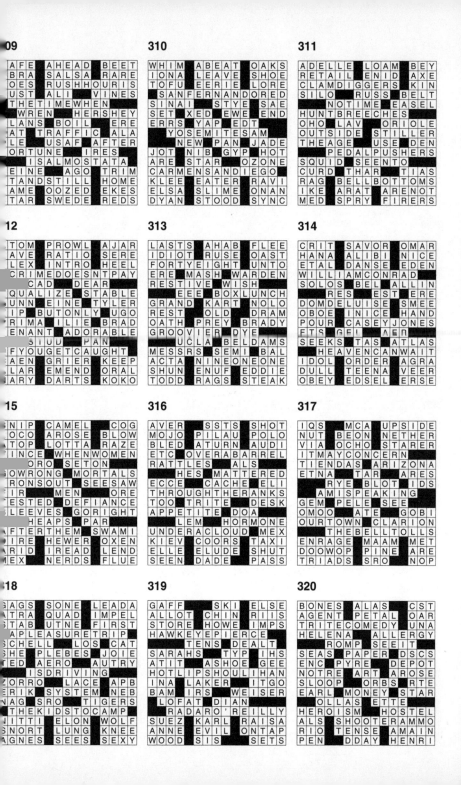

309

```
AFE AHEAD BEET
BRA SALSA RARE
OES RUSHHOURIS
UST ALI  VINES
THETIMEWHEN
 WREN  HERSHEY
LANS BOIL  ERE
AT TRAFFIC ALA
LE  USAF AFTER
ORTUNE  IRES
ISALMOSTATA
EINE AGO  TRIM
TANDSTILL HOME
AME OOZED EKES
TAR SWEDE REDS
```

310

```
WHIM ABEAT OAKS
IONA LEAVE SHOE
TOFU EERIE LORE
 SANFERNANDORED
SINAI STYE  SAE
SET XED EWE END
ERRS YAP  EDT
 YOSEMITESAM
  NEW PAN JADE
JOT NIB GYP HOT
ARE STAR  OZONE
CARMENSANDIEGO
KLEE EATER RAVI
ELSA SLIME ONAN
DYAN STOOD SYNC
```

311

```
ADELLE LOAM  BEY
RETAIL ENID  AXE
CLAMDIGGERS  KIN
SILO  RUSS  BELT
  NOTIME  EASEL
 HUNTBREECHES
OHO LAV  ORIOLE
OUTSIDE STILLER
THEAGE USE  DEN
 PEDALPUSHERS
SQUID  SEENTO
CURD THAR  TIAS
RAG BELLBOTTOMS
IKE ARAT ARENOT
MED SPRY FIRERS
```

312

```
TOM PROWL  AJAR
AVE RATIO  SERE
LEX INTRO  HEEL
CRIMEDOESNTPAY
  CAD  DEAR
QUALIZE STABLE
UNN EINE  TYLER
IP BUTONLY UGO
RIMA ILIE  BRAD
ENANT ADORABLE
  SIUD  PAN
FYOUGETCAUGHT
AEN GRIER  KEEP
LAR EMEND  ORAL
ARY DARTS  KOKO
```

313

```
LASTS AHAB FLEE
IDIOT RUSE OAST
FORTYEIGHT UNTO
ERE MASH WARDEN
RESTIVE  WISH
 EEE  BOXLUNCH
GRAND KART NOLO
REST  OLD  DRAM
OATH PREY BRADY
GROOVIER  DYE
 UCLA  BELDAMS
MESSRS SEMI BAL
ACTA NINEONEONE
SHUN ENUF EDDIE
TODD RAGS STEAK
```

314

```
CRIT SAVOR  OMAR
HANA ALIBI  NICE
ETAL DANSE  EDEN
WILLIAMCONRAD
SOLOS BEL  ALLIN
   RES  EST  ERE
DOMDELUISE SMEE
OBOE INICE  HAND
POUR CASEYJONES
ETS  GEI   AEN
SEEKS TAS  ATLAS
HEAVENCANWAIT
IDOL ORDER  AGRA
DULL TEENA  VEER
OBEY EDSEL  ERSE
```

315

```
NIP CAMEL   COG
OCO AROSE  BLOW
TOP LOTTA  RAZE
INCE  WHENWOMEN
ORO SETON
OWRONG MORTALS
RONSOUT SEESAW
IR  MEN    ORE
ESTED DEFIANCE
LEEVES GORIGHT
HEAPS  PAR
AFTERTHEM SWAMI
IRE HEWER  OXEN
RID IREAD  LEND
EX  NERDS  FLUE
```

316

```
AVER SSTS SHOT
MOJO PILAU POLO
BLED ATURN AUDI
ETC OVERABARREL
RATTLES  ALS
 HES  MATTERED
ECCE CACHE ELI
THROUGHTHERANKS
TOO TRITE  DESK
APPETITE DOA
 LEM  HORMONE
UNDERACLOUD MEX
KIEV COORS TAXI
ELLE ELUDE SHUT
SEEN DADE PASS
```

317

```
IQS MCA UPSIDE
NUT BEON NETHER
VIA OCHO STARER
ITMAYCONCERN
TIENDAS ARIZONA
ETNA TAR  ARES
 RYE BLOT IDS
AMISPEAKING
GEM PELE SEE
OMOO ATE  GOBI
OURTOWN CLARION
THEBELLTOLLS
ENRAGE MAAM MET
DOOWOP PINE ARE
TRIADS SRO  NOP
```

318

```
AGS SONE LEADA
TRA QUAD IMPEL
TAB UTNE FIRST
APLEASURETRIP
SCHELL LOS  CAT
HE PLEBES JOIE
ED AERO  AUTRY
 ISDRIVING
ZORRO LACE  APB
ERIK SYSTEM NEB
NAG SRO  TIGERS
THEKIDSTOCAMP
ITTI ELON  WOLF
SNORT LUNG KNEE
AGNES SEES SEXY
```

319

```
GAFF SKI  ELSE
ALLOT CHIN RIIS
STORE HOWE IMPS
HAWKEYEPIERCE
 TENS  DEALT
SARAHS TYP  IHS
ATIT ASHOE GEE
HOTLIPSHOULIHAN
INA LAKER  ITGO
BAM IRS  WEISER
LOFAT DIAN
RADARO'REILLY
SUEZ KARL RAISA
ANNE EVIL ONTAP
WOOD SIS  SETS
```

320

```
BONES ALAS  CST
AGENT PETAL OAR
TRITECOMEDY UNA
HELENA ALLERGY
ROMP  SEEIT
SEAS PAPER DSCS
ENC PYRE  DEPOT
NOTRE ART  AROSE
SLOOP ORBS  RTE
EARL MONEY STAR
OLLAS  ETTE
HEROISM HOSTEL
ALS SHOOTERAMMO
RIO TENSE AMAIN
PEN DDAY  HENRI
```

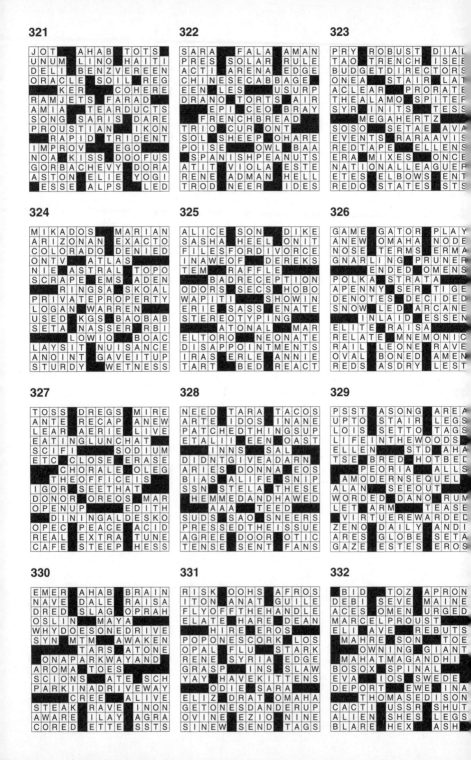

321

```
JOT   AHAB  TOTS
UNUM  LINO  HAITI
DELI  BENZVEREEN
ORACLE  SOIL  REG
   KER     COHERE
RAMJETS  FARAD
AMIA   TEARDUCTS
SONG  SARIS  DARE
PROUSTIAN    IKON
  RAPID  TRIDENT
IMPROV    EGO
NOA  KISS  DOOFUS
GORBACHEVY  DORA
ASTON  ELIE  YOGI
 ESSE  ALPS  LED
```

322

```
SARA   FALA  AMAN
PRES  SOLAR  RULE
ACTI  ARENA  EDGE
CHINESECABBAGE
EEN  LES    USURP
DRANO  TORTS  AIR
   EPI  CEO  BRAY
  FRENCHBREAD
TRIO  CUR  ONT
SOL  SHEEP  OHARE
POISE    OWL  BAA
 SPANISHPEANUTS
ATIT  VIOLA  ESTE
RENE  ADMAN  HELL
TROD  NEER  IDES
```

323

```
PRY  ROBUST  DIAL
TAO  TRENCH  ISEE
BUDGETDIRECTORS
ONEA   STAIR  LAT
ACLEAR   PRORATE
THEALAMO  SPITEF
SYR  INITS  TESS
   MEGAHERTZ
SOSO  SETAE  AVA
EVENTS  RARAAVIS
REDTAPE    ELLENS
ERA  MIXES   ONCE
NATIONALLEAGUER
ETES  ELBOWS  ENT
REDO  STATES  STS
```

324

```
MIKADOS   MARIAN
ARIZONAN  EXACTO
COLORADO  DENIED
ONTV  ATLAS
NIE  ASTRAL  TOPO
SCRAPE  EMS  ADEN
   RINGSA  SKOAL
PRIVATEPROPERTY
LOGAN  WARREN
USED  KGS  BAOBAB
SETA  NASSER  RBI
   LOWIQ    BOAC
LAYSIT  NUISANCE
ANOINT  GAVEITUP
STURDY    WETNESS
```

325

```
ALICE  SON   DIKE
SASHA  HEEL  ONIT
FILESFORDIVORCE
INAWEOF   DEREKS
TEM  RAFFLE
  BADRECEPTION
ODORS  SECS  HOBO
WAPITI    SHOWIN
ERIE  SASS  ENATE
STEREOTYPING
 ATONAL    MAR
ELTORO   NEONATE
DISAPPOINTMENTS
IRAS  ERLE  ANNIE
TART   BED  REACT
```

326

```
GAME  GATOR  PLAY
ANEW  OMAHA  NODE
NOSE  TERMS  ERMA
GNARLING  PRUNER
  ENDED  OMENS
POLKA  STRATA
APENNY  SER  TIGE
DENOTES  DECIDED
SNOW  LED  ARCANE
  INLAID  ESSEN
ELITE  RAISA
RELATE  MNEMONIC
RAIL  LEONE  RAVE
OVAL  BONED  AMEN
REDS  ASDRY  LEST
```

327

```
TOSS  DREGS  MIRE
ANTE  RECAP  ANEW
LEAR  AERIE  LIVE
EATINGLUNCHAT
SCIFI    SODIUM
ETC  CLOSE  ERASE
  CHORALE  OLEG
 THEOFFICEIS
IGOR  SEETHAT
DONOR  OREOS  MAR
OPENUP    EDITH
 DININGALDESKO
OPEC  PEACE  ACID
REAL  EXTRA  TUNE
CAFE  STEEP  HESS
```

328

```
NEED  TARA  TACOS
ARTE  IDOS  INANE
PATCHEDTHINGSUP
ETALII  EEN  OAST
  INNS  SAL
DIDNTGIVEADARN
ARIES  DONNA  EOS
BIAS  ALIFE  SNIP
SSN  STELA  THESE
HEMMEDANDHAWED
 AAA  TEED
SUDS  SAO  SNEERS
PRESSEDTHEISSUE
AGREE  DOOR  OTIC
TENSE  SENT  FANS
```

329

```
PSST  ASONG  AREA
UPTO  STAIR  LEGS
LOIS  SETTO  TAGS
LIFEINTHEWOODS
ELLEN   STD  AHA
TSE  BRED  HOTBED
  PEORIA  ALLS
 AMODERNSEQUEL
ALAN  SEEOUT
WORDED  DANO  RUM
LET  ARM  TEASE
VIRTUEREWARDED
ZENO  DAILY  ANDI
ARES  GLOBE  SETA
GAZE  ESTES  EROS
```

330

```
EMER  AHAB  BRAIN
NAVE  DALE  RAISA
DRED  SLAG  OPRAH
OSLIN  MAYA
WHYDOESONEDRIVE
SYN  MTM  AWAKEN
 TARS  ATONE
ONAPARKWAYAND
AROMA  TOES
SCIONS  ATE  SCH
PARKINADRIVEWAY
 CREE  ALIVE
STEAK  RAVE  INON
AWARE  ILAY  AGRA
CORED  ETTE  SSTS
```

331

```
RISK  OOHS  AFROS
ITON  ANAT  GUILE
FLYOFFTHEHANDLE
ELATE  HARE  DEAN
 HIRE  EROS
POPONESCORK  LOS
OPAL  FLU  STARK
RENE  SYRIA  EDGE
GRASP  INS  SLAW
YAY  HAVEKITTENS
 ODIE  SARA
ELIZ  DRAT  OMAHA
GETONESDANDERUP
OVINE  EZIO  NINE
SINEW  SEND  TAGS
```

332

```
BID  TOZ  APRON
DEBI  SEVE  MAINE
ACES  OMEN  URGED
MARCELPROUST
ELI  AVE  REBUTS
MAHRE  SON  TOE
OWNING  GIANT
MAHATMAGANDHI
BOSOX  SPINAL
EVA  IOS  SWEDE
DEPORT  EWE  INA
 THOMASEDISON
CACTI  USSR  SHUT
ALIEN  SHES  LEGS
BLARE  HEX  ASH
```

333

```
MAP CAMP ASTER
OLO ARIA TAHOE
RIS LENS OMENS
ACTSMACHINES
LESH EAVE AFL
ES ARP ESCUDO
AMOEBAS ARID
OSTUMERSERVICE
NTO PROTEUS
EANCE ANN CPA
AR OREO USHER
GROSSPROPHETS
HAUL TROD EERO
UZIE EASE ASON
MEND SHES REL
```

334

```
APBS ABASE ACRE
SLOT DARED SHED
HANA MIENS PINA
EYEDMONSTER POM
NATION LOBS
UNITE SOUTER
CALM SELF STORE
ALE CHEMIST CIA
FATHA MOST SKED
ESTERS SHINE
EXEC FINEST
HER ROSEOFTEXAS
OLDE PEALE CUTA
ELAN ETTAS ADAR
RAYS SHAFT SENS
```

335

```
SCAB CLARE CREE
ARNE HELIX OILY
NEGATIVIST NOSE
DELTA OVERACTER
SLEEVE ERASE
NERO SPRAWL
ISU RINGO TREE
SHRINKINGVIOLET
MUSS TURIN OKS
SLALOM ENDO
ABASE SINGES
TENNISPRO REEVE
IZOD COMPLAINER
EIRE ORATE LONG
ROAR TESSA LATE
```

336

```
IELD ELCID ILKA
ZIO LEONE TOIL
RLO IMPECCABLE
AIR JOY OOLONG
JEAN GRAY
HEATH FLAX PAM
KARMA SLOT HERA
NABLETOBEEATEN
OSS GORE DRANO
IE MYRA CELLAR
WIPE PANE
RRANT SEN QUIT
YACHICKEN UTAH
ANK ALIVE INGE
ANDY NUDES NEON
```

337

```
AHAS PATER MASH
TOWN LORRE ARLO
TWOFAKIND RIIS
ALLOUT WAKEME
PEER TITTLES
ERA LAO ENOW
ZEROSUM DEPARTS
REED IAMA
ALADDIN PRINTER
CINE REM END
STROPHE SCAB
THEUSA EGOISM
EARP BODYDOUBLE
ANAL IRATE TEUT
MENE TENDS STES
```

338

```
JADE ALSOP CHEW
ORAL LOIRE OATH
SKIFALLCRESSLOO
ESS POLK KIMONO
OPUS NATO
PIGLET CUBE CBS
AROMA KATO ALEC
COLORPISTOLGATE
ENDS INKY AARON
RYE ANTS MUTANT
HIKE GERE
CLOUDS KALE ABE
LOGMELONPOLOBED
ARLO IVIED FLAG
PEER PATSY FETE
```

339

```
RAB HEAL ASCAP
MOLE ILSA BOOLA
VELDTHATS ENNIS
REALITY OGEE
MPORT SALMONS
MILO SIS LOAM
ANAME DALLY IMP
OIST ONO ARNIE
SSN HILTS LAINE
READ ASH RUER
CHANNEL ALAMOS
APD MALARIA
SPIC TABLEVINE
STEVE HILO ICON
PAREE STEW SYNE
```

340

```
MAPS GAMMA SCAM
ABEL ORION PUMA
REAR SILTY ORES
ETC ATALOWPOINT
HALAS HIKED
REFLAG GWENS
AGUES QUARK NOD
GAZE OUTRE SOMA
ADZ AVAST DOTED
ELEGY CASINO
MOTOR HERON
CASHUPFRONT PAD
LILI ALERT ALPO
ALEC SENSE BAEZ
WARS SEDER EYRE
```

341

```
SAGAS JERICHO
TRENT TAXATION
OPENER HIAWATHA
PEN TOTELL LYON
SLAP NHL TOY
SDI REMISS WAS
ANGOLAN RAITT
LAVERNE&SHIRLEY
OXIDE FLEECED
YES ASTORS AFC
ETC UTA SLAM
HEAL RAISIN ONE
ORDINALS DARWIN
PIZZAPIE BUENO
ICEAGES STREW
```

342

```
HARE BLED MOTEL
EDEN YALE EVADE
LOLA LISA DEBIT
RACTICALNURSE
SEXTON TESS
REST PATTON
MOTTA ORCA URGE
NEWHOFALLSFORA
MUNI NAME AFTER
SPASMS POND
TOES EASYAS
WEALTHYPATIENT
MAYBE ROOT LAIR
GIRLS ERLE ARTE
SLEET DEER SNAP
```

343

```
OOMPAH JOB SAG
STOOGE HALE NIL
LIPTON AVES ALI
OSSA NEWAGE FED
TWYLA ETUDE
HANOI FIASCO
ELECTS INCHOATE
ESTH PLATO TURN
POSITION TESTED
PINUPS RIOTS
QUEST USAGE
URN ADONIS PEER
AGA NARC POODLE
SEC INCH ESPIED
IST CSA NESTED
```

344

```
DEARIE DEPARTS
INBORN ENTREAT
MADAMESOUSATZKA
AMUSE HOCUS OER
YORE ARMEE INIT
ONE SLIPS KNELL
RDS PENH SADDLE
LIRE SPRY
ABSENT SHAM ORB
DIODE OHARA NEA
EZRA TRUNK SOLD
LAG BHANG APRIL
MRHULOTSHOLIDAY
ARUSTLE AWAKEN
NEMESES INSERT
```

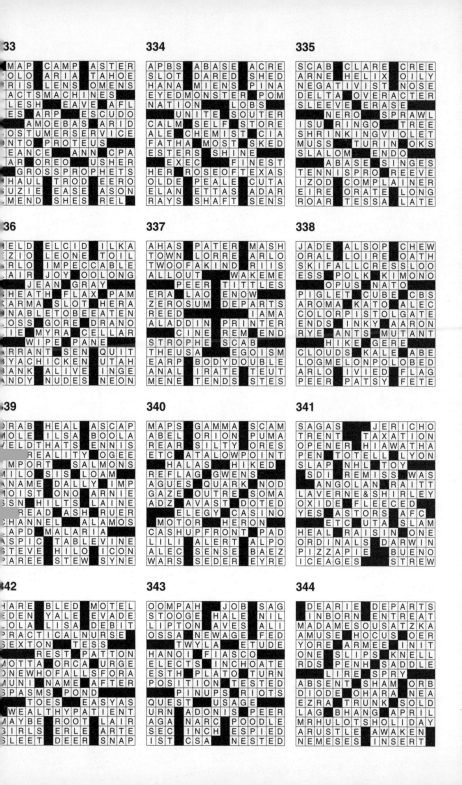

345

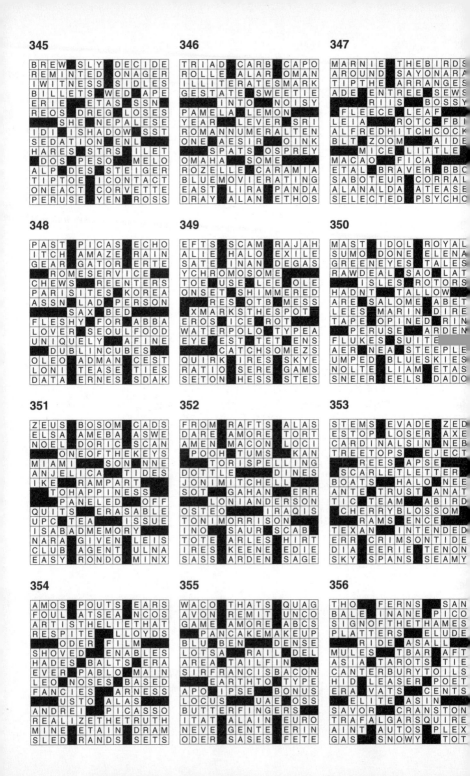

346

347

348

349

350

351

352

353

354

355

356

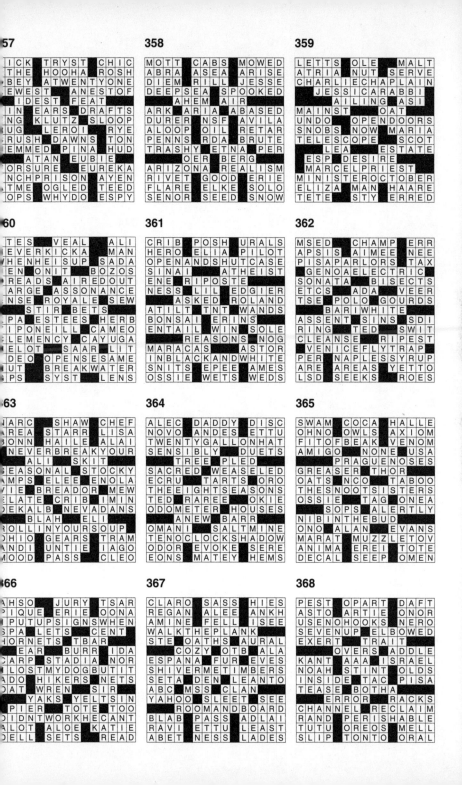

57

```
ICK TRYST CHIC
THE HOOHA ROSH
BEY ATWENTYONE
EWEST ANESTOF
IDEST FEAT
IN EARS DRAFTS
NG KLUTZ SLOOP
UG LEROI RYE
RUSH DAWNS TON
EMMED PINA HUD
ATAN EUBIE
ORSURE EUREKA
NCHPRISON AYEN
TME OGLED TEED
OPS WHYDO ESPY
```

358

```
MOTT CABS MOWED
ABRA ASEA ARISE
DIEM RILL JESSE
DEEPSEA SPOOKED
AHEM AIR
ARK ARIA ABASED
DURER NSF AVILA
ALOOP OIL RETAR
PENNS RDA BRUTE
TRASHY ETNA PER
OER BERG
ARIZONA REALISM
RIVET GOOD ERIE
FLARE ELKE SOLO
SENOR SEED SNOW
```

359

```
LETTS OLE MALT
ATRIA NUT SERVE
CHARLIECHAPLAIN
JESSICARABBI
AILING ASI
MAINST OAT
UNDO OPENDOORS
SNOBS NOW MARIA
TELESCOPE SCOT
LEA ESTATE
ESP DESIRE
MARCELPRIEST
MINISTEROCTOBER
ELIZA MAN HAARE
TETE STY ERRED
```

60

```
TES VEAL ALI
EVERKICKA MAN
WHENHEISUP SADA
EN ONIT BOZOS
READS AIREDOUT
ARGE ASSONANCE
NSE ROYALE SEW
STIR BETS
PA ESTEES HERB
IPONEILL CAMEO
LEMENCY CAYUGA
ELOT SAAR LIT
DEO OPENSESAME
UT BREAKWATER
PS SYST LENS
```

361

```
CRIB POSH URALS
HERO ELIA PILOT
OPENANDSHUTCASE
SINAI ATHEIST
ENE RIPOSTE
NESS LIL EDGIER
ASKED ROLAND
ATILT TNT WANDS
BONSAI ERINS
ENTAIL WIN SOLE
REASONS NOG
MARACAS ASTOR
INBLACKANDWHITE
SNITS EPEE AMES
OSSIE WETS WEDS
```

362

```
MSED CHAMP ERR
APSIS AIMEE NEE
PISAPARLORS TAX
GENOAELECTRIC
SONATA BISECTS
ETCS ADA VEER
TSE POLO GOURDS
BARIWHITE
ASSENT SINS SDI
RING TED SWIT
CLEANSE RIPEST
VENICEFLYTRAP
PER NAPLESSYRUP
ARE AREAS YETTO
LSD SEEKS ROES
```

63

```
ARC SHAW CHEF
AREA STARR LISA
BONN HAILE ALAI
NEVERBREAKYOUR
ALI SKIT
SEASONAL STOCKY
AMPS ELEE ENOLA
VIE BREADOR MEW
LATE CRIB IMIN
DEKALB NEVADANS
BLAH ELI
ROLLINYOURSOUP
OHIO GEARS TRAM
ANDI UNTIE IAGO
MOOD PASS CLEO
```

364

```
ALEC DADDY DISC
NOVO ANDES ETTU
TWENTYGALLONHAT
SENSIBLY DUETS
TREE PLED
SACRED WEASELED
ECRU TARTS ORO
THEEIGHTSEASONS
TED RAREE OKIE
ODOMETER HOUSES
ANEW BARR
OMANI SALTMINE
TENOCLOCKSHADOW
ODOR EVOKE SERE
EONS MATEY HEMS
```

365

```
SWAM COCA HALLE
OHNO OWLS AXIOM
FITOFBEAK VENOM
AMIGO NONE USA
PRAGUENOSES
GREASER THOR
OATS NCO TABOO
THESNOOTSISTERS
OSSIE TAG ONEA
SOPS ALERTLY
NIBINTHEBUD
ONO ALAN EVANS
MARAT MUZZLETOV
ANIMA EREI TOTE
DECAL SEEP OMEN
```

66

```
AHSO JURY TSAR
PIQUE ERIE OONA
PUTUPSIGNSWHEN
SPA LETS CENT
HORNETS TBAR
EAR BURR IDA
CARP STADIA NOR
LOSTMYDOGBUTIT
ADO HIKERS NETS
OAT WREN SIR
YAKS YELTSIN
PIER TOTE TOO
DIDNTWORKHECANT
ALOT ALOE KATIE
DELL SETS READ
```

367

```
CLARO SASS HIES
REGAN ALEE ANKH
AMINE FELL ISEE
WALKTHEPLANK
STE OATHS AURAL
COZY OTB ALA
ESPANA FUR EVES
SHIVERMETIMBERS
SETA DEN LEANTO
ABC MSS CLAN
YAHOO SLEET SEE
ROOMANDBOARD
BLAB PASS ADLAI
RAVI ETTU LEAST
ABET NESS LADES
```

368

```
PEST OPART DAFT
ASTO ARTIE ONOR
USENOHOOKS NERO
SEVENUP ELBOWED
EXERT TRAIT
OVERS ADDLE
KANT AAA ISRAEL
NOAH STINT OLDS
INSIDE TAC PISA
TEASE BOTHA
ERROR RACKS
CHANNEL RECLAIM
RAND PERISHABLE
TUTU OREOS MELL
SLIP TONTO ORAL
```

369

```
S L I D   M O I R A   C R A B
L O C I   E L T O N   H U G O
O N E S   M A S O N   A S E A
B I R D S O F A F E A T H E R
      A I R     S A M E
T H E I L I A D   L I A B L E
R Y A N   A G E S   C U R E R
E D T   F L O C K T O   E V A
E R I C A   G O Y A   S E E S
S O N A T A   R E K I N D L E
      T A N S   E L I
A N E W L Y W A S H E D C A R
T A R A   H E L L O   E L L A
O P A L   O D I U M   L E E J
M A S K   W E D G E   Y M C A
```

370

```
B E T T E   C R A T   P T A S
E T H A N   A O N E   O H N O
T H E I C E M A N C O M E T H
A N T   E K E D     P A T I O
S O W S   G O T O   E C U
      E P A   S O M B R E R O S
E L L E N     S A K E   N N E
L O V E A T F I R S T B I T E
L I E   C A E N     T E N O R
A N C H O R A G E   A N G
      H A N   T A L E   S P A T
B O A R D   P I C A   O L E
I M I T A T I O N O F L I F E
L O R E   A C R O   R E N I N
L O S S   B E E R   O A T E S
```

371

```
M A S H   A S T I   Q U I T S
I D L E   L O A M   U R G E S
A J A X   P L O P   A S N E R
  O N E W H O S E T R A I N
B U D D H A   D I T   T A B
A R E   I B I S E S   V E G A
S N R   F E S T     W A D E D
    O F T H O U G H T
C A S K S   O L L A   O T T
R I M S   H E L M E T   R A V
O R E   I B N   A D A G I O
  H A S N O T E R M I N A L
M O R A L   A L A I   S N O E
E L E N A   I M I N   E Z R A
T E D D Y   L O N G   L A S T
```

372

```
B A S S E S   F R I E D M A N
A L T E R S   R E T R I E V E
C L O V I S   O D O M E T E R
K O P E K   M M C   A N I S E
S P O R   A T A   E T I
E A V E S D R O P   L I R A S
A T E   L I S P   Z E N
T H R O U G H T H E H E A R T
    W E S   O O N A   N E A
A P R E S   A B H O R R I N G
R O O   L O O   E M I L
T U N E D   I T S   A M A T I
I N D I R E C T   P L A T E N
S C E N A R I O   R E D O N E
T E L E G R A M   E X E R T S
```

373

```
L E V I   L I M O S   G O A T
O V E N   I N A N E   O M N I
W A S H I N G T O N S T A T E
E S T A T E   A R A C H N I D
      L O O M     T O I
  J E F F E R S O N C I T Y
W H A R F   D E T R E   T A E
H O D S   F I L E S   W A L L
I R E   A L A I N   K A L E L
  M A D I S O N C O U N T Y
      R I P     S P E E
A N T I D O T E   P E R S I A
R O O S E V E L T I S L A N D
A N N E   E L I O T   O L G A
B E G S   R E E D Y   O K A Y
```

374

```
R A J A H   C H E F   S E P T
O H A R A   R O L L   E L L E
M A M M Y   O L E O   A L A N
E B B   F R A M E O F M I N D
    A L E U T   R A I S E S
R E L I V E   S L I D E
A G A P E   A M E N   R H E A
G A Y   R U L I N G S   O R F
E D A M   N A T O   A D U L T
    U G L I S   A D O R E S
S I E S T A   S W I N G
T H E C O W S I L L S   L B C
E A R L   F I N E   T I A R A
E D I E   U R G E   I N S E T
R A E S   L E E K   C A S T S
```

375

```
D E N Y   A B C S   S A M B A
A R I A   G O A T   U N A U S
M I C H A E L M O R I A R T Y
S C O O P   D E L E   I T E
    L O P E   R O C K F E S T
S S W   A M M O N   I L L
E L I   L I O N   L E H U A
M A L C O L M M C D O W E L L
I G L O O   I T E M   M A E
I R S   A T O N E   I N C
D R A M A T I C   S T A N
O H M   A S H E   E L G A R
R O S C O E L E E B R O W N E
A D O R N   E L L E   N A T E
S A N T E   S L Y E   E Y E D
```

376

```
D R A B   M A T T E   J A W S
A I D E   E L R O Y   U L A N
S T E A K D I A N E   D I K E
H E N R I   S P I L L O V E R
      U T A   E T E S   E N D
C R E P E S U Z E T T E
R A T   R I S E   S H E L
A R T I S A N   A P P E A R S
M A U L   A G A R   R I A
E G G S B E N E D I C T
P D Q   E A T S   E L I
H O U S E P E T S   I N S E T
O M I T   P E A C H M E L B A
T E T E   E L I O T   R O A R
O D O R   D E N T S   S E N T
```

377

```
J E T E   C N U T   A R O M A
A V I D   L O P E   D E L I S
M I T E   I N O N   D R A F T
B L I N D M A N S B L U F F
      I B M     E E N
A P I A N   E T C H   S A Y A
B U N G E E   I H A D   S U I
A L T E R N A T I V E R O C K
S S E   O R A L   E V I N C E
H E R E   A H E M   O C E A N
      L E G   I C U
I C E B E R G L E T T U C E
S H O V E   S A I L   A S I A
D O T E R   V I E T   L E T S
S P E N T   P L U S   C R E E
```

378

```
B O M B     C A P P   D R O P
E V I L   C O R E A   E E R O
L A L O   U N I O N   P A C K
A L L W O R K A N D N O P A Y
      G R R     S A Y S
B E Q U E A T H   S N A C K S
A R U N   N E A L   E L E N A
B O A   S T C R O I X   C O L
A D L A I   H E W N   T I L T
R E M I N D   M E G T I L L Y
      L U I S   E O N
M A K E S A H O U S E W I F E
A J A R   D I D S T   O R A L
R E N O   E R I E S   R A Z E
S T E N   M E N D     K N E E
```

379

```
A S C A P   T A B S   A C T S
D A R L A   A L A S   T H A T
A L T A R   B A R T S T A R R
      N A N A S   S P A R T A
A L A W   A R K   A R M A S
S A R A H A D A M S   S R S
P L A T A     G A F F
A S T H M A   S C A R A B
    S A A R     R A G A S
M S S   G R A H A M N A S H
A P P A L   R A H   S R T A
D R A F T S   G N A S H
C A R L S A G A N   T A M P A
A T K A   G A L A   A L B A N
P S S T   A M A H   T S A R S
```

380

```
  B O A R   B I T   A G A
B E L L A   U N E   A B O V E
Y O G I B E R R A   C A B O T
O N A B I N G E   S E D A N S
B E S I D E S   B A T A N
      E L S   D A T A B A S E
S T U D Y   S I B I L A N C E
H O N   I T C A N   A I R
E M B A S S I E S   B A S S O
A B A T T E R Y   G O B
    L A I R S   N E B U L A R
A R A B L E   B O O B T U B E
B A N A L   B U L L Y T R E E
C Y C L E   I R T   B E I L L
  S E S   B Y E   O D D S
```

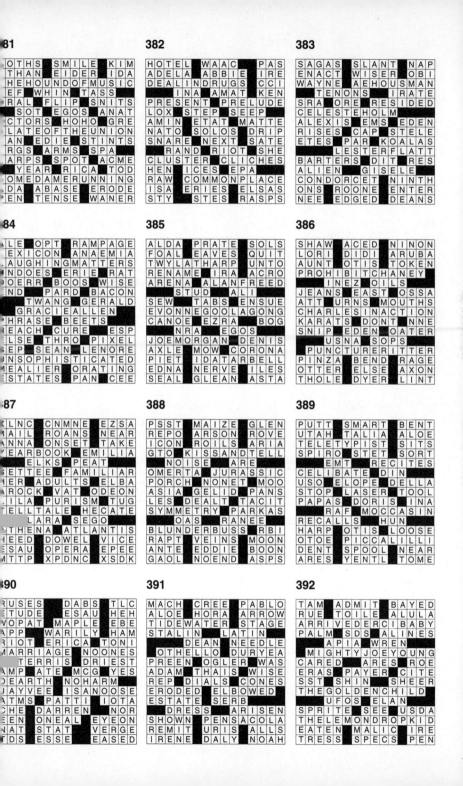

381

```
OTHS SMILE KIM
THAN EIDER IDA
HEHOUNDOFMUSIC
EF WHIN TASS
RAL FLIP SNITS
SOT EGOS ANAT
CTORS HOHO GRE
LATEOFTHEUNION
AN EDIE STINTS
RGS ARMS SPA
ARPS SPOT ACME
YEAR RICA TOD
OMEDAMERUNNING
DA ABASE ERODE
EN TENSE WANER
```

382

```
HOTEL WAAC PAS
ADELA ABBIE IRE
DEALINDRUGS CCI
INA AMAT KEN
PRESENT PRELUDE
LOX STEP SEEP
AMIN ETAT MATTE
NATO SOLOS DRIP
SNARE NEXT SATE
RAND RIOT SHE
CLUSTER CLICHES
HEN ICES EPA
RAW COMMONPLACE
ISA ERIES ELSAS
STY STES RASPS
```

383

```
SAGAS SLANT NAP
ENACT WISER OBI
WAYNE AEHOUSMAN
TENONS IRATE
SRA ORE RESIDED
CELESTEHOLM
ALEXIS EMS EDEN
RISES CAP STELE
ETES PAR KOALAS
LESTERFLATT
BARTERS DIT RES
ALIEN GISELE
CONDORCET NINTH
ONS ROONE ENTER
NEE EDGED DEANS
```

384

```
LE OPT RAMPAGE
EXICON ANAEMIA
AUGHINGMATTERS
NDOES ERIE RAT
OERR BOOS WISE
ND PARD BACON
TWANG GERALD
GRACIEALLEN
HRASE BEETS
REACH CURE ESP
LSE THRO PIXEL
EP SEAN LENORE
NSOPHISTICATED
EALIER ORATING
ESTATES PAN CEE
```

385

```
ALDA PRATE SOLS
FOAL EAVES QUIT
TWYLATHARP UNTO
RENAME IRA ACRO
ARENA ALANFREED
STUD ALI
SEW TABS ENSUE
EVONNEGOOLAGONG
CANOE EZRA BOG
NRA EGOS
JOEMORGAN DENIS
AXLE MOW CORONA
PIET IDATARBELL
EDNA NERVE ILES
SEAL GLEAN ASTA
```

386

```
SHAW ACED NINON
LORI DIDI ARUBA
AUNT OTIS TOKEN
PROHIBITCHANEY
INEZ OILS
JEANS EAST OSSA
ATT URNS MOUTHS
CHARLESINACTION
KARATS DONT NNE
SNIP EDEN OATER
USNA SOPS
PUNCTURERITTER
PINZA BEND RAGE
OTTER ELSE AXON
THOLE DYER LINT
```

387

```
KLNC CNMNE EZSA
RAIL ROANS NEAR
ANNA ONSET TAKE
YEARBOOK EMILIA
ELKS PEAT
SETTEE FAMILIAR
HER ADULTS ELBA
AROCK VAT ODEON
ILA PURISM TUG
TELLTALE HECATE
LARA SEGO
ATHENA ATLANTIS
HEED DOWEL VICE
ESAU OPERA EPEE
MTTP XPDNC XSDK
```

388

```
PSST MAIZE GLEN
REPO ARSON ROVE
ICON ROILS ARIA
GTO KISSANDTELL
NOISE ARE
OMERTA JURASSIC
PORCH NONET MOO
ASIA GELID PANS
LES DEALT TACIT
SYMMETRY PARKAS
OAS RANEE
BLUNDERBUSS RBI
RAPT VEINS MOON
ANTE EDDIE BOON
GAOL NOEND ASPS
```

389

```
PUTT SMART BENT
UTAH TALIA ALOE
TELETYPIST SITS
SPIRO STET SORT
EMT RECITES
CELIBATE DIN
USO ELOPE DELLA
STOP LASER TOOL
PAPAS DORIS INA
RAF MOCCASIN
RECALLS HUN
HARP OTIS LOOSE
OTOE PICCALILLI
DENT SPOOL NEAR
ARES YENTL TOME
```

390

```
RUSES DABS TLC
ETUDE ESAU HEH
VOPAT MAPLE EBE
APP WARILY HAM
RIOT ERICA TONI
MARRIAGE NOONES
TERRIS DRIEST
AMP ATE MCG YES
DEARTH NOHARM
JAYVEE ISANOOSE
ATMS PATTI IOTA
CHE DARREN NOR
EEN ONEAL EYEON
NAT STAT VERGE
TDS ESSE EASED
```

391

```
MACH CREE PABLO
ALOE HORA ARROW
TIDEWATER STAGE
STALIN LATIN
DEAN NEEDLE
OTHELLO DURYEA
PREEN OGLER WAS
ADAM THAIS WISE
REP DIALS CONES
ERODED ELBOWED
ESTATE SERB
DRESS ARISEN
SHOWN PENSACOLA
REMIT URIS ALLS
IRENE DALY NOAH
```

392

```
TAM ADMIT BAYED
RUE TOILE ALULA
ARRIVEDERCIBABY
PALM SDS ALINES
APIA WREN
MIGHTYJOEYOUNG
CARED ARES ROE
ERAS PAYER CITE
SST SHIN SHEER
THEGOLDENCHILD
UFOS ELAN
SPRITE SEE USDA
THELEMONDROPKID
EATEN MALIC IRE
TRESS SPECS PEN
```

393

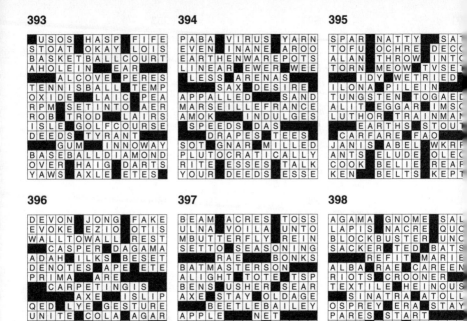

```
U S O S █ H A S P █ F I F E
S T O A T █ O K A Y █ L O I S
B A S K E T B A L L C O U R T
A H O L E I N █ █ E A R █ █ █
█ █ █ A L C O V E █ P E R E S
T E N N I S B A L L █ T E M P
O X I D E █ █ L A I C █ P E A
R P M █ S E T I N T O █ A E R
R O B █ T R O D █ █ L A I R S
I S L E █ G O L F C O U R S E
D E E D S █ T Y R A N T █ █ █
█ █ █ G U M █ I N N O W A Y
B A S E B A L L D I A M O N D
O V E R █ H A I G █ D A R T S
Y A W S █ A X L E █ E T E S █
```

394

```
P A B A █ V I R U S █ Y A R N
E V E N █ I N A N E █ A R O O
E A R T H E N W A R E P O T S
L I N E A R █ E W E R █ W E E
█ L E S S █ A R E N A S █ █
█ █ █ S A X █ D E S I R E
A P P A L L E D █ █ S A N D
M A R S E I L L E F R A N C E
A M O K █ █ I N D U L G E S
S P E E D S █ D A S █ █ █
█ D R A P E S █ T E E S █
S O T █ G N A R █ M I L L E D
P L U T O C R A T I C A L L Y
R I T E █ E S S E S █ T A L K
Y O U R █ D E E D S █ E S S E
```

395

```
S P A R █ N A T T Y █ S A T
T O F U █ O C H R E █ D E C O
A L A N █ T H R O W █ I N T O
T O R N █ M E O W █ T V S E T
█ █ █ I D Y █ W E T R I E D
I L O N A █ P I L E I N
T U N G S T E N █ T O G A E D
A L I T █ E G G A R █ I M S O
L U T H O R █ T R A I N M A N
█ E A R T H S █ S T O U
C A R F A R E █ F A O
J A N I S █ A B E L █ W K R P
A N T S █ E L U D E █ O L E O
C O O K █ B E L I E █ R E A P
K E N █ B E L T S █ K E P T
```

396

```
D E V O N █ J O N G █ F A K E
E V O K E █ E Z I O █ O T I S
W A L L T O W A L L █ R E S T
█ C A S P E R █ D A G A M A
A D A H █ I L K S █ B E S E T
D E N O T E S █ A P E █ E T E
P R I M A █ A R E █ █ █
█ C A R P E T I N G I S █
█ █ A X E █ █ I S L I P
Q E D █ L Y E █ G E S T U R E
U N I T E █ C O L A █ A G A R
A C R O S S █ R I S I N G
S I N K █ H A R D T O B E A T
A N D A █ E R I E █ N U R S E
R O L Y █ L I N D █ E L S I E
```

397

```
B E A M █ A C R E S █ T O S S
U L N A █ V O I L A █ U N T O
M B U T T E R F L Y █ R E I N
S E T T O █ S E A S O N I N G
█ █ R A E █ B O N K S
B A T M A S T E R S O N
A L I G H T █ T O T E █ T S P
B E N S █ U S H E R █ S E A R
A X E █ S T A Y █ O L D A G E
█ B E E T L E B A I L E Y █
A P P L E █ N E T █ █
C L E O P A T R A █ H A S T A
T A N K █ T H E B E E G E E S
O N C E █ N O B L E █ R A M P
R T E S █ O U S E L █ A L P S
```

398

```
A G A M A █ G N O M E █ S A L
L A P I S █ N A C R E █ Q U C
B L O C K B U S T E R █ U N C
S A C K E R █ T E D █ B A T S
█ █ R E F I T █ M A R I E
A L B A █ R A E █ C A R E E N
R I O T S █ C R O O N E R
T E X T I L E █ H E I N O U S
█ S I N A T R A █ A T O L L
O S P R E Y █ E R A █ S T A Y
P A R E S █ S T A R T █
E L I S █ A L I █ A R A B L E
N I N █ I C E C U B E T R A Y
E N G █ K E E L S █ A N O D E
R E S █ E S T E S █ T O W E D
```

399

```
C A S T E █ R E L A P █ T A J
U T U R N █ A L I B I █ I D O
S H I E D █ T I M E L A P S E
S E T S O F T A B L E S █
E N O █ R A E █ █ S H A R K
D A R C █ I R A N I █ T R A P
█ H E R █ R E S P R A Y S
█ P L A Y W R I G H T A B E
T H E P E A C E █ M A Y █
V I A L █ Y A L T A █ S A M S
A L D A S █ █ E E L █ A A A
█ I T C H Y A L L E R G Y
B E A N E R I E S █ A L O N E
O A F █ N O V A E █ M I N E R
A R T █ S P E N T █ A S S T S
```

400

```
R E C A P █ A G A R █ A M I D
A R O M A █ W A R T █ L A C E
J A M E S J O Y C E █ O R A L
A T E █ S O L E S █ A N K L E
S O S O O N █ I D S █ █
█ J U G H E A D J O N E S
H E L O T █ E D D A S █ A X E
A R I █ T R I M S █ S I T
D E A █ C O T T A █ M E A T S
J I M M Y J O H N S O N █
█ I S O █ I N D E N T
T W I X T █ D R A C O █ L O O
H I V E █ J O E J A C K S O N
A F A R █ U L N A █ L I A N A
T E N S █ D E E R █ E D S E L
```

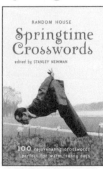

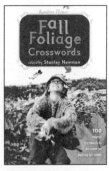

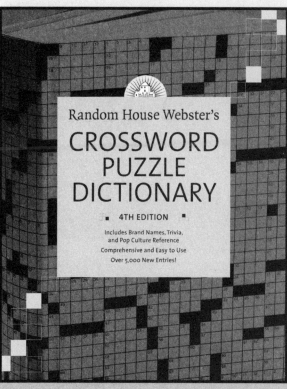